D1761267

FORGING A
KINGDOM
THE GAA IN KERRY
1884–1934

RICHARD MCELLIGOTT is a native of Stacks Mountain, Kilflynn, County Kerry. He completed his PhD on the early history of the GAA with the School of History and Archives, University College Dublin in 2011. He currently works as an occasional lecturer with the School. He is also chairman of the Sports History Ireland Society. A passionate GAA supporter, Richard decided to chronicle the early history of the GAA in Kerry as compensation for the fact he was the worst underage hurler and footballer north Kerry had ever seen.

www.sportshistoryireland.com

For Danny. Up the Rossies!

FORGING A
KINGDOM
THE GAA IN KERRY
1884–1934

The Collins Press

First published in 2013 by
The Collins Press
West Link Park
Doughcloyne
Wilton
Cork

Typesetting by Patricia Hope
Typeset in Sabon
Printed in Malta by Gutenberg Press Limited

CONTENTS

LIST OF FIGURES AND TABLES

ACKNOWLEDGEMENTS

This work has taken up most of the past five years of my life. Yet I know I could not have got through one week without the help, support and encouragement of so many people. I can only hope the finished product proves worthy of their faith in me.

First and foremost, I am forever grateful to Dr Paul Rouse. During the past five years, he has pushed me and constantly challenged me to make this work worthy of its potential. For all the pats on the back and the occasional (and deserved) kick up the behind, I am indebted. Thank you, Paul, for everything.

I wish to thank Professor Mike Cronin, Dr Catherine Cox, Professor Diarmaid Ferriter, Dónal McAnallen and Dr Declan Downey for all their kind help and guidance during my research.

A heartfelt thanks to my sisters Karen and Brenda, my brother, David, and my friends Neil Trebble, Maureen Sweeney and Fiona Martin for their long and tireless hours of proofreading and editing my often confused, long-winded and barely legible drafts. I am indebted to Sandra Boyd for her sterling work in proofreading and editing much of this work. Thanks also to my sister Theresa, for often providing me with a bed!

On a wet evening in Dublin in August 2007, I sat with my friend Keith Smith and, over a pint, breathed a heavy sigh of relief after Kerry somehow overcame a brave Monaghan team in the All-Ireland quarter-final. I would like to thank him for providing me with a eureka moment by suggesting that I write a book about the Kerry GAA, seeing as I talk about it so much!

Thanks to Donal Coffey, Charlie Solan and Conor Curran for their friendship and advice.

I am grateful to Conor Mulvagh, Steven O'Connor and Cathal O'Brien for providing an impromptu and lifesaving support group over much of the past five years.

I am indebted to the advice, direction and generosity of Weeshie Fogarty and Alan Groarke of *Terrace Talk*, J.J. Barrett, Tom Fox, John Keogh of Dr Crokes GAA, T.J. Flynn, Der Brosnan and John Lennon of Fitzgerald Stadium, Barry Houlihan of the NUIG Archives, Eoghan Corry, Fr Tom Looney, Paul Brennan of *The Kerryman*, Seán S. Ó Conchubhair, and Julia O'Driscoll Mitchell of Castleisland Desmonds GAA. A very special thanks to Seán Mac an tSíthigh and Frank Burke for all their generous help in providing some photographs for me.

I am thankful for the assistance of Mark Reynolds of the Croke Park Archive, Michael Lynch of the Kerry Archives and Griffin Murray of the Kerry County Museum.

My gratitude to the staff of the National Library, the National Archives, the UCD Archives, UCD Library, Kerry County Library and Archives for all their assistance in locating research material for this work.

I am indebted especially to Aonghus Meaney and all at The Collins Press who put so much effort into publishing my work.

Finally and most especially, thanks to my parents Tom and Kitty. I am eternally grateful for all the sacrifices they have made to allow me to indulge in my passion. For their constant and unwavering support throughout, I can't express enough gratitude. I love you very much.

INTRODUCTION

The foundation of the Gaelic Athletic Association in November 1884 ushered in a sporting revolution in Ireland. The association initiated the mass participation in organised sport among ordinary Irishmen. But more than this, the GAA, throughout its existence, became a profound influence on Irish social, political and cultural life. Yet despite its importance, the history of the GAA has only ever received relatively limited attention. Even when it has become the subject of investigation, the works have often failed to be comprehensive. From T.F. O'Sullivan's *Story of the GAA* through to P.J. Devlin's *Our Native Games*, the first histories of the Gaelic Athletic Association were dominated by the organisation's relationship with Irish nationalism and in particular physical-force nationalism.[1] These studies were celebratory in tone and the authors seemed intent on writing the GAA into the story of the creation of the Irish state.[2] In the 1980s, historians such as Marcus de Búrca and W.F. Mandle did little to dispel such conclusions, even if they sought to place the development of the GAA in a broader social context.[3] De Búrca and Mandle focussed on the national, often Dublin-centric, development of the association; they wrote about the politics of the GAA most usually, rather than its place within Irish life. Also in the 1980s – to tie in with the centenary of the establishment of the GAA, a cascade of club histories were published, detailing in greater or lesser detail the histories of many clubs across the country. These were often little more than extended records of matches played and facilities developed.

The 1990s saw the emergence of a generation of cultural and sport historians in Ireland who, influenced by what had been developing in British and American academia, sought to place the history of the GAA in the wider international context of the Victorian sports revolution. Work by Tom Hunt, Dónal McAnallen, Mike Cronin, Paul Rouse and Mark Duncan, among others, further sought to move the historiography of the GAA away from politics and place it within the broader context of Irish social, economic and cultural history.[4] In turn, this work has influenced – and been influenced by – those examining the broader narrative of Irish society. For example, Diarmaid Ferriter's excellent study on twentieth-century Ireland placed the role of Irish sport in its proper social context and wrote the story of sport into the history of modern Ireland.[5]

The historiography of the GAA then has traditionally been precariously balanced between two points. One focussed almost exclusively on the national history of the association and emphasised its political role in the creation of an independent Irish state. The other is the numerous local club histories which, invariably, only tell a broad story of a particular club's local development. Between both strands, however, lies a rich vein of material on the social and cultural role of the association in Irish life, which has yet to be fully explored. Serious studies on the association remain almost non-existent on a county level. It is true that various county histories were published in the 1980s – again to link in with the centenary commemoration of the establishment of the GAA – but these books invariably failed to place the GAA within any meaningful social, cultural and economic context. As Gearóid Ó Tuathaigh argued, 'detailed, scholarly case studies of the GAA's history in the context of wider social development [at a county level] are still awaited'.[6]

And yet it is a simple fact that the county is a fundamental foundation of the GAA's national organisation. Clubs are organised on a county basis to play local competitions, and teams representing counties are an essential element of the sporting life of the GAA. More than that, the idea of the Irish county is intrinsically linked to the GAA. Though originally developed by Norman invaders as part of the process of conquering and colonising Ireland, the county structure was only solidified as the major administrative and territorial unit in Ireland at the end of the nineteenth century.[7] Yet within a couple of decades the significance of the Irish county had surpassed any mere administrative function. From its origins in 1887 as an ad hoc club competition, the GAA's All-Ireland championship had, by the 1920s, evolved into the inter-county contest we know today. The reputation of county teams rose in unison with the prestige of the All-Ireland competition within the Irish sporting media. Today, it is the county that stands as the prime badge of identification among members and supporters of the GAA.

This work is an attempt to fill a significant void in Irish historiography. It is the first attempt to outline the establishment and development of the GAA in a rural county; William Nolan's work on the GAA in Dublin, published in 2005, remains the only attempt to look at the establishment of the GAA in such a local context.[8] Kerry is, arguably, the most successful county in the history of the GAA in terms of national success and local organisation. The presence of the GAA in Kerry is ubiquitous – it has woven itself into the fabric of life in the county in such a way as to leave it almost unimaginable that it should not exist. This work tells the story of the origins and development of the GAA in Kerry through its vital first fifty years. By the end of this period, the modern nature of the GAA in Kerry – its organisation and its success – was firmly established.

The intention is to examine how a sporting organisation was founded and developed and, in turn, what factors shape that development. How does a sporting body like the GAA fit into the life of a rural county like Kerry? How is that organisation influenced by the county it develops in and how does this, in turn, influence the greater story of that county? The history of the GAA in Kerry, likewise, feeds into the national story of the progress of the association in this fifty-year period. It also puts the history of that organisation in a local, as well as national and international, context. It places the development of the GAA in Kerry in the wider social, cultural, political and economic history of Ireland between 1884 and 1934.

This work utilises the GAA as a medium to shy away from the stale historical narrative of the state, the Church, trade unionism and their respective leaderships and to focus on the ordinary Irish people's perspective of this critical period of Irish history. It will investigate the relationship between the GAA and the major political, religious and social movements in these fifty years.

This raises many questions. How much did the association's officialdom, both in a local and nationwide context, use the GAA to school and influence ordinary members to their political, cultural or social beliefs? Conversely, how much did the GAA itself choose to be a vehicle for influence and reform among its members? From its fight for temperance, its notions of a muscular Gaelic Christian manhood, its enthusiasm for cultural revival, the preservation of the Irish language and the forging of a distinct sense of Irishness, what ideals did the GAA hope to transfer to its members about who they were and the kind of society they aspired to live in? As Ireland emerged as an independent nation, I will surmise how much influence either internal rhetoric or outside influence actually had on the GAA membership in Kerry.

This work will also examine the role the GAA played in the creation of a local and, specifically, a county identity. In regards to Kerry, was such a process already in motion before the advent of the GAA or was the explosion in popularity of inter-county contests in the early twentieth century a major factor in the development of a county identity in modern Ireland?

The impulse to play and watch sport is as old as human civilisation itself. By applying the lessons of the 'sports revolution' in contemporary Britain to its own traditional games, the GAA, within fifty years, was in a position to dominate the sporting landscape of the majority of Irish people. I will argue that by 1934, the strength of the GAA was not, nor indeed ever had been, its role as a recruiting ground for the various political and socio-economic forces in greater Ireland. Rather, in areas like Kerry, it was the association's ability to develop and then dominate the sporting landscape while destroying the threat of rival sporting codes which was the real cause of its success.

Was this, in essence, what made the GAA, excluding the Catholic Church, the largest national organisation in twentieth-century Ireland? Despite all the political sparring within its boardrooms, all the heady ideals and various attempts to paint its facade with another ideological coat, is the same basic appeal of the GAA as real today as it was in 1885, the joy of playing in or watching the games? That sense of pride and place in lining up for your team, your club, your county.

1

FOUNDATIONS, 1885–1890

'We won't have Kerry Moonlighters here.'

Fr E. Sheehy, Tipperary delegate at the GAA Annual Convention, Thurles, 23 January 1889

The GAA emerged in an Ireland assailed by agricultural depression, agrarian unrest and chronic emigration. Thus, in order to understand the organisation's origins it is necessary to examine the social, cultural and political situation in Ireland into which the association was born. Likewise in Kerry, it is impossible to examine its development without placing the association in the context of what was occurring in the county's society at this time. The 1880s witnessed the outbreak of the Land Wars and the collapse of the agricultural economy in Ireland. Politically, the establishment of the Land League and then National League and the growing support for Charles Stewart Parnell and the Home Rule movement were all important factors in Irish society at this time. In addition, to understand the emergence of a body like the GAA it is necessary to examine the development of Victorian leisure and sport in this period and its impact on sport in counties like Kerry. The sporting landscape of Kerry in the years before 1885 saw the decline of the older traditional Gaelic pastimes and their replacement by those modern sports which were developing across Britain at this time. However, the arrival of the GAA in Kerry in 1885 as a consequence of the first large GAA athletics meeting in Tralee in June of that year was a seminal moment in the history of the association. The political fallout from the event and its impact on the GAA both locally and nationally was of great significance. Yet despite the success of the event, Gaelic activity in Kerry all but ceased during the 1886–7 period. Indeed, it was only through the energies of key personalities in the county that a proper GAA structure was introduced in late 1887 and 1888, culminating in the first county championships and inter-county games. The reasons for the success and evolution of the GAA in Kerry at this time are varied and worthy of some attention, as is the relationship between the GAA and its main sporting rivals during the association's formative years in the county.

Kerry in the 1880s

Sport does not exist in a vacuum untouched by the particular space and time it occupies. Rather, sport, like a body of water, both adjusts to and reflects the physical, political and socio-economic world around it. The GAA's establishment in Ireland was part of a much larger sporting development across the British Isles in the later nineteenth century known as the 'Victorian sports revolution'.[1]

The Victorian sports revolution was the gradual process that turned traditional games across the western world into organised, codified and administered national and international sports. Tied in with this process was a myriad of changes taking place within wider Victorian society such as the decline of rural life and growing urbanisation, the civilising process of society and withdrawal of the gentry from the countryside, the development of the railway, the decline in average working hours and a sharp definition of work versus leisure time, increasing levels of per capita income, rising standards of literacy and the growth of the popular press.

The spread of public school and university education meant that by the end of the nineteenth century society was exercising an increasing social restraint on the upper classes who attended such institutions. Victorians saw an opportunity to turn schoolboy games into forms of social control and discipline to prepare young men physically and mentally for the challenges of the modern industrialised world.[2] The theories of the naturalist Charles Darwin, which filtered into educational opinion in the later nineteenth century, gave further impetus to anxiety about the strength of youth and created a sense of need for physically strong and mentally tough young men who would be required to administer and defend the ever-growing British Empire. Sports participation was seen as the perfect method by which to develop such traits. Through public schools the evolution of games like rugby and soccer began in the 1860s/70s. Many historians argue that a downward social diffusionist model can be used to explain the spread of these new codified games across Victorian society. Thus, games passed from elite schools through to universities and then onto the more modest grammar schools and eventually down to ordinary school level. As young men left their schooldays behind them they brought such sports to the colleges they attended, setting up the first clubs in those institutions and writing down the initial rules and regulations for the games. It was ex-public schoolboys and university men who instigated the formation of the English Football Association (FA) and the English Rugby Union (RFU) and devised the first common set of rules for the sports. In Ireland, Trinity Rugby Club was founded in 1854 from students bringing back what they had seen in public schools in England.[3]

Meanwhile, as British society became increasingly urbanised, millions left the land and entered the sprawling industrial cities to work. Numerous government acts introduced in the late nineteenth century decreased and regulated working hours. This increased the time available for recreation and also separated more sharply than ever before working and leisure hours. Thus, a shared period of leisure time was created for working-class communities, enabling the development of mass participant and spectator sports from the informal recreations of previous generations. Uprooted from the traditional, identifiable units of parish and village, they began to look to the factories and the streets where they worked and lived as the areas which anchored them in this new world. It was around these units that working-class sports clubs evolved.

The effects of this revolution in organised, codified sports were staggering. One of the clearest indications of this revolution was the dramatic increase in the range of sports. In the 1860s and '70s, the separate sports of association football and rugby had evolved from traditional folk football. By 1910, there was anywhere between 400,000 and 650,000 registered soccer players in England and Scotland. Attendances at FA Cup finals rose from 2,000 in 1872 to 110,000 in 1901.[4] By 1909, in England alone, one million people were reckoned to attend soccer matches on Saturday afternoons.

Kerry was to experience the spread of the Victorian sports revolution but the nature of that experience was coloured by the social and economic situation in the county. In 1891, the county's population stood at 179,136.[5] By then, its largest town, Tralee, was a thriving commercial port and also an important regional market town, mainly for butter and pigs. The relatively prosperous conditions for farmers in north Kerry up until the early 1880s ensured that a number of large general merchants located in the town thrived. Some of these leading merchants had begun to expand their businesses, opening new stores, mills, bakeries and even a small foundry.[6] Two woollen mills existed in the town but outside of these Kerry had little industry except for some publishing and printing offices, sawmills and smaller agriculturally based concerns, including flour and meal merchants.[7] Killarney, the county's second town, had begun to develop a flourishing tourist and tertiary sector by the 1870s. Meanwhile, other large towns like Listowel and Castleisland survived principally as local market towns for the agricultural produce of the surrounding hinterland.

Kerry remained a predominately rural county. In 1891, only 10.2 per cent of its population (18,394) lived in one of the three principal towns of Tralee, Killarney or Listowel. Agriculture was by far the dominant industry in the county. Of the total male workforce of 51,966 men in Kerry in 1891, 37,709 or 72.5 per cent worked in agriculture.[8] Kerry was a dairy county. It had the wettest climate in Munster and this constant dampness was favourable for grass growth.[9]

By the mid-1880s, the press described the county as 'the most criminally disturbed, the most evicted, the most rack-rented county in all of Ireland'. Land agitation had gripped the county with such force that for most of the decade, Kerry was at the forefront of agrarian disturbance and subsequent government coercion to eliminate it. The factors which caused this eruption of agrarian violence were varied. One was the county's continued high population. Kerry experienced a proportionally lower population loss than any other county in Munster between 1851 and 1901.[10] Yet the county contributed its equal share to emigration. The Irish Register General reported that between 1851 and 1885, 143,100 people had emigrated from Kerry. What made the county stand apart was its extraordinarily high birth rate. In the 1860s and '70s, it had the highest birth rate in the country. Pre-Famine marital customs remained intact, and marriage continued to occur at a relatively early age.[11]

After the Famine, the great estate owners continued to dominate Kerry life. As late as 1876 a mere twenty-six proprietors possessed over three-fifths of total land area in the county between them. Butter and beef continued to be Ireland's principal exports, and agricultural expansion between the 1850s and '70s had seen average prices for both rise by 45 and 138 per cent respectively. In consequence, many landlords considered that it was time rents reflected the more prosperous economic situation. Many, like Lord Lansdowne in his barony in Iveragh, chose prosperous harvests before 1877 to augment their revenues.[12] However, just at this moment the agricultural economy began to collapse. By the late 1870s, agricultural depression had set in, caused mainly by American competition in butter markets.[13] The depression was equally severe in Britain. Therefore, the earnings of the migrant population, upon which many Irish families, especially in the impoverished west and southwest of the country, relied, fell sharply. Between 1875 and 1879, butter prices fell by 27 per cent, while the value of principal crops fell by £14 million.[14] The harvest of 1879 was perhaps the worst in the entire century and butter prices fell a further 47 per cent.[15] Soon thousands of tenants were falling into arrears and evictions began to increase sharply.[16]

The sudden collapse of the butter market and the subsequent economic depression were a prime stimulus for agrarian unrest. By the late 1870s, tenant farmers were widely motivated by a strong desire to defend and preserve the substantial economic gains made in the previous twenty years. They did not see why they should stand by and endure, as their forbears had done in 1847, the worst effects of the catastrophe.[17] When the Land War erupted, the recent increase in rents, often combined with the resentment of a poor population slow to change its accustomed patterns of life against progressive and wealthy landlords, furnished powerful motive factors for a fervid agitation, punctuated by sensational violence.

Kerry, for most of the 1880s, had the highest eviction rates in Ireland.[18] Yet, due to the economic depression in Britain, the safety valve of emigration slowed in this period. The economic collapse had made many people's situation desperate. The minutes of the National Famine Relief Committee of 1880 indicate that on 1 March some 15,000 people were in distress in north Kerry alone. Kerry's tenants were poorer than those in any other part of Munster. In 1881, the county had the highest proportion of agricultural holdings (67 per cent), valued for Poor Law purposes at £10 or less.[19] With so many in the mire of poverty, tenants had little to lose and much to gain by taking on the landlords. Agrarian violence became common, especially around areas like Castleisland.

Demographic factors also help explain the rapid manifestation of land violence in the county. The 1870s had seen the abrupt appearance of delayed marriage, which outside the county had occurred earlier and more gradually. In the fertile lands of north Kerry, the number of single young men rose by 30 per cent, whereas those married fell by 40 per cent. Kerry was to the forefront of agrarian violence for much of the 1880s because, especially in the north of the county, there was a large population of socially frustrated young men whose numbers would continue to rise at an alarming rate during the last two decades of the nineteenth century.

Additionally, the decline of farm labourers as a societal class in the nineteenth century meant that the Irish tenant farmer was the most 'numerous, significant and homogenous part of the population of Ireland'.[20] This homogeny helped create a sense of a common bond among tenant farmers. Furthermore, Irish society after the Famine saw the separation, yet increasing dependence, of both urban and rural society on each other. This helped forge strong links across Ireland between townspeople and their neighbours in the rural hinterland. To mobilise their political potential rural society required leadership, propaganda and organisation on a nationwide scale. In October 1879, Michael Davitt established the Land League, a national political movement that seized the opportunity to tie into the immediate economic interests of the majority of the population.[21] Charles Stewart Parnell, the leading Irish nationalist politician of the 1880s, became its president.[22] The League's first branch in Kerry was established in Tralee on 25 September 1880. Yet despite its influence, agrarian violence continued to increase. In Kerry in 1880, 291 violent incidents related to the land struggle were reported. By 1881, that number had increased to 401.

With the agrarian situation worsening, the British Prime Minister, William Gladstone, decided to take decisive action. In January 1881, he introduced a new Land Act that effectively conceded the basic demands of Land League agitation: the 'three Fs' of fair rent, fair sale and fixture of tenure.[23] Despite the Land League being outlawed by a new government Coercion Act, Parnell's popularity was such that in October 1882 he established the new Irish National League, closely linked with the Irish Parliamentary Party (IPP) and effectively under its control.

The National League was a countrywide nationalist body set up to both advocate and defend tenant farmers' rights and to press the government for land and political reform.[24] The League began to expand substantially in Kerry. One of the main factors contributing to its spread was that it, like the Land League before it, was championed by the local nationalist paper, the *Kerry Sentinel*. The *Sentinel* had been established by Timothy Harrington in 1878.[25] By now, Timothy Harrington had become an MP and had risen to the position of secretary to the Central Committee of the National League. His brother, Edward, took over as editor of the paper and was himself elected president of the Tralee League when it was formed on 15 February 1885. The paper became the propaganda organ for the League, detailing reports of all its meetings in the various branches on a weekly basis, along with the evictions and outrages sweeping the county.[26] The organisation spread rapidly in Kerry and by the time of its first County Convention on 19 November 1885, fifty-seven branches were represented. Unlike its predecessor, the National League was in effect controlled by the Central Committee of the IPP. It put Home Rule to the forefront of its programme and relegated land reform to second place. The clergy quickly threw their support behind the League. In addition to the 277 delegates present at its first County Convention in November 1885, there were sixty priests.

By June, 1885 Parnell and his Irish Party, holding the balance of power in Westminster, had aligned with the Conservatives and the new government immediately dropped the Coercion Act and instituted a new scheme of land purchase called the Ashbourne Act. However, the economic situation deteriorated to its greatest extent since 1879. Store cattle prices suffered a substantial decline as a sharp industrial depression hit Britain and working-class consumption of Irish beef contracted.[27] Between 1883 and 1886, there was a 20 per cent drop in the price of butter and a 31 per cent drop in the price of cattle. The problem for Irish farmers throughout the later nineteenth century was that they were almost totally dependent upon conditions in the British market and this left them incredibly exposed when it contracted. Agricultural prices began to fall by more than the judicial rent reductions set up under the 1881 Land Act. Lack of credit meant evictions rose, and with the Coercion Act dropped, outrages increased at an alarming rate.[28]

William Gladstone, as leader of the Liberal Party, became convinced that Home Rule was the only solution to the Irish problem in British politics.[29] Having been enticed by this new prospect of Home Rule, the IPP pulled out of their alliance with the Conservatives and formed a new coalition with the Liberals in early 1886. However, Gladstone's plans for Home Rule were defeated by a split in his own liberal party, with the Liberal Unionists, anxious that Ireland be kept as an integral part of the United Kingdom, defecting rather than see the measure introduced.[30] In the aftermath of this defeat, a general election was called and the Conservatives were returned to power. With Home Rule dashed and the economic condition worsening daily, tenants were more and more unwilling to meet rent obligations. Despite many landlords offering abatements, the terms were refused by tenants.[31] Boycotting continued to be the most effective protection against eviction. Due to this, no one would dare defy the League and rent or work on evicted lands.[32] As a consequence, the process of eviction was often immensely loss-making for the landlord. In October 1886, this tactic was escalated, with the National League's 'Plan of Campaign' being launched in the pages of the *United Ireland* newspaper. Timothy Harrington was believed to have devised the scheme and been the main force behind its operation. The plan advocated that tenants act as a body to gain rent reductions and if they were not forthcoming, they would pay rent into a fund for the evicted instead.[33]

Yet the torpedoing of Gladstone's Home Rule Bill in June 1886 undoubtedly had a negative effect on the League's influence in Kerry. Secret societies, often Fenian backed, had been prevalent in north Kerry since 1879 and the League was slower to grow there as opposed to south Kerry. This is one of the reasons why north Kerry continued to be a hotbed for violence even into the 1890s. A special report on Kerry in the *Daily Mail* on 31 October 1886 stated:

> Absentee landlords and harsh agents are responsible for the state of the county. Rents are far too high . . . Boycotting is regarded as the only way in which the peasants can protect themselves . . . Where the Land League is strong there is little or no disorder . . . The Land League is weak in Kerry and therefore moonlighting is strong. There is a secret society in Kerry and there is little doubt they drill in barns and on the hillside.

It reported that this 'society' was made up mostly of young men, the sons of farmers and tradesmen.

Due to the extraordinary violence and unrest in Kerry, Major General Sir Redvers Buller, commanding a special force of 300 extra policemen, was appointed head of the military and civilian forces in the county and martial law was declared.[34] Buller quickly set up a special network of detectives and used informers to effectively undermine moonlighters. His tactics of using large-scale forces of Royal Irish Constabulary (RIC) to insist on evictions began to take its toll.[35] In August 1887, the Conservatives introduced the Perpetual Crimes Act and proscribed the National League. In order to counterbalance this, the Ashbourne Act was extended by the advance of a further fund of £5 million to make it easier for tenants to buy out their holdings from their landlord. In November 1887, Kerry was specially proclaimed under the terms of the Crimes Act. Copies of the proclamation, banning the League in the county, were posted around Tralee and on the Sunday the RIC occupied the National League rooms to stop meetings taking place. Police targeted the ringleaders of the organisation along with nationalist newspaper editors and newsagents. The Harrington brothers were arrested for publishing reports of suppressed meetings in Kerry in the *Sentinel*. The twin tactics of coercion and concession were working, and as early as June 1887 branches such as Dingle were failing to renew subscriptions from its members, indicating the growing weakness of the League.

The solidarity of the League was also weakened by the improving economic situation. After the disasters of the 1886 and '87 harvests, an upturn in the agricultural sector began in 1888 and continued until 1890. Heavy rainfall in the summer of 1888 caused an abundant grass crop and livestock prices made a strong recovery. A resurgence in British industry led to an increasing demand on Irish agriculture. The result was stronger prices in the British market for Irish cattle. By mid-1890, the coercing policies of the government, along with the extension of the Ashbourne Act and the economic improvement, had to a great degree silenced agitation in Kerry.

Dominated by an agricultural economy and its problems, Kerry was nevertheless linked into the wider Victorian world. Though isolated and distant from the heart of Victorian Britain and its Industrial Revolution, the effects of this great change were beginning to trickle into the county. Many, like the introduction of the railway, would be instrumental to Ireland's own sporting revolution.

The arrival of the railway transformed transport in Kerry. On 10 August 1853, the Great Southern and Western Railway (GSWR) opened its Mallow to Killarney line. The Waterford and Limerick Railway (W&LR) company opened the last stretch of the Limerick to Tralee line between Newcastlewest and Tralee on 20 December 1880. Over the next thirty years, the railways in Kerry were gradually extended, both for commercial reasons and as relief work for the thousands of unemployed within the county. The Railways (Ireland) Act of 1890 introduced free grants towards the construction of railways in remote parts of the country. On 15 January 1885, the Killarney line was extended with the opening of the Killorglin to Farranfore section. In north Kerry, the Lartigue light railway was opened between Listowel and Ballybunion on 29 February 1888 at a cost £33,000 for the ten-mile track.[36]

This expansion of the rail network facilitated the development of another feature of the Victorian Age. The railways began to revolutionise tourism.[37] The visit of Queen Victoria to Killarney in August 1861 was the event that put Kerry, and more specifically Killarney, on the Victorian tourist map. Two powerful local families, the Lords of Kenmare at Killarney House and the Herberts of Muckross House, seeing the obvious prestige and potential for tourism that a visit from the queen would bring, had exploited old family connections to ensure Killarney was one of the few stops on the queen's tour.[38] The royal visit meant Killarney became an area which any self-respecting Victorian traveller had to visit. Its spectacular lakes, mountains and woodlands came to be seen as a throwback to the fast-disappearing pre-industrial world of the British countryside. As a consequence, the local tourist industry rapidly expanded. Railway companies appreciated its potential and strategically located hotels at their train termini in order to maximise profits. Local gentry, like the Kenmare and Herbert families, did all they could to develop the industry further as it provided a valuable financial lifeline for landed families so often faced with the relatively futile task of earning a profit from farming the mountainous and boggy land in the district. Tourism became increasingly important to the economy of the region. Only later, with the introduction of paid holidays, would the tourist market become accessible to the masses. However, railway companies exploited a substantial market for day trips. For example, the GSWR advertised cheap excursion railway tickets every Sunday during the summer. A third-class train fare was charged at 2s (shillings) 6d (pence) day return from Listowel and 3s from Tralee. This afforded even the more modest members of Kerry society an opportunity to travel within the county. The development of rail transport in Kerry would have a major impact on the nature of sport there.

Kerry's Sporting Landscape Before the GAA

Sport in Kerry by the 1880s was influenced by both the ancient traditions of the countryside and the new games of the British Empire. Ireland, like Britain, witnessed an increasing trend towards the regulation and civilising of society as the nineteenth century progressed. In rural Ireland, traditional Irish fairs and festivals, such as the 'patterns' (festivals celebrating local patron saints), were in steady decline. They were often associated with heavy drinking, immorality, gambling, violence and other excess.[39] Patrick Begley, one of the founding members of the Laune Rangers GAA club in Killorglin in the 1880s, described how the traditional game of caid was often played at such fair and market days and the trouble that ensued from heavy blows inflicted on the field play, especially after the effects of cheap drink at 2d a pint.[40]

The Catholic Church in Ireland had experienced a profound revival. As the nineteenth century progressed, its rise to dominance in Irish society was one of the most striking features of post-Famine Ireland.[41] As in England, the Church sought to exert a far greater social control over its members and desired its congregations to be orderly, sober and respectable. The excesses of traditional celebrations were an obvious target, and zealous church officials were at the forefront of the campaign to destroy them.[42]

By the second half of the nineteenth century, the recreational element in rural life was disappearing. In addition, the entertainment element of fairs was giving way to more serious, commercial purposes. As in England, the development of free mass national school education further led to the increasing regulation of Irish society. The century also saw the development of the first professional police force in Ireland, the Royal Irish Constabulary, and its introduction contributed to a major decline in crime in the latter part of the century. Church and civil authority crusades to civilise Irish life spelt the death knell for many traditional forms of Irish sport. Even the old customary games of the Kerry peasantry, like hurling and caid, began falling into decline.

As with much of the south of Ireland, an ancient form of hurling called iomán was played in Kerry from at least the late seventeenth century.[43] The game allowed the ball to be handled or carried with a wooden ash stick and was played usually in summer.[44] Often this ball consisted of old hair plucked from cattle, carefully combed out, then steeped in water and rolled on the hands until it became perfectly round and quite hard. In the late 1700s, hurling enjoyed a boom period in the south and was sponsored on a semi-professional basis by some Anglo-Irish landlords who pitched their peasant hurling teams against those of neighbouring gentry.[45] This situation is strikingly familiar to the contemporary role the rural gentry played in England organising and maintaining cricket teams.[46] The O'Connells of Derrynane were one such family who patronised hurling in Kerry.[47] In Kilmoyley, tradition held that such contests originated in Ahabeg bog where young male tenants on the Crosbie estate met during the annual compulsory turf-cutting week in late spring and issued hurling challenges to the tenants of other parishes on the estate.[48] This early form of hurling was still popular into the early 1840s. The Halls describe one such match in south Kerry in 1841, with the teams being made up of fifty or sixty aside.[49]

By the mid-1800s, the disastrous effects of the Famine, coupled with the increasing regularisation of Irish life, had led to a catastrophic decline in hurling. This was heightened by the withdrawal of the gentry's patronage of the game. After the Famine, hurling retracted into a compact area in north Kerry bounded between the Casher, Feale and Smerlagh Rivers[50] and survived only in isolated regions such as Kilmoyley.[51] To this day that region represents the traditional heartland of Kerry hurling. It has long been questioned how the game survived in such a defined area within what became a Gaelic football-dominated sporting landscape. Kevin Whelan has shown that regions that have a traditional dominance of hurling in southern Ireland coincide with areas of level, well-drained terrain, seldom moving off the dry sod of a limestone rock bed, which also produces the best material for hurleys – ash. It is closely linked with distribution of big farms where a relatively comfortable lifestyle afforded the leisure time to pursue such games. The Halls in their description mentioned that the nature of the game required 'a level extensive plain'. Yet Whelan's theory needs much more detailed work if it is to be considered an accurate hypothesis for the survival of hurling in such defined areas. Nonetheless, there are aspects of his argument that can be observed around the traditional hurling areas of Kerry. Certainly, the hurling heartland of north Kerry coincides with some of the most fertile, level, well-drained and limestone-rich lands available in the county. For example, by 1881 40 per cent of the land holdings in the Tralee Poor Law Union and 39 per cent of land in the Listowel Union were valued at over £10. In contrast, the percentage of land valued similarly in the Cahersiveen and Dingle unions was 16 per cent and 23 per cent respectively. This indicates the better quality of land in north Kerry.[52]

Tenant farmers and labourers there had a more comfortable lifestyle and thus could afford the leisure time to play the traditional game even as late as the 1870s. In 1874, the *Tralee Chronicle* reported that the Kilmoyley hurlers had a 'great victory' against a team of the united parishes of Kilflynn, Abbeydorney and Killahin. In even more isolated parts of the county, hurling proved resilient and survived into the 1880s. Tomás O'Crohan described how on Christmas Day and throughout the Christmas season the islanders on the Great Blasket would play hurling matches on the strand.[53]

Caid, or 'rough and tumble', was the other traditional game popular with the Kerry peasantry. It used a ball made of farm animal skins with an inflated bladder within, giving it an oval shape.[54] If hurling was a summer game, caid was played in the winter months when the crops had been harvested off the fields.[55] Matches were usually played between teams of men from two neighbouring parishes, the ball being thrown up among them at an agreed central point. The game was played cross-country over fields and hedges, and tripping, pushing and wrestling or 'handi-grips' were all recognised methods used to try an impede the progress of opponents. Fast runners were often placed on the outside of the large crush of men wrestling for the ball to enable them to gain ground quickly when their side succeeded in moving the ball out to them. The winning team was the one that first managed to bring the ball 'home' to their own parish. The game evolved so that by the late 1870s contests were often confined within the boundaries of a field with even-numbered teams on both sides. Boughs of sally trees in the form of an arch became the goal into which the ball would be placed to register a score. This form was becoming increasingly popular in the Dingle Peninsula, as well as around Tralee and Killorglin.[56] As late as 1885 a team from Ballymacelligott was issuing challenges through the pages of the *Kerry Sentinel* for a match of football 'twenty one each side according to the Gaelic rules, or in rough and tumble, with any parish in the province of Munster'.[57] Agricultural prosperity helps to explain why, even though the games of hurling and caid were not as prevalent heading into the 1870s, they were still played on a relatively widespread basis across the county. However, the collapse of the agrarian economy in the late 1870s and the increasing politicisation of the Kerry peasants led to growing anti-landlord sentiment. Patronage collapsed and the time and energy which needed to be devoted to such games was unable to be sacrificed as the economic situation worsened. With the decline of such traditional sports, the codified creations of the Victorian age were able to enter the vacuum and gain a foothold among certain sections of Kerry society.

One sport that was rooted in the land and old traditions of rural society, but which had become increasingly affected by the Victorian sports revolution, was horse racing. Though its development from gentrified riding contest to a mass spectator sport had been ongoing before the advent of the Victorian age, by now horseracing had become one of the most popular pastimes shared by all classes throughout the British Isles. This was helped by the rise of literacy and the increasing phenomenon of dedicated sports papers in both countries.[58] By the 1890s, at least twelve newspapers chiefly concerned with sport were being published in Ireland. Many, such as *Sport* (an Irish weekly newspaper dedicated to sport and founded in 1880), dealt primarily with horse racing.[59] In 1790, Ireland set up its own governing body known as the Turf Club and started to publish the *Irish Racing Calendar*, detailing the courses in Ireland where meetings were held. Tralee was first mentioned in the publication in 1805.[60] The Tralee races continued throughout the century, lapsing in the 1860s only to be revived again at a track in Mount Hawke in October 1876. Due to agricultural depression, they again went into decline in 1879. However, *Sport*'s horse racing correspondent, 'Lux', was delighted to announce their revival, 'after having been allowed go into decay', in August 1884.[61] The first races held on the island track in Listowel were on 5/6 October 1858 and they continued to be held in late September or October into the 1880s. In Killarney, meetings had been held since the 1750s. Races were also reported in Ballyheigue, Dingle, Ballyduff, Ballylongford, Ballybunion and Abbeyfeale.[62] It was often the landed interest which sought to promote the sport in Kerry. For example, an advertisement for the Tralee Races in 1885 shows the prominent landlords Lord Kenmare, Lord Listowel and Lieutenant Colonel Edward Denny among the stewards, as was Sir Henry Donovan, head of one of the largest firms in the town.[63]

As in England, the development of railways was vital to the success of horse racing. Race tracks were established in towns that were serviced by rail lines, such as Tralee, Killarney, Listowel and Abbeyfeale. The opening of the Tralee to Limerick line in 1880 was a massive boost to the race meeting in Listowel. The railway companies were quick to see the benefits to their business due to horse meetings. The L&W railway company advertised special trains at special return rates leaving Tralee for the Abbeyfeale meeting in 1888. Horse racing seems to have been the only pre-Victorian sport that continued to be relatively little impacted by the economic, cultural and political changes affecting Kerry society in the 1880s. Other sports like hunting were not as lucky. Growing land agitation and pressure from the local Land League forced the popular Milltown hunt club to be disbanded in 1881. At a meeting of the Listowel National League a resolution was put to members to oppose and boycott fox hunting by gentry in the area.

Another introduction into the sporting landscape of Kerry was cricket. The *Annual Handbook of Cricket in Ireland 1871* showed Kerry was one of the last counties to establish a cricket club some time within the previous two years.[64] Studies suggest the spread of the game in many counties was due to a combination of the influence of locally garrisoned British regiments and the sons of local gentry returning from their studies at Trinity or English colleges, bringing back knowledge of the game and organising teams among tenants on their own estates.[65] In Tipperary, Kilkenny and Westmeath, cricket appeared to have been a relatively popular and widely played game among the rural population, at least up until economic collapse in the late 1870s. There is little evidence for such widespread popularity in Kerry. A survey of the *Sentinel* from 1885 to 1890 shows only eleven county combinations of teams involved in matches.[66] This is in contrast to forty-three club teams recorded in Tipperary by 1876. Yet the evidence seems to confirm that the spread of the game was similar in Kerry to that in Tipperary and Kilkenny. The gentry's influence can be seen in the fact that Colonel Denny lined out on the County Kerry Amateur Athletic and Cricket Club (CKAACC) team which played

Killorglin in September 1885.[67] The military influence is also
apparent from the match report, as it is stated Killorglin, though
victorious, 'made a complaint that they had to play a combination
team of the military and County of Kerry Club in place of the
County Kerry team as arranged'.

The Killarney Cricket Club, founded in April 1887, had Lord
Kenmare as patron and rented their grounds from him. As was the
case in England, local gentry often patronised teams made up of
their tenants. Such an example could be seen to survive the fraught
tenant–landlord relations in Kerry in the 1880s when a match
between a pre-existing Killarney cricket team and Major Henderson's
XI came off in the lawn opposite the major's residence in Glenflesk.
It was reported that Killarney played two match tests with the
Middlesex Regiment stationed in Buttevant, Cork in 1888.[68] This
again can be seen as the influence of English regiments spreading
the game by playing teams within travelling distance. The Anglo-
American Cable Company Cricket Club and Valentia Atlantic Cable
Company are both reported as being involved in cricket games in the
county.[69] This shows that employees of the foreign companies had
begun to set up clubs in the area, possibly teaching locals how to
play to augment numbers. The Valentia Cable Company was willing
to pay rent for a nearby field to have a permanent pitch.[70] In the
case of Tipperary, the popularity of cricket was due to the prosperity
and stability the county enjoyed in the 1870s. This allowed tenant
farmers the financial freedom and leisure time to devote to the game.
With the collapse of the rural economy in the 1880s, the game there
was devastated. While cricket may have been more popular in the
1870s in Kerry, the small number of clubs shows it was never
seriously taken up by the rural peasantry. By the turbulent 1880s,
the game had become confined principally to the gentry and military
elements in the county.

The game of rugby began to make an appearance in Kerry in
the 1880s, spreading among the larger towns.[71] Tralee Rugby Club
was founded in 1882. It seems to have been the only club in the
county to become officially affiliated to the sport's new governing
body, the Irish Rugby Football Union (IRFU).[72] It was the only
Kerry club mentioned in the 1880s as taking part in the Munster
Senior Cup, which was first held in 1886.[73] Dr John Hayes of

Tralee Rugby Football Club (RFC) seems to have been Kerry's star player throughout the 1880s. When the Munster interprovincial team was picked for their clash with Ulster in January 1889, Hayes was selected in the starting fifteen.

Based on newspaper reports of the *Sentinel* and *Sport* in the 1885–90 period, there is evidence of seven separate teams or clubs playing matches between themselves and clubs outside the county.[74] It is clear there were enough enthusiasts in Tralee to form two teams from members of Tralee Rugby Club: the Emmentines and the Unicorns, who played a match in February 1885.[75] With the exception of Listowel and Castleisland, most of the large towns in the county had a rugby team of some sort by the mid-1880s. How the game spread through Kerry is difficult to establish with accuracy. Certainly in the case of the Killarney rugby team one of its star players, 'The MacGillycuddy of the Reeks', had learned the game playing with Trinity College and Cambridge University. It is possible, just as was often the experience in Britain, that former pupils of such institutions, once they moved home, brought with them knowledge of the sport to local men in the area. Similar circumstances may explain the growth of the game in towns like Tralee. Medical graduates like Hayes, who attended university, were likewise introduced to the game.[76] When they returned home they took with them knowledge of the sport and were influential in setting up teams among the enthusiastic young men of their social circle. Another factor in the spread of the game comes from a report in the *Tralee and Killarney Echo* of what appears to have been a rugby match between the crew of the war steamer *Racoon* and a team from the island of Valentia.[77] It is possible, given the presence of the Anglo-American Cable Company on the island from the 1860s onwards, that British employees of the company, familiar with the game, introduced it to some of the islanders to form a team. This is further supported by Patrick Begley who, in writing about the formation of Laune Rangers, stated that when the club played rugby they beat 'the telegraphers in Valencia'.[78]

Another reason for rugby's spread was that both it and the traditional game of caid shared similar characteristics. Early descriptions of rugby are very similar to those of caid. Both games involved running with the ball in hand and scrimmages of men attempting to gain possession of the ball before passing to the more fleet-footed players hovering on the wings. Likewise, both were played with an oval football. It seems likely that the rules for rugby as they evolved were having an increasing effect on caid. More and more areas began to forgo the cross-country element and, due to the influence of rugby, played the game within a set boundary of a field against evenly numbered teams. This could be a plausible explanation as to why a team like Laune Rangers was formed to take up the sport.

In addition to horse racing, rugby and cricket, athletics was also popular in Kerry. On Tuesday 17 June 1884, the CKAACC held its annual athletics meeting at the sports ground in Tralee. The attendance was described as 'extremely large', and in addition to the grandstand being packed with the upper class of Kerry society, the working and rural classes took up their positions inside the wooden palisade of the grounds to watch the events. Yet athletics in its formative years in Ireland was mostly confined to the military and gentry. As Paul Rouse observed, the Irish peasantry were initially condemned to remain behind the ropes of the Victorian sporting revolution and watch their class betters participate on the field. Mass participation in sport remained poor in the Irish countryside. The tenant farmers, labourers and shop assistants who crowded into Tralee Sportsground to witness athletics would see men like R.D. Dobson, who won the open mile bicycle race, competing. His family ran Dobson and Co. Seedsmen and Implement Agents in Castle Street, Tralee. He was captain of Tralee RFC in 1885 and also played on the Tralee cricket team. In 1887, he was on the committee of the CKAACC and was also a member of Tralee Bicycle Club. J.E. Hussey, son of the notorious land agent Sean Hussey (one of the wealthiest men in the county), was another star of this athletics meeting, winning the long jump and quarter-mile bicycle race. Such men represented an elite, possessing the leisure time and financial security to compete seriously at athletics. Opportunities for any but the most talented sportsmen from the Irish peasant and lower middle classes were rare, an exception being John Patrick O'Sullivan, the legendary Laune Rangers captain who would become one of the greatest Irish athletes of the 1880s and early 1890s. However, the mass of Kerry's population remained untouched by the 'sporting revolution', while traditional games further declined. This situation would soon change and the man responsible was Michael Cusack. Through his new organisation, the GAA, the manner in which formal sports clubs were organised in Kerry became emblematic of who would play the games in the coming decades. This was a movement for the many, not the few.

The Arrival of the GAA: The Tralee GAA Sports, 17 June 1885

On 1 November 1884 at Hayes' Hotel, Thurles, County Tipperary Michael Cusack presided over a meeting to establish the Gaelic Athletic Association for the Preservation and Cultivation of

The Trinity Rugby Team. Second from left in the front row is Michael Cusack. Though by 1884 committed to the preservation of Ireland's indigenous Gaelic games and a staunch advocate of opening up Irish athletics to the ordinary Irishman, this photo illustrates that for most of his sporting life Cusack was in fact an Anglophile who enthusiastically participated in various sports that had evolved in Britain during the Victorian Sports Revolution. *(Courtesy of Special Collections and Archives, James Hardiman Library, NUI Galway)*

National Pastimes. As a young man he had been a successful athlete in his own right and by the early 1880s was a familiar and respected athletics official on the Dublin sports circuit. Cusack justified the need for such an organisation, stating that, increasingly in Irish athletics,

> . . . labourers, tradesmen, artisans and even policemen and soldiers [are] . . . excluded . . . The law is that all athletic meetings shall be held under the rules of the Amateur Athletics Association of England . . . the management of nearly all the meetings held in Ireland since has been entrusted to persons hostile to the dearest aspirations of the Irish people. Every effort has been made to make meetings look as English as possible – foot-races, betting and flagrant cheating being their most prominent features.[79]

Prior to the establishment of the GAA Irish athletics had no governing body; rather, events where occasionally run under the laws of the English Amateur Athletics Association (AAA). By the early 1880s, Ireland saw a growing tendency for local, traditional athletics meetings being supplanted by meetings run by clubs under the auspices of the AAA. These new formalised athletics meetings increasingly excluded the ordinary athlete from high-level competition. For example, a 'mechanics' clause in the rules of athletics competitions before 1882 specifically barred 'all mechanics, artisans or day labourers' from events in Ireland.[80] Cusack 'abhorred' this tendency of sporting organisations moving towards elitism. As more and more athletics meetings across Ireland became organised under AAA rules, he resolved to act.

Cusack, it is argued, saw the increasing anglicisation of Irish sport as part of a deliberate plan to spread British cultural imperialism. This may seem hypocritical given that as late as 1882 Cusack himself was a fully fledged member of the 'Anglocentric world' of sport in Dublin. Indeed, for several years few Irishmen seemed as committed to participating in and promoting English sports as Cusack. Not only did he play cricket during his time as a teacher in Blackrock College but when he set up his own school in 1877 he founded a rugby team and acted as both trainer and secretary, as well as playing in the forwards. What brought about the dramatic rejection of English games in favour of the establishment of a native sporting organisation to promote both Irish athletics and traditional pastimes is difficult to ascertain. Certainly the political backdrop of the early 1880s, with the unfolding Land War crisis and the real possibility of Irish legislative independence, was a factor.[81] Another motivation may have been Cusack's dubious talent for creating enemies everywhere. As Paul Rouse has commented, Cusack was more properly born to serve on a one-man committee.[82] As abrasive as he was brilliant, Cusack's inability to work with others may have had a significant bearing on his decision not to try to reform athletics from within, but rather to create and run his own organisation to take control of popular athletics in Ireland.

In any event, by 1884 Cusack was endeavouring to found a body that would open up organised sport to the ordinary Irish man and play a central role in creating and sustaining a new, distinct Irish identity.[83] He enlisted the support of Maurice Davin, who was perhaps Ireland's first internationally famous athlete. With Davin's help, he organised the first meeting of what would become the GAA. The assembly in Thurles was a small affair with between seven and thirteen present.[84] The meeting did little bar establish the Gaelic Athletic Association in name and request the patronage of Charles Stewart Parnell, Michael Davitt and Archbishop T.W. Croke.[85] However, through securing the support of these three pillars of Irish Catholic nationalist society in the 1880s (land, Church and political), Cusack ensured his new body would automatically have the attention of Irish nationalist opinion.

On 27 December 1884, a second meeting of the GAA was held in Cork. At this meeting a local group of prominent home rulers, along with some Irish Republican Brotherhood (IRB) members, attended. The IRB was a secret revolutionary organisation dedicated to the overthrow of British rule in Ireland.[86] Both they and the Irish Party saw potential in this new organisation and sought to gain influence within its ranks. At this meeting the IPP succeeded in getting a resolution adopted drafting the entire organising committee of its National League organisation onto the GAA's executive committee. Though it was never acted upon, the motion began to arouse suspicion among others involved in Irish athletics that the GAA had a more political aim than merely an interest in the cultural revival of native pastimes.

As 1885 dawned, rival parties became unnerved by the rapid progress Cusack's association was making; within ten days of its formation it had held the first athletics meeting under its auspices. In January, the GAA announced that after St Patrick's Day no athlete would be allowed to compete in a GAA event if they had already competed elsewhere under the rules of another athletics body.[87] Five days later the Irish Cyclist Association (ICA) met and one delegate called on Irish athletes to unite 'to quash' the GAA.[88] It is easy to understand the fury of delegates when someone who until recently had been part of their clique was now suddenly striking out on his own and attempting to pull the rug of Irish athletics from under their feet. This was only exasperated by the fact that several prominent athletics club representatives in Dublin had a personal dislike for Cusack over past disagreements. In response to the GAA's draconian legislation, athletics club representatives gathered in Dublin on 21 February 1885 and formed the Irish Amateur Athletics Association (IAAA), with John Dunbar as its honorary secretary, to contest the GAA's claim for control of Irish athletics.[89] The war to govern Irish athletics had begun. Cusack had already decided on the first battleground on which to fight the IAAA and it would be Tralee, County Kerry.

Cusack planned to use local nationalist support in Tralee to fix a GAA athletics event on the same day that the local CKAACC had advertised for their annual sports, Wednesday 17 June 1885. Cusack chose the town as a show of strength against the anti-GAA body for several reasons. Kerry was an area known for considerable cooperation between nationalists and unionists in sport. In Tralee, the CKAACC committee included among its members the local landlord Colonel Denny and his two sons, along with Edward Harrington, president of Tralee's National League and editor of the nationalist *Kerry Sentinel*.

Another reason was that the CKAACC had hoped to remain neutral in the battle for the supremacy of Irish athletics.[90] An explanation as to why the Tralee club decided not to affiliate with the IAAA was due to their past experience with its secretary, John Dunbar. Dunbar had been the official handicapper at their annual games in 1883. He had, however, been deemed unsatisfactory due to his arriving late and then leaving to catch the train back to Dublin when the event was little more than halfway completed. The following year another handicapper was employed and Dunbar, taking offence, had travelled to Tralee and at the sports was heard to remark that 'he would take good care the Kerry fellows should not win anything in Limerick'. The next day several Kerry club members travelled to compete at the Limerick athletics, at which he officiated as official handicapper. They subsequently 'much to their astonishment found themselves handicapped out of everything'.[91] This event had naturally soured the relationship between Dunbar and the Tralee club. Munster at this time was seen as the traditional powerhouse of Irish athletics. Clubs such as the Limerick AA, Queen's College Athletics Club, Cork, and Mallow Athletics Club were among the first to affiliate with the IAAA. Tralee was thus the largest athletics centre in this vital province for the control of Irish athletics, which had remained neutral.

Meanwhile, the Tralee Sportsground (on the site of the present-day Austin Stack Park) was widely regarded as among the finest in the country. *Sport* claimed Tralee 'possesses the best ground in all of Ireland', which was much larger than even Lansdowne or Ballsbridge. The CKAACC committee, backed by such wealthy men as Colonel Denny and Sir Henry Donovan, had been able to raise an estimated £1,200 to develop the ground. During the first months of 1885, the committee had begun laying down a cinder track for foot and cycling events and a new stand and palisade was being erected. For Cusack, Tralee presented a fantastic opportunity for a show of strength. If a GAA-organised event could mobilise popular sentiment to usurp such a previously successful athletics meeting courted by a rival body in one of the premier grounds in Ireland, the future success of his organisation could be secured.

Through his column in *United Ireland*, Cusack began to rigorously promote his rival GAA meeting.[92] Enlisting local nationalist support, he proudly proclaimed that in the National League rooms in Tralee a meeting was held to establish the first branch of the association in Kerry. Cusack boasted that the meeting declared it would boycott the CKAACC event 'under the auspices of the selfish foreign faction'. The members also pledged that any person patronising the event was 'not worthy of the name Irishman'.[93] The principal men who formed this branch and acted as promoters for the GAA event included prominent local members of the National League such as the old Fenian and Land Leaguer William Moore Stack and local IRB officers Batt O'Connor Horgan, Michael Power and Maurice Moynihan.[94] Edward Harrington, a promoter of the CKAACC sports, was incredulous at this action. Harrington was a prominent constitutional nationalist, having been elected as the first president of the Tralee branch of the National League when it was formed. He strongly believed that sport had no role as some 'political football' within the League.[95]

In his editorials in the *Sentinel*, Harrington began to attack a certain section of local nationalists for establishing the GAA to boycott the CKAACC sports and using 'vindictiveness under the name of sport to injure men who for no political or party reason had invested their money in providing a recreative and pleasant amusement ground for all classes of Tralee'. In response to the boycott, the local gentry did all in their power to hinder the event. When Horgan, elected president of the Tralee GAA, 'had the audacity' to apply at a petty sessions hearing in Tralee for an occasional licence to have alcohol sold at their event Sir Henry Donovan, the current president of the CKAACC, was able to use his power as chair of the sessions to deny such a licence.[96]

Cusack travelled to Tralee a week before the event to enlist the support of the local clergy, including Fr M. McMahon, parish priest of Boherbee, and to help the local GAA promote their meeting. As a result, the GAA sports, held in Rathonane near the present-day Greyhound track, proved an extraordinary success. *United Ireland* reported:

> Money was subscribed most liberally . . . Not counting those who entered for hurling and football, the entries amounted to the unprecedentedly large number of four hundred and sixty four. On the morning of the sports the people came swarming and trooping in from every part of the country . . . Every mode of conveyance would seem to

have been utilised and when neither vehicle or [*sic*] beast of burden was available the people walked in . . . Every artery of the town poured its stream of human life into the great tide which flowed noiselessly towards the hurling ground in Rathonane paddock.[97]

The *Kerry Weekly Reporter* commented that all 'the varied attractions of the [County Kerry] A.A. & C.C. could not bring together attendance, whereas the concourse assembled to witness the Gaelic sports was countless'.[98] It was stated that upwards of 10,000 people had attended.[99] That same evening at Ahamore outside Tralee, a hurling match was organised by the local GAA featuring the townlands of Rattoo and Kilury versus Abbeydorney and Killahan, each team comprising twenty-five men aside.[100]

The CKAACC sports, in contrast, were a financial disaster, with only a few hundred of the local gentry and their associates attending the events. The *Kerry Evening Post* reported:

The attendance on the ground was not at all what it should have been, though the large stand was well filled with the elite of the county. Outside the stand, however, there was a marked absence of the public who usually support the Athletic Meeting. This was caused no doubt by the action of those men who wished to merge athletic meeting into political meetings and who held opposition sports on the same day. So well had those men stumped the county putting false issues before the people, that though thousands of country folk entered town that day, they were drawn away to the opposition sports by the strain of a few brass instruments and the shrill fifes playing national airs. As an example of the issues placed before the country people, I can vouch for the fact that one fair maid from the country was heard asking another of her class whether she was going to the Protestant sports or the Daniel O'Connell sports. It should be also mentioned that a vast amount of intimidation was also introduced to prevent the people from attending the sports and it was really ridiculous to see some prominent

members of the opposition standing on the road leading
to the club grounds with a notebook and pencil taking
down the names of those proceeding to the sports. This
kind of intimidation . . . was calculated to do a great deal
of harm.[101]

We can see that the local GAA organisers and Cusack himself were
not above intimidation or playing on sectarianism to ensure the
success of the Rathonane event. From this position of strength the
local GAA continued to flex its muscles. John Stack, president of
the Listowel National League, held a meeting on 27 June 1885 to
establish a GAA branch there. Over the next two months, athletics
events under the GAA were held in Listowel, Castleisland and
Killarney, where the meeting opened with a hurling match between
the men of Kenmare. Early events in Kerry thus followed a similar
pattern to the rest of the country in the formative years of the
GAA. The rules of hurling and football, though published in
January 1885, remained ambiguous. It was far easier to organise
athletics meetings that had more standardised and accepted rules
governing them. Cusack's ambition to secure the GAA's
permanence in athletics meant that initially football and hurling
played only a secondary role to athletics events.[102]

Following on from the astounding success of the Tralee sports,
the GAA swiftly gained control of popular athletics at a provincial
level as the IAAA retreated to its urban strongholds of Dublin and
Belfast. Throughout the remainder of the summer, the vast
majority of sports meetings reported in the national press were run
by the GAA.[103] At an IAAA meeting that November it was
reported that 150 athletics events had been held under the auspices
of the GAA that year.[104] The IAAA could not hope to match such
popularity. Though it would continue to exist as a formal body
for another thirty-seven years, it would never again seriously
challenge the dominance of the GAA's control of Irish athletics on
a national level.[105] However, the events of 17 June 1885 would also
have another lasting effect on the association. In the aftermath, a
local political dispute developed into a national controversy whose
fallout led to the official link between the National League and the
GAA being permanently severed.

At a meeting of the Tralee National League a week after the event, Edward Harrington was stripped of its presidency and expelled from the branch. He was accused of using his paper to promote landlord games in deference to nationalist attempts to support traditional Irish sports. At the meeting, Batt Horgan, president of Tralee GAA, stated that Harrington had come to Tralee as a stranger and the people of the town had lifted him on their shoulders, but by his writings in the paper 'he had kicked the ladder by which he had ascended'.[106] In this it is easy to detect a streak of jealousy at the popularity of Harrington, especially among the older nationalists and IRB element which made up the GAA opposition to the CKAACC sports. In *The Freeman's Journal*, Harrington defended his actions, stating he

> . . . declines to [associate with] . . . those men who, he alleges, have organised this malicious conspiracy against him and the interests of his paper, merely because he tried to keep the League free from the introduction of irrelevant matter into it.[107]

In response, Cusack sent a letter to *Freeman's* editor declaring that on 20 October 1884 he canvassed Harrington to use both his personal and his paper's influence to support the revival of Irish games which Harrington had duly sworn to do. The following April Cusack again wrote to him and sent a copy of the new rules of the GAA but stated Harrington now 'took no notice whatever of me or the rules'.

The squabbles of local nationalists had quickly snowballed into a national debate played out on the pages of Ireland's nationalist press. This was probably inevitable since Edward's brother, Timothy Harrington, was a sitting MP and one of the most influential members of the Irish Party. Timothy wrote to the press to disclaim officially any link between the organising committee of the National League and the GAA. He stated they had never identified themselves with any athletics association and that those who had used the name of the National League in connection with the GAA 'have done so without authorisation and, as I believe, for personal purposes'. J.F. O'Crowley, the official handicapper of the GAA and a member of the National League, responded by saying that it took Harrington a long time to repudiate the connection between the two bodies. It was not until his brother 'had opposed the popular feeling had any attempt been made to do so'. The *Sentinel* next printed a letter from Archbishop Croke to Edward that stated: 'When I recommended the revival of our national sports, I had no idea of extending or even discouraging all other sports whatever, or any of them'. The next day the *Weekly Reporter* published a letter Cusack sent to Michael Power, the prominent local National League and GAA organiser. In it, Cusack stated he had discussed with Timothy Harrington the upcoming GAA event in Tralee. Cusack claimed Harrington described the crowd setting up the GAA event as no better than 'corner boys'. He also warned Cusack to 'beware of those getting up the Gaelic Sports in Tralee' and that if he really knew who the parties were he 'would have nothing to do with them'. In addition to political differences, it is possible to detect an element of class bias in these dismissive remarks. Harrington, an affluent businessman and politician, may have regarded the local GAA as little more than a playground for the baser elements of the county's lower class.

On 5 July 1885, matters came to a head at a National League meeting in Abbeydorney. Both Timothy and Edward Harrington attended and addressed the crowd. The *Weekly Reporter* described the attendance as split between hostile, friendly and neutral. When Edward rose to speak he could not be well heard owing to the constant booing of a section of the crowd. He was then stopped by the arrival of Power and other members of the Tralee National League. Power confronted Timothy Harrington about his comments in Cusack's letter. Harrington responded that the letter was 'a tissue of falsehood'. He asked why members of the Tralee League had stripped his brother of its presidency using the pretext of the GAA sports when Cusack had said his association belonged to no political organisation. In support of this argument, Harrington pointed to the example of a speech Cusack had recently given in Kingstown where he commenced by saying he belonged to no political organisation.[108] With this, the Harringtons left.

It seems that Harrington's local political leadership was resented by some Tralee nationalists. Many, like Stack and Power, were perturbed that their particular brand of physical-force nationalism was being usurped by 'blow-ins' from outside the county, taking control of popular national sentiment in Kerry. A general election was expected, and with the recent extension of the electorate nationalist candidates could be fully confident of significant success.[109] If his position as president of the Tralee branch was maintained, Edward would undoubtedly be one such candidate, as he enjoyed much popular support within the organisation in Kerry. The Harringtons had misjudged the popular sentiment the local IRB element had been able to galvanise behind the GAA event. They, however, knew well the dangerous potential of the IRB to monopolise nationalist movements and corrupt them into their own political aims. Yet Power, Stack and Horgan were guilty of even greater misjudgement. To dismiss the brother of the secretary of the Central Committee of the National League was naive, but to then disrupt a League rally in the secretary's presence was pure folly. On 13 July 1885, the Central Committee met in Dublin and dissolved the Tralee branch. Despite this, a resolution was passed by the branch unanimously stating its work should continue on as normal. At the meeting, its chairman, Thomas O'Rourke, stated it was their duty to propose election candidates for an upcoming County Convention and asked was it the job of the League to have 'candidates for Kerry manufactured by the League in Dublin'. In spite of this bullishness, it was clear that popular sentiment was against the local IRB-controlled branch. A letter from 'A Nationalist in Castleisland' to the editor of the *Evening Post* complained of the disgraceful treatment of Edward Harrington by them.[110] The lack of support in the county and isolation of the branch brought its members to their senses. On 30 August 1885, Stack announced the resignation of the entire executive of the Tralee League in order to elect new officers who would be recognised by the Central Committee. In early October, the branch was allowed to resume its meetings as it was once again 'in unison with the wishes and obedient to the dictates of the authority of the Central League'. At a further meeting later in the month, Harrington was re-elected president while a new executive was formed. The old officers such as Power and Stack where absent from the attendance of the newly formed branch.[111]

At the League's County Convention Edward Harrington was proposed and selected as the Irish Party candidate to contest the West Kerry seat in parliament in the upcoming general election. In the subsequent election, Kerry brought back a clean sweep of IPP candidates. In the West Kerry seat, Harrington won by an overwhelming majority. His popularity was such that when the results were confirmed all the houses in Tralee were brilliantly illuminated and the local Temperance and Boherbee Fife and Drum bands paraded the street till an early hour. This would not be the last time that success within the GAA did not equate with success in broader Irish politics.

Further, despite the success of the Kerry GAA sports in June 1885, by the following January the association there was dormant. Undoubtedly the effect on the local Tralee branch as a result of the fallout between the town's National League and Harrington was a factor. More importantly, the worsening economic climate and massive increase in agrarian disturbance meant that for the very people most receptive to the message of the GAA, harsh economic reality had taken over. For the next eighteen months the GAA remained stillborn in the county. Stack was among the delegates at the adjourned National Convention of the GAA in Thurles on 28 February 1886. However, this is the last reference to any Kerry delegate at a GAA convention until January 1888. Yet there was another interesting outcome to events. In June 1886, the annual CKAACC athletics were now run under the rules of the GAA and ICA.[112] But this is the only reference to any local GAA event in the *Sentinel* that year. Popular history holds that Dr Crokes was formed after a meeting between nineteen men in the town on 2 November 1886, though they did not affiliate with the GAA at the time.[113] The start of 1887 saw little Gaelic activity in the county. General Buller's campaign of coercion was taking effect and evictions where on the rise as the worsening economic climate continued unabated.[114] That summer the CKAACC again held its annual sports under GAA rules, with Frank Dineen, the GAA's national handicapper, present as handicapper along with Timothy O'Riordan, the joint secretary of the GAA.

O'Riordan was a Tralee man and worked as a reporter for the *Cork Herald*. It may well be due to his influence that the GAA's central executive decided to hold its third annual athletics sports in Tralee in late July. Preparations for the Tralee event began with both the GSWR and L&W railways offering extensive train arrangements for the two-day meeting held on 31 July and 1 August 1887. Hurling, football and tug of war competitions were arranged for the Sunday, while athletics and dancing events were held on the Monday. Both British and Irish athletes of renown were promised to be competing.[115] Around 3–4,000 people were in attendance on the Sunday but this fell to little over 2,000 on the Monday, despite the fine weather.[116] *Sport* remarked that this could be attributed to the admission price of 1s which 'was a rather prohibitive charge'.[117] The central executive was well represented on Sunday, with leading GAA officials P.T. Hoctor, J.E. Kennedy and F.R. Moloney attending along with the GAA's secretaries O'Riordan and John Wyse Power. The rise of J.P. O'Sullivan as a major athlete continued as he won the hop, step and jump event and some weight events. The lack of Gaelic activity in Kerry can be gauged from the fact that the hurling and football matches were contested by teams from Clare and Cork. In the hurling, St Finbar's club Cork played Cork National hurling club for a set of twenty-one silver medals, the latter winning 4-5 to 0-4. In the football, Clare's Newmarket-on-Fergus played out a 0-3 to 0-3 draw with the Lee football club.[118] Another indication that the GAA had not taken root in the county is suggested from a statement in the *Sentinel*. The paper regarded the fact that Sunday's crowd was seen as a disappointment as due to 'Sunday sports [being] . . . an innovation in Tralee and indeed, in any other part of Kerry and this, perhaps, was also another factor that militated against a really good attendance'. *Sport* described the meeting in athletics terms as a 'complete failure', stating that due to the remoteness of Tralee, none of the English athletes who attended the event in Dublin the previous year bothered to travel. However, the meeting was a success in one regard. *Sport* itself commented: '[W]e understood that one of the principal reasons for holding the meeting in Tralee was that it would be the means of stirring up and organising in the ranks of the GAA a county upon whose sons Nature has been particularly lavish in the matter of physical qualities.'[119]

The GAA in Kerry Reborn, 1887–1889

By this time, the IRB, who had supplied two of the original seven founding members of the GAA, had begun to infiltrate and gain control over its central executive. Though Cusack had been dismissed as secretary of the GAA in 1886, Maurice Davin remained on as president.[120] However, the IRB strength was such that P.T. Hoctor, who was a well-known Tipperary IRB official, was elected vice-president of the association in September 1886. Tensions between the IRB members under Hoctor and moderates under Davin grew. At an executive meeting in February 1887 the IRB succeeded in pushing through a raft of changes to the rules of the association, such as banning of RIC members from competing and a rule allowing members of the executive council to also become members of county committees.[121] This ostensibly meant that control of any county committees, which were restricted to seven members, could be exercised by the thirteen members of the executive if they so wished. On the back of this, an outraged Davin resigned, leaving the IRB to take full control of the governing level of the GAA. Timothy O'Riordan was part of this IRB faction on the executive and retained his place even after the special convention in January 1888, at which a compromise between moderates and the IRB was reached and Davin was re-elected president. Many of the original founders of the GAA in Tralee such as Maurice Moynihan and William Stack, along with other known IRB men in the town, like Thomas Slattery, acted as stewards for the central executive's athletics meeting held there in July 1887. It appears clear that the IRB-controlled executive had used this meeting to re-establish contact with the IRB/GAA element in Tralee with a view to reorganising the association on a county scale. O'Riordan, Hoctor and Kennedy, all IRB men, were reported as being the only members of the executive to stay on for Monday's event.

In this endeavour they were successful, and the first embers of a newly reorganised GAA began to flicker in the darkening winter months in Kerry. At the GAA's Annual Convention in Thurles on 9 November 1887, when the IRB attempted to take fully effective control over the body, no representatives were documented from Kerry. However, within days the Tralee branch of the GAA had been reorganised. Maurice Moynihan, the local

National League secretary, urged the necessity of establishing a branch in the town and 'thereby falling into line with the rest of athletic Ireland'. It was hoped the example they were setting would be followed throughout Kerry and 'that very soon a club would be in existence in every parish'.[122] The following month at a general meeting of the Gaelic club in Killarney affiliation to the GAA was discussed and John O'Leary, the honorary secretary, was authorised to contact Timothy O'Riordan in Cork to forward the names of the committee and the affiliation fee of 10s.

The new year finally saw the beginnings of a countywide spread of the association. In January 1888, Killarney officially affiliated as the Dr Crokes branch of the GAA, adopting orange and green as their colours.[123] The following month the members of the newly affiliated Tralee John Mitchels branch met to elect their officers. Thomas Slattery was elected the club's president with J. Burke as vice-president. Michael Hanlon was selected to be the club treasurer and Moynihan and P. Kennelly were appointed its honorary secretaries. That same month Slattery was provisionally appointed to the central executive of the GAA, having power to act as soon as at least five clubs from the county had affiliated. The following Sunday the county's first 'official' Gaelic football match was played at Rathass outside Tralee, when Mitchels met the Ashill Alderman Hoppers from Ballymacelligott in front of several thousand spectators.[124] As we have seen, the game of caid was popular in Ballymacelligott until at least 1885. Moynihan, being a Ballymacelligott native, possibly took a role in organising a Gaelic football team in the area which was among the first in the county. The spread of football was particularly strong in the Tralee–Castleisland region. In March, Mitchels played home and away fixtures with the newly established Castleisland Desmonds club. A sense of the pageantry and excitement that such matches brought for perhaps the first time in generations to parishes can be gleaned from the description of the return game in Tralee. The Castleisland players arrived into the town in a convoy of decorated horse cars, followed by their supporters, and were met by the Boherbee Fife and Drum band. The band then marched the team in parade through the town towards the sports field. They were followed by a large concourse of people who gathered to watch

Maurice Moynihan. The 'Godfather' of the GAA in Kerry. It was Moynihan's press campaigns during 1887–8 which led to the formation of the first county board and a countywide GAA structure in Kerry. In 1891, he was rewarded for this work by being appointed general secretary of the GAA. *(Courtesy of Liam Brosnan, Killarney)*

the throw-in at 3.15 p.m. Castleisland won by a goal to no score.[125]

Gaelic football began to spread, even into the previously traditional hurling regions that survived in south Kerry. In Kenmare, an 'exciting and well contested football match was played in a field near the town'. Some 5,000 spectators attended this game between Kenmare and Kilgarvan. The report in the *Sentinel* remarked that football here was 'an innovation on the more ancient use of the 'cummaun' at which the men of South Kerry were unmatched experts in days gone by'. Each side had seventeen men and the game lasted two hours, the final score reading an astonishing 2-17 for Kenmare to Kilgarvan's 0-16. Playing conditions in the early days of the GAA usually negated high-scoring games but perhaps the fewer numbers on each side, closer to the modern day fifteen, along with unfamiliarity of the rules and length of the contest, allowed for such impressive scoring. However, hurling was quick to reorganise itself in the area. In September 1888, a large meeting was held in Kenmare to affiliate officially a hurling club with the GAA.[126]

The same month, in conjunction with the CKAACC, a GAA athletics meeting was held in the Tralee Sportsground. The railways were contacted to provide cheap excursion rates for trains heading to Tralee from Limerick, Killarney and Killorglin. The admission price to the event was 6d for the ground and a further 6d for the stand. An 'immense concourse' attended entertained by the Kilmoyley brass band. The schedule included sixteen athletics events for various prizes. For example, J.P. O'Sullivan won the hop, step and jump and was presented with a silver cup. He also won the football place kick and received a silver medal. In addition, the new strength of the GAA in the county was demonstrated when a football match between two teams from the county was part of the programme. Dr Crokes and Mitchels played for a silver cup with Tralee winning 0-6 to 0-1. Familiarity with the finer points of the sport spread slowly, however, with the *Sentinel* stating that both teams were 'evidently deficient in the rules'. The success of this locally organised GAA event prompted Maurice Moynihan to take a more active role in organising the association in the county. He began his campaign through the pages of the *Sentinel*, which by now had resolved its differences with the local GAA to become the official organ of the association in the county. In a letter to its editor, he wrote:

> Our county is one of the most, if not the most, backward in Ireland in the ranks of the Gaelic Athletic Association. There were two causes at least in operation to which may be traced this deplorable result and those were emigration and moonlighting . . . [they] are the twin offspring of landlordism, for as surely have our kith and kin been banished by the infernal system so likewise have its crimes

caused our downtrodden peasantry to turn like the trampled worm and have recourse to the wild and foolish and impolite methods which have unfortunately for some time obtained. Moonlighting begot a diseased and unsettled state of society and there was little chance of popularising the Gaelic Athletic Association in Kerry, or placing it in [*sic*] anything like a firm footing. This great evil has now happily died out and the reaction has long since set in; and though the normal condition of the public mind has not yet been fully restored, there seems an opportunity of planting the seeds of the GAA and of getting Kerry to fall in line with the rest of athletic Ireland.[127]

In October 1888, a locally run National Monument Fund tournament in aid of nationalist memorials for Glasnevin cemetery attracted a large attendance to Tralee to witness the hurlers of Kilmoyley play Ballyduff. Afterwards, the newly constituted Laune Rangers football club from Killorglin played Ashill. The *Sentinel* described Rangers as dominating the game and winning 1-4 to no score, helped by the team refusing to let Ashill players play in their bare feet. Members of the Mitchels club had organised the event and at a subsequent meeting they reported that, after paying the Cork Barracks Street Band £15 to entertain the crowds, they had £18 10s of profit from the event to forward to the monuments committee. Buoyed by the success of the event, Moynihan again issued a rallying cry to the Gaels of Kerry:

A short time ago you gave publication to a letter of mine on the above subject and I am glad to say that it bore a considerable share of fruit. Our county is, however, still backward in Gaelic matters . . . There are at present the requisite number of clubs, namely, fifteen, affiliated to entitle the formation of a County Board and with that end in view I am, with the authority of our local committee here, issuing circulars to the different clubs to send delegates to the County Convention arranged to be held at the rooms of the Young Ireland Society, Tralee on

Wednesday, the 7th November. There is no reason, however, why we should rest satisfied with the bare number necessary to establish a governing body, especially when, I think, there are many parishes which only merely want to have the way pointed out to them to put themselves into line . . . When Ireland's National pastimes had died out, or were dragging out a lingering existence in other counties, the manly games of hurling and football were being actively cultivated in many parts of Kerry. Shall it be said then that when there is a general revival all over Ireland, Kerry is the only county which gives a faint and half-hearted answer to the call! . . . I would say to the young men of Kerry, join the ranks of the Gaelic Athletic Association . . . Do it because it is your duty; do it out of pride; do it for any motive, because it is an association which deserves well of the people and because it is at present a great force and is bound to become a much greater one in the athletic, social and political life of this country. There are Dingle, Castlegregory, Annascaul, Keel, Milltown, Firies, Currans, Scartaglin, Brosna, Knocknagoshel, Ballybunion, Ardfert and other places in which there ought to be no difficulty in forming clubs if only one or two men in each place put the task before them . . . I hope this action will be taken immediately as there is not a single day to lose.

At this first Annual County Convention of the Kerry GAA the *Sentinel* reported that the congregation bore testimony 'to the fact Kerry has awoken from its lethargy and that the speedy and successful development of the GAA throughout its every parish may be safely counted on'. Delegates arrived from nineteen separate clubs. Thomas Slattery was elected chairman of the new Kerry County Board, while Maurice Moynihan was elected as secretary. On Moynihan's motion, it was decided that the county be divided into five districts: North, South, East, West and Mid Kerry. A county board committee of eight members was elected comprising of delegates from each district.[128] In December, Laune Rangers and Tralee played home and away fixtures. An enormous crowd was reported at the first match to witness Rangers winning 2-3 to 0-1. The *Sentinel* proclaimed that nobody 'can fail to perceive the vast strides that have been made, even in Kerry, both as regards discipline and the science of play, during the short time that has elapsed since the association was practically introduced into the "Kingdom"'. However, the speed of the association's advance was not quick enough for some. 'A would be member of the GAA (if he got the chance)' complained of the lack of GAA branches in the Iveragh barony.[129]

Despite a degree of unevenness in its initial spread, the GAA in Kerry had witnessed remarkable growth. In the space of twelve months, the number of affiliated clubs had risen to nineteen. Assisted by the central executive under Hoctor and O'Riordan, Moynihan, the county secretary of the Kerry IRB,[130] had spearheaded the revival of the association in the county. It was no surprise that Kerry's first elected representatives to the GAA's Annual Convention in 1888 were the IRB officers Moynihan and Slattery. The IRB influence is further evidenced by the timing of the development of the association in Kerry. The period of its most rapid growth between late 1887 and summer 1890 was the exact time when the IRB had managed to gain total control over the GAA's executive.[131] Though the moderates under Davin and the IRB under Hoctor had been able to compromise and work in an uneasy alliance throughout 1888, events by the end of the year altered matters.[132] At the Annual Convention for 1888, which was held on 23 January 1889, Davin was personally held responsible for the GAA's dire financial situation.[133] The meeting split and some thirty delegates, many clerical, left to set up a rival meeting. The main body, deciding Davin had resigned, elected Peter Kelly, an IRB officer from Loughrea, as president. *Sport* reported that Slattery, along with some others, then entered the rival meeting but were told by its chair, Fr E. Sheehy, '[we] won't have Kerry Moonlighters here'. The Kerry delegates then left to rejoin the main meeting.[134] What is interesting to note is why Fr Sheehy used the term 'moonlighters'. It is possible he was referencing the particular politics that the Kerry delegates subscribed to, which would be better serviced by remaining under the IRB-dominated executive. The fallout from this convention led to a split within the GAA, with several counties severing their links with the executive. The clergy began to turn its back on the

League of the Cross Dingle Brass Band. The band was affiliated to one of the first GAA clubs in Dingle, which shared its name. A sense of the pageantry and excitement Gaelic contests brought to rural Ireland can be gleaned from the image of bands such as this accompanying parading teams to grounds and entertaining the crowds between matches. *(Courtesy of Fr Jackie McKenna and Seán Mac an tSíthigh)*

IRB-dominated association. Kerry, however, remained loyal to the executive and declared as much at a subsequent county board meeting. The year 1889 represented the strongest yet for the GAA in Kerry, with thirty-three clubs listed as affiliated that November.[135]

Both Marcus de Búrca and W.F. Mandle have argued that Kerry represents a perfect example of where IRB influence from above was the major factor in the spread of the GAA in the county. They highlight its relative weakness there before 1888, compared with its sudden transformation into a bastion of the association by the end of 1889.[136] Such an argument implies that the growth of the GAA is inextricably linked to the spread of the IRB within the county. While no doubt many of the leading officials within the county board had links to the secret organisation, many other officials, and more importantly rank and file members, had none.[137] An RIC report in February 1888 states that in Kerry the IRB were practically limited to Tralee, Listowel, Killarney and Castleisland.[138] This does not help explain how the GAA spread across the rest of the county.

The economic situation was a major factor. After the disasters of the 1886 harvest, an upturn in the agricultural sector started in 1888 and continued until 1890 as cattle prices rose and the market for Irish beef expanded in Britain. Coupled with the economic growth was the political situation. The introduction of the Perpetual Crimes Act across Ireland to quell agrarian violence had a telling effect on Kerry. By mid-1887, the majority of the county had become far quieter as land agitation was curbed. The National League was proclaimed and lost much of its political force. A calmer countryside and, more importantly, one with rising incomes for tenant farmers, labourers and, by extension, town traders and white collar workers meant people had more time and financial freedom to become involved with Gaelic sports. Moynihan, in his first letter to the *Sentinel*, makes reference to the fact that the economic situation was the main factor negating the development of the association there. Despite IRB influence, it was unlikely the GAA in Kerry would have witnessed such growth if the economic and political climate had remained so unstable.

The formation of GAA clubs was a far more complex and varied process than the arguments that branches of the association were little more than fronts for IRB organisation which, until relatively recently, have been prevalent among some historians. Modern sport in Ireland, as elsewhere, 'was a product of modernisation' and in the case of the GAA it was both a reaction against and consequence of this process.[139] As with other sports in the Victorian era, the newly codified games of Gaelic football and hurling were spread through similar processes. For example, the role of publicans has been identified as vitally important to the establishment and spread of soccer in urban centres in England, with clubs such as Tottenham Hotspur and Manchester United being just two examples. Publicans likewise played an important role in establishing Gaelic clubs in Kerry. The president of Dr Crokes, C.W. Courtney, was a publican, as was one of its committee members, P. Spillane.[140] It is stated that the initial discussion to form a GAA club in the town happened in O'Mahoney's public house on College Street. By 1890, the role of publicans had become so great that the RIC were reporting that the association in Kerry, then in decline, was only being kept alive as a result of their efforts.[141]

Evidence of a diffusionist model which has been used in Britain to help explain the spread of sports like rugby can also be seen in Kerry. A fascinating insight into how one of the most famous football clubs in the early years of the GAA was formed can be gleaned from the letter written by Patrick Begley about the formation of his own club in Killorglin. Though originally the game of 'rough and tumble' was prevalent in the district, this gave way to rugby, which was played by a local club calling itself the Laune Rangers from at least 1885. Later an attempt was made to start a Gaelic club in the town among the young men, but the real impetus to form a properly affiliated club came when two teachers from Dublin arrived:

> In 1886 Father Lawlor built six new schools, three male and three female. The next move was to find staff of teachers . . . and among the teachers selected were two young men, just finished training in Dublin, whose names were Jack Murphy and Tom Cronin. During their training in Dublin those two young men were playing members of the Erin's Hope club and they had learned all the rules and tricks of the game. When they came to Killorglin what did they find, but the game was rugby. They saw there was a Gaelic club in name only and some teachers playing rugby . . . So, wholeheartedly, but after weeks of debate, it was decided rugby would be dropped and that they would join the Gaelic club, already existing. A general meeting was

Erin's Hope Football Team, Dublin County Champions, 1887. Tom Cronin (middle row, second from right) and Jack Murphy (front row, second from right) were responsible for the establishment of Laune Rangers GAA club when they took up teaching positions in Killorglin. *(Courtesy of Dónal McAnallen)*

called . . . J.P. O'Sullivan was to be captain and Bill O'Brien secretary and the two new teachers were to give instructions of the rules. All were invited to turn out and train.[142]

The team itself played its first official game in the Monuments tournament in October 1888.[143] The spur of new teachers, bringing with them knowledge of the rules and nuances of the game from the highly successful Erin's Hope club (the St Patrick's training college football team), was the catalyst that led to adoption of the game among the young men of the town and the abandonment of the rugby code. The role of young men educated in the larger city educational institutions and bringing knowledge of the game to the localities where they were assigned can also be seen in the example of Reenard GAA. Pat McGillicuddy of Reenard was also on the

Erin's Hope team that won the first Dublin football championship in 1887. After his studies, he returned to become principal of Knockeens National School in 1890 and immediately set about organising Gaelic football in the locality. It is interesting to note that the club first affiliated and took part in the county championship that year.[144] These new coaches often gave their teams a distinct tactical advantage. In Patrick Begley's description of Rangers' first game against Ashill, he states that they had fifteen well-trained rugby men while 'Ballymac were spoiling each other by too much bunching around the ball'. Evidently they were still unsure of the rules of the new game and reverted back to the old tactics of caid while Rangers employed the concept of positional play and used it to good effect to beat them. Begley commented that the ball did not cross into the Rangers half of the pitch for the entire match.

Evidence of the survival of the older tradition of landlord patronage may also be found in Kerry. One member of the gentry in Cahersiveen, J.F. Fitzgerald of Mineigh House, gave use of his ten-acre field for a football game between Waterville and Fitzgerald's selection, a team comprised of tenants from his estate.[145] The spread of clubs may also have been influenced by more emphasis being placed on Gaelic football and hurling rather than athletics meetings. By now, the GAA was securely in control of most athletics events while the two field sports took on an increasing significance, the first All-Ireland championships being instigated in 1887.

Though the IRB's influence could be clearly seen among some of the more prominent officials within the GAA, the association was home to other politics besides those that advocated a brand of physical-force nationalism. Nationally, the leadership of the IRB had given their broad support to Parnell's political programme. They had resisted deliberate efforts to gain influence within the National League and instead had concentrated on gaining control of the GAA. The National League had publicly disclaimed any official connection with the GAA in 1885. Despite this, at a local level there was still a great deal of interaction between the two organisations in Kerry. This was not surprising. Many of the factors that led to the development of sport in Britain, such as mass industrialisation and the rise of a more rigidly defined class structure, were absent in Ireland, especially in rural agrarian economies like Kerry. In this situation, one of the principal reasons for the success of the association was its appropriation of political nationalism as part of its function. Without the streets or factories of large industrialised cities, around which the working class in Britain formed sports clubs, the GAA had to find Irish alternatives to graft their clubs onto, be they political or clerical. In early 1888, the association published its constitution and its fifth article stated that only one club per parish was allowed. Thus, the GAA grafted itself onto an existing and durable ecclesiastical territorial structure. Likewise, the administrative structure of National League branches provided a ready blueprint for GAA clubs. It is noteworthy how throughout 1888, as the League was becoming increasingly inactive, the GAA in the county was rapidly expanding. As reports of club meetings appeared in the *Sentinel* they resembled League meetings in structure, with committees established and resolutions proposed and adopted. Even the format of the reports was identical with those of League branches and they often appeared alongside each other.

There was also a widespread cross-membership between the organisations. For example, six of the founding members of Killarney's Dr Crokes were also members of the local National League.[146] Meanwhile, Michael Egan was honorary secretary of both the Castlegregory GAA club and the town's National League branch. The overlap in membership was such that meetings of the town's GAA club would start once the local League meeting was over. In Tralee, a comparison between the officers and committee of Mitchels GAA and members of the local National League showed at least ten men being dual members.[147] Local GAA meetings frequently passed resolutions commenting on the political situation in the country or condemning the government's policy in Ireland. The Dr Crokes branch was particularly vocal, decrying the government suppression of the National League as 'the only weapon the Irish people have to fight with against the cruel landlordism'. Often their meetings would end with cheers for the League, political prisoners, Parnell and singing of nationalist songs such as *God Save Ireland*. Political sentiment was not restricted to club meetings. After the end of a championship football match, the O'Brennan team was escorted by a crowd to the train station in Castlegregory with cheers raised for them, the local Castlegregory team, the political prisoners and the Plan of Campaign.[148] At a juvenile match between Ballyferriter and Dingle it was discovered that one of the Ballyferriter players was the son of a farmer 'who had recently turned grass grabber'. Dingle refused to play as long as he was part of the opposition's team, and after some 'considerable' booing from the crowd the Ballyferriter team left.[149]

With the League officially outlawed in Kerry, there were examples of Gaelic games being used as a cover under which League business was transacted. The *Sentinel* reported that during the match between Castleisland and Mitchels in Tralee Sportsground, a meeting of the suppressed Tralee League branch was held in the Pavilion under the stand, spoiling RIC attempts to disrupt it.[150] Certainly the RIC in Killarney suspected the local GAA branch was more than it appeared. At least three of its meetings were interrupted by the police in early 1888, with the local RIC Sergeant Murphy declaring at one that its members were acting illegally if they were attempting to hold a meeting of the National League. The next week the *Sentinel*, under the heading 'More Intimidation', reported the RIC observing the team as it practised that Sunday in its playing field adjacent to the town.[151] Many members of GAA clubs remained politically active in the League and were arrested and imprisoned on account of this.[152] Dr Crokes passed a resolution in support of their secretary when he was imprisoned for advocating the Plan of Campaign on the Kenmare estate. Rathmore GAA club expressed its 'utmost indignation towards the savage, cowardly and revengeful conduct of [government] agents' who sentenced their secretary, Daniel O'Keefe, and team captain John Moynihan to six months in prison. The two men had been caught cheering for the Plan of Campaign as the victorious Rathmore team returned through Headford station after a match.[153]

RIC reports in 1888 noted that the 'fusion' between the National League and the GAA in Kerry was so complete that 'in some cases the distinction is hardly distinguishable'.[154] However, as with the charge of the GAA being a mere front for IRB activity, the evidence for this is more apparent than real. GAA events were used as cover for some League meetings but no more than other tactics to fool the police.[155] With the National League suppressed, nationalists in Kerry were denied the platform the organisation provided to voice their legitimate and popular concerns at the current political situation. The same strata of population that had been denied a political voice had also up until now been denied the opportunity to participate in a popular national sports movement. No wonder that the tenant farmers, labourers, etc. who made up GAA teams deprived of the chance to speak out against the evils of the landlord system on the local League platform would use the meetings of their GAA club to voice their concerns. Such incidents do not prove that the GAA was an overtly political organisation, any more than Sunday Mass was overtly political, though the priest might condemn the political plight of Ireland from the pulpit. Rather, it was an organisation whose members shared a similar political sentiment with the broader nationalist society in Ireland.[156] This sentiment was seen across other sporting occasions. For example, at the Abbeyfeale races in 1887 the four-race card included the 'Plan of Campaign' Plate for £15 and the 'Home Rule' Plate for £10. There is much evidence for an overlap in membership between the League and the GAA during the latter's formative years in Kerry. However, such an overlap was inevitable given the shared agricultural class membership of small farmers and tenants that made up both organisations. The actual degree of this overlap varied from area to area in Kerry.

Some have argued that the naming of GAA clubs was a process for the constructing of an identity that stressed and publicised such clubs' links as sportsmen to the nationalist mission, the embrace of all things Irish and the rejection of the tainting influences of Britain.[157] Yet names like Lispole Emmets or Tralee John Mitchels did not in themselves signify some readiness to support the physical-force nationalism that these men had advocated. When the members of Lixnaw formed their GAA club they chose to call themselves the Sir C. Russell GAA club 'as a mark of gratitude and esteem to that distinguished advocate of the Irish cause'.[158] Like the names on horse-racing plates, these were expressions of popular political sentiment among the widespread community in Kerry and not signal posts indicating a duality of function by the GAA. Certainly the IRB used GAA events both as cover and to indoctrinate new members. The spy network established in the county by Major General Redvers Buller during

1886 meant that 'a constant knowledge' of IRB operations was obtained. In Kerry, six informers, four with GAA connections, were used to keep watch on the IRB within the association. One, Mary O'Sullivan, was paid £60 by Dublin Castle in 1889 for her information.[159] There were also reports that after games, the IRB approached and asked men attending if they wanted to join 'a higher club'.[160] However, for most rank-and-file members the GAA remained a sporting and not an overtly political organisation. This is evident in the spread of the games throughout parts of the county where, as has been seen, IRB organisation was weak.

TABLE 1.1.

KERRY GAA CLUBS THAT CONTESTED THE 1889 COUNTY CHAMPIONSHIP

Football	Hurling
Ashill Alderman Hoppers	Abbeydorney
Barraduff Daniel O'Connells	Ballyduff
Brosna	Kenmare Daniel O'Connells
Castlegregory William Allens	Kilgarvan Shamrocks
Castleisland Desmonds	Kilmoyley Robert Emmets
Irremore and Lixnaw	
Kenmare Daniel O'Connells	
Kilgarvan Shamrocks	
Killarney Dr Crokes	
Killorglin Harringtons	
Killorglin Laune Rangers	
Listowel Feale Amateurs	
O'Brennan	
Tralee John Mitchels	
Rathmore William O'Briens	

The year 1889 saw the first county hurling and football championships established in Kerry. At a meeting of the county board, the fifteen football teams and five hurling teams that had entered the competitions were announced and the draws were made for the first round.[161] Sunday 3 March 1889 saw the inauguration of the Kerry county championship. The competition began with three games at the Killarney GAA's ground a mile from the town on a bitterly cold day with a strong southeast wind. To generate interest in the competition, this first event was free of charge for all spectators. The Barraduff fife and drum band entertained the crowd as the teams and supporters marched to the field. Killorglin Laune Rangers and Barraduff Daniel O'Connells played the first ever championship game in Kerry, with Killorglin winning 1-3 to no score. Indicating Gaelic football was still slowly spreading across the county, the *Sentinel* reported this was only the second time Barraduff had been seen on the field of play and they still lacked the required fitness, judgement and science for football. The match was followed by a game between a second Killorglin team, The Harringtons, and Kenmare O'Connells and a final game between the Kilgarvan Shamrocks and Rathmore William O'Briens.[162]

Not every club that had affiliated necessarily thought themselves strong enough to enter the county championships. Some continued to organise friendly matches with neighbouring parish teams to increase their knowledge of the game or to lend assistance to newly established clubs. Dr Crokes played Aghadoe Lough Leane Rangers in a friendly 'to bring the newly formed club into practical knowledge of the rules of GAA'. The need for such practice to hone the skills of the game was obvious when Waterville played Cahersiveen in a game that when every 'real or supposed infringe-ment of the rules took place . . . [the referee] was immediately surrounded by both teams . . . this unseemly practice became so frequent that ten minutes play alternated with five minutes argument'. Both teams were described as 'utterly oblivious of the functions of the referee', and the official in question 'himself seemed fairly bewildered'. The finer points of Gaelic football, such as the concept of positional play, were also slow to spread across north Kerry. Lixnaw played Knockanure Volunteers and though the former were superior, winning 1-11 to no score, both 'lacked science and judgment and seemed to be in blissful ignorance of the knack of distributing themselves on the field. As a consequence the players were always in a clutter and when the leather did get out the Lixnaw men, who seemed to have more precaution in this respect, had little difficulty in sending it home.'

Disputes over scoring were another feature of early champion-ships. When O'Brennan and Castlegregory played in a first-round tie in 1889 the game ended level without a single score registered by either side in ninety minutes of play, including thirty minutes extra time 'where the only thing both sides succeeded in doing was bursting the ball'.[163] This fixture went to a second and then a third replay, where seven minutes into the second half Castlegregory scored a goal that the referee awarded but which O'Brennan disputed. The team walked off the pitch, refusing to play any more.[164] Such disputes became so frequent at county board meetings that in April 1889 a rule was passed that in future a fee of 5s must be accompanied with an objection 'which shall be forfeited in case of frivolous objections'. Yet it must be borne in mind that a dubiously awarded goal often meant the difference between the winning and losing of a match, as until the 1890s a goal outweighed any number of points scored during a game.[165] The haphazard nature of playing fields and problems resulting from a primitive transport system also hindered matches. When Waterville and Cahersiveen played a challenge match on neutral ground, the pitch had a considerable incline between the sidelines, 'which had the effect of confining the play to a particular portion of the field and, as an inevitable consequence, the constant kicking of the ball into touch'. Rathmore were unable to make their championship clash with Killarney on 28 April 1889 as they could not procure the necessary cars to transport the team to the venue.[166]

The inaugural Kerry county championship finals were held that May. On Sunday 19 May, the hurling final was contested between Kenmare and Kilmoyley Emmets before a large crowd at Fossa outside Killarney.[167] Though Kilmoyley were reported as the superior team as far as hurling and discipline were concerned, Kenmare succeeded in scoring a goal which the *Sentinel* thought was entirely accidental, giving them a 1-0 to 0-3 win. The rough nature of the game resulted in a Kilmoyley player breaking his leg and two of his teammates receiving severe injuries. Kilmoyley, feeling hard done by, sent an open challenge through the *Sentinel* requesting that Kenmare replay the game for the prize of £1 a hurley. In response, Maurice Moynihan, the Kerry GAA secretary, reminded Kilmoyley that the GAA was set up as a purely amateur organisation and under its constitution 'they will find betting is not permitted or money prizes allowed'. The football final on 26 May matched Laune Rangers against Dr Crokes at Tralee Sportsground. Special trains from the GSWR were secured from both Killarney and Killorglin and the admission price for the event was 3d. Moynihan was the referee for the match and in a game described as 'the finest game of football yet seen in Kerry', Rangers won 0-6 to 0-3 and became the county's first football champions.[168]

The year 1889 also marked the first appearance of Kerry clubs in the All-Ireland football and hurling championships – at that point it was the winning club team and not an all-county representative selection which contested the competition. Kerry's first foray into the Munster championship had mixed results. On 28 July 1889, the county's hurling and football champions were drawn to meet the Cork champions at a pitch outside Mallow. Special trains brought the four teams and their supporters to the venue. In the first match, Inniscarra met Kenmare in hurling. Though the 'former team were the superior hurlers luck was against them and [Kenmare] . . . were declared winners after a stiff match'. Kenmare, behind by five points to one, scored a goal from a free in the last minute to give them victory. The football match between Laune Rangers and Midleton was described as 'a magnificent exhibition of football, so well sustained to bring forth almost continuous applause from the spectators'. Rangers lost 0-2 to 0-1. However, they were evidently unhappy with the GAA's arrangements for the game. J.D. Foley complained at the treatment of his teammates when they had reached Mallow. They arrived off the platform that afternoon to find no one to greet them or provide refreshments, even though they had not eaten since breakfast at 8 a.m. They had to try and find the field of play themselves as no one was on hand to direct them. Eventually, after a weary trek they happened upon it on top of a hill, 'three miles from the station house'. They had to play the match on an empty stomach and, as play continued until 6.15 p.m., had to rush to bundle up their clothes to catch the train home, meaning they did not eat all day until they returned home at 11 p.m. that night. For all this they had been obliged to give a guarantee of £40 to GSWR for a special train to Mallow.[169]

Despite Kenmare's success, they found themselves in the unique position of being undefeated in the Munster championship, yet still losing the competition. They were next drawn against Tipperary champions Moycarkey but the latter failed to show and Kenmare were awarded the match as a walkover. Yet the GAA's executive council reversed the decision. Moycarkey had beaten Tulla Emmets of Clare, who had previously beaten the Limerick champions, Liberties, by 5-1 to 2-2. However, the Moycarkey versus Tulla match was ordered to be replayed. Moycarkey refused and Tulla were declared Munster champions even though the Kerry team remained unbeaten. At the GAA Convention in Thurles in November, Maurice Moynihan raised the fact that it had cost Kenmare £20 to get to the match against Moycarkey. He stated that the council had no right to reverse the decision of the referee and that Kenmare should be Munster champions. Despite his arguments, the GAA upheld the decision to award the Munster title to Tulla.[170]

Regardless of such disputes and teething problems, the GAA in Kerry continued to prosper. On 23 October 1889, Kerry held its second annual GAA Convention. The secretary's report listed the financial position of the county board, which gives an early insight into the finances of the association there. The balance sheet showed an income of £55 16s 8d. Expenditure was £23 11s 3d, mainly spent on two sets of county championship winners' medals as well as other smaller expenses.[171] By November, thirty-three clubs had affiliated and their names were published in the *Sentinel*. Members were reminded that those who continued to play with non-affiliated clubs would make themselves liable for expulsion.[172]

The GAA, within a few short years, had placed itself at the centre of Ireland's parallel 'sporting revolution'. Yet what was the relationship between the GAA and other codified games such as cricket and rugby? There appears, particularly in southern Kerry, to have been some hostility between cricket, Gaelic games and the clubs involved. For example, at the founding of the Kenmare GAA branch one of its members, J. White, proposed a resolution that was unanimously adopted – that the games played 'be purely Gaelic and that all imported games be vigorously excluded'. While giving arguments for this he spoke at length about the game of cricket being barred from their field. During 1890, the Killarney Cricket Club had an ongoing dispute with their patron, Lord Kenmare.[173] The dispute rumbled on until settlement was reached in November, before the case was brought to court. The club agreed to pay nominal rent of 1s a year for a new cricket field provided by the lord on his stipulation in a new contract that 'the political association known as the National Gaelic Association under any pretext whatever are not to have access to the field'. The club at their subsequent meeting accepted these terms of lease. In its next editorial, the *Sentinel* commented that as Dr Crokes had their own field and never requested access to the cricket field, this clause 'was purely a piece of gratuitous malevolence'.

Using match reports involving the CKAACC cricket teams in Tralee between 1885 and 1890 and comparing them to various Tralee John Mitchels teams in the same period, there is no evidence of any individual representing both. Likewise in Killorglin, comparing its cricket team line-up in 1885 with the Laune Rangers football team line-ups reported in the *Sentinel* in the 1887–90 period, there is again no evidence of players representing both clubs. This is in direct contrast to the experience of counties like Kilkenny where there is evidence of substantial overlap between GAA and cricket players. Yet despite this, there is an intriguing report of a cricket match between a Dr Crokes XI and Mr Rice XI in July 1888. R. Rice was the captain of the Killarney Cricket Club team but seeing as Crokes won the game 113 to 87, one would suspect, especially as this is the only reference to a Crokes cricket team, that it was evidently not the proper cricket club team that they played. No team line-ups are given, so it is impossible to know the men on either team. However, it does appear that, at least that summer, the local GAA club had members with sufficient knowledge of the game to challenge another team selection in the town.

Whereas the relationship with cricket was sometimes acrimonious, the relationship between Gaelic football and rugby in Kerry was often blurred. This is not surprising given the similarities between caid, rugby and early Gaelic football. For example, a comparison between the last match report of a Killorglin rugby team in February 1888 and the Laune Rangers team in the 1890 county championship shows that ten men represented both teams.[174] Rugby was popular enough that at a meeting of the Tralee Mitchels GAA club some members enquired about forming their own rugby club in the town. They were reminded of rule six of the GAA constitution which stated that members of other sporting bodies could not be members of the GAA. Evidently this did not deter some from the attractions of the game. At a meeting of Mitchels the following February a charge was brought against four members for playing rugby in the town. Only one member turned up to answer the charge and after apologising and promising to stay clear of the game was allowed back 'in the good graces of the members'. The other three who failed to show were expelled. Clearly, the Dr Crokes club was not so strict. After playing Dr Crokes in the 1890 county championship, Cahersiveen lodged an objection, stating that a rugby player, E. Bernard, had lined out for their opponents during the match. The *Sentinel*'s GAA reporter stated that Bernard had previously been expelled from the GAA by the county board for playing rugby. Refuting this, a special meeting of Crokes stated that when Bernard had last lined out for the local rugby club he was not a member of Crokes but on leaving them he had since joined Crokes and had paid his subscription for the year.[175] In response, the *Sentinel* dryly observed that Crokes must be 'very accommodating indeed' to allow this man, who played for them in the championship last year, to resign as soon as the rugby season started in winter 'and then was taken back when the Gaelic season returned'.[176] It is likely such a situation was not uncommon in the early days of the GAA in the towns of Kerry that had both rugby and Gaelic football teams.

The GAA in the county had seen remarkable growth since November 1887. But what was so unique about the association to explain this success? Neal Garnham has put forward a number of theories. He argues that the GAA's popularity was a reaction to the effective exclusion of nationalists from other sporting bodies. A growing Catholic 'petty bourgeoisie' was frustrated at their failure to be admitted into areas of life reserved by Protestants. By the 1880s, Catholics were reaping the benefits of the Liberal government's policy of a more open society. For example, in 1874 the civil service introduced a single open competitive examination system for admission in Ireland and between then and 1911 the numbers in service rose from 5,888 to 23,000. Many of these new recruits where young, lower-middle-class Catholics, products of the national school system introduced in October 1831.[177] In addition, the Intermediate Education (Ireland) Act of 1878 provided public funds for secondary schools for Catholics. Kerry boasted around ten secondary schools by the start of the twentieth century. Nationally, numbers attending these rose to 35,306 by 1901 and were comprised mostly of the children of better-off tenant farmers, teachers, professionals and shopkeepers in Ireland. Concurrently, the expansion of the Irish electorate combined with the effective party machine of the National League meant that Catholics were gaining an increasing voice in local government.[178] Catholic nationalists were thus achieving both education and power. They now sought the opportunity to join sporting bodies, which previously had been largely denied them. The men who crowded the rooms of the League were the same men who assembled in the GAA's meeting halls. The fact that the *Sentinel* was the mouthpiece for both associations is revealing. Dublin Castle reports on readers of provincial newspapers show the *Kerry Sentinel*'s readership was comprised of 'nationalists' drawn in the main from farmers and farm workers, shopkeepers and clerks of the towns.

Allowing for the presence of politics, it is argued that the GAA was more relevant and accessible to the majority of the Irish population whatever their politics. As has been shown, athletics in Ireland, as in England, actively discriminated against the lower classes. The vast majority of the Irish population were employed in agricultural and service industries (the country's industrial workforce even by 1907 only made up 5 per cent of the total UK industrial force). Thus, for both industries the only day of rest and leisure was Sunday, the day that sports such as cricket, rugby and soccer barred members from playing on. The GAA was relevant to most simply because it catered for people's longing to participate in sports at the only leisure time during a working week that was convenient to them.[179]

In addition, the GAA often represented the best value for money. For most sectors of the Irish workforce, rising incomes were a matter of fact by the late nineteenth century. Between 1850 and 1900, the wages paid to farm labourers doubled in numerical terms, although their purchasing power did not, given inflation, etc.[180] Despite this, Ireland remained a poor country and incomes rose conspicuously slower than elsewhere in the UK. Rise of disposable income was one of the key factors in the sports revolution, but in Ireland, where this trend was less marked, the GAA was an adaptation to fit in with the country's particular economic situation. For example, the Kerry County Board charged a club affiliation fee of 10s. This was in contrast to the £1 Tralee RFC had to pay to affiliate with the IRFU. The membership fee for Dr Crokes was 2s 6d in 1890, whereas the contemporary fee for cricket members in clubs in Ireland could be 10s. While spectators would have had to part with 1s to see a club rugby game, the admission to Kerry's first county football final was 3d. For patrons the GAA also offered more entertainment per admission, and match days often comprised several events. In contrast to a single rugby match at international or club level, Kerry's first football final had, in addition to the main event, two challenge games and a juvenile match as part of the programme. Frequently, such important matches were accompanied by several bands to entertain the crowds, and all this provided a far greater and more colourful spectacle than the more austere occasion of a cricket game. Likewise, during the early years of the GAA, festivities were often arranged after the conclusion of matches. Despite the fact that the O'Brennan team walked off the pitch in their third replay against Castlegregory in April 1889, after the game refreshments were laid out for the two teams and both 'spent an enjoyable evening dancing and singing'.[181]

The early success of the GAA cannot be solely tied to its embrace of nationalist politics. The association was fully affected by the sporting revolution taking place across the UK. Like other sports, it sought popularity and spectator interest to further its organisation. When Maurice Davin first published rules for hurling and football there were incredibly few, with only ten for football. As for properly regulating a match, they bordered on the farcical. No mention was given as to how the ball could be propelled during the game, so naturally in areas like Kerry where caid had been played and rugby was known, the ball was often picked up and run with. This forced Michael Cusack in April 1885 to state that the ball could not be carried. Cusack was attempting to differentiate his game from another Victorian code. The GAA found it had to redefine the rules of hurling and football regularly to distinguish them from other contemporary sports to ensure the success of its own games. Thus, the GAA invented football and hurling in the same way that soccer and rugby were derived from older traditional sports. Rule changes were adopted as the GAA wanted to show its sports were serious and acceptable rivals to soccer, cricket and rugby. This required the association to adapt its games to bring them more in line with the contemporary thinking on sport, which emphasised greater order and control. Tied in with this emphasis on the minimising of rough play was the promotion of the good-natured conduct of players and supporters to make the sport more attractive to potential spectators. In this the GAA took its place among other sports in the Victorian era. Match reports across the country invariably included some generic comments about the friendliness and order of the crowd and players on the field.[182]

The GAA also endorsed concepts of muscular Christianity, which were prevalent arguments behind the uptake of sport in Britain. Emphasis was put on the assumed intellectual and physical superiority of the Gaelic athlete over his English counterpart.[183] An article in the *Gaelic Annual* of 1907–8 stated:

> The ideal Gael is a matchless athlete, sober, pure in mind, speech and deed, self-possessed, self-reliant, self-respecting, loving his religion and his country with a deep and restless love, earnest in thought and effective in action.

It is interesting to compare this with the *Ideal of the English Cricketer* which was set out by Rev. James Pycroft, the first cricket historian, in 1851. He stated that cricket 'calls into requisition all the cardinal virtues . . . the player must be sober and temperate. Patience, fortitude and self denial, the various bumps of order, obedience and good-humour, with an unruffled temper are essential.'[184] When the formation of the GAA was announced the *Irishman*, regurgitating Victorian concepts of Darwinian theory, wrote:

> If any two purposes should be brought together it should be politics and athletics . . . the exigencies of our situation force us into perpetual war with England . . . While fighting the enemy in the byways which are called constitutional, we must maintain a certain degree of readiness to meet our enemy in the field, when the occasion offers. Our politics being essentially National so should our athletics . . . We must maintain a stout physique and cultivate a hardy constitution. A townsman unexercised in the field is stiff-limbed, short-winded and unable to endure hardship and privation . . . This defect would tell heavily against a townsman in a war with any recognised army . . . If we are corporally weak, our mental power will grow feeble . . . In physique and intellectual ability Ireland cannot lag behind the foremost nations without losing all hope of recovering her independence.[185]

Despite an area like Kerry never going through the processes of industrialisation or mass population displacement, the basic emotions of sport held true as much for a farmer in Moyvane as an industrial worker in Manchester. The camaraderie of being on a team and of participating in a common event such as a match was the same across the local sporting world in Britain and Ireland. Being part of a team led to bonding and shared experience. The experience of representing your local area was relevant across all sports. As Neal Garnham argued, tying the club structure to a parish system exploited long-held traditional local allegiances and rivalries. Thus, the GAA became an integral part of local community almost immediately.

2

'A GOOD SHIP GOING DOWN WITH THE TIDE':

THE COLLAPSE OF THE GAA, 1890–1898

The GAA is torn with internal dissension and if the breach is not very soon repaired, it will become inseparable.

Monthly Report of RIC District Inspector Jones, Southwestern division, 2 February 1891

Within little more than three years, the GAA had witnessed remarkable growth in Kerry. The local popularity of the association was such that at the beginning of 1890 the *Kerry Sentinel* had introduced a dedicated column in its paper for both local and national GAA matters under the title 'Gaelic Notes' by the reporter 'EMON'.[1] However, events both within and outside the organisation soon conspired to bring about the GAA's near downfall. The 1890s witnessed the almost fatal decline of the association both in Kerry and Ireland generally. The reasons why a sporting organisation like the GAA was so susceptible to collapse at this time were varied, but a return to agricultural and economic depression in the 1890s, coupled with the reoccurrence of mass emigration, had a devastating impact on the association. In addition, the political fallout over Parnell and his affair with a married woman had a catastrophic impact on the GAA. The incident split Irish nationalism and its effects reverberated throughout the GAA, robbing it of a coherent leadership at a time when it faced unprecedented challenges due to the economic situation. In the aftermath, the Catholic Church began to cut its ties with the GAA and in areas like Kerry the change in clerical attitudes had a demoralising effect on the association there. Though Kerry won its first All-Ireland title in 1892 in hurling and reached the All-Ireland football final the following year, the GAA quickly disintegrated thereafter in the county. By the mid-1890s, this dearth in Gaelic activity allowed rival sports such as rugby to gain unprecedented popularity in the county.

Economic Depression and the Parnell Split, 1890–1894

A major factor in the decline of the GAA in the early 1890s was the broader economic situation facing Ireland. By the summer of 1890, an economic depression had descended on the country, leading to a long downward slide in livestock prices which lasted over four years. This was exaggerated by the reappearance of the potato blight.[2] It was reported that in parts of Kerry the blight was so bad in the harvest of 1890 that little over a quarter of the potato crop was saved. As early as July the RIC district inspector for Kerry stated that a partial famine was almost inevitable in south and west Kerry.[3] In October, the editor of the *Sentinel* lamented the desperate situation facing the county as winter approached. Not only the potato, but the grain crops were also reported as destroyed due to the heavy rain and flooding. Any hay saved was said to be 'seething and reeking in rottenness'. 'Fuel famine' was dreaded almost as much as the potato blight, and 'from the great quantity of turf we see still stretched or only footed in the bogs, we are convinced that there will be a dearth of fuel in the coming winter'.[4] The potato blight not only affected the poorer, marshier lands of west and south Kerry but also the more prosperous farms in the north of the county. In some parts, its appearance completely destroyed the potato crop. Over the next five years, Kerry, like the rest of rural Ireland whose economy was dominated by agriculture, would witness a prolonged depression, interspersed with frequent potato crop failures. In January 1895, Abbeyfeale's parish priest wrote that the local people were verging on starvation.[5] In 1896, a report on the harvest noted that it was the wettest on record since 1841. The oat crop was the worst ever seen and the potato crop an almost complete failure.

As has been previously outlined, agriculture was the dominant industry of the vast majority of Irishmen. Nationally, direct employment in agriculture accounted for at least 61.8 per cent of GAA members.[6] This is not including the thousands of men employed in the commercial, retail and skilled or unskilled labour sectors whose business in rural counties like Kerry was heavily geared towards a supporting role for the agricultural economy. As occurred previously during the late 1880s the effects of a large-scale depression in what was the most dominant industry in Ireland was a major factor in the decline of the GAA both locally and nationally during the 1890s.

The economic situation led to the reappearance of mass emigration as a feature in rural Irish life. The striking increase in emigration amounted to some 716,000 people leaving Irish shores between 1881 and 1900.[7] The 1891 census reported that the population of Kerry had declined by 10.9 per cent since 1881.[8] Nationally, the population decreased by a further 5.3 per cent over the following ten years. Better economic opportunities in Britain and, more especially, in North America for those families decimated by the agricultural situation in Ireland accounted for this steep rise.[9] The *Sentinel* reported that 83.7 per cent of those who emigrated in 1896 were aged between fifteen and thirty-five.[10] This was exactly the age group of young rural men upon which GAA membership largely depended.[11] The flow of emigration, which had slowed to a trickle in the late 1880s, had become a torrent. Emigration had a devastating impact on the association. As the lifeblood of many clubs began to seep away, the GAA nationally was already fighting a losing battle to maintain its popularity.

In February 1890, the Kerry County Board met to make the draw for the county championship that twenty-four football and five hurling clubs had entered.[12] Due to the number of disputes and frequency of players playing for more than one club in the previous championship, the board decided to stop this practice of clubs 'borrowing' men. Therefore, any team fielding players that belonged to another club would automatically forfeit a game. In the Munster championship, Kerry, receiving a walkover from their arranged match with the champions of Clare, qualified for the Munster finals for the first time. The finals were played on 28 September 1890 at Ratheen, north of Limerick City. Special trains brought some 4,000 to the ground. In the hurling final, Aghabollogue of Cork beat their 'plucky' Kilmoyley opponents 2-0 to 0-1. The football match between Laune Rangers and Midleton was a 'more stubborn contest . . . The Cork champions were not, as a rule, so powerfully built as their opponents, who, from the athletic captain down, were a veritable team of giants.' No score was recorded by half time and during the second half the ball burst. There being no replacement, a replay was called. This occurred on 19 October at Banteer, County Cork, with Rangers losing heavily, 1-4 to 0-1.[13]

The result seemed to be emblematic; already the GAA in Kerry was showing the effects of the broader economic reality. In November EMON in his column wrote:

> What is the meaning of the apathy which pervades the Gaelic clubs in Kerry this year? The annual affiliation fee was due on the 1st of October and, in fact, the County Convention should have been already held, but as yet only half a dozen clubs have sent on the fee.

He mused over a number of reasons for such apathy. Disputes during the last two championships, decisions by the county board against certain clubs and the recent defeat of Kerry teams in Munster may have cast a 'dampener' over the association there. The fact that players were growing tired of bearing the travel expenses of their club out of their own pockets may also have been a factor. In response, he urged clubs to expand membership and let expenses be paid out of the club exchequer, 'which ought in most places [to be] supplemented by voluntary donations'.

Due to the difficult economic climate, EMON suggested that to increase affiliation, smaller clubs should amalgamate. The 'efficiency of the club will thereby be increased, its status will be raised and the working expenses will be spread over a more extended constituency'. He suggested clubs such as Lixnaw and Irremore, Ballymacelligott and O'Brennan, Kilmoyley and Lerrig, and Knocknagoshel and Brosna could unite. At the County Convention on 19 November 1890 club affiliation was reported to have fallen to twenty-one, with only sixteen clubs represented and twenty-nine delegates present.[14] RIC reports noted that across Ireland the GAA was 'crumbling'.[15]

Nationally, the number of GAA clubs fell by 438 in the three years up to the end of 1891, with the most severe declines being in the west and southeast of the country. In Mayo alone, branches fell from thirty to three. The total number of GAA clubs in the southwest was now put at 142, as opposed to 197 in 1889.[16] Maurice Moynihan, who had done so much to establish the GAA in Kerry, had been rewarded for his efforts by being elected joint honorary secretary of the association at its Annual Convention in November 1890. In an early attempt to check what seemed like a terminal decline in the popularity of the GAA, Moynihan wrote to all counties to attend a general meeting of the association in Dublin:

> . . . consisting of one member of each affiliated club during the year 1890 and now in existence, for the purpose of taking into consideration the present position of the Association, with the view of re-organising and uniting all its scattered forces in a solid phalanx for the preservation of the National pastimes: and also to take such action as may be deemed advisable under existing circumstances in support of the integrity of the National cause.[17]

The proposed meeting came off in the Rotunda Hospital on 22 July 1891 but no Kerry clubs were reported as present. The meeting agreed to appoint a paid secretary to look after the organisation and running of the GAA nationally. By the following October, however, Moynihan had resigned as secretary to the central executive and left his position in the Kerry GAA, moving to Cork for business reasons. Deprived of his immense talents as an organiser, administrator and gifted journalist, the Kerry GAA, sympathetic with the national experience, further decayed. At the GAA's 1891 Annual Convention, held in January 1892, only six counties were represented, while only one club each from Cork, Dublin and Kerry entered that year's All-Ireland hurling championship. The financial position of the central executive was said to be dire, the sixth annual All-Ireland athletics championship, held the previous August in Tralee, being a particular financial disaster. P.P. Sutton, the Gaelic correspondent for *Sport*, stated:

> Among the causes which have contributed to the decline
> of the Association in general may be mentioned emigration,
> expenses of teams contesting for championship and
> tournament honours; and last though by no means least,
> the bad management of the County Committee. County
> Boards are largely responsible for the disappearance of
> many clubs, which, smarting under the bungling and unjust
> treatment of the governing body, became disorganised and
> eventually disbanded.

Emigration, he argued, had been the 'deadliest enemy of all'. In
the south, he claimed, between 20 and 50 per cent of the 'old
hands in clubs' were now missing from their teams.[18] Nationally,
a report on the estimated strength of the GAA in January 1894
found that only thirty-eight branches survived in the midlands,
thirty-three in the southwest and a further twenty-nine in the
western division of the country. In the entire north of Ireland, only
one branch of 100 members was reported, in Belfast. Thus, all of
Ulster, along with Carlow, Clare, Kilkenny, Laois, Leitrim, Limerick,
Longford, Louth, Mayo, Meath, Offaly, Roscommon, North
Tipperary, Wicklow and Wexford were said to have no active
branch of the GAA.[19] In Kerry, clubs affiliating to the county board
dropped from twenty-eight in 1891 to a mere ten in 1894 (see
Appendix IV).[20] Likewise, the number of GAA matches reported in
Kerry fell from thirty-nine in 1891 to sixteen by 1894 (see
Appendix VII).

The decline can be further understood in Kerry if we examine
the actual playing population of GAA members in the county. A
police report on the association in Kerry in early 1891 identified
twenty-four active GAA clubs within the county. The report
estimated the total combined membership of these clubs at 1,286,
an average of fifty-three members per club. According to that
year's census, the male population of Kerry between the ages of
fifteen and forty stood at 38,101.[21] Thus, in early 1891, 3.37 per
cent of the male population were members of the GAA. In
contrast, taking fifty-three as an average club membership, the
GAA membership in Kerry in 1889 amounted to 4.6 per cent of
the male population. By 1894, membership numbers had fallen

further to 2.2 per cent of the total male population. The 1890s, coinciding as it did with the reappearance of large-scale emigration and the stagnation of the Irish economy, presented a challenging environment for any sporting organisation. Indeed, throughout the Munster region there was a noticeable decline in both rugby and association football clubs in this period. Yet outside of the major economic or social factors, there was a myriad of secondary reasons as to why the GAA specifically found itself in such terminal decline.

One explanation as to why the GAA was so vulnerable to the effects of emigration or economic depression was the nature of the vast majority of its clubs. Despite the association advocating a one parish/one club dogma, it is evident that across Ireland in the early decades of the association several clubs did coexist in the same parish or district. Though county boards tried to enforce the parish rule, many, such as the Cavan County Board, found it impossible to police and that earlier inter-parochial divisions proved too resistant to such change. Indeed, during the early years of the association people much more readily identified their sense of place with their local townlands than with their parish. At the heart of rural Ireland there existed a system of informal alliances between members of the farming community within such small territorial units like townlands. These alliances were used to pool resources during times of intense labour, such as the threshing season. Thus the nucleus of many early rural GAA clubs can often be traced from such farming alliances. Utilising such townland networks as the principal basis for young men to form Gaelic sides inevitably led to rural GAA clubs having a much more transient and ad hoc nature.[22] As a result, most early teams were 'ephemeral combinations', coming and going almost in an instant rather than being permanent organised clubs.[23] Their experience may be contrasted to those clubs that were formed with a local village or town acting as an anchoring point.

In most counties, a Gaelic club hierarchy developed, whose base consisted of these transient non-affiliated clubs. At its apex stood a small group of semi-permanent formally constituted clubs such as the Tralee Mitchels or the Killorglin Laune Rangers in Kerry. Many rural Gaelic clubs were often at a severe disadvantage compared to their sporting rivals. Unlike sports such as cricket, Gaelic games, due to their implied nationalist outlook, did not attract the patronage of local landlords and gentry. In stark contrast to areas like central Scotland, where 89 per cent of club patrons and presidents were either members of the nobility or large landowners, patronage of GAA clubs by such groups was almost nonexistent.[24] For example, the Killarney Cricket Club boasted the patronage of the Lord of Kenmare and played out of a cricket field in his own demesne for which they were able to afford to pay a rent of £10 per year.[25] Such clubs had their own meeting rooms and dedicated secretaries and treasurers. This was a far cry from the experience of rural GAA clubs in Kerry, often formed from a core group of athletic neighbours. Some larger urban clubs like Tralee's John Mitchels managed to acquire their own rented grounds and club rooms and had their own elected officers. Many of these officers were white-collar workers employed in some of the bigger firms in the town.[26] As such, they had acquired a certain standing in the community and exerted a natural air of leadership and authority among the younger members of their clubs. Yet the membership of the GAA in market towns like Tralee was so closely tied with the agricultural fortunes of their country brethren that, especially in economically bleak times such as the 1890s, such clubs could never match the financial clout of their cricket and rugby counterparts. GAA clubs were also far more vulnerable to the effects of emigration. Dr Crokes' lacklustre performance in the 1890 county championship was put down to the emigration of its 'crack players'. The loss of even one of the more talented players or organisers from smaller rural clubs often had a devastating effect. The Lispole St John's GAA club mourned the departure of their member James Casey when he left the village to seek a new life in America. The young man was described as giving 'impetus to his favourite game which enabled the Lispole team to enter the field with any other and often the . . . team carried off the laurels of victory which must, in justice to Jim Casey, be ascribed to him and the interest taken by him' in the club. No record of this club was uncovered in the months and years after his departure and it is assumed, like so many clubs before it, that St John's simply disbanded through want of organisation and interest.

Along with the loss of key personnel through emigration or death, a lack of success on the field or disputes with county boards often contributed to club disbandments. EMON, writing in January 1890, suggested that the Kerry County Board should give prizes for second-placed clubs to encourage them to compete in the competitions. 'It is a fault peculiar to many individuals as well as to clubs that, seeing no fair prospect of becoming champions, they throw up the game in disgust . . . [the] word "perseverance" should be written large in every club room.' Forty-one Gaelic games matches were reported as having taken place in Kerry in the 1890 season, including nineteen county championship matches.[27] However, no fewer than eighteen games were either awarded as walkovers owing to a team not turning up, or ended before the allocated time as disputes over a scoring decision or the sending off of a player erupted and county board objections were sought. That same year the RIC reported that the GAA, which had once threatened to expand widely in Kerry, was rapidly declining owing to clubs openly quarrelling with each other.[28]

From the viewpoint of the spectator it is easy to understand how early Gaelic games failed to stimulate the interest of the vast majority of patrons, especially given their quality. A noticeable feature of games in the first years of the championship was often their low-scoring nature. The fact that a goal outweighed any number of points conceded naturally led to an attritional game. This and the crowded nature of the playing field resulted in a heavily defensive game with physicality encouraged, the basic tactic being to prevent a team scoring a goal. The poor-quality playing fields, deep grass, unskilled players, winter and early spring playing season, the heavy water-absorbing football, use of everyday footwear and the crowded nature of a forty-two-man game all combined to ensure matches were kept to low scores.[29] In what was praised by the press as the best match of the 1890 Kerry football championship, Tralee beat Ballymacelligott in the quarter-final by a meagre 0-2 to no score!

The early standard of refereeing could also be a concern, with teams quick to exploit any hesitancy on the official's part. Tuogh and Laune Rangers played a match which, EMON stated, 'if I called it a football match I would probably leave myself open to an

action for libel'. The game lasted two hours and in all that time
there were not five minutes of uninterrupted play. Rangers scored
a goal and their opponents were about to walk off in protest when
the referee then disallowed it. After that, Tuogh disputed every
score by Rangers, seemingly under the impression that they could
get every score cancelled by ganging up on the referee. When
Rangers managed another goal, Tuogh refused to play on and
walked off. Often disputes like this led to courtroom-like battles
between representatives of the clubs involved being played out at
county board meetings and in the rigorous exchange of letters to
the local papers, which could continue for weeks on end.
Objections and counter-objections to the awarding of matches
would be a feature of local and national contests throughout the
1890s and beyond. It is perhaps not surprising that supporters of
games quickly became disheartened by witnessing decisive results
on the field of play being subsequently overturned on a technicality,
the inevitable result being a replay. Often this was taken to farcical
extremes. One championship match in Kerry was left unfinished
when the Keel team walked off in protest of a foul committed by
the Aghadoe captain on a member of their side. At a subsequent
county board meeting their objection was upheld and it was
decided that the last ten minutes of the match should be replayed
in Killorglin in two weeks' time. The Keel club duly undertook the
eleven-mile journey to the match venue only to find Aghadoe had
failed to turn up, and were awarded a walkover.[30]

The frequent holding of fixtures, especially inter-county
contests, at those times of the year most vulnerable to the effects of
unseasonable weather also contributed to a growing lack of
enthusiasm among supporters. When Laune Rangers became the
first Kerry football team to win a Munster senior title in 1892 they
did so in the depths of winter, playing the final in a foot of snow.[31]
At the following month's annual Kerry GAA Convention concern
was raised that the playing months for hurling and football were
extending throughout the calendar year. A resolution was adopted
declaring:

> that the recurrent and general violation of the rule which
> restricts the playing of football and hurling matches to

stated periods of the year is in our opinion, and for the following reasons, a cause of serious concern to the GAA. That it injuriously affects the sports of the association by in very many cases preventing general athletic training; that ultimately it creates a reaction against football and hurling, which diminishes the number of clubs, as teams become disgusted with the necessity of playing through the whole year.[32]

The constant poor quality of matches, the bad weather in which they were often contested and the incessant disputes over match decisions tested the commitment of even the most enthusiastic GAA follower. Yet, along with these specific causes, there appeared to be a growing apathy for the games of the association themselves. The GAA was established in counties like Kerry on a wave of popular enthusiasm. Its momentum was fuelled by the association being viewed as something new, unheralded and distinct. As has been argued previously, it brought a colour and pageantry to Irish life seldom seen in the decades before it. It became a focal point for communities to congregate and celebrate the athletic prowess of their men. By the early 1890s, this initial burst of enthusiasm seemed to have faded. P.R. Cleary, a former secretary of the GAA's central executive, articulated as much when writing to the *Sentinel* in 1892:

No matter how magnificent or imposing anything earthly may be, people weary of admiring it in the end. It was the same with the GAA. We admired the games; we grew excitedly enthusiastic in our admiration of them, but it being the same thing every day, we ultimately failed to go see a match.

Cleary saw that the novelty of the GAA had worn thin among the people of Ireland and hence it found itself in such a precarious position by 1892.[33]

Another contributing factor in the growing indifference towards the GAA was the often dangerous nature of the games for both players and public alike. During a triple-header of championship games played in Tralee Sportsground in May 1891, the palisading in the grandstand gave way under pressure from the crowd behind and some 100 spectators fell onto the crowds standing in the terrace below. Rumours swept the town that people had been crushed to death and maimed in the accident. Relatives and friends of those attending the matches converged on the scene, adding to the confusion. No fatalities occurred but several people were badly injured, including William Moore Stack, one of the original founders of the GAA in Tralee, who suffered a dislocated hip.

Though the *Sentinel* had previously declared that the GAA had effectively 'killed that spirit of factiousness which unhappily used to signalise football and hurling matches in the days not so remote', the reality was that such passions ran deep. The closing stages of the 1890 county championship brought the association there into disrepute. The hurling semi-final at Tralee Sportsground between Kenmare and Kilmoyley degenerated into a mass brawl between players and some of the 3,000 spectators present. The unionist *Kerry Evening Post* accused the GAA of bringing 'desecration of the Sabbath' in the fallout from the game.[34] In a subsequent letter to the *Sentinel*, John O'Shea, the honorary secretary of Kenmare GAA, stated that it was the intention of the Kilmoyley team to injure the Kenmare players from the start. This was in retaliation for a Kilmoyley player having his leg broken during their corresponding match the previous year. O'Shea claimed that the Kilmoyley supporters congregated by the Kenmare goal and could be heard shouting, 'Remember Killarney and the broken leg' and 'Give them the timber ye devils'.[35] Kenmare refused to replay the match in Tralee and so Kilmoyley met and defeated Ballyduff in the county final on 15 June 1890 by 2-2 to no score.[36] In Glin near the north Kerry border, a vicious fight broke out after a football match between supporters of the local team and those of the travelling Abbeyfeale side, resulting in a Glin native having his hand stabbed. For players, GAA matches could sometimes prove fatal. In a football match in Kilflynn in 1897, a seventeen-year-old player, John Enright, was knocked to the ground and trampled. The injuries he received to his stomach were so severe that he died from his wounds that night before medical assistance could arrive. Though the death was believed to be accidental, two men, Hayes and O'Leary, who participated in the match were arrested and questioned about the incident.[37] In a football match in west Limerick between Doon and Cappamore, an outsider rushed from the crowd and stabbed a Doon player called Connell through the heart, killing him.[38]

It is a particular irony for Kerry that the loss in popularity of Gaelic games and the decimation of its membership came at a time of unprecedented success for Kerry clubs in inter-county contests. In May 1891, Ballyduff won the Kerry hurling championship, beating the favourites Kilmoyley 1-0 to 0-1 in the county final. In Killarney that September, they entered the Munster championship, easily overcoming the Cork champions, Blackrock, by 2-6 to 0-3. They thus qualified for the Munster final against the Limerick Treaty Stones club. The tie was played in Newcastlewest where the Limerick side emerged victorious by 1-2 to 1-1. However, at a subsequent meeting of the central executive in Dublin Thomas Slattery and William O'Connell, representing the Kerry Board, supported Ballyduff's objection that the referee had unfairly disallowed an equalising point scored just before the allotted hour had elapsed. They argued that there was uncertainty about the way the time was kept during the game and produced written statements from impartial observers that confirmed the score was in time. Considering the evidence, the executive decided to replay the match.[39] On 31 January 1892, the replay duly took place at the Inch Racecourse near Abbeyfeale. A huge crowd arrived by special trains from Tralee and Limerick and it became quickly apparent that Kerry had the superior team, 'their manipulation of the *camán* being distinguished by considerable scientific execution and dash'. Ballyduff won 2-4 to 0-1. The victorious team (so far the only hurling side from the county to win a senior Munster hurling title) was led to the Abbeyfeale train station by the local brass band playing 'Hail the Conquering Hero'. When the team returned home every house in Ballyduff village was illuminated to celebrate their achievement and bonfires were lit. A crowd met the players outside the village and proceeded to march with them behind the Ballyduff band. Having become the first Kerry team to win a Munster title, Ballyduff qualified for the All-Ireland hurling final held on 28 February 1892 in Clonturk Park, Dublin. They met and defeated the Crossabeg club from Wexford in the only All-Ireland hurling final ever to go to extra time. *Sport* reported that for the ninety minutes the encounter lasted the atmosphere was at boiling point. With both sides level, Crossabeg were awarded a free, sending over a point, which they thought had won them the match. However, it was claimed the ball was only being lifted as the referee blew full time and thus the subsequent score did not count. Though Ballyduff were reluctant to do so, they were persuaded to play thirty minutes of extra time, eventually winning 2-3 to 1-5. When news arrived of the result, bonfires blazed on the surrounding hills of Ballyduff village, a large bonfire was lit outside the town and dancing continued until a late hour.[40]

Yet perhaps no episode summed up the growing disenchantment many players felt towards Gaelic games better than the aftermath of this All-Ireland success. Seven months later, this Ballyduff team, the reigning All-Ireland champions, failed to contest the Kerry hurling final against Kilmoyley, the latter being awarded a walkover. The *Sentinel* reported:

> The absence of the Ballyduff team – especially as it had been arranged to present them with [their All-Ireland] championship medals on the field – is exceedingly strange and no explanation of their action [has been given] . . . but it has been suggested that the cause for it lay in the fact that Ballyduff were so wearied after their hard fight for the championship last year that they did not train for this year's contests.[41]

The reason for this apathy was much more fundamental. The players on that Ballyduff team, rather than being fêted, found that winning an All-Ireland had done nothing more than severely drain their pockets. The team, comprising twenty-six players made up of farmers and farm labourers from Lixnaw, Ballyduff and Kilmoyley, had each had to pay sixteen shillings in expenses for transport and accommodation for the final. This was at a time when the average wage which an agricultural labourer in north Kerry earned was between one and two shillings a week.[42] The team received no financial assistance from the county board and this was identified as the root cause of their failure to show for the county final in 1892 and the general decline in hurling in Kerry in the years thereafter.

Such a situation is not unique to the early days of the GAA. Studies of contemporary soccer clubs in Northumberland in England showed how despite the level of on-field success a club had achieved, financial considerations alone determined whether clubs grew or perished.[43] Paddy Carr, a survivor of the Ballyduff side, described years later how the team 'celebrated' their achievement. Directly after the game they hastily made their way to Kingsbridge to catch the train home and did not arrive back in Tralee until 3 a.m. on Monday morning. There was no one there to greet them and the players went up to Tom Slattery's pub in Rock Street 'where we killed the time until 11 a.m. and then took the train to Lixnaw. And indeed there was no day off when we got home, we all had to turn into work as if nothing had happened.'[44] The team had to walk the several miles that morning from Lixnaw station to their homes and then prepare for a full week's work. Disillusioned by this experience, only eight of that All-Ireland-winning side ever again played in a hurling county championship in Kerry.[45] Rather than acting as a spur for the sport in Kerry, the experience of winning an All-Ireland had a detrimental effect on the game of hurling there. Affiliated hurling clubs in the county dropped from a mere five in 1892 down to three in 1894 and two in 1897. No hurling combination of any sort was reported as having played a match in 1898. As early as 1893 *Sport* was lamenting that the camán 'had been cast aside in Kerry',[46] while the Kerry hurlers' performance in the following year's defeat to Tipperary in the Munster final was described as 'exactly what was anticipated' by the players themselves. 'They had not practised during the past season and had no hope of being able to make anything of a decent show against such crack hurlers.'[47]

In regard to football, in September 1892 Laune Rangers beat Ballymacelligott in the county football final and qualified to represent Kerry in the Munster series. Rangers beat Clondrohids of Cork and then defeated Waterford's Dungarvan in the subsequent Munster final, setting up a tie with Dublin's Young Irelanders for the 1892 All-Ireland final. The game, played in Clonturk Park on

26 March 1893, resulted in defeat for the Kerry side by 1-4 to
0-3. However, the *Sentinel* claimed that the match

> . . . was not fought on anything like equitable terms. The
> representatives of Kerry had, in the first place, to
> perform a tedious tiresome train journey of over two
> hundred miles . . . while their opponents were able to
> walk fresh into the field . . . [yet this was not the only
> mitigating circumstance against the Kerry team as] to the
> indelible disgrace of the Dublin crowd which lined the
> Park be it said, that they acted towards the Kerrymen,
> and towards the Southern teams for that matter, in a
> scandalous and utterly un-Irish fashion. In the midst of
> play they did not content themselves with cheering for
> the Dublin men, but actually indulged in vigorous
> hooting and groaning of the Kerrymen, the inevitable
> result of which was, of course, to take the spirit out of
> them.[48]

Numerous attempts were made by J.P. O'Sullivan, the Laune
Rangers captain, in both the national and local papers to arrange a
rematch with the Dublin side owing to the 'unsatisfactory' manner
in which the All-Ireland was contested. Despite this, however, no
offer of a rematch was forthcoming, even though the Young
Irelanders team initially indicated that they would accept such an
invitation. In the years after this All-Ireland appearance, football in
Kerry suffered a noticeable decline, though not to the same level as
hurling (see Appendix V). An observer calling himself the
'Cahersiveen Beagle' identified in the *Sentinel* the real reason for
such decay in Gaelic affairs in Kerry. It was obvious, he wrote, that

> . . . our Kerry Gaelic clubs and the county organisation
> generally wants considerable toning up. With proper
> central guiding and assistance, there is no reason why
> every village in the county should not have a football or
> hurling club . . . The want of these clubs, the lack of
> proper grounds, apathy among the players themselves
> and the short supply of funds to meet necessary current

expenses, costs of locomotion, etc., are one and all directly traceable to the want of a vigorous and capable county board, with its members working in harmony with one another and with the right men in the right places.[49]

The survivors of the Laune Rangers 1892 All-Ireland side, pictured in May 1935. Note the men wearing their original blue jerseys. In the years after this defeat the GAA in Kerry steadily declined, until the county board itself collapsed in 1898. *(Courtesy of Fitzgerald's Stadium Collection)*

While the economic situation took its toll, the downfall of Charles Stewart Parnell as leader of a united Irish Party also had huge implications for the association both nationally and in Kerry. In November 1890, Parnell's affair with his married mistress, Kitty O'Shea, made headline news across Britain and Ireland. The scandal caused outrage among many political and Church leaders in Ireland. On 6 December, after several days' debate on the question of Parnell's continued leadership of the party, Justin McCarthy MP, who opposed his leadership, asked all those members who agreed with him to leave the meeting. Forty-three did so, leaving Parnell and twenty-seven others behind.[50] The action split not just the party, but Irish nationalist opinion. Like other sections of Irish society, the GAA became deeply divided on the issue. The patrons of the GAA were themselves opposed, with John O'Leary, the noted former Fenian leader, in the pro-Parnellite camp while William O'Brien and Michael Davitt, both leading Irish political figures in the land agitation of the 1880s, supported the opposing side. The *Sentinel*, which was Kerry's main nationalist paper, stood firmly behind its leader, stating: 'For us then Parnell is the word and Parnell is the man. Our confidence in him has never been higher.' At a meeting of Castlegregory GAA club a motion was unanimously carried that the club 'place its implicit confidence in the leadership of Charles Stewart Parnell, [and] that we condemn the action of the Irish Party who severed their connection with him'. At a well-attended gathering of the Dingle GAA a similar resolution in support of Parnell was carried almost unanimously.[51]

However, disunity was appearing within the ranks of the local GAA. At a meeting of Dr Crokes, D. Guerin proposed that members support the club's president, the MP J.D. Sheehan, in his decision to vote for the temporary retirement of Parnell from the leadership of the Irish Party. J. Corcoran, Dr Crokes' secretary, objected to this and a heated debate ensued with members jostling and shoving each other around the floor. The motion was passed by a majority, but when the chairman tried to unite the division by calling for three cheers for Parnell he was meet by cheers and boos and an opposite cheer for Tim Healy.[52] There were similar scenes at Tralee John Mitchels where a special meeting was held for the purpose of adopting the resolution that the club 'express our unaltered and unabated confidence in Charles Stewart Parnell, as leader of the Irish nation'. Maurice Moynihan, the club's secretary, asked for it to be carried unanimously but Thomas Slattery, as the club's chairman, stated that while Parnell had been a great leader for the Irish cause, he had come to the conclusion that he could no longer support him. Slattery gave his casting vote against the resolution and it was defeated amid great excitement.[53]

Nationally, the IRB decided to use its influence among the upper echelons of the GAA to throw the support of the association behind Parnell.[54] Yet despite IRB members holding every position on the Kerry County Board in 1890, support for Parnell was not unanimous.[55] A vote of confidence in Parnell's leadership, proposed at the first Kerry GAA Board meeting of 1891, was refused by the chairman Thomas Slattery and treasurer M. Hanlon. This was despite the fact that Slattery was the District Centre, or commander, of the IRB in Tralee and Hanlon was another prominent IRB member. However, on the same day Dingle and Castlegregory met in a football challenge match after which the crowd and players gave cheers for Parnell and Home Rule. Many prominent GAA officers who were also IRB members became involved in the formation of Parnell Leadership Committees in towns across Ireland.[56] In Kerry, Maurice Moynihan helped form the Tralee branch, while the Kilmoyley captain, John Quane, and Kerry Board representative, Mortimer Galvin, became members of the Abbeydorney branch at its inaugural meeting. When Moynihan organised his national general meeting of the GAA in Dublin in July 1891 the representa-tives present agreed to pledge their support to the leadership and ideals of Charles Stewart Parnell. Some saw this moment as the definitive break from the cautious former politics of the GAA hierarchy. They had now declared themselves not only in favour of Parnell but also in full sympathy with the Fenians and physical-force men. While this view drastically oversimplified the political views among GAA members and completely overstated the influence the IRB had within that membership, it did result in the alienation of those in the GAA opposed to Parnell. Nationally, police reports claimed that the association was being torn asunder due to internal dissension and if this breach was not soon repaired it would become inseparable. Indeed, District Inspector Jones of the RIC's Southwestern division regarded the Parnell split as giving the previously popular GAA its *coup de grâce*.[57]

Throughout 1891, Parnell conducted a whirlwind tour of Ireland in an attempt to retain popular support for his continued leadership of Irish political opinion.[58] However, despite his best efforts, the Parnellite camp lost three by-elections in Ireland that year. Becoming more desperate, Parnell even began to court the support of those of the physical-force persuasion, appealing to 'the hill-side men' of Fenian tradition. Yet this rigorous campaigning broke his health and, exhausted, he passed away in October 1891. At his funeral in Dublin the support of the GAA remained firm to the end. Six GAA officials shouldered his coffin into Glasnevin cemetery.[59] As many as 2,000 GAA members were prominently placed in his funeral cortège. Each one carried a hurley draped in black and held to resemble a rifle. Over a hundred representatives of various nationalist bodies, such as the GAA and the Parnell Leadership Committee, attended from Tralee alone.

Nevertheless, Parnell's death brought little resolution. The political fissure that cut open the Irish Party would continue to haunt Irish nationalist politics throughout the remaining years of the decade. Its effects on the GAA proved to be as catastrophic as those of the economic climate in which it took place. The Parnell split had a brutal impact on the GAA precisely because it denied the association a strong coherent leadership at the very time that the GAA needed it most. Only with such unity could the association have hoped to face and overcome the extraordinarily difficult challenge that the social and economic condition of the country posed for a sporting organisation like itself. Without that unity, combating the broader social and economic reality became extremely unlikely. However, the withdrawal of clerical support of the GAA at this time made it impossible.

The GAA and the Catholic Church
The Parnell split had a chaotic effect not only on the GAA as an organisation but on every facet of nationalist political opinion in Ireland. The IPP's National League remained loyal to Parnell, while his detractors in 1891 created their own body, the Irish National Federation. Yet the party's internal wrangling had a disastrous effect on the influence of both organisations in areas like Kerry. By 1893, the RIC claimed that only one branch of the National League operated in Kerry and though its opponent had sixteen branches, they were all said to be inactive. The IRB, having sided with the Parnellites, was said to have disintegrated to such an extent during the previous two years that its power was 'almost broken'.[60]

As 1892 dawned, the rival Irish political camps were preparing for a bitter struggle in that summer's general election.

Many within the GAA remained loyal to their 'lost leader'. However, the Parnell scandal had already aroused the ire of the Catholic Church in Ireland. It now turned its full force against the Parnellite camp and in particular its allies in the GAA. Already reeling from internal strife and seeing its membership melt away, the hostility of the Church would deal a near-mortal blow to the association.

During the second half of the nineteenth century, the Catholic Church had risen to a position of unheralded power and influence in Irish society in what Emmet Larkin termed 'the devotional revolution'. Larkin argued that the profound collective physiological effects of the Famine on Ireland, coupled with a massive exodus of the poorer elements of Irish society, left what remained of that society far more susceptible to the Church's influence.[61] Whereas in the years before the Famine there were simply not enough priests or churches to accommodate Ireland's Catholic population, when the population shrank, the numbers of clergy remained constant, increasing in real terms per head of population. Thus, a bolstered clerical machine found itself better able to control and influence its parishioners. The Famine also accelerated the destruction of the native language and culture, a process which hastened as the nineteenth century progressed. Communication in both the written and spoken word was increasingly geared towards English, while in education, business and politics British models were adopted for use in Ireland. The country was being effectively anglicised 'or, perhaps more appropriately, West Britonised'.[62] Aware of losing their identity, the Irish people embraced Catholicism with profound zeal as this 'provided the Irish with a substitute symbolic language and offered them a new cultural heritage with which they could identify and be identified and through which they could identify with one another'.[63] By the 1880s, the Catholic Church was perhaps the most dominant and influential body in Irish popular opinion. Any movement, political or cultural, would have been advised to court its blessings. The GAA was no different in this regard, though in the years before the Parnell split the relationship between the two had often been fraught.

When he founded the GAA Michael Cusack had been quick to enlist the patronage of Archbishop Croke of Cashel, almost instantly identifying his fledgling association with the prestige of the Catholic Church. Indeed, statements from the clergy in support of Gaelic games were common throughout the first years of the association's existence and received widespread publicity in those newspapers which supported the GAA.[64] Yet this harmony did not to last long. At the GAA Annual Convention on 8 November 1887 two IRB officers in the GAA's central executive, P.T. Hoctor and Patrick N. Fitzgerald, moved to secure control of that body for the IRB. The IRB had effectively rigged the convention, piling in its own members by claiming them to be representatives of fictitious clubs. This enabled the swelled IRB representation to elect one of their own to the presidency of the GAA. The decision caused uproar, especially among the clerical representatives and constitutional moderates within the association. As fist fights broke out on the floor, one representative, Fr John Scanlan of Nenagh, attempted to stop the election. At this the IRB supporters began hurling insults and some 'hustled him about'. In response, Scanlan, his clerical colleagues and around 200 of his supporters withdrew from the meeting.[65] In the fallout from the convention, Croke publicly disassociated himself from the new executive. Letters to the press from outraged clergy accused this new executive of being against Croke and the priesthood of Ireland.[66] It looked for a time that the GAA would disintegrate but Croke and the association's other patron, Michael Davitt, held negotiations with the IRB-dominated executive and the crisis was quickly resolved. At a special convention in January 1888 Maurice Davin was re-elected president and only two officers from the IRB remained in place on a newly elected executive.[67] Despite this, many within the Church remained hostile to the Fenian element they associated with the GAA.[68] That same month in Armagh, Archbishop Michael Logue in a sermon strongly condemned the workings of the GAA. He declared that while he did not object to boys engaging in a few hours of play on Sunday afternoon, 'he was opposed to their going away to play in places where they would have to mix with members of secret societies'.[69]

As previously outlined, during the delayed GAA Annual Convention for 1888 the IRB made a second attempt to take control of the GAA's central executive. Clerical delegates and their supporters, disgusted at the takeover by the physical-force faction, left to set up a rival meeting in an adjacent room. The fallout from the convention would have a serious effect on the popularity of the GAA in many counties. Clerical opposition spread almost countrywide as the Church sought to denounce the GAA and urged clubs not to affiliate with it. The result was bedlam in many counties. Both Cork and Limerick actually had two rival county boards, one staying loyal to the central executive, the other supporting the clerical-led moderates. At the Annual Kildare GAA Convention delegates refused to recognise the authority of the newly elected GAA central executive. Across Ireland, GAA clubs fell into opposing clerical- and 'Fenian'-controlled factions.[70] The RIC remarked that the GAA was continuing to diminish in both strength and discipline. They attributed this to the clergy's influence being brought to bear against the organisation once it became clear that the IRB was using the association to entrap the youth of the country into their secret society. In an interview with *Sport* in August 1889, William J. Walsh, the Archbishop of Dublin, stated he was fully aware that efforts were being made in some parts of Ireland to engraft upon the GAA a secret society of a political character.[71]

Despite the prevalence of clerical hostility towards the GAA, the Church in Kerry was reported 'as standing aloof' and on the whole taking little interest in the association.[72] This is not to say there was no evidence of Church participation in Gaelic events. For example, one of the first 'official' Gaelic football matches played in Kerry, between Tralee Mitchels and Castleisland, in March 1888 was refereed by the local parish priest, Fr McDonnell. In 1889, the League of the Cross GAA Athletic Club was formed in Dingle with the local reverend, C. Scully, as its president. Often in Kerry priests attending matches were asked to lend their moral authority to act as crowd stewards. During the aforementioned 1890 hurling semi-final between Kenmare and Kilmoyley, a number of priests swiftly managed to restore order among those players and supporters engaged in the mass brawl, allowing the match to resume.[73] However, despite such connections, the fallout from the Parnell split brought the full force of Church opposition to bear against the GAA in Kerry. This would prove almost fatal for the association there.

Members of the Central Executive, 1888. This is the earliest surviving photograph of the GAA's Central Executive. It was at the 1888 Annual Convention that the bitter split between the clergy and the IRB first occurred. *(Courtesy of Frank Burke)*

To understand the influence the Church held in Irish politics it is necessary to chart its relationship with the Irish Party. In October 1884, an informal alliance between Parnell's IPP and the Irish bishops, as a body, had been arranged. In exchange for the bishops being given control of all matters of educational policy in Ireland, they recognised the IPP as the bona fide medium for decisions on acceptable solutions to the land question and Home Rule.[74] By 1886, this understanding had evolved so that the Church had also established its individual right to be consulted as to the suitability of IPP parliamentary candidates selected by local conventions within their spiritual jurisdiction, as well as clearly defining the clergy's role in their approval of those candidates at such conventions. Yet this alliance was tested when senior clergy refused to back the IPP's 'Plan of Campaign' in the late 1880s as a result of the pope's condemnation of it. As a consequence, lay influence in political organisations like the National League grew while the clerical influence within the IPP began to diminish.[75] By

1890, the Church found its voice becoming eroded within the political sphere of Irish politics. To counter this, in October 1890, the bishops of Ireland met to radically reorganise the way they functioned as a body. Under the guidance of Archbishop Walsh of Dublin they set up a standing committee that could be convened at any time (on his initiative). This effectively made Walsh, with Rome's blessing, the head of the Irish Church. The Church emerged from this meeting a more effectively organised body than ever before, acquiring a single, strong voice with which to express its views. It did not take long for this committee to prove its effectiveness.

As the divorce crisis erupted, Parnell fought desperately to retain leadership of the IPP. His refusal to bend to the will of the clergy or to pressure from the IPP's British allies (William Gladstone and his Liberal Party) who called for his resignation instigated the split in Irish politics. The clergy quickly turned their backs on Parnell and his supporters. In January 1891, the *Kerry Sentinel*, at the request of Archdeacon O'Sullivan of Kenmare, published a list of clergy in the diocese who had declared themselves against Parnell's leadership on 'moral and political grounds'. The list included priests from almost every parish in Kerry. Because the *Sentinel* was an avowedly Parnellite paper, many clergy ceased to purchase it and some had even threatened to denounce it as 'immoral literature' if it was continued to be read by members of their parishes.[76] Despite Parnell's own death, clerical opposition to the Parnellites became increasingly acrimonious during the 1892 general election.[77] During polling for the election in Tralee, a priest took up position near the polling station and challenged every voter who passed, cautioning them under 'all sorts of penalties' not to vote for Parnellite candidates. In Dingle, a priest was heard to tell parishioners that voting for Edward Harrington, the Parnellite candidate, was 'voting against God'. Reports of similar intimidation came in from every village in Kerry.[78]

Throughout the election, the Parnellite camp fought a losing battle. All the weight of the clergy was against them and with the prospect of a liberal victory and the introduction of a Home Rule Bill in exchange for Irish MP support, it was hardly likely the electorate would endorse the Parnellite repudiation of the liberal alliance. The election resulted in seventy-one anti-Parnellite MPs under the leadership of Justin McCarthy being returned, as opposed to nine Parnellite MPs. In Kerry, all four constituencies returned anti-Parnellite candidates. The clergy there responded with glee. In Abbeydorney, the local priest, welcoming the formation of a Liberal/Irish MP coalition government, attacked with venom the failure of the Parnellite faction, remarking that locals who had supported them were nothing more than 'bastard makers'. Gladstone, with Irish MP support, pressed ahead with plans to introduce Home Rule to Ireland to finally bring about an end to the Irish Question which had dominated British politics for so long. However, his IPP allies were so truly demoralised by their own internal divisions that they could not cease quarrelling, even while the Home Rule Bill itself was at stake in 1893. The bill was quickly vetoed by the House of Lords, and Gladstone resigned as Prime Minister in 1894.[79] With his retirement, the Liberals ceased to make Irish reform a major element of their party's policy. Meanwhile, the Conservatives, who would govern Britain for the next ten years, sought to 'Kill Home Rule with Kindness', a policy of conciliation designed to address and remedy popular Irish grievances such as the land question. Home Rule was dead, and with Irish nationalist political opinion split down the middle, a sense of depression descended on Irish nationalism. A malaise set in across the political landscape for much of the remainder of the decade which seemed to hold Ireland itself under a cloud.

The decision of the GAA's ruling body to declare in favour of Parnell ensured the Church's hostility was also directed at the association. While the clergy had shown little interest in the GAA in Kerry before the Parnell scandal, in its aftermath they put considerable energy into opposing what they had begun to see as little more than a Fenian cover organisation.[80] The association's stance deprived the organisation of the support of the local priesthood. In April 1891, it was reported that two football matches in the Kerry county championship, due to have taken place in Annascaul, were not held on account of the Camp and Annascaul GAA teams being warned by their respective parish priests not to participate in GAA competitions. The Kerry GAA Board strongly condemned the local priest's 'unaccountable interference' with the county championship and voted not to fix any more matches for the Annascaul venue. However, clerical hostility began to have a definite effect on the local GAA. Following the IRB takeover of the central executive in 1889, the RIC in Kerry reported in mid-1890 that there were only two GAA clubs there that firmly sided with the clerical opposition to the IRB-dominated executive. Yet within nine months, fifteen of the twenty-four clubs then affiliated in Kerry were described as being under the control of the clerical opposition.[81] According to the RIC's Midland division, after the nationalist split the clergy redoubled their vigilance and their denunciations against Parnellism and secret societies: 'Through fear of the clergy many Gaelic Clubs, whose members were Parnellites and Extremists, were [being] reorganised under the patronage and personal conduct of the clergy and now they support the [opposing] side.' When GAA members were forced to choose between clerical denunciation and non-involvement in the GAA the pro-clerical choice proved by far the most popular. Nevertheless, bitterness towards the Church, especially among the advanced nationalists who made up the GAA's ruling body, remained strong. When Parnell was laid to rest in October 1891 the GAA's central executive laid a wreath on his grave. It was sure to be read by those who in their opinion had destroyed Parnell. It quoted the Apostle Matthew and read 'an eye for an eye, a tooth for a tooth'.[82]

However, many within the association realised that if the organisation was to survive, some attempt had to be made to heal the wounds left by Parnell's fall and the Church's opposition. At Kerry's Annual GAA Convention in 1893 the chairman, Thomas Slattery, pointed to the example of the Cork GAA Board which could claim that the success of the association in their own county was due to the absence of party politics, something that could not be said for Kerry. He urged his colleagues

> . . . to rigidly exclude all political matters from the association and let their chief aim and endeavours be directed entirely towards the promotion and interests of the GAA . . . [for] when they have their own Government watching over the interests of their country . . . then they would stand up as Irishmen against the common foe, hurl

them from every ditch . . . and finally kick them into the
Boyne.[83]

With the parliamentary party in disarray and the GAA a spectre of
its past glories, the IRB slipped away into the background of Irish
nationalism for much of the 1890s, biding its time until the
popular mood in Ireland would be more congenial for plans for an
IRB-led insurrection. By 1893, police reports showed that in Kerry
and Cork the GAA was operating without any noticeable IRB
influence and that the latter organisation was thoroughly
disorganised.[84] The clergy retained their enmity towards the
association for much of the remaining years of the decade.
However, in 1895 a dispute between the Kerry GAA and the local
Catholic Church provided an opportunity for the central executive
to extend the hand of friendship once again towards their
estranged patron, Archbishop Croke.

In April 1895, a Gaelic tournament was organised in Killarney
in conjunction with the Kerry County Board to aid the Sisters of
Mercy Holy Convent in the town. The promoter and organiser of
the event was a Tralee man, S.B. Roche. Two hurling matches were
to be held, the first between two north Kerry hurling selections,
the second an inter-county challenge between the Blarney and
Kenmare hurling clubs. Yet the holding of this tournament erupted
into a full-scale national controversy between the hierarchy and
the GAA. At the Kerry Annual GAA Convention, held the week
after the tournament, Roche was present to explain what had
transpired. Around six weeks previously he received a letter from
the Sisters of Mercy stating that they had got permission from the
Bishop of Kerry, Dr John Coffey, to host the event. Roche then set
about organising the tournament and got Lord Kenmare's
approval to use a pitch on his demesne to stage the matches. A few
days later, Roche, to his great surprise, received notice that the
bishop had withdrawn his support on the grounds that it would be
held under the auspices of the GAA. Roche wrote to the bishop
stating that the preparations for the event were at an advanced
stage and that it could not now be cancelled without disappointing
a large number of people. The bishop replied that as he believed
the GAA was connected with secret societies, 'he would on no

account give his consent to charity that would be worked under its patronage'. In consequence of the bishop's stance, Lord Kenmare refused the use of his field. Roche concluded his report by stating he had never known the association to be connected with any secret organisation and that as a good Catholic he saw 'nothing derogatory or disrespectful' to the faith in holding a GAA tournament.

In response, Denis Bunyan, secretary of the Kerry GAA, declared there were 'higher dignitaries of the church at the head of the Gaelic Association than the Bishop of Kerry and they have never found fault with it or withdrawn their patronage (hear, hear)'. Tom Slattery, as chairman, retorted that there was a belief among certain people that 'none but the higher class of society should enjoy themselves with sports of any kind'. It was better for them, he claimed, to see those young men 'who had no opportunity of amusement other than on a football or hurling field on a Sunday, lounging at the gable end of a house or sitting on a ditch trying to while away the time card-playing or otherwise'. Slattery obviously felt the bishop's stance was nothing but an attempt by some elements among the Church and gentry to tar all members of the GAA with a Fenian brush and preserve the patronage of organised sports for those who shared their own political views. Nonetheless, as a result of Dr Coffey's opposition the tournament was a financial failure. Roche, after some difficulty, was able to secure a second field for the tournament but this was some distance from the town and as a result the attendance was much smaller than expected.[85]

In the days after the tournament, Roche referred the matter to the GAA's Central Council. In consequence, a deputation from the Central Council headed by its president, Frank Dineen, waited on Archbishop Croke at his residence to lay before him the statement of the Bishop of Kerry. The meeting was fully reported in the national press. When Croke received them, Dineen spelled out the serious consequences of the bishop's statement for all those connected with the GAA if it was left unchallenged in public. He further declared to Croke that the GAA was purely a sporting organisation and 'while admitting that a strong political feeling existed among members some time ago, he was glad to say that was now replaced by a desire among members of the Association to promote the interests of the Association and its interests alone'. Croke responded that 'as far as he knew the Association was purely an athletic body'. Members of the association, he warranted, had taken sides in the recent political dispute, 'and that was natural'. With regard to the bishop's allegations, Croke said he was totally unaware of any foundation to back up the bishop's claim and moreover 'did not believe' Coffey's assertions. Croke also mentioned his 'surprise' that Coffey had made such a statement. Dineen assured the archbishop that the members of the GAA's councils, though they differed in politics, placed the interest of the association above and beyond all political and other matters. On the invitation of Dineen, Croke attended the All-Ireland championship match being played in Thurles that day and the captains of both teams were introduced to him.[86]

The above episode and its fallout marked a definitive break in the political controversy that so rocked the relationship between the Church and the GAA during the previous seven years. The GAA's president pledged to its clerical patron that all matters of politics, which had ruptured their relationship in the past, had been set aside. The time had come for both sides to move on and the GAA was striving to rebuild itself in a more harmonious apolitical model. Croke's public acceptance of the GAA's open act of contrition allowed many of the Irish clergy to again re-establish connections with the GAA at local level. That July the association joined in with the celebrations of Dr Croke's episcopal silver jubilee. During the event, an address was read to him from the GAA, signed by the members of its Central Council.

In Kerry, however, the controversy rumbled on. While the association nationally strove to heal the rift between itself and the Church, locally the episode continued to have a damaging effect on the already weak position of the GAA there.[87] It fuelled the scepticism of many clergymen that the association in Kerry remained merely an IRB front. Despite the public rebuke from his superior, Coffey stated that his opinion remained unchanged. An RIC report gives an insight as to why Coffey may have refused to change his opinions. It remarked that in Kerry, 'it is significant to find that the four branches of the association now existing in that county are under Fenian control and that all the officers are either known or suspected Fenians . . . In no other county of the division, however, does this state of things prevail'. The author noted there was little doubt that the action of the Bishop of Kerry had materially weakened the efforts to reorganise the association there and it had undoubtedly caused much 'uneasiness already among the parents of a good many young men in Kerry connected with the movement, who are most anxious that they should sever their connection with it'.[88]

For much of the first fifty years of the association, the relationship between it and the Catholic Church remained tense. The clergy was caught between not wanting to assist an organisation that might be misused by violent societies like the IRB and not wanting to completely cede control of that organisation to such societies. Yet in spite of the political wrangling which dominated much of their early history, many members of the hierarchy saw the potential of the association to promote their ideals of what a healthy, moral, orderly and Christian society should be. Some, like Archbishop Croke, perceived in a national body like the GAA a medium to tackle several issues prevalent among young men in Irish society. One such issue was alcoholism. The problem of intemperance was rife in Irish society. This was not surprising given the proliferation of public houses in Ireland in the late nineteenth and early twentieth century.[89] For example, in 1900, Killarney, which had a population of 2,212, boasted ninety-seven licensed premises, or one pub for every eleven men.[90] Such statistics demonstrate the enormous power publicans wielded in areas such as Kerry. Indeed, a parliamentary report in 1891 showed that in the previous year, 3,729 arrests for drunk and disorderly behaviour were made in Kerry, the largest number in any district in Munster.[91]

With a drinking culture already so prevalent within Irish society, it is perhaps unsurprising that those who were members of the GAA were any less disposed to the draw of the pub. Indeed, the very nature of GAA events may have made the members of the organisation more susceptible to the lure of alcohol than others in general society. In 1878, Church-led campaigns for temperance secured a measure of victory when a government act was introduced forcing the complete closure of establishments on

Sundays. It must be remembered that for the vast majority of the Irish working population Sunday was the traditional and only day of rest and as such usually the busiest day of the week for Irish publicans. One way to circumnavigate the law was by means of the 'bona fide traveller clause'. Under the act, anyone travelling more than three miles from his place of abode the previous day was entitled to be served at a pub or inn. Journey distances to rival parish and inter-county GAA matches were usually more than enough to ensure a legal drink was available on Sundays for players and spectators alike.

Drinking at matches or tournaments became much practised and much condemned in the association's first decades. Priests throughout the country loathed this excessive consumption of alcohol which was all too frequently connected with games held on the Sabbath. In his pastoral letter written in early 1888, Archbishop Logue of Armagh condemned the GAA's links with intemperance and their desecration of the Sabbath. That same year a number of parish priests in the diocese wrote to the bishop condemning the negative impact of the GAA with regard to its drink culture, its use as an opportunity for interaction between the sexes and its effect on church attendance among young men. In Laois, the local Bishop of Ossory issued strong denunciations of the alcohol consumption prevalent around Gaelic matches and ordered the faithful to avoid its games.[92] RIC reports from Kerry revealed that the popularity of the organisation there was much in debt to the 'excretions of the publicans whose trade is benefited by movement'.[93] Indeed, Thomas Slattery, chairman of the Kerry Board for so many years, was himself a publican with an establishment in Rock Street, Tralee. This sporting enthusiasm on the part of publicans was plainly in self-interest, it being reported that the various matches 'bring together large numbers of "bona fide travellers" whose custom goes to aggrandise the publicans'.[94] Drinking quickly became an accepted part of GAA culture. Indeed, the frequent examples of crowd rowdiness and pitch invasion in the early years of the association may have owed much to patrons indulging in the attractions of the public house before a match.

Yet even as the GAA was being viewed as an opportunity for

the publicans to grow their business, conversely it was seen by the clergy as a means of stamping out the culture of intemperance in Irish society altogether. In 1838, Fr Theobald Mathew of Tipperary formed the Total Abstinence Society, which pledged its members to live a life of total sobriety.[95] The movement grew with force throughout the nineteenth century as literally millions of people both in Ireland and abroad took the temperance pledge. For men like Archbishop Croke the GAA presented a perfect vehicle to drive home the message of temperance and abstinence. At the GAA's Annual Convention in January 1888 Croke sent letters urging the GAA to ban the sale of alcoholic drinks at or near GAA meetings, not to hold such meetings near public houses, not to accept prizes from publicans and not to hold meetings on days of obligation or before two o'clock on Sundays. The convention resolved that these proposals should indeed become law.[96] That same year the Cavan GAA Convention passed a motion that required each club to appoint three or four men to take charge of match arrangements for their teams and to ensure good conduct of their players and supporters on match days.[97] In March 1890, with the 100th anniversary of the birth of Fr Mathew drawing near, Croke wrote to the national press encouraging all members of the GAA to join the new Temperance Societies being formed across Ireland to celebrate the centenary.[98] In 1895, the Listowel branch of the Temperance Society actually affiliated a Gaelic football team to the Kerry Board and took part in that year's county championship. Ironically, the history of Listowel Temperance Society football club was both short and tempestuous. Their first ever championship match against Tralee Mitchels ended in controversy, with play abandoned due to two players getting injured. At the subsequent replay, finding themselves outplayed and seeing no hope of beating their more illustrious opponents by football means, the Listowel players began 'at every opportunity' to foul their Tralee opponents, actions that resulted in a mass brawl among the players. The supporters of the Listowel team then invaded the pitch and started to attack the Tralee players as they tried to leave the ground. At a subsequent county board meeting a resolution was unanimously passed throwing the team out of the competition in consequence of the disgraceful conduct of their players and supporters 'who

Archbishop Thomas Croke. Croke was the first patron of the association and one of the few leading church officials in Ireland to see the potential of the early GAA in spreading the Church's message of temperance in Irish society. *(Courtesy of Frank Burke)*

had brought discredit on the Association here'.[99]

In its drive for temperance through the medium of a sporting organisation, the Catholic Church in Ireland acted no differently from its contemporaries. In Britain, concern over how the lower classes amused themselves became increasingly acute at this time. The role of sporting organisations such as the English Football Association and the Rugby Football Union was seen by the English Church and lay authorities as having a vital role in a wider programme of moral reform within society. Just as the Catholic Church in Ireland sought influence in the GAA to promote its ideals, so many early sports clubs in England were Church-based and founded with the initial intention to promote rational and controlled recreation under middle-class supervision.[100] Indeed, the frequency in which temperance societies and Church organisations participated in the establishment of sporting clubs in Britain makes it clear that many who founded these clubs believed sport served the purpose of diverting men's attention away from drink and crime.

However, as was the case in Ireland, working-class sports inevitably revolved around a pub culture. It was a meeting at the Freemason's Tavern in London in October 1863 which led to the foundation of the FA. This set the seal for the pub's role in fostering the transition from traditional sports of the past to those that would be codified, regularised and orderly.[101] It was frequently the case in Britain that enterprising publicans established a connection with the growing sport of soccer by renting out the land next to their establishments for use as club grounds. They also rented space in their pubs for use as changing and meeting

Despite the hostility of the Church towards the GAA during the 1890s, in the years after the formation of the Free State both organisations would develop strong bonds, which remain to the present day. For much of the twentieth century this relationship was cogently expressed in the tradition of the ball for important matches being thrown in by a bishop or other important Church dignitary. In this photo from the 1929 All-Ireland final, both team captains prepare for the Bishop of Kildare, Rev. Dr Cullen, to do the honour. *(Courtesy of terracetalk.com and T.J. Flynn)*

rooms for local clubs.[102] Despite the best efforts of right-minded reformers both in Ireland and the UK, the pub was often the central nexus that bound sports teams together. The GAA was little different than other codes in this regard. Although because of its more ruralised society the pub may not have been the major nucleus for early GAA clubs in Ireland in the way it was for soccer or rugby teams in the industrialised cities of England, nevertheless the local pub became just as much a focal point for Gaelic teams.[103] The drinking culture which was so prevalent within the GAA was never going to be eradicated entirely by the zealousness of the Catholic Church. Yet the temperance crusade shows how, despite their views on the leaders of the GAA, the Church frequently used the association as a means to spread its own message of social control. The hierarchy's disputes with those who ran the organisation did not sever entirely the connection between the Church and the GAA's popular membership. Rather, throughout these first decades of coexistence the Church had a deep and profound concern for the welfare of its congregation who were members of the association.

Threat of Foreign Games, 1894–1904

The first half of the 1890s almost destroyed the GAA as a functioning body in Kerry. The long-term agricultural depression, coupled with the huge increase in the numbers of young men emigrating, robbed the association there of its grass-roots membership. Those few clubs that carried on had been wracked by internal divisions caused by the wider split in Irish nationalism over Parnell's downfall. Worse yet, the full force of the Catholic Church had been brought against the GAA nationally for its support of the Parnell cause. Deprived of the influential support of the local cleric, clubs were robbed of a natural ally, patron and organiser. In 1894, only sixteen GAA matches were reported as taking place in Kerry. The local situation reflected the national decline. A report at the beginning of that year put the national total of GAA clubs at a mere 118, with a combined membership of just 5,183.[104] With the GAA in such a weak state, it found itself in an increasingly desperate battle for the hearts and minds of young athletic men. While the GAA in Kerry struggled to continue as a viable sporting body, a number of rival sports were already set to capitalise on its demise.

In Kerry, the 1890s witnessed the emergence of a number of new codified sports which had spread throughout the British Isles over the preceding twenty years. For example, golf had begun to make an appearance in the county in the late 1880s. The game had evolved in Scotland before spreading across the UK and North America in the late nineteenth century. The first record of a golf club in Kerry was the Dooks Golf Club in 1889. In Ireland, its popularity exploded after 1891 and some 103 golf clubs were established nationally by the end of the decade.[105] The game became the preserve of the gentry, landlords, clergy, merchant classes, officers in the British Army and higher professions – in short, a recreation for members of the establishment and a mirror to the lifestyle of the Ascendancy. The Killarney Golf Club was formed in 1893 with Lord Kenmare as its patron and president, while its first captain was Walter Butler, head of the town's Munster and Leinster Bank branch. Frequently, the Tralee club played host to contests between British Army officers stationed in the town's barracks and some of the more senior RIC officers stationed there. By 1897, Kerry boasted eight golf clubs: Killarney, Dooks, Castlegregory, Fenit, Tralee Town Park, Ballybunion, Derrynane and Ardfert, where there was an eighteen-hole course owned privately by the Crosbie family. The rapid growth of the game in Ireland, albeit confined to a certain section of Irish society, led some to view the nation's golf clubs as places where the Anglo-Irish elite retreated following the collapse of Parnell and the dashing of Home Rule.

On Saturday 3 February 1894, a large local crowd turned out on the grounds of the Commercial Cable Company in Waterville to watch a match between the company's employees and the Durham Light Infantry Regiment stationed in Tralee. The sides drew 2-2.[106] The event marks the first definite recorded match of association football in Kerry. Nationally, by 1890 there were 124 clubs affiliated to the Irish Football Association. Though destined internationally to become the most popular sport in the world, the game in Ireland was slow to spread. Of the above 124 clubs, the vast majority were based in the larger urban centres such as Belfast and Dublin and there was little rural representation outside of Ulster. In this, the development of soccer as an urban sport, principally in larger industrial cities, mirrored its origins and development in Britain. Kerry, like much of the rest of rural Ireland, lacked the large urban centres and industrial workplaces from which many soccer clubs originated. Indeed, in the 1890s only six soccer matches involving teams from Kerry were recorded.[107] It is obvious that the impetus for the game in Kerry, as was the case for cricket before it, was from the military regiments such as the Durham Light Infantry stationed in Tralee, or from employees of some of the big international wireless companies like the Commercial Cable Company in Waterville. British workers from the latter who were acquainted with the game began to organise matches with local men. The Company team was reported as playing a side from nearby Cahersiveen in March 1894 and a team from Waterville village that September. However, the sport never achieved any great popularity in Kerry at any time before the Second World War and initially remained confined to military and foreign worker elements in the county.

Hockey was another sport novel to Kerry in the 1890s, with the Tralee Hockey Club being formed at a meeting in St John M. Donovan's merchant store in November 1895. Despite a record of the club being formed, reporting of hockey matches in the *Sentinel* only began in 1899. But a report of the club's record for the 1898 season showed they played nine matches – winning five, losing three and drawing one.[108] Hockey was one of the first examples of competitive sport in Kerry in which women participated. In February 1899, a ladies' team from Kenmare played a Tralee selection in the Tralee Sportsground, with the game ending level. Hockey clubs were recorded in Killarney, Tralee, Kenmare and Listowel, indicating the urban-based nature of the game. The Tralee Hockey Club took part in the Munster Hockey Cup in 1899. The membership list for clubs like Tralee shows that, similar to cricket and golf before it, hockey was the preserve of a certain well-to-do section of Kerry society. Indeed, the men who formed the Tralee club were also heavily involved with the local Tralee Athletic and Cricket Club. There is no evidence of any rural combinations being formed or of the sport ever becoming popular among those who may otherwise have played Gaelic games. The reporting of the game in the local Kerry media was also sporadic, another indication of its niche appeal.[109]

One surprise in looking at the development of other sports in Kerry in the 1890s is the definite increase in the popularity of cricket during the decade. Though only sixteen matches were recorded in the county between 1885 and 1890, seventy-five matches were reported in the ten years between 1891 and 1901. Nevertheless, the situation in Kerry in the 1890s, albeit on a much smaller scale, corresponds to what was happening in counties such as Kilkenny and Westmeath where the game was much more established and popular. In both areas, the sport, which due to the agrarian unrest of the late 1880s had suffered a dip in fortunes, quickly reasserted itself and reached its peak of popularity between 1894 and 1900.[110] A similar situation prevailed in Kerry, with cricket reaching a peak of popularity in the middle of the decade (see Appendix VIII). The numbers of county combinations recorded rose from eleven in the 1880s to twenty-nine during the 1890s.

It is difficult to explain the expansion of cricket during this time in Kerry. With reference to Kilkenny, Michael O'Dwyer speculated that the sport's growth there in the 1890s could be explained by the lack of GAA activity, with many of the association's players switching over to play cricket. There is little evidence in Kerry of former hurlers or footballers turning to the game because GAA clubs were disbanding.[111] Yet there are indications that some secondary schools might have been responsible for extending the sport's popularity in Kerry. In Listowel, the clergy who founded St Michael's College in 1879 quickly introduced the game to its pupils and cricket became the first team sport played by the school. This undoubtedly influenced the popularity of the code in the town and a senior cricket club was indeed established in Listowel in 1899 which probably included several past pupils of the college.

It was the RIC that seemed to play a key role in the expansion of cricket in the middle years of the decade in Kerry. District Inspector J.E. Holmes was a major force in the establishment of the RIC Cricket Club in Tralee, first recorded in 1895. Along with other senior local RIC officers, like S.A. Waters, he took a leading role in the organisation of matches. Often these were played against military teams either from the town's garrison or the Buttevant garrison in Cork. They also played an extensive programme against civilian teams from Tralee, Killarney, Ardfert and Glenbeigh as well as the Cork County Cricket Club. Both men were the star players of the RIC team and when the club played practice matches each man captained the opposing sides. Holmes was transferred from Kerry in 1896 and this seemed to have an impact on a number of matches the RIC arranged thereafter. The financial clout such local cricket clubs possessed was demonstrated in 1897 when the honorary secretary of the Tralee Cricket Club informed members that they had secured the services of a professional cricket player from England, one Mr Coleman. During the upcoming cricket season, he would be available to coach teams every day in the local sports ground.

The weight of evidence would suggest that the same professional, business and military classes that patronised cricket in Kerry in the 1880s were the major source for players and patronage again in the 1890s. This may help explain why cricket was able to attain a level of popularity previously unseen in the county. The professionals and military that played the game were unlikely to have been greatly affected by the agricultural depression that was having such an impact on the small farmers and labourers who made up the majority of the GAA. Likewise, emigration did not affect them to anywhere near the same degree as GAA members. Such men's social class ensured they had a stable, secure income and were much more likely to be married. The young men who were members of the GAA were largely single. Having no family responsibilities, emigration drew on them the most. For example, 90 per cent of those emigrating from Ireland in the late nineteenth and early twentieth century were single and unskilled.[112] It may also have been the case that in the absence of Gaelic games, newspapers became more interested in covering cricket to fill the void in their sports pages and this could be another reason for a seeming jump in participation.

Although the GAA continued to diminish, most of the rival sports which existed in Kerry remained the preserve of a mostly well-off and urban upper class. For the GAA to fail in an area like Kerry, a rival popular code that could compete for players among the lower middle and working class would need to be established. This is exactly what happened in Kerry in the last years of the nineteenth century. Rugby union, within a short space of time, began to enjoy unprecedented popularity in the county. A major reason for this was the continued local decline of the GAA.

In the face of clerical hostility and internal divisions, the GAA had sought to distance itself from its connections with the IRB and promote itself as a more apolitical organisation. To bolster numbers it removed its ban on RIC members joining the organisation at its Annual Convention in April 1893. In 1896, the association revoked the ban on its members playing 'foreign games'. Yet in Kerry the decline only seemed to worsen. The year 1897 marked the worst harvests recorded in the county since 1846. The exceptionally wet weather heralded the return of the dreaded potato blight, which caused the devastating failure of the potato crops across Munster. A series of disastrous harvests continued into 1898 and 1899 and with the agriculture sector in Kerry in such desperate straits, agrarian unrest began to rise. Only a strong and driven county board could have hoped to keep Gaelic activity going during such desperate economic times. But the Kerry GAA received an almost mortal blow in March 1897 when Thomas Slattery, who had been president of the county board since its inception in 1888, refused to allow his name to go forward for re-election. Robbed of his energetic and forceful leadership, the GAA in Kerry practically ceased to exist.

In the midst of such difficulties, rugby thrived, particularly in larger towns like Tralee. Tralee RFC became the most successful provincial town club in Munster at this time and played seasonal challenge matches with senior clubs in Limerick and Cork and competed in the Munster Senior Cup.[113] Likewise, the club was able to augment its regular season of fixtures by playing home and away matches against local teams, such as a garrison team from Ballymullen Barracks in the town and the Dingle RFC. Players from the club were of sufficient standard to impress in a provincial trial game between North Munster and South Munster in January 1895. That same year Dr William O'Sullivan of Killarney captained Queen's College Cork to victory in the Munster Senior Cup and became the first Kerry man to be capped at international level against Scotland that spring. The removal of the 'foreign games' ban led to a definite upswing in rugby's fortunes in the county. No longer affected by any stigma associated with the sport and in the absence of Gaelic activity, those young men who were in a position to do so, crossed over.[114] Indeed, already the Kerry GAA was concerned at the growth of the sport. At its county convention in 1894 the Kilmoyley representative, J. Lawlor, asked if the GAA was being too 'conservative' in not allowing its members to play rugby. John Moynihan of Tralee Mitchels retorted that the class of men who run that game 'would poison and hang everything Gaelic' given the chance.[115]

The significant uptake in rugby, despite the harsh economic conditions, can be explained by a look at the social profile of rugby players in Kerry. By selecting a pool of thirty-two players from various Tralee and Killarney rugby combinations from 1897 to 1900 and matching them to census material from 1901, the results prove illuminating.[116] The approach uses broadly the same class categories employed by both the 1901 census and Tom Hunt in his study on the social composition of GAA clubs. Thus, we find that Class I, or professionals, amount to 17.5 per cent of rugby players in this sample. Class II, which were defined as those engaged in various commercial activities such as merchants, clerks, etc., totalled 42.5 per cent. Class III, those employed in agriculture, made up 2.5 per cent. Class IV was defined as those in industrial labour, of which 2.5 per cent were unskilled and 30 per cent skilled.

If we corroborate these findings with the survey of Kerry GAA players active between 1896 and 1905 (see Table 3.6 next chapter), we find an enormous disparity between the 40.7 per cent of GAA members engaged in agriculture and the 2.5 per cent of rugby players. Likewise, those in commercial activity are more than double those equivalents in the GAA: 19.2 per cent. More than three times as many professionals were involved in rugby as opposed to GAA: 4.7 per cent. Finally, both skilled and unskilled industrial labour amounted to 32.5 per cent of rugby players, strikingly similar to the 32.1 per cent for GAA members. While considering the small sample and the fact we are talking of mostly urban dwellers, the limitations of this survey need to be given due recognition. The simple fact remains that rugby players were less likely to be directly affected by the harsh agricultural situation. Many were also higher up the social echelon and had a more stable income compared to GAA members of this period. Thus, they could afford to play sport even in economically bleak times. With no organised Gaelic activity, men in large towns who may otherwise have played GAA turned to rugby.[117] Towards the end of 1898, public meetings were held in Killarney and Dingle to re-form rugby clubs there. It is fascinating to note that St Brendan's Seminary in Killarney, now a celebrated 'nursery' for Gaelic football in Kerry, actually had rugby as its principal sport during this time, it being introduced under R. Cruise, the well-known Garryowen player who taught there.

The status rugby had attained in Kerry is evident from the fact that Tralee was chosen as the venue for the interprovincial test between Munster and Leinster in January 1900. Reports of the game noted the large crowd that turned out and gate receipts that were 'beyond all expectation'. The town was selected by the Munster branch, 'which urged that such a match would tend to stimulate Rugby in the County Kerry'.[118] Directly after the game, four Tralee men were selected on the Munster team to play Ulster. The Tralee forward C.C.H. Moriarty became the second Kerry man to be capped for Ireland when he was selected to play against Wales on 18 March. Such was the local enthusiasm for the sport that for the first time the Great Southern and Western Railway advertised special excursion trains from Tralee and intermediate stations to Dublin in connection with the international against Scotland. That April, Tralee caused the shock of the Munster Cup by beating Cork Constitution in the semi-final. They therefore qualified for their first final appearance, losing to Queen's College, 17-0. The *Sentinel* commented that: 'Up to the present Rugby football in Tralee had a chequered existence . . . Now things have begun to look up, the list of members is very much longer than it ever had been and the interests taken in the club is keen.'[119]

By 1898 the GAA had effectively collapsed as a functioning sporting organisation in Kerry. With its local rival crippled, rugby revelled in a new-found popularity. Unchecked, this might have completely altered the sporting history of the county. However, nationally a cultural movement was beginning to evolve that would have a profound regenerative effect not only on the association there, but on Irish society as a whole.

3

REVIVAL, 1898–1905

There is not a county in Ireland that can produce finer types of
manhood than the gallant sons of Kerry. It would be a pity,
therefore, if the grand old games, in which our forefathers
excelled, before the sickening antics of English effeminates were
known in our land, should be neglected by the present generation.

Kerry Sentinel, 31 May 1900

By 1898, the association in Kerry had effectively collapsed.
Nationally, the organisation fared little better. Blighted by
internal disputes and continued church hostility, the GAA found
itself in seemingly terminal decline as the new century approached.
Yet within four years the association would again rise to national
prominence. The centenary celebration of the 1798 rebellion, the
outbreak of the Boer War in South Africa and the Gaelic Revival
would all play a major role in revitalising the ideas of a culturally
independent, sovereign Ireland. For the GAA, the effects of all
these movements were deeply significant. The rise of the Gaelic
League and the ideals of a new 'Irish Ireland' were a great impetus
to those wishing to rebuild the association and make it a force
again in Irish society. Against a backdrop of growing nationalist
sentiment, the association saw itself playing a prominent role
within this board movement. This would lead to the creation of a
new political and cultural ideology in the GAA at this time. In
Kerry, officials like Thomas F. O'Sullivan were deeply inspired by
these developments and put their energies into the rebirth and re-
establishment of a new county board. Gaining prominence within
the association quickly, O'Sullivan embarked on a series of press
and administrative campaigns and led the charge for a more
vibrant and nationalistic body, spearheading the reintroduction of
the controversial foreign games ban. The ultimate effect of this

campaign was to condemn rival sports codes in Kerry to a marginal existence.

The Gaelic Revival and the GAA, 1896–1904

The mid-1890s found nationalist aspirations at a low ebb. The economic and social situation in Ireland was mirrored politically in the dashing of Home Rule and the continued bitter split within the IPP and Irish nationalism generally. The fortunes of the GAA seemed to mirror this social malaise which had descended on Ireland. However, the remaining years of the decade would witness the emergence of a collective movement that would transform the entire cultural, political, economic and social fabric of Ireland – a development termed 'The Gaelic Revival'.

Throughout the nineteenth century, the process of extending the system of education for Irish Catholics and the opening up of the civil service to that system's graduates continued apace. Yet rather than creating a progressive, educated, native middle class eager to participate in the running of the British Empire, this development instead generated, among this same middle class, a new sense of cultural nationalism.[1] This manifested itself in the birth of two symbiotic movements, the Irish Literary Revival and the Irish language movement. Together they provided the impetus for the Gaelic Revival. Concurrent with these developments, the latter half of the nineteenth century coincided with a renewed enthusiasm for Irish history and culture. The Royal Irish Academy which was established in 1785 to investigate and preserve the culture and history of the island began to undertake extensive surveys of the western seaboard, touring and cataloguing sites, antiquities and the surviving traditional Irish culture in areas like the Dingle Peninsula and the Blasket Islands. The rich archaeological remains of the country were increasingly used to represent the ancient and long-established traditions of Ireland.[2] This scholarly research had a deep impact on a rising generation of Irish literary revivalists. For example, the playwright John M. Synge became spellbound by the culture of the Aran Islands. Likewise, poets like W.B. Yeats became fascinated by the Celtic sagas and myths, which were being rediscovered and translated into English. For such writers, artists and subsequently politicians, the west of Ireland, its people, language, culture and landscape provided a body of material from which 'they could forge a new, distinctive construct of national identity'.[3] In the process, the literary revival hoped to restore an Ireland that had been reduced to a demoralised provincialism.

Meanwhile, the fall of Parnell and the political vacuum that ensued caused many political thinkers to reject the IPP's brand of political nationalism. In 1900, the weekly periodical *The Leader* was established under D.P. Moran. For revivalists like Moran, the present divisions and decay in Irish society were not due to adherence to Irish customs, preserved now only among sections of the peasantry, but in their abandonment by native religious and political leaders for accepted, alien English norms.[4] Moran dismissed the IPP's Home Rule crusade, arguing that it would not lead to national regeneration. Instead he passionately argued for an independent Ireland in which Irish language and culture were dominant and Catholicism was the state religion.

Yet such intellectual and political discourse flew over the heads of the majority of Irish men and women. To the poor rural farmer or labourer, such debates emanating from cities like Dublin caused barely a ripple. The plays which were performed in Dublin's Abbey Theatre or the editorials written by D.P. Moran were of little help to a farmer in rural Ireland in his understanding of what it was to be Irish. However, many members within the GAA saw it as their responsibility to introduce aspects of this national cultural revival to its membership. In Kerry, GAA officials such as Maurice Moynihan were convinced that as well as its sporting aspects, the GAA had a much greater intellectual role to play in Irish life. Writing in the *Sentinel* in 1890, he argued that there was no reason why the GAA 'should not also be made the medium of inculcating a taste for wholesome National literature and thereby founding a Nationalism that would be established on reason, intelligence and knowledge of history'. In reference to this, he was delighted that the Castlegregory GAA club was about to establish a branch of the Young Ireland Society in association with the club.[5] An article from the *Labour World* that September echoed these sentiments and warned against GAA members starving their brain to develop their muscle:

. . . it would appear that the present inactive and depressed condition of the association is attributable to an overdose of athletics and the absence of those social and educating influences which cement and keep together what otherwise would be jarring elements . . . Men cannot be active participants in athletics for more than a few years, but their membership will continue with clubs if they have the reading-room to resort to.[6]

From its earliest years, then, many officials within the GAA saw the organisation as having a greater ideological message than the mere promotion of native games. Yet its poor standing during the 1890s meant this ideological mission could not be accomplished without impetus from the new emerging cultural organisations.

A major stimulus to the GAA nationally was the emergence of the Gaelic League launched by Douglas Hyde in July 1893.[7] Hyde pleaded with his countrymen to turn their collective backs on all things English before they lost forever a sense of their separate nationality. The Gaelic League aimed to reconstruct a populist rural Gaelic civilisation based on the language and customs of the half a million Irish-speaking peasantry inhabiting the western seaboard. In the process, it hoped to recover Ireland's perceived Gaelic golden age.[8] The Gaelic League aimed to preserve and revive the Irish language but also encouraged the study of existing Gaelic literature and the cultivation of modern literature in Irish.[9] Hyde, probably mindful of the fate of the GAA, insisted his new organisation would be strictly apolitical. The Gaelic League began to extend across Ireland and by 1908 it had 671 registered branches and had successfully initiated Irish teaching into national primary schools.

The connection between the Gaelic League and the GAA was almost immediate. Michael Cusack, a native Irish speaker, became a key member of the League when it was formed and was a regular contributor at meetings. Hyde, in a lecture he gave a year before the League was formed, remarked, 'I consider the work of the Association [GAA] in reviving our ancient national game of *camán*, or hurling, and Gaelic football has done more for Ireland than all the speeches of politicians for the last five years.'[10] Many in the GAA saw that the energetic idealism generated by such a movement had the potential to revive the ailing fortunes of the association. In May 1896, a great public convention was organised in Tralee under the auspices of the Gaelic League. A week before at a Kerry County Board meeting members unanimously pledged the full support of the local GAA 'to render every assistance in [its] power to make the proposed convention an unqualified success'.[11] The Kerry GAA chairman, Thomas Slattery, and county board members J.P. O'Sullivan and Maurice Moynihan (who had since returned to his native Kerry and had been reappointed secretary of the Kerry GAA) were among those who attended this public convention. The growing interest in the language was such that from November 1896 the *Sentinel*, Kerry's main nationalist paper, carried a dedicated Irish column on its back page, given over to Irish prose and poetry. Indeed, the paper was critical of the local GAA for not doing enough to promote the language and accused it of taking little interest in the progress of the mother tongue.

The organisation continued to grow in Kerry and the relationship between it and the GAA, especially among those on the county board, remained strong. At the inaugural Annual Convention of the Kerry Gaelic League held in Tralee in 1902 three of the delegates from the Tralee branch, Maurice Moynihan, Thomas Slattery and T. O'Flaherty, were officers on the Kerry County Board. Thomas F. O'Sullivan, then secretary of the county board, represented the Listowel branch of the League at the meeting. Meanwhile, the chairman of the convention was Thomas O'Donnell, MP for West Kerry and a member of the Killorglin Gaelic League branch. O'Donnell was also the Laune Rangers representative at that year's Kerry GAA Convention.[12]

The RIC reported that the Gaelic League was spreading rapidly in Kerry under the patronage of the clergy and hinted at the close bond between it and the GAA, with one 'educating the mind' while the other trained 'the body'.[13] A Dublin writer, Seagan Ó Ceallaigh, sent a letter to the editor of the *Sentinel* arguing that the GAA could not yet truly call itself a national organisation as long as English remained the spoken word of its boards and clubs. He asked why in Kerry, from where so many teachers and poets of the native tongue hail, 'cries of victory, encouragement and jubilation on the playing field are expressed in the language of our oppressors'. The writer saw in the two organisations a natural alliance and argued for branches of the League to be established in every parish in Ireland and attached to each one a hurling club. In the process, the author was quick to dismiss Gaelic football and stated that, of the three versions of football played (rugby, soccer and Gaelic), it was the most unscientific.[14] In this view, Ó Ceallaigh was not alone. The translation of Irish historical sources during this time provided a wealth of material which seemed to attest to the status and popularity of the game of hurling in ancient Ireland. The cultural atmosphere in which these sources were translated prompted a heavy blend of nostalgia and nationalism. Thus, a myriad of words in these texts for stick, ball, game, goals, etc. were translated under the catch-all term 'hurling'. This suggested to contemporaries a game of far greater antiquity than was actually the case.[15] Hence, advocates of the Gaelic League viewed the game of hurling, which Michael Cusack and others had codified, as a present-day link to the pure and ancient sport of the Irish nobility.[16] In Westmeath and its bordering counties, the Gaelic League played an instrumental role in the popularity of hurling there. Indeed, the present-day regional demarcation of the sport in areas like Westmeath could be a product of the presence or absence of Gaelic League activists.[17]

There is evidence that at least one GAA club in Kerry owed its existence to Gaelic League connections. In August 1901, a special meeting of those interested in hurling took place among members of the Tralee Gaelic League. John O'Connell presided over the meeting and was made president of the newly formed Tralee Celtic hurling club. Austin Stack, an employee of O'Connell and soon to be one of the most prominent figures within the Kerry GAA, was appointed secretary of the club.[18] The following April the club also formed a Gaelic football team. The vitality the Gaelic League brought to rural life in Ireland played an important role in the revitalising of the GAA. The cultural aspirations of the League found a kindred spirit in the association. The League's promotion of an independent Gaelic culture was a natural extension of the GAA's own primary mission to secure and promote native Irish games. However, other movements developing at this time would also have a significant impact on the resurgence of the association.

Gaeltacht team in 1933. Since the foundation of the Gaelic League, its members in the GAA constantly urged the association to help spread the use of everyday Irish among players and spectators. In 1933, the Kerry Board inaugurated a Gaeltacht league to preserve the language's use on the field of play. *(Courtesy of Gearóid Mac Síthigh and Seán Mac an tSíthigh)*

At the height of the Gaelic Revival Irish nationalists marked the centenary of the 1798 Rebellion. The year saw a huge outpouring of nationalist fervour, as across the towns and villages of Ireland '98 centenary memorial committees were set up and marches and celebrations were held to mark the occasion. In Kerry, such committees were formed in all the major towns in the early months of 1898. On 23 May, nationalists celebrated the anniversary of the outbreak of the rebellion. In Kerry, the towns of Tralee, Listowel and Castleisland were completely illuminated that night. Portraits of the rebel leaders were displayed from prominent buildings while large torchlight processions moved through the streets. The year-long celebrations provided a much-needed sense of enthusiasm among Irish nationalists. In addition, it stimulated reconciliation among the factions of Irish political nationalism. Commentating on the celebrations in Tralee, the *Sentinel* remarked that the sight of 'erstwhile rivals in politics . . . combining to do reverence to the memories of '98 was certainly a good augury for the future'. The paper hoped that soon the fissures in Irish politics would disappear 'before the force of patriotism'.[19] This remark proved perceptive. That same year MP William O'Brien formed the United Irish League to unite Irish politics and to breathe new life into the Home Rule movement.[20] Negotiations regarding such a reunion began in 1899 between the opposing sides of the nationalist split. Finally, in January 1900 the IPP reunited and elected John Redmond as its new leader.

The centenary was one expression of the complex forces that were beginning to change the direction of Irish political nationalism and would soon mark a revival in the fortunes of the 'physical-force' men.[21] The celebrations helped foster a militant anti-British sentiment which was conducive to a reorganisation of the IRB. Many '98 memorial committees were used as cover to mask Fenian activity. It was reported that across Ireland all the known organisers of the IRB had been active in organising '98 committees. The RIC stated that an enormous demonstration in celebration of the centenary held on 15 August 1898 in Dublin was organised 'almost entirely' by an extreme section of Irish nationalists and 'can hardly have failed to give a powerful impetus to the form of revolutionary agitation which this section favours'.[22]

As regards the GAA, the 1798 centenary also proved influential. In 1898, the association was offered two seats on the executive council of the '98 Centenary Committee. This body was set up by all sections of the nationalist movement to celebrate the rebellion and was mostly controlled by the IRB.[23] The invite sparked a heated debate during a meeting of the GAA's Central Council. Richard Blake, the association's secretary, regarded acceptance as violation of the GAA's anti-political stance. Conversely, Frank Dineen, the GAA's president, was in favour of the offer. Yet no resolution on the issue was reached at this meeting and the '98 Committee saw this indecision as a severe rebuff. However, even though there was no official GAA connection with the centenary, locally the GAA became actively involved in spite of the Central Council's hesitancy. Throughout Ireland, GAA members became prominent in local '98 committees and many county boards took on a leading role in the organisation of the celebrations due to local Irish Parliamentary Party apathy or weak local IRB organisation. When the Tralee branch of the '98 memorial committee was formed Maurice Moynihan was elected president, while John Moynihan of the Kerry County Board was named its honorary secretary.[24] Thomas F. O'Sullivan, secretary of the Listowel GAA, assumed responsibility for the celebrations in north Kerry. J.P. O'Sullivan, the famous Laune Rangers captain, was involved in organising celebrations in his native Firies. The Castleisland Desmonds GAA club was also conspicuous in the celebrations in its town. In February 1898, it produced a play based on events of the rebellion. Members of the club also headed the procession through the town on the night commemorating the outbreak of the rebellion, while from the windows of their club room a large portrait of Robert Emmet was displayed with the words 'Remember '98'.[25] Marcus de Búrca argued that in some counties support for '98 actually led to a revival of the GAA. This was not the case in Kerry, however, where Gaelic activity remained dormant. But as we will see, the 1798 centenary was influential in fostering an atmosphere of nationalist sentiment which provided a stimulus for the rebirth of the GAA there.

The nationalist fervour whipped up by the anniversary of '98 rebellion was kept alive in Ireland by events internationally. In October 1899, the second Boer War broke out between the British Empire and Dutch-speaking inhabitants of two independent Boer republics in South Africa. With the celebrations of '98 fresh in Irish minds, the struggle of the Boers, fighting on their own soil against the might of the British Empire, struck a powerful chord with Irish nationalists.[26] Many would readily associate, however inaccurately, this struggle with Ireland's own political plight. The war came to be seen as another example of British oppression against the people of a smaller nation. At the outbreak of the war, the Tralee Young Ireland society passed a resolution condemning 'the aggressive, infamous and tyrannical policy of England towards the Transvaal'. The members of Tralee Urban District Council (UDC) likewise condemned the British government's 'unjust war'.[27] Some unionists were quick to see the irony of this outpouring of grief towards the notoriously bigoted Protestant Boers. At a meeting of the Kenmare Board of Guardians Samuel T. Head, Chief Justice of the Police, dryly observed that if the Devil himself landed in England at the head of an army, nationalists would cry 'three cheers for the grand old devil!' Yet the growth of radical Irish nationalism, evident in the '98 centenary celebrations, became even more apparent during the Boer War.[28] Though the GAA continued to profess itself as a non-political organisation, aspects of this radicalised nationalism among its membership were already clearly visible.

Across Ireland, pro-Boer toasts became the norm at GAA conventions and meetings. The GAA quickly neglected its own constitutional rule of remaining non-political, which had earlier prevented it from being associated with the '98 centenary. In Kerry, the Tralee Kruger's Own GAA club was formed and named in honour of the Boer Republic's president, Paul Kruger. The club affiliated to the county board in 1900, along with the Killorglin Irish Brigade Transvaal, a GAA club named in honour of a military unit formed from Irish settlers that fought with the Boers. RIC reports noted that the disaffected classes in Ireland had seized upon the war to make public 'their undying animosity to British interests'.[29] A national Irish Transvaal Committee was set up in Dublin with a view to assisting the Boers in their struggle. A pamphlet that was circulated in Listowel and believed to be the work of the committee declared:

> Fellow-Countrymen, not a man and, so far as it is in your power, not a penny for any war of greed and conquest! . . . It should always be the guiding principle with Irishmen to seize every opportunity that offers to oppose England at home and abroad, in consequence of her infamous policy of persecution and plunder in Ireland.[30]

Events such as the outbreak of the Boer War and the '98 commemorations fostered a mood of renewed patriotism and nationalism, the currents of which would eventually sweep the GAA back to a position of eminence. Concurrently, important political developments afforded Irish nationalists a far greater say in the local political arena. As part of the Conservative government's strategy of killing off the Home Rule movement, they embarked on a policy of conciliatory measurers designed to appease Irish public opinion. Many were economic, but perhaps the most important political policy they introduced was the Irish Local Government Act, passed in 1898. This gave Ireland a system of local government along the same lines of the British model, with county councils, urban district councils and rural district councils. Prior to 1898 the right to vote in local elections had been confined to rate payers, therefore the more property one possessed, the greater the number of votes one had. Under the 1898 act, this multiple votes system was abolished. The act gave Ireland for the first time proper democratically elected bodies that were representative of their constituencies. These councils marked a revolutionary shift of power and influence across the country, away from the landlord ascendancy class and towards a democracy of Catholic lower middle class.[31] When the elections were held in 1899 the new councils became dominated by the Catholic and nationalist majority. These bodies provided nationalists with a valuable training ground for self-governance.

Movements like the Gaelic League, the '98 centenary and the United Irish League, along with the wider cultural revival in Irish society, provided a valuable stimulus for Irish nationalism. The implementation of the Local Government Act gave it the power to turn these aspirations into political reality. For the GAA the combination of these factors would revitalise the organisation, bringing into its committee rooms a new generation of officials who were determined to place the association at the heart of this nationalist revival. Their work was facilitated by internal developments within the GAA which had helped alleviate its decline and would, in time, enable it to ride on the crest of this rising nationalist tide.

As has been discussed, the GAA executive had sought to publicly distance itself from any connections with physical-force nationalism by relenting on its ban of police and military members in 1893. In 1895, it would go further still. At that year's Annual Convention, Richard Blake, chairman of the Meath County Board, was elected secretary of the association.[32] For several years, Blake had written openly about the flaws in the GAA's organisation and, most importantly, its governing rules. His influence on the playing rules of Gaelic games and the impact they would have on the sport's popularity nationally will be considered in the next chapter. Administratively, he had a profound effect on the fortunes of the GAA. Observing the poor health of the association and identifying the power the IRB exercised on its ruling body as the primary cause for this, Blake was determined not to let another political upheaval wreak havoc within the GAA. Only a month after his appointment, the GAA's Central Council declared the association to be non-political and non-sectarian. Likewise, a rule was passed stating that 'no political questions of any kind shall be raised at any of its meetings and no club shall take part as a club in any political movement'.[33] Blake's policies enabled the public reconciliation between Croke and the GAA that same year. In 1896, he led the association in removing the foreign games ban.[34] His energy salvaged the GAA at a time when it faced extinction. During his tenure, the number of hurling and football clubs affiliated to the association grew from 114 to 357, while income mushroomed from £284 to £1,176. Between 1895 and 1897, the GAA witnessed a mini revival in its fortunes. However, Blake's tenure was not to endure. A special meeting of the Central Council on 16 January 1898 discovered that the GAA was £300 in debt. Blake was dismissed on the grounds of his alleged mismanagement of GAA finances.[35] Yet both RIC reports and Blake's own pamphlet, *How the GAA was Grabbed*, claim this was only a pretext and in fact IRB elements within the GAA, led by its president, Frank Dineen, wanted him deposed because of his hostility to their own influence.[36] Deprived of his able and effective administration and despite the fervour in wider Irish nationalism, the GAA began to slip back into decline, temporarily at least. The number of GAA clubs fell from 360 in 1897 to 303 in 1899. The dismal financial situation of the association and the appalling potato crop failures that were resulting in near famine-like conditions over much of Connacht and Munster contributed to this decline.

Yet despite its administrative difficulties, the GAA had and would continue to play a major role in the Gaelic Revival. Indeed, it would have been hard for it not to. The Ireland that a generation of Anglo-Irish writers and Gaelic League activists longed for, an idyllic rural-based society populated by a proud and noble peasantry, was underscored by the strength and dominance of rural GAA teams witnessed in Gaelic competitions.[37] Gaelic games became a 'hallmark of the Gaelic Renaissance', with hurling and football producing images of Irish masculinity that both connected spectators with a perceived glimpse of Ireland's past and gave contemporary Irish society an image to be proud of. The qualities and character of the Irish peasant and the wider landscape of rural Ireland were embedded in the literature of the Gaelic Revival from its beginning. The dominant image of the GAA was of a rural pastime in which locals performed deft of skill and bravery that anglicised sports, tainted by their associations with professionalism and modernity, could never hope to equal. Such imagery fitted into the developing national consensus of the superiority of traditional Irish life over that of the modern and increasingly anglicised society.[38] The feats of GAA players and teams were immortalised in stories and song, further enhancing their status within Irish culture. The Folklore Commission's records, which in the 1930s sought to record the stories, myths and piseogs of a disappearing Ireland, are awash with GAA lore.[39] A recurring theme was of a prominent young hurler walking home on a moonlit night, crossing into a field to join the spirits of his long-dead relations in a game of hurling.[40]

Since the early days of Gaelic games, important matches and victories were also immortalised in song. Many located themselves in the emerging sporting culture of the GAA, which would continue to resist the dominance and encroachment of anglicisation. In 1888, a local bard penned a fourteen-line song entitled 'The Kickers of Lios na Caol Bhuidhe', about a match between teams from Castlegregory and Cloghane:

> If you could see our boys! Oh, 'tis they that were
>   sweet,
> Their well-compacted bodies, their straight and
>   strong knees,
> And they'd kick all before them, from here to
>   Tralee.[41]

When Ballyduff captured the All-Ireland in 1892 a local songwriter committed these lines to posterity:

> In Clonturk Park they fought, when the Boys of
>   Wexford thought,
> With their camáns to their credit they could spare,
> But they found out to their cost, when they fought
>   the fight and lost,
> That the boys from Ballyduff could beat them there.[42]

The Irish revival has been characterised as a time when art met propaganda with the politicisation of the language, literature and sport, with movements like the GAA providing the evidence of this. In the wake of the failures of political nationalism, a more radical political movement evolved, translating the cultural ideals of the romantic intellectuals into concrete programmes for national economic, social and political regeneration. The importance of the Gaelic Revival was that it fed into the GAA a new generation of such politically radicalised officials who rejuvenated the association in the years after 1900. The most outspoken of this new generation were fervent in the belief that the association should be primarily engaged in a project of national and cultural liberation. The GAA would sit alongside organisations such as the Gaelic League in an attempt to define a unique Irish identity.[43] This new generation redesigned the nationalist approach of the association. They cast aside the apolitical model promoted by officials like Richard Blake, replacing it with a more militant and adversarial outlook. In turn, the association was utilised as a platform to attack its cultural and political rivals. The greatest example of this can be seen in the reintroduction of the 'foreign games' and police bans between 1901 and 1905.

Revival: The GAA in Kerry, 1900–1904

Despite the stimulus given by the Gaelic Revival and the improving fortunes of the GAA's Central Council, the GAA in Kerry continued to languish. There were several reasons for this. One was the enduring tensions between the Kerry County Board and the GAA's Central Council which stretched back to 1894.

In August 1894, Kerry, represented by a Ballymacelligott/ Laune Rangers combination, defeated Tipperary in the Munster semi-final. Yet at a subsequent Central Council meeting Tipperary objected to the result and the Central Council, on rather dubious evidence, ruled that the match should be replayed.[44] The Kerry Board was incredulous at the decision and refused to contest the replay, allowing Tipperary to qualify for the Munster final.[45] This episode left a bitter taste with the Kerry County Board.[46] Tensions between the Central Council and the Kerry GAA escalated further in 1896. The Central Council had promised to schedule that year's Munster final for Tralee, arranged to help the county board pay off the large rent it was being charged to use the field. However, at the last moment the Central Council refixed the venue for Kilmallock in County Limerick. Despite strong protests from the Kerry Board to reconsider the venue, the final went ahead as planned.[47]

On account of this treatment and given its poor financial state, the Kerry Board refused to affiliate with the Central Council in 1896, only returning to the fold the following year.[48] Yet as we have seen, Thomas Slattery's decision to step down as president of the Kerry GAA in 1897 dealt a hammer blow to the organisation there. The slide in Kerry's GAA fortunes was dramatic. No Kerry team contested the Munster championship from 1897 to 1901. The county championship for 1897, owing to frequent delays and the terrible weather conditions, rumbled on until June 1898 when Tralee Mitchels were declared champions.[49] The Kerry Board elected in 1897 continued to meet under its new president, John Moynihan, until the championship had been run off. After that, no county board met for almost two years. No county conventions were held during the same period and Kerry sent no delegates to the GAA's Annual Convention. With no governing body in the county to affiliate to, GAA clubs fell into disrepair. Only ten locally organised matches were reported in 1898, the lowest in the decade.

While the Gaelic Revival was met with great enthusiasm by nationalists in Kerry, the GAA there was simply in no position to benefit from the stimulus it provided. One of the dominant themes of the Revival was of the rural landscape of western Ireland representing a present-day link to Ireland's heroic past, uncorrupted by English influence.[50] Though the ideal of the Gaelic rural athlete fell into this narrative, a poet's longing for such an Ireland was not going to bring about the formation of, say, a hurling club. In Kerry, organisations such as the Gaelic League were not able to fill the void left by a defunct GAA between 1898 and mid-1900. If they had been able to do so, one would expect far more hurling clubs to have been active in Kerry at this time given the League's preference and support for hurling. Instead, the vast majority of clubs remained exponents of football, while hurling, with notable exceptions such as the Celtic GAA club in Tralee, did not spread outside of its traditional base of north Kerry at any stage in the twenty years leading up to 1916. The reappearance of affiliated GAA clubs in Kerry was due to the re-emergence of an effective, organised and well-run local county administration. The revival of interest in Irish history, literature and mythology, a re-appreciation of the deeds of past Irish rebels, the uniting of the Irish political movement and the anti-British rhetoric stemming from the '98 centenary and Boer War outbreak were the preserve of those who advocated that Ireland should once more seek its own political and cultural identity. However, such ideals cannot be given as evidence for the formation of a single GAA club in this period. Rather, though the Gaelic Revival may not necessarily have had a major impact in club formation across Ireland, it fostered an atmosphere among the youth of the country that was conducive to the message of the GAA. Yet that message could only be heard if the organisation was in a position to articulate it. By 1899, plans were already in motion to bring about the revival of the Kerry County Board and spark a remarkable resurgence in the GAA in Kerry. The man responsible for this was Thomas F. O'Sullivan.

O'Sullivan was born in Listowel in 1874. After attending St Michael's College in the town, he was diverted into a career of journalism and became the Listowel correspondent for the *Sentinel* and other local papers. His interest in the GAA was almost immediate. He became secretary of the Listowel Temperance football team at the age of nineteen in 1895. The following year he was elected as the north Kerry representative to the county board. Ruefully observing the utter lack of organisation in Gaelic activity, he took it upon himself to keep the flame of the GAA burning within the district. In 1899, as secretary of the Listowel GAA he organised a football tournament in which fifteen teams from north Kerry and west Limerick participated.[51] The success of the tournament, in helping to reorganise several clubs in the north Kerry region, prompted P.K. Kelly, the honorary secretary of Laune Rangers, to write to the *Sentinel* countenancing a countywide attempt to revive the Kerry GAA Board.[52] O'Sullivan responded admirably to the challenge. In early 1900, he moved to awaken the county from its lethargy in Gaelic affairs. Through the local press he made an appeal to club secretaries to re-form the county board. Keenly aware of the progress rival sports were making in Kerry, O'Sullivan stressed that the 'necessity of safeguarding our national pastimes was never greater than at the present moment when the more "fashionable" imported sports are making such headway'.[53] The association's Central Council, anxious that Kerry should be brought back into the GAA's fold, dispatched two officials to help O'Sullivan organise the county.[54] Circulars were issued to all clubs to attend a Kerry GAA Convention in Tralee on 26 May 1900. This proved a huge success. Many of the stalwarts of the old county board such as Maurice Moynihan, Thomas Slattery, John Moynihan and J.P. O'Sullivan were in attendance. A new board was formed with John Moynihan elected as president and Thomas F. O'Sullivan as honorary secretary.

The new political and cultural ethos of the revived Kerry GAA was immediately apparent. Throughout 1899, numerous GAA tournaments had been held in counties across Ireland in aid of funds for a Wolfe Tone memorial. In the weeks before the Kerry Convention, Maurice Moynihan had been appointed as secretary to the Wolfe Tone memorial committee which was in charge of this national fund. At the convention Moynihan argued that the board's first order of business should be to organise a tournament in aid of the project. He stated that the GAA was formed not only to promote the national games but 'to promote a healthy Nationalist opinion among the young men of Ireland, to cultivate the mind as well as the body and make them Nationalists as well as athletes'. By July, twenty football and four hurling teams had formally affiliated to the new board.[55] This increased to thirty the

Thomas F. O'Sullivan (back, far left) with the Kerry team that won the 1903 Munster Championship on their way to their maiden All-Ireland victory. O'Sullivan was a staunch political nationalist and his loathing of the continued anglicisation of Irish society informed his crusade to reintroduce the Foreign Games Ban into the GAA in 1901. *(Courtesy of the National Library of Ireland)*

following year. Due to various delays, the 1899 All-Ireland championship had not commenced by the summer of 1900. However, due to the fact that it was only just reorganised, the Kerry Board informed the Central Council that they would not take part in the championship that year, promising instead to enter its inter-county teams when the 1900 championship started. On 24 June 1900, the county championships resumed in Kerry after an absence of two years with Tralee Kruger's Own playing the O'Brennan club. Instead of holding a dedicated Wolfe Tone tournament, the county board decided that receipts from its county championship matches would be donated to the fund. Rather than play a separate tournament, holding championship matches in aid of the Wolfe Tone Fund proved a valuable impetus to the popularity of the GAA in Kerry. It could be speculated that many spectators, influenced by the renewed spirit of nationalism sweeping across Ireland and the patriotic cause the admission price went towards, may have been swayed to attend these games, more so than if they were ordinary GAA matches.

At the GAA's Annual Convention in September 1900 O'Sullivan

attended as the Kerry representative. He proposed that the association should formally support the objectives of the Wolfe Tone Memorial Fund. The resolution was unanimously passed and proved significant as it once again aligned the GAA to a political cause, despite the earlier efforts of Richard Blake and others. The meeting also passed what would prove to be one of the GAA's most important pieces of administrative legislation – it approved the formation of provincial councils to deal with the running of the GAA in the country's four provinces. In Munster, delegates wasted little time in putting the ruling of the Central Council into action. On 14 October 1900, a meeting was held in Tipperary to form the first Munster council, which J.T. McQuinn attended as the Kerry representative.[56] The formation of these four councils led to a much greater degree of organisation and control at provincial level than the Central Council alone could provide. It was a key factor in the revival of the GAA nationally from 1900 onwards. In 1901, the GAA's Annual Convention decided to make a break with the past. Delegates elected two young energetic and able men to high office. James Nowlan of Kilkenny was appointed president, a post he would hold for twenty years, and Luke O'Toole of Wicklow was elected secretary, a position he would hold for almost thirty years. Thomas O'Sullivan was rewarded for his sterling work in Kerry by being elected onto the Central Council. The influence of a resurgent IRB may be seen in the elections of O'Sullivan and Nowlan, both known IRB members in their respective counties. All three men were determined to revive the fortunes of the association and each played an instrumental part in guiding the GAA to a period of real expansion. As O'Sullivan himself wrote, the foundation of the GAA as 'a well-officered, intelligently-governed and wisely directed national organisation . . . was laid in 1901. All progress dates from that year.'[57]

On a local level, the aptitude and organisational skills of men like O'Sullivan helped to set the Kerry Board's financial and administrative house in order. Approaching the 1901 Kerry Convention, the *Sentinel* noted with satisfaction that in spite of the 'uphill work of reviving the association in the Kingdom', the fact that the board was able to announce a profit of £10 3s 4d 'must be regarded as a decidedly satisfactory performance'. The running of a dedicated Wolfe Tone memorial tournament in the county that year also generated much enthusiasm for Gaelic games among the Kerry public. John O'Connell, a member of the Kerry Board, offered a cup to the winners of the tournament and this proved a powerful incentive for teams across Kerry to organise and contest in the patriotic competition. Likewise, to streamline the county championships laws were passed stating that no challenge or tournament matches in aid of local causes, which had so often in the past clashed with county championship games, were to be arranged without prior approval by the county board. Any teams that ignored the ruling would forfeit their claim to matches held under the auspices of the Kerry GAA. Under the efficient leadership of men like O'Sullivan, the GAA in Kerry became more organised, more controlled and more profitable. Steadily the match disputes, delays and objections which had crippled county championships in the early 1890s were being eradicated. While the 1897 county championships had taken a full thirteen months to complete, the 1900 championships were completed within six. At the 1903 Kerry Convention a law was passed declaring that if, at a meeting of the county board, the chairman presiding at a dispute between two clubs was a member of either, he was obliged to step aside, with his place being taken by an independent member of the board. If a vote was taken on such a dispute, neither the representatives nor any other registered members of the clubs involved were allowed vote. It was also agreed that before the start of championship games the respective captains would be required to hand a team list to the referee. Rules such as these went a long way towards eliminating the disputes and arguments that had preoccupied previous county boards.

In 1902, a number of GAA clubs in south Kerry decided to form their own South Kerry Board to promote Gaelic games in the remote Iveragh Peninsula. Within a month, ten football and two hurling clubs had been formed and affiliated in the district.[58] At the Kerry GAA Convention the following month the body gave full support to the project and the South Kerry Board was affiliated.[59] The guarantee of well-run and organised matches completed within a predetermined sporting calendar did much to entice clubs, players and supporters back into the local GAA.

Nationally, other developments helped generate interest in the association and helped attract young men into the GAA. In 1898, Arthur Griffith founded the *United Irishman* paper and began to preach a doctrine that would later become known as the Sinn Féin policy. Griffith was convinced Ireland must be politically free before it could be prosperous. He advocated a peaceful policy of non-cooperation. Irish MPs should withdraw from Westminster, assemble in Dublin and set up an Irish government that would simply take over the administration of the country, relying on moral authority to ensure obedience. As will be discussed, the Sinn Féin movement was to play an important role in the GAA in the years leading up to 1916. Griffith also advocated the promotion of Irish industry and believed that Ireland should be as self-reliant as possible. Such policies were taken up with vigour by the GAA. In January 1901, Thomas Slattery and John Moynihan addressed a meeting in Tralee convened to establish a branch of the Irish Industrial League with the aim of promoting home industry in the town. Slattery called on the businessmen and merchants of the town to give preference to Irish goods. This doctrine of self-sufficiency was heavily influenced by the ideals of the Gaelic Revival. At a meeting of the Kerry Board Maurice Moynihan proposed that instead of sets of medals, books of Irish literature such as the works of Thomas Davis be presented as prizes. Moynihan noted that for the price of one set of medals, fifty good books could be purchased and used by the Gaels of the winning locality. However, this proposal was defeated, with the *Sentinel* angrily proclaiming that the association ought to be 'the servitor of Nationality, by fostering and encouraging the manufacturers, the language, the literature as well as the pastimes of Ireland'.[60] At the GAA's Annual Convention in September 1901 John Moynihan, representing Kerry, had a resolution passed pledging the GAA's support in the cause of Irish industry and the Irish language.[61] After years of hesitancy, the GAA officially had begun again to take an active part in promoting Irish nationalist movements. It continued to organise tournaments in aid of the Wolfe Tone Fund as well as playing a prominent role in the commemoration of the centenary of Robert Emmet in 1903.

The fortunes of the association were also aided by a softening of clerical attitudes towards the organisation. With Archbishop Croke's death in 1902, his successor in the See of Cashel, Dr

Fennelly, consented to becoming a patron of the GAA. In February 1903, Archbishop Walsh of Dublin did likewise and wrote to the Central Council declaring he was 'most fully in sympathy with [the] Association and its objects'.[62] This aided the mellowing relations between the Church and the GAA and the clergy again started to become involved in the association at a local and county level. The Church's stance was helped by the association's diminished connection with the IRB. Though still an influence within the GAA, the IRB had learned the lesson of the early 1890s. It had begun to forgo any open recruitment of GAA members, preferring a more subtle strategy of using its influence to get members elected on the central, provincial and county boards. Police reports claimed that seven IRB men were elected to the Kerry County Board that re-formed in 1900.[63] While nationally there was some concern among the RIC about such IRB influence, by 1904 Kerry's county inspector was noting that the IRB seemed dormant in the county and the popularity of the GAA was solely down to the revival of hurling and football matches.[64]

By the mid-1900s, the GAA had managed to reassert its place in Irish society. Yet what were the motives behind individual members joining the association? What was it that lured them to the GAA in 1900 when so many had stayed away during the 1890s? There is evidence that compared to their predecessors of ten or fifteen years before, a new breed of Irish man was joining the GAA at this time. Within club and county boards especially, the previous dominance of the local big farmer or town publican and merchant was giving way to men drawn more from the educated lower middle classes of Irish society, such as teachers, clerks, local government officials and civil servants. The survey of Kerry GAA members presented towards the end of this chapter clearly shows an increase in the participation of professionals and those in the commercial classes between 1888 and 1916. This new class of enthusiastic and well-educated young men can help explain the marked increase in the fortunes of the GAA. Their professional skills and administrative talents created a much better-controlled local administration.

Why such a class was so prevalent can be explained by a look at social conditions in Ireland. One of the most significant developments in nineteenth-century Ireland was the spread of the middle class and the increasing demand for education of all levels as a means of social and economic advancement. By 1901, those attending secondary schools in Ireland numbered 35,306, while literacy levels rose from 39 to 89 per cent between 1861 and 1911.[65] A new educated middle class was emerging that was attracted to the cultural and political message of movements such as the Gaelic League, Sinn Féin and the GAA. Men like T.F. O'Sullivan were a prime example of this new breed. As a journalist O'Sullivan, more than most, would have come into contact with the new political and cultural movements flowering across Ireland in the late 1890s. He was heavily involved with the Listowel '98 memorial committee and the local IRB, as well as being an enthusiastic member of the Listowel Gaelic League branch. O'Sullivan was a product of the new political nationalism of his time and this outlook coloured everything he said or wrote. For him, the GAA was not merely a sporting organisation as was so often pleaded by Richard Blake. Rather, the GAA represented the nationalist cultural and political bastion in an ideological battle for Ireland's sports fields. It stood as a bulwark against the increasing anglicisation of Irish culture and the growing popularity of English sports like rugby. For O'Sullivan such sports embodied foreign British rule, which, through his Gaelic activities, he was in daily contact with. O'Sullivan wrote that the GAA's responsibility lay 'not only to develop Irish bone and muscle, but to foster a spirit of earnest nationality in the hearts of the rising generation . . . saving thousands of young Irishmen from becoming mere West Britons'.[66] To O'Sullivan, then, the GAA was a critical component in Ireland's struggle for nationhood. Without its own culture, political independence would be useless.

As has been argued, it seems unlikely that the vast majority of the GAA's membership would have taken from the cultural and political debates and writings, which bloomed under the Gaelic Revival, any sense of what it was to be Irish. Yet perhaps in the GAA clubs across the country a new generation of officers such as O'Sullivan developed a role as cultural facilitators. They used their understanding of the embryonic consensus of an 'Irish Ireland' to impart to ordinary members how their role in the GAA fed in to this great national movement. By wielding the camán as their ancestors had done for thousands of years, they were helping keep alive the traditions of Ireland's heroic past. The spurning of English games in favour of native pastimes was a patriotic act that would ensure the final triumph of Irish culture and society over the corrupting influence of anglicisation once Ireland's political freedom had been won. It is hard to quantify how such rhetoric actually affected GAA membership in this period. Likewise, it is hard to gauge whether most ordinary members of the association even cared about the greater cultural mission advanced by men like O'Sullivan. Yet the use of the media to encourage the popularity of Gaelic games while simultaneously attacking its sporting rivals played a crucial role in diverting large numbers of athletic young men into the GAA's ranks.

It is significant that the rapid rise in literacy levels coincided in Ireland with the explosion of the press industry there in the latter half of the nineteenth century. The use of the print media by GAA officials would have had a huge impact on the success and popularity of the GAA. As Eoghan Corry argued, media coverage of the association 'was arguably the most important catalyst in creating the GAA and sustaining it through its early crisis-ridden years'.[67] In the early twentieth century, a new breed of GAA correspondents not only reported on matches and meetings but attacked the corrupting influences of English games while celebrating the superiority of the Gaelic athlete. A prime example of this comes from the *Sentinel* in 1900:

> . . . there is not a county in Ireland that can produce finer types of healthy manhood – a better race, either physically or intellectually, than the gallant sons of . . . Kerry. In the golden ages of the past our chiefs and clans were noted for their prowess on many a hard-fought field . . . It were a pity, therefore, if the grand old games in which our forefathers excelled, before the sickening antics of English effeminates were known in our land, should be neglected by the present generation.[68]

From such rhetoric it is easy to understand how participation in the GAA became a vehicle for the expression of Irish identity. In contrast to the way countries such as South Africa embraced rugby and used it as an expression of nationhood when they competed and defeated their colonial master, England, on the rugby field, the GAA would promote Gaelic games to the exclusion of English games in an attempt to define its own sense of nationality.[69] Across the nationalist media in Ireland games perceived as British were challenged and their supporters stigmatised as 'West Brits'. In Kerry, T.F. O'Sullivan, by now the *Sentinel*'s official GAA correspondent, harried those who championed foreign games over their native ones. He wrote that those who would think to promote non-national games were

> . . . the British garrison, anglicised Irish men and thoughtless youngsters who never realise that they owe a duty to their country. Have any of these classes ever done an honest day's work for their country? . . . In fact, it were better they ceased to exist from a National standpoint, than existing they should be the means of corrupting and degrading others to their inglorious level.[70]

Whereas in counties like Westmeath cricketers bore the brunt of the attacks made by the Gaelic press, in Kerry, O'Sullivan attacked the county's rugby advocates with glee. Given the real danger rugby was posing to the pre-eminence of Gaelic games, this should not have been surprising. O'Sullivan referred to its followers as, variously, 'contemptible West Britons, shoneens, Anglicised Cads and un-Irish'. Moreover, they were men who never shied away from toasting the health of the English king. In Kerry, as will be discussed shortly, the threat of rugby was all but destroyed by the press campaigns of O'Sullivan.

Media campaigns such as these clearly had an effect on GAA membership and the dwindling of support among its rival codes. Likewise, as has been argued, the message and ideals of the Gaelic Revival, disseminated through organisations such as the Gaelic League and the GAA, may have been a powerful force in encouraging Irish youth to join the association. In addition, the sway the IRB traditionally had within the GAA, coupled with the anti-British political rhetoric stirred up by the commemorations of 1798 and the continuing war in South Africa, may have

influenced others of the physical-force persuasion to become
involved. However, it is important to remember when assigning
motives as to why men joined the GAA that the membership of
the organisation was not some static monolithic mass full of
impressionable minds ready to absorb the political or cultural
viewpoints of those who took it upon themselves to run and
administer the organisation. The men who entered the GAA in
such numbers at the turn of the twentieth century were
individually as varied and complex as their motives for joining. It
is perhaps easier for the historian to find evidence in RIC reports
and newspapers pointing to membership influenced by a desire to
become involved in physical-force nationalism or due to a swelling
of cultural and national patriotism. Invariably, then, it is those
motives that are emphasised. Yet as much as any other motive, the
simple recreational aspect of the GAA, the love of Gaelic games
and the fun of participation were what drove many into the GAA's
embrace. It must be remembered that in counties like Kerry the
vast majority of rival sports codes such as rugby remained urban
based, with clubs being formed only in the larger towns. There
was simply no other organised sport in Ireland that had managed
to successfully graft itself onto the patchwork of rural Ireland.
Despite all the difficulties experienced by the GAA throughout the
1890s locally, the games continued to be played, albeit on a more
restrictive scale. Regardless of the influences the Gaelic Revival or
the emergence of a stronger political nationalism had on Irish
society, it is likely, once the economic and social conditions for its
members began to improve, that the GAA would have seen an
upswing in membership and club growth. A strong, efficient and
well-directed association would have seen its popularity grow
regardless of whether the Gaelic Revival had occurred or not.

Members joined for a myriad of reasons. These reasons were
not static but fluidic and changed over time. Thus, the farmer from
Abbeydorney who joined his local club simply for the love of
hurling in time became dedicated to the ideals of Sinn Féin. The
clerk in Tralee who had a deep affection for his native language
may have been influenced by the local Gaelic League to join the
town's hurling club, later leaving as he became disenchanted by
the increasingly political nature of club meetings. The carpenter

in Killarney might have joined because the town's rugby club had disbanded and his only interest, until the day he retired, was where the next match was on.

Social Structure of the Kerry GAA, 1896–1905

It has been argued that precious little investigation has been conducted on the occupations of early GAA players or their social or class backgrounds.[71] Yet such information is vitally important to fully understand the types of men who were attracted into the GAA in any given region. In an effort to address the deficiency, this section will look at the social background of GAA players in Kerry between 1888 and 1916. A database of 910 players involved in hurling (216) and football (694) between the years in question was constructed. This was compiled using various sources, such as team listings from newspaper match reports, club meeting reports and local club histories. Where possible, these names were matched with data taken from the online 1901 and 1911 census returns for County Kerry. In all, 183 separate team line-ups from sixty-nine clubs across Kerry in this twenty-eight-year period were represented.[72] Eighteen of the clubs were hurling with the remaining 51 being football. Likewise, 24 of the clubs were from the main towns in Kerry, the remaining 45 being rural or village clubs. In total, 112 of the 183 teams represented were urban based, the remaining 71 being rural.

The 1901 and 1911 census classified the occupations of people into five specific categories. Class I was comprised of professionals, with Class II being made up of those in domestic service. Class III was formed by those employed in commercial activities, while Class IV consisted of those in agricultural employment. Finally, Class V was formed from workers engaged in industrial labour. In addition, for the purposes of this survey I have included a category for those GAA players who were still in education. Appendix I gives the classification of the 910 footballers and hurlers, most of whose occupations were identified.

Forty-eight of the players in the survey belonged to the professional class, 14 were domestic servants, 170 were employed in various commercial activities, 349 worked in agriculture, 303 were employed in industrial labour and 23 were still in education.

Dr Crokes Club Officials, 1913. Back (l–r): unknown, Jer O'Leary; middle (l–r): Joe O'Brien, Pat Mahoney, Micksey Hurley, unknown; front (l–r): Denis Doyle, Dick Fitzgerald, Jim Galvin. *(Courtesy of John Keogh, Dr Crokes GAA)*

The occupations of three players could not be identified. As is clear, players in agricultural and industrial employment made up almost three-quarters (71.6 per cent) of those identified in this study. Agriculture remained the highest employer but those in industrial labour were a close second. Players employed in various commercial activities comprised almost a fifth of the Kerry playing population in this sample.

If we compare this survey to the national statistics of employment by category in 1901, the results are noteworthy.

TABLE 3.1		
NUMBERS AND CATEGORIES OF EMPLOYEES AS RETURNED IN 1901 CENSUS[73]		
Category	Number of Employed	% of Total
Class I: Professional	98,361	6.95
Class II: Domestic servants	26,087	1.85
Class III: Commercial activities	92,863	6.57
Class IV: Agriculture	790,475	55.90
Class V: Industrial labour	406,157	28.73
Total	1,413,943	100

As can be seen from comparing both surveys, there are significant differences between the employment patterns of GAA members in Kerry and the national average at this time. In domestic service and industrial employment, Kerry players are broadly in line with the national average, with roughly 5 per cent more men within the Kerry GAA being employed in industrial labour than their colleagues nationwide. Professionals are slightly underrepresented but the really noteworthy results refer to the differences between Class III and Class IV. Those employed in the commercial sector were almost three times more likely to be involved within the Kerry GAA than their overall participation in the Irish workforce indicates. Meanwhile, players in agricultural employment were significantly underrepresented compared with the national average.

While it may be expected that there would be variances between the employment of GAA members and the working population in Ireland at large, the findings of the survey become even more significant when compared with Tom Hunt's study on the occupations of GAA players nationally between 1886 and 1905. The results of Hunt's survey of 500 players across Ireland are detailed below.

TABLE 3.2

CATEGORIES OF EMPLOYMENT OF GAA PLAYERS
NATIONALLY, 1886–1905

Class I:	Professional	2.2%
Class II:	Domestic servants	0%
Class III:	Commercial activities	21.2%
Class IV:	Agriculture	61.8%
Class V:	Industrial labour	14.8%

The differences between Kerry players and their national counterparts are pronounced. There were more than twice as many professionals playing Gaelic games in Kerry than the national average of 2.2 per cent. Likewise, while those employed in domestic service were negligible, evidence from Kerry shows men employed in that sector did participate in, and were members of, the GAA. Broadly the same percentage of men employed in the commercial sector had involvement with the GAA, both on a national and local level. However, the major surprise in analysing both samples is the variance between GAA members categorised as Class IV and Class V. GAA members principally employed in agriculture are over a fifth (22.95 per cent) less likely to have been involved within the association in Kerry than was the case nationally. On the contrary, almost a fifth (18.49 per cent) more GAA members in Kerry earned a living from industrial employment.

The reasons for such discrepancies are not easily explained. Kerry society, like much of the rest of western Ireland, was dominated by a rural economy. The county had no significant industrial base, and while Kerry contained several large towns, most of these served as market towns for the local agricultural produce. The vast majority of commercial and industrial activities in Kerry were heavily geared towards a supporting role for its agricultural economy. After agriculture, the main employers were fishing and, in more recent times, tourism. The under-representation of agriculture in this context is all the more baffling. Yet certain limitations of this particular survey, as well as the broader economic and social situation, need to be borne in mind. As has been stated, the majority of the team line-ups that have been obtained from this period are from urban combinations, with only half as many being identified as rural teams. This imbalance can be partly explained by the fact that in the days before the handing of official team line-ups to referees prior to a match became the norm, local press correspondents often based in their native towns would have been more familiar with their town's own players than with the players of more rural clubs. Thus, match reports involving a town side were often the only such reports at this time that were accompanied by team line-ups in the local press.

As has been shown, the economic depression in the agricultural sector and the devastating failure of the potato crops in the last years of the 1890s had a crippling effect on rural life, especially across the south and west of Ireland. Throughout Kerry, rural clubs began to disappear as the immediate priority of their members was to put food on the table and pay the landlord's rent. When the Kerry GAA began to revive after 1900 the initial stimulus came from urban clubs whose members were less directly affected by the problems in the rural economy. Of the GAA clubs reported as being active in Kerry at the end of 1899, all eight were based within the county's main towns. Such factors can help explain the underrepresentation of the agriculturalist within the Kerry GAA.

Though useful, the occupational divisions used by the census authorities can be too general. In his own study, Tom Hunt further subdivided the occupations of the players sampled into seven categories in order to give a greater insight into the occupational characteristics of early GAA members. The results are presented in Table 3.3 (opposite).

Employing similar subdivisions, the results of this analysis on the Kerry GAA players are shown in Table 3.4 (opposite).

For the purpose of these subdivisions, occupations such as general labourers were classified as unskilled workers. Various office clerks and shop assistants were grouped together. Professionals were made up mostly of accountants, solicitors, tax collectors, postmen and teachers. Also in the professional class were a priest, a fireman, a workhouse manager, three journalists, a dentist and a doctor. The merchant class was comprised of merchants and their sons, along with publicans, livestock sellers, butchers and bakers. Again, the major difference in occupation between players in Kerry and

TABLE 3.3

OCCUPATIONS OF GAA PLAYERS NATIONALLY, 1886–1905

Occupation	% of Total
Farmer/son	53.4
Agricultural labourer	4.8
Un/semi-skilled worker	7.6
Skilled	13.4
Shop assistant/clerk	16.2
Professional	2.2
Merchant/son	2.4
Total	**100**

TABLE 3.4

OCCUPATIONS OF KERRY GAA PLAYERS, 1888–1916

Occupation	Number of Players	% of Total
Farmer/son	254	27.91
Agricultural labourer	94	10.32
Un/semi-skilled worker	105	11.53
Skilled	199	21.86
Shop assistant/clerk	94	10.32
Professional	48	5.27
Merchant/son	65	7.14
Domestic servants	15	1.64
Fishermen	10	1.09
Students	23	2.52
Unknown	3	0.32
Total	**910**	**100**

those nationally remains the underrepresentation of farmers and their sons. However, in contrast with what Hunt's survey uncovered, the participation of agricultural labourers among players employed in agriculture is significantly higher in Kerry. There they formed 37 per cent of the players in this sector, as compared to only 8.2 per cent in Hunt's national survey.

To illustrate further any changes within the social make-up of GAA players in Kerry between 1888 and 1916, the sample above of 910 players was divided into three distinct surveys, the results of which are shown in Tables 3.5, 3.6 and 3.7 (and see also Appendix I). These indicate that while the numbers of GAA members coming from industrial labour in Kerry remained relatively constant, as did those of members employed in the commercial sector, there is a notable and steady decrease in the membership of those involved in the agricultural sector. Emigration and an increasing tendency towards urbanisation, discussed in Chapter 4, are undoubtedly a cause of this. The steady rise in the numbers of those from the professional class would indicate that movements such as the Gaelic Revival had some influence on the participation of the more educated members of Kerry society within the association. Such changes are outlined in Table 3.5, in which a database of 120 players, including thirty hurlers and ninety footballers from 1888 to 1895, was constructed and matched to census material from 1901.

TABLE 3.5
OCCUPATIONS OF KERRY GAA PLAYERS, 1888–1895

Occupation	Number of Players	% of Total
Farmer/son	45	37.5
Agricultural labourer	11	9.16
Un/semi-skilled worker	14	11.66
Skilled	26	21.66
Shop assistant/clerk	4	3.33
Professional	3	2.5
Merchant/son	13	10.83
Domestic servants	1	0.83
Fishermen	2	1.66
Students	0	0
Unknown	1	0.83
Total	**120**	**100**

Table 3.6 was constructed from a database of 380 players active between 1896 and 1905, of which 302 were footballers and seventy-eight were hurlers.

TABLE 3.6

OCCUPATIONS OF KERRY GAA PLAYERS, 1896–1905

Occupation	Number of Players	% of Total
Farmer/son	100	26.31
Agricultural labourer	55	14.47
Un/semi-skilled worker	47	12.36
Skilled	75	19.73
Shop assistant/clerk	39	10.26
Professional	18	4.73
Merchant/son	32	8.42
Domestic servants	6	1.57
Fishermen	2	0.52
Students	6	1.57
Unknown	0	0
Total	**380**	**100**

Table 3.7 was constructed by matching a database of 410 Kerry GAA players (108 hurlers and 302 footballers) active between 1906 and 1916 with online census material from 1911.

TABLE 3.7

OCCUPATIONS OF KERRY GAA PLAYERS, 1906–1916

Occupation	Number of Players	% of Total
Farmer/son	109	26.58
Agricultural labourer	28	6.82
Un/semi-skilled worker	44	10.73
Skilled	98	23.9
Shop assistant/clerk	51	12.43
Professional	27	6.58
Merchant/son	20	4.87
Domestic servants	8	1.95
Fishermen	6	1.46
Students	17	4.14
Unknown	2	0.48
Total	**410**	**100**

A notable feature is the steady decline in numbers of agricultural labourers involved within the association in Kerry, a process consistent with the numerical decline of that class in Ireland after the 1880s. There is an 11 per cent fall in the participation of farmers and their sons in the Kerry GAA after 1896, though after this sharp decline the numbers remain stable over the next twenty years. This again points to the effects of emigration and urbanisation in Kerry society at this time. The growing numbers of skilled workers, clerks, shop assistants and professionals within the Kerry GAA between 1896 and 1916 points to the increasing urbanisation of the association's sports, particularly football.

As a final example of the social profile of GAA membership in Kerry, a database of 212 club officials, drawn from the sixty-nine clubs in the above-mentioned survey, was constructed. Some 159 of the men were involved in the running of football clubs in Kerry, the remaining fifty-three being active with hurling clubs. These officials included club presidents, vice-presidents, secretaries, treasurers, captains, vice-captains and club committee members. The results are illustrated in the table below (and see also Appendix I):

TABLE 3.8

OCCUPATIONS OF KERRY GAA CLUB OFFICIALS,
1888–1916

Occupation	Number of Players	% of Total
Farmer/son	40	18.86
Agricultural labourer	5	2.35
Un/semi-skilled worker	6	2.83
Skilled	41	19.33
Shop assistant/clerk	35	16.5
Professional	32	15.09
Merchant/son	48	22.64
Domestic servants	0	0
Fishermen	3	1.41
Students	2	0.94
Total	**212**	**100**

In contrast to the findings regarding Kerry GAA players, the results for GAA officials show a far greater spread of members from the agriculture, skilled labour, commercial and professional classes. This is not surprising if we consider that officers and captains of GAA clubs were invariable educated men of high standing in their local community. The under-representation of agricultural labourers and unskilled/semi-skilled workers when compared with player returns further supports this.

The above survey on Kerry GAA players and officials also reveals some interesting insights into their age, religion, marital status and education standards.

TABLE 3.9 AGE OF KERRY GAA HURLING AND FOOTBALL PLAYERS, 1888–1916						
Age	Total	%	Hurling	%	Football	%
15	8	0.87	0	0	8	1.15
16–20	272	29.89	58	26.85	214	30.83
21–25	333	36.59	72	33.33	261	37.6
26–30	218	23.95	57	26.38	161	23.19
31–35	58	6.37	22	10.18	36	5.18
36–40	19	2.08	6	2.77	13	1.87
41+	2	0.21	1	0.46	1	0.14
Total	910	100	216	100	694	100

The average age of the Kerry GAA player, at 23.67 years, was slightly older than the national average of 23.2. More than half of Kerry players were under the national average age, while a further three-quarters were aged twenty-six and younger. The age of players in this survey ranged from fifteen to forty-two. There was no significant difference between the average age of Kerry footballers and hurlers. It was found that footballers in Kerry, like their national counterparts, tended to retire earlier from the game than hurlers. In contrast, the age profile of GAA officials was predictably older.

TABLE 3.10

AGE PROFILE OF KERRY GAA OFFICIALS, 1888–1916

Age	Total	per cent
16-20	29	13.67
21-25	47	22.16
26-30	55	25.94
31-35	28	13.2
36-40	18	8.49
41-45	8	3.77
46-50	9	4.24
51-55	7	3.3
56-60	6	2.83
61-65	2	0.94
66-70	0	0
70+	2	0.94
Total	**212**	**100**

The average age of a GAA club official in Kerry was 31.03 years. The age of the various club officers in this survey ranged from the 1905 seventeen-year-old captain of Dingle, James Barry, to the 73-year-old James Finucane, president of the Tarbert Rovers football club in 1904.

Tom Hunt's survey found that a mere 1 per cent of the GAA players he sampled nationally were married. Yet in Kerry, 6.2 per cent of the players identified in this survey were classified as married.[74] Moreover, almost 34.5 per cent of GAA officials were also recorded as married. This statistic is unsurprising given the significant difference in age between officials and the playing members of a club. Nonetheless, there is a significant decrease in the number of players married after 1905. Whereas 9.2 per cent of players were married between 1888 and 1905, this had fallen to 2.6 per cent between 1906 and 1916. James Donnelly has argued that for much of the nineteenth century Kerry stood apart from the rest of Ireland on account of its exceptionally high birth rate caused by the continuing practice of early marriage in the region. For example, in 1871, over 34 per cent of women aged between twenty and twenty-four were married. While, as has been discussed in Chapter 1, the practice of delayed marriage appeared in Kerry during the 1880s, it is possible the county still lagged behind the rest of Ireland in this social trend. Yet it is clear that by the end of the first decade of the twentieth century Kerry had indeed caught up with this social trend in the rest of Ireland. The 2.6 per cent of GAA players married is only 0.1 per cent higher than the 1901 national average of married men aged between fifteen and twenty-five.

Literacy levels among Kerry GAA players were excellent, with only twenty-five players (2.7 per cent) being categorised as illiterate, while a further six (0.6 per cent) had the ability to read only. Just one (0.4 per cent) GAA official could only read, while a further four (1.8 per cent) were illiterate. When one compares this with the Kerry illiteracy rate of 13.4 per cent in 1901, it indicates that, for the time, the average GAA player in Kerry was of a reasonably high standard of education. The players surveyed were almost all Catholic. Only 1.2 per cent in this survey identified themselves as Church of Ireland and there was no other religious denomination recognised. Finally, 298 players, or 32.7 per cent of the GAA players in Kerry surveyed, had proficiency in Irish. This proficiency fluctuated, standing at 49.1 per cent between 1888 and 1895, declining to 29.2 per cent between 1896 and 1905, before rising to 31.2 per cent between 1906 and 1916. Among GAA officials, proficiency in Irish was most advanced, with 115 of the officers recorded (54.2 per cent) being able to speak the language.

The GAA in Kerry and the 'Foreign Games' Ban, 1900–1905

By 1901, the GAA in Kerry had managed to resurrect itself but could not yet rest easy. The threat of rugby to its popularity remained. It was Thomas F. O'Sullivan who led a campaign against the sport which all but shattered its status in Kerry and cemented the county's reputation as one of the emerging bastions of the GAA. In the process, he was instrumental in the adoption of perhaps the most controversial piece of GAA legislation in the twentieth century, as it was from the rugby fields of Kerry that the GAA's 'foreign games' ban was born.

Ever since he joined the association, O'Sullivan seemed horrified by the growth of 'foreign games' in Kerry, especially rugby.

Commenting on the situation in December 1901, he stated that 'six or seven years ago rugby was almost an unknown quantity in Ireland'; but it had acquired supporters in most towns and it was necessary, O'Sullivan felt, that decisive action be taken before it spread into rural districts 'bringing with it the pestilential spirit of Anglicisation'.[75] A likely catalyst for this stance was the fact that during his last days in St Michael's College cricket and rugby were introduced to the school under its principal, Fr Timothy Crowley. These quickly became the official games of the college, the latter being most popular among students. Having managed to re-establish the GAA in Kerry on a sound footing, O'Sullivan next turned his considerable rhetorical and journalistic skills to crushing the threat of foreign sports. O'Sullivan as a journalist was aware of the immense potential of the press to reach and influence a far wider audience than at any time in Irish history. Almost immediately, as official reporter of GAA activity in the *Sentinel*, he began to attack the enemies of the association. In his first 'Gaelic Notes', he decried the practice of RIC members competing at GAA events:

> Are we at the present time all English in Kerry? Has the GAA degenerated to such an extent and has the spirit of Gaelic manhood become so far perverted, that our once popular organisation cannot exist except under the distinguished patronage of the officers of the military garrison and the police barrack?[76]

As has been argued, from 1901 the GAA found itself caught up in the all-encompassing political nationalism of the era. O'Sullivan would thus find a ready audience within the GAA for his nationalist views. At the adjourned meeting of the GAA's Annual Convention in December 1901 delegates passed O'Sullivan's motion:

> That we the representatives of the Gaels of Ireland, in Convention assembled, pledge ourselves to resist by every means in our power the extension of English pastimes to this country as a means of preventing the Anglicisation of our people. That County Committees be empowered to

disqualify or suspend members of the Association who countenance sports which are calculated to interfere with the preservation and cultivation of our distinctive National pastimes. That we call on the young men of Ireland not to identify themselves with Rugby or Association football or any other form of imported sport which is likely to injuriously affect the National pastimes which the GAA provides for all self-respecting Irishmen who have no desire to ape foreign manners and customs. That we call on the newspaper Press of the country which does not profess to support alien rule and on our public representatives and Nationalist organisations to sustain the Association in its struggle to *crush* English pastimes and in its patriotic effort to make our young men more thoroughly and essentially Irish and self respecting.[77]

This re-imposition of the ban on GAA members playing foreign games was a practical application in the realm of sport of the policy of de-anglicisation, which had been advocated by Douglas Hyde as far back as 1892 and by Arthur Griffith from 1899 onwards.[78] O'Sullivan wrote that the GAA could not 'be separated from the National idea. If it could we might substitute Rugby for Gaelic football and cricket for hurling and instead of helping the Wolfe Tone Memorial Fund we might raise a monument to Cromwell.'

Having secured the moral force of GAA opinion, O'Sullivan stepped up his press campaign to undermine and destroy the popularity of 'English pastimes' in Kerry. In response to a letter in the *Cork Examiner* arguing against a foreign games ban, O'Sullivan wrote to its editor:

In my humble opinion the persons who are promoting the extension of Rugby, Association and the other anglicising agencies, which are generating shoneenism and flunkeyism, are doing more to blot out our Nationality than the British Government. If our people were self-respecting, if they drew inspiration from native and not from foreign sources, if instead of hob-nobbing with the avowed enemies of their country and aping foreign manners and customs and as a result, degenerating from sterling Irishmen into contemptible West Britons – and instead of toasting the English King at their social functions they endeavoured to realise the passionate aspiration of nationhood, there would be no fear of the ultimate triumph of our National cause, the success of which is imperilled not by British treachery or brute force, but by the recreancy of un-Irish and anti-Irishmen . . . [We have] every desire to prevent our young men from becoming anglicised cads . . . Irish games which are superior from an athletic standpoint should be good enough for self-respecting Irishmen who have no ambition to renounce their nationality.[79]

In 'Gaelic Notes' the following February, he excitedly announced that at the next meeting of the county board a number of players from Listowel and Tralee would be reported for playing and encouraging rugby, contrary to the new rules. To counter any detractors over his stance on foreign games he argued that some Gaels 'are blind' to the GAA's national significance: 'If it were a purely sporting body' and not a nationalist organisation it 'would not justify its existence for twenty-four hours'. Further espousing his militant nationalism, he declared it would be from the membership of the GAA that 'the material may one day be drawn for striking an effective and manly blow at the whole accursed system of British domination in this country of ours'.

Following Tralee's latest defeat in the Munster Cup, O'Sullivan, with unmistakeable glee, inserted a mock obituary into his column. He proclaimed that the Tralee Rugby team had succumbed and 'died' on 17 March in Markets Field, Limerick 'after an hour's painful illness. Regretted by a large circle of shoneens – RIP'. A week later he proudly announced that before the game, members of Tralee RFC had written to a Listowel man who had become a convert to the GAA, asking him to provide half a dozen players to augment the Tralee team. His refusal resulted in their defeat and meant the club had effectively 'given up the ghost as far as rugby is concerned'.[80] The patrons of rugby in Kerry, lacking the countywide organisation of the local GAA and without a voice in the increasingly nationalist popular media, could not hope to fight off such a determined attack on its status. Rugby followers found it impossible to defend the sport against the charge of it being another extension of the 'British garrison' in Ireland. The game was unable to win the battle for the minds of an increasingly nationalistic local population.[81]

In November 1902, O'Sullivan's voice was influential in a more stringent resolution on foreign games being passed by the Central Council. This rendered it obligatory, and not optional as was previously the case, for county committees to expel Gaelic players 'participating in, or encouraging in any way, West-British pastimes like Rugby or soccer which are calculated to interfere with our national sports'.[82] In 1903, Munster council delegates, recognising his work in promoting the national games, elected him president of the Munster council. That same year O'Sullivan was instrumental in reintroducing the ban on members of the RIC and British armed forces joining the GAA.[83] In a final triumph at the delayed 1904 convention in January 1905, a large majority of delegates decided to enforce from 1 February a rule suspending for two years members who were caught playing soccer, rugby, hockey, cricket and 'other alien games'.[84]

Thanks in large part to the press and administrative campaigns of O'Sullivan, the GAA in Kerry was in a position to finally lay claim to the county's sporting heritage. The ban, which was introduced to ensure the success and popularity of Gaelic games, conformed to the political climate that dominated Ireland at the time. It presented the sporting enthusiasts of Ireland with a simple choice: play Gaelic and be seen to do your nationalist duty or reject it and your cultural heritage. The ban was seen as the ultimate expression of the GAA's close association with nationalism. Unlike its predecessors, the 1905 ban was motivated not by immediate, practical concerns but by a long-term desire to assist in the attempt to drive British rule and its infrastructure out of Ireland.

By 1904, the GAA in Kerry had risen from the ashes and regained a position of pre-eminence unmatched by any foreign sporting rivals. Within a year, Kerry had captured its first All-Ireland football title, in the process changing the fortunes of the association forever.

4

THE KERRY WAY, 1905–1915

WHO THE HELL SAID WE COULDN'T PLAY IN THE WET?

The Kerryman, 21 October 1905

Thanks to the efforts of men like T.F. O'Sullivan, the GAA was able to quickly re-establish itself in Kerry. Considering the weakness of the organisation in the late 1890s, this success is all the more remarkable. Between 1905 and 1915, the county came to dominate Gaelic football nationally to a degree unseen since the foundation of the GAA. Through its exploits on the national stage, Kerry forged a unique tradition in Gaelic football which continues to the present day. The county would play a decisive role in transforming the fortunes of the GAA nationally, helping it to become the largest national institution outside of the Catholic Church in Ireland. Kerry's victories propelled the association to unprecedented popularity among the Irish public, securing for its games a position of dominance within Irish sport that it has never since surrendered. In addition, the contemporary success of Kerry natives in the GAA in New York and North America generally provided another fillip to the emerging idea of a Kerry tradition in football. Meanwhile, prominent Kerry players such as Dick Fitzgerald who advocated a more scientific style of play, along with Kerry innovations such as dedicated training camps for players in preparation for finals, had a significant impact on the sport at large.

Yet in spite of this outward success, internally the GAA in Kerry remained weak. Football became dominated by two major clubs, John Mitchels of Tralee and Dr Crokes of Killarney. Elsewhere the growth of football clubs stalled, especially in rural areas. The GAA's structure in the county remained fragile and this contributed to the internal inertia in Gaelic affairs. Developments in transport at this time were of fundamental importance in the growth of the GAA at local and national level. Specifically, the role and impact of the rail network on the spread of clubs in counties like Kerry was crucial. Yet relations between the association and the various railway companies were never harmonious and the Kerry County Board's dispute with the GSWR over rail fares, leading to the county's refusal to contest the 1910 All-Ireland final and the subsequent fallout, was of major significance. Meanwhile, though a Kerry tradition was being forged, this tradition essentially abandoned the game of hurling in the county. In spite of numerous attempts to grow the game there, hurling continued to stagnate. The era also marked the first appearance of women in Gaelic games with the development of camogie and the establishment of the first camogie club in Kerry. Yet despite the significant role women continued to play within the GAA, the emerging Kerry tradition remained essentially a male-dominated one.

One Decade, Two Games, Redefining Football: the 1903 All-Ireland and the 1913 Croke Cup

It is important to remember that Kerry's unique success on the football field during these ten years was not pre-ordained. Indeed, following the Laune Rangers All-Ireland defeat in 1893 the county endured an unremarkable inter-county record for almost a decade. Between 1893 and 1902, Kerry only reached two Munster finals, in 1900 and 1902, and lost both. Reporting on the Kerry defeat in 1902, T.F O'Sullivan in his 'Gaelic Notes' commented on the recurring problem facing the Kerry team:

> There were not half a dozen good men in the combination and some of the worst third rate play it was possible to conceive was witnessed by them. Worst was . . . the majority [of the team selected] did not travel. Years ago a player represented to play for Kerry would have incurred every inconvenience to play the game, now it is different and the most trifling consideration is sufficient to keep them home by the fireside.[1]

General apathy and the inconvenience of travelling long distances to play inter-county matches all contributed to a dwindling enthusiasm among Kerry's best players to line out. However, with the re-establishment of the county board in 1900, a new generation of young, talented and eager officials decided to confront this situation. In the process, they would lay the foundations of Kerry's rise to inter-county glory. Foremost among this new generation was Tralee native Austin Stack.

Stack had been instrumental in forming the Tralee Celtic hurling club in 1901 and became its secretary. The following year he helped re-form the Tralee Mitchels GAA club and acted as their secretary as well as captaining the team in 1906. Mitchels went on to dominate the Kerry county championship, winning every title between 1902 and 1910. On the back of their extraordinary success, the county team's rise to pre-eminence was built. From 1904 Stack became a regular on the county team, usually playing at half-back.[2] He recognised that if Kerry was to compete for All-Ireland honours, the process of the county champion team solely representing the county on the inter-county stage would have to be altered. When the All-Ireland championship was inaugurated in 1887 it was open to all affiliated clubs in Ireland, who would first compete in county-run championships. The winners of these competitions would then proceed to represent that county in the All-Ireland championship. Yet increasingly, these winning county teams were being supplemented by players from other county clubs in the inter-county series. Advocating this approach, Stack, as secretary of Mitchels, persuaded its club officials to look beyond their own members and select the best players from across Kerry. The Kerry team that took to the field against Kildare to win its inaugural All-Ireland in October 1905 contained only eight Mitchels players.[3] In the weeks leading up to important inter-county games, Stack organised a series of training games against Kerry clubs and other inter-county teams as trials for those players in contention for the county team. After these games, the final team selection, entrusted to a selection committee headed by the Mitchels club, was published in the local press. The importance of Stack to Kerry's success in this period was demonstrated when after Kerry's All-Ireland victory in 1905 the county chairman,

Eugene O'Sullivan, declared that no one had done more to organise that victory than Austin Stack due to his extraordinary 'organisational skills, untiring energy and personality'.[4]

Thanks to such innovations, the Kerry football team became representative of the best players within the county. Instead of an untrained selection which assembled hours before a match, they honed their combination in a regular series of practice matches before taking to the field. Quickly, Kerry's fortunes on the inter-county scene began to change. In August 1903, Kerry defeated Cork in the Munster semi-final on the impressive score of 2-7 to 0-3 with a team made up of players from Mitchels, Dr Crokes, Castleisland, Ballymacelligott and Laune Rangers.[5] Kerry lost the subsequent Munster final to Tipperary. Yet the seeds of success had been sown and over the following two years they bloomed spectacularly on a national stage.

Kerry began the campaign for the 1903 Munster championship with a first-round win over the Waterford footballers in June 1904. They beat Clare in the subsequent semi-final, 2-7 to 0-2. On 30 October 1904, Kerry won the Munster football final for only the second time, defeating Cork 1-7 to 0-3. Beating a Mayo selection in the semi-final, they qualified for the 'home' All-Ireland final against Kildare, who had overcome Cavan.[6] The 1903 decider, arranged for 23 July 1905, represented the first time a Kildare team had qualified for the final, while it had been twelve years since Kerry's last appearance on this stage. Immediately, interest in the match was intense. Within Kerry, the pages of the local press were overtaken with items in relation to the final. A stream of letters was published in the *Kerry Sentinel*. In an edition of the newly established *Kerryman*, 'No Favour' wrote to its editor suggesting:

There are only three men who should be put off the [Kerry football] team. No. 1 is called Arthur Guinness; No. 2 is called 'No Practice'; No. 3 is 'Not deserving'. No. 1 and 2 should be on no team, though No. 3 is harder to deal with because he may not be a No. 1 or 2 but probably not what could be called a first-class player, yet for selfish motives is allowed on the team ahead of others. We want to become champions of Ireland, we have the men to do so and we want the best men on. The eyes of Kerry will be on the selection committee and they must do their duty. [Those selected] must be specially trained because the chance offered us now may not occur again in a generation.[7]

The final, played on a warm summer's day in Thurles, went down in the history of the association as one of the greatest matches ever witnessed. An enormous attendance, given contemporary standards, of 12,000 squeezed into the primitive grounds which offered no embankments or stands for spectators and only sported a rope around the pitch to keep out the throngs. The receipts from the game amounted to a record £123 13s 4d. Ireland's railway companies put in place extensive train arrangements to deal with the expected traffic to the game but the demand for services was such that the railways were forced to supplement their already ample provisions.[8] Two heavy excursion trains, one via Mallow, the other via Limerick, were put on from Tralee.[9] No Gaelic football match before it had so captured the imaginations of player and patron alike. Kildare entered the field in distinctive all-white jerseys and even had their playing boots whitewashed to complete the look.

The speed, skill levels and exciting nature of the contest amazed the journalists and spectators present. A frantic and close contest was fought across sixty minutes. The playing styles of the teams supplemented the contrast in their attire. Kildare played a short-passing game along the ground and by hand as was allowed at the time, while Kerry relied on overhead kicking and high fielding. *The Kerryman* remarked that Kildare showcased 'all the scientific modern methods in Gaelic football' and by employing this short-passing tactic they 'baffled' the Kerry team so that not a single pass was intercepted.[10] At half time Kildare had a slender lead of 0-2 to 0-1. The huge crowd encroached onto the pitch during the break and the restart was delayed as stewards attempted to clear spectators off the ground. For the second half Kerry played with the wind and with the pitch's slight incline in their favour. Within minutes of the restart, Kildare scored a goal and with ten minutes remaining had moved three points clear. Kerry redoubled their attacks and J.T.

Fitzgerald closed the gap to two points with a free. With two minutes remaining, Kerry launched a last, desperate attack up the wing. Kildare gave away a free and a seventeen-year-old from Killarney, Dick Fitzgerald, stepped up to take it. The kick fell short and the Kildare keeper reached to catch it under the posts. However, in so doing his feet went behind the goal line and the umpire raised the green flag to signal a goal. The Kildare players protested but Pat McGrath, the referee, awarded the goal to leave Kerry 1-4 to 1-3 in the lead. The excitement proved too much and Kerry supporters burst onto the pitch in wild delight at the score. With Kildare players still arguing the referee's decision, the official tried in vain to clear the pitch but to no avail. Failing to restart the game, he awarded the match to Kerry.

At a meeting of the Central Council that evening, the Kildare representatives formally objected to the result, stating the goal should not have been awarded. The referee appeared before the Central Council and acknowledged that he was not in an advantageous position to see the goal being scored but after consulting with the umpire decided to award the goal even though the second umpire disagreed with the decision. Considering that the umpires disagreed over the goal, the meeting moved that the game should be replayed.[11] As a consequence of the crowd invasion at Thurles, Cork was selected as the replay venue.

The replay took place on 27 August 1905. Another huge attendance of 12–15,000 crowded into the Cork Athletic Grounds. Judging by the demand for the drawn match, special trains were run on almost every line owned by the GSWR. Again, the match was characterised by a speed and intensity never before witnessed, being described as one of the most auspicious days in the history of the GAA. Such was the ferocity of the play that the ball being used in the match burst and had to be replaced. The pace of the match was so frantic that at the end of full time the referee, M.F. Crowe, collapsed from exhaustion. Kerry led 0-5 to 0-3 at half time thanks to a strong wind at their back. With five minutes remaining, Kerry still led by three points. However, Kildare were not yet beaten. Following an attack on the Kerry defence, the Kildare forward Jack Conlon managed to gain possession. Beating three Kerry defenders, Conlon sent a shot below the crossbar to tie the match, 0-7 to 1-4.[12]

The Pioneers, Kerry's first Gaelic football All-Ireland-winning team (1903). Back (l–r): E. O'Neil, D. Breen, D. Curran, D. McCarthy, M. Murray; middle (l–r): John O'Gorman, J.P. O'Sullivan, James O'Gorman, J. Myers, Con Healy, Rody Kirwan, M. McCarthy, Eugene O'Sullivan (president, County Board), T.F. O'Sullivan (secretary, County Board); front (l–r): W. Lynch, Dick Fitzgerald, F. O'Sullivan, Thady O'Gorman (captain), P. Dillon, J.T. Fitzgerald, Austin Stack; on ground (l–r): J. Buckley, D. Kissane. *(Courtesy of Frank Burke)*

For the first time in history the All-Ireland final went to a second replay. Interest in the match was unrivalled. Across Ireland national and local press attention became intense. The *Irish Independent* was flooded with letters arguing for locations for the replay in order that Gaelic followers from across Ireland would have a better opportunity of witnessing the event.[13] A meeting of the Central Council was held on 10 September to fix the venue, with T.F. O'Sullivan and Eugene O'Sullivan representing Kerry. The final was scheduled for 15 October and members voted for Jones Road due to the fact that Leinster had not staged a final for the past three years. At this decision T.F O'Sullivan handed in a letter signed by Stack threatening to withdraw Kerry from the championship if they were forced to play in Dublin. James

Nowlan, the meeting's chairman, then suggested Thurles and the delegates consented. Nevertheless, *Sport* reported that Kildare objected to this decision and would only consent to play in Jones Road.[14] At a further meeting of the Central Council it was decided that the request was unfair on the Kerry team and Cork was instead chosen as the venue.

An innovation pioneered by both Kerry and Kildare in the run-up to the second replay was the introduction of a systematic training programme for their inter-county teams.[15] This was a revolutionary step forward in the preparation for important matches.[16] The system of earlier practice matches conducted by Stack was expanded into training camps for the players. In order for the meagre finances of the Kerry Board to cope with the expense, they initiated

Thady O'Gorman, Kerry's first All-Ireland-winning captain, pictured in later life. *(Courtesy of Frank Burke)*

the creation of a public team-training fund. The *Sentinel*'s editor made a special appeal through his paper to the Kerry public

. . . for funds to enable them prepare for replay of the final fixed for . . . 15 October and to defray expenses already incurred by the first match. The intention of those connected with the team is to leave nothing undone to make the contest a victorious one for Kerry. In order for this our players must train honestly and conscientiously and the only way that can be done properly is by bringing the players together as often as possible in order that they may have an opportunity of playing a few practice matches between this and 15 October . . . We confidently expect that every patriotic Kerryman will ungrudgingly give his mite towards what is primarily a county object

and in the years to come he can proudly boast that he did
his share to win for Kerry her first All-Ireland.[17]

In the weeks before the replay, the Killarney and Tralee contingents
of the squad trained separately in their own towns before
alternatively travelling to the other by rail for collective training
and weekend practice games. These matches drew large crowds to
the match venues in Tralee Sportsground and Killarney.
Subscriptions for the training fund poured in and the local papers
published lists of those who had so generously contributed. The
Sentinel carried advertisements for Kerry v Kildare badges covered
with the Kerry colours of green and gold which could be purchased
for the 'modest sum' of 2d each at Miss Mollie McCarthy's, Upper
Castle Street, Tralee. The badges had the Kerry motto ('Up Kerry')
printed on their face.[18] In its issue before the final, *Sport* carried a
full supplement on the game featuring pictures of both teams,
action shots of the previous matches and portraits and
biographical notes on the players from both sides.

Interest in the game was so great among supporters and
neutrals alike that the superintendent of GSWR stated that all the
available stock of the company would be in use as special trains for
the day. An estimated 3–4,000 Kerry supporters travelled by rail
to Cork.[19] Reports suggested anywhere between 18,000 and
25,000 people attended, a record for a GAA match at the time.[20]
In a drizzling rain, Kerry ran onto the pitch and it 'seemed the earth
itself shook with the ring of "Up Kerry"', the county's newly coined
war cry.[21] The rain prevented the match reaching the standards of
the previous two encounters. Yet *Sport* remarked that the play of
many of the Kerry players, given the conditions, was 'astonishing',
with Dick Fitzgerald playing 'a really splendid game'. A close first
half ended with Kerry leading 0-3 to 0-2. However, the second half
witnessed a complete transformation. Play became confined to the
Kildare half with the Kerry forwards tormenting the Kildare
backline and it was 'simply astonishing the way in which the Kerry
players outclassed in every respect the Kildaremen . . . For fifteen or
twenty minutes before call of time Kildare was a well whipped
team.' Kerry claimed its first football All-Ireland title on a score of
0-8 to 0-2. The victory led to scenes of jubilation. News of the win

was received by special telegram to *The Gaelic American* in New York, where it was greeted with elation among Kerry emigrants. The *Sentinel* stated that Kerry now stood 'head and shoulders above any team in the Association'.[22]

> The greatest battle in the history of the Gaelic Athletic Association has been fought and won . . . For generations to come the matches . . . will be spoken of at our Kerry firesides as one of the most interesting events in the whole history of the county.[23]

T.F. O'Sullivan, writing some years later, described the matches as 'the most sensational played since the inception of the Association and did more . . . to develop Gaelic football than any previous contests for championship honours'. What is certain is that these encounters between Kildare and Kerry catapulted the GAA into the mainstream of Irish sport. The huge publicity and neutral interest surrounding the games marked the first time Ireland joined the worldwide sporting revolution. The games heralded the GAA's coming of age and Gaelic football claimed its place at the centre of Irish sporting culture. Close to 60,000 people witnessed the games and the standards of football exhibited exceeded anything previously seen on a Gaelic field.[24] The total gate receipts from the three matches came to nearly £600. The financial windfall ensured that for the first time in its twenty-year history the association was on a sound financial footing, a position that was never again to be threatened. On 12 November 1905, Kerry defeated London in Dublin by 0-11 to 0-3, officially becoming the All-Ireland champions. Following this victory, arrangements were made to hold a function in honour of the victorious Kerry team. At the Hibernian Hotel in Tralee in the week before Christmas a gala banquet and concert was given to salute the county's All-Ireland heroes. In recognition of the outstanding contribution the vanquished Kildare team had also made to the prestige of the GAA, the Central Council decided to award them with a set of gold medals.[25]

The Irish public had never before witnessed Gaelic matches of the skill and speed as those encounters between Kildare and

Kerry. But why should this have been the case? What was unique about these games that created such a forceful and lasting impression among the Irish public, propelling the GAA to such popularity? Simply put, these matches were contested between two well-trained, disciplined combinations that were the first inter-county teams to be in a position to fully utilise the evolving playing rules of the organisation to their full potential.

At its second meeting, in December 1884, the GAA's members formally adopted the rules for their newly codified creations of Gaelic football and hurling. With regard to giving an insight into how a match in either code was in practice played, the rules were vague in the extreme. Merely ten rules for football and twelve for hurling were conceived and most of these dealt only with the playing area, duties of officials and the length of a match, etc. Only four of the ten football rules actually dealt with the mechanics of the game, stating that a match must be between fourteen and twenty-one a side, no pushing or tripping was to be allowed, kicking the ball over the side or your own goal line would result in a throw-in for an opponent and that the greatest number of goals would win a match. Hurling's rules were similarly vague, with only an additional pronouncement that it was illegal to lift the ball from the ground with the hand. In 1888, the rules of both codes were revised. Point posts standing twenty-one feet away from the goals were introduced. A new law stated that the ball, in either code, could be caught off the ground or struck with the hand but once caught it must be kicked or pucked. Throwing or carrying the ball was not allowed, except in hurling where the sliothar could be carried on the camán.[26]

Yet the very vagueness of these rules continued to cause uncertainty among officials and spectators alike. For several years before he was appointed secretary of the association, Richard Blake had argued that the rules of football in particular needed to be clearly defined and uniformly enforced if the sport was to gain widespread popularity. The overcrowded nature of the playing pitch with forty-two players competing for a ball naturally led to mass scrimmages reminiscent of the days of caid. The numbers on the field militated against any sense of positional play. Also, seeing as goals decided games, it was a frequent tactic once a team had scored to crowd their own goal line. In response, Blake suggested that teams should be reduced to fourteen a side, thereby opening up the game and creating more scoring opportunities.[27] In 1893, writing to the editor of *Sport*, Blake suggested that the principal reason for the decline in popularity of Gaelic games was the inadequate rules for the game of Gaelic football compared to its rivals.[28] Leading up to his election as secretary, Blake became more forceful in his views. He declared that after ten years the game of football was still 'crude and imperfect and unworthy of the GAA'. It had a dozen rules

> . . . that anyone can take what meaning he likes out of . . . referees are . . . absolutely ignored, [their] duties are merely hinted at and the result is the referee in a Gaelic match is like the 'fool in the middle', his decisions degraded, because in the most cases they are the outcome of his right of private judgement.

In particular, he quoted Rule Ten under the 1888 provisions, which stated: 'The player must not carry or throw the ball.' What, he asked, was to stop a player throwing a ball a little forward? It says he must not carry the ball but what number of steps constituted a carry?

The Kerry County Board was already deeply aware of the deficiencies in the GAA's official rules. In particular, one law stated that the two umpires must be appointed from opposing teams. As has been seen in other chapters, frequent disputes over scores dubiously awarded or denied by biased officials led to many games ending with one side walking off the pitch in protest. To curb this, the Kerry Board in November 1889 passed a series of rule changes under which subsequent championship matches would be held. Among the major changes were the introduction of independent umpires and the reconfiguring of the scoring system so that a goal would in future be equal to five points. This resulted in the highest number of points scored winning a match.[29] Kerry was the first county to introduce such an idea into the games of the association.

After being elected as the association's national secretary in 1895, Blake immediately set about restructuring the playing rules for both hurling and football in order to eliminate any uncertainty over them. This, he hoped, would increase interest in the games at the expense of their growing rivals, soccer and rugby. Among the new changes was the reduction of inter-county teams to seventeen a side and equipping referees with whistles. Likewise, players who had been sent off were strictly to adhere to the decision.[30] Kerry's decision to award five points for a goal was applied nationally, and every club was charged with the responsibility for the conduct of its players, officials and, critically, supporters. Finally, in relation to the association's Playing Rule Ten, Blake clearly defined that the ball could be struck with the hand but not thrown. Once the ball was caught it must be kicked immediately and could not be hopped, thrown or carried. Carrying was defined as more than four steps with the ball in hand. Throwing the ball against the ground was deemed illegal. In 1896, the rules were altered to make one goal equal to three points. The changes pioneered by Blake led to a faster, more open and higher scoring game which could at last compete with its more illustrious and international rival sporting codes for public interest.[31]

Although Blake was dismissed from office in 1898, his zeal in reforming the GAA's playing rules had a major impact on the future success of the games. At the association's 1901 Annual Convention a committee was formed, of which T.F. O'Sullivan was a member, to re-examine the GAA's playing rules.[32] The Kerry versus Kildare saga of 1905 forcefully demonstrated to the public how two skilled and trained combinations employing their own unique styles of play could utilise the evolving rules to produce a spectacle to rival anything its contemporaries in soccer or rugby could produce. Indeed, these contests led to innovations like the toe-to-hand being first demonstrated. The rules governing football and hurling continued to evolve between 1905 and 1915. In the GAA's official guide for 1907, the modern-day parallelogram was introduced, stipulating that no player from an opposing team was allowed to enter it until the ball had done so during play. This immediately led to a vast reduction in instances of congestion of the goal area and curbed the tactic of forwards loitering by the goalmouth to 'sneak' a goal or harassing the goalkeeper as he attempted to claim the ball.[33] The noted referee, M.F. Crowe, advocated the introduction of goal nets to remove the indecision of officials over whether or not a goal had been scored.[34] These were introduced in 1910. Also in 1907, the laws on catching and carrying the ball were altered to allow a player to carry for four steps before the ball had to be kicked, struck with the hand or hopped off the ground once, but no more than once.[35]

These redefinitions of the rules did not solve every problem. The Limerick referee appointed for the 1909 Munster football final between Cork and Kerry was described as being from a solely hurling district of his county. It was quickly evident that 'he knew little' about football. 'The first incident to rouse the ire of spectators was when Con Murphy [the Kerry forward] fielding a high ball hopped it once and was whistled! Players caught and obstructed each other to their heart's content.' The second half was rough, with the referee allowing 'every latitude'. A Cork player lifted the ball straight off the ground and kicked it between the posts, with the referee allowing the score despite cries of 'foul' from the crowd. As a result, Kerry walked off the field in disgust. They were persuaded to return and did so under protest. The referee's performance was cited as the reason for Kerry's 2-8 to 1-7 defeat. Kerry successfully appealed the decision of the match and in the

1909 Kerry team. Kerry won its third footballing All-Ireland in 1909, beating Louth in the final. *(Courtesy of the National Library of Ireland)*

replay defeated Cork, going on to win their third All-Ireland, beating the coming force of Louth in the final.

At the 1910 GAA Annual Convention the modern-day H-shaped goal and point posts were first introduced.[36] Innovations like this, coupled with the development of lighter footballs, less cumbersome camáns and specialised footwear led to an increasing emphasis on skill and practice to bring off scores. At the 1913 convention delegates approved Harry Boland's (the Dublin GAA representative and later noted republican) motion to reduce inter-county teams to the modern-day fifteen a side. The steady process in the reduction of team numbers had a drastic impact on the quality and tactics of future matches. Coupled with the widespread use of lighter footballs, this meant players had to train for matches to reach the required fitness and skill to compete in a much faster and more open game. Field positions became all important in order for teams to cover the expanse of the field. As a result, the mass player scrambles for the ball became confined to history. The first inter-county game to demonstrate the new fifteen-a-side rule was the Croke Memorial Cup final between Louth and Kerry in May 1913. What transpired in both matches stunned veteran and virgin spectators alike. They would enter GAA history as perhaps the greatest games ever played and would secure for the association an unmatched level of popularity among the Irish sporting public which it holds to this day. In the process, the games would forcefully cement the status of Kerry as the unrivalled football power of the era.

With the death of its patron Archbishop Croke in 1902, the GAA's Central Council had been attempting to raise sufficient funds for a suitable memorial in his honour.[37] From 1910 various tournament matches were held in aid of this memorial fund, which at the start of 1913 amounted to £308. In December 1912, the Central Council decided to hold a special Croke memorial tournament in hurling and football in aid of the project.[38] The following January Kerry, Cork, Dublin, Louth and Antrim were drawn in the football tournament, the object of which was to acquire the £700 needed to bring the memorial fund up to a sum of £1,000. The first ties saw Louth defeat Dublin on 16 February 1913, setting up a semi-final with Antrim on 16 March. At the

1913 Kerry Croke Cup team. The intense media and public interest in the final and the match which Louth and Kerry produced for the drawn game signalled the moment when the GAA became Ireland's pre-eminent sporting body. Back (l–r): J. Moriarty, C. Clifford, T. Costello, P. Healy, J. Lawlor, J. Kennelly; front (l–r): Tom Rice, P. O'Shea, D. Doyle, R. Fitzgerald (captain), M. Donovan, C. Murphy, M. McCarthy, D. Mullins (goal) and J. Skinner. *(Courtesy of the National Library of Ireland)*

opposing end of the draw, Kerry met Cork also on 16 February and, led by Dick Fitzgerald, secured an exciting 2-3 to 2-0 win to qualify for the final. *Sport* reported every Gael in Ireland was hoping Louth would qualify for the final and they did not disappoint, beating the Ulstermen 2-7 to 0-1. Once news broke that Kerry and Louth were to face each other, the Irish sporting media and public went into a near frenzy. Quite simply this was a match four years in the making.

In December 1909, Kerry had defeated Louth in the latter's first ever All-Ireland final appearance by 1-9 to 0-6. However, Louth, dissatisfied with the result, appealed to the Central Council lodging four separate objections against the legality of five members of the Kerry winning side.[39] At the subsequent Central Council meeting, Louth produced evidence that one member of the Kerry team known as John Healy was in fact a John Casey who had earlier that year transferred from the Valentia GAA club to the Dublin Kickhams, which should have ruled him ineligible to play for Kerry. Austin Stack, as the Kerry representative, was able to rebuff this and two of the other objections with his own evidence and Louth, seeing they had not convinced the meeting's members, withdrew their remaining objections. The incident caused some degree of animosity in Kerry, with *The Kerryman* hinting that members of the Valentia club had supplied information to the Louth delegates in reprisal for a dispute between the club and the Kerry County Board.[40] The following November Kerry and Louth again qualified for an All-Ireland final but, as shall be discussed in detail later, owing to a dispute with the GSWR the Kerry team refused to travel and Louth were awarded the All-Ireland as a walkover. In 1911, Kerry succumbed to a shock Munster semi-final defeat to Waterford while Louth were eliminated in Leinster. The following year promised to finally bring about a rematch of the two erstwhile rivals. Kerry had qualified to meet Antrim in the All-Ireland semi-final and it was widely expected that they would handsomely qualify for the 1912 final.[41] But 'in perhaps the most sensational GAA result of all time', Antrim defeated Kerry 3-5 to 0-2.[42] Afterwards, there were suggestions that the Kerry team had stayed up until all hours 'merry-making' the night before, having been invited to attend the wedding reception of a prominent Kerry man in Dublin. Whatever the reason, Kerry and Louth were denied another chance to renew their rivalry.

Thus, when the Croke Memorial final line-up was known the most intense interest immediately surrounded the match. An extra dimension was added by the bad blood which had developed between both counties. After Louth were awarded the All-Ireland in 1910, Kerry issued a series of challenges to the Louth team to face them in a rematch of the abandoned final. A response, purporting to be from the Louth GAA, was published in the national papers stating that the Louth junior football team would accept the challenge and would serve as a sufficient test for the Kerry team. Though their county board subsequently claimed that such a reply had been unauthorised and was not the official position of the body, the letter was seen as a grave slur and an affront to Kerry football. *The Kerryman* declared that not 'since the inception of the GAA was such an insult heard of'.[43]

The Croke final was fixed for 4 May 1913 in Jones Road, Dublin. For weeks previously, a county board-appointed selection committee, chaired by Austin Stack, conducted a series of trial matches between different team combinations in venues around Kerry. A wave of enthusiasm was described as 'once more sweeping through the hills and valleys of Kerry'. An appeal by Diarmuid Crean, the county secretary, for training funds was readily subscribed to. Interest in the match took on a global dimension. The Kerrymen's Patriotic and Benevolent Association of New York sent Austin Stack $81 collected from among its members for the Kerry team training fund. A 'Kerry Exile' wrote home from Massachusetts declaring that 'his native heart throbbed' when he saw that Kerry was to be pitted against Louth. The Kerry people in the US, he emphasised, were 'watching and waiting'.[44] In the week before the final, *Sport* declared that 'there was never a contest under any code in this country that attracted so much attention, that was so eagerly looked for, or that has aroused so much interest as this match'. Admission prices were charged at 6d for the Canal End, 1s for everywhere else and demand was reported as unprecedented.[45]

An enormous crowd converged on Jones Road for the eagerly anticipated final. Approximately 25,000 people attended the game, smashing all previous attendance records for any sporting event domestic or international held in Ireland. Over 5,000 Kerry supporters were estimated to have made the long journey to the capital. A gate of £750 was taken and, to the obvious delight of the memorial fund organisers, a fiercely contested match ended level, Kerry 0-4, Louth 1-1. In the days after the event, letters from enthusiastic followers filled the national press, discussing and dissecting the match. The *Sentinel* remarked that all who attended the final agreed it was the fastest-paced match they had ever witnessed.[46]

A meeting of the Central Council set the replay for Jones Road on 29 June 1913. It was also agreed to grant £50 to both counties to defray their expenses in training their sides. This would prove a hugely significant decision by the GAA and heralded the official sanction of the practice of dedicated training camps set up to prepare county teams for such important matches. In preparation for the replay, it was reported that Louth had secured the services of two professional soccer coaches from Belfast to train their side. Not to be outdone, Kerry enlisted the help of Jerry Collins as coach and William O'Connor as trainer of their team. Both men where well known in local athletics and gymnastics circles. The Kerry players were put into special training camps that were held alternately in Tralee and Killarney.[47] Numerous businessmen across the county offered the use of their motorcars to the team for excursions to break the monotony of the camp. Such was the enthusiasm for the match that Dan McCarthy, a member of the 1905 All-Ireland-winning side, sailed home from San Francisco specifically to attend the match.

On the day of the replay, every rail track owned by the GSWR had a train running from each district on their line. The company estimated that 11,328 people travelled on their trains to the match and eleven specials ran out of Kerry alone. A crowd estimated to be anywhere from 36,000 to 50,000 strong somehow squeezed into Jones Road.[48] It should be remarked that the average attendance for a soccer cup tie in England in 1913 was 20,600. That major football matches in Ireland could have surpassed this despite the huge population difference (36 million in England versus 4.4 million in Ireland) gives a powerful indication of the appeal the GAA had achieved.[49] Such was the demand for entrance that a full two hours before throw-in, people had to be turned away from the turnstiles as there was no more room in the ground. The lack of stands meant that for many among the huge crowds, the only glimpse they had of the ball was when it was kicked high in the air. Kerry played their traditional game of long kicking and high fielding, while Louth employed their distinctive tactic of foot passing, soccer style, along the ground. Having been level at half time the Kerry team pulled away in the second half to win 2-4 to 0-5. The noted Gaelic games correspondent 'Carbery', writing for the *Cork Examiner*, declared the match 'epoch making' and its result a 'great triumph' for Kerry's traditional style of football over Louth's more modern tactics.[50] *The Kerryman* headlines read: 'Glorious Kerry! . . . Insults Effectively Wiped Out . . . The "Wee County" Made Really Small'.[51] As a consequence of these games, *The Freeman's Journal* argued that Gaelic football had proved

> . . . to be scientific in principle as well as exciting in practice and, played by two well-trained teams, proves that it has attractions equal in merit but greater in sentiment and association than any of the rival games which are in vogue. For raising the game to this preeminence in the athletic world we may justly claim that Kerrymen . . . deserve the highest praise.[52]

When news of the victory reached Kerry that evening scenes of wild euphoria erupted. In Tralee, streamers were placed across the streets and green branches were hung from houses. In Listowel, the hilltops for miles around blazed with bonfires and a massive fire was set in the town's square around which hundreds congregated to celebrate. When the Kerry team arrived into Killarney on Monday night a huge reception welcomed them home. Thousands thronged the streets, lit by torches and tar barrels. Dick Fitzgerald and his Killarney teammates were carried shoulder-high through the town as the Tralee players left to await similar scenes at Tralee station.

It can be argued that, more than the matches between Kildare and Kerry, the Croke final transported the GAA onto another plain of popularity in Irish culture. If in 1905 the GAA had come of age, in 1913 it became unsurpassed as the island's preeminent sporting body. The rise of Kerry as a football power, which had begun with its victory in 1905, became undisputed on the back of this victory. The intense media hype surrounding both events gave the county and its players a degree of popularity in football unmatched in any of the preceding decades of the association. However, the Croke final was to have another long-term consequence. The gate receipts for the replay alone came to an incredible £1,183. Hoping that the tournament would raise the GAA's Croke memorial fund to £1,000, the drawn final and replay had surpassed all expectations and the total fund stood at £2,365 11s 7½d. It was decided, in deference to the huge amount of money raised, to purchase a suitable sports ground to be named in honour of Archbishop Croke.[53] That September, after viewing several potential grounds, the GAA's secretary, Luke O'Toole, reported that the association intended to purchase Jones Road and rename it the Croke Memorial Park. The ground was purchased on 22 December 1913 for a total cost of £3,6641 8s 5d.[54] After twenty-eight years, the GAA had found a permanent home. From that time Croke Park became the great symbol of the association, a fitting legacy for Kerry's celebrated victory.

The Evolution of a County Identity and the Birth of the Kerry Tradition

On the back of Kerry's success on the national stage, the county was able to construct a unique sporting tradition. This tradition was enhanced by the sense of communal identity that had developed parallel to Kerry's success within the GAA. By 1913, playing for Kerry had acquired a new meaning. When fifteen men dressed in their distinctive green and gold jerseys ran out onto the sunlit pitch of Jones Road on 4 May 1913 to face their Louth opponents in vivid red, there was little need to proclaim where they had come from. For Gaelic followers across Ireland, the colours of those green and gold jerseys had become synonymous with the county of Kerry and its footballers. As the association passed its quarter-century anniversary, the administrative division of the Irish county had become the bedrock of the GAA's organisational structure and its most prestigious competitions. The exact role the GAA played in the creation or development of distinct county identities around the turn of the twentieth century remains poorly understood. Yet it did play a significant role, grafting a communal loyalty onto these artificial divisions of administrative convenience.

The county system was introduced into Ireland as part of the English crown's process of conquering and colonising the country.

These county boundaries were often nominal administrative partitions that did not translate from, and bore little relation to, the divergent customs of the region.[55] The county system was just another imagined geographical boundary placed on top of previous diocesan, parish and old Gaelic fiefdom divisions. In the era before the advent of the GAA, it is uncertain to what extent the populations within such county boundaries actually looked upon themselves as a distinct community. The triumph of the county as the dominant badge of local identity and government was by no means inevitable. Indeed, during the nineteenth century the British government had looked to the establishment of the Poor Law unions as the most effective means of local administration in Ireland and the future of local administration seemed to lie with them. However, the Local Government Act of 1898 restored the county as a major unit of local government in Ireland. In addition, the growth of political organisations such as the National League that were structured on a county basis impacted on the significance of county boundaries and these became the main areas of electoral contestation.

Though Kerry had traditionally been split by the ancient Gaelic kingdoms of Thomond and Desmond, by the second half of the eighteenth century such divisions were historical relics. Nevertheless, its imposed county bounds corresponded almost exactly to the boundary of the Kerry diocese, and the 'devotional revolution', to use Emmet Larkin's term, that swept Ireland in the decades after the Famine impacted on the significance of this boundary.[56] It has also been argued that the explosion of the print media in Victorian Ireland led to newspapers playing a significant role in the creation of a national identity. It has been observed that a shared sense of community and identity could be forged by the communal 'ceremony' of readership of a locality's newspaper.[57] Just as the national press promoted Ireland as a unique entity, so the local press could be seen to be influential in the creation of a unique county identity. It seems then that by the foundation of the GAA, the people of Kerry had a sense of this shared county boundary which, however nominally, connected the populations of Kenmare and Dingle with those of Tralee and Tarbert.

Yet however strong or weak a sense of county prevailed in Ireland at this time, there were few opportunities for a social or sporting communal experience to impart and enforce the idea of a shared county identity. Athletics at best pitted the best men of a parish against their neighbouring rivals. Traditional games such as caid were likewise fought out on a parish basis.[58] Meanwhile, the new codified creations of the Victorian sports revolution, such as rugby and cricket, had the club and not any territorial divisions at the heart of their games. Indeed, the GAA itself did little to foster county teams or identity during the first years of its existence. When it was initially founded the GAA used the parish as the building block for its first teams. As has been discussed, the parish itself often proved too artificial a concept, with many teams forming within the older and more traditional townland boundaries. The association's All-Ireland championships remained little more than club competitions over much of the first twenty years of their existence. However, county boards began to be organised across Ireland in the late 1880s to establish and administer the association's games within each county. By the beginning of the 1890s, there was a gradual move towards the county becoming the main competing component on the national stage, a process that those within the Kerry GAA often pioneered.[59]

Early in 1890 *Sport* carried the suggestion that the GAA should encourage proper inter-county Gaelic matches in which the competing teams were composed of the best players available within a given county. Maurice Moynihan, the Kerry secretary, became one of the first GAA officials to support the idea. He argued that '[S]uch matches, where all the clubs of each county would be directly interested, would be sure to further enhance and popularise one of the most beneficial associations ever established by Irishmen'.[60] Moynihan wrote to *Sport*'s editor stating that Kerry fully endorsed the proposal and, acting on the suggestion, they had decided to challenge the Gaels of Limerick to such a contest in football and hurling.[61] By the end of the month, the Limerick Board had formally accepted the challenge and the contests finally came off in early August. Moynihan proudly declared 'the Gaels of the county deserved the greatest credit for uniting to the man' to compete for their county's honour. No doubt the sweeping victories that the Kerry hurlers and footballers achieved in the games added to his cheer.[62] The idea of such inter-county matches continued to gain support. In October 1890, as Laune Rangers and Midleton contested the Munster final in front of a mediocre attendance, an immense crowd of 7–8,000 gathered that same afternoon at a nearby venue to watch a challenge match between the picked men of Cork and Limerick. Kerry continued its interest in such challenge matches. In February 1891, the county board met to select an all-county team in hurling and football to face Galway in another arranged match in Limerick. In front of a large attendance, the two counties contested their first ever inter-county clash.[63] Periodically, over the rest of the 1890s Kerry continued to arrange inter-county challenge matches, one example being against Limerick in Mallow in November 1895.

Kerry was also one of the first counties to adopt this principle of picking the best players available to represent the county on the All-Ireland stage. The Ballyduff team that claimed the All-Ireland in 1892 was composed of ten Ballyduff, five Kilmoyley, three Ardfert and three Lixnaw players. Once the county board was re-formed in 1900 it, in conjunction with the winning county champions, made a conscious effort to form selection committees in which the best talent available in the county was selected to represent Kerry in the Munster and All-Ireland championships.[64]

This practice certainly helped to strengthen the bonds of county loyalty in Kerry. Such a process was only enhanced following the county's remarkable success on the national stage between 1905 and 1915. The exploits of its athletes, drawn from across the county, beating all challengers in gallant contests, certainly infused Kerry people with a pride and deep satisfaction in their county identity. Whereas for much of the troubled 1880s and '90s Kerry had graced the national press only in reference to its agrarian lawlessness and crippling emigration, now it was esteemed for its sporting achievements. The rise in this civic pride, built on the back of GAA success, could also have been influenced by the growing importance of the administrative unit of the county. The newly introduced county councils were the first truly democratically representative bodies established in Ireland. Therefore, the prestige attached to winning such a seat was immense, especially at a time when Ireland was struggling for some form of legislative independence. Their introduction changed what was previously an exercise in administrative boundary-making into a tangible political entity.

By 1905, the county had overshadowed the club at the heart of public and media interest. In fact, the GAA was the curious exception to the developments of other sports around the world which placed the club at the centre. Club, parochial and urban–rural rivalries quickly became subordinated into a single loyalty at inter-county level. Paul Rouse argues that with borders of such artificial design, as in the case of counties such as Offaly, 'the importance of hurling and Gaelic football in shaping the identity of the county and in inspiring county loyalty is immense'.[65] The growing popularity of the GAA had begun to infuse meaning into such county boundaries that otherwise would have been ambiguous and arbitrary. However, it is evident that this process was slower in some counties than in others. Up until the early 1910s inter-county teams from Dublin, Mayo and Cork continued to be reported in the press in the name of their county championship-winning clubs. The *Gaelic Athlete* in February 1912 had argued that the practice of county champions charged with selecting the county side discriminated against players from other clubs and disinclined them from believing that they represented a broader county interest.[66] To curb the trend of discrimination against players from outside the county champion club, the paper believed county boards should decide on distinct patterns for their county jerseys.

The proof of this theory was evident in Kerry, where the green and gold jerseys became synonymous with the county's footballers. Yet the adoption of the colours green and gold was not a predetermined act. For example, when Kerry played Galway in 1891 they lined up in white jerseys.[67] However, in the nine Kerry county championships played between 1902 and 1911, Tralee Mitchels won eight.[68] Despite selection committees being established by the county board, Mitchels' representatives still had an influential voice in the selection of the team and of course the county footballers wore this club's colours of yellow and green. The dominance of the Mitchels players on the Kerry team, wearing the same Mitchels colours in an era when Kerry shot to national eminence, reinforced the association of the colours with an all-Kerry team. Although the Kerry team was described as winning the 1905 home final against Kildare in red and green jerseys, by the time they faced London the following month they were attired in what would become their traditional green and gold.[69] A rule from the 1907 GAA guidebook stated that all counties must wear distinctive colours and register them with the association. A communication from the Central Council in early 1913 made clear that the above rule was to be enforced and requested each county committee to provide a distinct set of jerseys for use by county teams in all inter-county matches. Such jerseys were to be left in the custody of the county secretary and were to be worn in all such matches. Subsequently, the Kerry Board informed the Central Council that its county colours would be green with a gold hoop across the chest.[70]

The familiar faces that dominated Kerry's first great football team helped seal the notion of them as a county rather than a club selection. By the 1905 final, the public and media talked only in terms of Kildare and Kerry as opposed to the Mitchels and Clane teams they were officially selected from. The advent of photography and the increasing practice of photographing a county team in the county strip with the county's name embroiled across the chest also led to a solidifying of county identities.[71] Matches such as the Croke final were among the first with widespread use of photography. *Sport*, in particular, carried extensive photographs of the match and teams in the days leading up to and after the games. All of this assisted in the establishment of a set county identity onto which the Kerry tradition could be grafted.

In the aftermath of back-to-back All-Irelands in 1905 and 1906, Kerry's footballers became the media darlings of the Irish sporting press. Over the next ten years, their victories and battles would lead to a growing acknowledgement of a unique tradition held by its footballers and the way they played. During this time, Kerry bestrode the inter-county scene like a colossus, winning five All-Irelands, appearing in nine All-Ireland finals and winning nine Munster titles. In the midst of this remarkable period of success, the Kerry football tradition was created.

The acknowledgement of Kerry's unique standing grew quickly on the back of her victory over Kildare in 1905. By the 1940s, the match had become established in the association's folklore as 'the game that made the GAA'.[72] Following this victory, huge crowds were guaranteed anytime Kerry took to the field in various inter-county championship or tournament matches. This was especially true anytime the team made the long journey to Dublin. As the reigning All-Ireland champions they took on Dublin at Croke Park in April 1906 for a match in aid of the Wolfe Tone Memorial Fund at which a crowd of 6,000 paid in to catch a glimpse of 'the most famous side in Ireland'. In July 1907, they again played Dublin, this time in a challenge match for the benefit of the City Drapers' Society. Having succumbed to a heavy defeat in the Munster semi-final to Cork two weeks earlier, the *Sentinel* marvelled that there was something about the Kerry side 'that despite this [defeat], the mere mention of the team playing was enough to pack Jones Road'. Following their victory in the Munster final in 1906, *The Kerryman* mused: 'If we take Kerry victories for some considerable time back one is justified in designating the team the All-Whites, the opposite colour being that applied to the invincible New Zealanders.' *Sport* was forced to acknowledge that in the aftermath of her maiden All-Ireland wins, the appearance of the Kerry team in the All-Ireland final 'can arouse unusual interest and arrest widespread attraction'.[73] By 1910, the same paper, in reference to another upcoming contest against Dublin, informed GAA supporters in the capital that they would soon have a chance to witness the 'now recognised Kerry style'. The county gained a formidable reputation for this 'Kerry style' and played a fast, open, high-fielding game – developing a tactic where a player catching the ball swung clear and played on rapidly to a teammate taking up an advantageous position. The success of their style was hailed by reporters after the Croke Cup final as a triumph of a more traditional and Irish tactic of play over the modern 'scientific' and soccer-like short passing of Louth. In the Christmas edition of the *Gaelic Athlete* in 1914, 'Carbery', reflecting in the wake of another Kerry All-Ireland victory, wrote of the team:

Those men from the Kingdom instead of being the big, burly chaps I anticipated, were a medium-sized, wiry, well-trained lot who introduced us to Gaelic football in a new and nobler raiment . . . Their Celtic faces were the faces of well-schooled, well-disciplined men, full of enthusiasm but also of self-control . . . They have evolved a method of football which is ever a pleasure to watch and have brought the game to a pitch of popularity and perfection which looked an impossibility prior to their advent. And the beauty of it all is that they are sportsmen every one. Never have foul, dishonest nor ungrateful tactics been associated with their name. On and off the field they behave themselves in a style which does credit to their county and the game they play . . . Never has a team been so loved by their county, by rich and poor alike, as these Kerry men are . . . With their county men's heart behind them, Kerry will long keep near the top of Irish Football.[74]

However, one may argue that there is a significant element of hype and flannel in evaluations like Carbery's. Contemporary writers on the GAA were adept at eulogising the association, its games and teams. In their battle to secure the support of the Irish sporting public, it served their interest to mythologise both the GAA's games and its most successful teams. It can be argued that contemporary journalists were actively cultivating a tradition around its most successful teams to enhance the prestige of Gaelic games over their foreign rivals. This could be seen as an early example of the process of the media fabricating and sustaining a sporting tradition, such as that surrounding the Munster rugby team of the 2000s.[75] As a consequence, the Kerry team became hugely popular and this popularity was enough to guarantee record receipts whenever and wherever they played. Various nationalist organisations, along with charities, beneficial causes and the association's Central Council, were quick to exploit the money-making ability of the Kerry senior football team. Throughout the 1905–15 period, Kerry played innumerable challenge and tournament matches across Ireland in aid of a multitude of causes against its great rivals: Kildare, Louth, Wexford, Dublin and Cork. Indeed, by 1914 the Kerry County Board had become sick of the practice and passed a unanimous decision that in future priority would instead be given to internal GAA matters.[76]

The development of this Kerry tradition in football was greatly influenced by the era in which it took place. Kerry became the most dominant team at a time of unprecedented growth in media coverage, which heralded the introduction and mass use of photography in the press and the development of film. The 1905 finals were among the first major GAA events that witnessed the extensive use of photography in the national press, in the build-up and aftermath of the games. The *Cork Examiner* was one of the first major papers in Ireland to use regular photographs when covering GAA matches. However, it was the launch of the *Irish Independent* in 1905 that really accelerated the use of photography for GAA events. Through this medium, the faces of Kerry's great players such as Dick Fitzgerald, Paddy Dillon and Johnny Skinner transferred from a local to a national stage and became familiar to Gaels across Ireland. Indeed, at the 1911 Munster Convention Kerry's delegate, Joe Harrington, enquired if any arrangements had been made with cinematographers in connection with filming Gaelic matches.[77] During a challenge match between Cork and Kerry in 1910, both teams were filmed before and during the game, a development that was reported as an innovation on a Gaelic field.[78]

But there were many in the GAA who thought the media did not give sufficient space to Gaelic matters. *The Kerryman* in 1908 acknowledged that some of our 'so-called national daily journals display a hostility to the Gaelic Athletic Association which has been a serious obstacle to the development of Irish games in Ireland'.[79] In a piece on media coverage of the association in the 1909 *Gaelic Athletic Annual*, the writer 'Deligmis' attacked the 'woefully unsatisfying' reporting of Gaelic matches in and among the nation's press.[80] Even *The Kerryman*, whose editor Maurice Griffin was a devout and enthusiastic supporter of the association, came in for scorn. Diarmuid Cronin, Kerry's Munster Council delegate in 1913, reproached it and other local nationalist papers for the fact that scarcely a third of the twenty or thirty championship matches played in the county in the past year had been, he claimed, reported on. He also remarked that in some papers a recent soccer match in Waterville received a full report while the Kerry county final played the next day only received four lines.[81]

The emerging Kerry tradition was greatly enhanced by the publication of Dick Fitzgerald's *How to Play Gaelic Football* in 1914. As a training manual on the skills of Gaelic football and Fitzgerald's and Kerry's philosophy on the game, this seminal publication became essential reading for players, trainers and supporters alike. The book was ground-breaking in its extensive use of photography to demonstrate the skills Fitzgerald wrote about. Throughout the work, Fitzgerald claimed that the game was superior and more scientific than its foreign rivals, declaring it to be both the most natural and skilful of the three major football codes in Ireland. Fitzgerald spent much of the work musing on the strength and characteristics needed by players in each specific position on a Gaelic football pitch. Therefore, a goalkeeper 'like a poet is born and not made'; a great full-back should be a strongly built man and this strength, more than speed, is vital; half-backs 'should be as hard as nails and able to take a good deal of rough abuse'; midfielders should have a 'vice-like grip of the ball'; the centre-forward should be 'the star of the side . . . a master tactician and in a fashion . . . General to the whole team', while the full-forward should be heavy and strong, 'a good kicker and resourceful'. The book constantly emphasised the great Kerry players who lived up to these characteristics, while celebrating Kerry's football philosophy. Thus:

> Attack is best form of defence so the forward men must never make the critical mistake of dropping back to help their defence, however hardly pushed the latter is. If the choice is between playing a weak man in a position in defence or attack, he must play in defence as a full force attack can always gain advantage.

Action shot from *How to Play Gaelic Football*. Dick Fitzgerald published this seminal tome in 1916. The book was revolutionary in the use of photographs, which showed Fitzgerald demonstrating his own skill as a guide for others. The work also constantly referenced and celebrated Kerry's footballing philosophy. *(Courtesy of Terracetalk.com and T.J. Flynn)*

Fitzgerald, as well as demonstrating the skills of the game such as fly-kicking, toe to hand and drop-kicking, also spoke authoritatively on training and match preparation. He suggested dietary plans and exercise routines to get players in prime fitness for games.[82] The work could be seen as a Gaelic games equivalent to Sun Tzu's *The Art of War*. Publications such as Fitzgerald's helped fuel the growing mythology of the Kerry tradition.

Another major boost to this tradition was the success of Kerry players and teams internationally. By the late 1870s, Gaelic games were played on a relatively regular basis in San Francisco, Boston, Chicago and New York, but it was not until the mid-1880s following the inception of the GAA that codified, organised versions of the games were contested here.[83] In June 1886, the newly formed Boston Kerry GAA club played in the first game of Gaelic football to be held outside of Ireland under the GAA's new rules. In 1892, Kerry emigrants in New York had established a Gaelic football team called the Kerry Rovers and reports of their games were reprinted in the *Sentinel*.[84] By 1904, *The Kerryman* noted that a remarkable revival in Gaelic games was taking place in the US. In New York, most of the Irish county organisations there had their own football or hurling side, with the Kerryman's Association boasting one of the finest Gaelic football teams in the country, which had vanquished 'the teams of all the other counties that had been matched against it'.[85] This New York Kerry team dominated the American GAA's Eastern championship, drawing huge crowds to Celtic Park in New York. On 30 October 1905, they defeated the city's Tipperary football team in front of 10,000 in what was described as the 'greatest match ever played' in the stadium.

Following its All-Ireland triumph in late 1906, rumours swept Kerry that the county footballers had been asked to tour America and play a series of matches against local opposition. *The Kerryman* declared: 'If they are successful in them, like Alexander of old they would set out for new worlds to conquer.'[86] In the wake of that All-Ireland win, three of the winning Kerry side, Dick Fitzgerald, Dan McCarthy and Paddy Dillon of Dr Crokes, accepted an offer to travel to New York to play for the city's Kerry team in the New York football championship. Their addition to the side made the New York Kerry team 'practically invincible'. A special banquet was organised by the city's Kerrymen's Association in honour of the contribution the three Killarney men had made to the team's winning of the city's football championship.[87] In 1907, the *Irish American Advocate* reported that the New York Kerry team's record was unparalleled in the history of the GAA in America. In three years they played fifty competitive matches, losing only twice. In 1913 the *New York Advocate* noted:

> Kerry and Gaelic football seem now almost synonymous terms. Ever since the inception of the GAA the county has taken a leading part in the movement and occupied a foremost place . . . Yes, other counties have All-Ireland honours, but it seems strange [Kerry] are always in the fray at each succeeding epoch.[88]

The constant references to the success of Kerry teams in America while their county men in Ireland continued to dominate the Gaelic football fields naturally fed into this growing belief in the Kerry tradition of Gaelic football. This tradition had already been firmly constructed and established as the First World War dawned.

Outward Success, Inward Stagnation: the Association within Kerry, 1905–15

It is one of the ironies in the history of the association in Kerry that at a time of unprecedented success on the inter-county scene, internally the GAA within Kerry had started to flounder once more. Indeed, the decade between 1905 and 1915 would witness a great degree of internal stagnation within the Kerry GAA. Despite the wave of enthusiasm with which the county board was re-formed in 1900, by 1905 the organisation's development had begun to languish there. T.F. O'Sullivan, at that April's Kerry Annual GAA Convention, outlined the state of the affairs in his annual report. The finances of £25 available had proved 'utterly inadequate to meet the requirements which such a various organisation demanded' and that much more was needed to extend the GAA into those parts of the county where the sports had either lapsed or needed to be reorganised.[89]

A major social factor that impacted on the growth of the GAA, especially in the more isolated parts of Kerry during this time, was the continuing trend of emigration. Though levels of emigration fell on a countywide basis between 1901 and 1911, 3.9 per cent of the county's population still emigrated during these ten years. In addition, Kerry's population at this time showed a marked tendency towards urbanisation, and Tralee and Killarney grew rapidly. While the county's inhabitants decreased by 7.5 per cent between 1891 and 1901, the population of Tralee rose by 5 per cent between 1891 and 1911.[90] There was an increasing tendency for young men to leave the rural villages of Kerry to look for work either in the county's large towns or further afield in America, Australia or Britain. Kerry's economic underdevelopment continued to be a major factor for emigration. As always, agriculture continued to be the dominant employer of young Kerry men, though by its very nature the work offered little in the way of job security and was often seasonal and low paid. Many had little choice but to take the boat overseas in such economically bleak times.

In 1905, the county board chairman, Eugene O'Sullivan, remarked that in the previous eight years numerous clubs had disbanded from the GAA, principally due to emigration, 'which most affected the class from which their hurlers and footballers were taken'. He listed Lixnaw, Abbeydorney, Ballyduff, Ballybunion, Causeway, Killorglin, Keel, Firies, Rathmore, Milltown, Cordal, Fossa, Listry, Glenflesk, Kilgarvan, Kilcummin, Gneeveguilla, Ballymacelligott and O'Brennan as clubs that 'had, unfortunately, one and all become disorganised or completely fallen away'. The Lispole GAA club was forced to write to the county board that summer stating it would be unable to affiliate as eight of their prominent players had emigrated in the past twelve months. *The Kerryman* commented that it was another 'forceful example of the havoc emigration is playing with this country!'[91]

Additionally, Kerry's success on the national stage, rather than spurring on interest and growth in the organisation, seemed to have had the very opposite effect. During his annual report to the

Early Tralee football team, 1903. The 1905 Kerry All-Ireland-winning captain Thady O'Gorman (with the ball) pictured with some teammates. *(Courtesy of terracetalk.com and T.J. Flynn)*

Kerry Convention in 1906, T.F. O'Sullivan declared that in spite of the great success of the Kerry team in winning the All-Ireland, as far as the county is concerned,

> . . . there has been no great accession to our standard and in my experience I have not seen such a general lack with regard to Gaelic pastimes since I became officially associated with the County Board on the occasion of its revival five or six years ago . . . Unless Gaels are determined to assist each other in the maintenance and development of the organisation . . . [it] shall fail to exercise a powerful influence on the regeneration of our race and those who come after us will not bless our memories for allowing the good ship to go down in the full tide of an Irish revival, with the shoals and rocks

passed and the harbour lights throwing their rays athwart our path . . . We appeal to all Irishmen, the clergy, national teachers and all interested in the Irish Ireland movement to throw in their lot with the GAA which is helping to cheek emigration by dispelling the dullness of rural life, promoting self respect among the rising generation and fostering and developing in our young men a love of their native land.

At a meeting of the county board the following month it was stated that no affiliation fees had been received from any club since the convention and O'Sullivan commented that 'the organisation in the county seemed almost paralysed'.[92]

An article in *The Kerryman* tried to unearth the causes of this apathy. Its author, 'MAC LIR', gave the example of the fictional club 'Ballymacsorley FC' where the young men of its district, after reading glowing reports of championship action in *The Kerryman* and eager to emulate famous Kerry players, decide to form a team. At first practice is a pleasure and they enter the county championship, only to be heavily beaten. They do so again for a few years but still come up against better teams and training turns from fun into a chore. 'Enthusiasm eventually dies', and when a club 'has lost consistently in the field the spirit of winning at all hazards becomes so strong that every match is followed by an objection. This is a certain sign of "rot" setting into the organisation.' As a result, clubs disbanded, bad feeling was created and stagnation within the GAA ensued. T.F. O'Sullivan himself reported to the county board:

It was an extraordinary but an indisputable fact that the year which witnessed Kerry's first triumph in an All-Ireland football final synchronised with the almost complete disorganisation of the county. The GAA was never, in his experience, at a lower ebb in Kerry than at the present moment and that was due to a considerable extent to the inter-county contests which dwarfed their county competitions into insignificance.

The county chairman was forced to agree and suggested the following year that the question should be considered of not letting a Kerry team enter inter-county competitions.[93]

The organisation of the Kerry GAA was further weakened when O'Sullivan, who had done so much to revive the GAA's ailing fortunes in Kerry, left his position on the county board to take up a post with *The Freeman's Journal* in Dublin.[94] Without his keen flair for administration, the county board swiftly collapsed and O'Sullivan's departure was widely cited as the cause of the neglect of Gaelic affairs in Kerry. Between August 1906 and September 1907, no board meetings were organised in the county.

As 'MAC LIR' highlighted, the lack of success for many Kerry clubs made them reluctant to compete. Between 1900 and 1915, football in Kerry became dominated by the two large urban clubs of Tralee Mitchels and Dr Crokes of Killarney. In that fifteen-year period, Mitchels accounted for eight titles while Crokes won four. The two clubs became the main feeder for the Kerry county team and almost inevitably the county final was contested between them. Both clubs had a large and growing pool of young male players to select from. Likewise, they could call on the services of players from a sprawling hinterland. It proved impossible for many teams to break their stranglehold on the county title, and with little prospect of success smaller club sides dissolved into apathy. Admiration for what the Mitchels and Crokes players achieved in the Kerry colours was mixed with the realisation that these sides were too powerful for any of Kerry's smaller clubs to compete within the county championship. Similarly, the constant delays and objections that continued to plague Kerry's county championships meant that in most years the championship was significantly behind schedule. Club sides beaten in the opening round of games had to wait months if not a couple of years in some instances for another chance at competitive action. At the 1907 Kerry Annual Convention Eugene O'Sullivan declared that Kerry's brilliant achievements on the field nevertheless 'had a very damping effect on the organisation of the county. The enthusiasm of all were centred on the [Kerry] team, with the result that though the Tralee and Killarney clubs were kept alive and active, the

Dr Crokes, 1901. Along with Tralee Mitchels, Killarney's Dr Crokes would dominate Kerry's county championship during the first great era of the Kerry GAA. The rivalry between the clubs was intense and often very bitter. *(Courtesy of John Keogh, Dr Crokes GAA)*

remaining clubs in the Kingdom became apathetic and received but scant encouragement.'[95]

The situation was not helped by the intense rivalry that naturally developed between Dr Crokes and Mitchels in the county championship. As the two big fish in Kerry's small pond, their contests took on an increasingly bitter animosity. During the 1902 county championship, their meeting in Kenmare led to Mitchels, while leading 0-7 to 0-4, walking off the pitch after a number of Crokes' supporters rushed the field and assaulted some of the Tralee players. After the game, there was further trouble at Kenmare station, with Killarney supporters stoning the carriage in which the Mitchels team was sitting, smashing several of its windows. Despite the pivotal role many of the Crokes players had in Kerry's first All-Ireland success, they were not spared any abuse by Mitchels' supporters. Following the 1904 county semi-final played in December 1905 the Killarney club condemned the actions of the Tralee supporters, 'who hooted and jeered at the gallant captain of the Killarney team, Dick Fitzgerald'.[96] In 1908, the appointment of Austin Stack as county chairman led to another dispute. Killarney delegates became despondent that their own member, Eugene O'Sullivan, the outgoing chairman, had been deposed amid claims there was a pre-conceived plan in place by Tralee's delegates to get one of their own men in. In protest, Dr Crokes refused to send its players to play with the Kerry team drawn to meet Dublin in a Croke Cup match in Jones Road the following month.[97]

In 1911, this rivalry had serious consequences for the Kerry county team. During another championship clash, this time in the 1910 county semi-final in Tralee, the match descended into scenes of chaos with blows freely exchanged between the two teams. 'Thus it continued until one half-defeated team [Killarney] curtailed this football parody by the disgraceful method of walking off the field.' Tralee was awarded the match but the repercussions of Killarney's actions would be serious. To stamp out this practice of teams walking off the field when decisions went against them, a committee appointed by the Central Council introduced a new by-law, coming into effect in 1911. This stated that any team or player leaving the field of play before the end of a game without the referee's permission would be automatically suspended for six months with no council or committee of the association having the power to modify this penalty. Killarney thus found itself and its players banned from all competitions until September 1911. Realising the implications of being without many of their star players for that year's Munster championship, the Kerry Board proposed a motion at that year's GAA Annual Congress to have the Killarney team reinstated. The motion failed and in the Munster semi-final that August Waterford caused one of the biggest upsets of the decade by beating a Kerry side, shorn of its Killarney contingent, 1-2 to 1-0.

Despite the return to inter-county success with the All-Ireland victory of 1913, Dr Crokes players were still guaranteed a hostile reception in Tralee. In a county championship tie held there against Mitchels, *The Kerryman* bemoaned the disgraceful conduct of the Tralee supporters, who hissed and booed the Killarney men as they took the field. Throughout the match, every mistake by Killarney's players was cheered and every score or brilliant effort heckled. In a letter to the paper following the match, one neutral observer wrote:

> The Kerry players' achievements and names have become known across the world and known in every home in Ireland. Yet in Tralee what do you see but Dick Fitzgerald, John Skinner, Con Murphy, etc. being hooted, hissed and roughly handled in the capital of Kerry . . . Kilkenny citizens vie with one another in offering their hurlers the Freedom of the Marble City. The Capital of the Kingdom offers its representatives its jeers and taunts.[98]

In order to stem the disorganisation that prevailed in the Kerry GAA, efforts were made to reorganise the county board. Austin Stack took the initiative and issued notices to the local press that a county convention would be held in the *Kerryman* offices on 20 October 1907, with circulars being posted to wherever a club was supposed to exist.[99] Stack, having captained Kerry in 1906, had retired from the game due to injury and now put his energy into the administrative side of the association. The convention proved a marked success. A new county board was elected with Eugene O'Sullivan appointed president and Stack vice-president. Stack's obvious administrative talents ensured that the GAA in Kerry was able to stem its decline and slowly over the next six years the association rebuilt its base in the county. In his annual report in 1908, county secretary F. Cronin stated that generally the position of the GAA was growing and while twelve months previously the few GAA clubs in Kerry that existed verged on extinction, there were now over a dozen football and seven hurling clubs affiliated.[100]

Laune Rangers, County Champions, 1911. Tralee Mitchels' domination of the county championship (they won eight titles in a row between 1902 and 1910) was finally broken by the Killorglin team. Yet such success ensured the Tralee club's players backboned Kerry's county sides during these years. Back (l–r): Mick Joy, Ted Mangan, John Riordan, Dan Teahan, Mossie Breen, Eddie Kennelly, John Foley, Tommy Corcoran, William Roche, Jerry Healy; middle (l–r): Jimmy O'Leary, John O'Shea, John Langford, Mick Moroney; front (l–r): Patie Flynn, Paddy Foley, Paddy Kennelly, Danny Hayes, Nicholas Flynn, Mossie Counihan, John Paul McCarthy; on ground (l–r): John O'Brien and Danny Clifford. *(Courtesy of the National Library of Ireland)*

The idea of a Kerry junior county championship for clubs that lacked the player base to compete with the likes of Mitchels and Crokes had been suggested as early as 1903. The new county board fully embraced the idea and the competition was re-formed in 1908. Batt O'Connor of Dingle suggested to the board that previously senior clubs should be allowed register as junior, as at present many clubs were discouraged from affiliating for fear of being heavily beaten in the senior championship, whereas a year playing junior football could give them the confidence to return to the senior fold.[101] The GAA in Kerry continued to grow steadily under Stack's presidency, which began in 1908. The secretary's 1909 annual report stated that club affiliations were again above the preceding years and throughout the county new clubs were springing to life.[102]

However, there were still problems in trying to strengthen and sustain the organisation in the county. Stack gave an outline of the difficulties facing the running of the GAA in Kerry in the 1909 *Gaelic Athletic Annual*:

> Kerry has been an almost impossible County to work from a Gaelic Athletic standpoint. It is so scattered and thinly populated. In the old days every town and almost every village and parish had its hurling or football team, but the great exodus to foreign lands has left us with only ten or twelve affiliated clubs . . . Where are those who made the summer eve re-echo from the playing field? Where are the boys and girls one looks for at the cross roads tipping it in the old Kerry dance? Ask the Emigration Agent – still unfortunately with us. Inquire of the Landlord – unhappily not yet quite exterminated. Worse still, look up the records of the British Army and the Police force. The wonder is that the race has not ere this died out.[103]

At the 1911 county convention the secretary's report echoed these sentiments, arguing that Kerry's size and topography made it difficult for a central body in Tralee to effectively administer for the entire county. Matters were not helped by Kerry's decision not to contest the 1910 All-Ireland or its early exit from the 1911 Munster championship. By December, *The Kerryman* was reporting that Gaelic matters had come to a complete standstill in the county and if this state continued for too much longer the GAA there 'would be dead'.[104]

Another major factor in the varying degrees of growth or decline in the number of GAA clubs in Kerry throughout this period was the issue of finance. Studies on organised sport in contemporary Scotland showed that financial circumstances had a key impact on the variations of growth between rival sports. The financial position of a sport was dependent on its level of popular support in a given region and more particularly on the supply and demand for that particular sport. As has been discussed, popular support for Gaelic games was declining in Kerry, while demand for matches receded as Dr Crokes and Tralee Mitchels became more and more dominant. Financially then, the Kerry GAA's gate receipts were declining sharply. Indeed, throughout its first fifty years the association in Kerry was in a precarious financial situation. Frequently the Central Council was blamed for this predicament. In 1896, the board cited the loss of £23 of its revenue due to affiliation and other expenses paid to the Central Council as the principal reason why it could not afford to affiliate to the Central Council that year.[105] As we shall see, the demands made by rail companies for train guarantees often stretched the meagre finances of the board to their limits.[106] In addition, Kerry officials held a long suspicion that their county board did not benefit enough from the profits enjoyed by Central Council despite the role the Kerry teams played in securing those profits. In July 1916, Kerry again withdrew from the Central Council due to the county's dire financial position. An article in *The Kerryman* argued that during the previous five All-Ireland finals Kerry had taken part in, the Central Council had earned £4,339, not including provincial gates. In return, all the Kerry team had cost them was a total of £75 in various training expenses, the cost of rail tickets to Dublin and hotel accommodation from Saturday night to Monday morning. The board meanwhile had incurred large debts from having to fund training camps for the Kerry team. It was stated that outside of the Tralee v Killarney matches, gates at county games did not usually make a profit. The Kerry Board had nothing, and 'in a nut-shell, we owe all around us debts through All-Ireland training'.[107]

Yet the intense media and public interest in Kerry's Croke Memorial final victory and its reclaiming of the All-Ireland in 1913 certainly proved a much-needed fillip to the organisation's popularity within the county. The association there was given further impetus by the formation of district boards in the more isolated regions of the county. In November 1906, a meeting was held in Dingle to form a West Kerry GAA Board to promote Gaelic games in the region. A letter was read from the county board stating that the divisional board would have full authority to conduct its own tournaments and affairs.[108] Such was the success of the West Kerry Board that a meeting of the Listowel GAA club suggested that Gaels in north Kerry should follow their lead and establish their own district board based in Listowel. The establishment of district boards in the county, both in the south and the west, greatly improved the organisation of the GAA in Kerry. The large but remote regions of the Dingle and Iveragh Peninsulas now had an effective local administration to promote and supervise Gaelic activity in their respective regions. In 1907, a letter in *The Kerryman* suggested that the association should be further reorganised in Kerry and district boards should be established in the north and east of the county to supplement those already formed in the west and south. It was suggested that each board should play its own championships in a league format and that the four district winners would then be drawn in the semi-finals for the county championship. Along with initiatives such as the formation of district boards, junior football and hurling leagues were established in Tralee and Killarney to promote the games among the young boys of the town.[109]

By 1913, a record twenty-eight clubs were reported as entering the county championship.[110] The increase in the county board's revenue also points to the significant growth of the organisation in Kerry. At the 1914 county convention the balance sheet showed that the GAA in Kerry operated with receipts of £304 16s, while expenses amounted to £283 11s 3d. This was almost a tenfold increase in the finances of the body in the seven years since 1906 when it reported a revenue of just £36 5s 6d and expenses of £27 16s 3d for the year.

Transport and the GAA, 1885–1915

On a more practical level, access to cheap and regular transport was of paramount importance throughout the first decades of the association's history in Kerry. The county's size and topography proved a significant challenge for those wishing to attend club and inter-county matches held either within the county or further afield. For any sporting organisation to grow and flourish, the problems posed by the often primitive transport system in such a rural region was a significant obstacle that needed to be overcome.

Kerry, like much of rural Ireland, had only a rudimentary road network of little more than dirt tracks for much of the nineteenth century. Before the widespread development of the railways, Irish transport was dominated by the horse-drawn carriage. In 1833, the first regular passenger service between Limerick and Tralee was established by horse coach. Throughout the early years of the GAA, the horse-drawn car would be the staple for teams travelling the short distances to neighbouring parishes for matches. In one of the first official GAA matches in Kerry, the Castleisland team and their supporters travelled the eleven miles to Tralee in a train of horse-drawn carriages which on arriving were welcomed by the Boherbee Fife and Drum Band which paraded the players in their cars through the town towards the match venue. Sometimes the occasion of a match could provide for the use of more exotic forms of transport. When the Dingle footballers played Valentia on the latter's home ground in the 1907 county championship the team and their supporters crossed Dingle Bay in a fleet of sailing vessels accompanied by the town's brass band.[111]

However, until the widespread use of the motor car or bus in the second half of the twentieth century, it was the railway that dominated the transport network of Ireland and for better or worse it became the main travelling option for GAA players and supporters alike. As was discussed in Chapter 1, the railway rapidly extended across Ireland in the latter 1800s, growing from 840 to 3,044 miles between 1850 and 1894. Its arrival was of huge importance to the development of sports throughout the UK and Ireland. The railways likewise had an enormous impact on the development and spread of Gaelic games. In Kerry, the railways expanded rapidly in the 1880s and 1890s. In 1891, a rail line was completed between Dingle and Tralee, connecting that remote region with the county's capital. The main Tralee-to-Killarney line was extended to Cahersiveen and then Valentia by 1893. In 1896, a new line was opened up between Headford and Kenmare which connected the town to Killarney. It is no coincidence that the formation of the South and West Kerry Boards and the expansion of GAA clubs in these districts coincided with the opening up of these remote areas to a regular and reliable train service. The benefit of a rail service that connected those regions with Tralee, Killarney and the greater Irish network finally allowed supporters and players to attend and contest matches in locations that would otherwise have involved unfeasibly long travel times.

The mass spread of the railway was perhaps the singular factor in the enormous rise in match attendances across Ireland between 1905 and 1915. Yet railway companies proved almost as much a curse as a blessing to the GAA, especially in Kerry. The major railway company that operated most of the Kerry lines was the Great Southern and Western Railway (GSWR). The popularity of the GAA proved a great boon for such operators. GAA followers provided a huge customer base and valuable business to these companies on their otherwise quieter operating days such as Sunday. Despite this, companies like the GSWR seemed determined to kill the GAA goose that laid such a golden egg. Irish railway companies' requirements for generous guarantees in case of damage to their property by the travelling GAA supporters was a constant bone of contention for county boards that so often struggled to balance their finances.

This tension was evident from the very beginning of the association in Kerry. EMON, the *Sentinel*'s GAA reporter, complained in 1891 that in south and east Kerry where the GSWR ran its lines, clubs had to apply for 'favours' to get special trains run. 'Ample guarantees . . . had always been given and though the trains usually earned double and not infrequently treble the figure guaranteed, [GSWR policy] continues inexorable'. That January, the company sought a £20 guarantee to run a special train from Killarney to Tralee for a GAA tournament. On the return journey, several windows were broken in the train carriages and the *Sentinel* reported that the action of a few 'blackguards' meant supporters in the town would not be afforded cheap excursions for some time to come. In May 1891, Irremore were due to play Ballymacelligott in a county championship match in Tralee but did not show up. In a letter to the *Sentinel*, the club's secretary, John Quilter, stated they had arrived at the Lixnaw train station to catch the 10.30 a.m. train to Tralee that Sunday morning. However, the stationmaster refused to open the ticket office so they could purchase tickets, leaving the team stranded on the platform. A Lixnaw passenger arrived shortly after and was allowed to purchase a ticket but when Quilter accompanied the man to the ticket office the stationmaster advised Quilter and his team to 'go to the devil'.[112] At the Kerry County Convention in 1893 D.P. Murphy, the Laune Rangers delegate, had a motion carried calling on the GSWR Company not to insist on train guarantees for GAA supporters as it discouraged the promoters of such matches 'and was originally imposed on account of damage done to the Company's property, which was not committed by members of the GAA'.

The precarious finances of the re-formed Kerry Board in the years after 1900 meant it faced a constant struggle with the GSWR to secure train services for matches. In 1903, the board was unable to guarantee paying rail travel expenses for clubs competing in the county championship. As a consequence, Laune Rangers failed to show up for their semi-final against Tralee in Killarney. With the GSWR still demanding substantial guarantees for trains, that November the county board decided, as a consequence of this and the extraordinary wet weather, to postpone until the new year all championship matches. The board felt there was a significant risk of not making enough of a return on the gate receipts from the small crowds brave enough to face the elements to cover these guarantees. This would have left the board severely in debt. In April 1904, the county championship semi-finals, scheduled to be played in Killarney, had to be rearranged as the GSWR required an exorbitant guarantee of £33 5s to run two special supporters' trains to the town. In response, at a meeting of the Kerry Board its chairman, Eugene O'Sullivan, declared that if such large guarantees were insisted upon they would cripple the GAA in Kerry. It was stated that in the past few years the cost of a train guarantee to secure a special train from Tralee to Listowel had doubled from £5 to £10. The board pointed to the injustice of such prices considering the GAA was providing the company with thousands of pounds a year in custom.[113]

Meanwhile, many supporters were unimpressed with the service they paid for. After the drawn 1905 All-Ireland final in Thurles, *The Kerryman* ridiculed the performance of the GSWR, whose fastest train took five hours to get there from Tralee, a 'munificent average of 18 miles per hour'.[114] The same paper in 1908 declared that the 'chief obstacle to the development of the GAA in this county is the Railways', with its demand for 'excessive guarantees'. At the 1910 County Convention county secretary Michael Griffin announced that the railways had hampered the development of the GAA in the country for years. He stated that it was found impossible to get a train to or from an area like Kenmare without a substantial guarantee being required, and '[U]nless something can be done in this respect I fear we shall find it very hard to organise and develop the GAA in the South of Kerry'.[115] Worse was to follow. Within seven months, a dispute between the GSWR and the Kerry Board erupted into a national controversy that ended with Kerry forfeiting a place in the All-Ireland final.

In the run-up to the 1910 Munster final, the Munster Council held a special meeting in Tralee to consider the question of train guarantees, the council believing it was not being fairly treated by the GSWR. The fares the company was charging were blamed for the reduction in crowd numbers in that year's Munster champion-ship. Having defeated Cork in the Munster decider, Kerry qualified to face Louth in a rematch of the 1909 final. The Wednesday preceding the final, the Kerry team selected was named in the press and train arrangements for the final were printed in the *Sentinel*. However, on Thursday evening the *Kerry Evening Star* reported that the All-Ireland, due to be held in Jones Road, had been abandoned as the Kerry team refused to travel.[116] When they travelled to the previous year's final the team had been granted its own carriage on the Saturday afternoon train to Dublin. Feeling that the arrangements had proved satisfactory, the county secretary had written to the GSWR asking if the Kerry team could again avail of these arrangements travelling on the 3.20 p.m. train from Tralee to Kingsbridge station, Dublin. Additionally, the county board asked that twenty officials and supporters connected with the team be allowed to travel with the players at the team's reduced ticket rates. In response, the GSWR stated there would be sufficient room on the 3.20 p.m. Saturday train to accommodate the players without the need to supply a special carriage. The team would be issued, as per usual, with cheap excursion-rate tickets. Nevertheless, no such tickets would be given to friends of the team or other officials. The company insisted they would have to pay the standard Saturday-to-Monday ticket prices. These stipulations meant that the Kerry players would now be facing a journey on a slow, generally overcrowded train which frequently arrived late into Dublin. In addition, without their own carriage, the players would be mixed up in small groups among ordinary passengers. The Kerry Board was incredulous at the railway's terms. *The Kerryman* declared:

> The circumstances explaining this sudden line of action fully justify the decision arrived at and the boys of the Kingdom would not be men if they followed any other course than the one they have adopted. The Great Southern and Western Railway Company have affronted the Kerry team in a manner which could not lightly be passed over. Considering that the Kerry footballers have been the means, for the past five years especially, of pouring some thousands of pounds into the coffers of the Company, the Company's action cannot be considered as anything but mean and despicable. Apparently the executive heads of this Company imagine that the Kerry boys are a species of human door mat and that they can wipe their boots on them with impunity.[117]

Efforts by the Central Council to make the GSWR reconsider led to the company relenting on the issue of supplying the Kerry team with their own carriage but they stood firm on not allowing twenty passengers to accompany the team at excursion rates. Even though the Kerry Board offered to reduce the number to twelve, the company would still not compromise. As a consequence the Kerry team decided not to travel to contest the final. Across the country there was widespread support for the Kerry Board's action. The Tralee Gaelic League passed a resolution at their meeting condemning the company and congratulating the Kerry team on their stance. The Ennis branch similarly congratulated the team for their courage in standing up to a company notorious for the 'scant courtesy' it had given to the national organisations in Ireland.[118] Louth were offered a walkover by the Central Council but refused to accept it and offered to play Kerry for the final in Cork or even Tralee. The Kerry team declined the offer, stating they had no argument with Louth but were making a stand against the GSWR.[119]

On the Saturday following the aborted final, a special meeting of the Central Council was called to discuss the situation. Austin Stack represented Kerry and explained why they had taken their actions. J. Harrington, the Cork delegate, stated that his county fully endorsed Kerry's actions but other support was not forthcoming. D. McCarthy of Dublin argued that Kerry should have travelled to fulfil the fixture regardless of the railway's terms. The Meath and Galway representatives were in agreement with him. McCarthy moved that Kerry be suspended from the association for five years. Mr Corrigan, the Belfast GAA delegate, declared that in the north they had an uphill fight against soccer and the present trouble only added to this. M.F. Crowe concurred, remarking that such controversy was the last thing the GAA needed. He cautioned that ever since the foreign games ban was reintroduced, the GAA had been in a 'wobbling condition'. It was only by the enthusiasm of some of its followers that it had been saved from disintegration. He asked that some penalty be brought against Kerry. It was decided to convene at a special meeting, on 4 December 1910, to discuss such a sanction.[120] *The Kerryman* stood by the team, declaring that even if Kerry was censured or suspended, they could find comfort in the fact that their stand had the support of all the people of Kerry.[121] At the reconvened meeting McCarthy handed in a motion to suspend Kerry for five years. D. Fraher, the Waterford delegate, defended Kerry's actions and argued that this was a glorious chance to get better terms from the GSWR. An amendment to McCarthy's motion that Kerry be suspended for six months also fell through, with the meeting's chairman, the GAA president James Nowlan, finding that there was no law in the GAA under which they had the power to suspend Kerry. A motion to rearrange the fixture was discussed. However, McCarthy stated that if this was done, the GAA would be open to the charge that they were sacrificing their principles for the sake of gate receipts. On a vote of seven to six, the council decided to award the match to Louth.

This entire episode had a disturbing effect on the Kerry GAA and, as has been shown, it did little to help the growth of the association in the county in the months that followed. Given the unsympathetic attitude taken by many Central Council delegates to the Kerry team's action, a suggestion was even made that Kerry should break from the association and form its own Munster body, independent of the Central Council. Nevertheless, Kerry's stance did lead to a radical change in the railway companies' attitude to travelling GAA teams. Having lost out on such a lucrative day's business, the GSWR was careful not to push teams and county boards too far in the years following the stand-off. As was evident from the extensive rail arrangements that surrounded Kerry's Croke final appearance in 1913, it appeared the GSWR had learned the value and financial benefits of accommodating the wishes of travelling teams.[122]

By then, railway companies had already become one of the great sponsors of Gaelic events. In 1905, the GSWR spent £50 on two Railway Shields which it presented to the GAA for a national interprovincial competition in hurling and football. As Munster provincial champions, Kerry was given the selection of the Munster football team to compete in the inaugural competition in 1905, losing the final to Leinster, represented by Kildare. Kerry redeemed themselves the following year, winning their first Railway Shield, beating Roscommon, who were representing Connacht, in the final. In September 1907 Kerry won the Railway Shield for the second time in seven months, defeating a Dublin-picked Leinster selection in Jones Road. As per an agreement with the GSWR, the province that won the competition twice in succession was allowed to keep the shield and it was presented to the Munster Council. At a subsequent Munster Convention it was agreed to hand over the trophy to Kerry as they had supplied the winning Munster teams.[123] In 1913, the GSWR supplied an enormous silver cup to be awarded to the All-Ireland winners. Kerry became its first holder in 1913 and when it retained the cup in 1914, having again beaten Wexford in the final, the trophy was awarded outright to the county for its achievement.

Hurling in Kerry, 1905–1915

While the ten years under review witnessed the spectacular rise of Kerry as a Gaelic football power, the situation for followers of hurling in the county remained quite different. Smothered by the overarching success of the Kerry footballers, the county's hurlers experienced a dismal record on the inter-county scene. The emerging Kerry tradition had effectively abandoned hurling. The popularity of football contributed to an ever-growing increase and spread of clubs across the county as the First World War approached. In contrast, hurling clubs remained confined to their traditional heartland of north Kerry, while interest in the game remained static.

Considering the county won its first All-Ireland in the code, the collapse of hurling in Kerry remains one of the most interesting questions about the early development of the GAA there. It was certainly not through want of ideas and effort that hurling remained in the shadow of its more illustrious brother. In the Munster final of 1900 played in May 1902, Kilmoyley, who selected the Kerry team, were defeated by Tipperary's Two Mile Borris by 6-11 to 1-9. The *Sentinel* was encouraged by the Kerry hurlers' display in their first final appearance since 1891. The paper predicated that the result would been much closer if six players from the Kenmare and Lixnaw clubs, originally selected on the team, had not refused to travel owing to Kilmoyley having selection control of the team. That September Kerry were heavily beaten, 3-12 to 1-1, in their opening-round fixture in the 1901 championship against Redmonds of Cork. Any degree of optimism over the previous performance against Tipperary was quashed. T.F. O'Sullivan, writing in his 'Gaelic Notes' column, was blunt. Kerry, he said, were 'outclassed in every portion of the field and did not present a very formidable appearance'. It was with relief, he declared, that they heard the referee's full-time whistle. The match proved that 'in hurling we have no inter-county material. Our players are false, slow and destitute of combination, without in fact an elementary knowledge of the science of the game.'[124] During the 1902 championship, Kerry secured an opening-round victory against Waterford. While pleased with the result, followers of the game were aware that Waterford were the second-worst team in the province behind Kerry. Apprehension grew about the chances of the team against Cork in the semi-final. O'Sullivan wrote that although the county could justifiably be proud of its

1891 All-Ireland, '[we] cannot at the same time disguise from ourselves the fact that the play which was responsible for that historic victory is now somewhat antiquated and would scarcely be sufficient to win a County Championship contest'. Great strides, he noted, had been made in the sport since then and he urged the hurlers to 'practise, practise, practise'. His words were to little avail, Kerry being heavily defeated by 2-11 to 0-3.

In the years after the Kerry GAA re-formed in 1900, the question of the standard of hurling in the county became a burning issue. The *Sentinel* openly queried why no one in Kerry was doing for hurling what Austin Stack had done for football:

> . . . get the best men in the Kingdom to compose the team and then see that they become properly trained and be not what they are to-day, to a considerable extent, a completely disorganised mob . . . Who will throw himself heart and soul into the work of achieving these results and win a second hurling All-Ireland for Kerry?

Even their attire seemed archaic compared with the best hurlers in other counties. The paper went on to complain that many Kerry hurlers still played barefoot and regularly fell on the slippery and wet surfaces during matches: 'Surely the players ought to provide themselves with suitable footwear and not present the shabby appearance they sometimes do on the field?'[125]

In an effort to develop and spread the game in Kerry, the county board decided to play the 1905 county hurling championship on a league basis. *The Kerryman* noted that among the public it had 'become the fashion of late years to indulge in cheap sneering at Kerry hurling, mainly because of the non-success of the county in inter-county contests'. However, the paper felt there was little need for such a disparaging view and a 'few earnest workers and organisers would . . . be able to show expert hurlers as the result of their work. The league system of the County Championship introduced this year is a step in the right direction.'[126] The formation of district boards also helped in some small way to spread the code. The South Kerry Board revived the game in the region and established teams in Valentia, Cahersiveen and Waterville in 1905. With the formation of the West Kerry Board, Dingle stated that they were taking immediate steps to form a hurling club to develop the game in the district. The club made its competitive debut against Lixnaw in Tralee in May 1908 in what was billed as an 'interesting contest in view of the fact it will mark the beginning of hurling in west Kerry'. Likewise, the league system introduced in 1905 had some success. The newly formed Killahan club caused the shock of the championship, beating Tralee Celtic, the reigning county champions. In 1906, a junior hurling league was formed in Tralee in conjunction with a similar football competition to try and increase the popularity of hurling in the town. Four sides – Rock Street, Boherbee, Strand Street and Mall United – took part, the winners receiving a set of medals or jerseys of their choosing.

1903 Tralee Celtic Hurling Club. Smothered by the overarching success of the county's footballers, hurling in Kerry struggled to gain any sort of parity during the early twentieth century. Back (l–r): D. Casey, G. Fitzgerald, P. Guerin; second row (l–r): T. Nolan (president), M. O'Sullivan (treasurer), D. Walsh, P. Griffin, M. Twomey, J. O'Connell, D. Nolan (hon. secretary); front (l–r): P. Lawlor, P. Ryle, P. Stack, M. Horan (captain), M. Murphy, P. O'Connor, P. O'Mahony; on ground (l–r): W. O'Connor and J. Young. *(Courtesy of the National Library of Ireland)*

Yet the situation, particularly at inter-county level, remained difficult. In the approach to Kerry's opening tie against Tipperary in the 1905 Munster championship, 'Green and Gold' wrote to the *Sentinel* to express his views on why the Kerry hurlers could not match the success of the county's footballers. 'We are the best in Ireland in the latter and I would not be surprised to hear that we are nearly the worst in the former.' In the letter, he outlined six reasons for such a situation:

1) There was a lack of proper organisation or concord between Kerry hurling teams.
2) There was an absence of hurling captains to match the calibre of men like Austin Stack and Dick Fitzgerald.
3) The Kerry hurlers seemed to be indifferent to inter-county honours.
4) Those who selected the team were often deceived as regards form and depended on men who are hurlers 'only by past reputation'.
5) There was an unusual degree of club jealousy as regards county representation.
6) County championships were not being pushed to a conclusion and the Kerry Board should ensure that all affiliated clubs play at least six matches a year.[127]

The match against Tipperary proved a 'farce', with the Kerry hurlers being humiliated by 4-21 to 1-3. In response, a reader to the *Sentinel* wondered in bewilderment how a county the size of Kerry could not produce seventeen players to compete successfully in Munster. He pointed to the example of Galway, a similar-sized county, which had between twenty and twenty-six hurling clubs. In 1908, the Kerry hurlers defeated Clare for the second year in a row in their opening match of the Munster championship. They therefore qualified for the Munster hurling final for the last time in the county's history. However, the match was never played. The familiar curse of apathy was evident, with only fourteen of the players selected travelling to the game. It seems some could not rouse an interest even when competing in a final. Being three players short to form a team, the match was awarded to Tipperary.

That championship, ironically, proved the high point in the inter-county record of the Kerry hurlers. At the County Convention in 1909 the board's secretary, F.J. Cronin, assessed the state of hurling in the county. He argued that many clubs beaten in the first round of the championship found themselves with no other games to play for the rest of the year. Consequently, they remained a beaten team for a whole twelve months. The natural result was that teams lost heart and fell away with time. He also felt that the practice of giving championship winners the privilege of selecting the team was 'objectionable and was responsible for the reverses which the Kerry hurling team had met for the past five or six years'. Austin Stack suggested that the board should return the championship to the league format first trialled in 1905. It would, he hoped, give more encouragement to beaten teams. However, some delegates objected to it, saying the format had been tried before and failed to produce any results as far as the county team was concerned. Many delegates complained that not a single creditable suggestion to remedy the state of hurling in the county had been forthcoming. Yet when M. Hurley, the Valentia delegate, suggested trophies should be offered for competition among losing teams, many demurred and the debate ended inconclusively with the matter being dropped.[128] It seems obvious that the county board had hit a wall in its attempts to promote hurling in Kerry.

The reasons why hurling failed to develop, despite the best efforts of the county board throughout this period, remain complex. There is no straightforward answer for the failure of hurling to achieve some level of parity with Gaelic football in Kerry. However, there are clues to its lack of success. Bar Kenmare and smaller examples such as Dingle and Cahersiveen, the majority of hurling clubs remained rural combinations, mainly tied to a townland such as Killahan or Bonane, or at most were village teams such as Lixnaw and Abbeydorney. The Tralee Celtic hurling club was the only such club in a large urban area in Kerry at this time. Though it achieved notable success, winning two county titles in a row in 1904 and '05, by 1906 the club was reported to be struggling to attract members to training, especially in the summer months 'when there are so many attractions to wean them away'. The club soon after seems to have collapsed. Kerry hurling clubs, especially those grouped around traditional townlands, retained the ephemeral nature of their predecessors throughout this period and often clubs appeared and then disbanded within months. For example, the Ardfert hurling club affiliated to the county board in 1903 but fell away in 1905, only to reaffiliate in 1906. The club failed to contest the 1910 championship and folded in 1911. A team from Tubrid emerged to fill the void. However, that side failed to line out against Kilmoyley in their only game in the 1912 championship and in 1913 they followed Ardfert into disbandment.

Given that the vast majority of hurling clubs were based in rural areas like north Kerry, agricultural workers dominated their membership to an even greater extent than in Kerry's football clubs. For example, 51.8 per cent of the 219 hurlers identified in the census survey of Kerry GAA members were involved directly with agriculture, as opposed to 33.1 per cent of the 694 footballers identified. Naturally the recurring problems in this industry, highlighted elsewhere, would have had an especially hard bearing on hurling players. Emigration remained a constant problem, robbing small rural hurling clubs of their best players. Austin Stack was keenly aware of this. Writing in the 1909 *Gaelic Annual* he stated:

> In the old days every town and almost every village and parish had its hurling or football team, but the great exodus to foreign lands has left us with only ten or twelve affiliated clubs. Nowadays only large towns can put a team on the field . . . [Emigration] has played havoc particularly in our hurling areas – Kilmoyley, Ballyduff, Kenmare, Ardfert, Lixnaw and Abbeydorney.[129]

Another factor that hindered the growth of hurling clubs was the small geographical area in which the sport was most popular. In north Kerry, the area extended roughly from Ballyheigue in the west to Lixnaw in the east and Ardfert in the south to Ballyduff in the north, a district of 17.5 km in length and 19.3 km in width. Into this small and thinly populated rural hinterland there was a yearly average of six to twelve hurling clubs, all vying for the attention of a shrinking young male population. This competition for the best players in such a small geographical area naturally led to disputes and bad feeling among rival clubs. Indeed, the instances of the larger hurling clubs effectively stealing players from their smaller counterparts had become so common that a meeting of the county board was called in 1905 to consider the question of enforcing the GAA's parish rule on a strict basis as far as hurling was concerned. At the meeting, the county secretary complained that Kerry had only five hurling clubs at present, one of which, Tralee Celtic, was composed of players from Abbeydorney, Lixnaw and Causeway, whose clubs had all fallen out of the GAA since the previous year.[130] It seems likely that the increasing tendency towards urbanisation among the rural population of Kerry was a major contributor to a hurling tradition surviving to any extent in Tralee.

This animosity between clubs spilled over whenever the question of a county team selection was raised. *The Kerryman* found that for 'a county that at one time could easily boast of more hurling than football clubs, it is astonishing how the games have deteriorated in Kerry', a situation caused by clubs not selecting good players because they were not from their own parish. Such a spirit of selfishness 'pervades those in charge' of the Kerry team and thus they were always beaten. The 'picking of relatives and "Has Beens" has had a very bad effect on the game'.[131] For the 1910 Munster semi-final against Limerick several members of the Kerry team selected to play refused to travel to the match. Though the Kerry goalkeeper went, he too refused to play, the result of which forced Kerry to put a man between the posts 'who had never played in that position before'. Limerick easily won, 6-2 to 2-0.

The lack of a large urban centre in which the game could have developed was another major factor in the secondary status of hurling in Kerry. The sport in Tralee had a chequered existence. The Tralee Mitchels club formed its own hurling team, which was represented at the delayed 1907 County Convention and won the delayed championships of 1908. It would also win the county championship in 1911 and 1912. It seems the initiative of the junior hurling league, begun in the town in 1906, persuaded the Mitchels club that there was sufficient hurling talent in the area to form such a team. However, the hurling club appears to have had a short life span. Rural male workers from north Kerry, moving to Tralee in search of work, were probably mostly responsible for the success of the side in the same way as such players had dominated the Tralee Celtic team before it. In a town dominated by football, there seemed precious little appetite for the game among the native population. This remained so even when a Tralee club was winning county titles. Likewise, hurling was virtually unknown in any meaningful competitive way in Killarney or Listowel. In contrast to football, which developed on the back of two strong clubs in the main towns of Killarney and Tralee, hurling clubs had to vie for scarce resources and lacked the large urban populations Tralee Mitchels or Dr Crokes could rely on. It is arguable that for much of the 1905–15 period Gaelic football was essentially an urban sport in Kerry and in the large towns there was no rival sporting codes with which it had to compete. This could well be a crucial reason why Kerry became so adept and successful at the sport in contrast to larger counties such as Cork or Dublin where rugby and association football competed for the attention of young men. Conversely, this is why hurling was never able to develop. In large towns, hurling clubs faced an uphill battle against the appeal of football, especially in the aftermath of the heroics of the Kerry county team. Kenmare remained too small and isolated a centre from which to effectively grow the game, while Tralee remained predominately a football town. By 1915, *The Kerryman* was reporting that hurling in Tralee, ever since the days of the Celtic club, had been a 'dead letter', and though sporadic efforts had been made to resurrect its appeal, 'no permanent good resulted and the game has relegated to a back position'.[132]

Added to the above factors was the mismanagement and often apathy of the county board. Though the question of hurling seems to have taken up a great deal of their discussions, precious few initiatives came from these. Many criticised the county board's inability to properly administer and run the county hurling championship. Michael O'Sullivan, the captain of the Ardfert hurling team, argued:

It is an undeniable fact that our fine old game of hurling is rapidly declining in Kerry. The day when Kerry might hope to secure All-Ireland honours in a hurling contest seems to have passed for ever . . . It is clearly not the men who wield the camán who are at fault but the system. The County Board could not summon up sufficient energy last year to bring the large number of four hurling teams to try conclusions. Had the board been guilty of complete apathy they could be accused on that one score alone, but it looks seriously like as if [*sic*] the wires were being pulled to favour one team beyond another. Kenmare and Ardfert were due to play but the former has failed to meet Ardfert on more than one occasion for the 1904 championship and the matter has been left open. Is it any wonder teams feel disgusted at this treatment? At a meeting in Ardfert they decided to give up the game altogether unless they got an opportunity at once to try conclusion with some team. Unless the board makes its mind up and brings into action those teams willing to play, I fear Kerry's small number of teams will get smaller still and before long it will be thrown in our face that the rattle of the camán is no longer heard in the Kingdom.[133]

The Kerryman was constantly complaining about the lack of interest in the hurling championship. In January 1910, it reported that the 1908 county championship had still not reached a conclusion. In 1913, another attempt was made to play the county championship in a league format and ten clubs competed that year. Yet the 1914 Annual Convention reported that though the competition opened to great fanfare, it was unable to attract the attention it deserved from the county board, whose whole time was occupied with the inter-county footballers.[134] A marked improvement was seen in 1914 with many new hurling clubs being formed, especially in the towns.[135] That same year a hurling committee was set up to promote the game and take over selection of the county side, with Austin Stack being appointed chairman. At a meeting of the committee to prepare for Kerry's first-round tie against Clare, Stack made it clear that players would only be picked on merit and a number of trial games were arranged between various Kerry clubs to help determine the county fifteen.

Yet despite the increased interest and even a degree of optimism over the results of this committee, Kerry slumped to a familiarly crushing defeat to Clare, 7-3 to 4-1. *The Kerryman* reported that the result proved the selection committee was a failure, as many of the team selected showed themselves to be complete flops.[136]

It is debatable whether this new attempt to bring Kerry hurlers up to the footballers' standards would have been successful, but the opportunity to further this initiative was denied. With the outbreak of the war in Europe and the rise of Volunteer activity in Kerry, the GAA became increasingly disorganised over the course of the decade. Any chance to remove hurling from the overbearing shadows of Kerry's footballers was lost forever. In the years that followed, the game was condemned to a slow, withering existence. There appeared to be no room in the emerging Kerry tradition for the county's hurlers.

Women and Gaelic Games

As with many of the sporting, political or cultural institutions of the time, the GAA was a male-dominated organisation. It remained for most of its first fifty years an association run by men, for men. As is often the case in the history of Victorian or early twentieth-century society, the role of women often went unremarked or remained hidden from the general narrative. The story of Kerry's rise to prominence in Gaelic sport was essentially a male one. Yet the male-dominated facade portrayed by the GAA concealed the significant role women played at the grass-roots level. A role often ignored, often unheroic, but nevertheless vital for the logistics of the association.

It was women who were trusted with the unspectacular duties of making and caring for jerseys for clubs across Ireland. When Kilmoyley contested its first county final against the Kenmare hurlers in 1889 the team wore saffron jerseys, long trousers and multi-coloured woollen caps. The wives and lady supporters of the team had knitted the caps and wore similar ones themselves the day of the game to differentiate themselves from the rival Kenmare female supporters. Nationally, women often provided the refreshments after matches to weary players at every level of the game. They also invariably organised and provided entertainment and receptions to celebrate victorious teams, while honouring the defeated. At the AGM of the Mitchels club in 1910 the secretary commentated on the benefits of their decision to rent club rooms in the town the previous year. Since they took possession of the rooms, they had been able to cater better for the amusement of their members. He also thanked the ladies of the town for their help in organising their dance club and for their assistance in holding several successful dances over the past year.[137]

Female attendance at Gaelic games was a feature of the GAA since its inception. Newspaper coverage of the earliest GAA occasions is awash with enthusiastic descriptions of the female presence at games.[138] The association actively encouraged the patronage of women and offered reduced and often free admission to its major matches and other events. Indeed, such was the demand for the Croke Memorial final in 1913 that the GAA was forced to issue a statement in the press regretting that its usual practice of free entrance for ladies was being withdrawn. At the 1909 Kerry GAA Annual Convention one of the delegates, A.J. Smith, responding to the secretary's report suggested that allowing ladies free admission into games in the county would be desirable. He stated that it was common practice in most other counties and by the managing bodies of other sports. The slight loss of revenue, he argued, would be compensated by the increased popularity of hurling and football resulting from the patronage of the fairer sex. 'It would too, the speaker thought, increase the attendance of the opposite sex (laughter and hear, hear)!'[139]

However, the period between 1905 and 1915 witnessed women leaving the sideline and taking their places upon the Gaelic pitches of Ireland. The emergence of codified and regulated male sports in the Victorian period stirred the interest of some women across Britain and Ireland to emulate them.[140] During the Victorian Sporting Revolution, an interest in women's participation in sport was built around Darwinian arguments that to have strong sons, strong healthy mothers were required to bear and nurture them.[141] In Britain, sports such as lawn croquet, badminton and tennis which developed in the late nineteenth century were unique in that they could be played by either sex.[142] In a male-dominated sporting world, middle-class women playing such games could be regarded as legitimate participants by men so long as they played to their own strengths and abilities and retained their 'womanliness'. If women participated in sports such as tennis, they had to do so within the bounds of accepted 'ladylike' behaviour.[143] Such games marked the beginning of a widespread female participation in sport.[144] Yet by the start of the twentieth century female involvement in more competitive sports was developing. As with their male counterparts, Catholic Irish women were entering secondary schools, the civil service and Irish universities in increasing numbers and looked to sport to shift societal perceptions of what they were capable of doing. Due to the recently reintroduced foreign games ban, however, sports such as hockey and tennis were tainted with Anglophobia. If Irish nationalist women were to take part in sport and gain approval for it, they would have to follow the GAA's example and innovate.[145]

The year 1903 marked the development of camogie, a female form of the game of hurling. Given the enthusiasm for hurling among members of the Gaelic League, it is not surprising that camogie originated from the socially acceptable women's membership of Gaelic League clubs.[146] The game first emerged that year in the Keating branch of the League in Dublin, where rules for the game were drawn up by the club. In July 1904, the first inter-club camogie match was played in Navan between Keatings and the Cuchullains, a second club formed in Dublin. That August, two Keatings teams played in a public exhibition of the game in Drumcondra. The match resulted in the establishment of a number of camogie clubs in the city and the inauguration of a city championship.[147] In 1906, Kerry got its first view of the new sport. At the annual Whit Sunday Killarney GAA tournament held under the auspices of the town's Gaelic League, a programme of hurling and football matches between Kerry and Dublin clubs also included a 'game of ladies hurling' between the Keatings and Cuchullains teams of Dublin. The *Sentinel* remarked:

> Great interest was manifested in this ladies hurling match and it was thought its novelty would be its chief feature; but it was a surprise to see the energy and accuracy with which the ladies entered into the game.[148]

The above exhibition was the only reference to the sport in Kerry for the next eight years.[149] Nationally, the sport went into decline in the countryside and stagnated in Dublin.

Nevertheless, efforts to revive the game led to a Camógaíocht Association being formed in 1911 to administer the game in Ireland. The first inter-county games were held in 1912, while in 1913 the Ashbourne Cup, an inter-varsity competition for camogie, was established. Around this time, the game seems to have first spread into Kerry. In August 1914, the women of Tralee organised a camogie club in the town.[150] Later in the year camogie clubs were established in Killarney and Ballymacelligott. In January 1915, the *Kerry People* reported on the first dance night organised by the women of the newly established Ballymacelligott camogie club. Evidently, its members did not stop with the breaking of previous social norms by just engaging in competitive sports:

> A new and novel feature of the dance was the selection of partners by the ladies. This rule was kept up until midnight. Of course, there were those who saw nothing wrong with it – the boys who were asked to dance – but there were those who thought it a cruel innovation – the boys who got no dance from the ladies. It seems rather strange, but it is true, nevertheless, that at almost every dance there are girls who get very few dances from the boys. The Ballymacelligott girls reversed the order for the first part of Saturday night and gave the boys, so to speak, a dose of their own medicine.

The reporter praised the efforts of the Ballymacelligott ladies, the dance being a most successful and enjoyable affair. It was a success in every way and 'proves that the social tendencies of Ballymacelligott are onwards and upwards'.[151] The following June Annie O'Sullivan wrote to *The Kerryman* from Cahersiveen expressing her delight that efforts were being made in the town to form a camogie club. She declared that, for the poor girls in small country towns, '[T]here is no form of outdoor amusement or pastime with which we can while away an hour in God's free

1929 Dr Crokes Camogie Team. *(Courtesy of John Keogh, Dr Crokes GAA)*

healthy open air. There is nothing in the evenings but the same mild monotonous walk in the boreen or a cycle on hilly dusty roads which to the health is more detrimental than beneficial . . . We must have exercise, variety and amusement.' Camogie, she declared, was the healthiest form of sport for girls.[152]

The turbulent years between 1914 and 1923 impacted significantly on the development of the game. However, soon after the Civil War a Central Council was established to administer the sport in Ireland, and in 1932 a special convention brought the camogie All-Ireland championship to life. In Kerry, many clubs began to form in the mid to late 1920s, attached to local Gaelic football and hurling clubs. In Killorglin, the game was introduced into the local national and intermediate schools in the 1920s. Around 1928 the town formed a senior camogie team that played challenge games against Dingle and Killarney. In June 1929, a special meeting was convened in Tralee to form a county camogie board under the chairmanship of Kate Breen, vice-chairman of Kerry County Council. Teams from Boherbee, Rock Street, Castlegregory, Dr Crokes, Ardfert, Crotta and Listowel soon affiliated. Dick Fitzgerald trained the Dr Crokes camogie team. After his death, its players formed their own separate club and renamed themselves the Dick Fitzgeralds in his honour. In August 1929, Kerry made its first appearance at inter-county level, when a Kerry selection played Cork in a friendly in Mallow.

For women across Ireland, especially in rural areas, camogie offered the first and often only chance to participate in local and national competition for much of the twentieth century. It remained the main Gaelic sport for women for most of the twentieth century, though in Kerry it was not as widely played as elsewhere. Only in the 1960s were attempts made in some counties to form women's Gaelic football teams, leading to the foundation of the Ladies' Gaelic Football Association in 1974.[153]

5
KERRY AND THE POLITICS OF SPORT, 1905–1915

I hope that the war cry 'Up Kerry' will resound in the trenches when German barbarism is dead and buried forever. I hope the cry will be heard when we make the last attack on the Germans' goal.

Captain Laurence Roche of the Munster Fusiliers, *Kerry Advocate,* 19 June 1915

During the first two decades of the new century, the GAA had seen a remarkable resurgence in Kerry. Despite internal flaws, on a national level the county had become synonymous with a winning Gaelic tradition. Yet parallel to the development of this tradition the organisation in Kerry had another dimension, which had little to do with sport. The local GAA became increasingly aligned with the broader nationalist political movement that emerged in these years. Not only was the Kerry GAA shaped by this heightened nationalism, the association in turn had a significant effect on this emerging movement. Organisations such as the Gaelic League and Sinn Féin developed close links with the local GAA, a fact highlighted by the overlap in membership between the GAA and those two bodies. As Ireland moved into the second decade of the twentieth century, a reorganised IRB began to gain an increasing hold on the leadership of the GAA. At the same time, the Irish Volunteers emerged as a new and powerful force within Irish nationalism. The increasing militarisation of Irish politics would likewise have a significant effect on the association and its members. Finally, the outbreak of the First World War would not only impact greatly on Irish society generally, but specifically too on the national and local GAA.

The Kerry GAA and the Gaelic League

As the early years of the twentieth century progressed, the close relationship between the GAA and the Gaelic League increased. Across the country in areas such as Kerry there was a growing call by members and officials alike for the greater use and promotion of Irish within the association. At a meeting of the Rathmore GAA club in December 1905 members impressed upon their countrymen the necessity of preserving the ancient tongue of the Gael, the 'hallmark of our Nationality'. In the weeks leading up to the 1906 Kerry Annual Convention, the *Sentinel* implored members of the League to become involved in helping to form and re-form clubs in every parish of the county. The Tralee Gaelic League responded to the challenge, forming its own football team which competed in matches against other town sides that year. 'MAC LIR', writing to *The Kerryman* on the association's progress in Kerry, argued vehemently that though the Irish public was in sympathy with the Irish language, many of them simply stopped there. 'Our language is all important . . . the first of those principles which give a people the right to claim a separate Nationality. If then the Gaels are brought into touch with the Gaelic League the rest will follow.' Irish, he argued, should be made the language of the game and all expressions during a GAA match should be communicated in it. Such an example should first be made by teams from Irish-speaking areas and once it was begun it would soon become the fashion among all clubs. The transition from players to public would be immediate. In addition,

> [it] would forever stamp the GAA as a factor in the making of the nation and would give Gaelic football the individuality it at present in some degree needs. Kerry is peculiarly favoured for this purpose. Many of the most regular and earnest attendants at Gaelic matches are veterans whose mother tongue is Irish.[1]

The Gaelic League experienced a significant spread in Kerry. By 1905, it had established itself in eight towns in the county, with the number of branches rising to thirty in 1910.[2] By 1908, the League had grown to 500 branches nationally and had posted 111 teachers in Irish communities.[3] Often officials within the Kerry GAA were adherent members of their local Gaelic League branch. Austin Stack, the county chairman, and county secretary F.J. Cronin were enthusiastic supporters of the Tralee Gaelic League and attended its AGM in 1909. Michael Griffin, a future secretary of the county board, became joint secretary of the Listowel Gaelic League when it was founded, along with T.F. Cotter who was the Listowel GAA county board delegate.[4] Given that GAA officials were frequently officers in their local League branches, it was hardly surprising that the association was used to further the League's objectives.[5] At the GAA's Annual Convention in March 1910 Patrick O'Daly, the general secretary of the Gaelic League, was invited to address delegates. Afterwards, a resolution was unanimously passed recommending to all county boards that they assist the League both in finance and organisation as much as they were able. The Kerry Board frequently sent forward teams to compete as part of the Gaelic League's extensive programme of feiseanna. The Killarney Gaelic League feis was held every Whit Sunday and was accompanied by inter-county contests between the Kerry footballers and hurlers and often those of Dublin or Cork. At the 1912 Kerry GAA Convention Griffin urged members of the League and the GAA in Kerry to strengthen their connections:

> Every Gaelic Leaguer should be a member of the local hurling or football club and every GAA man should be a member of the Gaelic League. Unfortunately this state of things is more the exception than the rule. Young players tell us they cannot find time for everything . . . but let me tell you, that within the scope of either of these organisations a boy or man will find the most efficient means of becoming a good, strong, healthy, sterling Irishman. I ask GAA members to give local League branches all their support and that Leaguers will do the same in return.[6]

At the 1914 Kerry Annual Convention the Castlegregory GAA club proposed a motion that the inscriptions on all medals awarded should be made in Irish and that the names of all players should likewise be registered in Irish. They urged the compiling of a list of field terms in Gaelic with a copy supplied to each affiliated club in Kerry. They also asked the convention to strongly represent to the Munster and Central Councils the necessity of showing in a practical way that they believe 'in making Ireland Irish'.[7]

Yet the Gaelic League, like the GAA, was not immune to the advances of republicans who sought to subvert its ideals. Around 1907 the IRB reorganised and began again to show a marked increase in activity. This coincided with the return to Ireland of the future 1916 leader Thomas Clarke, a chief figure in the Brotherhood. The clandestine organisation began to spread again into national movements such as the Gaelic League, Sinn Féin and indeed the GAA. As early as 1905 the RIC in Kerry claimed there was a noticeable increase in IRB activity and that the Gaelic League was fast coming under the influence of men 'of extreme views'.[8] The effects of the IRB's radicalisation of the local Gaelic League naturally filtered through the cross-membership it shared with the Kerry GAA.

In 1911, census statistics showed that Irish was continuing to decline in use as a language in spite of the Gaelic League's efforts. This fact shocked many on the body's national executive. Many had invested great energy and personal capital in an attempt to bring about a spiritual and cultural revolution through the campaign to revive the Irish language. Some younger men within the League called for a more decisive and politically revolutionary policy to tackle the issue.[9] The group became known as 'The Left Wing' and its members included the Ballylongford native and prominent republican Michael Joseph O'Rahilly (The O'Rahilly) and Thomas Ashe of Lispole. Ashe, who would become one of the commanders in the 1916 Rising, had been captain and chairman of the Lispole GAA club before transferring to a teaching post in Corduff, County Dublin in 1908. He had been heavily involved with the Gaelic League in Kerry and kept up a strong connection with it when he moved to Dublin. Like most of the men in this 'Left Wing', Ashe was also a member of the IRB. Tensions between the group and the more moderate members within the League's national executive reached a climax in 1913 when Douglas Hyde, the League's president, denounced Ashe and the other radical members of the organisation's governing body. Despite this, at the League's Ard-Fheis in 1913 O'Rahilly, along with Ashe and three other IRB men, were elected onto the League's ruling executive board.[10] The republican element within the body rapidly made its influence felt. At the Ard-Fheis in 1915 a resolution was passed declaring: 'The Gaelic League . . . shall devote itself to realising the ideal of a Gaelic-speaking and free Irish nation, free from all subjection to foreign influences.' The emphasis on securing a 'free Irish nation' marked a definite break with the non-political policy of Hyde, who subsequently stepped down as president. Hyde's cultural movement was becoming a shadow organisation for Irish republicanism.[11]

While the crossover between the GAA and the Gaelic League was certainly strong among some officials within the Kerry GAA, it is hard to gauge the level of dual membership among the association's rank-and-file members. Despite calls for a closer working relationship between members of the Kerry GAA and the local Gaelic League, the latter had trouble expanding widely in the county. In March 1908, an RIC county inspector report alleged that the organisation had become 'inactive' in Kerry.[12] Given the lack of hurling clubs established in the county due to Gaelic League activity, when contrasted with places such as Westmeath it seems likely the most significant crossover of members between both organisations occurred at officer level. However, given the close local connections between the leadership of both organisations, the radicalisation of the League would undoubtedly fuel an increasingly politically militant outlook among those at the head of the Kerry GAA.

Sinn Féin and the Kerry GAA

Just as the GAA became more aligned with the Gaelic League, so other nationalist organisations began to wield more of an influence on the association. On a local level, emerging groups such as Sinn Féin would have a significant impact on the political outlook of many within the Kerry GAA.

In 1906, Arthur Griffith launched a journal entitled *Sinn Féin* following the collapse of his previous paper, the *United Irishman*. That same year he wrote a pamphlet entitled *The Sinn Féin Policy*.

Sinn Féin Ard Fheis, c. 1914/15. Austin Stack is second from right, middle row. In front are Arthur Griffith, Éamon de Valera and Michael Collins (fourth, fifth and sixth from left respectively). Roger Casement is third from left, second row. (Courtesy of the National Library of Ireland)

Following on from this publication, Griffith founded a political party that adopted the ideals outlined in the document and it quickly became known simply as Sinn Féin. Griffith's political and economic policy advocated the protection of Irish industry and commerce, the establishment of national courts and a civil service, national control over transport, wastelands and fisheries, reform of education, a policy of non-consumption of articles paying duty to the British exchequer, a withdrawal of all voluntary support to the British armed forces and, finally, non-recognition of the British parliament. He sought to capitalise on the inertia of the Irish Parliamentary Party during this period and to harness the energies of a younger generation of Irish nationalists. Through his writings, which formulated the emerging cultural revivalist ideals of the

Gaelic Revival in terms of the aspirations of frustrated social groups, Griffith, like his contemporary D.P. Moran, succeeded in making cultural nationalism the dominant ideological force in Irish society between 1900 and 1906.[13] Though Sinn Féin advocated the re-establishment of an independent Ireland, the party when it was founded was not a republican organisation. Rather Griffith hoped for a non-violent, constitutional separation from the United Kingdom.[14] However, many of the young men and women attracted to the organisation had grown increasingly weary of the lack of progress by the IPP in its attempts to secure Home Rule for Ireland. Indeed, several members had become increasingly open to republican doctrines of a more extreme split with Britain.

Despite initial enthusiasm for the organisation, Sinn Féin rapidly went into decline. Though it could boast 150 clubs nationally between 1908 and 1910, the vast majority of these were small and rural. Lack of funds was another issue and this hampered its ability to canvass during general elections. The rise of republican activism following the IRB reorganisation in 1907 also robbed the party of many existing and potential adherents.[15] Yet to the establishment it remained a dangerous organisation. Rather erroneously, in the years leading up to and after the 1916 Rising, British authorities began to group all separatists and republican activists under the catch-all term of 'Sinn Féiners'.[16]

The party spread into Kerry, with four branches being formed in the county by December 1906. The two nationalist Kerry papers the *Kerry Sentinel* and *The Kerryman* were enthusiastic supporters of the policy outlined by Griffith, albeit for different reasons. The *Sentinel*'s editor wrote: 'its principles are the basic principles of all progressive nations; they mean self-help, self-respect and self-support. Without these a country must remain provincial and dependent', but cautioned that the IPP's objective of obtaining legislative freedom 'is absolutely necessary to the success of the Sinn Féin idea'. In contrast, the more radical *Kerryman* advocated support of the party's policy, 'as any student of Irish politics can conclude with little difficulty that Ireland has had about enough of Parliamentarianism'.[17]

Throughout this period, members of Sinn Féin saw the benefits of using the national and local apparatus of the GAA to further the party's cause and popularity. Many of the new generation of officials who entered the association around the turn of the century were advocates of the Sinn Féin message. The likes of Dublin County Board official Harry Boland, GAA president James Nowlan and GAA secretary Luke O'Toole were prominent national Sinn Féin activists. In Kerry, there were similar connections between county board officials and the movement. Michael Griffin of Listowel was a founding member of the town's Sinn Féin club. In Killorglin, Pat Teahan of the famous 1893 Laune Rangers became president of the Killorglin branch, while the town's county board delegate, Tadhg Mangan, was also a member. In the years before 1916, the GAA began to align itself with Sinn Féin. Despite this, as far as divergent forces of Irish nationalism were concerned, the association adopted a neutral policy, welcoming members who still supported the constitutional efforts of the Irish Party as well as those who were beginning to advocate a more extreme form of nationalism. The vast majority of GAA members, like the Irish public at large, continued to support the IPP in its attempts to secure legislative independence for Ireland. For example, Eugene O'Sullivan, the former Kerry County Board chairman, stood for election as an IPP candidate in the East Kerry constituency in the 1906 and 1910 general elections.

Yet aspects of the Sinn Féin policy began to gather increasing support within the membership of the GAA. The association saw itself as protecting the national heritage and pastimes of Ireland and so it saw a kindred aspiration in Griffith's promotion of native Irish industry. In January 1905, the GAA passed a motion agreeing that in future all contract work done by the association would use only Irish material. Kerry's Annual Convention called on all Kerry GAA clubs to support the Irish Industrial Revival Movement and to promote and purchase only goods of Irish manufacture.[18]

The Sinn Féin doctrine had a growing effect on the emerging Irish republican movement. Nominally a non-political and neutral organisation, Marcus de Búrca argued that the GAA could never police the activities of its individual members, many of whom counted themselves as members of other political organisations. Often, when these members spoke out the impression created (and often intended) was that the speaker's opinions were also those of the association. Thomas F. O'Sullivan, a member of the IRB and a man who held an extreme nationalist outlook, was adept at arguing the case for radical nationalism in such a way as to suggest the GAA supported such views.[19] As has been seen, this was particularly the case in his arguments for the reintroduction of the ban on RIC and British military personnel becoming members of the GAA. At the GAA's Annual Convention in 1901 O'Sullivan declared that the police and military in Ireland were the embodiment of 'the vile system of Government whose sole object was to maintain subjection of our native land by fair means or foul' and stated that the fact the police were Irishmen or at least born in Ireland (which did not necessarily mean the same thing) should have the effect only of increasing Gaels' detestation of them.[20]

The British authorities certainly highlighted the growing connection between Sinn Féin and the GAA. For example, Dublin Castle reports throughout this period equated the GAA's ban on soldiers and the RIC as being part of the greater Sinn Féin policy of anti-enlistment. The RIC inspector general's report from May 1906 noted that anti-recruitment to British forces was one of the principal planks of the Sinn Féin movement and that the distribution of seditious anti-enlistment literature was becoming an increasingly common occurrence at GAA matches. A more hostile attitude was also being taken to the presence of members of the British armed forces at GAA events. In November 1906, two uniformed soldiers who had paid to attend a hurling tournament in Tullamore, County Offaly were assaulted by members of its organising committee after they refused to leave the ground.[21] The RIC observed that an attempt by moderates at the GAA's 1908 Congress to have the police and military ban altered was defeated by the 'Sinn Féin element' that was increasing its control over the association. A report the following year claimed that this extreme Sinn Féin constituent was daily extending its influence over the GAA's membership and gaining many adherents.[22] Indeed, many officials openly took pride in the association's purported role in the noted decrease in British Army recruitment within Ireland. Writing in the GAA's 1907 *Gaelic Athletic Annual*, M.F. Crowe remarked that though many men and organisations had taken credit for the decrease in numbers of Irish recruits, it should not be forgotten that the GAA had branches where political organisations had little influence and where anti-recruiting literature never found its way. He declared that the GAA's ban had been instrumental in curbing recruitment to the British Army.[23] Within two years, the voice of those advocating anti-enlistment within the GAA had become even more virulent. In its 1909 annual, 'Buille in Aipce' wrote:

> If the armed forces of England never had a footing here would Ireland now be in subjection? Would our martyrs have perished? Would the 'Famine' have desolated and depopulated Erin? Would our homes have been left fireless and voiceless? Would imprisonment follow the use of our native tongue? Is there any but one negative reply to these questions? Are not then the armed forces of Seaghan Buidhe, Ireland's greatest enemies and direst evil? Is their presence in Gaelic ranks anything but an outrage and a disgrace? Stop recruiting for England. Stop it by practice, by precept, by ostracism and not alone do you release one arm for Éire, but you paralyse one of England's too.[24]

The rank and file of the association's membership in areas such as Kerry seemed to share these sentiments. At half time in the 1908 Croke Cup final between Kerry and Mayo in Dublin a member of the RIC (and evidently a Mayo follower) walked onto the pitch to impart some wisdom to the team. On seeing the uniform, the crowd grew increasingly hostile, with shouts of 'throw him out' echoing around the ground. Once the officer recognised the jeering was directed at him, he made towards the stand, his pace increasing as the howls grew louder until finally as a barrage of oranges was flung at him he began to sprint off the field and disappeared into the crowd.[25] Likewise, the RIC in Tralee reported that the 'advanced members' of the GAA in the town were believed to be instrumental in distributing and posting a number of anti-enlistment notices at matches there. Though the majority of GAA members still supported the conservative parliamentary methods of the IPP, increasing support for the cause of anti-enlistment within the local GAA pointed to a growing extreme nationalist sentiment that had begun to filter through the association. The full effects of this would not become apparent until the rise of the Irish Volunteers between 1914 and 1915.

The Kerry GAA and the Birth of the Irish Volunteers, 1913–1915

The four years leading to the outbreak of the First World War proved to be a remarkable period in Irish history. The long-held dream of Irish self-government in the shape of Home Rule was on the cusp of being introduced due to the lobbying of the Irish Parliamentary Party under John Redmond. However, the prospect of its very introduction threatened civil war in Ireland. The nation was caught up in what Diarmaid Ferriter called 'the growing cult

Dr Crokes, Kerry County Champions, 1912–14. Under the captaincy of Dick Fitzgerald, the Killarney club began to dominate club football in Kerry in the years leading up to the First World War. *(Courtesy of John Keogh, Dr Crokes GAA)*

of militarism' which swept Europe at this time.[26] As nationalists and unionists began to arm, events far off in Europe were to drag human civilisation into the greatest conflict yet witnessed. These events, both national and international, would have a profound effect on the GAA and its membership in Kerry.

In the British general election of December 1910, the Liberal party under H.H. Asquith lost its overall majority in the House of Commons. To keep power, Asquith became reliant on the support of the IPP and its seventy-four seats. In return, he had no choice but to agree finally to Redmond's demands to introduce Home Rule for Ireland. To pave the way for its introduction the Parliament Act was passed in August 1911 which broke the power of the House of Lords to veto legislation passed in the House of Commons.[27] In May 1914, the Home Rule Bill was finally passed through the House of Commons amid wild cheers and celebrations. However, in Ulster the prospect of being ruled from a Dublin parliament filled the unionist majority with dread. Under the unionist MP Edward Carson a militia force calling itself the Ulster Volunteers was established to oppose Home Rule by force if necessary.[28] In response to this threat to Ireland's aspirations of self-government, Eoin MacNeill, Professor of Early Irish History at University College Dublin, urged that Irish nationalists should follow the Ulster Volunteers' example and create a similar force to protect their right to Home Rule. Following this, Maurice P. Ryle, editor of the short-lived *Kerry Advocate*, delivered a speech in Tralee and declared: '[I]f Ulster can give him [Carson] 90,000 drilled men, what could not the rest of Ireland be able to give?' Ryle stated that members of the GAA 'whose prowess have been proved on many a hard-fought field' could easily form Volunteer clubs and drill in the use of arms.[29] The RIC was equally worried about the potential of such a force, commenting that if it was established, 'the Gaelic Athletic Association could supply an abundance of first-class recruits'.[30] Their fears proved justified. On 22 November 1913, a large public meeting was held in the Rotunda in Dublin at which the Irish Volunteers were formally established.[31]

Across Ireland the Volunteers spread rapidly as nationalists, determined that Home Rule be realised, filled the ranks to protect its implementation from unionist aggression. In Kerry, the first Volunteer corps established was in Killarney at a meeting of the town's Gaelic League.[32] Yet almost immediately local GAA officials were prominent in setting up the organisation. Tadhg Kennedy, a member of the Kerry County Board and secretary of the Tralee

Gaelic League, was contacted by the Volunteers in Dublin and asked to arrange a meeting to discuss the formation of a corps in the town. Kennedy enlisted the support of the Kerry GAA president Austin Stack to organise the assembly.[33] Thomas Slattery, a former president of the Kerry GAA, chaired the meeting, at which a branch of the Irish Volunteers was established.[34] Over the next six months, Volunteer companies were established across the county. By April 1914, the RIC reported that over a thousand men were active members of the Volunteers in Kerry.

In June 1914, Redmond moved to establish his authority over the rapidly expanding force. He wrote to the Provisional Committee of the Irish Volunteers demanding that they accept twenty-five new members onto their board who would be nominated by the IPP. The committee reluctantly acquiesced. With the Irish Party having formally embraced the Volunteers, the organisation received the official sanction of the Irish Catholic Church and enlistment in the force rose dramatically.[35] In Kerry, small farmers, shopkeepers' assistants and labourers were reported as joining the Volunteers in droves and thirteen branches had been established, with the clergy giving the force its full backing in many areas.[36] In July 1914, the Irish Volunteers moved to arm themselves and a shipment of weapons was successfully landed at Howth, County Dublin. It was reported that the Tralee Volunteers had received from the shipment an allocation of 200 rifles, which they distributed among their members.[37] Yet attempts such as the Howth gun landing to arm the Volunteers widely highlighted the fact that despite Redmond's nominal leadership, the IRB and other extreme nationalists had successfully infiltrated the movement for their own ends.

As the Volunteers became more widespread and started to recruit young and active men, it was inevitable that a large proportion of its members would be drawn from the GAA. The extent of this dual membership only increased as the Volunteers grew. The situation was little different among the GAA membership in Kerry. Yet it is hard to determine the loyalties of those GAA members who enlisted to the opposing strands of nationalism and how much the infiltration of the Volunteers by republican elements had affected them. Certainly, a majority fully supported Redmond. His achievement of securing Home Rule had only increased his own prestige and that of his party. Redmond had appeared personally at the replay of the Croke Memorial final in 1913 and was given a 'rapturous' welcome from the crowd.[38] When Kerry contested the Munster semi-final against Tipperary in Limerick in October 1913 the attendance was described as minuscule owing to a massive Home Rule demonstration, which Redmond addressed, being held in the city at the same time.

Nevertheless, a growing militancy and rejection of constitutional nationalism was becoming evident among many Kerry GAA supporters in the months leading up to the formation of the Irish Volunteers. In March 1913, Eileen O'Hara, a journalist with *The Kerryman*, reported on a Gaelic games tournament between teams from Kerry and Limerick that had been held on St Patrick's Day in Ardfert. On the train to the match, a lively discussion on the approach of Home Rule began:

> It is so sad [some said] that the present generation is prepared to accept a subordinate legislature and forget the wrongs, the cruel devilish, fiendish wrongs of well nigh eight hundred years. 'Never,' says a pale faced, but youthful, occupant . . . It was a loud, lusty, defiant NEVER! The debate now became hot, one man shouted Redmond was leader of the Irish people. 'He is the leader of the old section,' came the retort quickly . . . [As we enter the ground] the scene reminds me of old times – the days when men were fearless and heroic . . . and when they played the national games, not so much because they were national but because the games made them physically strong to meet the common enemy – England – in the open plain, if the chance came. That was the sole intention. The men of today had better wake up.

After the match, O'Hara noted the ground was littered with slips of paper. Evidently some radical nationalist literature had been distributed among the crowd during the event. The papers read, 'England! D[am]n your concessions. We want our country and come what may we mean to have it.'[39] It was clear that for some within the association in Kerry, men and woman alike judging from the reporter's own strongly republican views, the appeal of Redmond's constitutional nationalism was waning.

At an official level the relationship between the Volunteers and the GAA remained ambiguous. The Central Council refused the Irish Volunteers permission to use Croke Park for drilling purposes in December 1913.[40] Colonel Jeremiah J. O'Connell, in his unpublished account of the Irish Volunteers, was of the opinion 'that the Volunteers did not receive the help they expected from the GAA and to which later on they might fairly be considered entitled'.[41] In a letter to the *Gaelic Athlete*, a member of the Volunteers complained that while in the previous year the association had held a successful national tournament in aid of a memorial to Archbishop Croke, they were now failing in the more pressing duty of holding a national tournament to help raise funds to arm the Volunteers.[42] Despite this, at the GAA's Annual Congress in 1914 Robert Page, representing the executive of the Irish Volunteers, obtained leave to address the delegates. He stated that, like the GAA, the Volunteer movement 'was a purely National body, non-political and non sectarian, though they were more a militant body. They did not ask Congress to take any official action, but they asked delegates when they went back to their clubs to recommend the objects of the Volunteers movement.'[43] Notwithstanding this, the association's leadership stepped back from endorsing the movement and it was clear that the Central Council was not prepared to risk the association's popularity as a sporting body through open political commitment. However, this did not stop prominent GAA officials from associating themselves with the movement. James Nowlan, the GAA's president, addressed a crowd of GAA followers in Wexford and recommended that every member should 'join the volunteers and . . . learn to shoot straight'.[44] Meanwhile, one of the speakers at the inaugural meeting of the Irish Volunteers in Dublin had been the GAA's secretary, Luke O'Toole.

Despite the association's cautious approach to the Volunteers on a national level, locally in Kerry there was a significant degree of interaction. As has been highlighted, many officials within the Kerry Board were deeply involved in the setting up of the Irish Volunteers in the county. When a corps was formed in Castleisland in April 1914 James McDonnell, the board's vice-president, John Collins, the Kerry GAA handicapper and Jerry Collins, the Kerry football team trainer, were prominent in the attendance. John Moran, the county board's treasurer, was a member of the Listowel Volunteers committee.[45] In Castlegregory, Kerry's midfielder Pat O'Shea was instrumental in forming a Volunteer corps and stated that the local GAA club was used extensively as a recruiting ground for members.[46] In Killarney, Eugene O'Sullivan, the former president of the Dr Crokes club and chairman of Killarney's urban district council, addressed several Volunteer rallies while Dick Fitzgerald, the Kerry captain, was an officer in the Killarney corps.

At a meeting of the Kerry Board in March 1914 its secretary, Diarmuid Crean, was reported to have made a stirring and well-received speech putting forward the claims of the Volunteers to the delegates present.[47] The Kerry Board also argued for a greater degree of cooperation between the two organisations. At a board meeting that September Michael Griffin, who had become prominent in the Listowel Volunteers, proposed a resolution requesting that the Central Council summon an immediate National Convention. He suggested that at this convention the association should amend its constitution to allow for the affiliation of rifle clubs in the same manner as hurling and football clubs were affiliated. He also recommended that the Central Council should promote rifle competitions among the GAA's membership.[48] The *National Volunteer*, the official journal of the Volunteers, declared that the Kerry GAA

> . . . has done excellent work in furthering the idea of rifle competitions under the auspices of the Gaelic Athletic Association and we trust that the characteristically patriotic attitude of the Central Authority will do everything possible to make the new move a success . . . Kerry, true to its traditions, has made a good start and has indicated the proper co-ordination of the Volunteers with Ireland's national pastimes. It was, of course, inevitable that sooner or later the GAA should play a conspicuous part in the regeneration of Ireland and the golden opportunity is at hand.[49]

Yet some of the dilemmas facing those within the GAA who openly supported the Volunteers were becoming evident. At a board meeting in August 1914 D.J. Griffin of the Castlemaine GAA club enquired if retired soldiers might be allowed to compete at sports meetings. When the county secretary responded that the rules of the GAA's ban on such individuals was clear, Griffin interjected and argued that many such men were giving tremendous help in training Volunteers across the county. The secretary reaffirmed the association's rules and commented that the Kerry Board had never asked such men to train the Volunteers and that this was an individual matter for each Volunteer corps.[50] W.F. Mandle argues that on a local level the Volunteer movement was wholeheartedly espoused by the GAA.[51] While there is much evidence for this assessment in Kerry, nationally this was not uniformly the case. Colonel Jeremiah O'Connell wrote that while many of the Volunteers' best officers were captains of GAA teams, the athletic activities of such men too often conflicted with their military duties and 'when a match and a parade or a field day clashed too often the parade or field day was put into the background'.[52]

Nevertheless, the relationship between the local Volunteers and the Kerry GAA continued to grow. The blurring lines of political nationalism were evident when Kerry travelled to New Ross for a rematch with their All-Ireland rivals Wexford in June 1914. Over 22,000 attended the eagerly anticipated clash, which was the centrepiece of a two-day Gaelic League feis and industrial exhibition in the town. Diarmuid Crean, in his role as county secretary, used the match as cover to secure a shipment of arms for the Tralee Volunteers. Meeting The O'Rahilly, he was able to purchase twenty to twenty-five rifles from him, for a sum of £200.[53] Volunteer companies also became prominent at local Gaelic events in Kerry. That July another match between Wexford and Kerry was organised in Tralee. When the train carrying the Wexford team arrived in Tralee around 700 Volunteers were drawn up outside the station. The local band struck up 'The Boys of Wexford' as the train entered the station and the Wexford players were conveyed to the positions allotted to them in the ranks of the Volunteers. A torchlight procession headed by the band marched them through Nelson Street and Castle Street to the team's hotel. When the Kerry footballers returned victorious from the All-Ireland in December a large contingent of armed Volunteers in uniform lined the platforms at Killarney and Tralee stations and marched the players through both towns in triumph.[54]

By now an undeniably powerful and united force, the Irish Volunteer movement found itself shattered by the outbreak of the First World War. In September 1914, the implementation of the Home Rule Act was suspended due to Britain's declaration of war on Germany and Austria-Hungary. In parliament, Redmond offered the British government the use of the Irish Volunteers to defend Ireland, allowing British troops stationed there to be transferred to the continent. This offer was swiftly rejected. Yet Redmond was determined that the Irish Volunteers should play some role in the war. Like many, he envisaged the war lasting only a few months. He hoped that when the hostilities ended his party would be in possession of a properly armed, military-trained force to leverage against the increasing likelihood of Ulster partition once Home Rule was enacted.[55] Redmond also wanted to make a 'blood sacrifice' of Irishmen to prove to the British Ireland's loyalty in return for the granting of Home Rule.[56] At a speech to Volunteers in Woodenbridge, County Wicklow Redmond urged the Volunteers 'to go where ever the firing line extends, in defence of right, of freedom and of religion in this war. It would be a disgrace forever to our country otherwise.'[57]

His call for open enlistment to the British Army split the Volunteers. The vast majority of its members, some 158,000, endorsed his position but 12,000 were bitterly opposed. This might well have been one of his motives: to try and establish a separate force within a force, free from the influence of the IRB.[58] The bulk of the Volunteers' membership joined Redmond's new 'National Volunteers'. However, four days after this speech, the majority of the Volunteers' original controlling executive issued a statement repudiating both Redmond and his nominees within the executive. Under MacNeill's leadership they retained the name the 'Irish Volunteers' and set up their own general council. However, MacNeill's split was an empty gesture as he had no real political alternative to the policy of Redmond. It was the IRB who held a substantial and growing influence within the splinter movement which would provide this alternative. In September 1915 the IRB appointed a Military Council to secure effective control over MacNeill's organisation in order to plan an insurrection. The continuation of the war offered them the opportunity and, more importantly, the time to execute it.[59]

Across Kerry local Volunteer companies held meetings in response to Redmond's speech in order to declare whether they were for or against him. In Cahersiveen, a meeting to discuss the situation ended in a split of the corps, thirty-seven voting to side with MacNeill's Irish Volunteers and twenty-seven opting to follow Redmond.[60] At a meeting of the Tralee Volunteers, called to decide which leader to follow, the Irish Party MP for West Kerry, Thomas O'Donnell, attempted to address the meeting but was heckled and forced to leave. A green flag was held aloft and those men who wished to join MacNeill were asked to move to the right of the hall. Around 300 did so, leaving only 20 to support Redmond. The former broke out in song and cheers while the latter left the hall, having Union Jack flags flung at them. Afterwards, a telegraph was sent to MacNeill declaring that Tralee 'stands firm for the old constitution'.[61] By December, the RIC calculated that nationally 93 per cent of the original Volunteers had stuck by Redmond. However, in Kerry, of the forty-eight branches known to exist, almost a quarter of their membership was reported to belong 'to the Irish Volunteers'.[62]

Members of the Kerry GAA within the Volunteers appear to have acted much like their non-Gael brethren. When the split came it was the constitutional Volunteers under Redmond who received the majority of support from within the national membership of the GAA. Despite the dominance of the IRB in the GAA's Central Council and their connections with the splinter Irish Volunteers, they had little influence on the loyalty of the grass-roots membership. The Central Council instead took the wise course of neutrality as far as the split was concerned, fearful that any open alignment with either section would cause a division among officials and rank-and-file members. When an extraordinary meeting of the Central Council was called in December to consider the Kerry motion to form rifle clubs in the GAA the Kerry delegates were persuaded to withdraw the motion after concerns were raised by their Cork counterparts that it would lead to a political rift within the membership of the association.[63] The following April at the GAA's Annual Congress in Dublin proceedings started at an early hour so those members who supported Redmond's National Volunteers could attend an Easter parade rally of the force that afternoon. However, despite such deference for the sake of keeping the organisation intact, unofficially the GAA's Central Council sided with the IRB-dominated splinter group. There is some evidence that the wider schism in the Volunteers permeated into individual clubs in Kerry. In 1914, the Laune Rangers club almost divided in two over reports of a dispute among its members due to the Volunteer split.

Despite the superficially neutral stance taken by the Central Council, the Kerry County Board seems to have clearly aligned with the Irish Volunteers. Indeed, a substantial group of GAA officials in Kerry, such as Austin Stack, Diarmuid Crean, M.J. Quinlan, Pat O'Shea, Michael Griffin and John Joe Rice, were members of the county's IRB network. Stack himself was the acknowledged head of the IRB organisation in Kerry. The Irish Volunteers there, no doubt as a consequence of the heavy GAA involvement, were organised using the same model. Just as each club in the county sent delegates to the Kerry GAA Annual Convention, so each company in the county was represented, often by the same delegates, at an Annual Convention of Kerry Irish Volunteers. The first such Volunteer convention was held in November 1914, at which a Volunteer county board was elected along GAA lines.[64] Support for the Irish Volunteers remained strong among the membership of the Kerry GAA. When Kerry played Louth in a challenge match in Dundalk on Easter Sunday 1915 the large crowd called for cheers for the famous Kerry team. However, Dick Fitzgerald, captaining the side, cried out for three cheers for Eoin MacNeill and the Irish Volunteers instead. In May 1915, Kerry played an inter-county challenge match against Dublin in Killarney. Afterwards, a parade of Kerry Irish Volunteers took place on the sports field and was reviewed personally by Eoin MacNeill. The *Kerry People* was in no doubt about the implications of this close alliance and published an article entitled 'Is Sinn Féin going to be the run and ruin of the GAA?' The paper regretted

... that the institution [the GAA], acting on the dictum of the controlling crowd in Dublin evidently, has seen fit to come into political works. It may be that those who are showing the way to the GAA are making a good bit out of the movement. It is certain that the men who make up the rank and file of the GAA get absolutely nothing beyond their railway expenses for their hard labours. That black-coated men who never played football should be running the GAA to suit their own purposes is very lamentable ... it is really a crying shame that those who are really nobodies should be allowed to exploit the GAA for their own ends.[65]

The split in the Volunteers and the energy increasingly devoted to drilling and military activity had a detrimental effect on the management of the GAA in many areas. In 1915, *Sport* reported that the GAA in Derry had fallen away 'to nothingness' owing to Volunteer activity.[66] Likewise, in Kerry, Volunteer activity significantly curtailed the operation of the association there. In January of that year, *The Kerryman* was complaining that meetings of the Kerry County Board were falling through due to lack of sufficient members present to form a quorum.[67] With so many prominent Kerry GAA officials and board members immersed in the Volunteer movement, the administration of the association on a local level suffered greatly. No County Convention was held in 1915 and few board meetings could be arranged. Likewise, no county championships were fixed for the year as the 1914 county championship remained unfinished.

The Great War and the GAA

The Great War had a profound effect on Ireland and its outbreak sent Irish nationalism hurtling on a course towards open rebellion against Britain. Around 210,000 Irishmen fought in the conflict, of which between 25,000 and 49,000 died.[68] Though Kerry was an isolated corner on the very western edge of the United Kingdom, the First World War and its repercussions would have a significant impact on the county, its people and the local GAA.

The effects of the war hit different strands of Kerry society in different ways. For a county dominated by agriculture, the war brought with it a huge demand for cereal and livestock. This resulted in an unprecedented economic boom for Kerry's farming community.[69] The British government offered incentives to farmers in areas such as Kerry to switch from their traditional cattle herding to cereal crop growth to cope with the huge demands for food produce. The move to a much more labour-intensive method caused a spike in demand for farm labourers and wages steadily increased. While the rural economy boomed, unemployment became the reality for many in Kerry's towns. In places like Killarney that were dependent on tourism, the outbreak of war and curtailment of travel had a devastating impact on the local economy, pushing many to the verge of destitution.[70] Likewise, rapid inflation of fuel and food prices led to great hardship, especially among the poorest living in areas such as Tralee. A meeting of the town's UDC in February 1915 called on the government to do something about the rapidly increasing prices and lack of employment.

Adequate recruitment to the British armed forces was a major concern for the British administration in Ireland throughout the war. It was inevitable that the local membership of the GAA would be among those targeted for enlistment. Kerry, and in particular Tralee, had a long-established military tradition, the town being the home barracks of the British Army's Royal Munster Fusiliers Regiment. It was to their ranks that the vast majority of Kerry men enlisted in the war. In a county of few economic opportunities, especially for the urban poor, the army provided a viable alternative for young men.[71] This was not to imply that Kerry men flocked to the British standard when the war broke out. On the contrary, Kerry actually had the lowest rate of enlistment of Catholic men employed outside of agriculture in the country, 3.3 per cent as opposed to a national average of 6.8 per cent.[72] Despite the RIC reporting a strong sense of anti-German sentiment in the county at the outbreak of the war, by October the authorities were dismayed that so few men in Kerry were enlisting. They also noted that virtually no members of the National Volunteers had joined up.[73] It seems that in Kerry, though many had stayed loyal to Redmond and his politics, this loyalty did not extend to them marching into the trenches of Flanders. This assessment also seems to reflect the attitude of Kerry GAA members within the original Volunteer movement, the majority of whom had subsequently joined Redmond's faction. Nationally, it was reported that a dread of military service was a major factor in a noticeable decline in National Volunteer membership. It was also reported that despite the best efforts of Redmond and the Irish Party to encourage men to enlist, the response to such appeals had been universally 'very poor'. Over the next twelve months, regardless of the attempts of Irish Party MPs to keep the organisation alive, the National Volunteers steadily declined in Kerry. With Home Rule already secured and no end to the war in sight, Redmond's force had little to offer nationalists but the prospect of being coerced into military service in the slaughter fields of France and Belgium. By October 1915, Dublin Castle was reporting that in Kerry the National Volunteers as an organisation was effectively dead.[74]

Recruitment drives became part of the wartime experience for counties such as Kerry. Irish Party MPs often took a leading role in these. The four sitting Irish Party MPs in the county were prominent in the recruitment tours organised by Irish regiments to try and encourage enlistment among the young men of the county. Thomas O'Donnell, the West Kerry MP, was particularly active. The unionist *Kerry Evening Post* was especially forceful in its support for the war and recruitment, its editorial in November pleading: 'Enlist. A single word conveys the whole duty at the present time of all men who are within the Army age limit.'[75] Yet such rallies were having a decidedly marginal effect on local enlistment rates as the months wore on. A growing sense of apathy towards the increasingly drawn-out conflict was already becoming evident. The exact number of Kerry men who joined the colours during the First World War is unknown.[76] However, given that the deaths of Kerry servicemen number around 674, Alan Drumm suspects some 2,000 men may have joined up.[77] Over three-quarters of those who died came from the three main urban centres of Tralee, Killarney and Listowel, with the majority coming from Tralee.[78]

In counties such as Kerry, it is easy to understand why urban areas would have supplied the majority of recruits. With the agricultural sector booming, farmers and their sons were little interested in giving up such lucrative profits for the dangers and poorly paid duties of a wartime soldier. A military tradition such as that which existed in Tralee played a role in urban enlistment. Mostly, however, it was unemployed and unskilled urban labourers and those with little economic alternative who were forced to take the king's shilling. A survey of 264 Kerry men who fought in and survived the war showed that 123 were labourers, 42 were tradesmen and only one was a farmer.[79] Yet there were local exceptions to this pattern. In 1915, the *Sentinel* reprinted an article from the English *Daily Sketch* that told of the remarkable record of enlistment in the small village of Clieveragh outside Listowel. Out of a population of ninety-two, twenty-six men had or were serving in the present war, leaving only four able-bodied men under the age of fifty living in the village.[80] This might well fall into what some called 'the collective pressure' of enlistment, where in a close-knit community or work environment bonds of loyalty and friendship accounted for higher than normal levels of recruitment in certain localities and employment industries.[81]

As for national GAA membership, the effects of recruitment in the First World War are difficult to establish. Though the vast majority of GAA members supported Redmond's politics, it is unclear how willing this made them to heed his calls and join the war against Germany. Likewise, though the vast majority of GAA members who had joined the Volunteers sided with Redmond during the split, RIC reports make clear that this did not necessitate many of them rushing to join the Irish regiments in the fight. Certainly, the 210,000 Irishmen who served in the war included many GAA officials, players and supporters. In Clare, it was reported that one local hurling club was forced to disband because so many of its team had enlisted.[82] At the GAA's Annual Congress in 1915 the Laois County Board submitted notice for a motion proposing that 'volunteering in the Army for the present European war should not entail any disqualification from playing under the Gaelic Athletic Association'. Nevertheless, when the motion came up for consideration by delegates it was announced it had since been withdrawn.[83] The fact that Laois and other counties contemplated a proposal to lift the ban on GAA members joining the British Army for the duration of the war tends to lend credence to the suggestion that many GAA members did enlist.[84] In Westmeath, a local GAA tournament in Glasson that August was held in aid of funds for wounded soldiers.[85] The unionist *Irish Times* certainly saw the potential of the GAA's membership. In an article following Kerry's victory over Wexford in the 1914 All-Ireland, it wrote that '[T]housands of the strongest and most active of the young men of Ireland were to be seen in Dublin'. The final between the athletic men of Wexford and Kerry was followed with great enthusiasm and interest by 'upwards of 15,000 strong, healthy young men of military age'. It was 'apparently a matter of momentous importance that these sturdy young athletes should receive the support and encouragement of a crowd of upwards of 20,000 football enthusiasts'. As the reporter watched the match he could not help

> . . . wondering what it was that kept these young men from joining their brothers in maintaining and enhancing the honour of Ireland in the trenches in Northern France and Belgium. Fully 10,000 of the supporters, it is evident from their age and appearance, have no serious home ties to prevent them doing so . . . And the young men who jingled tin boxes round the football gates yesterday begging the money 'to buy a gun' are not representative of the true spirit of Irishmen and more particularly Young Ireland.

The authorities, the author concluded, were to blame for much of this as accounts of 'the gallant and heroic deeds of Irish battalions at the front' had been censored in the press and had not been able to inspire the young. The author further commented that if such reports had been read and discussed at the firesides, reading rooms and workmen's clubs, then such heroics would be commended with as much enthusiasm as the game's score. 'The question then is – how can the enthusiasm caused yesterday by the conduct of thirty footballers be evoked towards the filling of the vacancies in the Irish brigade?'[86]

In Kerry, some recruiters tapped into the local popularity of Gaelic games to encourage enlistment.[87] During the summer of

1915, as part of a fresh enlistment drive in Kerry, the Band of the Munster Fusiliers toured the major towns of the county holding recruitment rallies. In June, they held a large meeting in Tralee. Thomas O'Donnell addressed the rally and stated that so far the town had sent 1,200 men to the front. Afterwards, he introduced Captain Laurence Roche of Limerick to the assembled crowd.[88] Roche appealed to the men of Kerry as someone who had been a member of the GAA for the past twenty-eight years and who had been present at the birth of the association:

> Since it was started at Thurles he had played it . . . And since the days of the Laune Rangers, the Ballyduff hurlers and later on when Mitchels beat the doughty champions of Kildare, he had often heard the cry 'Up Kerry' – it had been ringing in his ears for years. He trusted in God that he would hear in the ranks of the Royal Munsters, not alone the cry 'Up Kerry' but 'Up Ireland and the Irish Brigade' (cheers).

He expressed hope that the war cry 'Up Kerry' would be heard in the trenches 'when German barbarism would be dead and buried forever' and he hoped to hear it 'when they made the last attack on the Germans' goal'.[89] Such appeals to the heart of GAA followers in Kerry and elsewhere undoubtedly had some effect. That November the *Sentinel* reported the death of James Rossiter, a solider with the Irish Guards. Before he enlisted, he was an active member of the GAA in Wexford and was the brilliant forward on the team that lost to Kerry in the 1913 and 1914 finals. In a letter home before his death, he wrote that he felt more nervous before those finals than he did before attacking German lines. In letters from the front published in the local press, the national heroics of the Kerry team were commonly used as a metaphor. One such letter came from Private John O'Sullivan and Corporal J. Nagle, soldiers of the 2nd Royal Munster Fusiliers and natives of Killarney. The men requested that copies of the local Kerry papers be sent out to them as there were currently thirteen Killarney men serving in the battalion who were anxious to keep in touch with the news at home. They concluded the letter: 'As the Kerry team have defended the honour of the old Kingdom in the All-Ireland contest, so we too are doing our utmost to defend the honour of our land.'[90]

In Ireland and across the British Empire, the collective enlistment of groups of men attached to various sports clubs was a common phenomenon.[91] Yet the evidence suggests that recruitment among GAA members remained the exception rather than the rule. An argument to the contrary remains unlikely until a nationwide study of GAA enlistment can be conducted. Certainly in Kerry there is a clear lack of evidence for any level of enlistment by Kerry GAA members in the First World War. Johnny Mahony of Dr Crokes and the Kerry senior football team is one exception. He appeared alongside Dick Fitzgerald in many of the photographs in Fitzgerald's *How to Play Gaelic Football*, demonstrating the skills that were being described. In 1915, he emigrated to America and joined the US Army when it entered the war before returning home and captaining Kerry in the 1923 Munster championship.[92]

Given its support for the Sinn Féin policy of anti-recruitment in the years leading up to the First World War and the retention of the ban on military personal becoming members, it is hardly surprising that the GAA as an organisation was hostile to army enlistment during the war.[93] Reporting on the Munster final in Tralee in October 1914, *The Kerryman* mused:

> Recruiting sergeants and their sympathisers must have looked with envy and longing on the fine body of Irishmen who were assembled in the field. They undoubtedly would have made good food for powder but the rules and principles of the GAA have a different object than supplying recruits for [Lord] Kitchener's Army. They stand as form the beginning for a united Ireland and they have never yet gone back on their early teachings.[94]

Commenting on the poor recruitment figures in March 1915, the RIC reported that the rules of the GAA must militate against recruiting, 'and they appear to be designed with the intention of, as far as possible, preventing intercourse between members of the society and forces of the Crown'. These rules 'deter many young men enlisting in Kitchener's army'.[95] Indeed, the potential impact the GAA's ban had on recruiting was raised in the House of Commons in April 1915. Sir Frederick Banbury MP asked the Under-Secretary for War, Harold Tennant, whether he was aware that the rules of the GAA excluded from its membership soldiers and sailors, as well as pensioners of both. He further enquired if the maintenance of this rule by an association 'claiming to be one of the largest national organisations in Ireland operated against the enlistment of members of the Gaelic Athletic clubs'. In response, Tennant stated that it was difficult to judge the effect on recruitment but at present no action was being contemplated by his office, to which an Irish Party MP asked if the honourable gentlemen were aware that 'the majority of reserve men and recruits who have joined in Ireland have been members of the Association'. Tennant replied that his office had little information on the GAA and was unaware of the claim that the majority of recruits were from the association.[96]

For the most part, the first two years of the war had relatively little impact on the national or local GAA and its affairs. Its initial outbreak led to the government outlawing railway usage for anything but vital services and for some weeks this caused widespread disruption to local and national fixtures. At the end of August 1914, the Central Council sent a deputation to meet with the heads of railway departments with a view to reinstating the running of trains for Gaelic matches as quickly as possible. Although the provision was relaxed, some curtailments were kept in place. In 1915, the Munster GAA Council reported a £600 fall in income on account of the lack of train facilities due to the war. Also, British troops had occupied the Cork Athletic Grounds and Limerick's Markets Field, which caused a further loss of revenue.[97]

Between the turn of the century and the outbreak of the First World War, the association in Kerry was actively shaped by the broader nationalist movement that was emerging. Its officials and rank-and-file members took an active and often prominent role in the emerging political movements such as the Sinn Féin party and the Irish Volunteers. In turn, the association helped to shape those movements both nationally and at a local level in Kerry. The prominence of many local county and club officials within the higher echelons of the Kerry Gaelic League, Sinn Féin and Irish

Volunteers certainly impacted on the spread and support for those organisations among the GAA's membership. As 1916 approached, many within the Kerry GAA had been brought in contact with the increasingly radical and political nationalism emerging from these cultural and political organisations. It is evident from the anti-enlistment campaigns orchestrated by the association at this time that such militant sentiment was increasing among its grass-roots membership. In Kerry, this is further supported by the total lack of evidence for British Army recruitment during the war. However, it would be wrong to suggest that by now the GAA counted itself as a home for republican, physical-force nationalism. On the contrary, the majority of the GAA's membership in Kerry and elsewhere largely followed the political views of wider Catholic, nationalist Ireland. Support for Redmond and his parliamentary party remained strong, though admittedly this support did not stretch to GAA members actively enlisting in great numbers. Yet in this they merely replicated the poor recruitment figures recorded among young men throughout rural Ireland.

6
WAR AND PEACE, 1916—1923

We want our men to train and be physically strong [so that]
when the time comes the hurlers will cast away the camán for
the steel that will drive the Saxon from our land.

Future GAA president Dan McCarthy, *Wicklow People*, 21 January 1911

In January 1916, Ireland presented a peaceful appearance. RIC
reports noted the 'settled and satisfactory' general condition of
the island.[1] Indeed, thanks to the war, rural Ireland was experiencing
an unprecedented economic boom, with acute labour shortages
becoming common. Doubts over the question of Ulster's standing
if Home Rule was granted remained, and war weariness over the
continuing conflict in Europe was becoming evident. Despite the
best efforts of the IPP, the National Volunteers' influence was
already waning, while the Irish Volunteers remained a relatively
small splinter organisation. In the circumstances, the vast majority
of Irish nationalists seemed content to wait for an end to the war
and hoped for a rapid implementation of Home Rule once peace
was concluded. Nationally, the GAA carried on as best it could.
Volunteer involvement and wartime restrictions on rail travel
hampered its effectiveness in many counties but on the whole the
association seemed relatively untouched by the impact of the
Great War.

Within a few months, this illusion of peace was shattered as
the most serious revolt to British rule in Ireland since 1798 erupted
in O'Connell Street, Dublin and ultimately led to a political
revolution that lasted into the 1920s. The GAA, through its
members and by association, found itself dragged into the heart
of this maelstrom. The years after 1916 witnessed the political
radicalisation of many members of Irish society, a process that

gave birth to the Irish Revolution and the subsequent establishment of the Irish Free State. At both a national and local level GAA members played a significant role in the unfolding conflict. All the while, the association struggled to operate in a time of war and could not but be impacted by the broader political reality. In areas such as Kerry, the brutality of the Civil War had lasting effects on the association, while its aftermath laid the foundation for perhaps the most successful era in the history of the Kerry GAA.

The Road to Easter: the Kerry GAA and the 1916 Rising

From the start, leading members of the GAA in Kerry had an active input into the planning of the 1916 rebellion. After the Volunteer split, the IRB's influence within the anti-Redmond faction continued to grow. Three prominent IRB members secured vital posts within the Irish Volunteers' central executive.[2] Among them was Patrick Pearse, who was appointed Director of Military Organisation. Pearse had become convinced that Irish nationalism needed a new cult of dead martyrs to prompt it into a full-scale war of independence against a British government distracted by the Great War. In September 1915, the IRB set up a Military Council to plan a rebellion in Ireland against British rule. Meanwhile, Roger Casement, one of the founders of the Volunteers, had been sent to Germany to enlist its support if Ireland declared its independence.[3]

As the Military Council continued to make preparations for a national rising they became increasingly fearful that their intentions would be uncovered by British intelligence. They therefore kept their plans for revolt so secret that even the IRB's ruling Supreme Council was unaware of them.[4] Likewise, the Military Council gave those provincial leaders of the Irish Volunteers in favour of rebellion only a general notion of what their role would be. Kerry would play a vital role in the rebellion. It was arranged that an arms shipment, secured from the German government, would be landed there in the days before the outbreak, to be distributed nationally by the local Kerry Volunteers.

As Kerry was a lynchpin in the success of the venture, close links were established with the Volunteers' leadership there, many of whom were local GAA officials. By 1914, Austin Stack, the

Austin Stack in Volunteer uniform. By November 1915, Stack
had been appointed head of both the IRB and Irish Volunteers
in Kerry. *(Courtesy of Seamus O'Reilly)*

Kerry GAA chairman, had become the acknowledged head of the
IRB in the county. That organisation acted as a kind of inner circle
within the Kerry Volunteers.[5] In October 1915, Pearse visited
Tralee to appoint Stack formally as brigadier in the Irish Volunteers.
This placed control of the Kerry Volunteers under his direct
leadership. At this time Pearse first informed Stack of the IRB's

plans for revolt. Members of the GAA, particularly in Kerry, played a significant role in the IRB's preparations for the Easter 1916 Rising, an insurrection that provided the catalyst for the Irish Revolution. Shortly after Stack's meeting with Pearse he arranged for the purchase and transport of a large consignment of weapons for the Kerry Volunteers. Stack used the occasion of the upcoming All-Ireland final between Kerry and Wexford on 7 November 1915 as cover for this operation. Tadhg Kennedy, a lieutenant in the Tralee Volunteers and a member of the Kerry County Board, was dispatched by train on the Saturday of the final. He was in charge of a group of Volunteers ostensibly travelling as supporters to the match.

The morning after the final, Kennedy and his men organised two cars to take them from their hotel to the residence of Kerry native The O'Rahilly at 40 Herbert Park, Dublin. O'Rahilly, who had since become the Irish Volunteers Director of Arms, was to meet Kennedy's men there to hand over the weapons. However, as Kennedy recounted, one of their number, Tadhg Horgan, a painter from Killarney, had spent much of the Sunday night drowning his sorrows over Kerry's defeat. He emerged early the next morning feeling the effects of the previous night and proceeded to make a racket, breaking one of the car windows as he stumbled into it. Kennedy, deciding he would be of little use in the operation, bundled him into the back of the car and drove off for Herbert Park. Being in such a state, Horgan was ordered to stay behind and keep watch over both cars as his companions entered the house to secure the guns. When the Volunteers emerged they were stunned to find that one of the cars, and Horgan, had disappeared. Kennedy managed to load all the weapons into the remaining car and drove to Kingsbridge station, where the arms were smuggled aboard the returning supporters' train to Tralee that evening. Horgan subsequently resurfaced in Killarney several days later.[6] The weapons were distributed among the Volunteers in Kerry and provided the bulk of their armament during Easter week 1916. Michael Spillane, a member of the Killarney Volunteers, noted that during Easter week his company was armed with fifty-two rifles, ten shotguns and fifteen revolvers, all purchased from The O'Rahilly in November.[7]

On a national level, the growing connection between some of the leadership of the GAA and the Irish Volunteers was apparent when on the night of that All-Ireland final an informal conference between Volunteer leaders and the GAA's Central Council took place. The RIC was in no doubt that the Irish Volunteers were fully supported by extremists within the GAA and that many of the association's members were enlisting in the organisation.[8] However, it is difficult to say how much this cross-membership between the GAA and the Irish Volunteers was an indication of the former's support for physical-force nationalism. It is as likely that many GAA members enrolled in the Volunteers simply to protect themselves from the ever-increasing prospect of British Army conscription. Yet Sir Morgan O'Connell, the senior magistrate in Kerry, had little doubt as to what the GAA in the county increasingly represented. In a letter to *The Irish Times*, he complained that at a recent British Army recruitment meeting in Killarney a 'Sinn Féin' mob, headed by a band and a member of the town's Rural District Council (RDC), marched past the assembly booing and yelling. In response, James O'Shea, chairman of the Killarney RDC and the accused leader, stated the 'mob' was in fact a team of Tralee footballers on their way to a match in the town.[9] At a Gaelic football match in Farranfore in January 1916, 113 Irish Volunteers, eighty-two of whom were armed, attended and managed to raise £16 for the purchase of arms.[10] This again illustrates the growing relationship between the two organisations in Kerry in the prelude to the rebellion.

On 26 February 1916, Pearse visited Tralee and on the following day he reviewed a force of 250 local Volunteers.[11] That night Pearse revealed to Stack the date and general plan for the 1916 Rising. A large German arms consignment would be brought ashore at Fenit harbour from a German ship, the *Aud*, which would arrive in Tralee Bay during the Easter weekend. Once the arms were onshore they would be distributed among the Volunteers in Kerry, Clare, Cork and Limerick. Meanwhile, the Tralee GPO, railway station and military barracks would be seized by the local Kerry Volunteers in order to control communications in the county and disarm the local RIC and military. Posters announcing the proclamation of an Irish Republic would be posted throughout the county to inform the people. The Kerry Volunteers would then link up with their colleagues in Cork, Limerick, Galway and Clare and hold positions in a line running roughly down the Shannon through Limerick, east Kerry and onto Macroom in Cork.[12] In cooperation with Volunteers in Leinster, they were then to devote themselves to disrupting communications and preventing the movement of British reinforcements from the country into Dublin.

However, this general plan was mere 'fantasy'. The Volunteers lacked the heavy weapons to enable them to tie down British forces.[13] Stack was charged with formulating the plan to land the German weapons and distribute them across Munster. He effectively used his local GAA connections to assist him. About three weeks before the Rising he asked Patrick O'Shea of the Castlegregory Volunteers and an All-Ireland winner with the Kerry team to provide a trusted harbour pilot with whom to rendezvous and guide the *Aud* into Tralee Bay when it appeared off the Kerry coast.[14] Around this time he also informed his adjutant, Patrick Cahill, a member of the Tralee Mitchels who had played with Kerry in 1912, that the Rising was due to begin on Easter Sunday. In keeping with the obsession for secrecy among its planners, however, Stack failed to give Cahill any detailed plans of what was expected of the Kerry Volunteers once the rebellion broke out. Likewise, the majority of the other officers in the Kerry Volunteers had little knowledge of the arrangements. On 11 April, Stack visited the Military Council in Dublin and informed them of his plans to land the arms, which were subsequently approved.[15]

Though there was significant involvement by members of the Kerry GAA in the planning of the Rising, it must be stated that the vast majority of GAA members nationally and locally had little idea what was being planned. Even those members who were part of the Irish Volunteers' rank and file had little notion of what their leadership in the Military Council were undertaking. Instead, the months before the Rising saw the Kerry GAA conducting its business as best it could despite the wartime conditions. The 1914 Kerry county championship was not completed until January 1916 when Dr Crokes defeated Mitchels in the final. The Kerry footballers competed in that year's Wolfe Tone Cup and qualified for its semi-final in February. In late March, Kerry played Galway in the junior All-Ireland semi-final in a match that was abandoned due to heavy snow. Harry Boland, who was prominent in the fighting in the GPO less than a month later, refereed the game.[16]

Indeed, many within the GAA in Kerry were dismayed by the apathy that had enveloped its county board. In March, *The Kerryman* stated that football was effectively dead in Kerry. Due to the lack of interest from local GAA officials, the senior and junior teams, about to compete in inter-county action, were left to their own fate. The paper complained that in the past year any county board meeting held had been sparsely attended. Two days before the outbreak of the Rising it was reported that another meeting had fallen through owing to a lack of a quorum, with only three members attending. Its 'Gaelic Notes' contributor asked: '[H]ow long are the Gaels of the country going to stand this kind of humbug; in my humble opinion they have stood it too long.' In the same paper, 'Ciarraidhe', writing an article entitled 'The GAA in Kerry', bemoaned the fact that only one game had been played in the county championship in the past year. Furthermore, there were only two teams presently active in the county, Tralee Mitchels and Dr Crokes. The rest had fallen away due to the lethargy of the board.[17] There is little doubt that much of this apathy was due to the preoccupation given to Volunteer activity by Stack and other prominent board officials.

However, nationally the GAA's Annual Congress was held as normal in City Hall, Dublin on Easter Saturday.[18] The majority of delegates were unaware of what would erupt on the city's streets over the coming days.[19] It was the following Monday evening before most members realised what was transpiring. On his way home to Kilkenny that evening, the GAA's president, James Nowlan, was arrested for his role in the Sinn Féin movement, which the authorities now believed was rebelling against them. Like the general Irish public, the 1916 uprising had caught the GAA completely by surprise.

The Rising would prove a failure in military terms and its repercussions would have serious consequences for the association in Kerry. The Military Council's plans for the revolt began to fall apart almost as soon as they had been committed to action. On 6 April, the Military Council informed Roger Casement in Germany that the Rising was to take place on Easter Sunday and that the arms should be landed by then. By this time, Casement had become convinced that the Rising was doomed to failure.[20] He resolved to return to Ireland to stop the revolt before it ended in slaughter.[21] On the evening of Thursday 20 April, the arms shipment arrived in Tralee Bay on board the *Aud*. The Military Council had not expected the arms to arrive until the morning of Easter Sunday, 23 April and so the *Aud* found itself in Tralee Bay with no one among the Volunteers aware of its arrival. On Friday 21 April, the vessel was intercepted by British warships whose curiosity was aroused by its strange actions.[22] To avoid capture, its captain scuttled the ship and both it and the arms were sunk.[23] Stack and the leaders of the Kerry Volunteers remained blissfully unaware of all this.

On the Friday morning, Roger Casement, Robert Monteith, an ex-British officer and IRB member who had been sent to Germany to aid Casement, and Julian Bailey, an Irish prisoner of war who had joined up with Casement in Germany, landed from a U-boat on Banna Strand in north Kerry. Feeling ill, Casement remained in hiding near the strand as Monteith and Bailey headed to Tralee to contact the local Volunteers. From Monteith, Stack learned that the German arms shipment was nowhere near what had been promised. While they talked, the local RIC, alerted by British intelligence of the plan to land weapons in Kerry, conducted a massive police search of the Banna area.[24] Casement was discovered, arrested and charged with attempting to smuggle weapons into the county. He was brought to Tralee before being transferred to Dublin under heavy guard.[25] On hearing this, Stack called a meeting of the Tralee Volunteers and informed them of the IRB's plan for the Rising. Stack told them that he had orders that no trouble should occur in Tralee before the arms were landed. As a result, he decided against attempting to rescue Casement. After the meeting, Stack told Cahill that he would visit Tralee Barracks. Upon entering he was immediately arrested and found to have a number of incriminating documents on his person.[26] Within half an hour, Stack seems to have divulged in full the plan for the arms landing in Fenit.

In Dublin, Eoin MacNeill, the head of the Irish Volunteers, had been advised of the Military Council's plan for the Rising and had given it his broad support.[27] Yet on the evening of Easter Saturday, hours before the Rising was to be declared, MacNeill learned that the *Aud* had been sunk. Convinced the Rising was doomed, he issued orders countermanding any Volunteer activity arranged to take place the next day. By the Saturday morning, a large military force was drafted into Tralee to patrol its streets.[23] Despite being greatly outnumbered, the local Volunteers made ready with plans to march to Fenit, where they still expected to find the *Aud* in wait. Yet at around 11 a.m. on Easter Sunday a messenger arrived from Limerick informing the Kerry Volunteers that MacNeill had called off the Rising.[29] The Volunteers, who that morning had assembled, now disbanded and returned home, ending the county's involvement with the insurrection. Though some leading figures in the Kerry GAA, such as Stack, O'Shea and Cahill, had been intimately involved in the plans for the Rising, the overwhelming majority of the GAA membership in the county, many of whom were also members of the Volunteers, had no idea of their plans and took no part in the aborted arms landing.

Despite MacNeill's countermanding orders, the Military Council met on Easter Sunday morning and decided to press ahead with their plans for revolt the following day. MacNeill's intervention ensured there would be no countrywide rebellion, and once the *Aud* and its arms were scuttled there was no military justification for proceeding with the insurrection. It was clear by then that the Military Council was more anxious for a Rising to take place than for it to be successful.[30] On Monday 24 April 1916, Volunteer forces under Pearse's command seized control of the GPO and several other buildings in central Dublin and proclaimed an Irish Republic. Hopelessly outnumbered, the Volunteers managed to hold out for several days before finally surrendering on 28 April. In Kerry, as in much of the country, little information was forthcoming and the week passed off peacefully.[31] The Rising came as a huge shock to public opinion in Ireland. In all, some 450 people were killed and 2,614 wounded.[32] Among the dead was The O'Rahilly, killed on Moore Street near the GPO.[33]

Like the greater Irish public, the membership of the GAA was caught off-guard by the Rising. Nevertheless, as we have seen, many of its members played a prominent role in its build-up and implementation. One of the leaders of the rebel forces in Dublin was Thomas Ashe, the former Lispole team captain and secretary who had represented the club at Kerry's Annual GAA Convention. Ashe had now become a major figure in the Dublin IRB and Irish Volunteers. On Easter Monday, Pearse instructed him to disrupt and destroy enemy communications in north Dublin. With a force of sixty men, Ashe commanded one of the most successful actions of Easter week. On Friday 28 April, he attacked a large RIC force of fifty men in Ashbourne, County Meath, killing ten officers, wounding a further eighteen and capturing the rest with the loss of only two Volunteers.[34] He surrendered to the British the next day on being informed that Pearse had agreed to the unconditional surrender of rebel forces in Dublin. In all, five of the fifteen men executed for their part in the 1916 Rising had GAA connections.[35] Other prominent rebels captured, such as Stack, Harry Boland, Michael Collins, J.J. Walsh and Ashe, had been prominent local and national administrators within the organisation. Some 300 members of the Dublin GAA took an active part in the Easter Rising. There is evidence of a large degree of participation by individual Dublin GAA clubs, with sixty-nine members of the St Laurence O'Toole Gaelic football club alone taking part in the fighting.[36] In Galway, 500 Volunteers assembled on Easter Monday and carried out some limited attacks on local police barracks. The majority of these men were hurlers and members of local GAA clubs.[37] Meanwhile, in Wexford, Volunteers led by prominent local GAA men Sean Etchingham and Seamus Doyle used the pretext of an Easter Sunday GAA match in Wexford Park to cover their turnout for the Rising.[38] They managed to advance upon and hold Enniscorthy for several days before surrendering.

Nevertheless, most of these prominent GAA rebels were radical nationalists, in the main IRB men, long committed to the overthrow of British rule in Ireland. They neither represented nor reflected the political views of the national membership of the GAA in 1916. Yet despite the apparent contradiction, the overlap between radical nationalists and GAA members is perhaps easy to explain. Because of their political outlook, men such as Ashe would naturally have joined any movement with nationalist credentials, either to cement their own identity or to use as cover for recruitment into the IRB.[39] Thus in addition to attaining office in the GAA, such men were just as likely to be fervent supporters of bodies such as the Gaelic League. Historically, many prominent officials within the association were given to delivering pronouncements that seemed to support a brand of physical-force nationalism and the impression given (and often intended) was that the speaker's views were also those of the GAA.[40] The tenor of such declarations could only serve to attract men of the physical-force persuasion into the association and those advocates often became proportionately more prominent in the affairs of the GAA than, for example, the moderate constitutional nationalist supporters of the Irish Parliamentary Party.

The Radicalisation of the GAA, 1916–1919

In the immediate aftermath of the Rising, public opinion across Ireland was set firmly against the rebels. Likewise, the vast majority within the membership of the GAA censured their actions. The revolt was seen by many as an attack on democratic Irish opinion and indeed on the Irish themselves. At High Mass in Killarney, following the surrender, the Bishop of Kerry denounced the actions of the rebel leaders. He called on young men in the Irish Volunteers to follow the example of their leader Eoin MacNeill and not allow themselves on any account 'to be drawn into illegal courses by evil minded men affected by Socialistic and Revolutionary doctrines'.[41] The monthly meeting of Tralee UDC passed a resolution stating that its members

> . . . deplore with horror the outbreak in Dublin which brings the blush of shame to every honest Irishman. We have every confidence in John Redmond and the Irish Parliamentary Party by constitutional means bringing Ireland into the full possession of her rights.

A meeting of Kerry County Council also condemned 'the criminal folly in Dublin'.[42]

Yet the months after the Rising saw the GAA and its members becoming increasingly politically radicalised. This radicalisation was in part due to the response of the British authorities to the association in the aftermath of the revolt. This response had serious repercussions for the sporting activity of the organisation in Kerry. Martial law was proclaimed across the country and the holding of matches or sporting tournaments was strictly prohibited. As a result, Gaelic games were suspended, an early victim being the first-round Munster championship clash between Tipperary and Kerry due to have been played in Cork on 30 April.[43] Some 3,400 men across Ireland were arrested and deported in the days following the Rising for their supposed involvement with the rebellion. The vast majority of these were known or suspected Volunteers or IRB members but many of the young men taken had little or no involvement with the planning or execution of the Rising. Because of the close connection between some leading members of the GAA and the Irish Volunteers, those targeted for arrest included hundreds of ordinary members of the association. On 9 May 1916, large-scale arrests of known Volunteers were conducted in Kerry. The *Sentinel* and *Kerryman* carried lists of those detained. Among them were a significant number of local GAA officials and county players such as Michael Griffin, Paddy Cahill, Dick Fitzgerald, D.J. Griffin of Castlemaine, Harry Spring of Firies, Patrick Launders of Listowel, William Mullins of Tralee, M. Connell of the Castlegregory GAA and J.F. O'Shea, the Portmagee captain.[44] Many found themselves deported to special internment camps such as Frongoch in north Wales. There were fifty-seven Kerry men held in this camp, fifteen of whom were from Tralee.[45] However, far from hindering the Volunteers or the IRB, this policy of mass internment only succeeded in increasing the strength of both organisations. The detention of so many young men, many with little previous involvement in these organisations, brought them into contact with the emerging revolutionary political doctrine. Due to their shared incarceration, many GAA members also became politically radicalised. Internment proved an excellent training camp for the Volunteers. It allowed officers to subject their men to proper military drill. The realities of incarceration also turned them into a mentally tougher force. As Colonel Jeremiah O'Connell observed, '[T]he man who was released from Frongoch at Xmas 1916 was a professional soldier – quite another man from the enthusiastic nationalist who turned out in Easter week.'[46] William Mullins, an internee and footballer with the Tralee Mitchels, concurred:

> I am fully convinced that Frongoch made our whole organisation into what it eventually reached. The comradeship that developed in Frongoch and the knowledge we got of each other from different parts of the country, the military aspect of things and being brought into close contact with men whom we used only hear about previous to that was a binding force in the future. John Bull made an awful blunder when he put us all together there.[47]

Due to the numbers of Gaelic players interned in the camp, Gaelic football contests were arranged to keep up the discipline, fitness and morale among prisoners. Dick Fitzgerald and Michael Collins, a former member of the London GAA who had fought in the GPO, organised a series of GAA tournaments. Two matches were played daily and a league competition was also organised among four teams, with each competing in six games. The teams were called after the leaders of the Rising. The fourth team, nicknamed 'The Leprechauns' due to the small stature of their players, was coached by Dick Fitzgerald and actually won the competition.[48] Inter-county contests were also arranged and the main pitch in Frongoch was renamed Croke Park. In the final of one tournament, the Kerry and Louth internee teams renewed their county rivalries, with Kerry winning the consequent match by a point.[49] If Frongoch became a school of revolution, it is significant that Gaelic games were predominant. The concentration on Gaelic games was intended as a symbolic and deliberate statement 'of the prisoners' commitment to Irish nationalism and a rejection of Britain'.[50]

The GAA quickly came to the public attention of the British authorities in their attempts to discover the cause of the rebellion. In May, a Royal Commission on the Rising was set up by Sir Matthew Nathan, the under-secretary to Dublin Castle. Nathan laid the blame for the rebellion at the feet of the Irish Volunteers and asserted that their entire leadership consisted of separatists drawn mainly from four anti-British bodies of which the GAA was one.[51] The Castle's Director of Intelligence repeated this allegation, stating that the Irish Volunteers had practically full control over the association and the Gaelic League. It is easy to understand why a government inquiry would have targeted the association as an active participant in the rebellion. Many leading figures in its central and provincial councils were men of extreme nationalist views. Men such as Stack, Boland and J.J. Walsh, Cork's GAA president, had been arrested and sentenced for their role in the Rising. As we have seen, the GAA, since its inception in November 1884, had been actively identified as a semi-seditious body by British authorities. Given the continued IRB element within the GAA's higher echelons, it was only natural that in the political climate following the Rising the authorities would investigate the role of the association in connection with the rebellion.

Yet as a consequence of the government's internment of the more extreme nationalists within the association, it was the moderates within the Central Council who were left to deal with the charges levelled by the commission. At a special meeting of the Central Council on 28 May the GAA drew up and issued a press statement vehemently denying the accusations of Nathan's inquiry. In the statement, the GAA reaffirmed it was a strictly non-political organisation and protested strongly at the misrepresentation of its aims and objectives by the Royal Commission. In the political climate of the time, it was obvious that the GAA wished to disassociate itself as much as possible from the Rising to avoid any further government crackdown towards it or its members. The statement was devoid of any sympathy for the rebels or their deaths. The GAA, like every other major nationalist body in Ireland, showed no immediate empathy with those who took part in the rebellion, or their cause.[52] Indeed, far from discussing the fallout from the Rising, the Central Council meeting had been convened to discuss the British government's attempts to impose an entertainment tax on Gaelic events to help fund its war effort. The IPP did not consider the GAA as having played any role in the rebellion. In parliament, the Irish MP Thomas Lundson called on the Prime Minister to compel the military authorities in Ireland to let GAA games resume in those parts of the country unaffected by the Rising in Dublin. A proposed meeting of the Munster Council that Sunday in Limerick was stopped by the city's police, who served notice that it was not to take place.[53] However, the following week the *Sentinel* reported that restrictions on GAA activity had at last been withdrawn in Kerry and elsewhere and the county's footballers and hurlers were again at liberty to play. Yet some within the Kerry GAA were proud that the authorities had implicated the association, an act that seemed to reaffirm its nationalist credentials. After an absence of several years, the former Kerry county secretary Maurice Moynihan began once again to write for the *Sentinel*. Moynihan noted that any national organisation in Ireland worthy of its name had been drawn into the Nathan Inquiry and it would 'be most uncomplimentary to the Gaelic Association if it were omitted'.[54]

Between July and August 1916, the majority of the internees were released. By now, Irish public opinion had begun to turn against the British establishment. The Irish public was appalled by the executions of the rebel leaders. The trial and public hanging of Roger Casement in London also struck a powerful chord, particularly in Kerry. A growing cult of martyrdom emerged around the executed leaders, with frequent commemorative Masses being held in their memory.[55] This public reaction was influenced by the mass arrests and internments without trial, as well as the continued imposition of martial law and the undiminished fear that Irishmen would soon be forced into conscription for the British Army.[56] The outcome was that the government's actions had failed to destroy the Irish Volunteers or the IRB as effective organisations, merely driving both underground. As early as June the RIC was reporting a shift in nationalist opinion in Ireland towards empathy with the rebels.[57]

Once restrictions on Gaelic events were lifted, GAA matches in areas like Kerry provided some of the earliest instances for this growing surge of sympathy with the rebels. By September, the authorities were noting that '[A] discontented and rebellious spirit is widespread and though to a great extent suppressed, it frequently comes to the surface at Gaelic Athletic Association tournaments when large numbers of young men of military age are assembled together'. The RIC believed Sinn Féin were exploiting such GAA matches to organise the movement. The Kerry county inspector observed:

> As practically all members of the GAA are Sinn Féiners, I believe [their] matches are held more for the spread of sedition than for sport. If teams remain in any place after darkness there is always a certain amount of disorderly conduct by shouts of 'Up Sinn Féin', 'Up Germany', etc. The wearing of Sinn Féin badges is still very much in evidence and there is no sign as yet of any decline in the sympathy for Sinn Féin.[58]

With the lifting of martial law, the association in Kerry tried to resume activity. In early July, though still missing many prominent players including their captain Dick Fitzgerald, Kerry played Tipperary in a rearranged Munster championship match in Cork, beating their footballers 2-2 to 0-1. The following week the Munster Council sat for the first time since the Rising. They had received a letter from the Kerry Board stating it had decided to withdraw all its teams from the Munster competitions. Despite this, the Kerry senior hurlers and junior footballers met their Tipperary counterparts as arranged the following Sunday, with Kerry losing the hurling but winning the football. At a subsequent meeting of the county board, its treasurer, Con Clifford, explained why they had withdrawn. He stated the board was in a dire financial position and as a consequence Kerry had decided to remove its teams from national competition in order that they may play matches for their own board's benefit within the county.[59]

Despite this, the Kerry Board decided it would fulfil its commitment in the Wolfe Tone tournament that August. Just a few days after his release from prison, Dick Fitzgerald lined out for a cobbled-together senior Kerry side which duly lost the semi-final in Ennis to Mayo. Fitzgerald did not enjoy his freedom long as both he and M.J. Moriarty, another footballer from Dingle, were rearrested on 22 September and sent back to Frongoch. There was even a rather incredible rumour around Kerry that the arrests had been engineered by other Kerry internees in the camp in order to guarantee their success in the football competition there. The county board organised its Annual Convention in early August 1916, with P.J. O'Connell being elected chairman. The attendants followed the Central Council's lead and officially condemned Nathan's findings that the GAA was responsible for the Rising.[60] At the end of that month, Kerry defeated Westmeath in the delayed 1915 junior football final in Athlone.

In the months following the rebellion, the British authorities conducted a campaign of harassment towards the GAA as an organisation on both a local and national level. The government was still determined to impose its proposed entertainment tax on Gaelic events. In July, the GAA advised all county boards to resist any local efforts to levy the tax.[61] The government responded by stating it would exempt the association from the tax if the GAA removed its ban on foreign games and British military personnel and police becoming members, a proposition which was unanimously rejected by the Central Council. In September, the Kerry Board fixed the opening round of matches for the county's 1916 championship for Listowel. However, during these matches the town's head constable and six other uniformed RIC officers demanded entrance to the ground. Despite having no tickets, they reasserted their right under the government's imposed Defence of the Realm Act to enter the grounds. To avoid any trouble, members of the county board present consulted and allowed them to enter.[62] Following the incident, the Kerry GAA sent a letter to the Central Council requesting their advice should such a situation arise again. At a subsequent meeting, the association decided that a deputation led by its secretary Luke O'Toole would wait on the RIC's inspector general and ascertain from him under what statute the police claimed they had the right to attend football and hurling matches at enclosed venues without paying the ordinary charges for admission. They also sent a letter back to the Kerry Board reiterating that all police officers would be obliged to pay entrance fees into GAA events regardless of their demands.[63] The arrest and harassment of the association's members by the authorities had begun to harden many members' views of the British government. The rise of the Sinn Féin party between 1917 and 1918 would provide the catalyst for the political radicalisation of Irish society at large and with it the Kerry GAA.

The Rising had been greeted with disbelief and anger by the Irish people. The membership of the association in Kerry had overwhelmingly shared these sentiments. However, the brutal repression by the authorities swiftly changed public perception and generated a renewed hatred of British rule in Ireland. With popular opinion moving against Redmond's Irish Party and its links with the British government, Sinn Féin was in a unique position to capitalise on the new national mood. Though Arthur Griffith's organisation had no involvement with the Rising, the Home Rule press and British government succeeded in investing his Sinn Féin party with a role of authority in Irish nationalism it had never achieved by itself by simply branding all rebels as 'Sinn Féiners'. Moderates like Griffith thus had an opportunity to exploit this new-found, if misplaced, fame for the small organisation.[64] The incredible growth and popularity of Sinn Féin in the months and years after the Rising has to be seen in light of its alternative, the Irish Party. With Home Rule already on the statute books, the party could offer the Irish people little except to wait until the European war finally ended and hope that Home Rule would be enacted shortly afterwards.[65] Yet by the autumn of 1916, the inspector general of the RIC was reporting the widespread belief among the Irish population 'that one week of physical force did more for the cause of Ireland than a quarter of a century of constitutional agitation'. The increasing reality for many was that political freedom from Britain could be achieved quicker by adopting the Sinn Féin policy of defiance rather than the old Irish Party policy of cooperation.[66]

The Sinn Féin movement grew rapidly between late 1916 and 1917, though for much of this time it represented more of a popular mass movement than a coherent political party. It tried to gain as much publicity as possible while whipping up hatred of Britain by exploiting its clumsy errors of government and at the same time discrediting the Irish Party. In the process of supplanting the Irish Party, Sinn Féin readily took over the local organisational model the former had devised.[67] In 1917, Sinn Féin secured three by-election victories in Roscommon, Longford and East Clare. Across Ireland, local government bodies, such as the Killarney RDC, passed resolutions calling on Irish Party MPs 'to resign their seats in the House of Commons as they no longer represent the people of Ireland'.[68] In June 1917, the British government bowed to pressure and commuted the sentences of all those arrested after the Rising. Austin Stack and Thomas Ashe were given a hero's welcome when they returned to Kerry.[69]

Thomas Ashe, the former Lispole captain and representative of the Kerry County Board, was one of only two leaders in the 1916 Rising to be spared execution. His arrest and death while on hunger strike in 1917 inflamed Irish public opinion and led to a huge surge in membership for the Sinn Féin party. *(Courtesy of the National Library of Ireland)*

In the weeks that followed, Stack and Ashe toured Kerry and the rest of Ireland, appearing at public meetings and eulogising the Sinn Féin message. At one such meeting in Tralee, Stack implored the town's young men to re-form the Volunteers there and make it a powerful force again. Such appeals were the beginning of an attempt within Irish nationalism to unite the Irish Volunteers under the Sinn Féin banner. At the party's Ard Fheis in October 1917, Éamon de Valera, one of the sole surviving leaders of the 1916 Rising, replaced Arthur Griffith as president of Sinn Féin, with Stack being elected its honorary secretary. De Valera was also formally elected president of the Irish Volunteers, ensuring that from now on both bodies would run in tandem under the same leadership.[70] In August, both Stack and Thomas Ashe were arrested for making seditious speeches in public.[71] Numerous public bodies, including the Kerry County Board, passed resolutions condemning their imprisonment and demanding all political prisoners be immediately released.[72] Both men were transferred to Mountjoy prison where by mid-September they were joined by thirty-seven other Sinn Féin activists. Seeking prisoner of war status, they refused to cooperate with the prison authorities and in protest began a hunger strike on 20 September. On the fourth day of the hunger strike, Ashe suffered severe internal injuries due to attempts by prison officers to force-feed him. He died shortly afterwards.[73]

Across Ireland, the news was received with shock and outrage. Nationalist public opinion in Ireland was enormously resentful of his death, and his killing provided an even greater boost to the emerging republican movement than the executions in 1916. Mock funerals were held in towns and villages throughout the country to commemorate him. Those within the local GAA were similarly appalled by the death of their former member. The Dublin County Board issued a damning statement 'deploring the killing' and resolving to have representatives of every GAA club in the city at the funeral.[74] His public funeral in Dublin was the largest ever seen in the city.[75] Some 30,000 people took part in the funeral procession, which stretched for three miles. Over 500 wreaths were laid at his grave by various Sinn Féin clubs, GAA and Gaelic League branches, nationalist organisations and other public bodies. Following the Rising, Ashe had become the head of the Supreme Council of the IRB. With his death, the Brotherhood had no recognised leader and threw in its lot with Sinn Féin under de Valera's leadership. Ashe's death was a major catalyst for a huge expansion of the Sinn Féin movement across Ireland. By December, the RIC reported that nationally the party had over 1,000 clubs and 66,000 members.[76] In Kerry, Sinn Féin membership had risen to 44 branches and 3,270 members by November 1917.

By 1917, it was apparent that the transformed political landscape had impacted on the membership of the GAA. As such a large nationalist body, the GAA could not be immune from the new political reality. In fact in Kerry, GAA matches frequently showed the first evidence of this changing political mood. In

January 1917, a Lispole supporter coming from a match in Dingle was arrested and sentenced to six weeks' hard labour for shouting 'Up the Sinn Féiners, up Germany; the Germans are winning and they'll win.' That August, a football match between Glenflesk and Kenmare was preceded by a procession of the teams and supporters behind a girl holding the Irish tricolour. Such a display of nationalist political sentiment immediately caught the attention of the local RIC, who climbed over the fences of the ground and kept the day's proceedings under a watchful eye.[77] By May 1917, the RIC's inspector general was forced to concede that Sinn Féin's popularity was becoming so great it now 'virtually dominates' the GAA.[78] It is also clear that the death of Ashe had just as profound an effect on the membership of the GAA as it had on broader Irish nationalism. Increasingly resentful of British authorities' attempts to curb the popularity of Sinn Féin, many of its adherents within the association used their influence at both national and local level to indoctrinate members into the new political grouping. Peter Hart has argued that there was a significant correlation between GAA and Sinn Féin membership throughout 1917, while David Fitzpatrick acknowledged that the GAA bequeathed an army of zestful followers to the movement.[79] In Clare, the county board began the process which saw de Valera nominated to contest the by-election for Sinn Féin in July 1917. During the same year, the Clare footballers entered their matches under a banner proclaiming 'Up de Valera'. The support for Sinn Féin among many in the GAA hierarchy was implicit in the association's enthusiastic championing of the dependants' fund set up in 1916 to provide relief for families of those killed or arrested because of the Rising.[80] The association, through its organisation of national and local tournaments, became a promising source of income for the most important prisoner support organisation, the Irish National Aid and Volunteer Dependants' Fund. Supporting the fund was an activity which allowed mainstream nationalists to indicate a certain degree of sympathy for radicals, without becoming entirely identified with their aims.[81]

With the reorganisation of Sinn Féin and the election of de Valera as its president in October 1917, prominent GAA officials such as Stack, along with Harry Boland and J.J. Walsh of the Cork

County Board, were appointed onto its ruling executive. At the Kerry Annual GAA Convention the previous March, delegates had unanimously elected the imprisoned Stack as their chairman in recognition of the years of service he had contributed to the Kerry GAA and Irish nationalism. The association also hoped to capitalise on the new patriotic spirit that was enflaming Irish public opinion. At a meeting of the Kerry County Board in October, a letter was read from the Central Council about reorganising the association throughout the country. Each county committee was to make efforts to re-found clubs no longer in existence 'and take advantage of the present feeling throughout the county by establishing such clubs with the object of wiping out soccer and other foreign games'.[82]

However, the rising tide of Sinn Féin nationalism did not lift all GAA boats. There is evidence that in some clubs in Kerry there was resentment towards the status Sinn Féin had achieved by undermining and destroying the popular support of the Irish Party. For example, 1917 marked the reappearance of widespread agrarian disturbances in rural Ireland as thousands of farm labourers and uneconomic landholders became both increasingly politicised by the Sinn Féin movement and increasingly envious of the wartime profits which many farmers were accumulating. As fears of food shortage grew, the government introduced a compulsory tillage order requiring landowners to free up more land for food production.[83] Violence erupted over demands for the break-up and redistribution of such tillage land among small farmers and labourers.[84] Within the Keel GAA, differences arose between the younger farm labourers who fully supported and advocated the Sinn Féin policy and older members, mostly local farmers, who had greatly profited from the prosperity the war had brought them and were happy with the political status quo. Such men retained a strong allegiance to Redmond and his party. The dispute resulted in the club splitting in 1917. The Sinn Féin supporters renamed their team the Keel Sinn Féiners in deference to their political allegiance.[85] It was also recorded that similar differences arose in the Ballylongford GAA, with some of its members transferring to the nearby Tarbert club. The Farranfore Plunketts football team, most likely made up of supporters of Sinn

Féin, defeated the Keel Sinn Féiners in the 1917 county championship.

Nationally, the GAA's competitions continued to suffer due to the lack of railway facilities. The Munster Council was forced to abandon its junior championships due to transport difficulties, with the Central Council following suit and cancelling the junior All-Ireland championships in 1918.[86] As a consequence of the government's decision to suspend all unnecessary rail travel, the Kerry Board was forced to abandon its 1916 county championships. However, as the hurling championship was at such an advanced stage, it was decided to complete the competition, Tullig winning it that June.[87] Fourteen teams affiliated to the Kerry Board in 1917. It was decided that for that year's championship, the teams that were most geographically convenient to one another would be drawn to meet. As the Kerry GAA had only been able to complete one county championship since 1914, its finances remained in an abysmal state. The board decided against affiliating its inter-county teams in an attempt to cut back on its expenses.[88]

The GAA's control of its own revenue was still being threatened by the British authorities as the dispute over the imposition of an entertainment tax rumbled on. At the 1917 GAA Annual Congress, held behind closed doors for the first time in its history, its secretary Luke O'Toole reported that the association would resist the imposition of the tax by every means possible and if any attempt was made to force the GAA to pay, it would call an all-Ireland convention to consider a united action to oppose it. Such a convention was called in August as a consequence of the excise authorities' attempts to levy the tax on the Dublin County Board. The Kerry secretary, Din Joe Bailey, was elected to represent Kerry at the convention. A meeting of the Kerry Board noted that if the tax was imposed, £37 of their previous year's revenue would have been lost. At the subsequent convention, the delegates unanimously passed a resolution stating that no individual, club, committee or council of the GAA should pay any tax whatsoever.[89]

Though 1917 had not proved a successful year for the Kerry GAA, by concentrating on their internal championships the county board was able to run off its year's programme satisfactorily. Tubrid were declared hurling champions for 1917 that November, while the football championship ran into 1918. Yet 1918 would prove to be a hugely significant, if disruptive, year for the association. The Central Council found that conducting its sporting affairs was becoming increasingly difficult in the new political climate. The attempted imposition of conscription would complete the process of the political radicalisation of Irish society. This in turn had a huge impact on the political outlook of the ordinary membership of the GAA in Kerry. In the months that followed, the leadership of the GAA would be forced to orchestrate one of the greatest acts of public defiance against British rule in Ireland. This would forcefully demonstrate the power and influence the GAA could mobilise in support of the national cause.

In March 1918, Kerry was unrepresented at the Munster Annual Convention. However, the meeting's chairman, J. O'Brien, said he had learned that Kerry were considering reaffiliating for the coming season and proceeded to draw them against Clare in the first round of the Munster championship. At the Kerry Annual Convention the following week, the delegates noted with satisfaction the secretary's report on the body's finances, it being a noticeable improvement on former years. At the meeting, a decision to re-enter the Kerry hurling and football teams in the Munster championship met with significant opposition from a section of delegates who thought the interests of the county's GAA would be best served by firstly clearing all the outstanding debts owed by the board. Many delegates felt it was the matches held for various national causes in Dublin over the past few years which were the principal reason for the debts with which the Kerry Board had been straddled. In late March at the GAA's Annual Congress, Austin Stack and Dick Fitzgerald, the Kerry delegates, informed the meeting that unless the Central Council immediately granted a sum of £100 to the Kerry Board it would be unable to field any county teams for the coming season. Deprived of a team of the popularity of Kerry for the past two years, Congress agreed to the motion. It also decided to organise a national tournament between Kerry, Dublin, Wexford and Louth to raise funds for the Kerry Board.[90] By mid-April 1918, *The Kerryman* noted with satisfaction that the previous Saturday's meeting of the county board was one of the largest attended for some time. Club affiliations in all districts were said to be a great improvement on the previous two years and several older clubs had decided to reaffiliate to the board. An extensive list of fixtures for the 1918 county championships was made, with sixteen football and fourteen hurling clubs entering. Permission was also given to a Dingle representative to re-form the West Kerry Board in the town. A letter from the treasurer Con Clifford was printed in the local press, urging all affiliated clubs in the county to take advantage of the impetus of the Central Council's national tournament in aid of Kerry and make a determined effort as regards organisation and training. Clifford assured readers that there was enough playing talent 'twice over' in Kerry to enable them to regain the All-Ireland that year so long as it was properly nurtured by the clubs.[91] It seems that Kerry were laying the foundations for a successful year of GAA activity. However, the national political situation would rob them of this opportunity.

In the wake of a massive German offensive on the western front, the British government passed the Third Military Service Bill in mid-April which extended conscription to Ireland. This caused outright revolt among representatives of all shades of Irish national opinion. The Irish Party walked out of parliament in protest once the bill was passed. On 14 April 1918, a special meeting of the GAA's Central Council was held, after which the association unanimously adopted the following resolution:

> That we pledge ourselves to resist by any and every means in our power the attempted conscription of Irish manhood and we call on all members of the GAA to give effect to the terms of the following resolution.[92]

Large public demonstrations were held across Ireland to resist conscription. In Tralee on 17 April, around 7,000 people crowded the market square for a public meeting organised by Dr Mangan, the Bishop of Kerry. The platform was shared by prominent local Sinn Féin, Redmondite and even local unionist figurers, all of whom in turn asked the people to unite in their resistance.

In an editorial, the *Sentinel* warned the authorities that if they tried to enforce conscription, it could only end in 'bloodshed and disaster hitherto unknown in the history of Ireland'.[93] The warning proved prophetic. On Saturday 13 April, seven members of the Ballymacelligott Volunteers, under the command of Thomas McEllistrim, attacked the nearby Gortatlea RIC barracks in a raid aimed at securing weapons to properly arm the local Volunteers in their resistance to conscription.[94] The attack on Gortatlea resulted in the deaths of two of the Volunteers involved, Richard Laide and John Browne.[95] Some within the local GAA were sympathetic of their actions. At a meeting of the local Ballymacelligott GAA club, a resolution of sympathy was passed on to the families of the two dead Volunteers. Their public funerals in Tralee attracted a massive crowd of mourners. Following Gortatlea, a spate of similar arms raids was recorded across Ireland as the Irish Volunteers tried to arm themselves to resist conscription by force. However, the Catholic Church quickly stepped in and took effective control of the resistance, and the threat of national violence rescinded. On 23 April, a mass general strike was called across Ireland. Trains and postal services were halted, businesses closed and the country effectively ground to a halt. In the face of such mass public resistance, the British government postponed the implementation of the Conscription Bill in Ireland indefinitely.

The attempts to enforce conscription led to a huge uptake in enlistment to the Irish Volunteers. This in turn fed a large number of Kerry GAA members into the movement. By May, the RIC were reporting there were twenty-two companies of Irish Volunteers, with a membership of 2,898, along with sixty Sinn Féin branches with a membership of 6,642 in Kerry.[96] Local GAA matches were frequently used as cover for renewed Volunteer activity there. In Causeway, it was reported that hurling matches in the village were being used to mask the convening and drilling of several local Volunteer contingents.[97] In May 1918, in an attempt to paralyse the power of the Sinn Féin movement, the British authorities arrested seventy-eight of its better-known members. Seeing the unjust arrest and deportation of many of their elected leaders, public support for the party only increased.[98]

In the midst of all this unrest, the GAA in Kerry tried to carry on. In late May, the Kerry team defeated Louth in the semi-final of the Kerry Board GAA tournament in Croke Park by 1-5 to 0-6.

They qualified to meet Wexford in the final. However, on 14 June the two RIC officers responsible for the deaths of the two Ballymacelligott Volunteers the previous April were attacked in Tralee in revenge for the killing. In response, on 24 June 1918 British forces declared Tralee a 'Special Military Area'. The *Sentinel* reported how this proclamation in effect had turned the town into a huge jail in which the entire population was imprisoned. All roads to Tralee were barricaded and special permits were required from the local RIC barracks to allow anyone to enter or leave the town. A strict curfew was likewise imposed on all pubs and businesses.[99] The final of the tournament in aid of the Kerry County Board was played the following Sunday but the Kerry team were forced to travel without their Tralee contingent, who were unable to obtain special permits to leave the town. Weakened, the Kerry side lost the game 0-5 to 0-1 in front of a 12,000-strong crowd. The Kerry Board was forced to write to the Munster Council to delay the county's opening match in the Munster championship as it could not avail itself of its Tralee players. The military restrictions around the town were not lifted until 16 August.

In the face of growing political unrest in Ireland, emergency rule had been introduced in June 1918. On 4 July, the Lord Lieutenant of Ireland issued a special proclamation banning all public gatherings and political rallies unless a special police permit was obtained from the RIC. In addition, the Sinn Féin party was proscribed along with the Irish Volunteers, Cumann na mBan and the Gaelic League. The Lord Lieutenant's statement declared that he was satisfied such bodies both encouraged and aided persons to commit crimes and promoted and incited acts of violence and intimidation.[100] It can be argued that the absence of the GAA from the list of proscribed organisations is evidence that though the association's membership undoubtedly overlapped with Sinn Féin, up until this point the GAA was able to officially maintain a recognisable distance between itself and the party.[101] Yet the English *Daily Chronicle* argued that the authorities had made a grave error in not proclaiming the GAA 'an eager and lively organisation of revolutionary propagandists'.[102]

Though the GAA was not suppressed, the rules banning public

gatherings were framed in such a way as to include GAA matches. Within a week, games run under its auspices were being raided by the RIC and broken up. In counties Down and Offaly, several games were dispersed by RIC baton charges. The Ulster championship semi-final between Armagh and Cavan was declared illegal and police and military took possession of the venue at Cootehill to prevent it taking place. To circumvent the law, the local promoters of a championship match in Kerry between Cahersiveen and Portmagee falsely advertised the venue for the game as Ballinskelligs. While the local RIC were busy dealing with a decoy match there, the real teams contested the game at a pitch in Portmagee some seven miles away.[103] In Rathmore, attempts by the town's RIC to suppress matches at the local GAA field on two occasions in July resulted in a tense stand-off between the local hurling teams involved, their supporters and the force.[104]

The Central Council held a special meeting on 20 July to discuss the proclamation. The association's secretary, Luke O'Toole, told delegates that after an interview with Castle officials he was informed that no GAA matches could be held without first obtaining a permit. It was unanimously decided that no permit would be asked for under any circumstances. This decision was made known to all provincial, county and club boards and no member of the association was allowed take part in any competition where such a permit had been obtained. Anyone who disobeyed this rule was automatically and indefinitely suspended. Central Council also instructed all county boards to hold special meetings within ten days, to consist of one delegate from each affiliated club. At this meeting they would be informed of the stance on the permit issue. In addition, all clubs and county boards represented at these meetings would arrange an extensive programme of Gaelic matches to be held across every county on Sunday 4 August.[105] This mass protest of games, soon to be dubbed 'Gaelic Sunday', initiated a trial of strength between the government and the GAA. It was a fight the GAA was determined to win. At 3 p.m. on Sunday 4 August, between 1,500 and 1,800 matches arranged in every county in Ireland by both county and local club boards threw in concurrently. *Sport* reported that as many as 4,000 teams participated in the matches and that practically every affiliated hurling and football club in the country was involved. The paper concluded:

> The proceedings of the day, the good order among the crowds, the perfection of organisation and the magnificent response made by every team and club throughout the country, constituted at once a vindication of the Gaelic Athletic Association and its objects and a demonstration of the popular hold which the Gaelic games have on the interest and the sympathy of the Irish people.[106]

In Cork over forty matches were arranged and played off. In Kerry, a large programme of events was mapped out to contribute to the demonstration. However, torrential rain forced the cancellation of most of these games in the county. Even so, in Tralee Sportsground the organisers made a determined effort to hold two matches. Unfortunately, the first, a football game between the men of the upper and lower sections of the town, had to be abandoned fifteen minutes before the finish due to a heavy downpour. In Killarney, a Gaelic League Oireachtas went ahead despite the proclamation, and a hurling match between Kenmare and Kilgarvan was played as part of the Gaelic Sunday demonstration.[107] No interference came from the town's military, though a large number of RIC were on duty near the ground. Indeed, faced with such mass disobedience nationwide, the Castle authorities were powerless to resist. Afterwards, the authorities tried to save some credibility by declaring that the ban on Gaelic matches was only intended where meetings were followed by seditious political speeches. The success of the event put an end to the British government's interference with the running of the GAA and by the following week, Gaelic matches had resumed as usual. Just to emphasise the point, the Castleisland Sinn Féin branch decided to organise its own football tournament in the town between teams representing Sinn Féin clubs in Castleisland, Cordal, Currow and Dysart. As play opened, a large force of police and military arrived and remained until the onlookers had dispersed. Yet no attempt was made by them to interfere with the matches.

Marcus de Búrca makes a convincing argument that Gaelic Sunday represented the largest, most widespread and successful act of public defiance against British rule in Ireland in the 1916–22 period. While this can certainly be argued for, it must be highlighted that the GAA as an organisation had failed to take up any political cause officially until the conscription crisis of 1918. And as W.F. Mandle elaborates, Gaelic Sunday was more specifically a protest by a sporting body against a perceived unjust interference with its sporting activities. Certainly, many of its officials and members, including those in Kerry, were arrested for their political activities but they were arrested as individuals and not GAA members. It is also noteworthy that the occasion on which the association acted with greatest vigour and unity to oppose the British state occurred when the state threatened the very business of the GAA – its games.[108] Until now, it seemed clear that despite the changing political stance of many within the association, at an official level the GAA had remained cautious of committing itself too strongly ahead of the political opinions of the majority of Irish nationalists for fear of alienating its own more moderate members. By the summer of 1918, this position had altered significantly. The aftermath of the conscription crisis highlighted the extent to which a broad swathe of Irish society had become fundamentally opposed to the continuation of British rule. The protests and strikes held that April had shown the way forward for those within the association who hoped to utilise the organisation to discredit the British administration in Ireland. Emboldened by this example, the GAA followed the same template and began to organise its own mass, peaceful protest.

With interference from the authorities now at an end, the GAA nationally sought to quickly play off its present year's schedule. In late August, Kerry met Clare in the first round of the Munster championship, losing in hurling but winning the football 5-3 to 1-3 and qualifying to meet Tipperary in the Munster final. This was Kerry's first appearance in the decider since 1915 but they were beaten 1-1 to 0-1. *The Kerryman* stated that the news of defeat was received with incredulity in Tralee. It complained that some of Kerry's best men, including the young star forward John Joe Sheehy, were left to sit on the bench until the last fifteen minutes, whereas if they had started, victory would have been assured.[109]

During the last months of 1918, many within Kerry hoped

that after the summer of disruption the Kerry GAA would be able to complete their county fixtures. The end of the First World War and the lifting of railway restrictions looked like it might further aid a return to sporting normality. However, this would not prove to be the case. During the summer of 1918, Ireland registered its first victims of the 1918 flu epidemic (what would popularly become known as the Spanish Flu).[110] Between 1918 and 1920, the disease claimed between 50 and 100 million deaths internationally and spread to the four corners of the world.[111] The scarcity and high price of food due to the First World War caused a noticeable weakening of the resistance to disease in many nations' populations, especially among the urban poor. This lowered resistance was seen as a major reason for the devastating impact of influenza in western European countries like Ireland. In Kerry, the first reports of the influenza came from Valentia in July 1918 where eighty inhabitants of the island were reported to be suffering from it. By November, it had spread to such an extent that the Killarney Medical Board requested all schools and public buildings be closed to contain its spread, while similar actions were taken in Listowel and Dingle. In contrast to most flu outbreaks, which predominantly affect juvenile, elderly, or weakened patients, the 1918 epidemic attacked healthy young adults. As such, GAA players were among the sections of Irish society which suffered disproportionately higher instances of contraction and death due to the disease.[112] The epidemic had a significant impact on the activity of the Kerry GAA and its membership. In September, a county championship match between Laune Rangers and Farranfore went ahead despite some of the Laune Rangers team being struck down with the disease. In November, a tournament game between Tipperary and Kerry had to be postponed as most of the Tipperary team were suffering from the virus.[113] William Keating of Ballinskelligs, a well-known footballer and former member of the Kerry football team, succumbed to the disease in late October. In November, the deaths of Kerry GAA members due to the virus included the county board secretary, M.J. Quinlan, John C. Barrett, the treasurer of the recently formed Rock Street GAA club, and Patrick O'Sullivan of the Listowel football club.[114] Laune Rangers lost three of its players to the epidemic before Christmas:

Mossie Counihan, Tim O'Connor and John O'Shea. Jeremiah Murphy, in his memories of growing up in Kerry during those years, noted that 'few people escaped the "flu" and the medical profession seemed powerless against it'.[115]

At the same time as Ireland struggled to cope with the outbreak of the disease, its political landscape underwent a comparable upheaval. In unison with greater Irish nationalist opinion, the broad membership of the GAA fully supported this power shift within Irish politics. After the attempted introduction of conscription by the British government, the IPP lost all public credibility. In the general election held in December 1918 after the conclusion of the war, Sinn Féin won 48 per cent of the popular vote nationally but 65 per cent of the vote in the twenty-six counties.[116] The party returned seventy-three MPs as against the seven Irish Party candidates elected. The results effectively destroyed the Irish Party as a political entity. With the attempted imposition of conscription, the Church, which for so long had been one of the staunchest supporters of the Irish Party, finally accepted Sinn Féin as the leading political force of Irish nationalism and its bishops gave the party their official backing. Before the election, RIC reports noted that a comprehensive Sinn Féin victory was inevitable.[117] In Kerry, Sinn Féin returned a clean sweep in all four seats, with the imprisoned Austin Stack being elected in West Kerry. Following on from their electoral promise, the twenty-nine free Sinn Féin representatives refused to attend Westminster. On 21 January 1919, they assembled at the Mansion House in Dublin and established Dáil Éireann, dedicating to work to establishing a free Irish Republic. That April Éamon de Valera, the Sinn Féin president who had recently escaped from prison, was formally elected as Príomh Aire or Prime Minister of the Dáil.

With the broad base of Irish nationalism now fully in support of Sinn Féin, the GAA began to firmly align itself within the movement. During the same week that de Valera took his place at the head of Ireland's new legislative assembly, the association held the final of its tournament in aid of the Republican Prisoners' Dependants' Fund at Croke Park.[118] De Valera was in attendance and received a rapturous reception from the crowd of 25,000 present. He also donated a special cup for the match, which was presented to the victorious Wexford team. Further evidence of the

GAA's Sinn Féin leanings, especially among its leadership, was provided by the civil service controversy in early 1919. As part of a clause of the Defence of the Realm Act introduced in 1918, all of Ireland's civil servants now had to take an oath of allegiance to the King. Naturally, this affected hundreds of GAA members who were in the employ of the British state. At a special meeting of the Central Council, a motion was unanimously passed stating it was 'incompatible with the principles of the association for any member to take the oath of allegiance and any member having done so is hereby relieved of membership, pending the next All-Ireland Convention'.[119] The following February, matters came to a head in Dublin. Two GAA clubs, the O'Tooles and Geraldines, decided to continue to play an arranged tournament match in the city, despite being told they were not permitted to do so by a Dublin Board official because one of the O'Tooles players had already taken the oath. The event sparked widespread debate across the GAA. At the Annual North Tipperary Convention, delegates voted unanimously to condemn the Central Council's ruling.[120]

At Kerry's County Convention in March, the question of the county's stance on the issue was hotly debated. A letter was read from ten members of the civil service who belonged to various Kerry clubs which opposed the Central Council's ruling. The signatories noted that Michael Cusack himself had tutored prospective civil servants as part of his profession. They protested that under the Central Council's rules they had no choice but to take the oath or 'clear out and starve', and argued:

> There was no doubt the decision to administer the oath was the outcome of a section of men who were bitterly opposed to Ireland and Irish men and who felt that Irish Civil Servants were too closely identified with movements which helped to keep alive the spirit of nationality. The Central Council seems to think otherwise and by their excessive rule has endeavoured to misrepresent their position but were the Gaels of Ireland going to allow a half dozen Irish men to throw these Civil Servants out of a large branch of the Irish Ireland movement for an act not of their seeking or desiring?

Humphrey Murphy, the Dr Crokes delegate, proposed the convention vote against the Central Council's ruling, stating it was well known that civil servants 'had been the backbone of the GAA and the Gaelic League since the start'. Murphy asked if such men chose to leave the service, would the Central Council be willing to support them? He related one case where a civil servant on £300 a year was dismissed and got a redundancy of £20. The association promised him a benefit match but it never came off. However, the county secretary, Din Joe Bailey, was in favour of the association's ruling. After much debate, it was decided to leave the matter open to Dick Fitzgerald and Bailey, Kerry's delegates to the Annual Congress. They were allowed to vote whichever way they thought fit after hearing the debate on the issue.[121] At the subsequent Congress, GAA delegates voted by fifty votes to thirty-one to endorse Central Council's ruling to disqualify members who took the oath.[122] The ban was an instance of the GAA being used directly as a weapon against the British state in Ireland. However, the substantial opposition of ordinary members, as evidenced in Kerry, suggests it was the upper echelons of the GAA that were the more radically minded.[123] Yet the episode clearly shows how those in control of the association had adopted elements of the ostracising policy which was being advocated by Sinn Féin. They used it against sections of their own membership whom they saw, by their employment, as contributing to the British administration in Ireland. In view of such polices, there can be little doubt that by 1919 the GAA had taken an increasingly radical position.

With the War of Independence already under way, it is ironic that this year proved to be the most successful for the GAA in some time. By the end of February 1919, the previous year's All-Irelands had been played and, remarkably, on a national level the GAA's schedule had been brought up to date. The lifting of restrictions on rail travel undoubtedly had a major influence on this and local and national championships were brought off with renewed vigour.

The year 1919 would also prove to be the most complete and successful one for the Kerry GAA in the 1916–24 period. With rail travel again available, the Kerry Board was able to press ahead with its delayed county championships. Indeed, it could be argued that the lack of train facilities strengthened the position of the GAA locally in Kerry. Deprived of the opportunity of meeting teams outside their own districts, many areas in Kerry decided to form their own town and district leagues. Gaelic activity was kept alive by these competitions between local teams, which did not have to rely on the railway. In November 1918, representatives from four football teams in Tralee – Rock Street, Strand Road, Abbey Street and Boherbee – met to form a league competition for the town. The county board did its part, offering a set of medals to the winners.[124] It was reported that the former Kerry keeper Dan Mullins, together with Dick Fitzgerald, was training the Boherbee side in the competition. The league was such a success that *The Kerryman* observed that the talent uncovered in the town would ensure that Tralee sides would be prominent in the coming year's championship. Following on from Boherbee's victory, the paper noted with delight that Gaelic games had gained more popularity in the town in the previous six months than would have been thought possible. On the back of the league's success, the Tralee Mitchels club re-formed after several months of inactivity.

In north Kerry, a district league was established and run under a board set up by the Listowel GAA club during 1919.[125] The competition was praised for instilling a new passion for native games in a region previously all but 'dead' to Gaelic football. By November 1919, the league was comprised of the Listowel, Dromlought, Ballydonoghue, Newtownsandes, Ballylongford, Duagh, Faha and Tarbert clubs. *The Kerryman* remarked that the region could now boast 'football material as good as anywhere in Kerry'.[126] Such competitions benefited from the new social reality in Ireland during the war years. Due to the wartime restrictions on international travel and the unsettled condition of Ireland in the years immediately afterwards, emigration had effectively ceased as an option for many young men in rural counties such as Kerry. For example, although nearly 40,000 people left Ireland in 1901, this had dwindled to 2,111 people in 1917 and a mere 980 in 1918. *The Kerryman* noted that this was a fundamental reason for the success of these town and district leagues. They benefited from the energy idle young men redirected into the competitions to escape the drudgery and boredom of their daily lives.[127]

That the Kerry GAA could find itself in so strong a position given the upheavals of the previous three years owed much to the competency of its officials. In 1916, Din Joe Bailey of Ballymacelligott was first elected as county secretary. A talented footballer, he was a regular on the Kerry senior football team during this time. Bailey proved himself an able and enthusiastic administrator. A telling example of his efficiency is witnessed in his report to the Kerry Convention in 1919. Despite the lack of rail facilities and the imposition of emergency rule the previous year, Bailey had been able to balance the Kerry Board's accounts, even declaring a profit of 6d. Moreover, he informed the meeting that the Kerry GAA was still waiting on £50 of the £100 promised the previous year in a grant by the Central Council and on £29 12s 9d owed by the Munster Council as its share of the gate from Kerry's Munster final appearance. His work during this difficult time was praised both by the convention and *The Kerryman*, which reported on the meeting.[128] The financial situation of the Kerry Board was greatly improved the following month when at the Annual Congress, the Central Council handed over £277 to the Kerry GAA from the profits generated by the association's tournament organised in their aid.

By October 1919, the county's 1918 championship had finally been played off, with the Ballymacelligott footballers and the hurlers of the Tralee Parnells emerging victorious.[129] By that stage, the 1919 championships were well advanced. In May, the county board reported that seventeen football and fourteen hurling sides had affiliated for the year. It was decided to run both senior and junior championships in each code and affiliated teams were classified under each category. On 25 May, Kerry defeated Tipperary, the defending Munster champions, in what was described as Kerry's best display in years. In the ensuing Munster final, Kerry claimed its first Munster title in four years, beating Clare 6-11 to 2-0. Expectations were high for a resolute assault on the All-Ireland. However, Galway held Kerry to a draw in the All-Ireland semi-final later that month in Dublin. Determined that the Kerry team should regain its past glories, the county board issued a passionate appeal to the Kerry public to support a training fund to bring the players together in a training camp to prepare for the replay.[130] The public responded admirably and over £60 was raised in Tralee alone for the fund. Yet such efforts were in vain. On 14 September 1919, Kerry's remarkable record in replays failed them and they lost to Galway, 4-2 to 2-2. It would be almost five years before the county would again appear in Croke Park.

Yet whether nationally or in Kerry, the association could not remain immune from the day-to-day reality of Irish life as the country slipped into war during 1919. RIC reports from Kerry stated that though it was dominated by Sinn Féiners, the local GAA was 'showing much more enthusiasm for their sports'.[131] Nevertheless, the association continued to noticeably align itself with nationalist causes. One of the most striking aspects of the Irish Revolution was the spread of trade unionism and the organisation of labour. A unique feature of what was internationally an urban movement was how it was capable of expansion among labourers and the poorly paid in rural areas like Kerry. This was undoubtedly due to strong links between the local labour movement and the county's nationalists. In April 1919, in response to Limerick being placed under martial law, the city's trade unions called a general strike and formed themselves into the self styled 'Limerick Soviet'. Some 14,000 workers downed tools and the body even began to print its own currency. The action received enthusiastic support among the GAA. At its Annual Congress, representatives from the soviet asked members for their support and the Central Council responded, granting the striking workers £100 while also arranging for several matches to take place in May in their aid.[132] On 4 May, Kerry and Cork played such a match in Tralee and spectators were charged an entrance fee of 1s to help support the Limerick workers and their families. The game received huge support in the town and a large crowd contributed a gate of £63 in aid of the workers. A nationwide strike was held in their support on 1 May and the response in Kerry was overwhelming. As a consequence, the authorities in Limerick City relented and the general strike was called off.

Given the now close connection between the local GAA and Sinn Féin, the British authorities continued to disrupt and harass Gaelic events in Kerry when they saw fit. In June, the RIC proclaimed a number of feiseanna being held under the Gaelic

League at which prominent Sinn Féin leaders were to speak. In Killarney, one such feis, which was to include a football match between Dr Crokes and Tralee Mitchels as part of its programme, was proscribed. The arrival of the two teams in the town caused a great deal of tension. As they marched to the sports ground, the players and spectators were baton charged by the waiting RIC and military. Four of the Tralee players were reported to have received severe wounds.[133]

In the three years after Easter 1916, the GAA, as with greater Irish nationalism, had gone through a process of political radicalisation. The widespread support base of the IPP had been destroyed and in its place support of republican aspirations for an independent and free Ireland was overwhelming. As 1919 progressed, Ireland descended into open conflict with the British Empire. Meanwhile, at a central and local level the GAA tried desperately to keep itself alive as a functioning sporting body. However, the Anglo-Irish War would have a dramatic impact on the association in Kerry, but by the actions of its members it would, in turn, shape that conflict.

The Kerry GAA and the Anglo-Irish War, 1919–1921

On 21 January 1919, as Dáil Éireann convened for the first time, an RIC patrol was ambushed by local Volunteers at Soloheadbeg, County Tipperary. The action resulted in the deaths of two RIC officers and is seen as the traditional start of the Anglo-Irish War.[134] For much of 1919 the war was fought on a small scale, amounting to little more than local ambushes and raids on RIC barracks by the re-formed Irish Volunteers now styling themselves the Irish Republican Army (IRA).[135] In areas such as Kerry, such small-scale action had little impact on GAA activity and the association managed to conduct its business as normal. However, within months Britain had been provoked into a full-scale conflict with the IRA principally due to the military policy advocated by Michael Collins, the Volunteers' Director of Organisation. Throughout 1919, Collins hoped to incite such a war with Britain by conceiving a broad plan to undermine Dublin Castle through the destruction of its intelligence system.[136] Yet the more moderate members who retained the leadership of the Dáil preferred a policy of 'social ostracisation' against serving RIC officers.[137] In effect, the RIC was to be boycotted by the Irish public and anyone seen to do business with them locally was to receive a similar fate.[138] As the primary eyes and ears of British control in Ireland, it was essential that the RIC be undermined both socially and morally. Along with this, the Dáil advocated a policy of passive resistance among the Irish people towards the British administration. Taxes levied by the British government were instead to be paid to the provisional government in Dublin and the country's British legal system was to be ignored and supplanted with a system of Sinn Féin arbitrary courts.[139]

During 1919, the Volunteers began a widespread process of reorganisation. A sizeable number of the force now consisted of local GAA members. In Kerry, the local Volunteers were structured into three brigades.[140] However, for much of the war the control exercised by the IRA's general headquarters (GHQ) in Dublin was often precarious. The men who organised and commanded local IRA companies were strongly resistant to interference from Dublin and deeply immersed from the start in parochial traditions and parochial loyalties. Such an example could be seen in Kerry, where battalions remained fiercely independent and resentful of control from Dublin.[141] As attacks on RIC patrols increased, the British responded to the deteriorating national situation by proclaiming nine counties under its new Crimes Act. In addition, the Sinn Féin party was banned, its headquarters raided and the Dáil was suppressed. This played into Collins' hands by weakening the authority of moderates within Sinn Féin, many of whom would soon be arrested. Collins was thus able to take effective control over the Dáil's war policy. In September 1919 his position was further strengthened when he was appointed as the IRA's Director of Intelligence.

Despite the IRA's problems in forging a cohesive central command structure, they nevertheless intensified their campaign against the RIC during 1920. In Kerry, the early months of the new year saw attacks on the barracks in Camp, Ballybunion, Gortatlea, Annascaul, Ardea, Ardfert, Ballinskelligs and Fenit. On the night of 3 April, a massive national coordinated attack on over 100 rural barracks was carried out.[142] The RIC found that it lacked the manpower to effectively defend the more than 1,500 barracks situated across Ireland.[143] Vast tracts of the countryside fell under the effective control of the IRA, as the RIC retreated into the towns and only ventured out in increasingly heavily armed patrols. Faced with an overstretched and morally undermined police force, the British government moved to redress the balance. During the summer of 1920 a force of ex-British Army servicemen dubbed the 'Black and Tans' began to arrive in Ireland to supplant the native RIC.[144] They were further reinforced by the establishment of the 'Auxiliary Division' of the RIC, again made up of ex-British Army officers. Lacking the training of a regular police force, these units acted more like an occupying army.[145] Their arrival effectively put a halt to Gaelic games activity in Kerry. In reaction to the IRA's attacks, they commenced an unofficial campaign of terror. As a consequence of this it became impossible, in areas like Kerry, for the local GAA to continue to hold its sporting fixtures. The actions of the Black and Tans there were especially severe. In response to the local IRA's killing of seven RIC officers on the night of 1 November 1920, Black and Tan forces burnt parts of Abbeydorney and Killorglin, where some of the attacks had taken place.[146] In Tralee, the military laid siege to the town for nine days. All businesses, schools and public facilities were closed and the movement of people and foodstuffs in or out of the town was prohibited. A strict curfew was imposed and, frequently over the next week, Black and Tan and Auxiliary forces raced through the streets in convoy shooting indiscriminately at buildings and people, killing several innocent civilians. Numerous homes and businesses of suspected Sinn Féin and IRA activists were attacked and burnt. The sacking of the town was headline news internationally, making the front page of the *New York Times* on 5 November 1920. The siege of Tralee would prove to be one of the worst episodes of the military terror which enveloped Ireland during the month of November 1920.[147]

Nevertheless, the severity of the British government's response enacted by forces such as the Black and Tans actually shaped the IRA and the GAA membership within into a more powerful and cohesive military force. By driving them from their homes, the British invariably produced a class of full-time rebels who had the time and inclination to develop military capability. The IRA's small, embattled 'flying columns' were far better suited to fighting a war than the vast, cumbersome Volunteer organisations out of which they had emerged.[148] Meanwhile, public outrage over the Black and Tan reprisals banded people together with the local IRA. By 1921, the war had entered its final phase, characterised by larger-scale actions of mobile flying columns conducting hit-and-run tactics against large convoys of crown forces.

Kerry followed a similar pattern, with the IRA's GHQ sending down staff officers to help step up attacks on enemy patrols in the county. On 21 March 1921, a force of thirty IRA guerrillas attacked a train carrying a detachment of British military at Headford Junction station. This action would be the largest engagement of the Anglo-Irish War in Kerry.[149] In the months leading to the truce, the IRA in Kerry was growing bolder and more daring. By April, RIC reports noted how flying columns in the county were moving around committing outrages with ease and that the IRA was losing no opportunity 'to murder policemen'.[150]

The IRA's guerrilla war was only one aspect of a broader revolutionary campaign during the conflict. To achieve an Irish Republic, the Dáil set about supplanting the British apparatus of government with its own institutions. The IRA's campaigns had by late 1920 destroyed much of the British administration in Ireland. In its place, the Dáil formed its own. On several occasions, national general strikes were called to disrupt British rule in Ireland. A large demonstration was held in Tralee on 23 April 1920 which demanded the immediate withdrawal of the 'British Army of Occupation'.[151] That summer, rail workers refused to work on trains that carried British military arms or personnel, further impeding the effectiveness of British military control.[152] Likewise, by 1920 virtually all bodies of local government were in the hands of Sinn Féin. Patrick Sugrue, a member of the Kerry IRA, was elected Kerry County Council chairman and passed a resolution that the body 'hereby acknowledges the authority of Dáil Éireann as the duly elected Government of the Irish people and undertakes to give effect to all decrees duly promulgated by [it]'.[153]

By the early summer of 1921, both sides acknowledged that the military situation was in stalemate. Pressure was increasing on the British Prime Minister Lloyd George from a British public growing weary of the situation in Ireland. They would not tolerate an escalation of the conflict. Tension was also growing within his own cabinet, with some fearing the reaction of American popular opinion if Britain continued much longer with the war. As a result, attempts were made to contact the IRA to secure a negotiated settlement.[154] Following negotiations, a formal truce was declared, coming into effect at noon on 11 July 1921. The Anglo-Irish War was over.

Given the deteriorating situation across the country during 1920–1, the GAA nationally tried to function as an effective sporting organisation as best it could. On the day before its 1920 Annual Congress, *Sport* remarked that the association

> . . . is cast upon the troubled waters of Irish democracy; it is tossed by every popular current and exposed to every social storm. Stout and seaworthy, it has weathered six and thirty years' turmoil and trouble and is still as trustworthy a ship as ever.[155]

The Kerry Annual Convention was held as normal in February 1920, Dick Fitzgerald presiding. The accounts of the board were again in a precarious position. Due to the expense of preparing the Kerry team for the previous year's drawn and replayed All-Ireland semi-final, the board had incurred a loss of £115. Adding this to their other outstanding liabilities, the total debt of the body was put at £159 10s.[156] Before the arrival of the Black and Tans in July, the military situation in the county proved far more subdued. As such, the board was somehow able to play off the outstanding matches in its 1919 county championship. In March, Kerry played Cork in the Athletic Grounds in a tournament organised to raise funds to help the Central Council redevelop Croke Park, with Kerry being heavily beaten. Due to the IRA activities of some of its best footballers, Kerry were understrength, yet the writer of 'Gaelic Notes' in *The Kerryman* had little interest in this, stating that never in his memory had a Kerry football team been 'so whipped' as these men who 'misrepresented' their county.

At the end of April, Tralee Mitchels defeated Dingle in the 1919 county championship final.[157] The Kerry Board continued in fairly rude health and began making preparations to hold its 1920 competitions as normal. No Munster Convention was held in 1920 as many prominent officials within the Munster GAA had been interned or were on the run. The GAA's Annual Convention was held on 27 March but only twenty-seven delegates attended and there were no representatives from Connacht, Ulster or Munster.[158] Nevertheless, Kerry was drawn against Cork in the Munster championship semi-final that summer. Due to their financial situation, the Kerry Board was unable to give any assistance towards the training of the team. The Kerry players were left to their own devices and trained privately at home. There was much apprehension about this as both Cork and Tipperary were said to have strong teams for the coming championship. However, in their hurling tie the Kerry team surprised many and only lost by 2-5 to 2-3 against the reigning All-Ireland champions. The football proved better from a Kerry perspective, with the county defeating Cork 2-6 to 0-4. Kerry qualified to meet the winner of Waterford and Tipperary in the other semi-final but the game was not played until February 1922.

Due to the appearance of the Black and Tans and Auxiliary forces in the county, the Kerry Board suspended activity and after the summer of 1920 did not meet. Given the increasingly ferocious conflict being fought out between British military forces and the IRA, it is likely that Gaelic games, if they continued to be held locally, would have provided a convenient nationalist target for unofficial British reprisals. The Munster hurling final between Cork and Limerick was fixed for the first Sunday in September. Yet, given the conditions countrywide, the Cork County Board took the decision to suspend all fixtures under its control indefinitely and the final was postponed. *Sport* commented that not since the days of the Parnell split had the association's games been so disrupted by greater outside events. No one, it said,

> . . . can dissent from the decisions taken which have decreed a truce to play while the nation is stricken by tribulation and so many gallant Gaels are suffering and pining in alien durance. This suspension of popular pastimes is an index to the depth and intensity of racial

passion which cannot be misunderstood by those whose business it is supposed to be to measure the feeling of 'small nationalities'.[159]

In November, an attempt was made to play the delayed 1920 Munster semi-final between Tipperary and Waterford but the match was proclaimed by the military. By December, *Sport* reported that nationally all Gaelic games had been suspended and only in a selected few local districts were some matches still being played. On 10 December, Kerry, along with Cork City, east and west Cork, Tipperary, Limerick county and Limerick City was put under martial law, with the holding of any public gathering strictly prohibited. Until the truce of July 1921, Gaelic games activity in the province ceased.

The campaign of terror begun by British paramilitary forces in Ireland reached a crescendo with the attack on Croke Park in November 1920. Faced with the national suspension of Gaelic activity, the Central Council decided to fix a challenge match between Dublin and Tipperary for Croke Park on 21 November. The need for the association to survive and function, however limitedly, as a sporting organisation during the troubled days of late 1920 became of paramount importance to its Central Council. Staging the match was an attempt at imposing some semblance of normality in the middle of a war.[160] *Sport* was welcoming of the event, stating that in the suspension of national competitions, 'this fixture is certain to secure a big measure of public support . . . And for the time it will be the only break in the prevailing inaction'.[161] However, in reprisal for a series of assassinations carried out by the IRA in Dublin that morning, a convoy of British military forced entry into the ground during the match. In a few moments, 'scenes of wild confusion' broke out as they began firing into the crowd. Reports from eyewitnesses claimed that the troops gave no prior warning to the crowd before they opened fire. By six o'clock, it was reported that ten people had been killed and a further sixty to seventy wounded. Among the dead was the Tipperary right-corner-back Michael Hogan, shot through the mouth while he ran for cover. The Bloody Sunday massacre would go down as one of the most infamous examples of British reprisal and brutality during the Anglo-Irish War and its effects on the historiography of the association would be profound. Some have argued that the GAA received its position of pre-eminence in Irish history not as a result of its sporting credentials but because events such as Bloody Sunday and the actions of some of its members in the war allowed it to be seen as an important component of the national struggle, standing ready to support the IRA. Yet the GAA had no part and was not privy to the IRA's plans or its activity in Dublin that morning.[162] The Irish War of Independence had a huge impact on both the running of and legacy of the association. However, both nationally and in Kerry, the GAA actively shaped the conflict through the participation of its members in the war.

Various studies of the Irish Revolution have concluded that there was no direct link between the local strength of the broader 'Irish Ireland' movement and violent republicanism in the 1916–21 period.[163] A strong GAA was not necessarily a prerequisite if an area was to develop into a centre of revolutionary activity.[164] For example, County Longford was perhaps the most active in terms of IRA activity outside Dublin and Munster between 1916 and 1923. Yet police reports only showed a county GAA membership of 500, all of them in football clubs with hurling virtually non-existent. Indeed, the Volunteer Director of Organisation in the area, Seán Mac Eoin, actually saw Gaelic activity as an unnecessary distraction to Volunteer activity and one of his first actions was to ban local Gaelic matches.[165] However, it can be argued that such police reports underestimated the strength of the GAA in a given area. In January 1920, RIC reports noted that the GAA in Kerry had only ten active clubs and around 610 members. Yet a survey of the local papers shows there were twenty-five clubs or teams affiliated to the county board that year. In Sligo, the situation was more complex than in Longford, with the GAA being very popular in the years leading up to War of Independence. An average of twenty teams competed in the county's championship in the years 1917–20. The escalation of war in mid-1920 caused a severe drop in activity, with the county's 1920 championship being abandoned. After the ceasefire, Gaelic activity quickly re-established itself before being abandoned again due to the Civil War. However, the reawakening of Gaelic activity in Sligo after the

Civil War came mostly from clubs in the south of the county, the area least affected by the fighting.[166]

One cannot dismiss or deny the involvement of hundreds of Gaelic players, officials and supporters in the armed struggle for independence. As has been previously argued, there were close links between the Volunteer movement and the Kerry GAA in the years leading up to the 1916 Rising. Such links were maintained after the Volunteers began to reorganise in 1917. It seems inevitable that many of the leaders of local Volunteers companies would be young men of some local social stature. These 'natural leaders' were in many cases the captains of the local Gaelic team.[167] Such an example in Kerry was Michael Leen, captain of the Castleisland hurling team who reorganised the local Volunteer Company in 1917.[168] The close relationship between the Kerry GAA and the Kerry Volunteers was again evident when the latter was restructured on a county-wide basis in early 1919. Patrick Cahill, the former Kerry and Mitchels player, took command of Kerry No. 1 Brigade centred on Tralee. The brigade had seven battalions, the 4th, based in Listowel, was under the command of Patrick Launders, who played on the Kerry team in 1909 and was a member of the Listowel GAA. Kerry No. 2 Brigade was centred on Killarney and Humphrey Murphy of the Dr Crokes club, who also played senior football for Kerry in 1918, was its quarter-master. Murphy also commanded his local Firies Battalion and gave excellent service during the war, being involved in numerous actions. His ability was recognised by IRA headquarters in Dublin, who promoted him to command of the Kerry No. 1 Brigade in 1921 in place of the ineffectual Cahill. Another Dr Crokes and former Kerry player, John Joe Rice, commanded the Kenmare Battalion of the IRA under the control of the No. 2 Brigade. County board member Tadhg Kennedy was appointed Intelligence Officer for Kerry No. 1 Brigade in 1919 and reported directly to Michael Collins in Dublin. Under his leadership, a counter-intelligence network was built up by the IRA in the county, often supplied by sympathetic or disillusioned RIC officers.

Dozens of other Kerry GAA members were caught up in the national struggle. As part of the Dáil's policy of supplanting the apparatus of British administration, courts held under British judiciary in Ireland were targeted and boycotted in favour of those set up by Sinn Féin. William Nolan, vice-captain of the Ardfert IRA and secretary of the Kilmoyley hurling club, commanded an ambush party in an attempt to assassinate Kerry's resident magistrate Edward Wynne as he drove to sit at a local petty session in Causeway on 11 May 1920. However, Wynne was armed and managed to shoot Nolan dead in the ambush attempt before escaping.[169] In November 1920, an effort was made to blow up the bridge over the Shannow River in Abbeydorney to hamper the armoured patrols of Black and Tans in north Kerry. The local Abbeydorney Company was commanded by Georgie O'Shea who, along with another local IRA comrade, Stephen Fuller, had set up the Tullig Gamecocks hurling club which won the county title in 1916. O'Shea took charge of the operation but as his force advanced on the bridge they were surprised by a British convoy coming from Tralee and after a sharp battle were forced to retreat without destroying their target.[170] That same month Eddie Crowley, the secretary of the Rathmore GAA club, was seized on suspicion of being involved in an attack on the local RIC barracks. During his imprisonment, Crowley discovered that an eighty-year-old local blind man, Thomas O'Sullivan, was passing off information to the locally stationed Black and Tans. On his release, Crowley informed the IRA, which ordered O'Sullivan's execution, one of the more controversial episodes of the republicans' campaign in Kerry during the war. Having been seized by the Rathmore IRA, O'Sullivan was shot and his body left on the road as a trap for the Black and Tans. An ambush party waited as a patrol from the barracks was called out to investigate the finding of the body. As they approached O'Sullivan's corpse, the IRA opened fire, killing three Tans and mortally wounding two more.[171] In reprisal, homes in the village were burnt by the military the following night.

On 26 January 1921, RIC District Inspector Tobias O'Sullivan was gunned down in Listowel. Four men from the Newtownsandes IRA were responsible for the killing, including Con Brosnan, the Newtown GAA and future Kerry captain. Brosnan was subsequently arrested for his suspected involvement and deported to an internment camp in Britain where he remained until the end of the war.[172] In March, a number of GAA members were involved in the IRA's attack at Headford Junction, among them Humphrey Murphy and John Joe Rice.[173] The only IRA fatality of the action was Jim Bailey of the Ballymacelligott IRA and GAA football team. On 24 March 1921, William McCarthy, from Lixnaw and the adjutant of the IRA's 3rd Battalion in the No. 1 Brigade, was recognised and arrested by a Black and Tan patrol at Tralee station. After being questioned in the local RIC barracks, he was taken to Tralee Town Park where his body was found the following morning. The RIC reported he had been shot while trying to escape their custody as they marched him through the park, though most suspected he was merely shot for being a known IRA officer.[174] McCarthy was a prominent hurler and a popular member of the Lixnaw hurling club. His death and the suspicious manner surrounding it caused much consternation among the Kerry public and his funeral was attended by a massive crowd in Tralee.[175] In reprisal, RIC Head Constable Francis Benson was shot dead by a squad of Tralee IRA members led by John Joe Sheehy, who by now had established himself as Kerry's star forward, and also included the future Kerry All-Ireland winners Joe Barrett and Gerry 'Pluggy' Moriarty.

One of the last major actions of the IRA in Kerry was the assassination of Major John Mackinnon, the local commander of the Auxiliaries. His killing was in reprisal for the shooting of two unarmed Volunteers, Mossy Reidy and John Leen, in Ballymacelligott immediately after their capture by a force under the command of Mackinnon on Christmas Eve night 1920. Sheehy planned the assassination and would remain a committed republican throughout his long association with the Kerry GAA. As commander of the Boherbee Company of the Tralee Battalion, Sheehy was put in charge of the operation.[176] On Friday 15 April, a local IRA detail which included the future Kerry and three-time All-Ireland-winning goalkeeper Johnny O'Riordan gunned down the major as he played a round of golf on Oakpark golf course.[177] In reprisal, the local Auxiliaries went on a destructive orgy in Ballymacelligott, burning much of the village. On the night of his funeral, the Auxiliaries burnt numerous shops and business premises in Tralee, including the offices of *The Kerryman*, which remained out of print until August 1923. One of the final acts of war in Kerry was the ambush and killing of five RIC officers on patrol near Castlemaine. GAA members were again heavily involved, among them Garry Fernane who was a member of the Tralee Rock Street club, Donnchadh O'Donoghue, who played football for Kerry and lined out in the historic Kerry versus Kerry Internees game of 1924 and Jerry Myles, a future secretary of Kerry County Board.[178]

The 1926 Kerry hurling team that beat Waterford in Tralee. Included are several active members of the Kerry IRA in the War of Independence and Civil War, such as Johnny O'Riordan, who was in the ambush party that killed Major MacKinnon, J.J. Sheehy, Joe Barrett and Gerry 'Pluggy' Moriarty, who were all involved in the shooting of RIC Head Constable Benson, and Humphrey Murphy, who helped plant the mine in Knocknagoshel which killed several Free State troops. *(J.J. Barrett)*

With the declaration of a ceasefire, Gaelic activity slowly and tentatively resumed in Ireland while diplomats on both sides made ready to thrash out a settlement to the question of Ireland's independence. In Kerry, GAA events only began to resume on a small scale in August 1921. This is not surprising given the number of local GAA officials who took an active part in the IRA's campaign. In Annascaul, a football tournament was organised to raise funds for the local Sacred Heart church. A Kerry select team which included John Joe Sheehy was picked to face a combination selected from among the clubs in the West Kerry League, a competition that had been suspended in 1920. The Tralee and Dingle Rail Company offered special excursion rates in connection with the match, and so great was the demand for tickets that hundreds were refused travel, owing to a lack of seats. It seems that after the long months of suffering, the townspeople were desperate for a return to normality. A week later, two football matches between Tralee and Keel and Farranfore and Killorglin were organised in Milltown. The *Kerry People* observed that the 'reaction which has set in after the strenuous and tragic days of Irish war was very marked on Sunday . . . Fun and frolic succeeded gloom and bitterness and death'.[179]

The association made a determined effort nationally to play off the backlog of inter-county matches and bring the championships up to date. In August, the Leinster championship was resumed and the hurling semi-final for 1920 was played. However, the situation in Munster proved different. At a meeting of the Munster Council convened on 3 September 1921, Pat McGrath, the Tipperary delegate, argued that it was the wish of many Gaels in Munster that the active work of the council should be resumed as quickly as possible and pressed for the 1920 football championship to be completed. He stated that Tipperary, Waterford and Kerry were eager to proceed in this regard. Despite this, a telegram was received from a member of the Cork Board stating that it was 'unthinkable' at present that the county could participate in any matches. Another Tipperary delegate, Thomas Ryan, protested, stating that he could not see how Cork could not fulfil its fixtures if Kerry and Tipperary could. He informed the meeting that the Leinster Council had been busy playing its games in Croke Park in recent weeks. At this, Austin Brennan, the meeting's chairman, retorted, 'I don't take much notice of Leinster as they were enjoying themselves when we were fighting in Munster.' McGrath reminded him that, unlike Munster, most of that province had not been under martial law but Brennan still thought it 'queer' that

Leinster was holding games. McGrath pointed out that nationally the GAA's fixtures were out of kilter as Munster had still not completed its 1920 championship. However, Brennan responded that he agreed with the Cork Board's decision:

> It was the first duty of the Gaels and he was glad that that duty was being observed, to stand by Ireland. He knew that the Gaels no matter what happened would continue to discharge that duty. The attitude of Cork was that if hurling and football were resumed at the present time that the interest of the young men might be taken into sport and that the national fight might be neglected by them . . . It would be advisable not to resume activities until their national freedom had been secured.

Many agreed with this assessment. Limerick's delegate stated that if Cork could not play, Limerick would not force the issue. It was decided that the Munster championship in both codes would not be resumed under the prevailing conditions.[180] The following week, a deputation from Central Council met with the Munster Board and after discussion agreed to adhere to Munster's decision to suspend championship matches. In this decision the Munster delegates were fully aware of the attitude of the IRA towards the truce. There was great fear throughout that the peace negotiations which had begun in London on 11 October would break down and the war against the British would be resumed.[181] That September, an RIC report noted how the IRA across Ireland was engaged in widespread drilling and re-arming, with many training camps being formed in case hostilities were resumed. In October, Richard Mulcahy, the IRA's Chief of Staff, reported that his army was in rapid training for war, while the Irish government was involved in peace negotiations. He declared that the IRA had to be prepared for any and all outcomes of the upcoming talks.[182]

The Kerry GAA and the Irish Civil War
On 6 December 1921, the Anglo-Irish Treaty was signed between representatives of the British government and those of the Irish Republic. The treaty established the Irish Free State as a self-

governing dominion within the British Empire. It guaranteed Irish control over its own law, revenue, police and military forces. Crucially, however, the treaty excluded the six counties of what became known as Northern Ireland and also stipulated that any member of the Irish parliament would be required to take the Oath of Allegiance to the British monarch. Immediately, its conditions split opinion within the IRA, Sinn Féin and among wider Irish society. Likewise, the membership of the GAA both nationally and in Kerry bifurcated over its terms. For Michael Collins, the settlement was 'freedom to achieve freedom', but Éamon de Valera vehemently rejected it as he believed it represented the acceptance of colonial status with all the trappings of imperialism.[183] Throughout the last weeks of December, the treaty and its implications were hotly debated in the Dáil. In Kerry, opinion was already divided.[184] On 7 January 1922, the treaty was ratified by Dáil Éireann by sixty-four votes to fifty-seven. De Valera resigned his position in protest.[185] On 11 January, a new government cabinet was elected and Arthur Griffith replaced de Valera as the provisional president of the Irish Free State.

Evidence suggests that in Kerry there was a strong anti-treaty feeling among the county's population.[186] This manifested itself among those prominent in the local GAA. For example, Austin Stack, who served as Minister for Home Affairs, regarded the treaty as 'an unmitigated disaster' and did everything in his power to prevent its ratification. Tadhg Kennedy, the Kerry IRA's Director of Intelligence, remarked that though he personally favoured the treaty, his friendship with Austin Stack influenced his opinion to side with those on the anti-treaty side.[187] It does appear that Stack's reputation in Kerry on account of both his GAA and republican credentials was so great that his influence carried huge sway among the Kerry people. In March, de Valera visited Kerry in order to secure popular support against the ratification of the treaty. While addressing a large rally in Killarney, he warned that civil war was the likely outcome if the treaty was endorsed. In April, Collins visited Kerry to secure the county's vote for the establishment of the Free State. Though de Valera had encountered no trouble on his visit, Collins was not so lucky. The local IRA was strongly anti-treaty and posters were put up in Tralee before his visit warning people to stay off the streets as the meeting had been proscribed.[188]

The treaty likewise split the republican movement. The IRB's Supreme Council voted to accept its terms. Stack, the leading figure of the organisation in Kerry, was disgusted with this decision and his fellow IRB members in Kerry followed his example.[189] The treaty also caused division within the IRA. Nine members of its general headquarters staff in Dublin favoured the treaty, while a number of diehard IRA commanders such as Rory O'Connor and Liam Mellows rejected it. Outside of Dublin, most of the more able IRA commanders such as Liam Lynch, head of IRA Southern Division, did likewise. On 26 March 1922, those officers who rejected the treaty held their own IRA convention. A new IRA executive was formed and Liam Lynch was appointed the IRA's new Chief of Staff. With this move, political leaders such as de Valera found themselves sidelined from the leadership of the anti-treaty section. In Kerry, the majority of the IRA in the county's three brigades strongly backed the new executive. Those who were also GAA members followed suit. Tadhg Kennedy commented that '99 per cent' of the men he served with in Kerry No. 1 Brigade were against the treaty.[190] Likewise, Humphrey Murphy and John Joe Rice of the Kerry No. 2 Brigade rejected it.[191]

With both sides of the republican movement seemingly heading for open conflict, the association tried to ignore the broader political climate and concentrated on its sporting responsibilities. At a meeting of the Munster Council in January 1922 it was decided to resume activity and play off the unfinished 1920 provincial championship. Tipperary beat Waterford in February and thus qualified to meet Kerry in the much-delayed 1920 Munster football final. At the Cork Athletic Grounds in front of a large attendance, Kerry succumbed by 2-2 to 0-2. The GAA held its Annual Congress on 16 April and in view of the delay with the 1920 championship it was decided to drop the All-Ireland competitions for 1921 for the present time.

In Kerry, the county board slowly reorganised itself. On 15 April 1922, it held its first Annual Convention since 1920. All outgoing officers from the previous county board were re-elected, including Austin Stack who was again voted in as chairman. The convention made arrangements to play off the remaining fixtures in the interrupted 1920 county championship.[192] However, rising political tensions were already starting to affect the ability of the Kerry GAA to resume its games. The most visible effect of the treaty was the sight of RIC and British military personnel evacuating barracks and garrisons across the country. Local IRA units took possession of these installations as soon as the British vacated them. Yet it often depended on local circumstances as to whether they did so in the name of the newly established Free State or the anti-treaty section. One such incident occurred in Listowel. Troops of the newly formed Free State Army took up billets in the town once the RIC left. In response, on 29 April the local IRA took possession of several other buildings and stated they would not leave until Free State forces had withdrawn. The Listowel football club was due to travel to Tralee the next day to fulfil its championship fixture with Castleisland but was unable to leave the town due to the tense stand-off and the match was awarded to Castleisland.[193] In late May, the Kerry Board convened for what few realised would be its final meeting for more than a year. An extensive programme of matches was arranged to finally finish off the 1920 county championship. But these were never fulfilled as the Irish Civil War erupted in Dublin that June.

Gaelic activity ceased in Kerry until the summer of 1923 as a brutal and bitter struggle for supremacy was fought out in the county. In Cork, some areas managed to play club games and even its county board was able to keep meeting until September when Free State forces arrived en masse in the county. However, by late autumn the military situation was such that it proved impossible to conduct Gaelic events across the province. Only in Leinster, where the fighting had died down, was the provincial council able to play off some championship matches in late 1922.[194]

The catalyst for the conflict was the outcome of elections held across Ireland in June 1922 to form a constitutional assembly to pave the way for the formal establishment of the Irish Free State.[195] The elections resulted in the pro-treaty candidates winning fifty-six seats to the anti-treaties' thirty-six.[196] Nationally, the results showed the vast majority of people were in favour of giving the treaty a chance. Nevertheless, the anti-treaty IRA refused to accept the result. Rory O'Connor at the head of a force loyal to the newly appointed IRA executive took possession of the Four Courts in Dublin. He threatened that the IRA would invade the six counties and reignite the Anglo-Irish War in the hope of securing a 32-county Republic. Michael Collins knew that the majority of the IRA's most capable commanders supported O'Connor and that units under their command were already mobilising. He therefore hoped to avoid conflict as long as possible in order to gain time to build up the government's own Free State Army. However, his hand was forced by the British Cabinet. On 22 June 1922, two IRA members assassinated Sir Henry Wilson, a retired British field marshal, in London.[197] The British government believed the killing was ordered by the anti-treaty IRA. It issued an ultimatum to the Irish provisional government to act against the IRA garrison in the Four Courts.[198] On 28 June, Collins gave the order to begin the shelling of the Four Courts. It fell after a two-day siege. The tragedy of civil war had descended across Ireland.

The course of the war can be broken up into two distinct phases. During July and early August, it consisted of a number of large-scale confrontations between anti-treaty IRA, or 'Irregulars' as they became known, and Free State forces. The most significant of these occurred in Dublin but large battles also took place in Limerick City and Cork. By mid-July, Dublin had been secured by Free State troops. The Irregulars next moved into their Munster heartland and tried to establish a defensive line running from west Limerick to Waterford which was styled 'The Munster Republic'.[199] That August, Collins, who took over as Commander-in-Chief of the Free State Army, launched an amphibious assault against north Kerry, effectively attacking the Irregular lines from the rear. The gambit succeeded to a degree that not even Collins could have expected.[200] On 2 August 1922, a force of 450 men, under the command of Brigadier Paddy O'Daly, landed in Fenit. They met with little opposition and advanced on Tralee supported by an armoured car.[201] The Tralee IRA, under the command of Kerry footballer John Joe Sheehy, managed to inflict some casualties on the approaching troops. However, the landings had taken the Tralee IRA completely by surprise and they had no time to organise an effective defence. In the circumstances, Sheehy ordered the IRA to retreat and the town was captured within a matter of hours.[202] Another Free State landing took place in Tarbert and, once ashore, the troops advanced on Listowel.[203] As with Tralee, the landings took the local IRA by surprise and they quickly abandoned the town. Over the next week, Free State troops advanced and captured Killarney, Killorglin, Kenmare and Castleisland. By mid-August, all the major centres of population in Kerry were under state control. Given that Tralee was now occupied, it would have proved impossible for the Kerry County Board to continue meeting even if it so wished.[204]

With the occupation of the larger towns in areas like Kerry, the war entered its second and final phase as the Irregulars were driven into the countryside and conducted a hit-and-run guerrilla campaign similar to those used against the British. By then, the forces ranged against the IRA were overwhelming. At the start of the war, the IRA may have outnumbered the embryonic Free State Army by as much as four to one. Collins though was able to recruit rapidly for his new force.[205] Before long, the Free State Army numbered some 53,000. However, this new army was 'a motley crew', with heavy drinking and indiscipline a characteristic feature. For the most part, Collins was able to keep the discipline of his forces in check, but on 22 August 1922 he was killed in an ambush at Béal na mBláth in west Cork. Without his firm leadership, discipline in the ever-expanding Free State Army became a major issue and the consequences of this on the war in Kerry would quickly become apparent.[206] Collins' death increased the bitterness of the Free State towards those on the republican side and contributed to the war descending into a cycle of assassinations, atrocities and reprisals. In November, the Dáil, which had convened in September and elected a new government, authorised the execution of anyone found in possession of unauthorised firearms. That same month, the Free State began the execution of republican prisoners captured in the fighting.

Perhaps nowhere was the brutality which typified the conflict as apparent as in Kerry. Though many people in the county may have personally supported the treaty, this did not lead to any significant recruitment for the Free State Army among the young men of Kerry. Many Kerry IRA veterans and the GAA members among them simply took the guidance of their commanding officer, most of whom backed the anti-treaty campaign.[207] This meant that Kerry found itself in a unique situation, with the vast majority of Free State forces who served in the county being outsiders.[208] The troops that landed in August comprised the newly formed Dublin Guards. This was an elite unit within the army that included many members of Collins' infamous Dublin-based 'squad'.[209] The Free State commander in Kerry, Paddy O'Daly, had himself been a senior figure in this squad. This meant Free State troops had little or no empathy with either the Kerry people or indeed their republican adversaries. The IRA in Kerry, due to its poor service record during the Anglo-Irish war, was regarded by the Guards Regiment as having done little to achieve national independence but was now doing its utmost to put the gains won at risk.[210] O'Daly therefore fretted little over the severity of their actions in dealing with the IRA in the county or of people suspected of harbouring Irregulars. The bitterness of the conflict in Kerry was only enhanced by the fact that the Free State forces were regarded as – and behaved like – an occupation force in the county. Consequently, local republicans received much support even from pro-treaty supporters in Kerry.

By January 1923, the county was effectively cut off from the rest of the country. After the loss of the towns, the Irregulars' guerrilla campaign consisted of concentrated attacks on the road and railway networks of the county. Soon rail services ground to a halt. Given the wartime conditions prevalent in Kerry since the preceding August, it had proved unfeasible for even locally arranged Gaelic matches to be conducted. The military situation had reached a stalemate and mirrored the prevailing conditions at the end of the Anglo-Irish War. Free State forces occupied all the major towns but their control extended little beyond them and much of the countryside was left in IRA hands. On the other hand, the Irregular commanders in Kerry were unable to dislodge Free State troops from the towns and large attacks on towns like Kenmare proved costly failures.[211] While nationally the Free State was on the verge of triumph, in Kerry its forces were unable to seal this victory in the opening months of 1923. In their frustration they became all the more ruthless.[212]

On 6 March 1923, five Free State Army officers were killed by a mine explosion near Knocknagoshel. The IRA had tricked a large Free State force into believing the location of the mine was actually a local IRA hideout. The killings at Knocknagoshel marked the beginning of the bloodiest period of the Civil War in Kerry. In reprisal, local Free State troops, without official state authorisation, removed nine IRA prisoners being held at Tralee Barracks and drove them to Ballyseedy Wood near Ballymacelligott. The men were ordered to stand around a pile of rocks in which the Free State soldiers had earlier placed a mine. They were then tied together and the mine was detonated, blowing them to pieces.[213] On 12 March at Cahersiveen, a further five IRA prisoners were placed on a mine, shot in the legs to prevent their escape and then blown up by the local Free State garrison.[214] Such actions clearly illustrated the depths of savagery to which the conflict in Kerry had descended. In all, between November 1922 and May 1923 some seventy-seven anti-treaty prisoners were officially executed by the Free State. In the overwhelming majority of cases, such executions were carried out under orders by local Free State commanders without any sanction from the Free State Army headquarters, which effectively turned a blind eye to their actions.[215] In March alone, twenty-eight people died due to the war in Kerry.[216]

On 10 April 1923, Liam Lynch, the IRA's Chief of Staff, died of wounds sustained in a firefight in Clonmel. Realising the hopeless situation facing the IRA and in the face of overwhelming Free State numbers, Frank Aiken, Lynch's replacement, issued an order for all IRA units to stand down from noon on Monday 30 April.[217] That September, a general election was called with the new pro-treaty party, Cumann na nGaedheal, taking power and forming the first official Free State government.

When the Civil War broke out the association nationally was faced with a dilemma. Though many of its leading officials were pro-treaty, any clear alignment between the organisation and the Free State government would most likely have split its membership in counties such as Kerry between pro and anti-treaty factions along the same lines as Sinn Féin or the IRA. The implications of such a split for a sporting organisation like the GAA would have been disastrous and might have ultimately destroyed it. As such, the association took what was probably the only viable course open to them and insisted on a strict policy of neutrality during the war. In order to maintain this neutrality, the GAA had to twice pass legislation to ban the selling of political literature at its games in 1923. It also had to ban collections for political purposes taking place outside its grounds on match days. However, this neutral stance came close to being jeopardised on occasion. In December 1922, the Cork Board wrote to the Central Council calling on them to organise a special congress to discuss the political situation in Ireland and the possibility of negotiating a peace settlement between the Free State and the IRA. At a meeting of the Central Council on 7 January 1923, the motion by Cork was discussed. The council decided to send a deputation to prominent members of the GAA on both sides to assess their views on the possibility of a peace settlement being negotiated. The deputation reported back to a meeting of Central Council that there was little appetite for such an intervention by the association.[218] Fearing that such an event would only give public airing to the deep divisions within its membership over the war, the association abandoned its plans to hold the special congress in an attempt to preserve its outward appearance of neutrality. Nevertheless, splits within the GAA during the war arose in some counties. In Clare, serious resentment was felt when two prominent and popular county players, Con MacMahon and Patrick Hennessy, were executed by the Free State due to their IRA activities in Limerick in early 1923. At a subsequent Clare County Board meeting several officials resigned when a motion condemning the killings failed to pass. The body split and in 1924 anti-treatyites representing twenty-five clubs set up a rival county board. The two boards continued to conduct their own affairs until unity was restored in 1925.[219]

With much of the fighting confined to Munster by early 1923, the Central Council was able to contemplate the completion of its delayed championships. In March the 1921 hurling final was played in Dublin. On 12 March, the Munster Council held its Annual Convention. As the Civil War was reaching its bloody climax in Kerry, no delegate from the county was present. The meeting fixed 25 March as the date for the Munster final for 1921 between Tipperary and Kerry. It also drew fixtures for the 1922 championship, with Kerry drawn to face Limerick on 15 April. Kerry was unable to send a side to contest either of the matches and Tipperary were declared the Munster champions.

Though the Civil War had probably affected Kerry more than any other county in Ireland and the GAA in the county had effectively ceased to exist during its duration, the re-establishment of Gaelic activity so soon after the IRA ceasefire is testimony to the popularity and durability of the organisation in the county. On 15 July 1923, Kerry made their reappearance on the inter-county scene to contest their first-round match against Limerick for the 1923 Munster championship. *Sport* was unable to pass much comment on Kerry's prospects due to the prevailing uncertainty of the condition of the Kerry players after such a long period of inactivity. In the ensuing matches the Kerry hurlers went down to their Limerick counterparts but the Kerry footballers, senior and junior alike, were victorious, prompting *Sport* to comment that the results were an encouraging sign for the reappearance of 'this great Munster football county'.[220] In October, Kerry defeated Tipperary in Tralee in the 1923 Munster final by 0-6 to 0-3. In the build-up to that game, the county board managed to reorganise and decided on a series of league matches among the clubs currently active in the county – Dingle, Listowel, Tralee Mitchels, Dr Crokes and Castleisland – from which the Kerry team would be selected. *The Kerryman* noted that, due to the political strife, a large number of Kerry's recognisable stars of the past were absent, many having been interned by the Free State while others were still on the run. The paper reported that the team that ran out against Tipperary was a 'youthful, clean-shaven lot', not of the 'veteran battle-scarred type which have done duty in the past for the county'. Regardless, its Gaelic reporter looked on the result with optimism. As supporters left the ground, a violinist struck up 'The Rocky Road to Dublin'. 'Yes', he commented, 'tis a rocky road, but we've got over the most rugged rock in Tipp.'[221]

7

THE PHOENIX FROM THE FLAME, 1924–1934

The game was robust, at times too much so and was marred by the large numbers of fouls which ensured the referee was kept busy.

Description of the famous Ex-Internee versus Kerry team game,
The Kerryman, 16 February 1924

Despite the ending of the Civil War, large numbers of Kerry republicans, many of whom were also GAA members, remained interned in various prison camps in Ireland. When these men were eventually released a team of ex-internees challenged the Kerry senior football team to a series of matches. The games got huge public attention in Kerry and from them was forged a team which would become the greatest of its era. This Kerry side, politically divided yet united, became the symbol Irish society craved in its search for closure on the wounds of the Civil War. Yet the reality was far more complex. Kerry remained a political hotbed for republicanism and this continually manifested itself among the hierarchy of the GAA there in the decade after the Civil War. Many IRA officers in Kerry, who often held prominent positions with the Kerry GAA, used their influence to manipulate the association for their own ends. The refusal of the Kerry senior team in 1924 to contest matches until republican prisoners were granted release was such an example. In 1927, the Kerry team set out on a tour of the US, an event almost solely orchestrated between the IRA in Ireland and New York to raise funds for the Republican Army.

Yet this period was also characterised by a great expansion of club football in Kerry. Learning from the experience of the previous seven years, the county board established several district boards and leagues in the county to promote and grow the game. The move away from reliance on the railroads and the availability of motor transport cut down travel costs and opened up access to the more remote areas of the county. Despite this, hurling continued at a low ebb and various attempts by the county board to advance its popularity inevitably led to failure. Nationally, the introduction of the Railway Cups, the National Leagues and other competitions added to the prestige of the GAA. Also at this time, the association concentrated on promoting its games within the Irish education system. Dr Éamonn O'Sullivan of Killarney was a hugely significant figure in the introduction of national and secondary school competitions on a county and inter-county basis. Also in the 1920s serious attempts were made by the Kerry GAA to acquire and build their own stadiums, culminating in the opening of Austin Stack Memorial Park in 1932 and the completion of the Fitzgerald Stadium project in 1936.

As the 1930s dawned, political unrest once again began to sweep Kerry. Following on from the Fianna Fáil election victory of 1932, the IRA initiated an intensive campaign of recruitment and activity. This led them into open conflict with the Blueshirt movement of General Eoin O'Duffy. Within the Kerry GAA, tensions mounted as members fell under the sway of the rival paramilitaries. Despite both being eventually outlawed, the significant influence of the IRA within the Kerry County Board remained. The manifestation of this culminated in the withdrawal of all Kerry teams from inter-county competitions in protest at the arrest of several Kerry IRA officers in 1934. However, not only did this campaign ultimately fail to secure the release of these men, it ended up only weakening the GAA in Kerry while alienating support for the IRA within its ranks.

As the GAA's fiftieth-anniversary year began, writers and journalists grappled with the role the association played in the life and development of the young nation. The celebrations surrounding its first half-century allowed those within the GAA to construct an identity and history for the association, one which was both very influential and often very different from the reality.

Healing the Wounds? The Kerry GAA, 1924–5

With the end of the Civil War, the association in Kerry attempted to resurrect its county championships. Yet many of the county's best young footballers, such as Joe Barrett from Tralee, remained unavailable, being among those interned for their IRA activity. As a means of keeping up fitness and discipline, an intense programme of Gaelic football training was introduced by officers in the camps for their men.[1] By July 1923, some 11,316 political prisoners were still held in prison camps by the state.[2] That autumn, the new Free State government, under W.T. Cosgrave and his Cumann na nGaedheal party, began the slow release of the men.[3] In late December, with the liberation of the majority of prisoners, *The Kerryman* reported on the dominance of Kerry internees in Gaelic football teams and competitions organised in the camps. With freedom came an eagerness to represent Kerry in the following year's Munster championship, many considering they had a fifteen more than capable of beating the current Kerry side.

In January 1924, a group of Kerry ex-internees duly challenged the Kerry team to a contest. It is significant and an acknowledgement of the status that football had achieved in Kerry society that the ex-IRA prisoners chose a football match to embarrass what they regarded as a Free State combination. On 12 January, *The Kerryman* reported that the Kerry team had accepted the challenge, which was fixed for Tralee on 10 February. The paper noted that the ex-internees believed the Munster champions 'haven't a ghost of a chance of standing up against, much less defeating, the picked men from the different camps'. The county board had decided to use the match as a trial to select players for the Kerry side due to play Cavan in the upcoming All-Ireland semi-final. Over the following weeks, both teams trained, with the ex-internees conducting sessions every morning in Tralee in the two weeks leading up to the match. Before a large attendance on a damp February afternoon, the two sides lined the pitch of the Tralee Sportsground. Those on the internees' team were politically opposed to many on the Kerry side, such as the Kerry captain Con Brosnan who had actually served as a Free State captain during the recent Civil War. This ensured the game would be something of a grudge match. The fact that the contest was being used as a trial for the Kerry team only heightened its importance. For the internees, the match was an opportunity to prove a point to those on the opposite side of the political wire. As a sporting occasion, the event had a considerable political undercurrent. In the circumstances, it came as little surprise that *The Kerryman* found the game to be 'robust and at times too much so', marred by a large number of fouls, ensuring the referee was kept busy. The match was a tight affair with little to separate the teams, the Munster champions winning by a narrow 0-5 to 1-0.[4]

Their pride dented, the internees requested a replay, which was duly played on 23 March. This time the contest was much more open and noticeable for the clean spirit in which it was played. The internees grasped their final opportunity to impress the Kerry selection committee and won a commanding victory, 4-4 to 0-4. As a result, a much-changed Kerry side to that which had beaten Tipperary the previous October contested the All-Ireland semi-final on 27 April 1924. This was Kerry's first appearance in Croke Park in five years. *The Kerryman* noted the changes which had occurred to the famous ground since then. The stadium now boasted two magnificent covered stands packed with spectators trying to escape the day's heavy rain which had turned the pitch into a marsh. Soon

> . . . a youthful brigade in their early twenties stalked upon the field . . . On entering the field the Kerry team proceeded to the spot where Hogan, the Tipperary player, was shot on 'Bloody Sunday'. They knelt in silent prayer on the fatal sod while the spectators maintained a respectful silence. This action on Kerry's part was warmly appreciated by the crowd. As the Kerry team walked to the centre, the cheering was long and loud.

Many have seen huge significance in this simple gesture of respect to a murdered Gael killed as part of the fight for Irish Independence. For the writer J.J. Barrett, the sight of this newly formed Kerry team, composed as it was of men from either side of a bitter political divide, kneeling united in prayer was an indication that they regarded themselves once more as brothers. After the trauma the Civil War had inflicted on Kerry society, 'the healing process had begun'.[5] Yet the reality was that the divisions and hatred built up in the previous two years could not be so easily wiped clear either within the Kerry dressing room or among the greater Kerry public. A deep resentment over the atrocities conducted during the Civil War remained among members of the Kerry GAA long after the fighting ceased. Such political differences would resurface time and again in the club and county boardrooms of Kerry over the following fifteen years. One of the most notable disputes would occur just weeks after this game.

By the summer of 1924, there were still some 2,000 republican prisoners held by the Free State. Among their number were Éamon de Valera and Austin Stack, the Kerry County Board president. In early June, Patrick Cahill, the former Kerry player and now Sinn Féin TD, published a letter in the local press calling on all local bodies in Kerry to secure the release of these prisoners. He stated that, along with de Valera and Stack, there were at least thirty other Kerry men still in internment camps, two of whom, Humphrey Murphy and Moss Galvin, were members of the Kerry team. As a protest to secure their release, Cahill called on the Kerry Board not to send a team to contest the upcoming All-Ireland final with Dublin. Cahill was supported by his former IRA comrade and fellow TD Tom McEllistrim. Tomas Ua Murcada, the chairman of Currow GAA club, wrote to *The Kerryman* asking it to publish the club's resolution in support of Cahill's letter. The next Sunday posters circulated around Kerry, printed by the Kerry County Standing Committee of Sinn Féin, calling on the team and the Kerry Board to refuse to contest the fixture.[6]

Many disgruntled republican advocates within the association utilised the dispute in Kerry to publicise their views. Though the GAA had presented a facade of neutrality during the war, the fact that many dominating personalities on the Central Council happened to be in favour of the treaty meant that the association developed a close relationship with the Free State government. This was evident when in 1924 the Free State authorised a substantial loan of £7,500 to the Central Council to help fund what had been a pet project of the association for many years, the Tailteann Games.[7] Many GAA members from the republican side realised that the loyalty of the association's ruling body lay with the Free State but chose not to show their opposition by defection, except in isolated instances such as in Clare. After the war, the IRA hoped to use its influence among the membership of the GAA to continue its struggle against the Irish government. Indeed, for a brief period the IRA even gave serious thought to attempting to gain control of the GAA.[8] Paddy Cahill had the support of Moss Twomey, the new IRA Chief of Staff, in his call for the boycott. Because of the close relationship between the membership of the republican movement and the GAA in Kerry, Twomey saw the Kerry GAA as the perfect vehicle for the IRA to get its political message across.[9] As Twomey noted, there were nine ex-republican internees on the Kerry side on whose support they could depend. He chose to exert this pressure now as he felt the media attention of an All-Ireland final would be the perfect time to introduce the question of the political prisoners to the wider Irish public. Cahill informed Twomey that following the publication of his letter to the press, the Tralee Mitchels and Parnells clubs had held meetings at which they unanimously supported the motion. Five other clubs in Kerry were reported as following suit. Twomey noted that even if the Kerry Board decided to contest the final, eight players on the team, including Sheehy 'who is their best player', would not play. In such circumstances 'Kerry's display will be hopeless if the crowd, who at present boss the county board, beat us and decide to send a flapper team'. Twomey however, expected the Kerry Board 'to fall into line'.[10]

At a meeting of the Kerry team and selectors on 10 June, a decision was taken not to contest the All-Ireland final until all political prisoners were released. The county secretary, Din Joe Bailey, and John Joe Sheehy (who was still on the run and wanted by the Free State over his IRA activities) were dispatched to Dublin to inform the Central Council of their decision. It appears Sheehy was able to convince his teammates that supporting the boycott was the only option to preserve the unity of the team. In a statement to the *Kerry Reporter*, he said he was certain that if the match had gone ahead, some of the team would not have played and it would have resulted not just in defeat in the final but in the splitting of the GAA in Kerry.[11] Doubtless, men like Con Brosnan were persuaded by this argument for unity among the players, though they probably had no idea that the IRA had effectively engineered the situation for its own political ends. In the days that followed, Twomey sent orders to all IRA volunteers across the country to approach members of county teams and county boards to obtain resolutions calling for the prisoners' release. Teams were to be asked to withdraw from competitions in protest. If they refused, republicans were to threaten them with boycott. The IRA felt that if it could gain sufficient control and influence over the GAA it would be possible to severely embarrass the Free State by organising a complete GAA boycott of the upcoming Tailteann Games until its demands were met.[12]

The action of the Kerry team split opinion locally and nationally. 'Referee' wrote to the editor of *The Kerryman* from Dublin, arguing that politics must be kept out of sport. He observed that the contributions to the Kerry team training fund for the final could not all have come from one side and that the Kerry team should not allow itself to be used as 'propaganda for either party in this deplorable dispute'. From north Kerry, 'Anti-politics' wrote that the GAA in the county would never regain its former greatness if political questions were entertained. In his district, he wrote that the thud of a football or the crack of a camán had not been heard for many years and such disputes would not help matters. However, a meeting of the Dublin Erskine Childers branch of Sinn Féin passed a resolution in support of the 'splendid action of the Kerry team'.[13] At a special meeting of the Central Council on 14 June, it was decided, in consequence of Kerry's actions, to award the final to Dublin. Dick Fitzgerald, the Kerry delegate who was to present the county's case, arrived late to the meeting, after the motion had already been passed. Yet as a result of the decision, the Limerick County Board followed Kerry's example and refused to meet Galway in the All-Ireland hurling final fixed for 6 July. In response, the Central Council decided to fix the junior hurling final between Cork and Offaly in its place but both county boards declared they would likewise boycott the match. At the same time, both Laois and Louth also declared their intention to boycott their Leinster championship matches. It appears that some residual anger towards the GAA hierarchy due to its close association with the Free State government may have been a prime motive for the support which Kerry received from other county boards. The Central Council threatened to suspend the three Munster counties and in response the Munster Council declared it would refuse to select football and hurling teams to represent the province in the interprovincial trial matches for the upcoming Tailteann Games. Undaunted, the Central Council selected its own makeshift Munster teams for the event. This again caused controversy in Kerry when it emerged that eight Kerry players were part of the Munster football team that played against Ulster. The players were all junior, as any senior footballers approached had refused to go against the boycott. However, one or two county board members purposely went against the wishes of that body as a whole and assisted the Central Council in selecting the men.[14]

By now, the boycott had become a moot point as in late July all remaining political prisoners were released by the Irish government. On 27 July 1924, a massive crowd turned out in Tralee to welcome Stack home after his release. Stack was accompanied by Cahill and McEllistrim as well as Humphrey Murphy, also released under the general amnesty. The strong connection between the GAA and republican politics was evident when, as part of the welcome home rally, a football match was organised between ex-internees of the Curragh Camp and a team of ex-internees from the other camps, along with other Kerry players. Paddy Cahill acted as referee while Murphy took his place in the Curragh Camp team. Faced with the prospect of six separate county boards in open revolt and the damage that could be done to the national Tailteann Games without a strong Munster contingent, the Central Council called a special congress on 10 August to discuss the dispute. In deference to the 'abnormal' circumstances which had prevailed in counties such as Kerry for the past couple of years, the meeting decided to wave or annul the penalties it had threatened to impose and recommended the completion of the interrupted championships.[15]

The amnesty certainly seemed to have taken the bite out of the argument and although many delegates had strongly conflicting opinions on the dispute, the proceedings were described as temperate and mainly conciliatory and the decisions taken were unanimous. The following day, a Munster football side which included nine senior Kerry players beat Ulster 2-4 to 1-4 in the interprovincial competition played as part of the programme of the Tailteann Games which commenced on 2 August. The All-Ireland football final of 1923 was refixed for 28 September. In the weeks preceding the final, the Kerry side underwent special training and again a training fund appeal was issued to the Kerry people. In front of an enormous crowd, Kerry lined out in their first All-Ireland final appearance since 1915. The game was described as one of the most exciting and strenuous finals ever witnessed. Yet Kerry could not stop Dublin winning three titles in a row and lost narrowly, 1-5 to 1-3.

The Kerry team unluckily defeated by Dublin in the 1923 All-Ireland final. Back (l–r): M. Galvin, T. Kelliher, C. Russell, J. Moriarty, J. Barrett, W. Landers, J. Sheehy, D. Donoghue, R. Stack, C. Brosnan; front (l–r): M. Murphy, J. Bailey, J.J. Sheehy, T. Mahony, P. Sullivan (captain), E. Moriarty, P. McKenna, J. Ryan, Jas Bailey. *(Courtesy of the National Library of Ireland)*

Writing in 1946, the author of *Sixty Glorious Years* noted:

> In the lure of their native games Irish men began gradually
> to forget their political differences and, standing side by
> side on the sports field, soon learned to look again on
> their brothers as brothers, not as enemies.[16]

However, this was an expedient argument which masked the
reality that tensions and political differences would continue to
haunt the GAA long after the Civil War had ended. The foreign
games debate was a perfect example of the underlying tensions
within the GAA in the 1920s. In 1923, as the Civil War was
nearing its end, a motion at Congress calling on the foreign games
ban to be rescinded was defeated by fifty votes to twelve. Despite
this result, in 1924 there was another groundswell of support to
abolish it. At the Cork GAA Convention in February, a large
majority voted in favour of abolishing the ban. In the run up to the
1924 Annual Congress, it was reported that the Tyrone, Sligo,
Tipperary and Dublin conventions had all voted to have the ban
rescinded. *The Kerryman* noted its surprise that such a divisive
issue was being considered in the present political climate. At the
Kerry Convention on 8 March, Dick Fitzgerald was in favour of
its abandonment, saying there was something 'hypocritical' in
some players 'objecting to a sport like soccer though they went to
dances and danced the jazz, the tango and the fox-trot'. Yet his
argument failed to convince the delegates and a motion to support
the withdrawal of the ban was lost.[17] At the GAA's Annual
Congress that April, all eyes were on the question of the fate of
the foreign games rule. A motion to overturn the rule was moved
by the Cork, Sligo and Wicklow delegates but was lost by fifty-
four votes to thirty-two. *Sport* noted that Congress 'did not think
that "Irish Ireland" is yet in a position secure and strong enough
to throw down all its defences'.[18] Indeed, the Central Council in
August 1924 approved the formation of special vigilance committees
to be formed in each county whose duty was to visit centres where
foreign games were contested and report on the attendance of
members of the GAA as players or spectators at such functions. It
also recommended to all boards that counter-attractions be

provided whenever foreign games were played. Nonetheless, the debate on the ban did not go away. In 1925, a motion to rescind the ban was again put forward but was defeated by sixty-nine votes to twenty-three at Congress that April.[19] In 1926, a similar motion at that year's Congress was again defeated.

It appeared that the debates for and against the ban were really nothing more than a symptom of the ongoing tensions between the pro- and anti-treaty sections of the GAA.[20] Many prominent GAA members in the Free State government such as Eoin O'Duffy, the head of the newly established An Garda Síochána, supported the abolition of the ban. Yet if the leadership of the GAA was seen to acquiesce to this pressure, it would lay itself open to the charge that it openly supported a government which many within the grass-roots of the organisation blamed for starting a bitter civil war. Throughout the debates, it was clear that the majority of the rank-and-file members of the association were against its deletion. Any change could therefore have split open the divisions in the association which Central Council had worked so hard to avoid during the Civil War. The foreign games ban debate would rumble on for another forty years. However, its retention in the mid-1920s saved the GAA from the possibility of another divisive and potentially crippling divide. As has been seen, the split left by the Civil War on the association and Irish society in general was not easily repaired. Tensions would remain for years afterwards, particularly among those in the Kerry GAA. Yet despite this, the Kerry team of the 1920s would become a forceful example to many of the triumph of sport over even the bitterest political entrenchment.

In 1924, the Kerry GAA, after years of disruption, was finally able to operate as normal. For the first time in four years county championship draws were made. To restore the popularity of its games, moves were made to re-establish district and local leagues. In north Kerry, a new football league was inaugurated while in Killarney the Dr Crokes club set up a town league similar to those which were run in Tralee. During the 1924 Munster championship, the Kerry footballers won both the senior and junior finals. The seniors qualified to meet Mayo in the All-Ireland semi-final on 7 December 1924, with Kerry emerging victorious by 1-4 to 0-1 in a poor contest.[21] That result set up a second All-Ireland final appearance against Dublin in nine months. The final was fixed for 26 April 1925, with Dublin hoping to claim a fourth successive All-Ireland.

The 1924 Kerry county championship had been frequently delayed over the previous season due to the All-Ireland boycott and unseasonable weather in the latter half of the year.[22] As a result, most of the Kerry players were desperately short of game time. To compensate, an appeal for training funds was made and the team came together for an improvised training camp for the ten days leading up to the match. Dr Éamonn O'Sullivan, a psychiatric doctor with the Killarney Mental Hospital who would become the legendary trainer of Kerry sides over the next forty years, began his long association with the team and prepared them for the game.[23] One of Kerry's best players, Mundy Prendeville, had not played in over a year as he was a clerical student studying in Maynooth. The college authorities banned him from playing in the final because he was shortly to be ordained. But on the morning of the game, Prendeville climbed over the college wall and made it to Croke Park where he lined out under an alias in what was his final appearance for the county.[24] *Sport* declared that the final 'aroused the wildest enthusiasm and evoked comparisons, in the minds of the older Gaels, with the tense historic contests of the past'. Some 28,000 spectators crammed into the ground to see the match. The interest from Kerry was such that 'Pat'o', writing in *The Irish Times*, declared that '[T]he game might as well have been played in Tralee so decisively did the Southern accents hit the ear among the good-humoured throng in the packed stands and terraces'.[25] Kerry made history, becoming the first county to win both the senior and junior football All-Irelands on the same day. The Kerry junior footballers beat Mayo 3-3 to 1-1. In the senior final, Kerry won a tight contest 0-4 to 0-3. Such was the interest at home and abroad that the *Kerryman* offices were immediately phoned with the result. Staff posted the scoreline on the walls outside its office for the anxious crowds who had congregated there to learn the outcome. Likewise, cables with the result were sent to the chairman of the Kerry Association in New York to be broadcast in America.

Kerry, 1924 All-Ireland champions. The victory of this politically divided Kerry team which secured the county's first All-Ireland in ten years marked the beginning of perhaps the most successful period in the county's GAA history. *(Courtesy of terracetalk.com and T.J. Flynn)*

The final of 1924 marked the beginning of perhaps the most successful period in the county's GAA history. Many have seen the success of what was a politically divided Kerry team as a metaphor for the power of sport to transcend political divides and unite a society still reeling, as Kerry itself was, from the effects of the Civil War. The role of the Kerry team in reuniting a community divided by war is the first and perhaps, with the exception of contemporary Northern Ireland, only example in Irish history of the power of sport to transcend a social divide caused by conflict. Many believed the success of the team was instrumental in breaking down the barriers of hate left by the war and that the GAA provided the Kerry people with an opportunity to unite in a common purpose and interest. Without the uniting force of Gaelic football, it has been argued, it is debatable whether the post-war bitterness would have been healed. At the very least it would have lingered far longer than was actually the case.[26] However, such arguments have

A medical officer with the Killarney Mental Hospital,
Éamon O'Sullivan prepared the Kerry team for the 1924
All-Ireland final against Dublin. This began his long
association with the team and he would go on to
become a legendary trainer of Kerry senior sides over the
next forty years. *(Courtesy of terracetalk.com and T.J. Flynn)*

been overplayed and became a convenient myth for those within
the association to downplay the very real divisions which
simmered within the GAA there.

Yet this is not to suggest that there is no evidence on which to
base such assertions. John Joe Sheehy, for example, had been
hiding near Ballyseedy on the day of the infamous massacre of
republican prisoners. Among the nine IRA men sent out to die
were Stephen Fuller and Georgie O'Shea, both enthusiastic hurling
organisers from Kilflynn. By some miracle, when the mine
exploded Fuller was blown clear and survived. It was Sheehy who,
investigating the scene, had found Fuller alive, hiding in a ditch,
and rescued him. It is testament to the spirit of the GAA that
Sheehy, knowing what atrocities had been carried out on his
brother Gaels and republicans in the name of the Free State, could

have shared a dressing room with a prominent local Free State officer such as Con Brosnan. Brosnan himself did all in his power to reach out to the republicans on the team. The 1924 Munster final had been played in the Markets Field, Limerick in October 1924. At the time, Sheehy, who had escaped internment after the war and was still on the run, was hiding out in north Kerry. Brosnan arranged safe passage for Sheehy to Limerick for the final. Although he was not named on the starting team, Brosnan informed a select inner circle of the team that he would be lining out. Sheehy made his own way to Limerick and entered the ground as a spectator. He then emerged from the crowd before kick-off in his jersey and boots to take his place in the forward line. Once the match was won, Sheehy disappeared into the throng of spectators on the pitch and was allowed to make good his escape from the city. Brosnan, though himself very politically active, did not allow any political discussion in the dressing room, which again spared teammates from falling out over their political division.[27] Yet the effects of such a divisive event like the Civil War could not be washed away so quickly. As has been argued, episodes such as the All-Ireland boycott threatened to tear open the wounds of the conflict among GAA members in the county. Several instances within the association in Kerry in the next fifteen years would prove just how strong the undercurrent of division was.

Continued Tensions: the IRA's Influence on the Kerry GAA, 1925–30

The GAA in the immediate post-Civil War period remained in a vulnerable state. Though obstinately neutral during the recent conflict, the leadership of the association had in fact been supportive of the Cumann na nGaedheal government. Its continued financial weakness for much of the 1920s meant it operated at a significant loss throughout the first half of the decade. This shortage of income forced the association into an even closer relationship with Cosgrave's government, which bankrolled a large loan to help keep the GAA financially viable. Furthermore, due to the casualties and interments of the previous eight years of unrest, the GAA had become deprived of many seasoned officials. This disruption to its administration had led to a notably poorer calibre of officials operating at all levels by the time hostilities had ceased. As such, by 1925 the association had a significant number of new and inexperienced men in charge. Of those experienced veterans who remained, many now held local and national political offices which began to divert their attention more and more. The inexperience of its administrators and the continued tensions which simmered within the organisation would lead to a range of objections and counter-objections within the national GAA in the first years after the Civil War. The most serious was the debacle of the 1925 All-Ireland football championship.

Having beaten Tipperary and then Cork in the Munster championship of 1925, Kerry were nominated to represent Munster in the All-Ireland semi-final as the Munster final was delayed.[28] On 23 August, the reigning All-Ireland champions welcomed Cavan to Tralee and after a close contest, Kerry emerged victorious 1-7 to 2-3. Immediately after the game, the Cavan County Board sent an objection to the Central Council stating that Kerry's captain, Phil O'Sullivan, had made himself ineligible to play for his county having already played competitive matches with two separate clubs in Dublin in 1925, which was illegal. The Central Council upheld the objection and Cavan were duly awarded the match.[29] Aggrieved, Kerry responded with a counter-objection of their own, stating that two players on the Cavan team were guilty of a similar offence. As a consequence, Cavan were also disqualified and the All-Ireland was awarded to Mayo, who had beaten Wexford in the other semi-final. Following the decision, the Cavan Board protested at the slander to which the Cavan GAA was allegedly subjected, stating that Pat McGrath, the Munster secretary, had referred to Cavan as a 'crowd of beggarmen', while Dick Fitzgerald was alleged to have remarked that 'Craig [Northern Ireland's Prime Minister] was not rubbing it in half hard enough to us'.

The Central Council's ruling drew scorn from many. *Sport* claimed the 'prestige and administration of Gaelic games has been shaken grievously by these revelations and objections . . . that this should occur at the most crucial and popular stages of the games is the devastating aspect of the whole business'. *The Kerryman* was similarly scathing at the decision made by the GAA's new president, Patrick Breen, who 'went one better than old King Solomon, for he allowed the All-Ireland infant to be cut in two and he can now distribute the medals to Mayo at the wake. His actions have reduced the 1925 championship to a fiasco and made the GAA a laughing stock.'[30] However, the farce was not yet complete. Like Kerry, Mayo had contested the All-Ireland semi-final, despite not yet being provincial champions. The following month, they duly lost to Galway in the Connacht final. Unable now to claim the All-Ireland, the Central Council was forced to award the championship to Galway, making them the first county from Connacht to win the title. This was despite strong protests from Mayo and Kerry, who had demanded that a special congress should be convened to investigate the debacle. The GAA tried to save face by organising a substitute competition between the four provincial winners for a set of gold medals. The Kerry GAA unanimously decided not to enter it in protest at how the All-Ireland was handled.[31] The competition was a comparative failure that attracted poor attendance for its two games, with Galway beating Cavan in the final in January 1926. The fallout from the 1925 championship was a serious, if temporary, setback to the prestige and image of the GAA, an episode that highlighted some of the animosities still rife within the organisation and the inexperience of many of its leading officials, such as Breen, who would serve only two years as the GAA's president.

The following year proved far more successful for the Kerry GAA on the national stage. Having retained its Munster title, Kerry gained their revenge on Cavan, *The Kerryman* gleefully reporting on the decisive 1-6 to 0-1 victory in the All-Ireland semi-final that August.[32] This set up a meeting with old rivals Kildare. A record crowd of 37,500 attended the contest in Croke Park which ended level. Kerry made no mistake in the replay, winning 1-4 to 0-4. However, this success masked the political tensions which continued to run high within the Kerry GAA. Though vanquished in the Civil War, the IRA remained unbroken. As we have seen, immediately after the conflict the IRA command had ordered its members in the GAA to organise in the hope of gaining influence and eventual dominance within the association. Yet their aim was thwarted because the IRA remained merely one of a number of political organisations to which members of the GAA continued to subscribe. There were as many Free State soldiers and Gardaí prominent in the association as dedicated republicans. The GAA membership was not some monolithic mass and, depending on location, they could be sympathetic to the IRA, as in the case of Donegal and Sligo, or openly hostile, as was the situation in Roscommon and Leitrim.[33] Indeed, Moss Twomey remarked that in many areas the GAA sought deliberately to divert young men from involvement with the IRA. However, as has been demonstrated, the link between the IRA and GAA remained particularly strong within the Kerry County Board and the Kerry team itself.

By November 1926, the IRA's national estimated membership had shrunk to 5,042, while in Kerry numbers had fallen to fewer than 500.[34] Despite this numerical weakness, on the night of 14 November the IRA organised a series of raids on Garda barracks across the Free State to gather intelligence and capture weapons. These raids were the closest it came to a coordinated military action in the late 1920s, with barracks being attacked in Kerry, Cork, Tipperary, Wexford and Meath. The action was a disaster and the deaths of two Gardaí ensured a swift response.[35] The ruling Cumann na nGaedheal government had an authoritarian nature, understandable to men being given the task of building a nation from the ashes of a Civil War. As such, they made little distinction between ordinary and political crime and treated the latter with great severity. In retaliation, the government proclaimed a state of emergency and some 110 republicans were rounded up and interned. In Kerry, John Joe Sheehy, who remained one of the principal IRA officers in Tralee, and John Joe Rice, the town's IRA commander, were among those arrested.[36] As a protest against their imprisonment, the Tralee GAA District Board refused to allow junior players from the town to travel with the Kerry team that was due to face Dublin in the All-Ireland junior semi-final. The Kerry Board approved the decision and informed the Central Council that in the circumstances it could not send any team to play Dublin. In response, the match was awarded to Dublin and the GAA suspended the Tralee players who had refused to travel.[37] Following the release of Sheehy, Dick Fitzgerald appeared before a meeting of the Central Council and correctly pointed out that the body did not have any power in its remit to suspend the Tralee players. After discussion, they agreed to reinstate the men and the delayed junior match was played in July, with Kerry losing to Dublin.[38]

Patrick Foley, the new GAA reporter for *The Kerryman*, was scathing of the conduct of the Tralee District Board and in particular its chairman, Patrick Campion.[39] Throughout the 1920s and '30s, Tralee remained the stronghold of the IRA in Kerry. It seems clear that the organisation had again used its considerable influence to put pressure on Tralee players and the Tralee Board to boycott a major game. Indeed, Connie Neenan, the IRA representative in New York, had already been in contact with republican members on the Kerry team to encourage them to protest against the inactivity of IRA units there during the recent raids.[40] Din Joe Bailey, the long-serving secretary of the Kerry Board, alleged that in the fallout over the suspensions, Campion and the Tralee Board had twice tried to get him voted out of office. Moreover, he accused the Tralee Board of being 'saturated with politics', which exercised 'a malign influence on the GAA in Kerry'. He also remarked that republicans within the Tralee GAA had refused an approach made in 1925 to have a Free State military team affiliated to the county board. Furthermore, in 1926 Sheehy, Campion and the Tralee Board rejected the proposed affiliation of a Garda team and threatened that their inclusion would lead to the disbandment of the Tralee League as no team in it would play them. This was despite the fact that some of Kerry's most prominent players, such as Jack Murphy and Paul Russell, were Gardaí while Con Brosnan and Phil O'Sullivan were serving army officers. Bailey remarked that while local Gardaí had subscribed to Kerry's training fund the previous year, Campion's sole contribution was 'destructive nagging criticisms'.[41] The Kerry juniors incident illustrates just how strained relations between those in the Kerry GAA could become over political matters. It also highlighted the strong influence the IRA as a body maintained on the Kerry GAA, particularly in Tralee, a town that would remain the stronghold for Gaelic football and indeed hurling in Kerry in the 1920s and '30s. This influence was reinforced by the IRA's involvement with the Kerry team's first football tour of the US in 1927.

In 1926 the victorious Tipperary hurlers became the first county team to tour America. Following this, at the beginning of 1927 preparations were made for Kerry, the All-Ireland champions, to tour the major cities of the US and play matches against their representative football sides. Ted Sullivan, a well-known baseball promoter and originally a native of Clare, was the enthusiastic supporter of the venture.[42] It was agreed that Sullivan would undertake to pay all expenses of the Kerry team in return for 60 per cent of the net receipts from matches. The rest would be handed over to the Kerry GAA. Extensive arrangements were made for the eleven-week tour, with the team scheduled to be present at a large

Con Brosnan, second from left, and Paul Russell, second from right, in 1946. Both men's political sympathies with the Free State caused concern among John Joe Sheehy and other IRA members planning Kerry's 1927 tour of the US. Also in the picture is Denny Curran, far left, who played on Kerry's first All-Ireland-winning football team, and Jerry Moriarty, who won All-Irelands in 1924 and 1926 before emigrating to the US. *(Courtesy of terracetalk.com and T.J. Flynn)*

banquet in their honour in New York on 26 May. Following this, it was hoped that Kerry would play matches in New York, Boston, Chicago, Detroit, St Louis, Cincinnati, Pittsburgh, Philadelphia and Washington DC, with the first being against a New York selection in the city's Polo Grounds on 29 May.[43] On 15 May, the Kerry team set sail from Cobh on their American adventure.[44]

However, the tour was beset with problems both on and off the field. In New York, the team played in front of huge crowds of between 40,000 and 60,000 but lost the two 'test' matches against the city's representative side heavily, 3-7 to 1-7 and then 2-6 to 0-3. Though victorious in their five other games outside New York, attendances were disappointingly small, with only 6,000 turning out in Boston to watch them. Following their first match against New York, a telegram – purported to have been sent by Dick Fitzgerald and which heavily criticised the performance of the referee, the former All-Ireland winning Tipperary footballer Ned O'Shea – was published in several national newspapers. It also alleged that the New York team were more interested in 'playing the man' and knocking 'our lads out' rather than playing the ball – and had duly been allowed to do so.[45] The statement caused consternation and the Central Council received a letter from the Eastern Division of the American GAA strongly condemning the accusations of unsportsmanlike behaviour by the New York players. Reporting on the tour to the Kerry Board upon the team's return, John Joe Sheehy clarified that it was in fact Dick's brother, Fr Fitzgerald, who had accompanied the team and who had penned the offensive telegram and sent it without the knowledge of Dick or anyone else. Sheehy put on record the team's surprise and disgust at the comments as they all considered that they had been beaten by the better team.[46] In addition to not enamouring themselves to the New York GAA, the touring party discovered that following their second defeat to New York, the tour's promoter had disappeared from the hotel they were staying in, taking with him the profits from the gate receipts. As a consequence, the players found themselves penniless, but thanks to the help of the local GAA and the New York Kerryman's Association they were able to secure enough funds to keep them going until they returned home.[47]

The 1926 All-Ireland-winning Kerry Team.
(Courtesy of terracetalk.com and T.J. Flynn)

However, perhaps the most interesting aspect of Kerry's tour was the significant role the IRA played in organising it. To quote Tom Mahon, 'the team represented the IRA as much as it represented Kerry in America'. In 1926, Moss Twomey had appointed his fellow Cork man Connie Neenan as his representative in New York. Neenan planned a covert takeover of the GAA in the city. It was believed that by controlling the New York GAA, the IRA would find it easier to recruit Irish emigrants into the organisation while IRA men holding elected offices in the GAA would acquire positions of influence and prestige among the local Irish-American community. Finally, gate receipts from Gaelic games there would prove a valuable source of funding for the IRA back home.[48]

In January 1927, the IRA managed to get two of their members elected as treasurer and vice-president of the New York GAA. In addition, Neenan was appointed onto the New York GAA's executive committee. Lacking the resources to organise matters himself, Neenan began to search for a promoter in order to arrange for the Kerry team to tour America.[49] Considering the close links between the IRA and many of the Kerry team, Neenan knew he would have their support and also hoped that having a team of Kerry's stature travel to America would ensure large gates at matches, the profits of which would go towards funding and arming the IRA. Neenan eventually agreed terms with Sullivan to promote the tour, although Neenan did not trust him and informed Sheehy, the main Kerry IRA contact for the tour, to do likewise. Neenan also wanted Sheehy to ensure that the contract the Kerry GAA signed with Sullivan would allow the team to play additional matches to benefit the IRA. Sheehy was told that when the contract was being signed, he should 'expressly reserve freedom of action after the matches contracted for, are played'. Neenan expected to be able to arrange at least one match in New York, Boston and Chicago whose receipts would go towards republican funds. Sheehy, in turn, felt most of the team would not object to playing games for the IRA's benefit and that eighteen out of the twenty-five travelling players had agreed to the proposals.

Neenan was aware that any public exposure of the IRA's hand in the tour could destroy their plans and warned Twomey to keep all references to the GAA and the Kerry visit in code, as any message that was deciphered and subsequently seized in a raid could ruin the plan. Aware that some members of the Kerry team, such as Con Brosnan and Paul Russell, had no republican sympathies, Twomey warned there could be friction on the tour if they uncovered what the purpose of some of the matches really was.[50] It is interesting to note that despite the well-worn myth of reconciliation embodied by this Kerry team, Brosnan and Sheehy remained deeply divided politically, if not personally, towards one another. Indeed, Sheehy even suggested to Neenan that a threatening letter should be sent to Brosnan from the States to warn him that it would not be safe for him to travel on the tour due to the republican sentiment among Irish-Americans. Neenan dismissed this as impractical given the possibility of Brosnan going public, and although Brosnan travelled, it is interesting to note that Paul Russell, who served in the Gardaí, was unable to do so.[51] It is quite possible that sufficient pressure was put on Russell by IRA

Kerry's legendary goalkeeper Dan O'Keefe displays the seven All-Ireland medals he won between 1931 and 1948. Despite the continued political tensions within the Kerry GAA, the county dominated Gaelic football like no other at this time. *(Courtesy of Frank Burke)*

elements within the Kerry GAA to force him out of the tour. Sheehy travelled to America not only as captain of the Kerry team but also as the appointed IRA Army Council representative to America. While most of the gate receipts went to Sullivan, the proceeds of the two matches in New York were reserved for the IRA. Neenan also looked after the team's social programme, which included dances attended by the team to help IRA fundraising and recruitment. In Boston, he arranged for Sheehy to meet wavering republicans to try and dissuade them from leaving the IRA and give their allegiance to de Valera and his newly formed Fianna Fáil party. In addition, Sheehy and those players who could be trusted to be sympathetic agreed to smuggle home in their luggage a cache of Thompson sub-machine guns owned by the IRA and held for safekeeping in

New York.[52] The 1926 boycott and 1927 US tour demonstrate that the Kerry GAA remained racked by dissension and political tensions throughout the last years of the 1920s. The IRA continued to enjoy huge influence within the local GAA, more so than in any other county in Ireland.

In spite of such politics, the years 1926 to 1933 saw the Kerry footballers claim the title as the greatest team of any era up to then. Despite being beaten by Kildare in the 1927 All-Ireland final and suffering a shock defeat to an unfancied Tipperary side in the 1928 Munster semi-final, the Kingdom rallied to become only the second team to win the four-in-a-row. Between 1929 and 1932, Kerry accounted for Kildare, Monaghan, Kildare again and Mayo in consecutive All-Ireland finals. Indeed, the 1929 All-Ireland final was the first sporting event in Ireland to officially break the 40,000 attendance mark. The final also marked the first time a Kerry captain, Joe Barrett, was presented with the famous Sam Maguire Cup.[53]

But success on the playing field could not entirely mask personal differences off it. John Joe (Purty) Landers was to become one of the stars of this Kerry side and made his debut as a twenty-year-old in 1927. An active IRA member, he vividly described the political differences and tensions between the various factions in the Kerry dressing room as 'most uncomfortable'. Indeed, Landers asserted that often the Free State advocates on the team would come to the game already togged out to avoid having to share the dressing room with the others. Another player, Tim O'Donnell, confirmed the tensions inherent in the group though he insisted this disappeared once they stepped out onto the pitch in the Kerry jersey.[54] However, it would be wrong to claim that this remarkable Kerry side did not at least offer some example of reconciliation in the post-Civil War period. Though interned due to his IRA activities in the Civil War, Joe Barrett was among those within the Kerry side who tried to reach across the political divide. When his club, Rock Street, won the Kerry football championship in 1930, Barrett was nominated to be Kerry's captain following the retirement of Sheehy. Instead, Barrett turned the captaincy over to his friend and ideological rival, Con Brosnan. Though he came under intense pressure from his own club and the IRA elements within the Tralee

GAA, Brosnan held firm on his decision before resuming the captaincy again in 1932.[55] Such a stand was doubtlessly made easier by the fact that Sheehy had retired from playing and his influence was no longer a factor within the dressing room. Yet the symbolism of this gesture cannot have been overlooked by those who remained on opposing sides of Kerry's political divide.

Champions of the World: Kerry's dominance of Gaelic Football, 1926–33

This Kerry team came to dominance at a time of renewed expansion in the national GAA. Following the upheavals of the revolutionary period and the controversies which marked much of the middle years of the 1920s, the last years of that decade saw the association cement its place as the largest sporting and cultural organisation on the island. Its prestige continued to grow and the organisation attracted thousands of new members into its ranks. Indeed, the numbers of affiliated clubs had grown markedly year on year from 1,051 in 1924 to 1,549 by 1929.[56] This coincided with a noticeable rise in the standard of Gaelic games across the four provinces, with Gaelic football now firmly established as the most popular field game in Ireland. That it was the Kerry team and not its particular star players that was feted in the national press should be no surprise. As Dónal McAnallen has argued, the GAA's ability to manage the boom in top-level games and retain a general amateur code owed largely to the prevailing national mood. Modesty, manliness and voluntarism were central themes of the Catholic ethos which would dominate post-independence Ireland. It was widely believed that for state-building purposes, popular participation in sport should be prioritised over the glorification of individuals. The appeal of great GAA players remained predominantly local. While their names became famous nationally, in the age before television their faces remained relatively unknown outside their own county. With photography in the press still the exception, their images were rarely seen and only around half a dozen games a year attracted more than 40,000 to watch these men in the flesh. Indeed, those who travelled to the national finals came more to support their county and enjoy the occasion than to see the best players display their skills.[57]

Johnny Riordan, the Kerry goalkeeper, and Joe Barrett leap to gather in a high ball in the 1929 All-Ireland final against Kildare. *(Courtesy of terracetalk.com and T.J. Flynn)*

The growth in popularity of the association's games was facilitated by the introduction of a range of new provincial and national competitions in the 1920s. The status the Kerry team achieved during this period was reinforced by its successes in each. At its Annual Congress in 1925, the GAA voted to establish the National Hurling and Football Leagues, which would run as a secondary competition to the All-Ireland championship. Initially, every county was grouped into four divisions – North, South, East and West – whose teams would play off against each other, the top two sides progressing to the quarter-finals. The new competition got under way that October.[58] It was hoped that the leagues would help raise the standard of hurling and football in weaker counties and this seemed to pay immediate dividends when the Laois footballers won the inaugural final in September 1926, defeating Kerry in the quarter-final along the way.[59] The competition lapsed for two years before being revived for the 1927/8 season. In April 1928, Kerry qualified for its first League final, having won the Southern division. In the match against their old enemy Kildare in Croke Park, Kerry were triumphant, winning 2-4 to 1-6. In its inaugural year, the competition had been a failure, characterised by poor attendance at matches. This was what had forced its initial abandonment. However, the interest in the 1928 final between the great rivals ensured that all doubts about the future of the competition were dispelled. The continued success of the League, argued *Sport*, was due to it forcing counties to start practising earlier with resultant improvements across standards of play and, consequently, the swelling of gate receipts. In October 1928, the National Insurance Company donated a £100 silver cup to be awarded perpetually to the winners of the Football League. In December 1929, Kerry were presented with the cup for the first time, having retained their title by again beating Kildare in the final 1-7 to 2-3 in what was regarded as one of the greatest games of the era. Kerry continued their dominance of the competition and after it lapsed again in 1930, the county went on to secure the next two titles, beating Cavan in the 1931 final and Cork in the 1932 decider.[60]

By now, the weak standard of football in Munster had become a source of concern within the province, with 'PF' arguing that it had a detrimental effect on Kerry as the team never faced a quality side until it reached Croke Park. By then, he contended, it was too late to counteract any weaknesses on the team, which were masked by the poor standard of opposition in Munster.[61] In an effort to improve the standard of football in the province, the Munster Council secretary, Pat McGrath, donated a silver cup for a football league competition among its counties. The inaugural McGrath Cup competition got under way in October 1925 and predictably Kerry annexed it at the first time of asking, beating Tipperary in the final in June 1926. Despite the good intentions of such a competition to raise the county standards of Gaelic games in Munster, many old problems persisted. Indeed, by 1927 an article on the future of Gaelic games in the *Irish Independent* suggested

All-Ireland and League Champions, 1929. This photo, taken after the Kerry team's victory banquet in December 1929, emphasises their dominance of national competitions. In the foreground are all the cups Kerry won that year, including the McGrath Cup, National League Cup, Munster Championship Cup and the Sam Maguire. *(Courtesy of terracetalk.com and T.J. Flynn)*

the elimination of the provincial system due to the dominance of Kerry in Munster, where the weakness of football was of no benefit to the team. It suggested an open draw for the All-Ireland, which would benefit weaker counties as teams would be pitted against rivals of similar ability.[62]

One of the most important developments in the GAA at this time was the inauguration of a new interprovincial competition that would be held annually on St Patrick's Day. This was a revival of the old Railway Shield competitions which had first been held in 1906. The Great Southern Railways Company, which had taken over the running of the rail network in the Free State, donated two large trophies for the competitions, which were first held in 1926.[63]

That November, a Munster football selection that featured twelve Kerry players, two from Tipperary and one from Cork defeated an Ulster selection in Cavan by 1-8 to 3-1 in the first game of the new Railway Cup. The three non-Kerry players were dropped for the subsequent final in Croke Park and on 17 March 1927 an all-Kerry fifteen representing Munster claimed the inaugural Railway Cup, beating the pick of Connacht by 2-3 to 0-5.[64] In 1931, another all-Kerry fifteen was responsible for Munster winning its second Railway Cup in football, beating Leinster in the final 2-2 to 0-6.[65] The Railway Cups would continue to grow in popularity, becoming one of the most prestigious and prized medals in Gaelic games. Up until the 1960s, the finals attracted crowds on a par with the All-Ireland finals themselves and became one of the most celebrated days in the GAA's calendar. Kerry's distinction of singlehandedly winning two of the competitions in this period was a forceful reminder of their dominance in the most popular Gaelic game. *Sport* summed up Kerry's winning mentality as a county which, drawing on limited resources, employed intelligent training combined with a consciousness of its fine football tradition.[66]

Kerry's status both at home and abroad was only enhanced by the successful tours it conducted across America. As we have seen, its excursion in 1927 brought mixed results. However, in 1931, the Central Council gave approval for the reigning All-Ireland champions to conduct a new tour of America under the auspices of the Eastern Division of the United States GAA. The trip was a triumph for Kerry football. At Yankee Stadium in front of a record-breaking 60,000 attendance for a GAA event in America, Kerry beat a New York selection by 0-9 to 0-6 in their first game. Throughout the rest of the tour, they remained unbeaten, vanquishing the New York team in two further matches, a Chicago selection twice and also beating selections from Philadelphia and Boston. After defeating New York in the final game, Kerry's captain, John Joe Sheehy, was presented with the magnificent McGovern Cup donated by an Irish-American firm in the city. Large crowds gathered at Cobh for the GAA's official welcome reception on their return, and once they reached Kerry, huge crowds congregated in both Tralee and Killarney to catch a glimpse of the team. *The Kerryman* described the scenes as 'an

Kerry's great four-in-a-row team, 1929–32. By 1933, the Kerry footballers laid claim to the title of the greatest team of any previous era. In the preceding decade the county won six senior All-Ireland titles, including a four-in-a-row, three junior and three minor All-Ireland championships as well as ten Munster senior football titles, two Railway Cups and four National Leagues. The team also conducted three tours of America. *(Courtesy of Seamus O'Reilly and T.J. Flynn)*

extraordinary manifestation of a county's interest and affection for their team who set out like Alexander of old to conquer new worlds and succeeded'.[67] At a meeting of the GAA's Central Council, the association's president, Sean Ryan, proposed a motion that 'the GAA was always indebted to Kerry and their tour of America has reflected credit on the Association'. Kerry 'had helped to bring the GAA to its present proud position and now, having won every honour in football conceivable, they might be termed champions of the world'.[68] In 1933, the Kerry team completed another successful tour of America, drawing one and winning five of their six matches.[69]

Yet Kerry's monopoly of Gaelic football was not universally lauded. Controversy surrounded their All-Ireland victory in September 1930. The final was dubbed a farce, with Monaghan, who were contesting their maiden All-Ireland, being completely ill-equipped to deal with a Kerry side that routed its Ulster opponents

3-11 to 0-2. Yet the match would enter GAA folklore as 'the last battle of the Civil War', not only due to the perceived associations of the Kerry and Monaghan teams with the republican and Free State sides respectively (the Monaghan team contained several officers in the Free State Army), but also because of the number of Monaghan players injured in the match and their accusations about the rough tactics of Kerry.[70] After the game, the Monaghan Board protested against 'the brutality' of Kerry's play and the supposed bias of the referee towards the southerners (it was said at one point he took no notice of three Monaghan players lying injured on the ground). At a meeting of the Central Council in December, the Monaghan GAA officially objected to the result, claiming the match resembled 'a Spanish bull-fight'. The meeting concluded that Monaghan's protests were unjustified.[71] However, a reputation for Kerry vigour seems to have persisted. Following their 1932 All-Ireland victory over Mayo, J. McCarthy, the Kerry secretary, complained about the conduct of the referee, Martin O'Neill. Before the throw-in, he had entered the Kerry dressing room and proceeded to insult the Kerry players, stating that as far as he was concerned they had been blackguarding in every game they played and threatened to stop play if they carried on like that during the match.[72]

This remarkable period of success for the Kingdom's footballers finally came to an end in August 1933 when Kerry succumbed to Cavan in the All-Ireland semi-final in Tralee. It was the first championship defeat since July 1928. Between 1923 and 1933, the county had won six senior All-Ireland titles, including a four-in-a-row, three junior and three of the newly created minor All-Ireland championships. Kerry had claimed ten Munster senior football titles, two Railway Cups, four consecutive National League titles and completed three tours of America.[73] Such dominance was unparalleled in the previous history of the sport. The repercussions of the Civil War would linger in Kerry society for decades to come. As we have seen, several instances within the association in Kerry proved just how strong that undercurrent of division was. Yet in spite of this, the successes of the Kerry team provided a powerful symbol of unity to which both sides of Kerry society in the post-war years could aspire.

Kerry captain Joe Barrett (left) and Mayo captain Mick Mulderrig renew rivalries in New York during Kerry's third triumphant tour of North America in 1933. *(Courtesy of Frank Burke)*

The Reorganisation of the Association in Kerry, 1924–34

Kerry's dominance of Gaelic football throughout this period was no accident. Following the Civil War, the GAA within the county was able to reorganise effectively and strengthen its administrative infrastructure, which had lain shattered following the upheavals between 1919 and 1923. Over the next ten years, various competitions were put in place and local and district leagues were developed. All this greatly aided the expansion of Gaelic football across Kerry and facilitated the emergence of more teams and affiliated clubs than at any point in the previous history of the Kerry GAA.

In 1925, in an effort to rationalise the administration of the GAA in the county and promote the spread of Gaelic games, the Kerry Annual County Convention voted to divide the county into five divisional boards – Tralee, North, South, East and West Kerry – each of which was to run its own district league and be subject to the governing body of the county board. Club affiliation fees to the divisional boards were set at 12s 6d, of which 2s 6d would

Action from the 1932 All-Ireland final against Mayo *(Courtesy of terracetalk.com and T.J. Flynn)*

go to the Kerry Board.[74] Within two months each of the new divisional boards was inaugurated at meetings in Tralee, Listowel, Killarney, Dingle and Cahersiveen and the draws for their respective leagues were made. By July 1926, the inaugural district league competitions had been completed and Boherbee,

Newtownsandes, Milltown and Kilcummin had won the Tralee, North Kerry, West Kerry and East Kerry leagues respectively.[75] However, the problem of spreading the game through south Kerry persisted, and though a South Kerry District Board had met in April 1925 and drawn teams for its inaugural league, no district competition was completed there until 1928. Reflecting on their introduction, 'PF' declared that, despite such problems, the district league system had proven an unqualified success and had unearthed many promising players for the county side.[76] The decision of the Kerry GAA to establish local divisional boards that could freely run their own competitions between clubs within their own vicinity proved a far more practical administrative structure than the previously ungainly county board system that held its meetings in distant Tralee and was expected to effectively promote and run competitions across the whole expanse of the county. The league system was soon credited with the massive expansion in Gaelic football clubs in the county and it was estimated that there were now up to five times as many clubs in Kerry than had existed under the old county championship. Indeed, the leagues' success was such that some complained that the divisional boards had effectively replaced the county board as the functioning administrative body in the county and that their leagues were detrimentally interfering with the county senior championship, which was constantly behind schedule.[77]

The 1925 senior county football championship was contested between five teams – Tralee, Cahersiveen, Killarney, Dingle and Listowel – which were selections made by each divisional board. However, the competition progressed slowly and was not completed until April 1927 when Tralee beat Listowel 1-5 to 0-4 at Tralee Sportsground. It had been almost exactly eight years since Kerry's last county football final was held. For the 1926 championship, it was decided that the winners of three of the active district leagues – Dingle, Listowel and Dr Crokes – along with another Tralee selection would contest the county semi-finals, with Tralee again beating Listowel in the final. The dominance of Tralee and Listowel led to claims that while the district leagues were a great success in Tralee and north Kerry, they had been far less successful in spreading the game in other regions.[78] In response, the Kerry Convention of 1928 decided for the purposes of that year's championship to split Tralee into three clubs, comprising the Rock Street, Strand Street and Boherbee sides that had dominated the town's own district league. It was also decided that North Kerry should enter three clubs – Newtown, Craughdarrig and Listowel – and East Kerry would enter Currow, Dr Crokes and Killorglin's Laune Rangers, which had recently re-formed. It was further decided that given the weakness of football in these areas, the West and South Kerry Boards could enter a representative side comprising a selection of the players in each district. In 1926, the Kerryman's Association in New York had forwarded a cheque for $200 to the county board to purchase a silver cup which would be competed for in the county football championship competition. A cup was purchased for £40 and was first put up for competition in 1928.[79]

By now, Tralee had become the undisputed stronghold of Gaelic games in Kerry. Despite attempts to make the county football championship more competitive by splitting the town in three, Tralee teams continued to dominate the competition, with Rock Street winning in 1928, 1930, 1931 and 1932 and Boherbee prevailing in 1929 and 1933. In 1931, Rock Street renamed itself Austin Stacks in memory of Kerry's iconic county board president. Soon after, the Strand Street club was rechristened the O'Rahillys and Boherbee resurrected the name of the club's illustrious predecessor and became John Mitchels. The successful Kerry teams of the era were backboned by players from the town, whose stars included the Rock's John Joe Sheehy, Joe Barrett and John Joe (Purty) Landers. Such was Tralee's dominance of football and indeed hurling at this time that a player such as Joe Barrett, in addition to the wealth of national titles won, would also retire with seven county football and three county hurling championships.[80] By the 1930 championship, the three Tralee clubs were entering a seven-team county senior championship against the pick of the four other divisional boards.

Yet despite this dominance by Tralee, by the beginning of the 1930s the new divisional board structure had succeeded in spreading Gaelic football and encouraging club affiliation across Kerry. In addition to the various senior and junior district leagues that were now running, a number of the larger towns such as Killarney, Listowel, Killorglin and Castleisland had followed Tralee's example and organised their own town leagues to promote Gaelic football among the young men in the area. Also, in 1933 permission was given for a Gaeltacht league in west Kerry, involving six teams, to help sustain and promote Irish in the region.[81] The spread of Gaelic football in more remote regions of the county was made far more viable by the increasing use of motor transport. No longer constrained to the railway companies and subjected to the high prices charged to transport teams, the use of buses and motor cars greatly reduced the burden on county and divisional board finances. For example, by 1934 the North Kerry Board could report that its transport costs for the previous year's district championship which comprised ten teams was a mere £18 15s, less than a fifth of its total expenditure.

By the late 1920s, the Kerry GAA had never been in a stronger position. In 1929, it was reported there were seventy affiliated clubs in the county, with eighty-six teams. By 1930, the Munster Council reported that club affiliation in the province had increased from 368 in 1925 to 410, with 12,000 playing members.[82] The expansion of competitions and the resultant explosion in club numbers in Kerry ensured that a constant stream of talent was being discovered and their skills honed in local and regional competitions. They provided a rich crop from which to sow further All-Ireland success.

Behind the Long Shadow: Hurling in Kerry, 1924–34

While the Kerry footballers continued to achieve unparalleled national success, for followers of hurling the game continued to stagnate behind football's imperious presence. Following the blueprint of district boards being established for football, a North Kerry Hurling Board was formed in April 1925 to promote the sport in its traditional heartland. The board decided to run a league competition for a set of medals with the runners-up receiving a set of jerseys. An affiliation fee of 12s 6d per team was set. The league was played throughout the year with teams from Abbeydorney, Ballyduff, Lixnaw, Causeway, Ardfert, Listowel, Finuge, Ardrahan, Ballyheigue, Ballyrehan and Addergown all entering. Abbeydorney and Ballyduff competed in the final that November, with Abbeydorney emerging victorious.[83] The standard in games steadily improved as the league wore on and hopes were high that its continued success could translate to the county side. *The Kerryman* noted with optimism that with the exception of Cork, the Kerry hurlers had pushed the All-Ireland champions Tipperary closer in their Munster semi-final than any other team in Ireland that year. In the newly created National Hurling League, Kerry were placed in the second division along with Offaly, Clare, Waterford and Wexford and the hurlers got off to a positive start, beating Waterford in November by 8-5 to 3-4.

Yet predictably, such progress proved another false dawn. As north Kerry and Tralee were the only areas playing hurling on any widespread basis at this point, the 1925 county championship consisted of one match between a representative side from north Kerry and one selected from players competing in the Tralee town hurling league. The match was played in July 1926, Tralee easily winning 8-5 to 2-3 with a team that was comprised of several noted Kerry footballers such as Sheehy and J.J. Landers. The North Kerry Hurling League continued in 1926, but despite this no senior county championship could be organised either then or in 1927. In the 1926 Munster championship, Kerry were outclassed by the Cork hurlers, 7-7 to 1-4. 'PF' lamented that it was the age-old story with Kerry hurling, the team selected lacking anywhere near enough practice games, and he argued that only by getting outside teams to play against them could they ever hope to compete.[84] In 1928, following on from the county's dismal performances and the overall strength of the game in the rest of Munster, the Kerry Board requested that the county be graded as junior and allowed to compete in that year's Munster junior championship. The county remained in the grade until 1931 when they again re-entered the senior championship.[85]

Initiatives were continually attempted to spread the game. Again, following the example made in football, an East Kerry Hurling Board was established and the North Kerry Board re-formed in 1928, while the decision to split Tralee into three separate clubs was also carried through for the town's hurlers. That year's county championship contained twelve teams: Rock

Street, Boherbee and Strand Street from the Tralee district, Kilflynn, Listowel, Lixnaw, Abbeydorney and Causeway from North Kerry and Killorglin, Rathmore, Kenmare and Killarney from the East Kerry district, with Rock Street winning the final in May 1929.[86] Over the next five years, these developments did increase the participation of clubs in the competition. However, interest and involvement in the game remained strongest in the traditional area of north Kerry and in the three Tralee clubs. Teams from east Kerry failed to have much impact on the county's senior championship and no steps were taken to try and promote the sport in south or west Kerry.

On a national stage, the county continued its unremarkable pedigree. Commentating on the decision to persist with grading the county team as junior, 'PF' argued that this grading had not led to any improvement and only serves

> . . . to make us . . . realise the low standard of camán wielding in the county. No changes to selection or any amount of training would materially alter the result. As long as Kerry is represented by footballers in hurling we cannot hope to secure hurling honours . . . it must be encouraged in the Kenmare area and north Kerry where the game is indigenous to the soil and where little football is played.[87]

In this assertion, Foley was being notably perceptive. In the ten years under consideration, hurling became dominated by the three Tralee teams in the same fashion as football. In the six county championships held between 1925 and 1934, Tralee teams won four. Discussing the pre-First World War problems of spreading the game in Kerry, it was noted that the lack of interest in the game in the major urban centres in the county was a fundamental hindrance to developing hurling there successfully. While it may seem ironic then that the dominance of Tralee at this time should also ensure Kerry's failure to progress in the sport on a national level, this is not so. Tralee remained a footballing town. The men who played on the Rock Street, Strand Street and Boherbee hurling teams were all principally footballers who turned their hand to the game when the football season permitted. Doubtless some showed real skill with the game, Joe Barrett who captained the Rock's hurling team and J.J. Sheehy who led the Boherbee hurlers being two notable examples (Sheehy had been selected on one of Munster's Railway Cup hurling teams). Yet due to their extensive commitments with the Kerry football team, such players could rarely play for the Kerry hurlers. The fact that three teams, comprising mostly footballers, could be so successful within the county's championship also points to the weakness of hurling in areas such as north Kerry at this time. By 1933, a meeting of the North Kerry Board was told that the division of the county into hurling districts had only benefited Tralee and in north Kerry 'decline, decay, apathy and retrogression' had made their position 'hopeless'.[88]

No doubt the ongoing problems relating to high emigration in the county continued to affect hurling disproportionately. A request form the Banna club to amalgamate with Ardfert was refused by the board as it felt it would have a fatal effect on hurling there. As ever, the familiar accusations citing a lack of attention towards the plight of hurling by the county board and its sole concentration on the wellbeing of the county's footballers continued to be raised. Yet in response, 'PF' commented that the hurlers themselves showed no desire to change matters. He noted with disgust that during a recent match against Waterford, one of the Kerry players 'left his place to light a cigarette, which he proceeded to smoke complacently on the field while his side was being trounced'. The familiar story of indifference to playing for the county team and the constant bickering between hurling clubs, he argued, was responsible for the state of the game there.[89]

To try to solve the eternal problem, it was suggested that serious steps be made to introduce hurling into schools in Kerry. It was acknowledged that the cost of camáns made the game a far less attractive prospect for the finances of hard-pressed national primary schools. As such, the Kerry Board submitted a motion to congress asking the Central Council to take steps to provide cheaper hurleys for Kerry clubs.[90] 'MAC', writing in the *Kerry Champion*, remarked that a hurler was fashioned at an early age and must be playing by the time he is twelve. 'I doubt if, with a later start, a first-class player can be produced. It is in national schools where the future of hurling must start.'[91] In February 1928, a meeting of schools in north Kerry decided to form a north Kerry school league to promote hurling in the region. Abbeydorney, Killahan, Ardrahan, Cappa, Kilflynn, Lixnaw, Dromclough, Clandouglas, Ballinclogher, Ballyduff and Ballincrusing schools all competed. In 1929, the competition was expanded to include teams from across Kerry, with Killarney St Brendan's winning the first such competition. In July 1933, a county hurling convention was held in Tralee and it was decided that the county should establish an independent county hurling board separate from the county board. Also initiated was a county hurling league made up of four representative teams: St Brendan's, drawn from Kilmoyley, Abbeydorney, Causeway and Banna; Pearses, drawn from Kilflynn, Lixnaw and Ballyduff; an east Kerry selection and a Tralee selection. However, after a year the competition disbanded. 'PF' decried that

> . . . outside Kenmare, which through lack of field has not been prominent in recent years, hurling has been suppressed by football in every town in Kerry. There is little public interest and outside local games in north Kerry, all championship matches are run at a loss. The football championship has been acting as a tractor for Kerry hurling for years.

He lamented that, across the county, large areas were alien to the game and even Ardfert, 'formerly sacrosanct to the camán', now had a football team. In response, he again urged that concentration should be given to the schools to help spread hurling, as had been done with success in Waterford in recent times.[92]

Throughout the rest of the 1930s, the strength of the game in Tralee decayed as north Kerry clubs again came to dominate the county championship, a position which continues to the present day. Indeed, it could be argued that the internment of many of the town's prominent GAA players due to their political activities was a major reason for the decline in hurling in Tralee at this time. However, the eternal problems of club apathy towards the county

The Dr Crokes Hurling Team, 1934 *(Courtesy of John Keogh, Dr Crokes GAA)*

team, the continued reluctance of the county board to devote enough attention to the sport in Kerry and the smothering success of the Kerry footballers on a national stage would conspire to condemn hurling in Kerry to a twilight existence, obscured by the radiance of its football tradition. But the county should not be singled out for this failure. Responding to attempts by the GAA in 1925 to have hurling designated an Olympic sport, *Sport* commentated that it would be far better for the Central Council to devise ways of spreading the game outside its traditional counties.[93] It is a challenge the GAA grapples with to this very day.

Making a Home: the Austin Stack Park and Fitzgerald Stadium Projects

Throughout the history of sporting organisations across the world, the acquisition of grounds or facilities has proven to be of fundamental importance to long-term viability. The GAA was no different. With the Central Council securing Croke Park as its permanent national base and home, county boards sought to emulate the example. They were fortunate to have an active supporter in their endeavours in the shape of Pádraig Ó Caoimh, who became general secretary of the GAA in 1929 and was a key figure in the development of GAA grounds across Ireland.[94] From the early 1930s, a host of new county stadiums, such as McHale Park in Castlebar, Cusack Park Ennis and the Gaelic Grounds in Limerick, were opened by those counties' respective GAA boards. In Kerry, the need for a county ground had long been recognised. *The Kerryman* complained in 1927 that there was no pitch or ground to hold a gathering of 10,000 and that serious thought needed to be given to acquiring its own arena.[95] In an era when the county's GAA finances often remained in a perilous state, the advantages of the Kerry Board owning and operating its own ground free from the significant financial drain of renting were obvious.

Since the inception of the GAA in Kerry, the Tralee Sportsground in Boherbee had been the epicentre of Gaelic activity in the county. By the early 1920s, the ground was leased to the Kerry Board and run by a committee headed by John Joe Sheehy. In 1927, the AGM of the Sportsground Committee showed that debts it had incurred through various improvements to the ground over the previous years had been cleared off. In addition, the lease arrangement for the field was due to expire. Serious plans were now made by the Kerry Board to raise sufficient capital to enable it to purchase the Sportsground outright. The principal reason for Kerry conducting its first tour of the US in 1927 was to raise £500 from the games' profits in order to purchase the stadium. When the tour's promoter reneged on his commitment, the Kerry Board had to come up with alternative sources of finance. While the Central Council was reluctant to approve such a large loan to enable the Kerry GAA to purchase the ground, the Munster Council was far more supportive and invested £400 of its own money in the project between 1928 and '29.[96]

The venture was given added impetus by the sudden death of Austin Stack in April 1929. A towering figure in the Kerry GAA where, since the re-formation of the Kerry Board in 1924, he had continued each year to be nominated unopposed as president, his death caused huge shock in his native Tralee. Following the precedent of such grounds as Croke Park, it was hoped the Tralee

Sportsground project would be a fitting monument to his memory. Through a combination of Munster Council investments and local collections, the Kerry Board raised the £500 necessary to purchase the arena in October 1929. But in addition to this purchase price, it was found that considerable cost would have to be incurred in order to bring the pitch, player facilities and stands up to approved standard. The 1931 Kerry tour to America managed to raise £500 towards the development work. Following the tour, the extent of the work required was laid out by John Joe Sheehy at a meeting in Tralee. The ground's oval pitch had to be converted into the standard 150 x 90 yard GAA playing field which, once completed, would allow the town to attract and stage some of the lucrative hurling ties between teams such as Cork, Tipperary and Limerick. Plans were made to raise a new stand and, beneath the concrete structure, dressing rooms, lavatories and shower baths were to be constructed for the players. Overall, £1,000 was required to complete the work, the cost of squaring the pitch alone being £150. Having raised £540 already, Sheehy suggested that a public appeal be made immediately to raise the remaining monies needed. A further meeting still found them £330 short of the required amount and it was decided to approach the Central and Munster Councils for the remainder.[97] The Central Council was less than helpful, agreeing to forward only £100, a decision which caused consternation in Kerry. This was seen by some as an insult, especially considering the amount of money Kerry teams had raised for the council historically. Despite this, with another grant of £100 in early 1932 and more public appeals, the required sum was raised. In December 1931, work on constructing a grandstand and extending and squaring the pitch began.

On 1 May 1932, the Austin Stack Memorial Park was formally opened. The Rev. Canon Breen of St Brendan's Seminary presided over the opening ceremony which was also addressed by Sean McCarthy, the GAA's president. In addition to work on the grandstand, two embankments were constructed which commanded a clear view of the pitch for all spectators. An attendance of 2,500 turned out for the ceremony, which included the staging of the Kerry football college final between St Brendan's and Tralee CBS and an exhibition match between a united university of Ireland team and the Kerry senior footballers.[98] After forty-eight years, the Kerry GAA had secured its first permanent home. Work to develop the ground continued over the next two years which increased the stadium's capacity to 20,000, with the newly erected stand being able to hold 1,000, the embankments 14,000 and the sideline 5,000. In 1934, Austin Stack Park was selected to host the All-Ireland semi-final between Kerry and Dublin. Further improvements were made to prepare the ground for the match, with volunteers from the Tralee clubs carrying out the work. The pitch was enclosed with a wire fence while the embankments were raised and widened around the ground. Inside the paling, sideline seats were installed to provide accommodation for 5,000.[99] A record attendance of 21,438 for an All-Ireland semi-final crowded into the new arena to see Dublin bring a definitive end to one of the greatest eras in the Kerry GAA, beating the home side by 3-8 to 0-6. At the same time that work on transforming the Tralee Sportsground had begun, the death of another iconic Kerry Gael would prove the catalyst for an even more ambitious stadium project in Killarney.

On 26 September 1930, the GAA community in Ireland was stunned by the sudden death of Dick Fitzgerald, the famous ex-Kerry captain. Following his death, thoughts turned quickly to a suitable memorial to honour him and his contribution to the Kerry GAA. Dr Éamonn O'Sullivan, by then head of the Killarney Mental Hospital, took the lead in this project. At a meeting of the Kerry Board in November, O'Sullivan proposed that a field be bought in Killarney and renamed Fitzgerald Park. In order to facilitate this, he suggested that the present ground used by the GAA in the town be sold and that profits, along with an additional £400, be used to purchase a new site. The county board unanimously agreed to the idea and a Fitzgerald memorial committee under Dr O'Sullivan was formed. Over the next five years, countless appeals to the Kerry public, both in Ireland and abroad, and to the Central and Munster Councils were made to help raise funds for the enormous project. In October 1931, a challenge match was held between Mayo and Kerry to finance the venture, while the Munster Council invested £400 and the Central Council £200.[100]

Having secured sufficient funds, a general meeting of the Dr

Construction work being carried out on Fitzgerald Stadium, Killarney
(Courtesy of Fitzgerald Stadium Collection)

Crokes GAA club in March 1932 recommended that a large field at Kilcoolaght be purchased for £750. It was quite probable Dr O'Sullivan had the final say in choosing the site. The land was directly adjacent and overlooked by the town's mental hospital where he worked. O'Sullivan's position as head of St Finan's Hospital played a huge part in the development of the stadium. Occupational therapy had been largely unheard of in such institutions at the time, yet O'Sullivan sought and gained permission in March 1933 to allow patients to work on developing the field. Though there was some condemnation for this in the local press, O'Sullivan was in no doubt that the work was of great therapeutic value to the patients.

Work on the ground proceeded apace throughout 1933 and 1934, with a large hillock in the centre of the pitch being removed and the soil used to build up the embankments around the ground. Though the total estimated cost of the development was put at £24,000, the work was completed for £3,000 as most of the labour was provided free of charge, many workers being actual patients of O'Sullivan's. Towards the end of 1934, *The Kerryman* devoted an entire page to the progress of the work, accompanied by panoramic pictures of the pitch and embankments, calling it 'The finest Gaelic Arena in Ireland'. The paper described the 12 acres of field enclosed by a concrete wall and the circular entrance specially designed by architect Michael Reidy. The pitch would be 15 yards longer and 13 yards wider than Croke Park and was surrounded by a banked cycle track. The 170-yard pitch was flanked on one side by a 30-foot natural slope, about the same gradient as Hill 16, and the paper estimated at least 28,000 would be accommodated here alone. It overenthusiastically projected the total capacity at 70,000.[101]

On 31 May 1936, Fitzgerald stadium was formally opened with a huge public ceremony in the town. A crowd of 28,000 converged on the ground, which was blessed by Dr O'Brien, Bishop of Kerry, in the company of the Archbishop of Cashel, Dr Harty. Kerry and Mayo lined out to play a challenge match for a set of gold

Poster advertising the opening of Fitzerald Stadium, May 1936
(Courtesy of Fitzgerald Stadium Collection)

medals to mark the occasion. Before the game, surviving members of Kerry teams going back to the Laune Rangers side of 1892 were paraded around the ground behind the bands for the opening ceremony. The following year, the stadium played host to the 1937 All-Ireland hurling final as Croke Park was unavailable due to improvement works. Kilkenny and Tipperary battled in front of an estimated crowd of 50,000.

In its quest to find a home for its Gaelic teams, the Kerry GAA proved singularly successful. By the mid-1930s, the county could boast two of the largest and finest stadiums available anywhere in Ireland.

Official opening of Fitzgerald Stadium, 31 May 1936. Canon Hamilton, the chairman of the Munster GAA Board, addresses the crowd as Dr Éamonn O'Sullivan (left) and Eugene O'Sullivan, chairman of Killarney UDC, listen intently. *(Courtesy of Fitzgerald Stadium Collection)*

The GAA and Education, 1905–34

The introduction of organised sport into the education institutions of society was fundamental for the development and mass appeal of any sport that was developed during the course of the Victorian sports revolution. By the turn of the twentieth century, Catholic orders such as the Christian Brothers dominated both primary and secondary education in Ireland. In the absence of a widespread system of fee-paying schools, similar to those in England, the GAA faced the challenge of how to develop its games among the country's youth given the lack of sport on the educational curriculum of Ireland's schools. In Britain it was only after 1906 that sport began to be organised officially within the national education system.[102] It was around this time that attempts were being made among schools in Kerry to organise inter-school hurling and football matches. Branches of the county's Gaelic League seemed to have taken the lead in this. In May 1905, a football match in Filemore was organised between the local Carhen and Teeromoyle national schools. The following year's South Kerry GAA Convention noted that some teachers in the Iveragh Peninsula had taken it upon themselves to organise matches between schools and the board hoped that every teacher would do likewise to establish a competition between all schools in the region. In 1908, the Munster Council decided to introduce a Munster Shield competition between secondary schools and colleges in the province.[103] In April 1909, the Kerry Board inaugurated its own school league competition.[104] Such school competitions continued to be played both on a county and provincial basis over the next six years, although because of the fluctuating fortunes of the GAA in Kerry they were not always run or finished in any given year and did not appear to be very successful. However, wartime restrictions, the effects of growing political nationalism on the GAA and finally the Anglo-Irish and Civil Wars effectively ended any attempts to promote games in the state's national and secondary school system.

The GAA, along with cultural intuitions like the Gaelic League, had been an enthusiastic supporter of the campaign to open up third-level education to the Catholic youth of Ireland, a campaign that dominated Church–state relations at the beginning of the twentieth century. It was into this emerging national, Catholic, third-level education system that the GAA made its first coordinated attempt to develop games within Irish education. In 1911, the GAA founded the Sigerson Cup, an inter-varsity Gaelic football competition to promote the sport in third-level institutions throughout Ireland. In 1912, the Fitzgibbon Cup was offered up for similar competition in hurling.

Yet it was only when the association emerged after the long years of revolution that any serious attempt to organise its games within the Free State's primary and second-level educational system was mounted. In 1926, Dr Éamonn O'Sullivan, the Kerry football trainer, moved to establish a permanent secondary schools football competition in Kerry.[105] In March, he arranged the inaugural meeting of the Kerry Colleges' GAA Board.[106] Dr O'Sullivan stressed the need for such a board because of the progress that rugby and other foreign games were making within the schools of Kerry which he felt was to the detriment of Gaelic games. At the next meeting of the Colleges' Board, affiliation fees were received from St Brendan's, St Michael's in Listowel, CBS Tralee, Tralee Central Technical School, CBS Dingle, the intermediate school in Killorglin, CBS Cahersiveen, Presentation Monastery in Killarney and the Jeffers Institute, Tralee. That June, the Tralee CBS junior team won the first Dunloe Cup, beating St Brendan's in the final 1-7 to 1-1. On 30 May, the St Brendan's senior team won the O'Sullivan Cup final, beating the Tralee Technical School.

Following on from his success in Kerry, O'Sullivan organised a meeting of representatives of the schools and colleges of Munster in February 1927. The meeting established a Munster Schools and Colleges Board and decided to run competitions for teams in the under-seventeen and under-nineteen grades in both football and hurling. The following year, Archbishop Harty of Cashel offered the Harty Cup for competition between senior hurling colleges in the province. In addition, the Munster Council Cup was put up for competition among senior football college teams. In May 1927, O'Sullivan was instrumental in forming an All-Ireland Colleges Council to promote school games on a national basis. At its inaugural meeting, O'Sullivan was appointed the body's secretary and representative to the Central Council.[107] That same year, he organised an All-Ireland football and hurling tournament based on a selection of school sides from each province. Only Munster and Leinster competed in its first year, but in 1928 all four provinces took part in the competition.

In 1927, the GAA's Annual Congress passed a motion proposed by the Cork County Board to establish minor All-Ireland championships for players under eighteen years of age.[108] In 1928,

St Brendan's Past Pupil Side, 1924. Back (l–r): Fr David O'Connor, Jim Flaherty, Dick Fitzgerald, unknown, Dr Éamonn O'Sullivan, Canon Breen (president, St Brendan's); middle (l–r): unknown, Jack Swell, Dan Carroll, unknown, Vincie Doyle, Paul Russell; front (l–r): Harry Turner, unknown, Con Healy, B. McSweeney, Jack Sheahan. Photo taken on town cricket field. *(Courtesy of John Keogh, Dr Crokes GAA)*

the first minor hurling All-Ireland championship was played, with Cork winning. Kerry was nominated to represent Munster in the football championship but the competition fell through. However, in 1929 the first All-Ireland minor football championship was held, with Clare emerging victorious. Kerry would dominate the grade in the early 1930s, winning three All-Ireland titles between 1931 and '33.

It is no surprise that Kerry's most dominant period in football coincided with the establishment of school competitions in the county. The O'Sullivan and Dunloe Cups would unearth and produce players who would continue to form the backbone of

Kerry's club and county sides. In the process, schools such as St Brendan's in Killarney and Tralee CBS would become renowned nurseries for Kerry's inter-county players. The influence of the church is apparent in the early pioneers of these competitions such as Canon Breen and Brother Turner of Tralee. In its wish to foster native games in education and produce healthy young males, the Catholic Church conjoined the twin forces of the 'Irish Ireland' movement and the broader developments of the Victorian sports revolution. Its success would become the powerhouse of the Kerry GAA for generations to come.

Politics and the GAA, 1930–4

Entering the 1930s, the GAA projected itself as a confident, vibrant and harmonious organisation. Yet as with so many times in its past, the association and its heterogeneous membership was not immune to the greater political and social climate in which it existed. The early 1930s witnessed a fundamental power shift in Irish politics that briefly threatened the entire stability of the Free State. In Kerry, where sport and politics could never easily be separated, the effects on the GAA were most marked.

By 1926, Éamon de Valera, president of Sinn Féin, had become disaffected with the political direction the party was taking. Because of its rejection of the treaty, Sinn Féin-elected TDs conducted a policy of abstention from the Oireachtas. This meant that the ruling Cumann na nGaedheal party was in the unusual electoral position of not needing or receiving a majority of the popular vote in order to govern.[109] As a result, the government operated without strong opposition within the Dáil, save for a small number of Labour TDs. De Valera had come to believe that gaining power was his best chance of securing an Irish Republic and ending the state's continued dependence on Britain. In March, he announced that he was in favour of entering the Dáil as a matter of policy, not principle, if the Oath of Allegiance was abolished. The Sinn Féin Ard-Fheis subsequently rejected this, leading to his resignation as president of the party. De Valera quickly established a new political organisation, Fianna Fáil, which was dedicated to securing a united Ireland while developing a native Irish culture and self-sufficient economy. Over the next year,

Sinn Féin rapidly lost ground to the new republican party and quickly diminished as a viable political entity. At the next general election in June 1927, Cumann na nGaedheal performed poorly, with Fianna Fáil managing to win forty-four seats, just three less than the government party.

As we have seen, in 1926 the IRA began once more to show signs of activity. In July 1927, the Minister for Justice, Kevin O'Higgins, was assassinated by three IRA members. In response, the government introduced a Public Safety Act, which authorised the death penalty for political crimes, and an Electoral Amendment Act, which required all elected TDs to take their seats. This forced Fianna Fáil's entry into the house in August. For the first time the Cumann na nGaedheal government would have to deal with vigorous opposition as two parties, which were in effect the political groupings of the opposing sides of the Civil War, clashed in the Dáil chamber.

Over the term of the next government, Cosgrave's support base gradually eroded. This was nothing extraordinary. As Diarmaid Ferriter argues, Cumann na nGaedheal was never very popular with the electorate and had maintained power principally due to the abstention tactics of the opposition. Because it was seen as the party of law and order, it was difficult for them to connect with voters once a sense of stability returned. In addition, it was often accused of being too quick to ape the manner of the former conquerors and indeed a noticeable feature of life in the years immediately after independence was the anglicisation of the higher echelons of Irish society. Fianna Fáil was able to attack, with great success, the government's poor economic performance. Cumann na nGaedheal favoured well-off and established businesses and clung to a belief that Irish economic development went hand-in-hand with agricultural development. As a result, only 14 per cent of the workforce was in industrial employment and emigration continued as a fact of life, with more than 166,000 leaving Irish shores between 1926 and '36.[110] At the general election in February 1932, Cosgrave was swept from office, with Fianna Fáil winning seventy-two seats to Cumann na nGaedheal's fifty-seven. Once in power, de Valera quickly set about cutting ties with Britain and in April the Oath of Allegiance was removed from the Irish constitution. In early 1933, de Valera called a snap election which succeeded in further enhancing Fianna Fáil's power in the Dáil.

With the rise of Fianna Fáil, the IRA began to emerge from the political shadows and threw their support behind the new party. That they did so should not be surprising given the spiritual status de Valera, a veteran of the 1916 Rising, had within the organisation. His party's stated aim was one and the same as that of the IRA: the cessation of partition and the establishment of a 32-county Irish Republic. By 1931, as Fianna Fáil's popularity among the electorate continued to grow, the IRA was again actively recruiting new members and in Kerry throughout 1930–1, there were several instances of republican arrests. In July 1931, eight men were charged by a military tribunal set up under the Public Safety Act for organising and drilling a group of 200 men in military exercises near Listowel.[111] In Kerry, there was much evidence linking endorsement of the IRA with the more generalised political support for republicans. Over 67 per cent of the popular vote in 1933 went to Fianna Fáil and it seems there was a direct connection between this result, support for the IRA and the region's history during the revolutionary period. It was believed that because the county had been so ruthlessly treated in the past, the Civil War would remain a bitter memory to many Kerry youths, which resulted in continued and active IRA support. Several years later, this theory was echoed when army intelligence examined why the IRA, which had almost vanished elsewhere, was able to maintain its organisation in Kerry. It was believed that the legacy of family tragedy in the Tan or Civil War was the main basis for this residual support.[112]

Following de Valera's election victory in 1932, the IRA's membership witnessed considerable growth. Its contribution to Fianna Fáil's election success and the enthusiasm this victory generated allowed the organisation to recruit relatively openly throughout that year. The growing confidence of the IRA's command was evident in orders such as those given to members in Tralee that they had 'an opportunity now that we have been looking for, for years and every advantage should be taken of it in order to improve the training and morale of our organisation'.[113] Enlistment was encouraged by Fianna Fáil's decision to release all

IRA members convicted by the military tribunals over the preceding five years. In addition, the law that banned the IRA was allowed to lapse, leading to an immediate resumption in drilling and recruiting. The increasing strength and exuberance of the organisation was manifested in the numerous public parades, drills and commemorations held by the IRA across Ireland. In Kerry throughout 1932, a series of memorials and commemorations to fallen IRA members in the Anglo-Irish and Civil Wars were unveiled across the county in large public ceremonies. Furthermore, events such as the sixteenth anniversary of the 1916 Rising were celebrated with renewed fervour across the county, with local IRA units often taking a leading part in celebrations. With Fianna Fáil's victory in 1933, the IRA's membership reached its post-Civil War high point and estimated its numbers at around 16,000.[114] However, this marked increase in IRA activity threatened to destabilise the political situation severely, as the IRA in Kerry and many other areas of rural Ireland was brought into open conflict with another paramilitary force, the Blueshirt movement.

In the lead-up to the 1932 election, the IRA began a campaign of intimidation against supporters of Cosgrave's party. Cumann na nGaedheal election meetings were increasingly raided and broken up by local IRA units. In response to local intimidation, the party organised its own defence force in the form of the Army Comrades Association (ACA). The new organisation grew steadily among supporters of Cumann na nGaedheal. However, what gave real impetus to the movement was the political emergence of General Eoin O'Duffy. Shortly after Fianna Fáil's election victory in 1933, de Valera sacked O'Duffy, a prominent supporter of the previous Cosgrave government, from his position as Garda Commissioner. In response, O'Duffy was handed the leadership of the ACA. Modelling it on his own admiration for Benito Mussolini and his fascist Blackshirt movement in Italy, O'Duffy adopted a blue shirt as the organisation's new uniform, a decision which gave rise to their popular name.[115]

Immediately O'Duffy set out on a national campaign of recruitment for the new body and during his leadership, membership increased enormously from 8,337 in October 1932 to 37,937 by March 1934. Despite O'Duffy's political views, it would be wrong to view the Blueshirts as some sort of Irish proto-fascist entity. In reality it was a rural-based and highly conservative movement whose image was coloured by O'Duffy's personal fascism. Indeed, an important appeal was the movement's strong embrace of an active social and sporting calendar.[116] Yet O'Duffy was a serious challenge to the authority of de Valera's government. After a summer of recruiting, he organised a mass march on the Dáil in August 1933 in the mould of Mussolini's famous 'March on Rome' which had toppled the post-war Italian government. In response to this show of force, de Valera moved decisively against him. Three hundred armed guards were posted outside Leinster House and raids were carried out on the homes of suspected Blueshirts across the city. As a consequence, O'Duffy was forced to abandon his march. On 23 August, the government banned the ACA. While opposition parties under Cumann na nGaedheal moved to re-form themselves into a new political party that would become Fine Gael, O'Duffy merely renamed his movement the National Guards and continued on recruiting.[117] Not everyone supported the increasingly militaristic trappings of the ACA under O'Duffy. In Kerry, Con Brosnan had initially been one of its principal supporters, being appointed to the post of organiser in the twenty-six counties. However, he soon became disillusioned with the path it had taken. In early 1933, he resigned when an executive meeting in Dublin rejected his motion that the movement declare itself non-political.

It was inevitable that the rise in Blueshirt activity would bring them into increasing conflict with the republican IRA. Between 1933 and '34, violence between the two private armies reached its height in the Irish countryside. It is likely that in areas such as Kerry the manifestation of violence between the Blueshirts, a movement comprised predominantly of large farmers and the middle class, and the IRA, an organisation consisting mainly of the rural poor, was in many respects the continuation of the agrarian struggles that had sporadically affected the county during the 1880s and early 1920s. Indeed, this is all the more likely given the economic environment in which it took place, with de Valera's Economic War against Britain having a devastating impact on the livelihoods of those in Irish agriculture during this time.

The emergence of ACA and the National Guards gave local

IRA units a focus for their energies and led to increased recruitment. The conflict was particularly intense in Kerry. This should not be surprising: as we have noted, the IRA's appeal in Kerry remained strong due to the legacy of the Civil War atrocities in the county. IRA leaders such as J.J. Sheehy argued that the Blueshirts should be crushed before they had a chance to do the same to the IRA. The majority of the IRA in Kerry was in agreement on need for confrontation. Whether this was because it was led by a man who made 'Kerry a graveyard in 1922' (during the Civil War, General O'Duffy had been one of the principal architects of the Free State Army's strategy of seaborne landings which had led to harsh subjection of Kerry from republican forces) or because they represented dictatorship is debatable. Yet in the end it meant the IRA was never likely to avoid a conflict.[118] The intensity of IRA violence towards it was influenced not only by the fact that the Blueshirts greatly outnumbered the IRA, but also because throughout 1933 in areas such as Kerry it had begun to make its presence felt. Thus, in Ballylongford, IRA members putting up posters to advertise the forthcoming Easter 1916 commemoration were set upon by groups of ACA members and severely beaten. In October 1933, O'Duffy attempted to address a large public meeting in support of the National Guards in Tralee. This resulted in a mass riot when a large IRA element in the crowd, which included several members of the town's local GAA clubs, attacked the platform and in the melee O'Duffy was struck in the head with a hammer. Only with difficulty were the local police able to restore order later that night.[119]

With the situation across the country becoming ever more volatile, de Valera realised that both groups would have to be dealt with. In February 1934, a bill preventing the wearing of private uniforms, badges, banners and the use of military titles was introduced by the Minister for Justice. Fianna Fáil also reinstated military tribunals to undermine both the Blueshirts and the IRA. By the end of 1934, the Blueshirts had effectively been broken as an organisation and by then violence between it and the IRA had decreased perceptibly. In addition, throughout 1935 arrests, internments and military tribunals began to have a telling effect on IRA activity. In 1936, after a series of three high-profile

John Joe Sheehy. This photograph illustrates the success Kerry achieved in the decade after independence. A diehard republican, Sheehy represented the IRA's continued influence on the county board during the politically volatile period of the early 1930s. *(Courtesy of Frank Burke)*

murders which shocked Irish public opinion, the IRA was officially outlawed and driven underground.

As Joseph Lee argues, the conflict between the IRA and the Blueshirts was the last spasm of the fever that had infected Irish social and political life since the Civil War.[120] In this context, it is easy to understand the intensity of the struggle in Kerry, a county that had been bitterly divided over the events of 1923. Both the IRA and Blueshirt movements recruited heavily in Kerry, with both organisations targeting young men. Though the conflict between the two forces did not permanently harm the national GAA, the unique situation in Kerry, where the IRA retained a powerful influence on the leadership of the Kerry GAA, ensured that the struggle would have a significant and detrimental impact on the association in the county.

By the 1930s, local IRA commanders such as Sheehy and J.J. Rice of Tralee were respected and influential members of the county board. In addition, more recent recruits to the IRA, such as Patrick Fleming, the IRA's commander in Killarney, were also actively involved in the association, with Fleming a prominent member of the recently formed Killarney Legion GAA club. As we have seen, Tralee remained a stronghold for IRA activity in the county throughout this time and the town's District Board and individual clubs reflected this strong republican element. For example, each of Tralee's three football clubs boasted individual IRA companies of over 100 men.[121] Yet outside Tralee, support for the republican movement within the membership of the Kerry GAA was far from universal. For instance, Con Brosnan had run as a North Kerry candidate for Cumann na nGaedheal in the 1933 general election. Brosnan was a popular and persuasive figure within the Kerry GAA, so much so that the IRA's leadership had brought the Kerry IRA to task for doing little to undermine his influence within the association there.[122]

If Tralee was a noted republican stronghold, then Listowel, due to Brosnan's influence, was a notable bastion of support for Cosgrave's party and, from 1932, the ACA and subsequent National Guards movements. In September 1932, the first branch of the Kerry ACA was organised in Listowel. Under the presidency of Brosnan, it became the headquarters of the movement in the county and branches spread rapidly across north Kerry so that by early 1933 there were over a thousand members in the district.[123] Support for the Blueshirts movement remained strong in the district even after Brosnan severed his links with the organisation in February 1933. Despite this, many local areas remained deeply republican. As Listowel was the seat of the North Kerry District Board, it seemed inevitable that the growing political tensions caused by the revival of the IRA would have ramifications for the body. In early 1932 a request was made by local republicans for the board and its affiliated clubs to participate in the upcoming Easter 1916 commemorations. The request was overruled as the board concluded that participation would contravene rule four of the association, which prevented the discussion of political matters and involvement in political events.[124] Yet this decision caused considerable unrest and resentment among some local clubs. Within a week, it was reported that certain clubs had withdrawn from the board's district league, forcing its abandonment. By June, GAA activity in the town was said to have ceased altogether and it was reported that several attempts to call a meeting of the North Kerry Board had come to nothing.[125]

Just as the IRA had always traditionally seen its influence on the GAA as a powerful weapon to exploit for its own means, so too the Blueshirts recognised the advantage of gaining sway within the association. That GAA clubs became identified with O'Duffy's movement is not surprising. O'Duffy himself had been a prominent official within the national GAA after the Civil War and when he took over leadership of the Blueshirts he actively promoted the organisation's sporting and social aspects to attract young members. Indeed, he frequently attacked the dominance of Fianna Fáil supporters in the GAA and demanded his members 'get in everywhere' to control local sporting bodies. He envisaged that soon his movement would be able to control and supervise the association.[126] In response to the political strife that was enveloping much of Ireland, the Central Council was forced to issue a statement to its members on the eve of its jubilee year urging them

> . . . to discourage and discountenance, in these difficult and harassing times, this fatal tendency which threatens to disrupt the good feelings and mutual cooperation which should animate all of us on the road to national and economic regeneration . . . The GAA is non-political, allowing freedom of opinion outside to its members in matters of public policy, but it is broadly national . . . Consequently, we appeal in all earnestness to the members of our movement to do their utmost to abolish the memories of past dissensions.[127]

The fight between the Blueshirts and the IRA in Kerry was particularly pronounced in the north of the county. As the conflict reached its height between 1933 and '34, the GAA in the region would find itself struggling to function. It was stated that across the region political activists were proclaiming affinities between their GAA clubs and the rival political organisations, leading to great antagonism. As a result, local clubs and their players became popularly identified and pilloried as either republican or Blueshirt. Throughout 1933, there were frequent complaints that the administration of the GAA around Listowel had been greatly retarded owing to political differences within local parishes.[128]

These political tensions soon began to manifest themselves on the field of play. The Listowel GAA split over its members' political differences and two rival teams, the Ashes and Pearses, both took part in the North Kerry League that year. During a North Kerry League game between Bedford and Clounmacon in Listowel in 1934, a riot broke out when three Clounmacon players assaulted their opponents. Players and spectators rushed to confront each other amid goads and shouts of 'Up the Blueshirts'. The referee was forced to abandon the game due to the large melee.[129] *The Kerryman* reported that the fight had started over politics, while the Bedford club strongly defended their conduct in the press, their secretary, T. Pelican, declaring that all their members were proud republicans who were in 'complete disagreement of the Blueshirt policy'. In June, eight prominent hurlers refused to play for the North Kerry Board's representative team against Austin Stacks in the county hurling championship. Investigating the matter, the board found that some of the players had been persuaded by a local prominent Blueshirt not to play in order to ensure the failure of matches organised under the county board. That same month, there were reports that the Newtownsandes team was preparing to withdraw from the North Kerry League over the political influence of republicans on its board.[130]

Not only clubs but individual players were being stigmatised. Johnny Walsh of Ballylongford recalls that tensions within the Kerry team dressing room were particularly high at this time, given that many players were associated with either the Blueshirt or republican movements. Walsh, himself a fervent supporter of Cumann na nGaedheal, had made his debut on Kerry's All-Ireland winning side in 1932. Yet his status as Kerry's newest star could not protect him from ill will towards his political stance. During Easter 1933, he was involved in an altercation with local IRA members in the village after which he was branded a Blueshirt, something which alienated him from much of his teammates. This reputation followed him across the Atlantic later that year when he lined out for Kerry against New York in the first match of the county's 1933 American tour. Because of his political leanings he was singled out by the opposition for particular rough treatment, with Tom Armitage, the New York captain who marked him, yelling, 'You Blueshirt, I'll send you back to Cosgrave in a coffin.' Walsh replied he had 'an hour to do it'. Yet Walsh felt that his political beliefs were the reason he was not selected for Kerry team in 1934 and, disillusioned, he turned to rugby before being persuaded to return in 1936 when the political situation had eased.[131]

With continued arrests and imprisonments already having a significant impact on the strength of the IRA, its leadership again decided to make the GAA in Kerry a weapon in its fight for legitimacy. Yet such actions caused major disruption to the county's sporting calendar and did significant damage to the IRA's image in Kerry. Following the riots that had erupted over O'Duffy's visit to Tralee in October 1933, fifteen men from the town were arrested and brought before a military tribunal for their political activities before being interned by de Valera's government. Those arrested were all members of one or other of Tralee's three GAA clubs. In response, the IRA pushed for clubs to stand down and for Kerry to withdraw from inter-county competitions in protest. As a result, the Kerry football team refused to travel for a scheduled National League fixture against Kildare and the hurlers declined to play a match scheduled in Abbeyfeale. There was initially much public support for this stance. Both the East and North Kerry Boards passed resolutions supporting the decisions of the Kerry teams and decided not to fix or play any fixtures until the political prisoners were released.[132] Support for prisoners seemed universal, with even Tralee Rugby Cub forgoing matches in solidarity with their GAA colleagues. At the Annual Convention of the Tralee District Board in January 1934, the gathering unanimously supported the decision of the Kerry team in continuing to refuse to play any matches. It is a noteworthy indication of the republican influence within the body that this decision was followed by a stirring rendition of 'The Soldiers' Song'.

At the following Annual County Board Convention, however, disquiet arose over the continued boycott. It is notable that the press reported the convention as being the smallest and least well attended of the previous decade. The Kerry chairman, Din Joe Bailey, called on members to remember the GAA was a non-political entity that should be tolerant of all political views. Afterwards, a letter was read from the prisoners that congratulated the Kerry hurling and football teams for their protest at the imprisonment of a number of their colleagues. The letter stated that Kerry's protest had brought about improved conditions for the prisoners, such as the abolishment of the rule enforcing silence and the policy of solitary confinement. As they had accomplished all that it was possible for them to do, the letter ended by hoping that the board would lift the boycott on Gaelic games in the county. Reacting to this, Sheehy argued that the Kerry GAA had made its protest and had succeeded in raising the issue to the wider public. He commented that in consequence of the letter, the board was now released from any obligation to continue the protest. Rice then proposed that the board resume its normal activities and this was agreed. He suggested that the board affiliate with the Central Council for the year as normal and if there was any punishment forthcoming over the boycott, so be it. He ended: 'We make no apologies for our actions up to the present and we are prepared to take the consequences.'[133] Following this, matches in the county resumed and the Kerry team re-entered national competitions.

Though the government was attempting to crack down hard on the IRA, police reports stated that republican activity and influence in Kerry continued to grow.[134] IRA commanders such as J.J. Rice constantly addressed public demonstrations, calling on young men to enter the IRA's ranks 'and train for the advancement and protection of the Republic'. In late November 1934, several local members of the Army Volunteer Reserve, an institution founded by de Valera in an attempt to divert recruitment of young men from the IRA, were attacked in Tralee by local IRA members.

In response, police arrested and imprisoned several well-known Tralee republicans. Among the men arrested was Patrick Drummond, the Austin Stacks full-back. As a consequence, the club informed the county board that it would not play as planned in the upcoming 1934 county football final against O'Rahillys.[135]

Whereas the IRA-influenced boycott in early 1934 had not caused any long-term harm to the GAA in Kerry, that which followed in 1935 caused widespread disruption to the local association and did extensive damage to the IRA's image in one of its strongest bastions of support. Clubs such as Tralee Mitchels and Austin Stacks stood down and vowed not to participate in any matches amid accusations that the men held were being subject to torture. At the Kerry County Convention it was decided by a majority vote that Kerry would withdraw from the Munster championship and all national competitions unless the lot of republican prisoners in the Curragh was improved, or until they were released.[136] Likewise, both the 1934 hurling and football championships were abandoned and it was decided to hold no championships for 1935. In response, the Munster Council put pressure on Kerry's Fianna Fáil TDs to persuade the government to give concessions to IRA prisoners and allow Gaelic games to resume in the county.[137] Yet rather than force any concessions from the government, the IRA-influenced boycott accomplished nothing more than a backlash against it by its own supporters in the Kerry GAA. Soon the IRA was blamed for reducing the status of football in Kerry 'to below zero' and it was stated that soccer and rugby had gained significant ground in Kerry because the GAA was leaving the field open to them. An indication of the unpopularity of the boycott was seen in May 1935 when IRA prisoners in the Curragh themselves called on the GAA in Kerry to resume activity. When concern mounted over the paralysis of the GAA, Sheehy bemoaned that the whole episode was a mess brought about by the IRA biting off more than it could chew.[138] When Gaelic games in Kerry returned to something like normality in 1936, the *Kerry Champion* reflected that while the association nationally had carried on as normal, the government had remained in office and prisoners still in jail, the only thing to have suffered was the GAA in Kerry itself. Though the IRA had the influence within the GAA in Kerry to bring it to a halt for political purposes, it alienated much support by its tactics and ultimately failed to attain its demands.[139]

The 1935 stand-down was the final example of IRA-motivated boycotts that had affected the Kerry GAA on numerous occasions since 1924. While the IRA had continually sought to use these as an effective tactic to highlight particular political issues to the broader Irish public, the events of 1935 and the damage they caused to the association in Kerry proved a bridge too far. Not only had the stand-down not achieved any political concession, it had ended up severely straining the relationship between the IRA and one of its most erstwhile supporters, the Kerry GAA. With the IRA being outlawed later that year, the organisation's influence within the local GAA appreciably diminished.

Fifty Years A-Growing: the GAA in 1934
As the GAA entered its jubilee year, it had never been stronger, encompassing almost a quarter of a million members. Out of the ashes of the Civil War, the association had grown and thrived. In the years following, a new generation of young, enthusiastic officials, who for the most part spurned party politics, had taken over the national administration of the association. This helped strengthen the position and influence of the national GAA as a body largely free from political commitments. Among the most influential were men such as Sean Ryan of Tipperary, who in 1928 became the youngest president yet of the GAA and remained an influential figure within it for the next thirty-five years. In addition, the appointment of Pádraig Ó Caoimh as general secretary proved enormously significant. Although it had operated at a loss for most of the 1920s, Ó Caoimh's appointment – and administra-tive skills – transformed the financial position of the GAA, turning it into a profitable organisation from then on. By 1934, assets exceeded £35,000 and the GAA had a bank credit of almost £40,000. During the ten years after 1924, the number of clubs rose from just over 1,000 to more than 1,600. It flourished in every county in Ireland and for many years branches operated successfully across the UK and the US.

The popularity and spread of its games was unmatched. Though it had taken nearly fifty years, by 1934 a thoroughly

competitive four-province All-Ireland had become a reality. The previous year had witnessed for the first time an Ulster and Connacht team meeting in the All-Ireland final, with Cavan becoming the first Ulster team to claim the title. By now the GAA comfortably held the record for sporting attendances in Ireland. In addition, £30,000 worth of developments were about to be begin to increase the capacity of Croke Park to 58,000, turning it into one of the largest stadiums in the British Isles. Since 1926, its major games had been regularly broadcast across Ireland by the state's radio station, 2RN. Furthermore, the formation of the *Irish Press* in 1931 led to a revolution in national sports coverage of Gaelic games. From the outset, the paper gave extensive and

The Kerry Tradition: the survivors of every victorious team from 1891. The group photo was taken in Killarney in 1953 when the golden jubilee of the 1903 All-Ireland football victory was celebrated. *(Courtesy of Frank Burke)*

sympathetic coverage to the GAA, and its sports section came to be regarded as superior to any of its rivals. As a result, competitors like the *Irish Independent* were forced to raise their own standards and devote more space to their sports columns.[140]

Befitting its status, the association organised several high-profile events to celebrate its half-centenary. To commemorate the anniversary, a special postage stamp was commissioned. The Central Council held its Great Jubilee Congress on 1 April in the association's spiritual home of Thurles. The extensive programme of events began with a reception for delegates and the presentation of addresses from dozens of public bodies. Afterwards, High Mass was celebrated in the cathedral at which the Archbishop of Cashel, Dr Harty, presided and priests actively connected with the GAA officiated. Following the service, there was a large procession through the town's streets to a platform outside Hayes' Hotel where a plaque commemorating the establishment of the GAA was unveiled. After an extensive lunch in the hotel, the Congress finally began at 3 p.m. Among the attendants were a number of special guests, including Michael Cusack's son, John and three surviving members of the Thurles team which won the inaugural hurling All-Ireland in 1887. The delegates passed a motion to host a national tournament in Thurles to celebrate the centenary.[141] In Kerry, a special jubilee tournament was organised by the Tralee District Board to mark the occasion.[142] That September in Dublin, a mass parade was held through the city to celebrate the GAA which ended at Croke Park, where 35,000 watched a series of school teams in action. Also that year, most of the leading national papers issued special supplements commemorating the history of the association.

The GAA was in self-congratulatory mood and this was reflected in the musings of officials, journalists and historians which appeared in the national press and in print throughout the year and beyond. During his presidential address to the Jubilee Congress, Sean Ryan proudly argued that 'the men of the GAA have played a manly part in resuscitating the Irish outlook and in maintaining the onward march to cultural, economic and general liberty'.[143] In this, Ryan was fervently arguing that the GAA had achieved the twin aims it had set itself in 1884 of reviving Ireland's traditional field games while also erecting a barrier to the tide of anglicisation that had been threatening to engulf the island. In his secretary's report to delegates, Pádraig Ó Caoimh concurred. The GAA, he argued, was not merely a successful sporting body. No, the association had taken up

> . . . the cause of native pastimes . . . to give them new vitality that would render their adherents a power in the re-erection of the Gaelic state to which they historically

belong. The physical wellbeing and social equality of the native race as a whole were its basic aims and in the circumstances prevailing in Ireland, these objectives imposed a paramount national purpose; since it would be mockery to bid a man exercise his limbs, unless you set them free.[144]

Addressing the Annual Munster GAA Convention a month earlier, W.P. Clifford, the council's president, had extolled that:

[A]t all times the GAA's members had shown an intense love of the motherland and the ideal of an Ireland, Gaelic, free and happy had never been absent for their minds . . . [her independence] . . . was sealed with the blood of its members throughout the various counties and doubly so with the blood of its players in Croke Park.[145]

In these sentiments, the officials in question were merely restating what many within the association and wider Ireland took as fact. Such speeches and subsequent histories of the GAA, such as P.J. Devlin's *Our Native Game* and P.D. Mehigan's *Hurling: Ireland's National Game*, portrayed the GAA as stirring a romantic and mythical notion of nationality which stressed sporting physical fitness as the route to securing national self-rule. The GAA was viewed both by contemporary historians and its own officials as a heroic underground movement which succeeded against huge odds to re-establish native political and cultural identity in the face of British oppression.[146] Highlighting the Bloody Sunday massacre, as Clifford had done, allowed the GAA to portray itself as being at the forefront of the gallant fight against British rule. With such incidents to reference, by 1934 the association could project itself to the new Free State as an organisation with unblemished nationalist credentials.[147] In part, this work has attempted to show that such sentiments were a historical construct, an easy and convenient truth to wash over the very real tensions and conflicts between various personalities and political groups within its membership which on occasion threatened to overwhelm the GAA both at a national and local level. The association was as varied and complex an organisation as the wide-ranging membership of which it was comprised. No one historical narrative, however well constructed or widely believed, could hope to tell its entire story.

Yet it is clear that by 1934 the GAA still faced huge challenges, some of which it still grapples with today. As the example of Kerry has shown, the failure to expand hurling in any meaningful or lasting way outside its traditional half dozen counties drew criticism which continues to this day. Likewise, there remained the failure of the association to attract active participation from non-Catholic communities both north and south of the border. In addition, the association continued, and in some sense still continues, to exhibit a marked insecurity when faced with the challenge of international sports such as soccer and rugby union. But despite these issues, there can be little doubt that by its jubilee year the association had become one of the resting pillars of the Irish Free State, a position it continues to hold.

The years surrounding the jubilee proved a testing time for the association in Kerry. Semi-final defeats in 1933 and '34 finally spelled the end of the great Kerry team of Sheehy, Brosnan, Barrett et al. Indeed, with the defeat of the Kerry footballers in the All-Ireland junior final that October, 1934 would be the first year since 1925 that Kerry had failed to win an All-Ireland title in any grade.[148] Political disturbances led to the abandonment of Gaelic games there throughout the following year. Yet the Kerry tradition, first established with renown on the fields of Thurles by the team of Thady O'Gorman and Dick Fitzgerald, could not be so easily disregarded. In January 1936, the Kerry GAA reorganised itself and re-entered its teams in national competitions. That April, the Kerry county championships were revived. By 1937, it had regained the All-Ireland, defeating Cavan in a replay after the drawn match had attracted a new record attendance of 52,000. In 1938, almost 70,000 people watched Kerry and Galway contest the All-Ireland final, which ended in a draw, Galway winning the replay. Of the five All-Irelands played between 1937 and '41, Kerry won four. The next chapter of its football dynasty was only beginning.

Conclusion

'What would Kerry be without football?'

In an essay on the GAA and its place in Irish society, Tom Humphries enquired, 'What would Kerry be without football?' Humphries was trying to convey to his readership the unique position the Gaelic Athletic Association occupies in counties such as Kerry. The association has never been a purely sporting body. Rather, it is an institution which has stitched its way into the very fabric of society in areas such as the Kingdom. Indeed, perhaps there is no county in Ireland whose greater history of the past 130 years has been so intertwined with Gaelic games activity.

By 1934, the modern GAA had been firmly established. This work has attempted to outline the social, economic and political factors in order to highlight how this process was achieved in Kerry. Of course, the establishment of the GAA in Ireland was part of the same progression of sports organisation, codification and administration that was occurring simultaneously across the British Isles. The association was a fully fledged creation of the wider Victorian sports revolution. Although the GAA was openly hostile to all things English and to the ever encroaching process of anglicisation, the association, its growth and early development bore all the hallmarks of its rival Victorian sports codes. Much of what it proclaimed to be distinctively Irish, such as its promotion of muscular Christianity and the advocating of self-control among its athletes, was in fact adapted from English methodology.[2] However, given the social and economic climate of areas such as Kerry, the GAA was a specific Irish adaptation to fit Irish circumstances.

With agricultural depression, agrarian unrest and chronic emigration all factors in Irish society throughout much of its formative years, the GAA's model of organisation had to reflect this social reality. As it emerged within a rural society, the GAA could not simply ape the factory or street club structure which its contemporaries of rugby or soccer were developing in post-Industrial Revolution Britain. Aware of the poverty of rural Ireland, the early administrators of the GAA grafted their organisation onto the Irish parochial system. At a stroke this provided the association with a durable territorial structure that at the same time harked back to the traditional townland organisation of teams in older sports such as iomán and caid. Likewise, the GAA utilised the administrative configuration of political organisations like the National League as a blueprint for their clubs.

Tying into its organisational framework was the economic reality for its membership. The GAA was specially founded by Michael Cusack to secure popular control of Irish athletics for that class of men most excluded by the increasing tendency of elitism among sports bodies in Victorian Britain.[3] The men who were first attracted into the association were those from the lower middle and working classes in Irish life. By offering participation in sport at a cost they could afford, while also insisting that events be held on Sundays, the main day of rest and recreation, Cusack's fledgling organisation was able to attract the support of the broad base of Irish society. In a rural area like Kerry that meant a membership dominated by farmers, agrarian labourers, white-collar workers, tradesmen and certain professionals such as teachers. Due to the nationalist political stance often taken by those within its leadership, members of the Irish gentry who were a vital financial support for sports such as cricket and rugby shied away from participation or patronage in the GAA. As a consequence, the average GAA club lacked the financial clout of its codified rivals. In their absence the formation and control of clubs in rural areas such as Kerry was often carried out by enterprising publicans, the local big farmer or national school teachers.

This very membership base was drawn from the same strata in Irish society that was becoming increasingly politically active and radicalised during the 1884–1934 period. A critical factor in this was the rise of cultural nationalism, crystallised in the Gaelic Revival movement which emerged in the mid-1890s. The emerging political and cultural organisations such as the Gaelic League and Sinn Féin had a radical impact on the men who ran the association both nationally and locally. It fed into the GAA a new generation of such politically radicalised officials, who rejuvenated the association in the years after 1900. The most outspoken of this new generation were ardent in their belief that the association should be primarily engaged in a project of national and cultural liberation. In counties like Kerry, officials such as T.F. O'Sullivan typified this new cultural nationalism. Like contemporaries in other counties, O'Sullivan orchestrated an extensive media campaign eulogising the playing of Gaelic games while decrying the corrupting influences of British sports. In the process, O'Sullivan and officials like him were instrumental in the reintroduction of the police and foreign games ban into the GAA. With such acts, the association began to take its place within the re-energised broader nationalist movement which advocated the end of British rule in Ireland.

Yet outside these higher notions of a political mission, the association still had to develop and function as an ordinary sporting body. A county like Kerry presented significant physical challenges which the local GAA was forced to overcome. Its very size, mountainous topography and poor infrastructure greatly hindered attempts to establish a viable, countywide structure to administer and run its games. Officials such as Austin Stack were keenly aware that Kerry's scattered and thinly populated hinterland greatly negated attempts at forming an effective, central controlling body for the association there.[4] A county board based in Tralee could not hope to be able to administer matches and events efficientlyin areas as distant and isolated as the Iveragh or Dingle Peninsulas. Throughout its first fifty years, the association in Kerry struggled to create a permanent framework of clubs in such areas. It was only with the introduction of innovations like district boards that this trend was reversed. Practical control of GAA activity in these regions was thus passed to bodies based in local towns such as Dingle and Cahersiveen. These proved far more suited to the administration of local GAA matters than a central county board based in a distant centre like Tralee. A lack of finance was another constant problem for the GAA in Kerry. Deprived of the patronage of wealthy backers and for so long without adequate facilities such as permanent sports grounds to ensure healthy gate receipts, the Kerry GAA faced an incessant struggle to raise sufficient funds to administer its games. This led to frequent and often bitter confrontations with the Central Council. The Kerry Board constantly claimed it did not receive a sufficient cut of the GAA's profits. In addition, the Central Council continually overlooked Tralee as a venue for inter-county matches. The loss of revenue to the Kerry Board on account of this, especially given the high rent the local GAA paid to operate the ground, again caused major tensions.[5] On a club level, adequate finance was a major factor in the transient nature of most rural clubs in counties such as Kerry. As has been seen, the collapse of the Ballyduff club after their All-Ireland success of 1891 was largely due to the financial cost of contesting that final.

Tied into the question of finance was the practical difficulty of the transport network in a rural region like Kerry. For most of its first fifty years, the Kerry GAA was at the mercy of the rail networks to transport club and county teams to various matches and tournaments. The demand for exorbitant guarantees for special trains to GAA events frequently crippled the meagre budget of the Kerry Board. In 1910, Kerry relinquished its place in the All-Ireland final to make a national protest against the treatment of the association by Ireland's main rail companies. Though controversial, the decisions led to a radical improvement in the treatment of the GAA by transport providers in the country in the years that followed.

Throughout much of its first fifteen years, the GAA locally struggled to attract spectators to its contests. Against the more defined and codified rules of rugby or soccer, Gaelic games, and in particular football, resembled little more than mass scrimmages with little in the way of tactics or concepts such as positional play. The election of Richard Blake as secretary of the GAA in 1895 coincided with a dramatic improvement in the sport as a spectacle. Blake's insistence that rules be shaped to avoid all ambiguity and be applied consistently by the sport's officials began the process of transforming the game. Between 1905 and '15, Gaelic football became the dominant sport in Ireland in terms of playing numbers, attendances and media interest. Kerry played a vital role in this popularisation of Gaelic games. By the use of such innovations as dedicated training camps, the county led the way in terms of preparation for inter-county matches. These systems were then adopted and adapted by other counties who sought to follow their successful example.

The eventual rise of the GAA as the pre-eminent sporting body in Kerry and Ireland would not have been possible without the effective leadership and administration of prominent local and national officials. The force of personality or its absence cannot be underestimated in the success or failure of the organisation in a local context. The progression of the association in Kerry in these fifty years, its expansion and contraction, can be linked to the presence or absence of men of such ability. Maurice Moynihan provided the first impetus for Gaelic activity, and his retirement from the Kerry Board in the early 1890s coincided with a near-fatal collapse of the association there. Though historical forces such as the Gaelic Revival provided an impetus for organisations such as the GAA, individuals mattered more. The remarkable revival and success that Kerry experienced between 1905 and '15 would not have been achieved without the dedicated work and able management of officials like Austin Stack and T.F. O'Sullivan. Both men ensured that a much more professional and united local administration replaced the ineffectual and politically divided leadership which preceded it in the 1890s.

On the back of their tireless efforts, Kerry became the dominant power in Gaelic football in Ireland. This success sparked an incredible advance in both media interest and public hype in the national game. Following its remarkable success, Kerry developed a unique sporting tradition which in turn shaped the county's own sense of identity. Kerry's football teams came to be seen as the embodiment of the 'Kerry tradition'. This tradition was enhanced by the victories of contemporary Kerry sides in the GAA in America and the international interest in the Kerry team by emigrant Irish communities. In addition, the county's most famous players, such as Dick Fitzgerald, became household names thanks to an explosion of media coverage of Gaelic games. Fitzgerald himself wrote a hugely influential manual on Gaelic football. This work had a profound effect on the coaching of Gaelic football and further added to the perception of Kerry as a place of sporting innovation.

Yet, paradoxically, unprecedented success on the national stage masked the numerous failures of the association within Kerry. The county's newly forged sporting tradition effectively abandoned its second biggest sport, hurling. The fate of hurling and its inability to grow outside its traditional power base in north Kerry was a forceful reminder of the inadequacies and limitations of the GAA's governing body there. Extraordinary success on the national stage also contributed to a significant fall off in support for club football in Kerry. As the county board increasingly devoted its attention to the needs of its inter-county football team, the organisation of club championships duly suffered. County football became dominated by the two large urban clubs of Tralee Mitchels and Killarney's Dr Crokes. In response, smaller clubs increasingly disbanded, apathetic of their chances of competing with such dominance on a local stage. For much of this period, the county had no secondary competition for weaker clubs. Added to this were the significant delays within county competitions which meant many clubs rarely played more than one or two competitive matches a season.

As well as these practical challenges, the evolving political situation in Ireland significantly impacted on the Kerry GAA. The rise of the Irish Volunteers, the Easter Rising of 1916 and the radicalisation of Irish nationalism in the years that followed greatly influenced its membership. The almost incessant political violence between January 1919 and April 1923 in turn had major consequences for its ability to function effectively as a sporting body. In addition, much of the GAA's national leadership saw the organisation as having a political as well as a sporting role. In counties like Kerry, the administration of the GAA was notably affected by the political activities of its membership. No county championship was held in 1915 as county board officers such as Austin Stack became increasingly engrossed in their leadership within the local Volunteer movement. A noticeable political radicalisation of the county's rank-and-file members was apparent in the years after the 1916 Rising. The rise of the Sinn Féin party and its policy of open opposition to British rule in Ireland filtered into the GAA. Anti-enlistment campaigns, the wearing of Sinn Féin colours and republican collections at Gaelic matches in Kerry were practical demonstrations of this.

With the outbreak of the Anglo-Irish War, Gaelic activity in Kerry ultimately collapsed. Dozens of its local membership took an active and often prominent part in the fighting, ensuring that as an organisation the Kerry GAA significantly shaped that conflict. GAA events were halted for fear that they would be used as a convenient nationalist target for British reprisals, as was the case at Croke Park in November 1920. Even with a truce and the start of negotiations on the Anglo-Irish Treaty, many within the Kerry GAA were wary of returning to ordinary sporting activity. Many concurred with the assessment of the Munster Board chairman Austin Brennan that the first duty of GAA members was to help secure the independence of Ireland. Sporting considerations, therefore, remained on hold until this was achieved. The ferocity and bitterness of the Civil War in Kerry made it impossible to contemplate Gaelic activity during those months. Numerous members of the Kerry GAA again found themselves as active participants in the war. Many were subsequently interned over their IRA activity and some of Kerry's best players remained in prison camps until the end of 1923.

As the GAA entered 1924, it did so in a radically altered political reality. Despite the upheavals of the previous eight years, the association had managed to survive as a sporting organisation. Reeling from the catastrophe of the civil strife that had ripped through Irish society, many officials and members approached their work within the GAA with a renewed vigour. The association nationally had taken the wise choice of neutrality during the Civil War. This ensured it provided a neutral ground where foes in the political arena could potentially meet as friends in that of sport. Tensions undoubtedly remained within its membership. These were demonstrated in the arguments over the retention of the foreign games ban which dominated the agenda at various Annual Congresses in the immediate post-Civil War years.

However, in an effort to wash over the Civil War, those writing about the GAA in the years immediately after the conflict

looked back to the role of the association in Ireland's War of
Independence. Events such as the Bloody Sunday massacre ensured
a level of popularity in the post-Civil War era by allowing the GAA
to be portrayed as victims of British brutality and martyrs to the
Irish cause.[6] In Kerry, the years after 1924 witnessed arguably the
most successful era in the county's football history. For a society
torn apart by a brutal civil conflict, the Kerry team, made up of
supporters of both the pro- and anti-treaty divide, was seen by
some as a metaphor for the power of sport to transcend politics.
The reality, though, was much more complex. While the GAA did
play a role in Kerry in helping to heal the wounds of civil conflict,
it could not wash away all that enmity through the process of
winning All-Irelands. Tensions and conflicts within the Kerry GAA
frequently threatened to split the association there in the fifteen
years following their All-Ireland success in 1925. However, in spite
of this, by 1934 the association had become a vital component of
Kerry society. This status was only enhanced by the county's
remarkable sporting success in the 1924–32 period. The transformation of the GAA from a mere sporting body into an active
force in Kerry's cultural, social and political story was complete.

Yet at present it is simply not possible to judge how typical
the development of the GAA in Kerry is compared to other
counties. At the moment, the only similar study is William Nolan's
work on the GAA in Dublin. Nonetheless, comparisons between
both places can be observed. Nolan highlights the significant
influence that the major political and cultural forces in Ireland had
in moulding the embryonic association in Dublin. As in Kerry, the
rise of cultural nationalism drew into the GAA a generation of
officials who both re-energised and redesigned the nationalist
approach of the organisation there. Members of the Dublin GAA
in turn actively participated in and shaped those contemporary
cultural and political movements. Nevertheless, one cannot lose
sight of the obvious social differences between a large urban centre
like Dublin and an isolated, sparsely populated and predominately
rural county such as Kerry. The communal forces that gave birth
to the organisation in Dublin were often far different from those
that shaped the formation of the GAA in Kerry.

How the Kerry experience compared to that of similar-sized

rural counties such as Donegal, Mayo or Galway remains unknown. In less successful counties was the GAA able to become such an active force in the social and cultural life of the region? Can similar reasons to those applied in Kerry be used to explain the present secondary status of hurling or, indeed, football, in various counties? Was the absence of local GAA officials of the capacity of men like Austin Stack a fundamental reason for the under-whelming record of many counties in Gaelic games? How much did the forging of a unique tradition, which Kerry achieved during this time, principally contribute to the subsequent growth and success of the association there over the next 125 years? Conversely, was the inability to create such a tradition a recurring theme in the failure of many other counties to match Kerry's record?

The answers to such questions can only be provided after a comprehensive study of the GAA in each Irish county has been completed. A rich and as yet unwritten story waits to be told, one that places the unique experience of every single county within the broader national history of the Gaelic Athletic Association.

NOTES

INTRODUCTION

1 T.F. O'Sullivan, *Story of the GAA* (Dublin, 1916); P.J. Devlin, *Our Native Games* (Dublin, 1935).

2 William Murphy, 'The GAA During the Irish Revolution, 1913–23', in M. Cronin, W. Murphy and P. Rouse (eds), *The Gaelic Athletic Association, 1884–2009* (Dublin, 2009), p. 61.

3 See Marcus de Búrca, *The GAA: A History*, 2nd edition (Dublin, 1999); W.F. Mandle, *The GAA and Irish Nationalist Politics, 1884–1924* (Dublin, 1987).

4 See Tom Hunt, *Sport and Society in Victorian Ireland: The Case Study of Westmeath* (Cork, 2007); Dónal McAnallen, David Hassan and Roddy Hegarty (eds), *The Evolution of the GAA: Ulaidh, Éire agus Eile* (Armagh, 2009); M. Cronin, M. Duncan and P. Rouse (eds), *The GAA: A People's History* (Cork, 2009).

5 Diarmaid Ferriter, *The Transformation of Ireland, 1900–2000* (Dublin, 2004).

6 Gearóid Ó Tuathaigh, 'The GAA as a Force in Irish Society: An Overview', in Cronin et al., *The Gaelic Athletic Association*, p. 237.

7 See Mary Daly, 'The County in Irish History', in Mary Daly (ed.), *County and Town: One Hundred Years of Local Government in Ireland* (Dublin, 2001), pp. 2–8.

8 William Nolan (ed.), *The Gaelic Athletic Association in Dublin, 1884–2000, Vol. 1: 1884–1959* (Dublin, 2005).

CHAPTER 1: FOUNDATIONS, 1885–1890

1 For two excellent studies on its development and process see Richard Holt, *Sport and the British: A Modern History* (Oxford, 1990) and Neil Tranter, *Sport, Economy and Society in Britain, 1750–1914* (Cambridge, 1998).

2 John Hargreaves, *Sport, Power and Culture: A Social and Historical Analysis of Popular Sports in Britain* (Cambridge, 1986), p. 41.

3 Edmund Van Esbeck, *Irish Rugby, 1874–1999: A History* (Dublin, 1999), p. 10.

4 Mike Huggins, *The Victorians and Sport* (London, 2004), pp. 9–10.

5 National Library of Ireland (NLI), Census of Ireland 1891, General Report (1892), Ir 310 c 1, pp. 528–9.

6 Paul Dillon, 'The Tralee Labourers' Strike of 1896: An Episode in Ireland's New Unionism', *Journal of the Kerry Archaeological and Historical Society* (*JKAHS*), Series 2, Vol. 2 (2002), p. 103.

7 Kieran McNulty, 'Revolutionary Movements in Kerry from 1913 to 1923: A Social and Political Analysis', *JKAHS*, Series 2, Vol. 1 (2002), p. 9.

8 *Census of Ireland, 1891. Part I. Area, houses and population; also the ages, civil or conjugal condition, occupations, birthplaces, religion and education of the people. Vol. II. Province of Munster*, pp. 414/484 [C. 6567], HC 1892, XCI, 1.

9 James Donnelly, 'Kenmare Estates During the Nineteenth Century', *JKAHS*, No. 21 (1988), p. 19. This work is an excellent general survey of the economic conditions in Kerry in the latter half of the nineteenth century.

10 For example, in 1871 its population declined by 2.6 per cent, as opposed to a Munster average of 8.8 per cent.

11 In 1871, 34 per cent of women aged between twenty and twenty-four were married in Kerry, as opposed to the national average of 16 per cent. Only 13 per cent of women in their early forties were single, as opposed to a national average of 26 per cent.

12 On Lansdowne's estate 300 tenants were required to pay an increase of 24 per cent in 1875, on rents last adjusted in 1858.

13 Jonathan Bell and Mervyn Watson, *A History of Irish Farming, 1750–1950* (Dublin, 2008), p. 246.

14 F.S.L. Lyons, *Ireland Since the Famine* (London, 1985), p. 165. This was mostly due to a decrease in the potato yield.

15 As butter was by now Ireland's largest agricultural export, the implications of such a decline were obvious.

16 J.C. Beckett, *The Making of Modern Ireland* (Norfolk, 1981), p. 385.

17 George D. Boyce, *Nineteenth-Century Ireland: The Search for Stability* (Dublin, 2005), p. 176.

18 One of the most notorious evictors in the county was George Sandes of Listowel, who was the land agent to Lord Ormathwaite, whose estate encompassed 8,900 acres in north Kerry.

19 *Return of agricultural holdings in Ireland, compiled by the Local Government Board in Ireland from returns furnished by the clerks of the Poor Law unions in Ireland in January, 1881*, pp. 4–6 [C 2934], HC 1881, XCIII, 793. In 1838, the Irish Poor Law system was set up to enable the poor to obtain relief from starvation in newly built workhouses. Kerry was divided into six unions and a Board of Guardians was set up to administer each union. They took on the responsibility for the general health and welfare of their area.

20 Labourers had decreased from 13.8 per cent of the population in 1871 to only 9.1 per cent in 1881.

21 Laurence Marley, *Michael Davitt: Freelance Radical and Frondeur* (Dublin, 2010), p. 41.

22 F.S.L. Lyons, *Charles Stewart Parnell* (London, 1977), p. 98.

23 The act established for the first time a system of dual ownership, by recognising the permanent interests of the tenant in his holding.

24 Alan O'Day, *Irish Home Rule, 1867–1921* (Manchester, 1998), p. 80.

25 It was printed twice weekly, first on Tuesdays and Fridays and then, from 1889 onwards, on Wednesdays and Saturdays.

26 Donnacha Lucey, *The Irish National League in Dingle County Kerry, 1885–1892* (Dublin, 2003), p. 9.

27 James Donnelly, *The Land and the People of Nineteenth-Century Cork: The Rural Economy and the Land* (London, 1975), p. 150.

28 Between 1884 and 1885 Kerry had the highest relative incident rate of reported agrarian crime in Ireland. K. Theodore Hoppen, *Elections, Politics and Society in Ireland, 1832–1885* (Oxford, 1984), pp. 374–5.

29 Ciara Breathnach, *The Congested Districts Board of Ireland, 1891–1923* (Dublin, 2005), p. 19.

30 Teresa O'Donovan, 'Ulster and Home Rule for Ireland, to 1914', *Éire-Ireland*, XVIII, 3 (1983), p. 8.

31 For example, Lord Ormathwaite offered a 15 per cent reduction on his estate in north Kerry, which his tenants refused.

32 Siobhán Jones, 'Land Agitation and Issues of Ownership in Southern Irish Loyalist Propaganda', in Úna Ní Bhroiméil and Glenn Hooper (eds), *Land and Landscape in Nineteenth-Century Ireland* (Dublin, 2008), p. 104.

33 F.S.L. Lyons, 'John Dillon and the Plan of Campaign', *Irish Historical Studies (IHS)*, XIV, 56 (1965), pp. 316–17.

34 *Kerry Sentinel (KS)*, 31 August 1886. By the end of the year Kerry would be the second most heavily policed county in Ireland.

35 For example, evictions rose from forty-three families in the county for 1885 to 306 families (1,766 people) in the first three months of 1887.

36 The line operated until October 1924.

37 Donal Horgan, *The Victorian Visitor in Ireland: Irish Tourism, 1840–1910* (Cork, 2002), p. 26. The royal party arrived in Killarney on Monday 26 August 1861 and spent three nights there before returning to England.

38 Though she reigned for over eighty years, the Queen only visited Ireland four times, making this coup all the more impressive.

39 Elizabeth Malcom, 'Popular Recreation in Nineteenth-Century Ireland', in Oliver MacDonagh, W.F. Mandle and Pauric Travers (eds), *Irish Culture and Nationalism, 1750–1950* (Canberra, 1983), pp. 45–6.

40 Patrick Begley's letter to Rev. John P. Devane, quoted in Patrick F. Foley, *Kerry's Football Story* (Tralee, 1945), p. 169.

41 Emmet Larkin, 'The Devotional Revolution in Ireland, 1850–75', *The American Historical Review (AHR)*, 77, 3 (1972), p. 625.

42 As early as the 1740s, the Bishop of Kerry was attempting to abolish the patterns and the number of church and local holidays was reduced from over thirty in 1700 to ten in 1830.

43 Kevin Whelan, 'The Geography of Hurling', *History Ireland*, 1, 1 (1993), p. 27. One such game, recorded in verse by the poet Eoghan Rua O'Sullivan, took place on St Stephen's Day 1770 on the banks of the Oweneecree River in Glenflesk, between the married and single men of the parish.

44 In the north, another variant which more closely resembled the Scottish sport of shinty was played in winter, often around Christmas time. Eoin Kinsella, 'Riotous Proceedings and the Cricket of Savages: Football and Hurling in Early Modern Ireland', in Cronin et al., *The Gaelic Athletic Association*, p. 19.

45 Marcus de Búrca, 'The GAA and Organised Sport in Ireland', in Grant Jarvie (ed.). *Sport in the Making of Celtic Cultures* (Leicester, 1999), p. 101.

46 David Underdown, *Start of Play: Cricket and Culture in Eighteenth-Century England* (London, 2000), p. 128.

47 Whelan, 'Geography of Hurling', p. 29.

48 Seán S. Ó Conchubhair, *Kilmoyley to the Rescue: A History of Kilmoyley and its Hurling Club* (Dublin, 2000), p. 95.

49 Mr and Mrs S.C. Hall, *Ireland: Its Scenery, Character etc*, Vol. 1 (London, 1841), pp. 256–8.

50 Seamus J. King, *A History of Hurling* (Dublin, 2005), p. 297.

51 Jim Cronin, *Munster GAA Story* (Ennis, 1986), p. 9.

52 *Return of agricultural holdings in Ireland, compiled by the Local Government Board in Ireland from returns furnished by the clerks of the Poor Law unions in Ireland in January, 1881*, p. 5 [C 2934], HC 1881, XCIII, 793. However, the problems with Whelan's theory on hurling are evident in the fact that in the Kenmare Union only 24 per cent of the land holdings there were valued at over £10, despite the strong tradition of hurling in this area.

53 Tomás O'Crohan, *The Islandman* (Oxford, 2000), pp. 133–5.

54 Pat O'Shea, *Trail Blazers: A Century of Laune Rangers, 1888–1988* (Killorglin, 1988), p. 2.

55 Carbery, *Gaelic Football* (Tralee, 1941), p. 15. An early record of such a match appears in an RIC report on the activities of Fenians in the Tarbert region. On 16 December 1866, a game of 'Foot-Ball' was played in the locality which the local RIC constable suspected was arranged for the purpose of bringing the local 'disaffected together without attracting the notice of the police'. Seán Ó Lúing, 'Aspects of the Fenian Rising in Kerry, 1867', *JKAHS*, No. 3 (1970), p. 39.

56 It was also played around Killarney. The *Cork Examiner* reported on a game between two teams of eighteen, one from the town and the other from the neighbourhood of Glenflesk in 1874. *Cork Examiner (CE)*, 24 April 1874.

57 *KS*, 27 March 1885. In the 1920s, the game made a brief reappearance in the county. Around Christmas 1926 the game was introduced to Gneeveguilla by Fr William Ferris, then curate in Rathmore. He arranged a match between Gneeveguilla and Knocknagree and around 250 people took part. Shortly after, the local parish priest banned the game due to safety concerns.

58 In 1861, 61 per cent of Irish people were illiterate. This had fallen to 12 per cent by 1911.

59 Paul Rouse, 'Sport and Ireland in 1881', in Alan Bairner (ed.) *Sport and the Irish: Histories, Identities, Issues* (Dublin, 2005), p. 10.

60 John Welcome, *Irish Horseracing: An Illustrated History* (London, 1982), p. 13.

61 *Sport*, 23 August 1884. The races continued on throughout the rest of the 1880s as a two-day festival in the town, usually being held in August.

62 Based on a survey of the *Kerry Sentinel* and *Sport* newspapers, 1885–90. In Ballyheigue, the popular Ballyheigue strand races can be traced back to 1853.

63 Due to such wealthy backers, the race meeting at Tralee was able to offer 'The Kerry Plate' for £100 to attract the best horses and help establish the meeting's name.

64 Gerard Siggins, *Green Days: Cricket in Ireland, 1792–2005* (Gloucestershire, 2005), p. 26.

65 See Michael O'Dwyer, *The History of Cricket in County Kilkenny: The Forgotten Game* (Kilkenny, 2006), p. 12; Patrick Bracken, *'Foreign and Fantastic Field Sports': Cricket in County Tipperary* (Thurles, 2004), pp. 6, 56.

66 Teams were: Anglo-American Cable Company, CKAACC, Dr Crokes XI, Killarney,

Killarney Athletic and Cricket Club, Killorglin, Listowel, Major Henderson's XI, Rice's XI, Tralee Garrison and the Valentia Atlantic Cable Company.

67 In Ardfert, the local landlord family, the Crosbies, were responsible for the introduction of the sport into the area in the nineteenth century.

68 *KS*, 16, 27 June 1888.

69 With the laying of the first transatlantic telegraph cable in 1865, Valentia became a centre for transatlantic communications between Europe and North America.

70 The Valentia club was also reported as playing matches against the smaller cable stations in Waterville and Ballinskelligs.

71 The game was the most popular sport in Killorglin at this time.

72 The IRFU was formed on 5 February 1880.

73 That year Tralee were drawn in the first round against Clanwilliam of Tipperary.

74 Teams were: Tralee Rugby Club, Dingle Rugby Club, Tralee Emmentines, Tralee Unicorns, Gallerus/Ferriter, Killarney Rugby Club and Laune Rangers Killorglin.

75 Hayes is reported as one of the players on the Unicorn team who distinguished himself.

76 Medical students were often among the first to set up rugby clubs in England.

77 The match was described as being played with goals set 106 yards apart.

78 Please note the spelling 'Valencia' and 'Valentia' were both used for the island until modern times. For clarity I have stuck with the modern spelling of 'Valentia'.

79 Michael Cusack, 'A word about Irish athletics', *United Ireland (UI)*, 11 October 1884.

80 Neal Garnham, 'Accounting for the Early Success of the Gaelic Athletic Association', *IHS*, XXXIV, 133 (May 2004), p. 70. In his history of the GAA, P.J. Devlin stated that by 1885 Irish athletics had become the preserve of 'un-Irish coteries' and needed to be recast among democratic lines. Devlin, *Our Native Games*, p. 12.

81 See Paul Rouse, 'Michael Cusack: Sportsman and Journalist' for a discussion on how the political and social climate of the 1880s, as well as other events, may have influenced Cusack's decision to found the GAA.

82 Paul Rouse, 'Gunfire in Hayes' Hotel: The IRB and the Founding of the GAA', in F. McGarry and J. McConnell (eds), *The Black Hand of Republicanism: Fenianism in Modern Ireland* (Dublin 2009), p. 77.

83 Mike Cronin, *Sport and Nationalism in Ireland: Gaelic Games, Soccer and Irish Identity Since 1884* (Dublin, 1999), p. 79.

84 Pádraig Puirséil and Joe O'Mahony have both erroneously claimed that one of those present at the meeting, RIC District Inspector Thomas St George McCarthy, was a Kerry man. However McCarthy, who was a former pupil of Cusack's, was born and raised in Tipperary. It was in fact his father, Lieutenant George Tomás McCarthy, who was born and raised in Tralee. See Pádraig Puirséil, *The GAA in its Time* (Dublin, 1984), p. 43; Joe O'Mahony, *The Kingdom: Kerry Football – The Stuff of Champions* (Dublin, 2010), p. 3.

85 Croke was a leading clerical nationalist and a champion of the Irish tenants' cause. Though a Cork man, his paternal grandmother owned a general store in Tralee and he spoke all his life with a Kerry accent, the result of spending much of his childhood in the county.

86 Owen McGee, *The IRB: The Irish Republican Brotherhood from the Land League to Sinn Féin* (Dublin, 2005), p. 15. It was founded on 17 March 1858.

87 As Paul Rouse argues, there was nothing intently nationalist about this action. Rather,

the ban was a weapon to ensure the growth of the GAA by asking athletes to give their undivided allegiance to the association and thus undermine its competitors. Paul Rouse, 'The Politics of Culture and Sport in Ireland: A History of the GAA Ban on Foreign Games, 1884–1971. Part One: 1884–1921, *International Journal of the History of Sport (IJHS)*, 10, 3 (1990).

88 *UI*, 24 January 1885.

89 The IAAA accused the GAA of being overtly political and guilty of 'monstrous conduct in daring to frame rules for athletics'. NLI, T.F. O'Sullivan Papers, Kerry GAA History, MS 15 385.

90 In a letter to the editor of the *Sentinel*, the secretary of the club, J. McGoff, stated: 'Heretofore the Tralee Sports were held under the rules of the Amateur Athletic Association (an English Club) and when the matter came to be discussed as to which of the three clubs the coming sports would be held under, the committee of the County Kerry Athletic and Cricket Club decided for the present to remain neutral and to adopt the rules of the AAA and not run under either the IAAA or GAA, leaving it open to parties who are to compete at the Limerick sports to be held under the IAAA and at [the] Cork sports under the GAA.' *KS*, 29 May 1885.

91 Letter from Lieutenant Colonel Denny, President of the County Kerry Amateur Athletics Club, to the Editor, *Sport*, 28 June 1884.

92 Indeed, as Paul Rouse argues, the row with the IAAA had already proved a blessing for the association, gaining for the GAA a level of publicity it could only have dreamed of following 'the damp squib' of its inaugural meeting. Paul Rouse, 'Journalists and the Making of the Gaelic Athletic Association, 1884–1887', *Media History*, 17, 2 (2011), p. 121.

93 In his own papers (O'Sullivan Papers, MS 15 385), T.F. O'Sullivan claims the first branch was formed on 2 June 1885. However, the reports in *United Ireland* and *Kerry Sentinel* clearly show it was formed on Sunday 31 May.

94 William Moore Stack was the father of Austin Stack. He had been imprisoned after the Fenian rising in the 1860s and again in the early 1880s for his involvement with the Land League in Kerry.

95 In a previous editorial, he had welcomed the decision of the National League in Listowel not to pass a proposed resolution boycotting fox hunting by the local gentry in the area. He stated: 'We cannot see any logical reason for interfering with "fox hunting" any more than for stopping lawn tennis, yacht racing, horse racing, pheasant shooting, or any pastime of the wealthier or more privileged classes, merely because it is they which indulge in them.' *KS*, 23 January 1885.

96 *Kerry Evening Post (KEP)*, 10 June 1885.

97 *UI*, 27 June 1885.

98 *Kerry Weekly Reporter (KWR)*, 20 June 1885.

99 Cusack reported Fr McMahon as stating that it was the largest meeting he had ever seen in the town except perhaps for Daniel O'Connell's meeting there in 1845.

100 A force of 100 RIC officers was drafted into Tralee for the event but the crowds behaved impeccably and gave the RIC 'no excuse to attack the people'.

101 *KEP*, 20 June 1885.

102 However, within two years the GAA, under Cusack's direction, began to revive hurling in earnest. Yet by doing so in a standardised fashion, the GAA accelerated the disappearance of local traditions such as iomán. Art Ó Maolfabhail, Roddy Hegarty and Dónal McAnallen, 'From Cú Chulainn to Cusack: Ball-Playing, Camán, Shinny

and Hurling in Ulster before the GAA', in McAnallen et al., *The Evolution of the GAA*, p. 77.

103 For example, Gorey, 8 August, Cashel, 15 August and Drogheda, 22 August 1885.

104 That same meeting was called to consider a letter from the CKAACC asking the organisation to amalgamate officially with the GAA. The situation was such that the IAAA sent a letter to the association enquiring as to their opinion on the proposal. In a further effort to end the dispute between both organisations, Dunbar himself sent a conciliatory letter to Cusack. He received the infamous reply: 'Dear Sir, I received your letter this morning and burned it.' *UI*, 19 December 1885.

105 In 1923, the GAA Athletics Council (formed in 1905) was merged with what remained of the IAAA into a new body, the National Athletic and Cycling Association of Ireland (NACAI) for the governance of Irish athletics. The famous Kerry team trainer Dr Éamonn O'Sullivan became the first Kerry president of the NACAI in 1929.

106 *KEP*, 24 June 1885.

107 *The Freeman's Journal (FJ)*, 23 June 1885.

108 *KS*, 7 July 1885.

109 The Franchise Act of 1884 and the Redistribution Act of 1885 resulted in an increase of the size of the electorate in Ireland from 4.4 to 16 per cent of the population. The immediate result was to give the vote to small farmers and landless labourers, thus augmenting the rural, tenant farmer base of the IPP's electoral support.

110 *KEP*, 1 July 1885.

111 *KWR*, 3 November 1885.

112 The CKAACC had written to the executive council of the GAA in June 1886 to ask permission to affiliate with the organisation. The GAA refused, stating there was already a branch of the association in the town, but gave permission for the club to hold its athletic events under GAA rules. O'Sullivan, *Story of the GAA*, pp. 32–3.

113 Fr Thomas B. Looney, *A King in the Kingdom of Kings: Dick Fitzgerald* (Cork, 2008), p. 15.

114 There were, however, some signs of activity. For example, a Gaelic football match, watched by a large crowd, was reported as being held in the Kerries between two teams from Strand Road and Spa Road in Tralee.

115 *KS*, 26 July 1887.

116 The event was the biggest athletics meeting in Ireland in 1887.

117 Maurice Davin was also in attendance.

118 *Sport*, 6 August 1887.

119 *KS*, 2 August, *Sport*, 6 August 1887. Michael Cusack, writing in his newly launched paper *The Celtic Times*, praised the central executive for choosing Tralee, 'to follow up the great blow struck there for National Pastimes in 1885 . . . it is now almost assured that Kerry will join hands with her neighbours, [and] take up the camán'. *The Celtic Times*, 6 August 1887.

120 Though it has often been claimed that Cusack was dismissed in an IRB-led heave, Paul Rouse argues convincingly that Cusack was removed because of his dubious talent for making enemies and alienating almost every section of the association. In addition, his administrative shortcomings were 'biblical'. Paul Rouse, 'Why the GAA was Founded', in McAnallen et al., *The Evolution of the GAA*, p. 81.

121 The ban on RIC members was ostensibly due to the fact that many prominent members of the GAA were being shadowed by detectives from Dublin Castle due to

suspected IRB involvement. Anon., *Sixty Glorious Years, 1886–1946: The Authentic Story of the GAA* (Dublin, 1946), p. 22.

122 *KS*, 15 November 1887. T.F. O'Sullivan stated that in the two years before this meeting the Tralee Gaels had contended themselves with affiliating with the GAA without organising any hurling or football. Hurling and football contests were played in the county but not by teams affiliated to the GAA.

123 *KS*, 16 December 1887, 6 January 1888. The decision by the club to affiliate was taken on 11 December 1887. At that meeting it was reported the club had received a copy of the rules of Gaelic football from the GAA's central executive and had played football for the first time under them, with both players and spectators appreciating 'the sport exceedingly'.

124 Official in the sense that it was the first stated to be contested by teams of twenty-one a side and also that a goal scored by Ashill was disallowed by the referee, who judged the player had infringed the rules by running a few steps with the ball before shooting. Ashill emerged victorious, 0-3 to 0-1. *KS*, 10 February 1888.

125 *KS*, 28 March 1888.

126 *KS*, 14 April, 26 September 1888. The club decided to name themselves after the locally born nationalist leader Daniel O'Connell. They also began to rent a large field near the town for use as a training field. For this they paid an annual rent of £5.

127 *KS*, 5, 19 September 1888.

128 *KS*, 27 October, 10 November 1888. Delegates were: Moynihan and Slattery, Tralee; John Callaghan and James McDonnell, Ballyduff; William O'Brien and J.P. O'Sullivan, Killorglin; M.K. Horgan and R. Finn, Castleisland; Denis Kelliher and John Langford, Killarney; Martin O'Sullivan and J. McGrath, Listowel; Timothy Gavin and Jeremiah McMahon, Ashill; Jerry Daly and John Healy, Barraduff; Laurence Egan and D. O'Kelly, Kenmare; P. Driscoll and John Slattery, Doon; William Quane, Kilmoyley; R. Dissette, Dingle; J.W. Scanlon and Cornelius Daly, Currans; Daniel Fitzgerald and Timothy Moore, Castlegregory; Maurice Scollard and Michael Tracy, Abbeydorney; William O'Halloran and Thomas McCarthy, Irremore and Lixnaw; Denis Moynihan and Thomas Keane, O'Brennan; Timothy Linihan and Dan O'Keefe, Rathmore. T. Mangan represented the CKAACC as it also affiliated.

129 *KS*, 19, 22 December 1888.

130 National Archives of Ireland (NAI), Crime Branch Special (CBS), District Inspectors' Crime Special (DICS), 521/W/8867.

131 Indeed, W.F. Mandle claimed that the IRB had as early as 1883 considered establishing a nationalist athletics movement and they were said to have approached Michael Cusack about the idea. W.F. Mandle, 'The IRB and the Beginnings of the Gaelic Athletic Association', *IHS*, XX, 80 (September 1977), p. 420.

132 Davin had pushed for the holding of the first Tailteann Games in the summer of 1889. This was to be the revival of a Gaelic form of the fabled Greek Olympics played in ancient Ireland. To finance it he came up with the idea of an athletics tour of fifty athletes to America, which would hopefully raise the estimated £5,000 necessary to fund the games. However, the tour, dubbed the 'American Invasion', turned into a financial disaster, incurring debts of over £400. Séamus Ó Riain, *Maurice Davin (1842–1927): First President of the GAA* (Dublin, 1994), pp. 164, 184.

133 Due in large part to the American tour fiasco, the GAA debt was reported as being over £700.

134 *Sport*, 26 January 1889.

135 *KS*, 30 November 1889.

136 See de Búrca, *The GAA*, p. 37; Mandle, *GAA and Politics*, p. 67.

137 An RIC report from April 1890 claimed that the eleven members of the Kerry County Board were all members of the IRB. NAI, CBS Index, 126S.

138 NAI, CBS, DICS, 521/W/7567.

139 Richard Holt, 'Ireland and the Birth of Modern Sport', in Cronin et al., *The Gaelic Athletic Association*, p. 34.

140 Likewise Dingle's representative at the first GAA county convention was Michael Dissette, a publican from the town. This practice mirrors what was occurring in contemporary British soccer teams, where many players in clubs such as Sunderland and Blackburn became publicans to supplement their wages. Tony Collins and Wray Vamplew, *Mud, Sweat and Beers: A Cultural History of Sport and Alcohol* (Oxford, 2002), pp. 13–14.

141 NAI, CBS, DICS, 521/S/889.

142 Foley, *Kerry's Football Story*, pp. 169–72.

143 In early November, a meeting of the club reported that its membership now stood at fifty. It also stated that the club was little over a month old, so that would put its formation as a GAA club at around late September or early October.

144 *KS*, 5 April 1890.

145 *KS*, 26 June 1889. Such cases are similar to those in Argyll in Scotland where the gentry's patronage of shinty survived well into the 1890s. See Lorna Jackson, 'Sport and Patronage: Evidence from Nineteenth-Century Argyllshire', *The Sports Historian*, 18, 2 (1998), pp. 96–7.

146 Éamonn Fitzgerald (ed.), *Dr Crokes Gaelic Century, 1886–1986* (Killarney, 1986), p. 13. James O'Leary, the club's secretary, was secretary of the town's National League, while J.D. Sheehan, the Irish Party MP for South Kerry, was president of both clubs. In Listowel, the MP for North Kerry, John Stack, had been behind the formation of a GAA branch there.

147 Based on a comparison of the General Meeting of Mitchels, League meeting of Tralee branch, and report of Mitchels delegates at the Annual National League convention.

148 *KS*, 17 January, 10 April 1889.

149 Evidently the boy's father had begun to rent the farm of a recently evicted tenant.

150 *KS*, 28 March 1888. At another football match between Kenmare and Kilgarvan, members of the RIC were reported as standing on the ditch above the field 'evidently having some other motive than the preservation of order . . . It is openly reported that they failed in their primary object, as a meeting of the principal leaguers of both parishes is said to have taken place in an adjacent field.'

151 *KS*, 6, 13 January 1888.

152 Maurice Moynihan was imprisoned for booing, hissing and laughing at the police who were keeping an eye on League activists at a GAA match in Tralee in February 1888.

153 *KS*, 5 January, 17 April 1889.

154 NAI, CBS, DICS, 521/W/7766.

155 At Ballyferriter, for example, some local men, determined not to let the local RIC discover a League meeting, started to march and counter-march for three hours 'through the most rugged parts of the parish cheering for O'Brien as well as other Nationalist leaders'. While the police were on a 'wild goose chase' after the young men through the bogs, a meeting of the National League was held, without interference, by the principal men of the parish.

156 In Scotland, a similar campaign for land reform in the 1880s led to the formation of the Highland Land Law Reform Association, many of whose prominent leaders were involved with traditional shinty clubs. Irene A. Reid, 'Shinty, Nationalism and Celtic Politics, 1870–1922', *The Sports Historian*, 18, 2 (1998), p. 119.

157 Mike Cronin, 'Enshrined in Blood: The Naming of Gaelic Athletic Association Grounds and Clubs', *Sport in History*, 18, 1 (1998), p. 96.

158 Russell was an English barrister and MP who supported the call for Home Rule by the IPP.

159 NAI, The British in Ireland Collection, CO 904, MFA, 54/107.

160 NAI, CBS Index, 296/S.

161 *KS*, 9 February 1889. It was decided the county should be divided into a north and south division, the final tie to be played between the victorious team in each. Draw was: South Kerry football: 3 March – Rangers v Barraduff at Killarney, 1 p.m., Harrington v Kenmare, same venue, 2 p.m., Kilgarvan v Rathmore, same venue, 3 p.m.; 10 March – Castleisland v Killarney at Killorglin, 2 p.m. South Kerry hurling: Kenmare v Kilgarvan, 10 March, same venue. North Kerry football: 10 March – Listowel v Irremore/Lixnaw at Listowel, 2 p.m.; 17 March – Tralee v Ashill at Tralee, 1 p.m., Castlegregory v O'Brennan, same venue, 2 p.m. Brosna got a bye. North Kerry hurling: 10 March – Ballyduff v Abbeydorney at Lixnaw, 3 p.m., Kilmoyley a bye.

162 *KS*, 6 March 1889. For a fixture-by-fixture record of every county championship played between 1889 and 1998, see Pat O'Shea, *Face the Ball: Records of the Kerry County Championships, 1889–1998* (Tralee, 1998), an excellently researched record.

163 *KS*, 23 February, 2 March, 25 September 1889.

164 In the following edition of the *Sentinel*, John O'Brien, umpire for O'Brennan, wrote to the editor and complained that the referee gave the score though he could not have been positive of it as 'he was not convenient to the goal post at the time'.

165 The 1886 GAA rules conferred on the referee the power to award a score if a shot destined for goal 'had not struck a bystander'. This indicates that spectators were often prone to attempting to intervene to stop or change the trajectory of rival teams' shots at goal, actions which often provided the catalyst for such disputes. Paddy Dolan and John Connolly, 'The Civilizing of Hurling in Ireland', *Sport in Society*, 12, 2 (2009), p. 204.

166 *KS*, 20 April, 8 May 1889.

167 The game was played in a field owned by farmer John Cronin at Lackabane. A hillside to the north provided spectators with a natural terrace.

168 *KS*, 22, 29 May, 8 June 1889.

169 Letter to the Editor, *KS*, 7 August 1889.

170 *KS*, 9 November 1889. At this Moynihan remarked that if Kenmare were not the Munster champions, then 'who beat them?'

171 Most income was derived from the affiliation fee of thirty-one clubs – £15 10s – entrance fee for twenty clubs for county championship – £2 10s – and receipts from matches in Tralee – £28 13s. In addition, the board had raised £101 18s 6d from the gate receipts of a second tournament in aid of the National Monument Fund held in September 1889. Of that, £40 was given to the fund and the rest went on expenses such as: £20 to CKAACC for use of the sports ground, £3 7s for hired men to steward matches, £19 10s 6d for the expenses of teams, including dinner and refreshments for four Limerick teams and refreshments for the home teams as well as for two bands,

9s for footballs, £2 for the Limerick Liberties train fare, 4s 6d for football pitch lining and £5 7s 6d for printing, advertising, letters and telegrams. *KS*, 26 October 1889.

172 *KS*, 30 November 1889. Clubs affiliated were: Abbeydorney, Aghadoe, Ballyduff, Ballymacelligott, Cahersiveen, Camp, Callinfercy, Castlegregory, Castleisland, Cordal, Currans, Dingle, Irremore, Keel, Kenmare, Killarney, Killorglin Laune Rangers, Kilmoyley, Knockanure, Knocknagoshel, Lispole, Listowel, Listry, Lixnaw, Milltown, Muckross, O'Brennan, Rathmore, Tralee Mitchels, Tralee Red Hughs, Tralee Amateur, Tuogh, Waterville.

173 It seems the original field which the club was renting from Lord Kenmare had been ploughed up without warning and repossessed by his agents in February 1890. *KS*, 15 February 1890.

174 The players were: J.P. O'Sullivan, Patsy Sheehan, Pat Hurley, Jim Curran, P. O'Sullivan, Moss O'Brien, Dan P. Murphy, M. O'Sullivan, Pat Teahan, Jim J. O'Sullivan.

175 *KS*, 2 February 1889, 19, 26 April 1890.

176 *KS*, 10 May 1890.

177 The national school system was introduced in 1832. By 1870, Kerry had 264 such schools.

178 By 1886, 244 of the controlling positions in all local Boards of Guardians in Ireland were in the hands of nationalists as compared with only 59 in 1877.

179 To illustrate, in 1889 the Ballybunion GAA athletics was held on a Wednesday to coincide with a local holiday, and despite the pleasant weather and the running of trains at reduced fares at hours 'suited to the convenience of the public', the attendance was extremely poor. The *Sentinel* complained that many from the surrounding districts and towns who would have liked to attend could not owing 'to their being engaged at their different occupations: whereas, if the sports had been held on a Sunday, when all business establishments would have been closed up and business suspended, the public in general would have an opportunity of enjoying themselves'. *KS*, 1 June 1889.

180 Neal Garnham, *Association Football and Society in Pre-Partition Ireland* (Belfast, 2004), p. 8.

181 *KS*, 10 April, 22, 25 May 1889.

182 For example, the *Sentinel*, commentating on a Laune Rangers versus Castlemaine championship game, stated that despite the huge attendance, 'the utmost order was preserved, without any extraordinary efforts being called forth from those responsible for the management'.

183 Alan Bairner, 'Civic and Ethnic Nationalism in the Celtic Vision of Irish Sport', in Grant Jarvie (ed.), *Sport in the Making of Celtic Cultures* (Leicester, 1999), p. 17.

184 Celt, 'The National Pastime', *The Gaelic Athletic Annual and County Directory for 1907–08* (Dublin, 1907), p.11; Derek Birley, *A Social History of English Cricket* (London, 1999), p. 94. Yet it is ironic that at the same time the association sought to stress the self-controlled and disciplined nature of its athletes, reports of matches invariably eulogised the physical prowess and manliness of their play. See John Connolly and Paddy Dolan, 'The Civilising of Gaelic Football', in McAnallen et al., *The Evolution of the GAA*, p. 156.

185 *Irishman*, 8 November 1884.

CHAPTER 2: 'A GOOD SHIP GOING DOWN WITH THE TIDE: THE COLLAPSE OF THE GAA, 1890–1898

1 EMON first appeared in the *KS*, 11 January 1890. EMON was a pseudonym used by county secretary Maurice Moynihan.

2 The failure of the potato crop in the west of Ireland was reported as the ninth reoccurrence of the potato blight since the famine of 1848.

3 NAI, CBS, DICS, 521/S/1065.

4 *KS*, 18 October 1890.

5 *KS*, 16 January 1895.

6 Tom Hunt, 'The GAA: Social Structure and Associated Clubs', in Cronin et al., *The Gaelic Athletic Association*, pp. 184–5.

7 E. Vaughan and A.J. Fitzpatrick (eds), *Irish Historical Statistics: Population, 1821–1971* (Dublin, 1978), p. 3.

8 NLI, Census of Ireland 1891, pp. 528–9.

9 See David Fitzpatrick, 'Irish Emigration in the Later Nineteenth Century', *IHS*, XXII, 86 (1980), p. 129.

10 *KS*, 20 March 1897. Of those reported to be leaving west Kerry, the largest percentage was of farmers' sons and daughters, the rest being chiefly from the labouring class.

11 The results of an age profile study of 910 Kerry GAA players between 1888 and 1916 showed that 97.6 per cent of those surveyed were aged between fifteen and thirty-five. See Chapter 3.

12 *KS*, 22 February, 8 March 1890. Clubs were: football – Brosna, Castlegregory, Listowel, Ballymacelligott, Killarney, Keel, Muckross, Valentia, Castleisland, Miltown, Cahersiveen, Rangers, Waterville, Tuogh, Castlemaine, Aghadoe, Tralee Mitchels, Tralee Red Hughes, Lixnaw, Cordal, Rathmore, Listry, Knockanure and Irremore; hurling – Ballyduff, Kilmoyley, Kenmare, Abbeydorney and Lerrig.

13 *KS*, 1, 22 October 1890.

14 *KS*, 1, 8, 22 November 1890.

15 NAI, CBS, DICS, 521/S/5433.

16 NAI, CBS Index, 4467/S: The GAA at the end of the year 1891, 25 February 1892. In the northern division, branches were reported to have fallen from a high of fifty-eight in 1889 to eleven. In the western division, club numbers fell from 129 in 1889 to fifty-seven in 1891.

17 *KS*, 11 July 1891.

18 *Sport*, 2 January 1892.

19 NAI, CBS, DICS, 7828/S. A previous report in 1893 also showed that there were no clubs active in Mayo or Clare. NAI, CBS Index, 6247/S.

20 Indeed, at the start of 1894 a police report stated there were only three GAA clubs at that time active in Kerry. NAI, CBS Index, 7828/S.

21 NLI, Census of Ireland 1891, pp. 340–1. As my survey of GAA players in Chapter 3 shows, 99.8 per cent of GAA players in Kerry were aged between fifteen and forty.

22 Tom Hunt, 'Parish Factions, Parading Band and Sumptuous Repasts: The Diverse Origins and Activities of Early GAA Clubs', in McAnallen et al., *The Evolution of the GAA*, pp. 87–8.

23 Dónal McAnallen, 'The Greatest Amateur Association in the World? The GAA and Amateurism', in Cronin et al., *The Gaelic Athletic Association*, p. 160.

24 See Neil Tranter, 'The Patronage of Organised Sport in Central Scotland, 1820–1900', *Journal of Sport History (JSH)*, 16, 3 (1989), p. 232.

25 *KS*, 15 February, 12 March 1890. Likewise, the presidency of the club was held by the local Justice of the Peace, Major Hewson. In addition, those individuals who made up the club's committee were either the owners of the most important businesses in the town or else prominent members of the town's professional and military classes.

26 For example, the Tralee Mitchels secretary, Maurice Moynihan, was a clerk in a butchers' buyer establishment in Tralee.

27 *KS*, 11 January, 1 November 1890, 28 September 1898.

28 NAI, CBS, DICS, 521/S/658.

29 Hunt, *Sport and Society in Victorian Ireland*, p. 153.

30 *KS*, 5, 19 April 1890.

31 *Sport*, 10 December 1892. However, as Tom Hunt points out, the preference for playing GAA matches at a time of year when weather conditions were least favourable had a practical basis. Clubs were dependent on the patronage of local farmers for use of a suitable playing field. During such months grass growth was essentially dormant, so meadows were not damaged by the actions of forty-two footballers competing in a small area. Tom Hunt, 'The Early Years of Gaelic Football and the Role of Cricket in County Westmeath', in Alan Bairner (ed.), *Sport and the Irish: Histories, Identities, Issues* (Dublin, 2005), p. 37.

32 *KS*, 21 January 1893.

33 *KS*, 10 September 1892.

34 *KS*, 24 May 1890. As was the case in Britain, there was an increasing trend for working-class people to use Sundays for recreation. This met with much disapproval among the relatively leisured, church-going middle and upper classes, who viewed it as unchristian behaviour. Neil Wigglesworth, *The Story of Sport in England* (London, 2007), p. 65.

35 *KS*, 4 June 1890.

36 *KS*, 21 June 1890. In celebration, a silken banner with the slogan 'Kilmoyley to the Rescue' was produced. In years that followed, the banner was marched at the head of the village brass band when it paraded.

37 *KS*, 6 August 1889, 10 February 1897.

38 *Sport*, 2 September 1893. The motive for crime was believed to be 'the fierce spirit of factionalism there'.

39 *KS*, 13 May, 23 September, 2 December 1891.

40 *KS*, 5 March 1892.

41 *KS*, 28 September 1892.

42 Report on the average wages paid to agricultural labourers in Kerry. *KS*, 29 July 1895.

43 Alan Metcalfe, 'Football in the Mining Communities of East Northumberland, 1882–1914', *IJHS*, 5, 3 (1988), p. 278.

44 Quoted in Ó Ruairc, Micheál, 'The Early Days of Athletics, Football and Hurling in Kerry', *The GAA in Kerry, Centenary Exhibition* (Killarney, 1984), p. 7.

45 Ó Conchubhair, *Kilmoyley*, p. 103.

46 *Sport*, 2 December 1893.

47 *KS*, 22 August 1894.

48 *KS*, 29 March 1893.

49 *KS*, 23 March 1895.

50 Frank Callanan, *The Parnell Split, 1890–91* (Cork, 1992), p. 53.

51 *KS*, 3, 17, 31 December 1890.

52 Tim Healy was an MP with the Irish Party and one of Parnell's sternest critics following the divorce scandal. Frank Callanan, *T.M. Healy* (Cork, 1996), pp. 257–9.

53 *KS*, 20 December 1890. It was said that Slattery had refused to allow seven or eight members of the club to speak in Parnell's favour, stating that they had not paid their subscriptions and were thus not technically members. He refused them a chance to speak even when they offered him their affiliation there and then. This was despite the fact that many who were allowed speak and had voted against the resolution were not members of the club nor had they paid their subscriptions. The *Sentinel* reported that if the vote had been allowed to take place unmolested, the pro-resolution side would have been confident of a large majority. However, on the day of the meeting, active canvassing by those who opposed Parnell had been conducted among the members of the club in order to defeat the resolution.

54 NAI, CBS, DICS Reports, Box 2, South Western Division: Monthly Report of DI Jones, December 1890, 1 January 1891, 521/S/2493.

55 NAI, CBS Index, 126/S.

56 These bodies were formed to fund the electioneering of the pro-Parnellite IPP faction.

57 NAI, CBS, DICS Reports, 521/S/2817/521/S/3563.

58 Parnell addressed a large meeting in Tralee on 18 January 1891 at which there was a sizeable contingent of local GAA officials in attendance, including P. Gould, secretary of Dingle GAA, and several officers from Tralee Mitchels, Killarney Dr Crokes and Killorglin Laune Rangers.

59 John Sugden and Alan Bairner, *Sport, Sectarianism and Society in a Divided Ireland* (Leicester, 1993), p. 31.

60 NAI, CBS, DICS, 6205/S/521/S/9062. Indeed, police reports in May 1892 reported that many prominent members of the IRB had sided against the Parnellite faction.

61 Emmet Larkin, 'Church, State and Nation in Modern Ireland', *AHR*, 80, 5 (December 1975), pp. 1253–4.

62 'West Briton' was a pejorative term which originated in the nineteenth century for an Irish person who was perceived as being too much of an Anglophile in matters of culture or politics.

63 The result of this process was that by the 1880s Mass attendance among Irish Catholics had jumped from 30 to 90 per cent and the terms Irish and Catholic had become as interchangeable as Catholic and nationalist. Emmet Larkin, *The Roman Catholic Church and the Creation of the Modern Irish State, 1878–1886* (Dublin, 1975), p. 395.

64 Mike Cronin, 'Fighting for Ireland, Playing for England? The Nationalist History of the Gaelic Athletic Association and the English Influence on Irish Sport', *IJHS*, 15, 3 (1998), p. 52.

65 *Celtic Times*, 12 November 1887.

66 *FJ*, 12 November 1887.

67 O'Sullivan, *Story of the GAA*, p. 63.

68 Indeed, an RIC report from early 1892 pinpoints the convention in November 1887 as the turning point which led to such a rapid decline in the fortunes of the GAA due

to this clerical opposition. NAI, CBS, DICS Reports, Box 2, South Western Division: Monthly Report of DI Jones, January 1892, 1 February 1892, 521/S/8031.

69 Simon Gillespie and Rody Hegarty, 'Camán and Crozier: The Church and the GAA, 1884–1902', in McAnallen et al., *The Evolution of the GAA*, p. 114.

70 An RIC report in 1890 counted 196 clubs across Ireland under clerical control, 502 under Fenian, with 149 unattached. NAI, CBS Index, 127/S: GAA, Approximate Strength under Clerical and Fenian Control by Divisions, 5 May 1890.

71 *Sport*, 3 August 1889.

72 NAI, CBS, Divisional Commissioners and County Inspectors (DC and CI) reports, 521/W/9660.

73 *KS*, 24 May 1890.

74 Emmet Larkin, *The Roman Catholic Church in Ireland and the Fall of Parnell, 1888–1891* (Liverpool, 1979), p. xvii.

75 James H. Murphy, *Ireland: A Social, Cultural and Literary History, 1791–1891* (Dublin, 2003), p. 32.

76 *KS*, 11 March 1891.

77 Police reports before the election stated that nationalists were 'daily becoming more bitter and pronounced in their hatred of each other'. NAI, CBS, DICS, 521/S/8837.

78 *KS*, 9 July 1892.

79 Alvin Jackson, *Home Rule: An Irish History, 1800–2000* (London, 2003), p. 85.

80 This is similar to the situation which developed in Ulster in the 1890s where the Catholic hierarchy began to oppose the GAA vehemently, seeing it as nothing more than 'a flag of convenience' for 'secret societies'. David Hassan, 'The GAA in Ulster', in Cronin et al., *The Gaelic Athletic Association*, pp. 80–1.

81 NAI, CBS Index, 792/S. Out of a total GAA membership of 1,286 in Kerry, 703 were members of clerical-controlled clubs.

82 *FJ*, 12 October 1891.

83 *KS*, 15 April 1893.

84 See NAI, CBS, DICS, 521/S/10816.

85 *KS*, 17 April 1895. In addition, the ground was not properly enclosed and was full of 'loopholes', so that more than a quarter of the crowd managed to gain access without paying the admission price.

86 *CE*, 22 April 1895.

87 The RIC reported that the parents of many young men in the GAA in Kerry 'are most anxious to have them sever their connection with that association since Dr Coffey's pronouncement on the matter'. NAI, CBS Index, 9854/S.

88 NAI, CBS, DICS Reports, Box 2, South Western Division: Monthly Report of CBS Officer, April 1895, 4 May 1895, 521/S/13760.

89 Between 1891 and 1892 alone the amount spent on alcohol in Ireland reached £13,014,771, while 100,528 arrests had been made for drunkenness. Diarmaid Ferriter, 'Sobriety and Temperance', in Shane Kilcommins and Ian O'Donnell (eds), *Alcohol, Society and Law* (Chichester, 2003), p. 8.

90 Likewise Tralee, a town with a population of 9,367, had 117 public houses – a ratio of one pub for every eighty people. Ferriter, *Transformation of Ireland*, p. 57.

91 *Criminal and judicial statistics, Ireland, 1890. Report on the criminal and judicial statistics of Ireland for the year 1890*, p. 71 [C. 6511], HC 1891, XCIII, 251. Some 226

arrests for being drunk on Sundays were also made in Kerry that same year, the fourth largest number in the country after Dublin city and county, Cork city and county and Belfast, including Antrim county. *KS*, 5 August 1891.

92 Pádraig G. Lane, 'Government Surveillance of Subversion in Laois, 1890–1916', in Pádraig G. Lane and William Nolan (eds), *Laois – History and Society: Interdisciplinary Essays on the History of an Irish County* (Dublin, 1999), p. 603.

93 NAI, CBS, DICS, 521/S/889.

94 NAI, CBS, DICS, 521/S/404.

95 Elizabeth Malcom, 'The Catholic Church and the Irish Temperance Movement, 1838–1901', *IHS*, XXIII, 89 (1982), p. 3.

96 *Sport*, 7 January 1889.

97 Hunt, 'Parish Factions', p. 96.

98 *KS*, 22 March 1890. At a Central Council meeting that May a letter from Croke was read to delegates urging them to do all in their power to influence members to join the movement.

99 *KS*, 7, 14 August 1895.

100 Tony Collins, *Rugby's Great Split: Class, Culture and the Origins of Rugby League Football*, 2nd edition (Oxford, 2006), p. 18.

101 Denis Brailsford, *British Sport: A Social History* (Cambridge, 1997), p. 69.

102 Tony Collins and Wray Vamplew, 'The Pub, the Drinks Trade and the Early Years of Modern Football', *Sport in History*, 20, 1 (2000), p. 6. For example, both the Everton and Blackburn Rovers football clubs were based out of local pubs in their early years. Pamela Dixon and Neal Garnham, 'Drink and the Professional Footballer in 1890s England and Ireland', *Sport in History*, 25, 3 (2005), p. 375.

103 In Dublin, the importance of the pub trade was reflected in the timing of games to suit bar workers. As late as the 1930s all games in the city had to start at 11 a.m. to ensure barmen could be at work on time at 1 p.m. David Gorry, 'The Gaelic Athletic Association in Dublin, 1884–2000: A Geographical Analysis', MLitt Thesis, University College Dublin, 2001, p. 103.

104 NAI, CBS, DICS, 7828/S.

105 Daniel Mulhall, 'A Gift from Scotland: Golf's Early Days in Ireland', *History Ireland*, 14, 5 (2006), p. 32.

106 *KS*, 10 February 1894.

107 Based on a survey of the *KS*. Teams involved were: Waterville Commercial Cable Company FC, Durham Light Infantry FC, Tralee FC, Cahersiveen FC and Waterville Village FC.

108 *KS*, 20 September 1899.

109 After 1899 only one other match, 1901, was reported on in the *Sentinel*. *KS*, 5 January 1901.

110 See Tom Hunt, 'Classless Cricket? Westmeath, 1880–1905', *History Ireland*, 12, 2 (2004), pp. 26–9; O'Dwyer, *Kilkenny*, pp. 54–62.

111 For example, though no senior GAA club was recorded in Castleisland in 1897, a meeting of the town's cricket club that summer indicated that cricket remained the preserve of the business and professional classes there. The membership included: the club president, Mr Meredith; manager of the local National Bank, Dr Rice; Mrs Meredith, Lamie and Patrick Broderick, all local solicitors; Bernard Roche BL;

Redmond Roche, the local Justice of the Peace, along with Dr Moore and Sergeant Conway of the RIC. *KS*, 14 July 1897.

112 Ferriter, *Transformation of Ireland*, p. 44.

113 Liam O'Callaghan, *Rugby in Munster: A Social and Cultural History* (Cork, 2011), p. 36.

114 Listowel founded its own rugby club in October 1899. The inaugural meeting was presided over by John Macaulay, one of the founding members of Garryowen RFC and a former Irish international who had moved to the town. Thomas Dillon, 'Listowel Rugby Club: 110 Years of History', in Listowel Rugby Club, *Listowel Rugby Club: Celebrating 110 Years, 1900–2010* (Listowel, 2010), p. 13.

115 *KS*, 17 April 1894.

116 Players names taken from the following teams: Tralee RFC 1897, 1899, 1900; Tralee Wreckers, 1900; Tralee Pioneers RFC, 1900; Killarney RFC, 1898, 1899; St Brendan's Seminary Killarney team, 1899.

117 In March 1900, a former junior football team in Tralee called the Pioneers changed codes to rugby. *KS*, 24 March 1900.

118 *KS*, 17 January 1900.

119 *KS*, 10 February, 17 March, 7 April 1900.

CHAPTER 3: REVIVAL, 1898–1905

1 John Hutchinson, *The Dynamics of Cultural Nationalism: The Gaelic Revival and the Creation of the Irish Nation State* (London, 1987), p. 115.

2 Elizabeth Crooke, 'Revivalist Archaeology and the Museum Politics During the Irish Revival', in Betsey Taylor FitzSimon and James H. Murphy (eds), *The Irish Revival Reappraised* (Dublin, 2004), p. 83.

3 Marie Bourke, 'Yeats, Henry and the Western Idyll', *History Ireland*, 11, 2 (2003), p. 32.

4 Advocates of the literary revival chose the vernacular emerging from bilingual peasantry, an English language infused with Irish idioms and rhythm, to construct this new Anglo-Irish culture. Hutchinson, *The Gaelic Revival*, pp. 119, 128.

5 *KS*, 18 January 1890. The Young Ireland Society was a national organisation set up to encourage the study of Irish history, as a means of developing a national self-consciousness. It had several branches in Kerry, most notably Tralee, where Moynihan acted as secretary and Thomas Slattery was also on its ruling committee.

6 The author further encouraged the Young Ireland Society to organise literary evenings in connection with local GAA clubs. Reprinted in the *KS*, 24 September 1890.

7 Timothy G. McMahon, *Grand Opportunity: The Gaelic Revival and Irish Society, 1893–1910* (New York, 2008), p. 2.

8 This past provided Irish nationalism with a historical legitimacy far more powerful than the tradition of token self-rule in eighteenth-century Ireland, propagated by the Irish Party in their search for Home Rule. R.V. Comerford, *Ireland: Inventing the Nation* (London, 2003), p. 141.

9 Tom Garvin, *Nationalist Revolutionaries in Ireland, 1858–1928* (Oxford, 1987), p. 79.

10 Brian Ó Conchubhair, 'The GAA and the Irish Language', in Cronin et al., *The Gaelic Athletic Association*, p. 138.

11 *KS*, 27 May 1896.

12 *KS*, 23 July, 12 November 1902. O'Donnell gained fame as being the first Member of Parliament in history to address the House of Commons in Irish.

13 NAI, CBS, IG and CI, 24242/S.

14 *KS*, 6 June 1900.

15 A.B. Gleason, 'Hurling in Medieval Ireland', in Cronin et al., *The Gaelic Athletic Association*, pp. 4–5.

16 In the earliest literary references to hurling, it is the sons of kings and other nobles who play the game. Art Ó Maolfabhail, 'Hurling: An Old Game in a New World', in Grant Jarvie (ed.), *Sport in the Making of Celtic Cultures* (Leicester, 1999), p. 154.

17 Hunt, *Sport and Society in Victorian Ireland*, p. 252.

18 Anthony J. Gaughan, *Austin Stack: Portrait of a Separatist* (Dublin, 1977), p. 20.

19 *KS*, 25 May 1898.

20 Philip Bull, 'The United Irish League and the Reunion of the Irish Parliamentary Party', *IHS*, XXVI, 101 (1988), pp. 51–2.

21 Peter A. Quinn, 'Yeats and Revolutionary Nationalism: The Centenary of '98', *Éire-Ireland*, XV, 3 (1980), p. 61. Indeed, Roy Foster argues the centenary itself sparked the revival of the IRB. R.F. Foster, *The Irish Story: Telling Tales and Making it Up in Ireland* (London, 2001), p. 221.

22 NAI, CBS, IG and CI, 16163/S, 17167/S.

23 Police reports stated that the Tralee '98 Centenary Committee was mostly comprised of local IRB suspects.

24 *KS*, 28 April 1898.

25 *KS*, 28 May 1898.

26 Daniel Mulhall, 'Ireland at the Turn of the Century', *History Ireland*, 7, 4 (1999), pp. 33–4.

27 *KS*, 4 October 1899.

28 Deirdre McMahon, 'Ireland, the Empire and the Commonwealth', in Kevin Kenny (ed.), *Ireland and the British Empire* (Oxford, 2004), p. 192.

29 NAI, CBS, IG and CI, 20125/S. In Kerry, it was reported that there were strong feelings among the lower classes in support of the Boers.

30 NAI, CBS Index, 2467/S.

31 Thomas Bartlett, *Ireland: A History* (Cambridge, 2010), p. 362.

32 *Sport*, 13 April 1895. Blake would be the first GAA official to fix the All-Ireland finals at Jones Road, Dublin, site of the present-day Croke Park. Devlin, *Native Games*, p. 31.

33 *Sport*, 4 May 1895. Despite this, Blake was not above getting actively involved in local politics. In 1895, he had been dismissed as chairman of the Meath Board for insisting the body be kept non-political while simultaneously issuing a pamphlet in support of the victorious north Meath anti-Parnellite candidate in that summer's general election. David Lawlor, *Divine Right? The Parnell Split in Meath* (Cork, 2007), p. 213.

34 Paul Rouse argues that the decision to rescind the ban was motivated by the desire to encourage the spread of native games as the rule was seen as limiting the growth of the GAA because it prevented the recruitment of rugby players and their ilk. Rouse, 'The GAA Ban', pp. 345–6.

35 Blake, *How the GAA was Grabbed*, pp. 4–6. Blake defended his record stating that the

debts were so high due to the shortfall in gate receipts on account of the finals of the 1896–7 championship having not been played. In addition, the 1897–8 championship had not yet started. He stated he would have needed only a few months to bring the competitions up to date and that by 1 June 1898 'every shilling could have been cleared off'. However, the GAA's Annual Convention in May 1898 found that the association's debts now amounted to a total of £403, the fault for which was levelled not at the organisation itself but at its officials, principally Blake. *Sport*, 28 May 1898.

36 NAI, CBS, Precis Box 2: Precis of information relative to Secret Societies etc, 11 February 1898, 15506/S. Blake claimed Dineen had engineered the meeting in Thurles by forging the required number of signatures of Central Council members needed to call such a special meeting. He also claimed that the resolution of no confidence in him, which passed by one vote, did so by means of two forged and bogus proxy votes presented by delegates in league with Dineen. Blake, *How the GAA was Grabbed*, pp. 4–6.

37 Patrick McDevitt, 'Muscular Catholicism: Nationalism, Masculinity and Gaelic Team Sports, 1884–1916', *Gender and History*, 9, 2 (1997), p. 269.

38 Such romantic views of hurling especially remained common with historians of the GAA well into the 1940s. 'Carbery', for example, credited the establishment of the GAA under Michael Cusack and the ensuing popularisation of hurling as bringing about the regeneration of Irish culture and the 'spiritual emancipation' of the Irish people. Carbery, *Ireland's National Game*, pp. 57–9.

39 One such story recounts the feats of the Tuogh hurler Con O'Shea. He was said to have such a powerful shot that if he hit a sliothar in the air he had time to unbutton his shirt before it came down. Once it did, he could strike it so hard that it was frequently never seen again. Years later, local men cutting turf in a bog five miles from Tuogh discovered a sliothar embedded in 10 feet of bog which they claimed was where O'Shea's sliothar had landed. Kerry County Archives (KCA), Department of Irish Folklore records: S135c, MSS433.

40 Similar stories abound in Irish folklore. Great hurlers and footballers were often taken away at night to play in matches between fairy teams. Such a motif stretches back to at least the twelfth century. Jimmy Smith, *Praise of Heroes: Ballads and Poems of the GAA* (Dublin, 2007), p. 7.

41 Pat 'Aeroplane' O'Shea, 'Football in Castlegregory in the Early Days', in Michael Lyne (ed.), *Kerry GAA Yearbook, 1975–6* (Tralee, 1976), p. 38.

42 Jack Harrington (ed.), *Ballyduff: A GAA History, 1888–1991* (Limerick, 1991), p. 19.

43 Paul Rouse, 'Empires of Sport: Enniscorthy, 1880–1920', in Colm Tóibín (ed.), *Enniscorthy* (Wexford, 2010), pp. 47–8.

44 *KS*, 22 September 1894. Patrick Regan, the captain of the Kerry team, stated that it was illegal for Tipperary to object as a referee's decision – with regard to scores in matches which have already been decided – in such matters was final. He also pointed out that no member of the Kerry Board was informed that this meeting of the Central Council was to go ahead until 8.30 the night before. Given the short notice, no Kerry delegate was in attendance when the ruling was passed. This again was illegal as no objections could be put forward without representatives from both sides being present.

45 *KS*, 24 October 1894.

46 At the Annual Kerry GAA convention the following March, the chairman opened by saying he was proud of the inter-county teams and was sure they would be holders of All-Ireland medals had they been better treated by Central Council. *KS*, 27 March 1895.

47 The *Sentinel* declared the GAA had broken 'its word of honour with a county which,

with the sister county of Cork, has kept afloat the banner of the GAA when other counties turned their backs on the sports and pastimes of their forefathers'. *KS*, 15 February 1896.

48 The financial situation of the county board was so serious that they had been unable to award medals to the previous year's county champions.

49 A dispute over the rent charged by the Tralee Sportsground committee was responsible for many of these delays.

50 W. Foster, 'Certain Set Apart: The Western Islands in the Irish Renaissance', *Studies*, No. 66 (1977), p. 264.

51 *KS*, 29 April 1899.

52 Kelly stated that at present there were eight football clubs active in Kerry (Listowel, Tarbert, Castleisland Desmonds, Killarney Dr Crokes, Cahersiveen, Tralee Mitchels, Milltown and Laune Rangers) and that representatives of each should meet together to reform the body. *KS*, 16 December 1899.

53 *KS*, 21 April 1900.

54 Croke Park Archives (CPA), GAA/CC/01/01, Central Council Minute Books, 1899–1911: 1 April 1900. The decision was taken at a Central Council meeting held in Thurles on 1 April. William Ahern of Cork and J. Dooley, GAA honorary treasurer, were the two officials selected to go.

55 *KS*, 12, 31 May, 14 July 1900.

56 *KS*, 15 September, 20 October 1900. This council would subsequently be declared illegally constituted by the GAA Central Council due to the fact that two delegates had not been granted permission to represent their respective boards. A further meeting was held on 27 January 1901 at which a new Munster Council was formed. Cronin, *Munster GAA*, p. 58.

57 O'Sullivan, *Story of the GAA*, p. 147.

58 *KS*, 3 May, 4 June 1902. The draw for the inaugural South Kerry championship was made on 21 June 1902. However, the championship was not completed until May 1904 with Cahersiveen beating Portmagee in the final.

59 *KS*, 23 July 1902.

60 *KS*, 3 November 1901.

61 CPA, GAA/CC/01/01: Annual Convention of the GAA, 22 September 1901.

62 CPA, GAA/CC/01/01: Annual Convention of the GAA, 1 February 1903.

63 NAI, CBS, Home Office Precis Box 2, 22189/S.

64 NAI, CBS, IG and CI, 29733/S.

65 Boyce, *Nineteenth-Century Ireland*, pp. 265, 275.

66 O'Sullivan, *Story of the GAA*, p. 1.

67 Eoghan Corry, 'The Mass Media and the Popularisation of Gaelic Games, 1884–1934', in McAnallen et al., *The Evolution of the GAA*, p. 100.

68 *KS*, 31 May 1900.

69 See Neal Garnham, 'Rugby and Empire in Ireland: Irish Reactions to Colonial Rugby Tours', *Sport in History*, 1, 23 (2003), pp. 107–14.

70 *KS*, 11 January 1902.

71 Hunt, 'Social Structure', p. 183.

72 Clubs were: Abbeydorney, Ardfert, Annascaul, Ballinskelligs, Ballinorig, Ballybunion,

Ballyduff, Ballydavid, Ballyferriter, Ballyheigue, Ballylongford, Ballymacelligott, Bonane, Cahersiveen, Caragh Lake, Castlegregory, Castleisland Desmonds, Castlemaine, Camp, Causeway, Cordal, Counanna, Crotta, Cuas, Currans, Currow, Dingle Gascons, Duagh, Dunquin, Farranfore, Finuge, Firies, Glencar, Glenflesk, Irremore, Keelduff, Kenmare, Kilgarvan, Killarney Dr Crokes, Killarney St Brendan's, Kilmoyley, Killorglin Laune Rangers, Lougher, Lispole, Listowel, Listowel Temperance Club, Listowel Young Irelanders, Lixnaw, Milltown, Portmagee, Rathmore, Renard, Rock Street Shamrocks (Tralee), Scartaglin, Tarbert Rovers, Tralee Celtic, Tralee Drapers, Tralee Grocers, Tralee Junverna, Tralee Kruger's Own, Tralee Mitchels, Tralee Parnells, Tralee Printers, Tubrid, Tullig Gamecocks, Valentia, Valentia Young Irelanders, Ventry.

73 Information obtained from Hunt, 'Social Structure', p. 184.

74 For all comparisons above, see Hunt, 'Social Structure', pp. 185, 192.

75 *KS*, 18 December 1901.

76 *KS*, 19 May 1900.

77 CPA, GAA/CC/01/01: Adjourned Annual Convention of the GAA, 15 December 1901.

78 De Búrca, *The GAA*, p. 71. P.J. Devlin, writing in the 1930s, insisted that the leaning of Irish men towards imported games was simply 'the desire, born of serfdom and all its venalities, to ape and pose as a superior castle'. Devlin, *Native Games*, p. 65.

79 'The GAA and English Pastimes', *Cork Examiner*, reprinted in *KS*, 11 January 1902.

80 *KS*, 8, 22 February, 29 March 1902.

81 In Donegal in 1905, a campaign to revive the GAA in the county shared remarkable similarities to T.F. O'Sullivan's work in Kerry. There, a prominent local member of the Gaelic League, Seamus MacManus, started his own press campaign to promote Gaelic games at the expense of the popularity of soccer in the county. See Conor Curran, *Sport in Donegal: A History* (Dublin, 2010), pp. 81–3.

82 CPA, GAA/CC/01/01: Annual Convention of the GAA, 30 November 1902. However, support for the ban was not universal in Kerry. RIC reports noted that the exclusion of the police from participating in local sports and the hostility to association football had not been approved of by the Gaelic clubs. 'A certain amount of friction has been the result.'

83 The ban on active members of the RIC, Army and Navy joining the GAA was reintroduced at the adjourned 1902 convention in January 1903 by twenty-four votes to twelve. O'Sullivan made a vigorous speech in support of this motion. That November at the 1903 Annual Convention, this decision at O'Sullivan's instigation was extended to include pensioners of the above forces. The ban also applied to events where police or military bands were playing. In Tipperary in 1904, a group of players were suspended for taking part in a match where the half-time entertainment was provided by a local military band.

84 CPA, GAA/CC/01/01: Annual Convention of the GAA, 8 January 1905.

CHAPTER 4: THE KERRY WAY, 1905–1915

1 *KS*, 9 September 1902.

2 See *KS*, 8 June 1904. That same year, he first represented Mitchels as their delegate at the Kerry GAA county convention. *KS*, 30 March 1904. Over the following twenty-three years, Stack held various positions on the board, being vice-president in 1907 and serving as chairman almost continuously from 1908 until his death in 1929.

3 *KS*, 11 October 1905. The team comprised: T. O'Gorman, J. O'Gorman, M. McCarthy,

D. Curran, J. Buckley, C. Healy, J.T. Fitzgerald, A. Stack (all Tralee Mitchels), R. Fitzgerald, P. Dillon, W. Lynch, J. Myers, D. Kissane, D. McCarthy (Killarney Dr Crokes), R. Kirwan, D. Breen (Castleisland), E. O'Neil (Cahersiveen).

4 *KS*, 15 February, 19August, 20 December 1905.

5 This result was hugely significant. Since the establishment of inter-county contests in 1887, Kerry had only beaten the Cork footballers on one previous occasion (1892), a remarkable statistic considering the subsequent history of this great football rivalry.

6 *Sport*, 15 July 1905. The GAA's Central Council decided to include London as a province to contest the All-Ireland in 1900. As such, between then and 1905 the All-Ireland final was actually played as two games. The 'home final' was contested between the two counties that qualified from within Ireland. The winners of this match would then play London to decide officially the All-Ireland title.

7 *The Kerryman (KM)*, 17 June 1905. General opinion and form going into the final suggested that Kildare were favourites. However, in an attempt to inspire his countymen and stoke the fires of animosity, the Gaelic games reporter for *The Kerryman* stated that 'the Leinster Champions despise the Kerrymen and utterly ridicule the idea that they have the remotest chance of success. He laughs best who laughs last and we are inclined to think that Kerry will have the best of the laugh.'

8 *Sport*, 29 July 1905. Even then, arrangements left much to be desired. The special train from Tralee only arrived in Thurles at 3.20 p.m., meaning its passengers only saw the second half of the match. Worse, the train left for Kerry at 6.15 p.m. sharp, stranding most of the Kerry supporters, who failed to make it back in time.

9 The latter contained twenty-three carriages and had to be pulled by two engines. The former had twenty-two carriages. A single special had been arranged from Dublin but so quickly did it fill that a second and then a third train had to be laid on to cope with demand.

10 *KM*, 29 July 1905.

11 CPA, GAA/CC/01/01: 23 July 1905. In the meantime, T.F. O'Sullivan, as secretary of the Kerry Board, succeeded in conveying a special meeting of the GAA's Central Council to rescind this initial decision. At the subsequent meeting the Kerry delegates argued that the original score should stand but were eventually persuaded to replay the match.

12 *KM*, 2 September 1905. *The Kerryman*'s correspondent was furious with the concession of this score. He declared that 'instead of blocking their quarter line to prevent any incursions whatever, they [Kerry] played loose and their whole defence fell to pieces. They failed to resort to what any mediocre seventeen in Ireland would have resorted to, when in such a position.'

13 Jones Road Dublin, Belfast, Limerick, Cork, Thurles and even London's Crystal Palace venue were all suggested.

14 *Sport*, 16 September 1905.

15 The Central Council had voted to give each team a grant of £25 above their usual expenses for the purpose.

16 For example, when Ballyduff won the All-Ireland in 1892 they had not trained for the final.

17 *KS*, 20 September 1905.

18 The paper observed that those 'visiting the great venue will have no possible excuse for not wearing the colours of their team and proving in a practical and manly manner their belief and confidence in the boys from the '"Kingdom"'. *KS*, 14 October 1905.

19 *Sport*, 14 October 1905. Every obtainable carriage was laid on for Cork station. Special trains from Dublin, Carlow, Thurles, Carrick-on-Suir, Kilkenny, Waterford, Tralee, Abbeyfeale, Limerick, Castleisland and Cahersiveen were all arranged to cope with the demand. Some 1,085 passengers travelled from Tralee alone. *KM*, 21 October 1905.

20 *Sport*, 21 October 1905. As Eoghan Corry has illustrated, even a conservative estimate of 18,000 put the matches close to breaking the 20,000 record for a sporting event in Ireland, held by the Scotland v Ireland rugby international in Belfast in 1898. Eoghan Corry, *Illustrated History of the GAA* (Dublin, 2005), p. 44. In addition, the gate receipts for the match amounted to an unparalleled £270. O'Sullivan, *Story of the GAA*, p. 163.

21 *KS*, 18 October 1905. During the local elections for the Kerry County Council in 1903 a prominent member of the Ascendancy class near Tralee was opposed in the election by James Baily of Ballymacelligott. His supporters published the poster 'Up Baily' and Kerry followers adopted the slogan, transforming it into 'Up Kerry', a cry soon to be heard 'at every crossroads in the county'. Foley, *Kerry's Football Story*, p. 29.

22 *KS*, 18 October 1905; *Sport*, 21 October 1905.

23 *KM*, 21 October 1905. 'JJ MC' wrote an article entitled 'Kerry's Day Out' to accompany the *Kerryman*'s report of the match. It stands the test of time as a powerful firsthand account of the experiences of a supporter attending an All-Ireland final. In it, he tracks his worries and concerns about the game. The long train journey found him fretting at the rain streaming down the window, raising concerns about Kerry's chances when faced with playing in the wet. The piece vividly portrays the almost unbearable tension for a spectator watching the match and a winning-team supporter's unbridled joy when the final whistle has gone: '[As] Kerry were led away in triumph you noticed a man coming across the field after the whistle who you knew and at home was much respected . . . you thought he was under the influence of drink but found he was only temporarily mad. He struck you on the shoulder and in what he intended for a shout, but was only a husky whisper, he slung the question at you: "WHO THE HELL SAID WE COULDN'T PLAY IN THE WET?"'

24 Writing nine years later, the noted GAA journalist 'Carbery' stated: 'My first experience of their play was a revelation . . . Many thinking men about this time were satisfied that Gaelic football was a poor thing. The championship ties were wretched, scrambling, disjointed contests – mostly rucks and rushes broken up by repeated whistle calls and frequent disturbances consequent on wrong interpretations of the rules. Some legislators were for throwing up the game and confining attention to the National pastime – hurling. Others suggested revolutionary changes in the governing laws. Many thought of adopting Rugby and beating other nationalities at their own game. But after the Kerry display against Kildare . . . we heard little of these things.' Carbery, 'The Kerry Footballers', *Gaelic Athlete*, Christmas issue, December 1914, p. 9.

25 CPA, GAA/CC/01/01: 10 December 1905.

26 Joe Lennon, *The Playing Rules of Football and Hurling, 1602–2010* (Gormanstown, 2001), pp. 10–11, 25–8.

27 *Sport*, 6 December 1890.

28 He argued this led to referees and officials constantly interpreting the rules for themselves. This varied interpretation by individual referees negated a common understanding, resulting in players losing all confidence in these officials while spectators were left bewildered by their decisions. *Sport*, 28 January 1893.

29 *KS*, 30 November 1889.

30 If the offending player refused to leave or attempted later to rejoin the match, the referee had the power to award the match to the opposing team.

31 However, the response to these changes was not always universally positive. 'A Kerry Gael' wrote to the *Sentinel* in relation to Blake's tampering, wondering if the Kerry Board would apply the revised rules for its upcoming county championships. He was at a loss 'to see the wisdom in the rule in banning hopping of the ball, the practice which beyond all others in the football field' distinguishes the Gaelic player. At a subsequent meeting of the Kerry Board, they decided against introducing the new rules for that year's championship. *KS*, 4, 15 May 1895.

32 Among changes it implemented was allowing the substitution of injured players during Gaelic matches. *KS*, 20 November 1901.

33 Mandle, *GAA and Politics*, p. 144.

34 M.F. Crowe, 'On the Field', *The Gaelic Athletic Annual, 1907–08*, pp. 27–8.

35 Lennon, *Playing Rules*, pp. 66–9. Yet, strange as it may seem, a motion at the 1903 GAA Annual Convention proposed that catching the ball during play be made illegal. It was defeated by eleven votes to twenty, despite support from the GAA secretary, Luke O'Toole. Had the motion passed, Gaelic football as we know it might have ceased to exist. CPA, GAA/CC/01/01: Adjourned Annual Convention of the GAA, 11 January 1903.

36 CPA, GAA/CC/01/02, Central Council Minute Books, 1911–1925: 1910 Annual Convention of the GAA, 27 March 1910.

37 They eventually decided upon erecting a statue in his honour in Thurles, the birthplace of the association.

38 CPA, GAA/CC/01/02: 16 December 1913.

39 *KM*, 22 December 1909.

40 *KM*, 8 January 1910.

41 The reason for this optimism was that Kerry had beaten Cork, the reigning All-Ireland champions, by the impressive score of 2-3 to 0-1 in the Munster campaign. That same Cork side had humiliated Antrim by nineteen points in the previous year's final.

42 *Sport*, 31 August 1912.

43 *KM*, 5 July 1913. In the months after the 1910 final, their Gaelic games reporter sneered at the 'paper' and 'gallant walk-over champions' of Louth. Commenting on a story that the Central Council had temporarily insufficient funds to award the All-Ireland winners a set of gold medals, he suggested that leather ones would be more appropriate. *KM*, 8 April 1911.

44 *KM*, 19 April 1913. Edward Courtney, a native of Castlegregory, wrote home stating he would not care if the Kerry team 'ever played again so long as they won'. *KM*, 3 May 1913.

45 *Sport*, 26 April, 3 May 1913. Recalling the event before his death in 1980, Kerry's Pat O'Shea, who played in the match, stated he could not remember during his lifetime 'any sporting event in the country which excited as much general interest'. Michael Lyne (ed.), *The Kerry GAA Yearbook, 1981* (Tralee, 1981), p. 37.

46 *KS*, 7, 10 May 1913. Despite this, several letters to *The Kerryman* blamed the poor performance of the Kerry forwards and their 'erratic shooting' for their failure to win. *KM*, 10 May 1913.

47 *KS*, 18 June 1913. While in Tralee, the player training programme involved an hour-long sprinting walk to Fenit every morning, followed by afternoon training in the Sportsground. A practice match was also held every Sunday against a local Kerry combination. *KM*, 7 June 1913.

48 *Sport*, 5 July 1913.

49 Mandle, *GAA and Politics*, p. 151.

50 *CE*, 30 June 1913.

51 *KM*, 5 July 1913.

52 *FJ*, 30 June 1913.

53 CPA, GAA/CC/01/02: 6 July 1913. The new ground was intended to function as a permanent base for the GAA.

54 CPA, GAA Annual Congress Minute Books, 1911–1927: 12 April 1914.

55 Paul Rouse, 'Sport and the Offaly tradition: The Gaelic Athletic Association', in Timothy P. O'Neill and William Nolan (eds), *Offaly – History and Society: Interdisciplinary Essays on the History of an Irish County* (Dublin, 1998), p. 889.

56 Also, as Mary Daly points out, when the county of Kerry was formed it was not considered part of the region of Munster. This may have strengthened a sense of community identity within its boundaries. Daly, 'County in Irish History', p. 2.

57 Benedict Anderson, *Imagined Communities: Reflections on the Origin and Spread of Nationalism* (London, 2006), pp. 34–5.

58 Often parish boundaries served as the 'goal lines'. Foley, *Kerry's Football Story*, p. 17.

59 P.J. Devlin states that it was 'unavoidable' that the county would become the main competitive unit of the GAA as, though it rarely corresponded to historical territorial divisions, it lessened the likelihood of perpetuating local faction feuds. Devlin, *Native Games*, p. 51.

60 *KS*, 15 February 1890.

61 *Sport*, 1 March 1890.

62 *KS*, 6 August 1890. The Kerry hurlers won 1-3 to 0-1, while the footballers won 0-9 to no score.

63 *KS*, 4 February 1891. The football side was composed of ten Laune Rangers, three Dr Crokes, three Tralee Mitchels and two Milltown players, along with one man each from the Tuogh, Ballymacelligott and Rathmore clubs. Meanwhile, the hurlers featured eight Kilmoyley, five Abbeydorney, five Ballyduff and three Kenmare men. Kerry brushed aside the westerners' challenge in football, winning 1-6 to no score. However, the hurling match was abandoned when the Galway men left the field in protest at one of their scores not being awarded by the referee.

64 When Kerry faced Tipperary in the 1900 Munster championship a selection committee of county chairman J.P. O'Sullivan, Maurice Moynihan, J. O'Connell (county board treasurer) and D. Shanahan of Abbeydorney, along with Laune Rangers captain E. Sheehan and Kilmoyley captain P. Rourke, was tasked with selecting the county's hurling and football teams. *KS*, 2 April 1902.

65 Rouse, 'Offaly', p. 889.

66 *Gaelic Athlete*, 24 February 1912. Yet in May 1912 the same paper called for the dismantling of the GAA's county system. The paper cited the irregular size and areas of different counties as its reason. It also noted that often, as in the case of Leitrim, the north and south of the county were serviced by two different rail companies. Thus, the obvious solution was to split the counties affected in this way by the railway lines. *Gaelic Athlete*, 4 May 1912.

67 *KS*, 31 January 1891. Folklore maintains that the green and gold colours were adopted in 1903 when Kerry played Waterford in a tournament in the county but travelled without any jerseys. Roddy Kirwan, the Kerry player and Waterford native, contacted the Kilrosanty club and asked them if Kerry could borrow their green and gold jerseys,

which they played in and hence adopted as their colour. Jimmy Darcy O'Sullivan, *Forged in Gold and Green: 125 Years of Kerry GAA* (Killarney, 2009), p. 18. Another tale is that the Tralee Rugby Club played in green and orange colours and lent a set of jerseys to the Tralee Mitchels GAA club when they founded, thus becoming the main colours of the county side. Gordon Revington (ed.), *Tralee Rugby Football Club, 1882–1982* (Tralee, 1983), p. 18.

68 Although it must be highlighted that in 1904 and 1909 the county football championships were merged with those of the following year, to alleviate the backlog of games.

69 *Irish Independent*, 13 November 1905.

70 *KS*, 8 March 1913.

71 Mark Duncan, 'The Camera and the Gael: The Early Photography of the GAA, 1884–1914', in Cronin et al., *The Gaelic Athletic Association*, p. 104.

72 Anon., *Sixty Glorious Years*, p. 51.

73 *KS*, 3 July 1907; *KM*, 13 January 1906; *Sport*, 29 May 1909.

74 Carbery, *Gaelic Athlete*, Christmas issue, p. 9.

75 For a discussion on the role of the media in the creation of the Munster Rugby sporting tradition, see Liam O'Callaghan, 'The Red Thread of History: The Media, Munster Rugby and the Creation of a Sporting Tradition', *Media History*, 17, 2 (2011), pp. 178–87.

76 The Kerry Board stated that, during the past year, they had expended £380 on their inter-county hurling and football teams, expenditure which only went towards the benefit of the Central and Munster Councils. Furthermore, the board noted that the men who constituted those bodies treated the claims of Kerry for more funding 'in a cavalier and offhanded fashion'. The county board had come to believe that Kerry was seen as nothing 'but a money maker for these councils'. In spite of this, Kerry still did not have any representation on the Central Council, despite all the county had done to put the GAA on a sound financial footing. *KM*, 25 April 1914.

77 A discussion on the merits of the new technology took place, at which delegates professed they were not against the use of film so that Irishmen abroad in the UK or North America would be able to watch their county footballers and hurlers on screen. It was acknowledged that the technology should be supported, as the association was 'living in an age of progress', though it was suggested some of the profits from these picture shows should be handed over to the competing teams who provided the entertainment. *KS*, 5 March 1911.

78 *KM*, 26 March 1910. However, the earliest known film of a Gaelic game was recorded at a Dublin hurling game in 1901. Seán Crosson and Dónal McAnallen, '"Croke Park Goes Plumb Crazy": Gaelic Games in Pathé Newsreels, 1920–1939', *Media History*, 17, 2 (2011), p. 160.

79 *KM*, 18 September 1908.

80 'Deligmis', 'The Press and the GAA', *The Gaelic Athletic Annual and County Directory for 1908–09* (Dundalk, 1909), pp. 30–1.

81 *KS*, 8 February 1913.

82 See Dick Fitzgerald, *How to Play Gaelic Football* (Cork, 1914), pp. 14–67.

83 Paul Darby, 'Gaelic Games and the Irish Diaspora in the United States', in Cronin et al., *The Gaelic Athletic Association*, p. 206.

84 *KS*, 6 August 1891.

85 *KM*, 20 August 1904.

86 *KM*, 6 August 1906. That November, the Knights of St Brendan, an Irish, Catholic religious order in Boston, had written to the Central Council to enquire whether the All-Ireland champions could be sent on a tour of America the following summer, to encourage the game in the US. They also wrote to the editor of *The Kerryman* to put the matter before the Kerry Board. However, nothing came of the invitation.

87 *KM*, 15, 29 December 1906.

88 Reprinted in *KS*, 17 September 1913.

89 *KS*, 5 April 1905.

90 See NLI, Census of Ireland 1901, General Report (1902) Ir 310 c 1, pp. 528–9.

91 *KM*, 6 May 1905.

92 *KS*, 14 April, 9 May 1906.

93 *KM*, 17 February; *KS*, 9 June 1906.

94 CPA, GAA/CC/01/01: 31 March 1907. O'Sullivan held a number of different positions for that paper, including a spell as parliamentary correspondent in London from 1916 until the paper's demise in 1924, during which time he covered the Anglo-Irish Treaty negotiations. He continued to work for a variety of Dublin papers until his death in 1950.

95 *KS*, 26 October 1907.

96 They found such unsportsmanlike conduct inexcusable, especially as it was the goal and point Fitzgerald scored five minutes from time that had 'saved Kerry against Kildare' in the drawn All-Ireland in Tipperary. *KS*, 9 December 1905. The replay of the match was not held until the following June and again the game was left unfinished, Killarney walking off the pitch in protest at a referee's decision. At a subsequent Board meeting Fitzgerald, representing Crokes, threatened to withdraw the town's football and hurling club from affiliation to the county board unless another replay was granted. *KS*, 9 June 1906.

97 *KS*, 22 August, 19 September 1908. This competition is not to be confused with the Croke Memorial Cup of 1913. The Croke Cups had been donated by Archbishop Croke to the GAA in 1896. From 1904 they were put up for competition on an inter-provincial basis in both codes, an early precursor to the Railway Cups. Kerry, representing Munster, won its first Croke Cup in November 1907, beating Mayo.

98 *KM*, 22 November 1913. In consequence of their treatment, the Dr Crokes club seriously considered withdrawing themselves from the Kerry Board and their players' services from the inter-county team.

99 *KM*, 12, 19 October 1907.

100 *KS*, 22 August 1908.

101 *KM*, 17 October 1908.

102 F.J. Cronin's honorary secretary's report to the 1909 Kerry GAA county convention. *KM*, 29 May 1909.

103 Austin Stack, 'In the Kingdom of Kerry', *Gaelic Annual, 1908–09*, p. 26.

104 *KM*, 2 December 1911.

105 *KS*, 28 March 1896.

106 Individual clubs were even more vulnerable. Kilcummin were forced to concede a walkover to Mitchels for the 1903 county final as the county board could not pay the team's travel expenses to the match venue in Killarney.

107 *KM*, 28 October 1916.

108 *KS*, 3 November 1906. Batt O'Connor of Dingle was elected its first chairman, Jeremiah Lynch of Ballydavid was elected vice-chairman, Jeremiah Moriarty was appointed as secretary and M. O'Connor of Ballyferriter was appointed treasurer. By December it was reported that the Dingle, Ballyferriter, Lispole, Dalcassians, Ballydavid, Milltown and Cuas clubs had all affiliated to the body.

109 See *KM*, 15 December 1906. The Tralee Football League in 1906 had five teams competing: Clahane, Scrahan, Boherbee, Rock Street and Strand Street.

110 *KS*, 8 February 1913.

111 *KM*, 8 June 1907.

112 *KS*, 31 January, 26 April, 20 May 1891.

113 *KS*, 11 November 1903, 13 April 1904. The meeting passed a unanimous resolution asking the GSWR to reduce its exorbitant rates for guaranteed trains, 'the existing rates being of such a character as to practically cripple the conduct of Gaelic sport'. They also requested that other local sports committees write to the company on the matter and asked the Irish newspapers to support them.

114 On the return journey the train left two and half hours late and took a further seven hours to reach Tralee. *KM*, 29 July 1905.

115 *KM*, 26 December 1908, 21 May 1910.

116 *Kerry Evening Star (KES)*, 10 November 1910.

117 *KM*, 12 November 1910.

118 *KM*, 3 December 1910.

119 *Sport*, 19 November 1910.

120 CPA, GAA/CC/01/01: 19 November 1910.

121 *KM*, 19 November 1910.

122 Pat O'Shea recalled that the railway authorities 'had experienced a wonderful change of heart since the 1910 debacle. Now we [Kerry] were accorded VIP treatment . . . travelling in a specially reserved coach. Lyne, *Kerry Yearbook, 1981*, p. 38.

123 *KS*, 19 February 1908.

124 *KS*, 17 May, 6 September 1902.

125 *KS*, 4 November 1905. Evidently things had not changed much. When Ballyduff won the All-Ireland in 1892, the team had played the game barefoot and in their everyday-working long trousers.

126 *KM*, 19 August 1905.

127 *KS*, 4 August 1906. The lack of matches was a huge problem in trying to keep club sides together. For example, the Ardfert team did not play a match between 1904 and June 1906, when the 1905 championship finally started. Tommy O'Connor, *Ardfert: A Hurling History* (Ardfert, 1988), p. 22.

128 *KM*, 29 May 1909.

129 Austin Stack, 'In the Kingdom of Kerry', *Gaelic Annual, 1908–09*, p. 26.

130 *KS*, 19 April 1905. Smaller clubs were just as active and inter-club transfers were common. In 1903, Patrick Riordan transferred from Abbeydorney to Ardfert, Daniel Driscoll transferred from Kilmoyley to Ardfert, while Martin Hennessey went in the opposite direction.

131 *KM*, 23 January 1915.

132 *KM*, 31 July 1915.

133 'M. O'S to Editor', *KS*, 20 May 1905.

134 *KM*, 14 March 1914.

135 The county board received affiliation fees from two clubs in Abbeydorney, two in Listowel, Causeway, Ballyduff, Tralee Mitchels HC, Ballyheigue, Kilflynn, Kilmoyley, Lixnaw Davis, Lixnaw Redmonds, Kenmare, Valentia and Shannon Rovers. *KS*, 1 April 1914.

136 *KM*, 16 May 1914.

137 *KS*, 28 September 1910.

138 Rouse, 'Journalists and the GAA', pp. 127–8.

139 *KM*, 29 May 1909.

140 Regina Fitzpatrick, Paul Rouse and Dónal McAnallen, 'The Freedom of the Field: Camogie Before 1950', in McAnallen et al., *The Evolution of the GAA*, p. 123.

141 Jennifer Hargreaves, 'The Victorian Cult of the Family and the Early Years of Female Sport', in Sheila Scraton and Anne Flintoff (eds), *Gender and Sport: A Reader* (London, 2002), p. 57.

142 Tom Hunt, 'Women and Sport in Victorian Westmeath', *Irish Economic and Social History*, Vol. XXXIV (2007), p. 37.

143 There was a commonly held belief that excessive sporting activity could lessen a woman's ability to have children. Jennifer Hargreaves, *Sporting Females: Critical Issues in the History and Sociology of Women's Sports* (London, 2003), p. 45.

144 Jane George, 'An Excellent Means of Combining Fresh Air, Exercise and Society: Females on the Fairways, 1890–1914', in Tony Collins (ed.), *Sport as History: Essays in Honour of Wray Vamplew* (London, 2011), pp. 4–5.

145 Fitzgerald, 'Camogie', p. 124.

146 Mike Cronin, 'More Than Just Hurling and Football: The GAA and its Other Activities', in Cronin et al., *The Gaelic Athletic Association*, p. 227.

147 By 1905, the game had spread to Cork, with the first club being formed in Cork City that summer.

148 *KS*, 6 June 1906.

149 In Tipperary, the sport was introduced through a similar exhibition between the Keatings and Árd Craobh teams of Dublin which was held in Nenagh on 12 August 1906. In contrast to Kerry, the exhibition proved the stimulus for the formation of a local camogie club in the town in the weeks that followed. Martin Bourke and Seamus J. King, *A History of Camogie in County Tipperary* (Naas, 2003), p. 11.

150 *KM*, 1 August 1914.

151 *Kerry People (KP)*, 5 January 1915.

152 *KM*, 19 June 1915.

153 Cronin et al., *A People's History*, p. 317. Kerry actually participated in the first ever inter-county ladies football match against Offaly in Tullamore in July 1973.

CHAPTER 5: KERRY AND THE POLITICS OF SPORT, 1905–1915

1 *KM*, 3 March 1906.

2 NAI, CBS, IG and CI, 538/S.

3 The League had been instrumental in a bilingual programme of education being

introduced into the national school system in 1904. By 1908, it had introduced the teaching of Irish into 3,000 schools in the country and had published some 200 Irish-language books of which 200,000 copies were selling annually.

4 See *KM*, 16 May 1908.

5 This cross-membership should not be surprising. Timothy McMahon, in his work on the Gaelic League, shows that 55 per cent of its members from 1894 to 1899 were comprised of lower-middle-class Catholics (i.e. clerks, shop assistants, skilled labourers and artisans). This correlates favourably with the 51 per cent of GAA members in Kerry from a similar background in the 1896–1905 period. Timothy G. McMahon, '"All Creeds and All Classes?" Just Who Made Up the Gaelic League?' in *Éire-Ireland*, XXXVII, 3–4 (2002), pp. 139–40.

6 *KM*, 23 March 1912.

7 *Sport*, 7 March 1914.

8 NAI, CBS, IG and CI, 501/S/43126.

9 Garvin, *Nationalist Revolutionaries*, p. 55.

10 During a visit to Kerry, Ashe reckoned that the elections at the Ard-Fheis would mean 'the Gaelic League will be kept straight for another while. Had we been kicked out, the Gaelic League would be stuck on to John Redmond's tail . . . as everybody in Ireland today are licking his heels for jobs. However, we won't be bought by any upholder of Empire.' NLI, Thomas Ashe Papers, Diary Kept During a Visit to Kerry in 1913, n. 4923, p. 4955.

11 As Tom Garvin argued, the League was the central nationalist institution in the development of the Irish revolutionary elite. Most of the leaders of the 1916 rebellion, the War of Independence and the Irish Civil War had been members. Garvin, *Nationalist Revolutionaries*, p. 78.

12 NAI, CBS, IG and CI, 1994/S.

13 Hutchinson, *The Gaelic Revival*, p. 168.

14 Kevin Rafter, *Sinn Féin, 1905–2005: In the Shadow of Gunmen* (Dublin, 2005), p. 43.

15 Sinn Féin, though nominally a political party, was before 1916 little more than a clique of Dublin journalists, minor politicians, politicised students and office workers who enjoyed limited contact with similar groups in the provincial centres. Tom Garvin, *The Evolution of Irish Nationalist Politics* (Dublin, 1981), p. 105.

16 J.J. Lee, *Ireland, 1912–1985: Politics and Society* (Cambridge, 1989), p. 38.

17 *KS*, 20 March; *KM*, 23 March 1907.

18 *KS*, 5 April 1905.

19 De Búrca, *The GAA*, pp. 94–5.

20 *KS*, 2 October 1901.

21 NAI, CBS, IG and CI, 769/S/1206/S.

22 NAI, CO 904, MFA 54/39, 2335/S.

23 M.F. Crowe, 'On the Field', *Gaelic Annual, 1907–08*, p. 26.

24 'Buille in Aipce', *Gaelic Annual, 1908–09*, p. 7.

25 *KS*, 25 November 1908.

26 Ferriter, *Transformation of Ireland*, p. 112.

27 The act limited the power of the Lords to a two-year delay of any legislation passed by the House of Commons.

28 By the end of 1913, Carson's Volunteers had a force of 88,000 men armed with around 17,000 rifles. NAI, CO 904, MFA, 54/53, 4769/S.

29 *KS*, 22 November 1913.

30 NAI, CO 904, 54/53, 4950/S.

31 *KM*, 22 November 1913. MacNeill, through his Gaelic League connections, enlisted the support of The O'Rahilly of Ballylongford, a member of the League's national executive. O'Rahilly was instrumental in organising the Rotunda meeting and played a prominent role in the Irish Volunteers, becoming its Director of Arms.

32 T. Ryle Dwyer, *Tans, Terror and Troubles: Kerry's Real Fighting Story, 1913–23* (Cork, 2001), p. 33.

33 NAI, Bureau of Military History Interviews (BMH), WS 135: Tadhg Kennedy, Tralee, p. 1.

34 Diarmuid Crean, the Kerry Board's secretary, acted as the meeting's secretary. *KS*, 13 December 1913.

35 National membership increased from 25,000 to 120,747 between May and June 1914.

36 NAI, CO 904, MFA 54/54.

37 *KS*, 1 August 1914.

38 *Sport*, 5 July 1913.

39 *KM*, 23 March 1913.

40 W.F. Mandle, 'The Gaelic Athletic Association and Popular Culture, 1884–1924', in Oliver MacDonagh, W.F. Mandle and Pauric Travers (eds), *Irish Culture and Nationalism, 1750–1950* (Canberra, 1983), p. 108.

41 NLI, J.J. O'Connell Papers, Autobiographical Account of events leading to 1916, MS 22, 114, p. 4.

42 Letter to the Editor, *Gaelic Athlete*, 1 August 1914. The writers noted that most of their provincial leaders were prominent members of the GAA and they should use their influence to get the GAA to provide funds.

43 CPA, GAA/CC/01/02: 12 April 1914.

44 *Gaelic Athlete*, 17 January 1914.

45 *KS*, 11 April, 6 June 1914.

46 NAI, BMH, WS 1144: Patrick O'Shea, Castlegregory.

47 *KWR*, 4 April 1914. Unfortunately no record of what this speech contained is to be found in any Kerry paper of the time. Crean left Kerry later that year to take up a position in the postal service in British-controlled Uganda. He was dismissed from his post in 1916 in the aftermath of the Easter Rising due to his previous connection with the Volunteers. He returned to Kerry in 1917. Joe O'Toole, 'Corcha Dhuibhne in 1916 and the First Kerry President of the Irish Republic', *The Kerry Magazine*, No. 17 (2007), p. 8.

48 *Tralee Liberator*, 5 September 1914.

49 Reprinted in *KS*, 23 September 1914. The *National Volunteer* was widely supportive of the GAA and carried a dedicated weekly Gaelic games column.

50 *KM*, 8 August 1914.

51 Mandle, *GAA and Politics*, p. 108.

52 J.J. O'Connell Papers, MS 22 114, p. 4. For example, in Clare in 1914, the first county inspection of the Volunteers was delayed for a week as it clashed with the All-Ireland hurling final which Clare was contesting. Murphy, 'The GAA and Revolution', p. 66.

53 NAI, BMH, WS 146: Diarmuid Crean, Spa, Tralee, p. 3.

54 *KS*, 8 July, 5 December 1914.

55 Paul Bew, *Ideology and the Irish Question: Ulster Unionism and Irish Nationalism,
1912–1916* (Oxford, 1998), p. 123. Bew also argued that by encouraging Irish
nationalists to enlist, Redmond hoped to provide a context for reconciliation between
unionists and nationalists which, he hoped, would avoid partition.

56 Jackson, *Ireland*, pp.169–97. On top of these reasons, it is argued Redmond genuinely
felt the war against Germany was a crusade of good against aggressive evil. D.R.
O'Connor Lysaght, 'The Rhetoric of Redmondism, 1914–16', *History Ireland*, 11, 1
(2003), p. 46.

57 *Irish Independent*, 21 September 1914.

58 Jackson, *Ireland*, p. 168.

59 Lee, *Ireland*, pp. 22–3.

60 *KS*, 24 October 1914. Some members were subsequently victimised for this stance. In
October 1915, Jeremiah O'Connell, the principal at Foilmore National School, was
dismissed from his post by the National Board of Education because he was a member
of the Cahersiveen Irish Volunteers. KCA, Cahersiveen Rural District Council Minute
Books, 1899–1925, RDC 48/A/6, 1912–1919: 20 October 1915.

61 *KM*, 17 October 1914.

62 NAI, CO 904, MFA 54/55. Indeed, by March 1915 it was reported that significant
numbers of the Redmond Volunteers in Tralee were anxious to rejoin the Irish
Volunteers. The Tralee Battalion committee, headed by Austin Stack, decided to write
to Volunteer HQ in Dublin about the feasibility of passing a rule 'to stop [such]
undesirables from again rejoining the ranks'. Kerry County Museum (KCM) Minute
Book of the Tralee Irish Volunteers, March 1915–April 1916, KCM 1994: 22, 22
March 1915.

63 CPA, GAA/CC/01/02: 19 December 1914.

64 *KM*, 28 November 1914.

65 *KP*, 25 May 1915.

66 *Sport*, 23 March 1915. A similar situation had developed in Tyrone where the recently
revived GAA virtually collapsed owing to large-scale Volunteer recruitment. Éamon
Phoenix, 'Nationalism in Tyrone, 1880–1972', in Charles Dillon and Henry A. Jefferies
(eds), *Tyrone – History and Society: Interdisciplinary Essays on the History of an Irish
County* (Dublin, 2000), p. 774.

67 *KM*, 23 January 1915.

68 The exact number is still disputed among historians; see Keith Jeffery, *Ireland and the
Great War* (Cambridge, 2000), pp. 33–5.

69 Thomas F. Martin, *The Kingdom in the Empire: A Portrait of Kerry During World
War One* (Dublin, 2006), pp. 64–7.

70 Alan Drumm, *Kerry and the Royal Munster Fusiliers* (Dublin, 2010), pp. 23, 70.

71 Martin, *Kingdom*, p. 81.

72 Kieran McNulty, 'Revolutionary Movements', p. 15.

73 NAI, CO 904, MFA 54/55, 6512/S/6769/S.

74 NAI, CO 904, MFA 54/57, 9856/S.

75 *KEP*, 4 November 1914.

76 The records pertaining to such information, kept in the British Home Office, were destroyed during the London Blitz in the Second World War.

77 Drumm, *Munster Fusiliers*, p. 21.

78 Martin, *Kingdom*, p. 81.

79 Drumm, *Munster Fusiliers*, p. 39.

80 Only two of the four men left where under forty years of age. *KS*, 12 May 1915.

81 David Fitzpatrick, 'The Logic of Collective Sacrifice: Ireland and the British Army, 1914–1918', *The Historical Journal*, 38, 4 (1995), p. 1017.

82 Sean O'Sullivan, 'The GAA and Irish Nationalism, 1913–1923', MA thesis, University College Dublin, 1994, p. 27.

83 CPA, GAA Annual Congress Minute Books, 1911–1927: 4 April 1915.

84 Murphy, 'The GAA and Revolution', p. 67.

85 Pádraig Griffin, *The Politics of Irish Athletics, 1850–1990* (Ballinamore, 1990), p. 29.

86 *The Irish Times*, 30 November 1915.

87 That they did is not surprising given that across the UK enlistment rates among sports clubs in general, and rugby clubs in particular, were strong. For example, Bristol Rugby Club alone lost 300 members in the war while nine Irish rugby internationals also died in the conflict. Gareth Williams, 'Rugby Union', in Tony Mason (ed.), *Sport in Britain: A Social History* (Cambridge, 1989), p. 324.

88 Roche was chairman of Limerick County Board and that county's representative at Munster Council before he became chairman of the Limerick City Volunteers. He sided with Redmond after they split and enlisted with the Royal Munster Fusiliers. Murphy, 'The GAA and Revolution', p. 67.

89 *Kerry Advocate*, 19 June 1915. Throughout the war the popular appeal of sport was used to recruit and motivate soldiers. On the first day of the Battle of the Somme, a captain in the 8th East Surrey Battalion provided his platoons with two footballs and offered a prize for the first platoon to dribble a ball as far as the German trenches. Mason, *Sport in Britain*, pp. 1–2.

90 *KS*, 20 November, 13 March 1915.

91 For example, in Dublin a group of rugby players, styling themselves the 'Dublin Pals', enlisted together in the days following the outbreak of war. Philip Orr, '200,000 Volunteer Soldiers', in John Horne (ed.), *Our War: Ireland and the Great War* (Dublin, 2008), p. 67. In Australia, recruitment among rugby league clubs resulted in a 44 per cent reduction in club numbers between 1914 and 1917. Rodney Noonan, 'Offside: Rugby League, the Great War and Australian Patriotism', *IJHS*, 26, 15 (2009), p. 2205.

92 Looney, *Dick Fitzgerald*, pp. 74–5.

93 Michael Wheatley observes that in Roscommon, the local county board was strongly anti-war and was a major influence in the county's poor recruitment. Michael Wheatley, *Nationalism and the Irish Party: Provincial Ireland, 1910–1916* (Oxford, 2005), p. 246.

94 *KM*, 10 October 1914.

95 NAI, CO 904, MFA, 54/56, 8388/S.

96 *KS*, 1 May 1915.

97 Cronin, *Munster*, p. 100.

CHAPTER 6: WAR AND PEACE, 1916–1923

1 NAI, CO 904, MFA 54/58, 10664/S.

2 The Irish Volunteers had been rapidly increasing in numbers on account of the continued fear that Britain would introduce compulsory conscription into Ireland. In May 1915, the Kerry RIC county inspector reported that the Irish Volunteers had twelve branches in the county, with 778 members. NAI, CO 904, MFA 54/57, 8805/S.

3 Lyons, *Ireland*, pp. 330–9. He was also expected to make arrangements to secure a large shipment of German arms from the German government.

4 The general aim was to seize a ring of fortified positions in strategic buildings in Dublin which could be defended against a full-force British attack. They chose the GPO in Dublin to be their central headquarters during the planned rebellion. Alvin Jackson argued its choice was to provoke maximum bloodshed and destruction in the hope of resurrecting Irish Anglophobia and regaining popular support for the discredited militant programme. Jackson, *Ireland*, p. 205.

5 Gaughan, *Austin Stack*, p. 30. Invariably the IRB centre in a given area was either the commanding officer or another high-ranking officer in the local Volunteer battalion. For example, in Listowel, Maurice Griffin was the town's IRB centre and Volunteer commander.

6 NAI, BMH, WS 135: Tadhg Kennedy, Tralee, pp. 3–4.

7 NAI, BMH, WS 132: Michael Spillane, Killarney; Michael J. Sullivan, New Street, Killarney, p. 2.

8 NAI, CO 904, MFA 54/58, 10893/S.

9 *KM*, 4, 11 March 1916.

10 NLI, *The Royal Commission on the Rebellion in Ireland, Minutes of Evidence and Appendix of Documents*, Ir 94109 12, p. 80.

11 *Tralee Liberator* (*TL*), 29 February 1916.

12 Michael Foy and Brian Barton, *The Easter Rising* (Gloucestershire, 2004), p. 43.

13 Lyons, *Ireland*, p. 353.

14 O'Shea was dubbed the 'Aeroplane' because of his fielding prowess. Joe Ó Muircheartaigh and T.J. Flynn, *Princes of Pigskin: A Century of Kerry Footballers* (Cork, 2008), p. 31.

15 Gaughan, *Austin Stack*, pp. 44–5.

16 *KS*, 29 March 1916.

17 KM, 11 March, 22 April 1916. Kerry were fixed to play Tipperary in the first round of the Munster championship the following week but still the county board was reported as not having met to select a team.

18 Harry Boland was a noteworthy attendant.

19 However, the Cork GAA president, J.J. Walsh, stated that as he made his way to the GPO on Easter Monday morning to take his place among the rebels, he was met by Nowlan and a few other GAA officials who were aware of what would transpire and gave him their blessing. J.J. Walsh, *Recollections of a Rebel* (Tralee, 1944), p. 36.

20 Dwyer, *Kerry's Fighting Story*, pp. 63–4. Instead of the 20,000 rifles with ammunition promised, Casement discovered that the Germans were sending nothing but a token arms shipment to Ireland and they had no intention of providing the Volunteers with the heavier weapons they had requested.

21 See NLI, Austin Stack Papers, MS 17 075, p. 3. Stack stated that Casement, once he

landed in Kerry, hoped to get him to send a message to the Military Council to call off the rebellion.

22 Since Thursday evening, the *Aud* had been sailing up and down the north Kerry coast near Fenit giving the agreed signal to alert the local Volunteers to its presence. However, as the ship was not expected for a further three days, there was no one to receive and reply to the signal. Dwyer, *Kerry's Fighting Story*, p. 67

23 Charles Townshend, *Easter 1916: The Irish Rebellion* (London, 2006), p. 131.

24 British naval intelligence had intercepted the IRB's signal to Germany to arrange the arms shipment, and as they had already broken the German naval code were fully aware of the plan to land the arms in Kerry.

25 *KEP*, 22 April 1916. Despite the fact that Casement was well known and photographs of him with his trademark long beard were circulated to the RIC some months earlier, he was not identified by the Tralee RIC for some hours as he was clean-shaven when arrested. Donal O'Sullivan, 'The Fate of John B. Kearney, District Inspector of the RIC and Superintendent of the Civic Guard', *The Kerry Magazine*, No. 9 (1998), p. 20.

26 J.A. Gaughan has argued that Stack purposely set out to be arrested. Being the well-known head of the IRB and Volunteers in the county, his arrest would hopefully have ensured that the police were not put on alert, thus enabling the German arms to be landed unhampered. Gaughan, *Austin Stack*, p. 62. T. Ryle Dwyer is more sceptical, suggesting that Stack's motive for being arrested was more to do with the fact that he saw the plans for the Rising quickly unravelling before his eyes. Dwyer, *Kerry's Fighting Story*, p. 81.

27 The Military Council made him aware of the famous 'Castle Document' on the Wednesday before the Rising. Though the document was based on real British plans to crack down on the Irish Volunteers, it had been 'enhanced' to make the plans appear imminent so as to get MacNeill to support immediate action. Charles Townshend, 'Making Sense of Easter 1916', *History Ireland*, 14, 2 (2006), p. 41.

28 The local Volunteers had a force of 300 men with only 200 of them armed, ranged against some 500 military troops and 200 armed RIC officers on full alert. Dwyer, *Kerry's Fighting Story*, p. 88.

29 Brian Ó Conchubhair (ed.), *Kerry's Fighting Story, 1916–1921*, 2009 edition (Cork, 2009), p.124.

30 Jackson, *Ireland*, p. 202. Pearse himself had long advocated that a blood sacrifice was the only means of freeing Ireland from English domination. See Joost Augusteijn, 'Patrick Pearse: Proto-Fascist Eccentric or Mainstream European Thinker?' *History Ireland*, 18, 6 (2010), pp. 34–6.

31 NAI, BMH, WS 1110: P Browne, Ballymullen, Tralee, p. 7.

32 Lyons, *Ireland*, p. 375.

33 He was shot while leading a charge against a British Army barricade in the street. NLI, The O'Rahilly Papers, MS 13 019.

34 From the *Daily Sketch*, reprinted in *KS*, 6 May 1916.

35 Mandle, *GAA and Politics*, p. 178.

36 Nolan, *The Gaelic Athletic Association in Dublin*, p. 126.

37 Fergus Campbell, 'The Easter Rising in Galway', *History Ireland*, 14, 2 (2006), p. 24.

38 Robert Brennan, *Allegiance* (Dublin, 1950), pp. 51, 64.

39 Mike Cronin, 'Defenders of a Nation? The Gaelic Athletic Association and Irish Nationalist Identity', *Irish Political Studies*, No. 11 (1996), p. 7.

40 For example, in 1911, the future GAA president Dan McCarthy stated that he wanted GAA men 'to train and be physically strong [so that] when the time comes the hurlers will cast away the camán for the steel that will drive the Saxon from our land'. *Wicklow People*, 21 January 1911.

41 *KS*, 3 May 1916.

42 *KS*, 10 May 1916; *KEP*, 6 May 1916.

43 *KS*, 29 April 1916.

44 *KS*, *KM*, 13 May 1916.

45 J.J. Barrett, *In the Name of the Game* (Wicklow, 1997), p. 53.

46 NLI, J.J. O'Connell Papers, Notes, MS 22 117.

47 NAI, BMH, WS 801: William Mullins, Moyderwell, Tralee, p. 1. Mullins was commander of the Tralee Volunteer cycle corps. KCM, 'Minute Book of the Tralee Irish Volunteers', KCM 1994: 2, 1 December 1915.

48 Looney, *Dick Fitzgerald*, p. 123.

49 *KS*, 22 July 1916.

50 Murphy, 'The GAA and Revolution', p. 71.

51 NLI, *Royal Commission on Rebellion in Ireland*, p. 3: Sir Matthew Nathan's Statement with Regard to the Insurrection. The IRB, Gaelic League and Sinn Féin were the other three organisations mentioned.

52 De Búrca, *The GAA*, p. 103.

53 *KS*, 7, 10 June 1916.

54 *KS*, 12 August 1916.

55 Writing in May to his brother Michael, serving in the British Army, John Moynihan (Maurice Moynihan's son) wrote '[the rebel leaders] are not really dead; the men who sought to destroy them only succeeded in giving them a power over the hearts and minds of men greater than ever they had before'. John Moynihan to Michael Moynihan, 21–22 May 1916, quoted in Deirdre McMahon (ed.), *The Moynihan Brothers in Peace and War, 1908–1918: Their New Ireland* (Dublin, 2004), p. 122.

56 As Paul Bew argues, the British reaction to the Rising was by their standards abnormally severe. 'It was an aberration generated by the pressure of total war.' Paul Bew, 'The Real Importance of Sir Roger Casement', *History Ireland*, 2, 2 (1994), p. 45.

57 NAI, CO 904, MFA 54/58, 11179/S.

58 NAI, MFA CO 904, 54/60, 12427/S.

59 *KS*, 26, 29 July 916.

60 *KS*, 9 August 1916.

61 CPA, GAA/CC/01/02: 9 July 1916.

62 *KS*, 20 September 1916. The Defence of the Realm Act was introduced at the outbreak of the First World War. It gave the British government wide-ranging powers to monitor and censure the public as part of the war effort.

63 *KS*, 23 September 1916.

64 As Michael Laffan argued, resentment at the rebels' conduct was overshadowed by resentment at their fate. Michael Laffan, 'The Unification of Sinn Féin in 1917', *IHS*, XVII, 67 (1971), p. 354.

65 David Fitzpatrick, *Politics and Irish Life, 1913–1921: Provincial Experience of War and Revolution* (Cork, 1998), p. 97. Paddy Cahill for one believed that this political

inertia was the principal cause of the discontent which led to the 1916 Rising. 'Paddy Cahill Correspondence', KCM 1994: 23.

66 NAI, CO 904, MFA 54/60, 12427/S.

67 Fitzpatrick, *Politics*, pp. 121–3. Sinn Féin clubs operated in much the same way as the old National League and they used the same system of county and national conventions.

68 KCA, RDC 104/A/19.

69 *KM*, 23 June 1917. A crowd of 10,000 greeted them when they arrived in Tralee.

70 Laffan. 'Unification of Sinn Féin', p. 375.

71 *KS*, 25 August, 1 September 1917. Ashe had made an inflammatory speech in Longford while Stack had addressed a meeting in Banna to mark the first anniversary of Casement's death.

72 *KM*, 1 September 1917.

73 At the subsequent public inquest into his death, the jury's verdict strongly condemned the prison authorities for their role in it. *The Death of Thomas Ashe: Full Report of the Inquest* (Dublin, 1917), p. 84.

74 *FJ*, 29 September 1917.

75 It was said that the funeral procession was so large, it took the entire cortège an hour and a half to pass any given point on the route. *KM*, 6 October 1917.

76 NAI, CO 904, MFA 54/62, 17685/S.

77 *KS*, 13 January 1917; *KWR*, 4 August 1917.

78 NAI, CO 904, MFA 54/62: IG and CI Monthly Confidential Reports May–December 1917, IG Confidential Monthly Report May 1917, 9 June 1917, 14679/S.

79 Peter Hart, *The IRA at War, 1916–1923* (Oxford, 2003), p. 55; Fitzpatrick, *Politics*, p. 112.

80 Maurice Moynihan had urged county boards to take the lead in this and that appropriate prizes would include the published works of the dead rebel leaders. Such tournaments, he argued, would both advance the GAA's standing in the country as well as provide much-needed support for this worthy objective. *KS*, 16 August 1916.

81 In November, the Central Council decided to run a national tournament in its support.

82 *KS*, 13 October 1917.

83 Sinn Féin had promised to end the 'Land Question' once and for all by means of exclusive control of Ireland's own resources by her people. Terence Dooley, *The Land for the People: The Land Question in Independent Ireland* (Dublin, 2004), pp. 31–4.

84 This agitation only increased as the War of Independence began. Such was the preoccupation with land disputes in Kerry that Austin Stack and his fellow Kerry TDs, elected in 1918, were forced in April 1920 to issue a circular demanding that disputes over the ownership of such land be put aside until the current armed struggle for an independent Ireland had been won. NLI, Austin Stack Papers, Land Agitation in Kerry in 1920, MS 17 085.

85 O'Connor, *Keel GAA*, p. 74.

86 CPA, Annual Congress Minutes: 31 March 1918.

87 *KS*, 30 June 1917. Though Tullig had in fact only won the 1916 junior hurling championship that day, the Kerry Board had only one set of medals to award. Tullig played the senior championship winners Kenmare and by beating them were presented with the medals and the title of 1916 hurling champions.

88 However, Dick Fitzgerald trained the Clare football team to its first Munster title in

1917 and the county reached the All-Ireland football final for the only time in its history, being defeated by Wexford. *Sport*, 15 December 1917.

89 *Sport*, 11 August 1917.

90 CPA, GAA CC 01/02: GAA Annual Congress, 31 March 1918; *KM*, 6 April 1918.

91 *KM*, 13 April 1918.

92 CPA, GAA/CC/01/02: 14 April 1918.

93 *KS*, 13 April 1918.

94 The Volunteers had been reorganising ever since the release of their members from British jails during late 1916 and 1917. The rise of the Sinn Féin movement and the dual leadership between it and the Volunteers on a national level had provided the impetuous for this reorganisation. Colonel Jeremiah O'Connell wrote that once the Volunteers reorganised they were assured of the support of the Irish public, which was 'the one solid national gain from the Insurrection of Easter 1916'. NLI, J.J. O'Connell Papers, MS 22 117.

95 *KS*, 20 April 1918. Having occurred nine months before the Soloheadbeg ambush, seen as the traditional start of the Anglo-Irish War, some Kerry historians have argued that this raid in fact marks the beginning of the conflict between the Irish Volunteers and the British government.

96 NAI, CO 904, MFA 54/64, 19917/S.

97 In Glenflesk, a football match was played between the Fermoyle and Ballinskelligs football teams, which were made up entirely of the local Volunteer half companies. *KM*, 8 June 1918.

98 By now many within the Irish Volunteers regarded it as just a matter of time until armed conflict broke out with Britain. Writing from Belfast Goal, Austin Stack proposed that the Volunteers should organise hidden food stores to use as rations for the force as 'John Bull' may find himself 'on the run on the Irish front ere very long'. KCM, Austin Stack Correspondence, KCM 1995.

99 *KS*, *KM*, 29 June 1918.

100 *FJ*, 5 July 1918.

101 Murphy, 'The GAA and Revolution', p. 68.

102 Quoted in *KS*, 13 July 1918.

103 *KS*, 3 August 1918.

104 Seán S. Ó Súilleabháin, *Aililiú Rathmore: A History of Gaelic Activities in the Parish* (Rathmore, 1990), p. 96.

105 CPA, GAA/CC/01/02: 20 July 1918.

106 *Sport*, 10 August 1918. It was estimated that between 50,000 and 100,000 players participated. Murphy, 'The GAA and Revolution', p. 72.

107 *KM*, 10 August 1918. The sides drew 2-0 apiece.

108 De Búrca, *The GAA*, p. 111; Mandle, 'The GAA and Popular Culture', p. 108; Murphy, 'The GAA and Revolution', p. 72.

109 *KM*, 28 September 1918.

110 The epidemic occurred in three waves, the last of which had receded by the summer of 1919. The spread of the disease was greatly assisted by the demobilisation of hundreds of thousands of soldiers with the ending of the First World War. Caitriona Foley, *The Last Irish Plague: The Great Flu Epidemic in Ireland, 1918–19* (Dublin, 2011), pp. 14, 25.

111 John M. Barry, *The Great Influenza: The Epic Story of the Deadliest Plague in History* (New York, 2004), p. 450. In Ireland, the epidemic claimed more than 20,000 lives and infected as many as 600,000 to 800,000 people, the vast majority within a six-month period around winter 1918–19.

112 Caitriona Foley shows how in Ireland the highest death rates from the epidemic were in young males aged between twenty-five and thirty-five. In addition, Kerry was one of the counties with the highest mortality rates from the disease in 1919. Caitriona Foley, 'The Last Great Irish Plague: The Great Flu in Ireland, 1918–19', PhD Thesis, University College Dublin, 2009, pp. 38, 296.

113 The All-Ireland football semi-final between Mayo and Tipperary also had to be postponed due to the outbreak. Foley, *The Great Flu*, p. 64.

114 *KM*, 2, 23 November 1918.

115 Jeremiah Murphy, *When Youth Was Mine: A Memoir of Kerry, 1902–1925* (Dublin, 1998), p. 114.

116 Michael Laffan, *The Resurrection of Ireland: The Sinn Féin Party, 1916–1923* (Cambridge, 1999), pp. 164–6.

117 NAI, CO 904, MFA 54/65 IG and CI Monthly Confidential Reports September–December 1918, IG Confidential Monthly Report December 1918, 11 January 1919, 22628/S. Another boost to Sinn Féin was the Representation of the People Act which was passed in February 1918. It gave votes to men over twenty-one and women over thirty. This dramatically increased the voting electorate in Ireland. In Kerry, at a stroke, the numbers of voters increased from 28,586 to 67,912. As Sinn Féin was predominately a youth movement, the implications for its election success were clear.

118 This was another political fund set up to support political prisoners jailed on account of their Sinn Féin activity.

119 CPA, GAA CC 01/02: 7 December 1918.

120 *Sport*, 8, 22 February 1919. Both the Limerick and Sligo conventions passed similar resolutions.

121 *KM*, 29 March 1919.

122 CPA, Annual Congress Minute Books, 1911–1927: 20 April 1919.

123 Murphy, 'The GAA and Revolution', p. 65.

124 *KM*, 2 November 1918. At a meeting of Laune Rangers in October a similar league was established for Killorglin to promote football among young men there.

125 *KM*, 3 May 1919. The competition was inaugurated on 4 May between eight teams.

126 *KM*, 15 November 1919.

127 *KM*, 15 May 1920. Though this surplus of young men benefited a nationalist organisation like the GAA, Peter Hart argues that any correlation between republican violence and lack of emigration opportunities during the revolutionary period has been overstated. Hart, *IRA at War*, pp. 50–1.

128 *KM*, 29 April 1919.

129 *KM*, 18, 25 October 1919. The Tralee Parnells was the name of the Tralee Mitchels club's hurling team.

130 *KM*, 6 September 1919.

131 NAI, CO 904, MFA 54/67, 25962/S.

132 CPA, GAA Annual Congress Minute Books, 1911–1927: 20 April 1919.

133 *KWR*, 14 June 1919.

134 Michael Hopkinson, *The Irish War of Independence* (Dublin, 2002), p. 25.

135 The IRA was formed on Easter Monday 1916 as the army of the proclaimed Irish Republic. John O'Beirne-Ranelagh, 'The IRB from the Treaty to 1924', *IHS*, XX, 77 (1976), p. 26.

136 T. Ryle Dwyer, *Michael Collins: The Man Who Won the War* (Cork, 2009), pp. 108–9. Collins realised the British would retaliate but without intelligence they would do so blindly against innocent Irish people, driving them into the arms of the republicans.

137 Such tactics frustrated Collins and by May 1919 he was complaining to Austin Stack that those in charge of Sinn Féin were becoming 'ever less militant and even more politically theoretical'. NLI, Michael Collins Papers, MS 5848.

138 W.J. Lowe, 'The War Against the RIC, 1919–21', *Éire-Ireland*, XXXVII, 3–4 (2002), p. 85.

139 Austin Stack, as Dáil Éireann's appointed Minister for Home Affairs, was responsible for the setting up of this system of courts. Mary Kotsonouris, 'Revolutionary Justice: The Dáil Éireann Courts', *History Ireland*, 2, 2 (1994), p. 32.

140 Dwyer, *Kerry's Fighting Story*, pp. 157–8. No. 1 Brigade was centred on Tralee and controlled Volunteer battalions in north and west Kerry. No. 2 Brigade was based in Killarney and controlled battalions around the south and east of the county, while No. 3 Brigade controlled the area of the Iveragh Peninsula.

141 Fitzgerald, *Politics*, pp. 169–71. This was particularly the case in relation to Kerry's No. 1 Brigade under the command of Patrick Cahill. Throughout the war, general headquarters frequently complained of the lack of discipline and organisation of the brigade and its unremarkable record of operations against the enemy. Cahill was eventually dismissed due to his failings as a commander in March 1921. Indeed, the 'Cahill influence' was seen by many veterans as the primary reason for Kerry's underachievement during the War of Independence. See Sinead Joy, *The IRA in Kerry: 1916–1921* (Cork, 2005), pp. 50, 62, 84–7.

142 The RIC's Inspector General stated that such attacks were regarded by the Volunteer leadership as legitimate military operations against an enemy force. Furthermore, they were committed in pursuance of a deliberate campaign to break the morale of the RIC, 'which is often referred to as the last obstacle in the way of the establishment of an Irish republic'. NAI, CO 904, MFA 54/67: IG and CI Monthly Confidential Reports May–August 1919, IG Confidential Monthly Report August 1919, 15 September 1919, 25962/S. Between the attack on Soloheadbeg and the truce, some 434 police officers were killed in Ireland. See Richard Abbott, *Police Casualties in Ireland, 1919–1922* (Cork, 2000), p. 7.

143 Between late 1919 and early 1920 almost a third of the total number of RIC barracks in Ireland were abandoned. Joost Augusteijn, 'Accounting for the Emergence of Violent Activism among Irish Revolutionaries, 1916–21', *IHS*, XXXV, 139 (2007), p. 330.

144 The first reports of their arrival in Kerry were from Tralee in July 1920. *KM*, 24 July 1920.

145 A hastily recruited force, the Black and Tans received only a six-week training course on arrival in Ireland, contrast to the six-month course which was the norm for RIC officers. Pádraig Ó Concubhair and Caitríona Lane, 'The Black and Tans in Ballylongford', *The Kerry Magazine*, No. 13 (2002), p. 39.

146 Up to that night only five RIC officers had been killed in the county since the 1916 Rising.

147 The siege was finally lifted on 10 November.

148 Ferriter, *Transformation of Ireland*, p. 223; Fitzpatrick, *Politics*, pp. 180–1.

149 Ó Conchubhair, *Kerry's Fighting Story*, pp. 256–9. The British death toll was believed to be between twelve and twenty-four. *KM*, 26 March 1921; Dwyer, *Kerry's Fighting Story*, p. 294.

150 NAI, CO 904, MFA 54/72, 501/41137/S.

151 *KM*, 17 April 1920.

152 See Charles Townshend, 'The Irish Railway Strike of 1920: Industrial Action and Civil Resistance in the Struggle for Independence', *IHS*, XXI, 83 (1979), pp. 266–9.

153 *KM*, 26 June 1920.

154 McMahon, 'Ireland and the Commonwealth', p. 207.

155 *Sport*, 3 April 1920.

156 *KM*, 21 February 1920.

157 *The Kerryman* declared that 'never in the history of the GAA here was a county final played under such peculiar circumstances'. Though the match was billed for 3.30 p.m. at Tralee Sportsground and a large crowd had already assembled there, the Mitchels team did not arrive until 5 p.m. There was still no sign of Dingle, so runners were sent down town to try and locate them. It was discovered that the large charabanc which the Dingle side had procured as their transport had broken down at Camp village. Someone arranged for a convoy of motor cars to collect the stranded Dingle men. Finally, at 7.30 p.m. in fading light the teams lined out to contest the final, Mitchels winning 3-3 to 2-2. *KM*, 1 May 1920.

158 CPA, GAA/CC/01/02: 4 April 1920.

159 *Sport*, 18 September 1920.

160 Michael Cronin, 'Defenders', p. 7.

161 *Sport*, 20 November 1920.

162 Cronin, *Sport and Nationalism*, p. 87.

163 See Joost Augusteijn, *From Public Defiance to Guerrilla Warfare. The Radicalisation of the Irish Republican Army: A Comparative Analysis, 1916–1921* (Amsterdam, 1994), pp. 16–22.

164 Murphy, 'The GAA and Revolution', p. 69. Hart states that in Cork the relationship between the Volunteers and subsequently the IRA and the GAA could be tenuous. Many Cork Volunteers were wary of GAA members and officials being 'talkers rather than fighters'. Peter Hart, *The IRA and Its Enemies: Violence and Community in Cork, 1916–1923* (Oxford, 1998), pp. 211–12.

165 Marie Coleman, *County Longford and the Irish Revolution, 1910–1923* (Dublin, 2003), p. 177.

166 Michael Farry, *The Aftermath of Revolution: Sligo, 1921–23* (Dublin, 2000), pp. 131–41.

167 Fitzpatrick, *Politics*, p. 169.

168 NAI, BMH, WS 1190: Michael Pierce, Castleisland, pp. 2–3.

169 *KM*, 15 May 1920.

170 Frank O'Donovan, *Abbeydorney: Our Own Place* (Abbeydorney, 1989), pp. 100, 169–71.

171 Ó Súilleabháin, *Rathmore*, p. 103.

172 *KM*, 22 January 1921.

173 Claire Turvey, 'Politics, War and Revolution: The Kenmare District, 1916–1923', *JKAHS*, Series 2, Vol. 6 (2006), pp. 98–137, at p. 114.

174 *KM*, 2 April 1921.

175 At his funeral there were scenes of wild excitement as armed Black and Tans forced themselves through the crowd and tore off the tricolour which was draped over the hearse. Diary of Christopher P. O'Grady, KCM 1993: 47.

176 Barrett, *Name of the Game*, p. 115.

177 *Kerry People (KPE)*, 23 April 1921.

178 Barrett, *Name of the Game*, p. 61.

179 *KPE*, 3, 20 August, 3 September 1921.

180 *CE*, 5 September 1921.

181 For a discussion on the IRA and Lloyd George's preparations for war in case the negotiations broke down, see S.M. Lawlor, 'Ireland from Truce to Treaty: War or Peace? July to October 1921', *IHS*, XXII, 85 (1980), pp. 51–62

182 *CE*, 4 October 1921.

183 Dermot Keogh, *Twentieth-Century Ireland: Nation and State* (Dublin, 1994), pp. 2–4.

184 Fionán Lynch, the South Kerry TD who had been secretary to the negotiating party in London, fully backed the treaty. In a speech to the Dáil during the treaty debates, Lynch refuted the claims of the opposition that Lloyd George had been able 'to put the wind up Michael Collins' and intimidated him into accepting the settlement. KCA, Fionán Lynch Papers, P/31: Speech to the Dáil, 20 December 1921.

185 Diarmaid Ferriter, *Judging Dev: A Reassessment of the Life and Legacy of Éamon de Valera* (Dublin, 2007), p. 69.

186 Christopher O'Grady noted that when the news arrived in Tralee that the treaty was ratified there was no jubilation and he personally considered the treaty 'bosh'. KCM, Diary of Christopher P. O'Grady, KCM 1993: 47, 7 January 1922.

187 NAI, BMH, WS 1413: Tadhg Kennedy, Ardfert. John Joe Sheehy of the Tralee IRA likewise rejected it, noting that many people in Tralee may have approved it but that Stack's supporters secured the town first.

188 *KPE*, 18, 25 March, 29 April 1922. Collins was due to address a public meeting in Killarney on 22 April but the platform erected for the event was burnt down by the local IRA. Collins instead gave his speech in the grounds of the town's Franciscan church.

189 John O'Beirne-Ranelagh, 'The IRB from the Treaty to 1924', in *IHS*, Vol. XX, No. 77 (1976), p. 28. The IRB continued to operate until November 1924 when, at a meeting of its remaining county centres, the decision was made to disband the organisation. It was felt that the IRA was a sufficient body to express its views and by now the need for a secret society had ceased. University College Dublin Archives (UCDA), The Irish Republican Brotherhood Papers, P21/9.

190 NAI, BMH, WS 1413: Tadhg Kennedy, Ardfert.

191 Joy, *The IRA*, pp. 114–18. Indeed, Sinead Joy claims that the IRA's stance there may have had more to do with personal circumstances than ideological differences. There was huge resentment over the fact that Paddy Cahill had been dismissed as commander of No. 1 Brigade by the IRA's GHQ during the war and this may have meant that a split with high command was inevitable regardless of the outcome of the treaty negotiations.

192 *KPE*, 22 April 1922.

193 *KPE*, 6 May 1922.

194 *Sport*, 25 November 1922.

195 For the election, a pact was made between the two opposing factions within Sinn Féin, led by Michael Collins and Éamon de Valera respectively. They agreed that regardless of the split over the treaty, the party would put forward candidates to the electorate in proportion to the existing treaty divide in the party. Assuming Sinn Féin won, they would then form a coalition government with ministers being appointed based on the proportional strength of the pro- and anti-treaty sides among the party's TDs. Michael Gallagher, 'The Pact General Election of 1922', *IHS*, XXI, 84 (1979), pp. 405–6.

196 In Kerry, there was an even split with Paddy Cahill and Austin Stack being elected for the anti-treaty section, while Fionán Lynch and Piaras Béaslaí were elected for the pro-treaty Sinn Féin. *KPE*, 24 June 1922.

197 The men, acting probably on their own initiative, killed Wilson in the mistaken belief that he had been responsible for a number of Catholic deaths in Belfast during the War of Independence. Peter Hart, 'Michael Collins and the Assassination of Sir Henry Wilson', *IHS*, XXVIII, 110 (1992), p. 170.

198 In Westminster, their presence in the Four Courts was stated to be in 'gross breach and defiance of the Treaty'. Ireland was warned that if the stand-off was not brought to a speedy end, the British government would regard the treaty 'as having been formally violated'. *KPE*, 1 July 1922.

199 Bill Kissane, *The Politics of the Irish Civil War* (Oxford, 2005), p. 78.

200 As T. Ryle Dwyer noted, the operation had a tremendous psychological impact on the Irregulars. Dwyer, *Kerry's Fighting Story*, p. 354. Tom Doyle agrees but argues that the task forces landed proved too inadequate numerically to hold the county at large, leading to the inevitable stalemate with IRA forces. Tom Doyle, *The Summer Campaign in Kerry* (Cork, 2010), p. 135.

201 Niall C. Harrington, *Kerry Landing, August 1922: An Episode of the Civil War* (Dublin, 1992), pp. 70, 104–5.

202 *CE*, 7 August 1922.

203 Doyle, *Summer Campaign*, pp. 46–7. The force of 240 men was able to disembark unopposed and quickly secured Tarbert. Patrick J. Lynch, *Tarbert: An Unfinished Biography* (Shanagolden, 2008), p. 339.

204 For example, once the Free State took possession of Tralee, the newspapers in the town were shut down. See *CE*, 23 September 1922.

205 A major source of recruitment were the huge numbers of unemployed – 150,000 men in the summer of 1922. Kissane, *Civil War*, p. 77. The new army was a hastily constructed composite force including veterans from the War of Independence and the First World War. There was also a great deal of recruitment among men from urban centres like Dublin who would traditionally have joined Irish regiments in the British Army. Jackson, *Ireland*, p. 266.

206 Keogh, *Ireland*, p. 11.

207 Joy, *The IRA*, p. 118.

208 Tom Doyle, *The Civil War in Kerry* (Cork, 2008), p. 319.

209 The 'squad' was a small band of Dublin Volunteers attached to Collins' Intelligence Department which acted as an assassination team targeting Dublin Castle spies and informers during the Anglo-Irish War in Dublin. Colm McInerney, 'Michael Collins and the Organisation of Irish Intelligence, 1917–21', *The History Review*, Vol. XIV (2003), p. 37.

210 Doyle, *Civil War*, p. 319.

211 The attack in February 1923 was led by the main IRA commanders in Kerry, Humphrey Murphy and John Joe Rice, both players for Dr Crokes.

212 Michael Hopkinson argues that the intensity of republican resistance in Kerry can be put down to the extreme unpopularity of outside Free State forces. Michael Hopkinson, *Green Against Green: The Irish Civil War* (Dublin, 1988), p. 240.

213 Dorothy Macardle, *Tragedies of Kerry, 1922–1923* (Dublin, 1991), pp. 16–17. That same day four more IRA prisoners were killed in similar circumstances at Countess Bridge, Killarney. On 7 April 1923, a military court held an enquiry into these deaths of Irregular prisoners in Kerry. All the Free State Army witnesses in connection with Ballyseedy claimed the eight prisoners killed had been ordered to remove the barricade and were proceeding with this work when the concealed mine inside went off. They all categorically denied the subsequent assertions made by the sole surviving prisoner of the explosion, Stephen Fuller, that the nine men had been bound and placed around the barricade before the device was purposely detonated. See NLI, *Proceedings of Military Court of Inquiry into Deaths of Republican Prisoners at Ballyseedy, etc., Co. Kerry with Associated Correspondence, etc.*, MS 22 956.

214 Dwyer, *Kerry's Fighting Story*, p. 371. However, the findings of the Military Court set up to investigate these incidents stated that the prisoners were killed 'in explosions while removing obstructions on the road, placed there by Irregulars'. NLI, *Proceedings of Military Court of Inquiry*, MS 22 956, p. 2.

215 T. Ryle Dwyer estimates that as many as forty republican prisoners in Kerry may have been summarily executed by firing squad or in incidents such as Ballyseedy. Dwyer, *Kerry's Fighting Story*, pp. 364, 372.

216 Barrett, *Name of the Game*, p. 13. Paddy O'Daly reported on 11 April that Free State casualties in the war in Kerry stood at sixty-nine dead, 157 wounded. NLI, *Proceedings of Military Court of Inquiry*, MS 22 956, p. 2.

217 Precise casualties on the short but bitter conflict are difficult to establish. Michael Hopkinson put pro-treaty losses at between 540 and 800, with Irregular losses considerably higher. Civilian losses were estimated as anywhere between 1,000 and 4,000, including combatants. Hopkinson, *Green Against Green*, pp. 272–3.

218 CPA, GAA/CC/01/02: 7/21 January 1923.

219 Daniel McCarthy, 'Citizen Cusack and Clare's Gaelic Games', in Matthew Lynch and Patrick Nugent (eds), *Clare – History and Society: Interdisciplinary Essays on the History of an Irish County* (Dublin, 2008), p. 488.

220 See *Sport*, 21 July, 4 August 1923.

221 *KM*, 13, 20 October 1923.

CHAPTER 7: THE PHOENIX FROM THE FLAME, 1924–1934

1 Barrett, *Name of the Game*, p. 16.

2 Government Statement to the Dáil, *KM*, 24 November 1923.

3 Keogh, *Ireland*, p. 17. However, by November numbers interned had dropped to 6,384. *KM*, 24 November 1923.

4 *KM*, 12 January, 2, 16 February 1924. The teams were: Kerry: D. Hurley (goal), T. Ryle, T. O'Connor, Phil Sullivan, J.J. Sheehy, T. Kelliher, D. O'Connor, C. Brosnan, D. O'Donoghue, T. Mahony, M. Walsh, P. Murphy, M. Graham, P. Donovan, J. Baily. Ex-Internees: J. O'Riordan (goal), J. Moriarty, J. Barrett, W. O'Gorman, J. Moriarty,

J. McMahon, J. Tangney, C. Mahony, T. O'Donnell, J. Ryan, B. Sheehy, C. Cronin, J. Murphy, M. Maher, P. Daly.

5 *KM*, 3 May 1924; Barrett, *Name of the Game*, p. 66.

6 *KM*, 7, 14 June 1924.

7 *KM*, 14 June 1924. When the Anglo-Irish Treaty was ratified, the first government of the Irish Free State resurrected Michael Davitt's proposal from the 1880s of reviving the ancient Tailteann Games. The government appointed J.J. Walsh as Director of the games. An organising committee representing every aspect of native culture was set up to contribute to the games. The GAA had generous representation on this committee, with separate nominees being allowed for football, hurling, athletics and handball. The Tailteann Games, staged in August 1924, proved a huge success. A full week's programme was held which included hurling matches involving Irish, Scottish, Welsh, English and American teams. A football international between the US and Ireland was also played, along with an interprovincial competition in both codes. Mike Cronin, 'The Irish Free State and Aonach Tailteann', in Alan Bairner (ed.), *Sport and the Irish: Histories, Identities, Issues* (Dublin, 2005), pp. 58–63; *Sport*, 2, 9 August 1924.

8 Brian Hanley, 'Irish Republican Attitudes to Sport Since 1921', in McAnallen et al., *The Evolution of the GAA*, p. 177.

9 The strength of the IRA in the First Southern Division (Kerry/Cork) in 1924 was said to be 2,904 men. Brian Hanley, *The IRA, 1926–1936* (Dublin, 2002), pp. 11–12.

10 UCDA, Moss Twomey Papers, P/69/43, pp. 57–9.

11 *Kerry Reporter* (*KR*), 14 June 1924.

12 UCDA, Moss Twomey Papers, P/69/145, p. 231, Adjunct General to O/C Divisions, 20 June 1924.

13 *KM*, 21 June, 5 July 1924.

14 Sport, 28 June, 5, 19 July 1924; *KM*, 26 July 1924.

15 CPA, GAA/CC/01/02: Meeting of the Central Council, 10 August 1924.

16 *Sixty Years*, p. 75.

17 *KM*, 23 February, 15 March 1924.

18 *Sport*, 26 April 1924.

19 CPA, GAA/CC/01/02: GAA Annual Congress, 12 April 1925. At the Kerry convention, delegates were unanimous in their opinion that the rule on foreign games should not be altered or interfered with in any way. *KM*, 4 April 1924.

20 Mandle, 'The GAA and Popular Culture', p. 109.

21 *Sport*, 13 December 1924.

22 In fact, the 1924 Kerry county championship was so disrupted that the county board subsequently abandoned it.

23 *KM*, 2 May 1925. O'Sullivan drew up an extensive programme of training for the Kerry team beginning at 8 a.m. and finishing at midnight. This was followed by a strict regime of eight hours' sleep every night. See Fogarty, *Éamonn O'Sullivan*, p. 178.

24 Barrett, *Name of the Game*, p. 69, *KM*, 2 May 1925. The young cleric paid for this indiscretion and others such as card-playing and smoking while in his studies and thus had to be ordained at Clonliffe College as Maynooth refused after such breaches of its rules.

25 *The Irish Times*, 27 April 1925.

26 Barrett, *Name of the Game*, pp. 73–4.

27 *Ibid.,* pp. 155–7.

28 Kerry won the facile match played two weeks after the All-Ireland semi-final by beating Clare 5-5 to no score. *KM*, 19 September 1925.

29 Cavan claimed Kerry's officials knew that it was illegal for them to play O'Sullivan, but had approached members of the Cavan Board before the match and asked them not to protest if they played him. *Anglo-Celt* (*AC*), 12, 19 September 1925.

30 *Sport*, 19 September 1925; *KM*, 19 September 1925.

31 *Sport*, 31 October 1925. Resentment towards Cavan remained strong, and at several coursing meetings over the next few months a well-known Rock Street player ran a dog called 'Cavan's Objection'. *KM*, 21 November 1925.

32 *KM*, 14 August 1926.

33 Hanley, 'Republican Attitudes', p. 177.

34 Hanley, *IRA*, pp. 11–12.

35 Tom Mahon and James J. Gillogly, *Decoding the IRA* (Cork, 2008), pp. 104–5.

36 *KM*, 27 November 1926.

37 CPA, GAA/CC/01/03: Special Meeting of Central Council, 11 December 1926.

38 *Sport*, 21 January 1927; *KM*, 16 July 1927.

39 Using the pseudonym 'PF', over the next forty years Foley would become one of the most eminent journalists on Gaelic games in Ireland and would go on to write the first history of the Kerry GAA.

40 UCDA, Moss Twomey Papers, P/69/183.

41 *KM*, 15 January 1927.

42 Tom Mahon, 'Up Kerry! Up the IRA! Kerry's 1927 American Tour', *History Ireland*, 18, 5 (2010), p. 39.

43 *KM*, 5 March, 7, 14 May 1927. Yet in spite of this impressive itinerary, the Kerry team would end up playing just seven games across New York, Boston, Chicago, Springfield, Hartford and New Haven.

44 The Kerry squad that travelled was: John Riordan, John Walsh, Pat Clifford, Paul Sullivan, Jas Sullivan, Joe Sullivan, John J. Slattery, Con Brosnan, Robert Stack, John Ryan, J.J. Sheehy (capt.), J.J. Landers, Thomas Mahony, James Baily, John Baily, Michael Coffey, Daniel J. Conway, Denis Connor, Jeremiah Hanafin, Cornelius O'Leary, Standish Kerins, Michael Murphy, Jack McCarthy, Jack Sheehy and Phil O'Sullivan. Dick Fitzgerald travelled as the Kerry manager while Joe Barrett, Paul Russell, Bill Gorman and Dennis O'Connell were unable to make the journey.

45 See *Sport*, 4 June, 9 July 1927; *KM*, 4 June 1927.

46 *Sport*, 27 August 1927.

47 *KM*, 27 August 1927. Sullivan later claimed he had lost money on the games but after representatives of the Kerry team went through the figures with Sullivan's manager, it was discovered that he had made a net profit of $11,000. Of that, after the team's expenses, Sheehy said the Kerry Board should have received at least £500 from the tour proceeds.

48 Mahon, *Decoding*, pp. 207–8.

49 UCDA, Moss Twomey Papers, P69/183.

50 Mahon, *Decoding*, pp. 212–13.

51 *KM*, 14 May 1927.

52 Mahon, *Decoding*, p. 216.

53 The Sam Maguire perpetual cup, valued at £150, was first awarded to the winners of the All-Ireland in 1928. It was named in memory of the veteran London GAA official. *KM*, 28 September 1929.

54 Barrett, *Name of the Game*, pp. 134, 148.

55 Ó Muircheartaigh and Flynn, *Princes of Pigskin*, p. 76.

56 CPA, Annual Congress Minutes, 1928–38: Annual Congress, 20 April 1930.

57 Dónal McAnallen, 'The Greatest Amateur Association in the World: The GAA and Amateurism', in Cronin et al., *The Gaelic Athletic Association*, pp. 166–8.

58 *Sport*, 10 October 1925.

59 *KM*, 27 March 1926. Kerry lost 1-6 to 1-5.

60 *Sport*, 7 December 1929, 7 March 1931; *KM*, 11 February 1933.

61 *KM*, 31 July 1926.

62 Reprinted in *KM*, 8 January 1927.

63 CPA, Annual Congress, 4 April 1926; *KM*, 26 March 1927.

64 Munster's Kerry selection was: J. Riordan (goal), J.J. Sheehy (capt.) J. Barrett, J. Slattery, J. Ryan (all Tralee), P. Clifford, James Baily (Ballymacelligott), P. Russell (Killarney), J. O'Sullivan (Dingle), E. Fitzgerald (Caherdaniel), R. Stack (Ballybunion), C. Brosnan, T. O'Mahony (Moyvane), J. Walsh (Asdee), Frank Sheehy (Listowel). *KM*, 26 March 1927.

65 *KM*, 21 March 1931. Team was: J. Riordan (goal), J.J. Sheehy (capt.), J. Barrett, T. Landers, E. Sweeney, J.J. Landers, M. Doyle (all Tralee), J. Walsh (Asdee), P. Russell, D. Connor (Killarney), T. O'Donnell (Camp), J. O'Sullivan (Dingle), C. Brosnan (Moyvane), R. Stack (Ballybunion), E. Fitzgerald (Caherdaniel).

66 *Sport*, 21 February 1927.

67 *KM*, 11 July 1931.

68 CPA, GAA/CC/01/04: Meeting of the Central Council, 4 July 1931.

69 *KM*, 24 June 1933.

70 Dónal McAnallen, 'Cén Fáth a Raibh Cúige Uladh Chomh Lag Chomh Fada Sin? Deacrachtaí CLG Ó Thuaidh, 1884–1945', in McAnallen et al., *Evolution of the GAA*. p. 145.

71 *AC*, 11 October 1930; CPA, GAA/CC/01/04: 20 December 1930.

72 *KM*, 5 November 1932.

73 Foley, *Kerry's Football Story*, p. 73.

74 *KM*, 4 April 1925.

75 *KM*, 19 June 1926.

76 *KM*, 1 January 1927.

77 *KM*, 7 January 1928.

78 *KM*, 7 January 1928.

79 *KM*, 4 February, 17 March 1928.

80 Barrett, *Name of the Game*, p. 168.

81 *KM*, 4 February 1933. Ventry, Ballyferriter, Marhin, Cuas, Dunquinn and Ballydavid took part.

82 CPA, Munster Provincial Council Minute Book, 1928–1938, GAA/MUN/01/01: 26th Annual Convention, 2 March 1930, p. 103.

83 *KM*, 14 November 1925.

84 *KM*, 17 July, 21 August 1926.

85 Cronin, *Munster GAA*, p. 153.

86 *KM*, 18 May 1929.

87 *KM*, 3 May 1930.

88 *KM*, 1 April 1933.

89 *KM*, 30 May 1931.

90 CPA, Annual Congress Minutes, 1928–38: Annual Congress, 27 March 1932.

91 *Kerry Champion* (*KC*), 29 December 1934.

92 *KM*, 8 July 1933.

93 *Sport*, 11 July 1925.

94 Cronin et al., *A People's History*, p. 126.

95 *KM*, 12 February 1927.

96 GAA/MUN/01/01.

97 *KM*, 18 April, 5, 26 September 1931.

98 *KM*, 7 May 1932.

99 *KM*, 1 September 1934.

100 CPA, CC 01/04, 5 September, 28 November 1931.

101 *KM*, 3 November 1934.

102 Holt, *Sport*, p. 139.

103 St Brendan's Seminary in Killarney became the first educational institution in the county to affiliate with the county board in order to participate in the competition. *KS*, 18 March 1908.

104 *KS*, 10 April 1909. Dingle CBS, Dingle Xian, St Brendan's, Tralee CBS, Tralee Xian, Tralee Jeffers Institute and Killarney Presentation all took part.

105 Michael Ó Ruairc, 'Dr Éamonn O'Sullivan and the Revival of our Games in the Schools and Colleges', in Michael Lyne (ed.), *The Kerry GAA Centenary Yearbook, 1884–1984* (Tralee, 1984), p. 68. Dr O'Sullivan secured the patronage of Charles O'Sullivan, the Bishop of Kerry, who donated a silver cup for the senior competition among the schools. In addition, Howard Harrington of Dunloe Castle offered a £20 silver cup for competition among junior school sides. Harrington was an American lawyer who bought and resided at Dunloe Castle near Killarney. He became the first president of the Irish Tourist Association founded in 1925. Michael Cronin and Barbara O'Connor (eds), *Irish Tourism: Image, Culture and identity* (Clevedon, 2003), p. 264.

106 The meeting took place in Tralee and was presided over by the Rev. Canon Breen, the president of St Brendan's Seminary College Killarney. Fr D. O'Herlihy of the Jeffers Institute Tralee, Br. P.T. Ryan of CBS Dingle, Br. T.S. Ryan of CBS Cahersiveen,   Br. Pascal Turner of Tralee CBS, J. O'Dwyer of the Intermediate School Killorglin, J. Moynihan, John Joe Sheehy, P. Foley, J. McCarthy and Dr Éamonn O'Sullivan attended. O'Sullivan was elected the honorary secretary of the new body and Canon Breen was elected its first chairman. KCA, Michael Ó Ruairc Papers.

107 *KM*, 19 February, 7 May 1927, 28 January 1928.

108 CPA, GAA Annual Congress Minute Books, 1928–1938: 17 April 1927.

109 Ferriter, *Transformation of Ireland*, p. 302.

110 *Ibid.*, pp. 300–14.

111 *KM*, 25 July 1931.

112 Hanley, *IRA*, p. 26.

113 UCDA, Moss Twomey Papers, P/69/155.

114 Hanley, *IRA*, p. 15.

115 Keogh, *Ireland*, p. 81.

116 Mike Cronin, 'Blueshirts, Sports and Socials', *History Ireland*, 2, 3 (1994), pp. 43–5.

117 Keogh, *Ireland*, p. 82.

118 Hanley, *IRA*, pp. 84, 89.

119 *KM*, 15 April, 7 October 1933.

120 Lee, *Ireland*, p. 184.

121 Barrett, *Name of the Game*, p. 138.

122 Hanley, *IRA*, pp. 62–3.

123 *KM*, 10 September 1932, 11 February 1933.

124 *KM*, 26 March 1932.

125 *KM*, 9 April, 1 June 1932.

126 Cronin, 'Blueshirts', pp. 44–6.

127 CPA, GAA/CC/01/05, Central Council Minute Book 1932–1934: Meeting of Central Council, 15 December 1933.

128 *KM*, 7 October, 23 December 1933.

129 *KM*, 14 July 1934.

130 *KM*, 21 July, 23 June 1934.

131 Barrett, *Name of the Game*, pp. 128–9. It appears Walsh got the better of their engagement, with Armitage being substituted just before half time after Walsh broke three of his ribs in a clash for the ball.

132 *KM*, 16 December 1933.

133 *KC*, 24 February 1934.

134 NAI, Department of Justice Papers, NA 2008 117/330.

135 *KM*, 7 April, 1, 8 December 1934.

136 CPA, GAA/CC/01/06, Central Council Minute Book s 1934–1938: Annual Congress, 21 April 1935.

137 UCDA, Frank Aiken Papers, P/104/2801.

138 *KC*, 9 February, 25 May 1935.

139 *KC*, 11 January 1936.

140 De Búrca, *The GAA*, p. 172.

141 CPA, GAA/CC/01/06: Annual Congress, 1 April 1934.

142 *KM*, 9 June 1934.

143 CPA, GAA/CC/01/06 CC: 1 April 1934.

144 CPA, Annual Congress, 1 April 1934.

145 CPA, GAA/MUN/01/01, 4 March 1934.

146 Cronin, *Sport and Nationalism*, p. 95.

147 Cronin, 'Defenders', pp. 10–11.

148 *KM*, 20 October 1934.

CONCLUSION: 'WHAT WOULD KERRY BE WITHOUT FOOTBALL?'

1 Tom Humphries, 'Gaelic Games', in Neil Buttimer, Colin Rynne and Helen Guerin (eds), *The Heritage of Ireland* (Cork, 2000), p. 199.

2 See, for example, Rouse, 'The GAA Ban', p. 33.

3 Cronin et al., *A People's History*, p. 19.

4 See Austin Stack, 'In the Kingdom of Kerry', *Gaelic Annual, 1908–09*, p. 26.

5 In 1896, the Kerry secretary complained that though they possessed one of the finest grounds in Ireland for Gaelic events for which they paid a rent of £25, the GAA's central executive had not seen fit to hold any inter-county contest there, which in his opinion was 'scandalous'. *KS*, 28 March 1896.

6 Cronin, 'Defenders', p. 9.

BIBLIOGRAPHY

PRIMARY SOURCE MATERIAL

GAA CROKE PARK ARCHIVES, CROKE PARK, DUBLIN

GAA Annual Congress Minutes: 1911–1927
GAA Annual Congress Minutes: 1928–1938
GAA/CC/01/01, Central Council Minute Books: 1899–1911
GAA/CC/01/02, Central Council Minute Books: 1911–1925
GAA/CC/01/03, Central Council Minute Books: 1925–29
GAA/CC/ 01/04, Central Council Minute Books: 1929–1932
GAA/CC/01/05, Central Council Minute Books: 1932–1934
GAA/CC/01/06, Central Council Minute Books: 1934–1938
GAA/MUN/01/01, Munster Provincial Council Minute Books: 1928–1938

KERRY COUNTY ARCHIVE, TRALEE

Annual Reports of the Local Government Board for Ireland, 1874–1908
Department of Irish Folklore Records Relating to Kerry Schools, S124–145
Fionán Lynch Papers, P/31
Kerry Grand Jury Presentments, 1874–1889
Kerry Grand Jury Presentments, 1892–1897
Michael Ó Ruairc Papers
Cahersiveen Poor Law Union Board of Guardian Minute Books, 1838–1922
Dingle Poor Law Union Board of Guardian Minute Books, 1838–1922
Kenmare Poor Law Union Board of Guardian Minute Books, 1838–1922
Killarney Poor Law Union Board of Guardian Minute Books, 1838–1922
Listowel Poor Law Union Board of Guardian Minute Books, 1838–1922
Tralee Poor Law Union Board of Guardian Minute Books, 1838–1922
Cahersiveen Rural District Council Minute Books, 1889–1925
Dingle Rural District Council Minute Books, 1889–1925
Kenmare Rural District Council Minute Books, 1899–1925
Killarney Rural District Council Minute Books, 1899–1925
Listowel Rural District Council Minute Books, 1889–1925
Tralee Rural District Council Minute Books, 1889–1925
Statutes – United Parliament, Public General Acts, 1802–1914

KERRY COUNTY MUSEUM COLLECTION, TRALEE

Austin Stack Correspondence, KCM 1995: 1, Letter from Austin Stack to Nellie Hurley, Belfast Gaol, 23 May 1918
Diary of Christopher P. O'Grady, January 1921–January 1922, KCM 1993: 47

Minute Book of the Tralee Irish Volunteers, March 1915–April 1916, KCM 1994: 22

Paddy Cahill Correspondence, KCM 1994: 23, Letter from Wakefield Prison, 1916

NATIONAL ARCHIVES, BISHOP ST, DUBLIN

Bureau of Military History Interviews, statements relating to activity in County Kerry

British in Ireland Collection, CO 904, Microfilm Archive, MFA 54/26–73 Inspector General and County Inspector Monthly Confidential Reports, January 1892–September 1921

British in Ireland Collection, CO 904, Microfilm Archive, MFA 54/8 Secret Societies, Register of Suspects, Home I–W, 1890–98

British in Ireland Collection, CO 904, Microfilm Archive, MFA 54/107, Register of Informers, 1882–1891

Census of Ireland, 1901, Online Returns Relating to County Kerry

Census of Ireland, 1911, Online Returns Relating to County Kerry

Crime Branch Special, District Commissioner and County Inspector Monthly Reports, Box No. 4, 1887–1898

Crime Branch Special, District Commissioner and County Inspector Monthly Reports, Box No. 9, South Western Division, 1890–1891

Crime Branch Special, District Inspectors' Crime Special Monthly Reports, Box No. 2, South Western Division, 1887–1895

Crime Branch Special, inspector General and County Inspector Monthly Reports, Box Nos 1–15, 1898–1920

Crime Branch Special, Precis Box No. 1, Home Office Crime Department Special Branch, Precis of Information on Secret Societies 1895–1897

Crime Branch Special, Precis Box No. 2, Home Office Crime Department Special Branch, Precis of Information on Secret Societies January 1898–December 1899

Crime Branch Special, Precis Box No. 3, Home Office Crime Department Special Branch, Precis of Information on Secret Societies January 1901–December 1905

Department of Justice Papers, IRA Activity in County Kerry in 1934, NA 2008 117/330

CRIME BRANCH SPECIAL INDEX

Crime Branch Special, Annual Report, South Western Division, 23 January 1893, 6205/S

Crime Branch Special, Estimated Strength of Various Nationalist Associations in 1893, 31 January 1894, 7828/S

Crime Branch Special, GAA, Approximate Strength under Clerical and Fenian Control by Divisions, 5 May 1890, 127/S

Crime Branch Special, GAA in 1892, Revised List of Branches, 1 February 1893, 6247/S

Crime Branch Special, GAA Returns, South Western Division, February 1891, 2792/S

Crime Branch Special, Nationalist Associations in 1891, Summary of Information Contained in Divisional Commissioners' Annual Reports for 1891, as to Progress or Decline of Above, 16 May 1892, 5006/S

Crime Branch Special, Pro-Boer Sentiment, Seditious Pamphlet, 25 May 1901, 2467/S

Crime Branch Special, RIC South Western Division, Connection between the IRB and GAA in Clare and Kerry, 15 April 1890, 126/S

Crime Branch Special, RIC South Western Division, Modus Operandi of Seducing One of the GAA into IRB Society, 14 April 1890, 296/S

Crime Branch Special, RIC South Western Division, The Bishop of Kerry and the GAA, 26 April 1895, 9854/S

Crime Branch Special, The GAA at End of Year 1891, 4467/S

NATIONAL LIBRARY OF IRELAND, KILDARE ST, DUBLIN

Austin Stack Papers, Account by Stack of his own Arrest with References to the Arrest of Casement, MS 17, 075

Austin Stack Papers, Land Agitation in Kerry in 1920, MS 17, 085

Austin Stack Papers, Memo to Third Dáil on Republican Casualties during Civil War and Treatment of Republican Prisoners, 1922, MS 17, 082

Census of Ireland 1891, General Report (1892), Ir 310 c 1

Census of Ireland 1901, General Report (1902), Ir 310 c 1

Colonel Maurice Moore Papers, Account of the Irish Volunteers in 1914, MS 8489

Description of County Kerry During the Civil War, September 1922, MS 10 781

Harrington Papers, Relating to Land Agitation in Kerry in 1888, MS 8579

Harrington Papers, Relating to Irish National League in Kerry 1880–1888, MS 8933

J.J. O'Connell Papers, Autobiographical Account of Events Leading to 1916, MS 22, 114

J.J. O'Connell Papers, Notes, Correspondence etc. Regarding the War of Independence, 1917–1922, MS 22 117

Michael Collins Papers, Letters to Austin Stack, 1918–1919, MS 5848

Proceedings of Military Court of Inquiry into Deaths of Republican Prisoners at Ballyseedy, etc., Co. Kerry with Associated Correspondence, etc., MS 22 956

Rules and Regulations for the County Committee of the Gaelic League for the County of Kerry 1910, MS 24, 428

The O'Rahilly Papers, Documents Relating to the O'Rahilly and Easter Week, 1916, MS 13 019

The Royal Commission on the Rebellion in Ireland, Minutes of Evidence and Appendix of Documents (London, 1916), Ir 94109 12

Thomas Ashe Papers, Correspondence with Nora Ashe, n. 5370, p. 5482

Thomas Ashe Papers, Diary Kept During a Visit to Kerry in 1913, n. 4923,   p. 4955

Thomas. F. O'Sullivan Papers, Kerry GAA History, MS 15 385

UNIVERSITY COLLEGE DUBLIN ARCHIVES

Austin Stack Papers, P149

Frank Aiken Papers, P104

Irish Republican Brotherhood Papers, P21

Moss Twomey Papers, P69

UNIVERSITY COLLEGE DUBLIN LIBRARY SPECIAL COLLECTIONS

Patrick Ferriter Manuscripts, MS 19: Political Notes of the Parnellite Period Including Resolutions against Priests in Kerry

PARLIAMENTARY PAPERS

Census of Ireland, 1891. Part I. Area, houses and population; also the ages,
civil or conjugal condition, occupations, birthplaces, religion and education of the people.
Vol. II. Province of Munster [C. 6567], HC 1892, XCI, 1

Census of Ireland for the year 1911 [Cd. 5691], HC 1911, LXXI, 641

Criminal and judicial statistics, Ireland, 1890. Report on the criminal and judicial statistics of Ireland for the year 1890 [C. 6511], HC 1891, XCIII, 251

Return, by provinces, of agrarian offences throughout Ireland reported to the Inspector General of the Royal Irish Constabulary between 1 January 1880 and 31 December 1880, HC 1881 (3), LXXVII, 595

Return, by provinces, of agrarian offences throughout Ireland reported to the Inspector General of the Royal Irish Constabulary between 1 January 1881 and 31 December 1881, HC 1882 (72), LV, 17

Return, by provinces, of agrarian offences throughout Ireland reported to the Inspector General of the Royal Irish Constabulary between 1 January 1882 and 31 December 1882, HC 1883 (12), LVI, 1

Return of agricultural holdings in Ireland, compiled by the Local Government Board in Ireland from returns furnished by the clerks of the Poor Law unions in Ireland in January, 1881 [C. 2934], HC 1881, XCIII, 793

NEWSPAPERS AND PERIODICALS

The Anglo-Celt
The Celtic Times
Cork Examiner
The Freeman's Journal
Gaelic Athlete
Irish Independent
The Irish Times
Irishman
Kerry Advocate
Kerry Champion
Kerry Evening Post
Kerry Evening Star
Kerry People
Kerry Press
Kerry Reporter
Kerry Sentinel
Kerry Weekly Reporter
The Kerryman
Sport
Tralee Chronicle
Tralee Liberator
United Ireland
Wicklow People

CONTEMPORARY PUBLICATIONS

Anon., *Sixty Glorious Years, 1886–1946: The Authentic Story of the GAA* (Dublin, 1946)

Blake, Richard. T., *How the GAA was Grabbed* (Dublin, 1900)

Carbery, *Gaelic Football* (Tralee, 1941)

Carbery, *Hurling: Ireland's National Game* (Dublin, 1946)

Devlin, P.J., *Our Native Games* (Dublin, 1935)

Fitzgerald, Dick, *How to Play Gaelic Football* (Cork, 1914)

Foley, Patrick F., *History of the County of Kerry* (Dublin, 1907)

Foley, Patrick F., *Kerry's Football Story* (Tralee, 1945)

Hall, Mr and Mrs S.C., *Ireland: Its Scenery, Character etc.*, Vol. 1 (London, 1841)

Harrington, Niall C., *Kerry Landing, August 1922: An Episode of the Civil War* (Dublin, 1992)

Murphy, Jeremiah, *When Youth Was Mine: A Memoir of Kerry, 1902–1925* (Dublin, 1998)

O'Crohan, Tomás, *The Islandman* (Oxford, 2000)

O'Donovan, T.M., *A Popular History of East Kerry* (Dublin, 1931)

O'Sullivan, Thomas. F., *Story of the GAA* (Dublin, 1916)

O'Sullivan, Thomas. F., *Romantic Hidden Kerry* (Tralee, 1931)

The Death of Thomas Ashe: Full Report of the Inquest (Dublin, 1917)

The Gaelic Athletic Annual and County Directory for 1907–08 (Dublin, 1907)

The Gaelic Athletic Annual and County Directory for 1908–09 (Dundalk, 1909)

Thom's Official Directory of the Kingdom of Great Britain and Ireland (Dublin, 1885)

Walsh, J.J., *Recollections of a Rebel* (Tralee, 1944)

SECONDARY SOURCES

Abbott, Richard, *Police Casualties in Ireland, 1919–1922* (Cork, 2000)

Allison, Lincoln, 'Sport and Nationalism', in Jay Coakley and Eric Dunning (eds), *Handbook of Sports Studies* (London, 2004)

Allman, Jerry, *Causeway Co. Kerry: Its Location, Lore and Legend* (Naas, 1983)

Anderson, Benedict, *Imagined Communities: Reflections on the Origin and Spread of Nationalism* (London, 2006)

Augusteijn, Joost, 'Accounting for the Emergence of Violent Activism among Irish Revolutionaries, 1916–21', *Irish Historical Studies*, XXXV, 139 (2007)

Augusteijn, Joost, *From Public Defiance to Guerrilla Warfare: The Radicalisation of the Irish Republican Army – A Comparative Analysis, 1916–1921* (Amsterdam, 1994)

Augusteijn, Joost, 'Patrick Pearse: Proto-Fascist Eccentric or Mainstream European Thinker?', *History Ireland*, 18, 6 (2010)

Austin Stack GAA Club, *The Street of Champions: Down Memory Lane with the Rock GAA Club* (Tralee, 1989)

Bairner, Alan, 'Civic and Ethnic Nationalism in the Celtic Vision of Irish Sport', in Grant Jarvie (ed.), *Sport in the Making of Celtic Cultures* (Leicester, 1999)

Barrett, J.J., *In the Name of the Game* (Wicklow, 1997)

Barrington, Ruth, *Health, Medicine and Politics in Ireland, 1900–1970* (Dublin, 1987)

Barrington, T.J., *Discovering Kerry: Its History, Heritage and Topography* (Cork, 1999)

Barry, John and Horan, Éamon, *Years of Glory: The Story of Kerry's All-Ireland Senior Victories* (Tralee, 1977)

Barry, John M., *The Great Influenza: The Epic Story of the Deadliest Plague in History* (New York, 2004)

Barry, Michael, 'The Lartique Railway, 1888–1924', in Ballydonoghue GAA Club, *The Grasses We Combed: A Collection of Remembrances* (Ballydonoghue, 1987)

Bartlett, Thomas, *Ireland: A History* (Cambridge, 2010)

Beckett, J.C., *The Making of Modern Ireland* (Norfolk, 1981)

Bell, Jonathan and Watson, Mervyn, *A History of Irish Farming, 1750–1950* (Dublin, 2008)

Bew, Paul, *Ideology and the Irish Question: Ulster Unionism and Irish Nationalism, 1912–1916* (Oxford, 1998)

Bew, Paul, 'The Real Importance of Sir Roger Casement', *History Ireland*, 2, 2 (1994)

Birley, Derek, *A Social History of English Cricket* (London, 1999)

Bourke, Martin and King, Seamus J., *A History of Camogie in County Tipperary* (Naas, 2003)

Bourke, Marie, 'Yeats, Henry and the Western Idyll', *History Ireland*, 11, 2 (2003)

Boyce, George D., *Nineteenth-Century Ireland: The Search for Stability* (Dublin, 2005)

Bracken, Patrick, *'Foreign and Fantastic Field Sports': Cricket in County Tipperary* (Thurles, 2004)

Brailsford, Denis, *British Sport: A Social History* (Cambridge, 1997)

Breathnach, Ciara, *The Congested Districts Board of Ireland, 1891–1923* (Dublin, 2005)

Browne, Éamon, 'More than a Game: A Study of the GAA and its Links with Politics in County Kerry, 1885–1935', *The Kerry Magazine*, No. 11 (2000)

Browne, Éamon, 'Tralee and its Links to the GAA', *The Kerry Magazine*, No. 12 (2001)

Bull, Philip, 'The United Irish League and the Reunion of the Irish Parliamentary Party', *Irish Historical Studies*, XXVI, 101 (1988)

Callanan, Frank, *T.M. Healy* (Cork, 1996)

Callanan, Frank, *The Parnell Split, 1890–91* (Cork, 1992)

Campbell, Fergus, 'The Easter Rising in Galway', *History Ireland*, 14, 2 (2006)

Carey, Tim, *Croke Park: A History* (Cork, 2004)

Carey, Tim and Marcus de Búrca, 'Bloody Sunday 1920: New Evidence', *History Ireland*, 11, 2 (2003)

Carmody, Vincent, *Listowel and the Gaelic Athletic Association, 1885–1985* (Listowel, 1985)

Coleman, Marie, *County Longford and the Irish Revolution, 1910–1923* (Dublin, 2003)

Collins, Tony, *Rugby's Great Split: Class, Culture and the Origins of Rugby League Football*, 2nd edition (Oxford, 2006)

Collins, Tony and Vamplew, Wray, *Mud, Sweat and Beers: A Cultural History of Sport and Alcohol* (Oxford, 2002)

Collins, Tony and Vamplew, Wray, 'The Pub, the Drinks Trade and the Early Years of Modern Football', *Sport in History*, 20, 1 (2000)

Collins, Tony, Martin, John and Vamplew, Wray (eds), *Encyclopaedia of Traditional British Rural Sports* (London, 2005)

Connolly, John and Dolan, Paddy, 'The Civilising of Gaelic Football', in Dónal McAnallen, David Hassan and Roddy Hegarty (eds), *The Evolution of the GAA: Ulaidh, Éire agus Eile* (Armagh, 2009)

Comerford, R.V., *Ireland: Inventing the Nation* (London, 2003)

Corry, Eoghan, *Catch and Kick: Great Moments of Gaelic Football, 1880–1990* (Dublin, 1989)

Corry, Eoghan, *Illustrated History of the GAA* (Dublin, 2005)

Corry, Eoghan, *Kingdom Come: A Biography of the Kerry Football Team, 1975–1988* (Dublin, 1989)

Corry, Eoghan, *The History of Gaelic Football* (Dublin, 2009)

Corry, Eoghan, 'The Mass Media and the Popularisation of Gaelic Games, 1884–1934', in Dónal McAnallen, David Hassan and Roddy Hegarty (eds), *The Evolution of the GAA: Ulaidh, Éire agus Eile* (Armagh 2009)

Cottrell, Peter, *The Irish Civil War, 1922–3* (Oxford, 2008)

Cronin, Jim, *Munster GAA Story* (Ennis, 1986)

Cronin, Mike, 'Blueshirts, Sports and Socials', *History Ireland*, 2, 3 (1994)

Cronin, Mike, 'Defenders of a Nation? The Gaelic Athletic Association and Irish Nationalist Identity', *Irish Political Studies*, No. 11 (1996)

Cronin, Mike, 'Enshrined in Blood: The Naming of Gaelic Athletic Association Grounds and Clubs', *Sport in History*, 18, 1 (1998)

Cronin, Mike, 'Fighting for Ireland, Playing for England? The Nationalist History of the

Gaelic Athletic Association and the English Influence on Irish Sport', *International Journal of the History of Sport*, XV, 3 (1998)

Cronin, Mike, 'More Than Just Hurling and Football: The GAA and its Other Activities', in M. Cronin, W. Murphy and P. Rouse (eds), *The Gaelic Athletic Association, 1884–2009* (Dublin, 2009)

Cronin, Mike, *Sport and Nationalism in Ireland: Gaelic Games, Soccer and Irish Identity Since 1884* (Dublin, 1999)

Cronin, Mike, 'The Gaelic Athletic Association's Invasion of America, 1888: Travel Narratives, Microhistory and the Irish American "Other"', *Sport in History*, 27, 2 (2007)

Cronin, Mike, 'The Irish Free State and Aonach Tailteann', in Alan Bairner (ed.), *Sport and the Irish: Histories, Identities, Issues* (Dublin, 2005)

Cronin, Mike and O'Connor, Barbara (eds), *Irish Tourism: Image, Culture and Identity* (Clevedon, 2003)

Cronin, M., Murphy, W. and Rouse, P. (eds), *The Gaelic Athletic Association, 1884–2009* (Dublin, 2009)

Cronin, M., Duncan, M. and Rouse, P. (eds), *The GAA: A People's History* (Cork, 2009)

Crooke, Elizabeth, 'Revivalist Archaeology and the Museum Politics During the Irish Revival', in Betsey Taylor FitzSimon and James H. Murphy (eds), *The Irish Revival Reappraised* (Dublin, 2004)

Crosson, Seán, 'Gaelic Games and "the Movies"', in M. Cronin, W. Murphy and P. Rouse (eds), *The Gaelic Athletic Association, 1884–2009* (Dublin, 2009)

Crosson, Seán and McAnallen, Dónal, '"Croke Park Goes Plumb Crazy": Gaelic Games in Pathé Newsreels, 1920–1939', *Media History*, 17, 2 (2011)

Curran, Conor, *Sport in Donegal: A History* (Dublin, 2010)

Curtin, Danny, 'Edward Harrington and the First GAA Event in Kerry', *The Kerry Magazine*, No. 11 (2000)

Curtin, Danny, 'Kerry's First Elected Ladies', *The Kerry Magazine*, No. 10 (1999)

Curtis Jr, L.P., 'Ireland in 1914', in W.E. Vaughan (ed.), *A New History of Ireland. Volume VI: Ireland Under the Union II, 1870–1921* (Oxford, 1996)

Daly, Mary, 'The County in Irish History', in Mary Daly (ed.), *County and Town: One Hundred Years of Local Government in Ireland* (Dublin, 2001)

Darby, Paul, 'Gaelic Sport and the Irish Diaspora in Boston, 1879–90', *Irish Historical Studies*, XXXIII, 132 (2003)

Darby, Paul, 'Gaelic Games and the Irish Diaspora in the United States', in M. Cronin, W. Murphy and P. Rouse (eds), *The Gaelic Athletic Association, 1884–2009* (Dublin, 2009)

De Búrca, Marcus, *The GAA: A History*, 2nd edition (Dublin, 1999)

De Búrca, Marcus, 'The GAA and Organised Sport in Ireland', in Grant Jarvie (ed.), *Sport in the Making of Celtic Cultures* (Leicester, 1999)

De Brún, Pádraig, 'Kerry Diocese in 1890: Bishop Coffey's Survey', *Journal of the Kerry Archaeological and Historical Society*, No. 22 (1989)

Dillon, Paul, 'The Tralee Labourers Strike of 1896: An Episode in Ireland's New Unionism', *Journal of the Kerry Archaeological and Historical Society*, Series 2, Vol. 2 (2002)

Dillon, Thomas, 'Listowel Rugby Club: 110 Years of History', in Listowel Rugby Club, *Listowel Rugby Club: Celebrating 110 Years, 1900–2010* (Listowel, 2010)

Dixon, Pamela and Garnham, Neal, 'Drink and the Professional Footballer in 1890s England and Ireland', *Sport in History*, 25, 3 (2005)

Dolan, Paddy and Connolly, John, 'The Civilising of Hurling in Ireland', *Sport in Society*, 12, 2 (2009)

Donnelly, Ambrose, 'The Days of Caid', in Gneeveguilla GAA Club, *History of the GAA in Gneeveguilla, From the Days of Caid to 1985* (Tralee, 1985)

Donnelly, James, 'Kenmare Estates During the Nineteenth Century', *Journal of the Kerry Archaeological and Historical Society*, No. 21 (1988)

Donnelly, James, 'Kenmare Estates During the Nineteenth Century', *Journal of the Kerry Archaeological and Historical Society*, No. 22 (1989)

Donnelly, James, 'Kenmare Estates During the Nineteenth Century', *Journal of the Kerry Archaeological and Historical Society*, No. 23 (1990)

Donnelly, James, *The Land and the People of Nineteenth-Century Cork: The Rural Economy and the Land* (London, 1975)

Doolan, Billy and Fitzgerald, Éamonn (eds), *Kilcummin GAA, 1910–1985* (Kilcummin, 1985)

Dooley, Terence, *The Land for the People: The Land Question in Independent Ireland* (Dublin, 2004)

Doyle, Tom, *The Civil War in Kerry* (Cork, 2008)

Doyle, Tom, *The Summer Campaign in Kerry* (Cork, 2010)

Drumm, Alan, *Kerry and the Royal Munster Fusiliers* (Dublin, 2010)

Duncan, Mark, 'The Camera and the Gael: The Early Photography of the GAA, 1884–1914', in M. Cronin, W. Murphy and P. Rouse (eds), *The Gaelic Athletic Association, 1884–2009* (Dublin, 2009)

Dunleavy, Janet Egleson and Dunleavy, Gareth W., *Douglas Hyde: A Maker of Modern Ireland* (Berkley, 1991)

Dwyer, Dermot, *The Alluring Call of the Leather Ball: CLG Chill Chuimín – Comóradh Céad Bliain, 1910–2010* (Kilcummin, 2010)

Dwyer, Dermot (ed.), *St Finan's Hospital Killarney: A Medical, Social and Sporting History, 1852–2002* (Killarney, 2002)

Dwyer, T. Ryle, *Michael Collins: The Man Who Won the War* (Cork, 2009)

Dwyer, T. Ryle, *Tans, Terror and Troubles: Kerry's Real Fighting Story, 1913–23* (Cork, 2001)

East Kerry GAA Board, 'History of Fitzgerald Stadium', retrieved from http://www.eastkerrygaa.com/history-stadium.htm [accessed 25 June 2012]

Egan, Thomas (ed.), *Milltown Parish: A Centenary Celebration* (Naas, 1994)

Farry, Michael, *The Aftermath of Revolution: Sligo, 1921–23* (Dublin, 2000)

Fennessy, Ignatius, 'Horse Racing at Killarney and Waterville Long Ago', *Kerry Magazine*, No. 10 (1999)

Ferris, Tom, *Irish Railways: A New History* (Dublin, 2008)

Ferriter, Diarmaid, *Judging Dev: A Reassessment of the Life and Legacy of Éamon de Valera* (Dublin, 2007)

Ferriter, Diarmaid, 'Sobriety and Temperance', in Shane Kilcommins and Ian O'Donnell (eds), *Alcohol, Society and Law* (Chichester, 2003)

Ferriter, Diarmaid, *The Transformation of Ireland, 1900–2000* (Dublin, 2004)

Fitzpatrick, David, 'Irish Emigration in the Later Nineteenth Century', *Irish Historical Studies*, XXII, 86 (1980)

Fitzpatrick, David, 'Militarism in Ireland, 1900–1922', in Thomas Bartlett and Keith Jeffery (eds), *A Military History of Ireland* (Cambridge, 1996)

Fitzpatrick, David, *Politics and Irish Life, 1913–1921: Provincial Experience of War and Revolution* (Cork, 1998)

Fitzpatrick, David, 'The Logic of Collective Sacrifice: Ireland and the British Army, 1914–1918', *The Historical Journal*, 38, 4 (1995)

Fitzpatrick, Regina, Rouse, Paul and McAnallen, Dónal, 'The Freedom of the Field: Camogie before 1950', in Dónal McAnallen, David Hassan and Rody Hegarty (eds), *The Evolution of the GAA: Ulaidh, Éire agus Eile* (Armagh 2009)

Fitzgerald, Éamonn (ed.), *Dr Crokes' Gaelic Century, 1886–1986* (Killarney, 1986)

Fogarty, Weeshie, *Dr Éamonn O'Sullivan: A Man Before his Time* (Dublin, 2007)

Fogarty, Weeshie, 'Dr Éamonn O'Sullivan Pioneers the Building of Fitzgerald Stadium', retrieved from http://www.terracetalk.com/articles/Dr-Eamonn-O-Sullivan/113/Dr-Eamonn-pioneers-the-building-of-Fitzgerald-Stadium [accessed 25 June 2012]

Foley, Caitriona, *The Last Irish Plague: The Great Flu Epidemic in Ireland 1918–19* (Dublin, 2011)

Foley, Kieran, *History of Killorglin* (Killarney, 1988)

Foster, Roy, *Modern Ireland, 1600–1972* (London, 1988)

Foster, Roy, *The Irish Story: Telling Tales and Making it up in Ireland* (London, 2001)

Foster, W., 'Certain Set Apart: The Western Islands in the Irish Renaissance', *Studies*, No. 66 (1977)

Foy, Michael T., *Michael Collins's Intelligence War: The Struggle Between the British and the IRA, 1919–1921* (Gloucestershire, 2006)

Foy, Michael and Barton, Brian, *The Easter Rising* (Gloucestershire, 2004)

Gallagher, Michael, 'The Pact General Election of 1922', *Irish Historical Studies*, XXI, 84 (1979)

Garnham, Neal, 'Accounting for the Early Success of the Gaelic Athletic Association', *Irish Historical Studies*, XXXIV, 133 (2004)

Garnham, Neal, Association *Football and Society in Pre-Partition Ireland* (Belfast, 2004)

Garnham, Neal, 'Rugby and Empire in Ireland: Irish Reactions to Colonial Rugby Tours', *Sport in History*, 23, 1 (2003)

Garvin, Tom, *Nationalist Revolutionaries in Ireland, 1858–1928* (Oxford, 1987)

Garvin, Tom, *The Evolution of Irish Nationalist Politics* (Dublin, 1981)

Gaughan, Anthony J., *Austin Stack: Portrait of a Separatist* (Dublin, 1977)

Gaughan, Anthony J., *Listowel and its Vicinity* (Cork, 1973)

Gaughan, Anthony J., *Memoirs of Constable Jeremiah Mee, RIC* (Dublin, 1975)

George, Jane, 'An Excellent Means of Combining Fresh Air, Exercise and Society: Females on the Fairways, 1890–1914', in Tony Collins (ed.), *Sport as History: Essays in Honour of Wray Vamplew* (London, 2011)

Gillespie, Simon and Hegarty, Roddy, 'Camán and Crozier: The Church and the GAA, 1884–1902', in Dónal McAnallen, David Hassan and Roddy Hegarty (eds), *The Evolution of the GAA: Ulaidh, Éire agus Eile* (Armagh 2009)

Gleason, A.B., 'Hurling in Medieval Ireland', in M. Cronin, W. Murphy and P. Rouse (eds), *The Gaelic Athletic Association, 1884–2009* (Dublin, 2009)

Griffin, Pádraig, *The Politics of Irish Athletics: 1850–1990* (Ballinamore, 1990)

Hanley, Brian, 'Irish Republican Attitudes to Sport Since 1921', in Dónal McAnallen, David Hassan and Roddy Hegarty (eds), *The Evolution of the GAA: Ulaidh, Éire agus Eile* (Armagh, 2009)

Hanley, Brian, *The IRA, 1926–1936* (Dublin, 2002)

Hargreaves, Jennifer, 'The Victorian Cult of the Family and the Early Years of Female Sport', in Sheila Scraton and Anne Flintoff (eds), *Gender and Sport: A Reader* (London, 2002)

Hargreaves, Jennifer, *Sporting Females: Critical Issues in the History and Sociology of Women's Sports* (London, 2003)

Hargreaves, John, *Sport, Power and Culture: A Social and Historical Analysis of Popular Sports in Britain* (Cambridge, 1986)

Harrington, Jack (ed.), *Ballyduff: A GAA History, 1888–1991* (Limerick, 1991)

Hassan, David, 'The GAA in Ulster', in M. Cronin, W. Murphy and P. Rouse (eds), *The Gaelic Athletic Association, 1884–2009* (Dublin, 2009)

Hart, Peter, 'Michael Collins and the Assassination of Sir Henry Wilson', *Irish Historical Studies*, XXVIII, 110 (1992)

Hart, Peter, *The IRA and Its Enemies: Violence and Community in Cork, 1916–1923* (Oxford, 1998)

Hart, Peter, *The IRA at War, 1916–1923* (Oxford, 2003)

Hayes, Victor, *Senan's County* (Mountcoal, 1990)

Henchey, Jimmy, *The Spirit of Tarbert* (Tarbert, 1986)

Hickey, Donal, *Queen of Them All: A History of Killarney Golf and Fishing Club, 1893–1993* (Killarney, 1993)

Hickey, Donal and Leen, T., *The Clear Air Boys: An East Kerry GAA History* (Tralee, 1986)

Holt, Richard, 'Ireland and the Birth of Modern Sport', in M. Cronin, W. Murphy and P. Rouse (eds), *The Gaelic Athletic Association, 1884–2009* (Dublin, 2009)

Holt, Richard, *Sport and the British: A Modern History* (Oxford, 1990)

Hopkinson, Michael, *Green against Green: The Irish Civil War* (Dublin, 1988)

Hopkinson, Michael, 'Negotiation: The Anglo-Irish War and the Revolution', in Joost Augusteijn (ed.), *The Irish Revolution, 1913–1923* (New York, 2002)

Hopkinson, Michael, *The Irish War of Independence* (Dublin, 2002)

Hoppen, K. Theodore, *Elections, Politics and Society in Ireland, 1832–1885* (Oxford, 1984)

Horgan, Donal, *Echo After Echo: Killarney and its History* (Cork, 1988)

Horgan, Donal, *The Victorian Visitor in Ireland: Irish Tourism, 1840–1910* (Cork, 2002)

Huggins, Mike, *The Victorians and Sport* (London, 2004)

Humphries, Tom, 'Gaelic Games', in Neil Buttimer, Colin Rynne and Helen Guerin (eds), *The Heritage of Ireland* (Cork, 2000)

Hunt, Tom, 'Classless Cricket? Westmeath, 1880–1905', *History Ireland*, 12, 2 (2004)

Hunt, Tom, 'Parish Factions, Parading Band and Sumptuous Repasts: The Diverse Origins and Activities of Early GAA Clubs', in Dónal McAnallen, David Hassan and Roddy Hegarty (eds), *The Evolution of the GAA: Ulaidh, Éire agus Eile* (Armagh, 2009)

Hunt, Tom, 'The GAA: Social Structure and Associated Clubs', in M. Cronin, W. Murphy and P. Rouse (eds), *The Gaelic Athletic Association, 1884–2009* (Dublin, 2009)

Hunt, Tom, *Sport and Society in Victorian Ireland: The Case Study of Westmeath* (Cork, 2007)

Hunt, Tom, 'The Early Years of Gaelic Football and the Role of Cricket in County Westmeath', in Alan Bairner (ed.), *Sport and the Irish: Histories, Identities, Issues* (Dublin, 2005)

Hunt, Tom, 'Women and Sport in Victorian Westmeath', *Irish Economic and Social History*, Vol. XXXIV (2007)

Hutchinson, John, *The Dynamics of Cultural Nationalism: The Gaelic Revival and the Creation of the Irish Nation State* (London, 1987)

Jackson, Alvin, *Home Rule: An Irish History, 1800–2000* (London, 2003)

Jackson, Alvin, *Ireland, 1798–1998: Politics and War* (Oxford, 1999)

Jackson, Lorna, 'Sport and Patronage: Evidence from Nineteenth-Century Argyllshire', *The Sports Historian*, 18, 2 (1998)

Jeffery, Keith, *Ireland and the Great War* (Cambridge, 2000)

Jones, Siobhán, 'Land Agitation and Issues of Ownership in Southern Irish Loyalist Propaganda', in Úna Ní Bhroiméil and Glenn Hooper (eds), *Land and Landscape in Nineteenth-Century Ireland* (Dublin, 2008)

Joy, Sinead, *The IRA in Kerry, 1916–1921* (Cork, 2005)

Kartakoullis, Nicos L. and Loizou, Christina, 'Is Sport (Football) a Unifying Force or a Vehicle to Further Separation? The Case of Cyprus', *International Journal of the History of Sport*, 26, 11 (2009)

Kennelly, Paddy, *Ballylongford O'Rahilly's GAA Club History* (Ballylongford, 1983)

Keogh, Dermot, *Twentieth-Century Ireland: Nation and State* (Dublin, 1994)

Kilberd, Declan, *Inventing Ireland: The Literature of the Modern Nation* (London, 1996)

King, Seamus J., *A History of Hurling* (Dublin, 2005)

Kinsella, Eoin, 'Riotous Proceedings and the Cricket of Savages: Football and Hurling in Early Modern Ireland', in M. Cronin, W. Murphy and P. Rouse (eds), *The Gaelic Athletic Association, 1884–2009* (Dublin, 2009)

Kissane, Bill, *The Politics of the Irish Civil War* (Oxford, 2005)

Kotsonouris, Mary, 'Revolutionary Justice: The Dáil Éireann Courts', *History Ireland*, 2, 2 (1994)

Laffan, Michael, *The Resurrection of Ireland: The Sinn Féin Party, 1916–1923* (Cambridge, 1999)

Laffan, Michael, 'The Unification of Sinn Féin in 1917', *Irish Historical Studies*, XVII, 67 (1971)

Lane, Pádraig G., 'Government Surveillance of Subversion in Laois, 1890–1916', in Pádraig G. Lane and William Nolan (eds), *Laois – History and Society: Interdisciplinary Essays on the History of an Irish County* (Dublin, 1999)

Larkin, Emmet, 'Church, State and Nation in Modern Ireland', *The American Historical Review*, 80, 5 (December 1975)

Larkin, Emmet, 'The Devotional Revolution in Ireland, 1850–75', *The American Historical Review*, 77, 3 (1972)

Larkin, Emmet, *The Roman Catholic Church and the Creation of the Modern Irish State, 1878–1886* (Dublin, 1975)

Larkin, Emmet, *The Roman Catholic Church in Ireland and the Fall of Parnell, 1888–1891* (Liverpool, 1979)

Larner, Jim (ed.), *Fossa & Aghadoe: Our History and Heritage* (Killarney, 2007)

Larner, Jim (ed.), *Killarney: History and Heritage* (Cork, 2005)

Lawlor, David, *Divine Right? The Parnell Split in Meath* (Cork, 2007)

Lawlor, S.M., 'Ireland from Truce to Treaty: War or Peace? July to October 1921', *Irish Historical Studies*, XXII, 85 (1980)

Leane, Michael, 'The Presentation Brothers in Killarney', *The Kerry Magazine*, No. 13 (2002)

Lee, J.J., *Ireland, 1912–1985: Politics and Society* (Cambridge, 1989)

Legg, Marie-Louise, *Newspapers and Nationalism: The Irish Provincial Press, 1850–1892* (Dublin, 1999)

Lennon, Joe, 'An Overview of the Playing Rules of Gaelic Football and Hurling, 1884–2010', in Dónal McAnallen, David Hassan and Roddy Hegarty (eds), *The Evolution of the GAA: Ulaidh, Éire agus Eile* (Armagh 2009)

Lennon, Joe, *The Playing Rules of Football and Hurling, 1602–2010* (Gormanstown, 2001)

Looney, Fr Thomas B., *A King in the Kingdom of Kings: Dick Fitzgerald* (Cork, 2008)

Lowe W.J., 'The War Against the RIC, 1919–21', *Éire-Ireland*, XXXVII, 3–4 (2002)

Lowe W.J., 'Who Were the Black and Tans?', *History Ireland*, 12, 3 (2004)

Lucey, Donnacha, *The Irish National League in Dingle, County Kerry, 1885–1892* (Dublin, 2003)

Lynch, Patrick J., *Tarbert: An Unfinished Biography* (Shanagolden, 2008)

Lynch, Peg and Sicat, Patty, *The History of Ballymacelligott and its People* (Ballymacelligott, 1997)

Lyne, Michael (ed.), *The Kerry GAA Yearbook, 1981* (Tralee 1981)

Lyons, F.S.L., *Charles Stewart Parnell* (London, 1977)

Lyons, F.S.L., *Ireland Since the Famine* (London, 1985)

Lyons, F.S.L., 'John Dillon and the Plan of Campaign', *Irish Historical Studies*, XIV, 56 (1965)

Lysaght O'Connor, D.R., 'The Rhetoric of Redmondism, 1914–16', *History Ireland*, 11, 1 (2003)

Lysaght, Paddy, *Duagh: Its Story* (Limerick, 1970)

McAnallen, Dónal, 'The Greatest Amateur Association in the World? The GAA and Amateurism', in M. Cronin, W. Murphy and P. Rouse (eds), *The Gaelic Athletic Association, 1884–2009* (Dublin, 2009)

McAnallen, Dónal, 'Cén Fáth a Raibh Cúige Uladh Chomh Lag Chomh Fada Sin? Deacrachtaí CLG Ó Thuaidh, 1884–1945', in Dónal McAnallen, David Hassan and Roddy Hegarty (eds), *The Evolution of the GAA: Ulaidh, Éire agus Eile* (Armagh, 2009)

McAnallen, Dónal, Hassan, David and Hegarty, Roddy (eds), *The Evolution of the GAA: Ulaidh, Éire agus Eile* (Armagh 2009)

Macardle, Dorothy, *Tragedies of Kerry, 1922–1923* (Dublin, 1991)

McCarthy, Daniel, 'Citizen Cusack and Clare's Gaelic Games', in Matthew Lynch and Patrick Nugent (eds), *Clare – History and Society: Interdisciplinary Essays on the History of an Irish County* (Dublin, 2008)

McDevitt, Patrick, 'Muscular Catholicism: Nationalism, Masculinity and Gaelic Team Sports, 1884–1916', *Gender and History*, 9, 2 (1997)

McGee, Owen, *The IRB: The Irish Republican Brotherhood from the Land League to Sinn Féin* (Dublin, 2005)

McGrath, John, 'Music and Politics: Marching Bands in Late Nineteenth-Century Limerick', *North Munster Antiquarian Journal*, Vol. 46 (2006)

McInerney, Colm, 'Michael Collins and the Organisation of Irish Intelligence, 1917–21', *The History Review*, Vol. XIV (2003)

McKenna, Jack, *Dingle* (Killarney, 1993)

MacMahon, Bryan, 'George Sandes of Listowel, Land Agent, Magistrate and Terror of North Kerry', *Journal of the Kerry Archaeology and Historical Society*, Series 2, Vol. 3 (2003)

MacMahon, Bryan, 'Sir Redvers Buller in Kerry', *The Kerry Magazine*, No. 14 (2003)

MacMahon, Bryan, *The Story of Ballyheigue* (Ballyheigue, 1994)

McMahon, Deirdre (ed.), 'Ireland, the Empire and the Commonwealth', in Kevin Kenny (ed.), *Ireland and the British Empire* (Oxford, 2004)

McMahon, Deirdre, *The Moynihan Brothers in Peace and War, 1908–1918: Their New Ireland* (Dublin, 2004)

McMahon, Timothy G., '"All Creeds and All Classes"? Just Who Made Up the Gaelic League?', *Éire-Ireland*, XXXVII, 3–4 (2002)

McMahon, Timothy G., *Grand Opportunity: The Gaelic Revival and Irish Society*, 1893–1910 (New York, 2008)

McMorran, Russell, 'The Mount Hawk Races', *The Kerry Magazine*, No. 15 (2005)

McNulty, Kieran, 'Revolutionary Movements in Kerry from 1913 to 1923: A Social and Political Analysis', *Journal of the Kerry Archaeological and Historical Society*, Series 2, Vol. 1 (2001)

McNulty, Kieran, 'Revolutionary Movements in Kerry from 1913 to 1923: A Social and Political Analysis', *Journal of the Kerry Archaeological and Historical Society*, Series 2, Vol. 2 (2002)

Mahon, Tom and Gillogly, James J., *Decoding the IRA* (Cork, 2008)

Mahon, Tom, 'Up Kerry! Up the IRA! Kerry's 1927 American Tour', *History Ireland*, 18, 5 (2010)

Malcom, Elizabeth, 'Popular Recreation in Nineteenth-Century Ireland', in Oliver MacDonagh, W.F. Mandle and Pauric Travers (eds), *Irish Culture and Nationalism, 1750–1950* (Canberra, 1983)

Malcom, Elizabeth, 'The Catholic Church and the Irish Temperance Movement, 1838–1901', *Irish Historical Studies*, XXIII, 89 (1982)

Mandle, W.F., *The GAA and Irish Nationalist Politics, 1884–1924* (Dublin, 1987)

Mandle, W.F., 'The Gaelic Athletic Association and Popular Culture, 1884 –1924', in Oliver MacDonagh, W.F. Mandle and Pauric Travers (eds), *Irish Culture and Nationalism, 1750–1950* (Canberra, 1983)

Mandle, W.F., 'The IRB and the Beginnings of the Gaelic Athletic Association', *Irish Historical Studies*, XX, 80 (1977)

Marley, Laurence, *Michael Davitt: Freelance Radical and Frondeur* (Dublin 2010)

Martin, Thomas F., *The Kingdom in the Empire: A Portrait of Kerry During World War One* (Dublin, 2006)

Mason, Tony (ed.), *Sport in Britain: A Social History* (Cambridge, 1989)

Metcalfe, Alan, 'Football in the Mining Communities of East Northumberland, 1882–1914', *International Journal of the History of Sport*, 5, 3 (1988)

Moran, Mary, *Cork's Camogie Story, 1904–2000* (Cork, 2000)

Moriarty, Gene, 'Gaelic Games in Fossa', in Jim Larner (ed.), *Fossa & Aghadoe: Our History and Heritage* (Killarney, 2007)

Morrison, Tom, *For the Record: A History of the National Football and Hurling League Finals* (Cork, 2002)

Mould, Daphne Pochin, *Valentia: Portrait of an Island* (Dublin, 1978)

Mulhall, Daniel, 'A Gift from Scotland: Golf's Early Days in Ireland', *History Ireland*, 14, 5 (2006)

Mulhall, Daniel, 'Ireland at the Turn of the Century', *History Ireland*, 7, 4 (1999)

Murphy, James H., *Ireland: A Social, Cultural and Literary History, 1791–1891* (Dublin, 2003)

Murphy, John, 'Cork: Anatomy and Essence', in Patrick O'Flanagan and Cornelius G. Buttimer (eds), *Cork – History and Society: Interdisciplinary Essays on the History of an Irish County* (Dublin, 1993)

Murphy, Junior, *History of Cahersiveen GAA from 1889–1999* (Killarney, 2000)

Murphy, William, *Richard Thomas Blake*, Dictionary of Irish Biography, retrieved from http://dib.cambridge.org/quicksearch.do [accessed 14 January 2011]

Murphy, William, 'The GAA During the Irish Revolution, 1913–23', in M. Cronin, W. Murphy and P. Rouse (eds), *The Gaelic Athletic Association, 1884–2009* (Dublin, 2009)

Nic Craith, Dr Mairéad, 'Primary Education on the Great Blasket Island, 1864–1940', *Journal of the Kerry Archaeological and Historical Society*, No. 28 (1995)

Nolan, William (ed.), *The Gaelic Athletic Association in Dublin, 1884–2000. Vol. 1: 1884–1959* (Dublin, 2005)

Noonan, Rodney, 'Offside: Rugby League, the Great War and Australian Patriotism', *International Journal of the History of Sport*, 26, 15 (2009)

O'Beirne-Ranelagh, John, 'The IRB from the Treaty to 1924', *Irish Historical Studies*, XX, 77 (1976)

O'Callaghan, Liam, *Rugby in Munster: A Social and Cultural History* (Cork, 2011)

O'Callaghan, Liam, 'The Red Thread of History: The Media, Munster Rugby and the Creation of a Sporting Tradition', *Media History*, 17, 2 (2011)

O'Carroll, Gerald, *The Pocket History of Kerry* (Tralee, 2007)

Ó Cléirigh, Nellie, *Valentia: A Different Irish Island* (Dublin, 1992)

Ó Conchubhair, Brian (ed.), *Kerry's Fighting Story, 1916–1921*, 2009 edition (Cork, 2009)

Ó Conchubhair, Brian, 'The GAA and the Irish Language', in M. Cronin, W. Murphy and P. Rouse (eds), *The Gaelic Athletic Association, 1884–2009* (Dublin, 2009)

Ó Concubhair, Pádraig, 'Comoradh '98: How Kerry Celebrated the Centenary of a Revolution', *The Kerry Magazine*, No. 10 (1999)

Ó Concubhair, Pádraig (ed.), *Sixty Years A-Growing: The North Kerry Board, 1924–1984* (Shanagolden, 1984)

Ó Concubhair, Pádraig and Lane, Caitriona, 'The Black and Tans in Ballylongford', *The Kerry Magazine*, No. 13 (2002)

Ó Conchubhair, Seán S., *Kilmoyley to the Rescue: A History of Kilmoyley and its Hurling Club* (Dublin, 2000)

Ó Conchubhair, Seán S., 'Roger Casement in County Kerry', *The Kerry Magazine*, No. 16 (2006)

O'Connell, J. 'The Rediscovery of Aran in the 19th Century', in J. Waddell, J. O'Connell and A. Koff (eds), *The Book of Aran* (Kinvara, 1994)

O'Connor, Maurice, *Keel GAA: A Club History* (Naas, 1991)

O'Connor, Tommy, *Ardfert: A Hurling History* (Ardfert, 1988)

O'Connor, Tommy, *Ardfert in Times Past* (Ardfert, 1999)

O'Day, Alan, *Irish Home Rule, 1867–1921* (Manchester, 1998)

O'Donoghue, Michael (ed.), *Glimpses from the Glen: Golden Jubilee of St Agatha's GAA Club, Glenflesk* (Killarney, 2001)

O'Donoghue, Thomas A., 'Educational Innovation in the Kerry Gaeltacht, 1904–22', *Journal of the Kerry Archaeological and Historical Society*, No. 19 (1986)

O'Donovan, Frank, *Abbeydorney: Our Own Place* (Abbeydorney, 1989)

O'Donovan, Teresa, 'Ulster and Home Rule for Ireland, to 1914', *Éire-Ireland*, XVIII, 3 (1983)

Ó Duibhne, Eoghan, *GAA: The Story of Camp Football, 1890–1953* (Camp, 2002)

O'Dwyer, Michael, *The History of Cricket in County Kilkenny: The Forgotten Game* (Kilkenny, 2006)

O'Flaherty, John, *The Listowel Races* (Listowel, 1992)

O'Hare, Patricia, 'The Herberts of Muckross', *The Kerry Magazine*, No. 12 (2001)

Ó Lúing, Seán, 'Aspects of the Fenian Rising in Kerry, 1867', *Journal of the Kerry Archaeological and Historical Society*, No. 3 (1970)

Ó Lúing, Seán, *I Die in A Good Cause* (Tralee, 1970)

O'Mahony, Joe, *The Kingdom: Kerry Football – The Stuff of Champions* (Dublin, 2010)

Ó Maolfabhail, Art, 'Hurling: An Old Game in a New World', in Grant Jarvie, (ed.), *Sport in the Making of Celtic Cultures* (Leicester, 1999)

Ó Maolfabhail, Art, Hegarty, Roddy and McAnallen, Dónal, 'From Cú Chulainn to

Cusack: Ball-Playing, Camán, Shinny and Hurling in Ulster before the GAA', in Dónal McAnallen, David Hassan and Roddy Hegarty (eds), *The Evolution of the GAA: Ulaidh, Éire agus Eile* (Armagh 2009)

Ó Muircheartaigh, Joe and Flynn, T.J., '*Princes of Pigskin: A Century of Kerry Footballers* (Cork, 2008)

Ó Riain, Séamus, *Maurice Davin (1842–1927): First President of the GAA* (Dublin, 1994)

Ó Ruairc, Michael, 'Dr Éamonn O'Sullivan and the Revival of our Games in the Schools and Colleges', in Michael Lyne (ed.), *The Kerry GAA Centenary Yearbook, 1884–1984* (Tralee, 1984)

Ó Ruairc, Michael, 'The Early Days of Athletics, Football and Hurling in Kerry', *The GAA in Kerry, Centenary Exhibition* (Killarney, 1984)

O'Shea, Donal, *A History of Kerry's Winning All-Irelands* (Ardfert, 1990)

O'Shea, Fr Kieran, 'Robert Finn, 1860–1935', in Éamon O'Sullivan (ed.), *Castleisland Desmonds GAA Club: Memories in White and Blue* (Castleisland, 1983)

O'Shea, Pat, *Face the Ball: Records of the Kerry County Championships, 1889–1998* (Tralee, 1998)

O'Shea, Pat, *Trail Blazers: A Century of Laune Rangers, 1888–1988* (Killorglin, 1988)

O'Shea, Pat 'Aeroplane', 'Football in Castlegregory in the Early Days', in Michael Lyne (ed.) *Kerry GAA Yearbook, 1975–6* (Tralee, 1976)

Ó Súilleabháin, Seán S., *Aililiú Rathmore: A History of Gaelic Activities in the Parish* (Rathmore, 1990)

O'Sullivan, Donal J., 'An Insight into the Life of an RIC District Inspector at Listowel in 1901', *The Kerry Magazine*, No. 8 (1997)

O'Sullivan, Donal J., 'Kerry's Tenuous Connection with the Foundation of the Gaelic Athletic Association', *The Kerry Magazine*, No. 20 (2010)

O'Sullivan, Donal J., 'Laying the Atlantic Cable', *The Kerry Magazine*, No. 11 (2000)

O'Sullivan, Donal J., 'The Fate of John B. Kearney, District Inspector of the RIC and Superintendent of the Civic Guard', *The Kerry Magazine*, No. 9 (1998)

O'Sullivan, Patrick, *The Farranfore to Valencia Harbour Railway. Volume I: Planning Construction and an Outline of Operation* (Manchester, 2003)

O'Sullivan, Jimmy Darcy, *Forged in Gold and Green: 125 Years of Kerry GAA* (Killarney, 2009)

O'Toole, Joe, 'Corcha Dhuibhne in 1916 and the First Kerry President of the Irish Republic', *The Kerry Magazine*, No. 17 (2007)

Ó Tuathaigh, Gearóid, 'The GAA as a Force in Irish Society: An Overview', in M. Cronin, W. Murphy and P. Rouse (eds), *The Gaelic Athletic Association, 1884–2009* (Dublin, 2009)

Orr, Philip, '200,000 Volunteer Soldiers', in John Horne (ed.), *Our War: Ireland and the Great War* (Dublin, 2008)

Phoenix, Éamon, 'Nationalism in Tyrone, 1880–1972', in Charles Dillon and Henry A Jefferies (eds), *Tyrone – History and Society: Interdisciplinary Essays on the History of an Irish County* (Dublin, 2000)

Puirséil, Pádraig, *The GAA in its Time* (Dublin, 1984)

Quane, Michael, 'Primary Education in Kerry a Hundred Years Ago', *Journal of the Kerry Archaeological and Historical Society*, No. 5 (1972)

Quinn, Peter A., 'Yeats and Revolutionary Nationalism: The Centenary of '98', *Éire-Ireland*, XV, 3 (1980)

Quirke, Michael P., 'A Centenary of Local Government: Kerry County Council', *The Kerry Magazine*, No. 10 (1999)

Rafter, Kevin, *Sinn Féin, 1905–2005: The Shadow of Gunmen* (Dublin, 2005)

Reenard GAA Club, 'Reenard Club History', retrieved from http://www.reenard.kerry.gaa.ie [accessed 15 April 2009]

Reid, Irene A., 'Shinty, Nationalism and Celtic Politics, 1870–1922, *The Sports Historian*, 18, 2 (1998)

Revington, Gordon (ed.), *Tralee Rugby Football Club, 1882–1982* (Tralee, 1983)

Rouse, Paul, 'Empires of Sport: Enniscorthy, 1880–1920', in Colm Toibín (ed.), *Enniscorthy* (Wexford, 2010)

Rouse, Paul, 'Gunfire in Hayes Hotel: The IRB and the Founding of the GAA', in F. McGarry and J. McConnell (eds), *The Black Hand of Republicanism: Fenianism in Modern Ireland* (Dublin, 2009)

Rouse, Paul, 'Journalists and the Making of the Gaelic Athletic Association, 1884–1887', *Media History*, 17, 2 (2011)

Rouse, Paul, 'Michael Cusack: Sportsman and Journalist', in M. Cronin, W. Murphy and P. Rouse (eds), *The Gaelic Athletic Association, 1884–2009* (Dublin, 2009)

Rouse, Paul, '*Sport* and Ireland in 1881', in Alan Bairner (ed.), *Sport and the Irish: Histories, Identities, Issues* (Dublin, 2005)

Rouse, Paul, 'Sport and the Offaly Tradition: The Gaelic Athletic Association', in Timothy P. O'Neill and William Nolan (eds), *Offaly – History and Society: Interdisciplinary Essays on the History of an Irish County* (Dublin, 1998)

Rouse, Paul, 'The Politics of Culture and Sport in Ireland: A History of the GAA Ban on Foreign Games, 1884–1971. Part One: 1884–1921', *International Journal of the History of Sport*, 10, 3 (1990)

Rouse, Paul, *Thomas F. O'Sullivan*, Dictionary of Irish Biography, retrieved from: http://dib.cambridge.org/quicksearch.do [accessed 18 May 2010]

Rouse, Paul, 'Why Irish Historians Have Ignored Sport: A Note', *The History Review*, Vol. XIV (2003)

Rouse, Paul, 'Why the GAA was Founded', in Dónal McAnallen, David Hassan and Roddy Hegarty (eds), *The Evolution of the GAA: Ulaidh, Éire agus Eile* (Armagh 2009)

Shanley, Frank and Kelleher, Mary, *Kilgarvan in the Beautiful Valley of the Roughty* (Kilgarvan, 1995)

Siggins, Gerard, *Green Days: Cricket in Ireland, 1792–2005* (Gloucestershire, 2005)

Smyth, Jimmy, *Praise of Heroes: Ballads and Poems of the GAA* (Dublin, 2007)

South Kerry GAA Board, *South Kerry GAA, 1902–2002: The Centenary Story* (Cahersiveen, 2002)

Spillane, Dr Milo, 'Queen Victoria in Killarney', *The Kerry Magazine*, No. 19 (2009)

St Senan's GAA, 'The History of St Senan's GAA: The Early Years of the GAA', retrieved from http://www.stsenans.ie/historydetail.asp?historyid=3 [accessed 16 February 2011]

Sugden, John and Bairner, Alan, *Sport, Sectarianism and Society in a Divided Ireland* (Leicester, 1993)

Tarbert GAA Club, *Tarbert GAA: A Century of the Red and Black* (Tarbert, 2000)

Townshend, Charles, *Easter 1916: The Irish Rebellion* (London, 2006)

Townshend, Charles, 'Making Sense of Easter 1916', *History Ireland*, 14, 2 (2006)

Townshend, Charles, 'The Irish Railway Strike of 1920: Industrial Action and Civil Resistance in the Struggle for Independence', *Irish Historical Studies*, XXI, 83 (1979)

Tranter, Neil, *Sport, Economy and Society in Britain, 1750–1914* (Cambridge, 1998)

Tranter, Neil, 'The Chronology of Organised Sport in Nineteenth-Century Scotland: A Regional Study. I – Patterns', *International Journal of the History of Sport*, 7, 2 (1990)

Tranter, Neil, 'The Chronology of Organised Sport in Nineteenth-Century Scotland: A Regional Study. II – Causes', *International Journal of the History of Sport*, 7, 3 (1990)

Tranter, Neil, 'The Patronage of Organised Sport in Central Scotland, 1820–1900', *Journal of Sport History*, 16, 3 (1989)

Turvey, Claire, 'Politics, War and Revolution: The Kenmare District, 1916–1923', *Journal of the Kerry Archaeological and Historical Society*, Series 2, Vol. 6 (2006)

Underdown, David, *Start of Play: Cricket and Culture in Eighteenth-Century England* (London, 2000)

Van Esbeck, Edmund, *Irish Rugby, 1874–1999: A History* (Dublin, 1999)

Van Esbeck, Edmund, *One Hundred Years of Irish Rugby: The Official History of the Irish Rugby Football Union* (Dublin, 1974)

Vaughan, E. and Fitzpatrick, A.J. (eds), *Irish Historical Statistics: Population, 1821–1971* (Dublin, 1978)

Welcome, John, *Irish Horseracing: An Illustrated History* (London, 1982)

Wheatley, Michael, *Nationalism and the Irish Party: Provincial Ireland, 1910–1916* (Oxford, 2005)

Whelan, Kevin, 'The Geography of Hurling', *History Ireland*, 1, 1 (1993)

Wigglesworth, Neil, *The Story of Sport in England* (London, 2007)

Williams, Gareth, 'Rugby Union', in Tony Mason (ed.), *Sport in Britain: A Social History* (Cambridge, 1989)

UNPUBLISHED THESES

Foley, Caitriona, 'The Last Great Irish Plague: The Great Flu in Ireland, 1918–19', PhD thesis, University College Dublin, 2009

Gorry, David, 'The Gaelic Athletic Association in Dublin, 1884–2000: A Geographical Analysis', MLitt thesis, University College Dublin, 2001

O'Sullivan, Sean, 'The GAA and Irish Nationalism, 1913–1923', MA thesis, University College Dublin, 1994

Quinn, Ruth-Blandina, 'Thomas Ashe: Analysis of an Insurrectionist', MA thesis, University College Dublin, 1989

SOCIAL PROFILES OF KERRY GAA PLAYERS AND OFFICIALS, 1888–1916

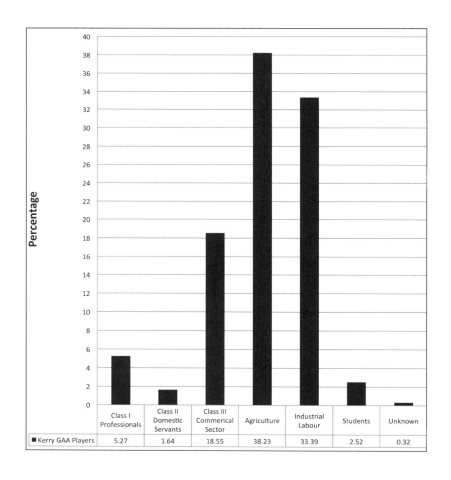

	Class I Professionals	Class II Domestic Servants	Class III Commerical Sector	Agriculture	Industrial Labour	Students	Unknown
■ Kerry GAA Players	5.27	1.64	18.55	38.23	33.39	2.52	0.32

SOCIAL PROFILE OF KERRY GAA CLUB OFFICERS, 1888–1916

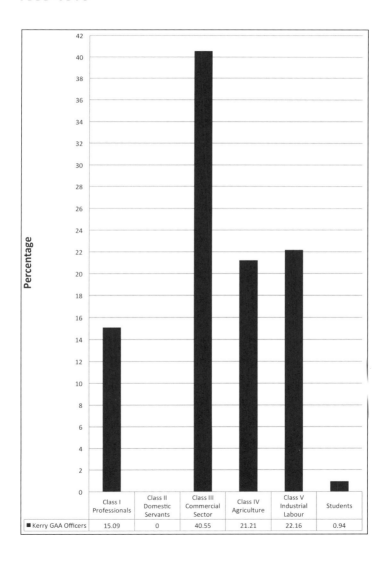

	Class I Professionals	Class II Domestic Servants	Class III Commercial Sector	Class IV Agriculture	Class V Industrial Labour	Students
■ Kerry GAA Officers	15.09	0	40.55	21.21	22.16	0.94

COMPARISON OF THE SOCIAL PROFILE OF KERRY GAA PLAYERS, 1888–1916

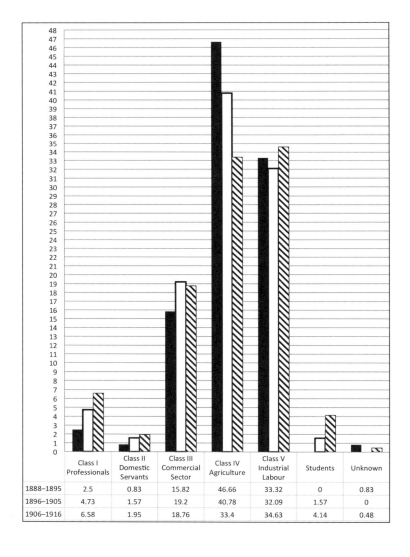

	Class I Professionals	Class II Domestic Servants	Class III Commercial Sector	Class IV Agriculture	Class V Industrial Labour	Students	Unknown
1888–1895	2.5	0.83	15.82	46.66	33.32	0	0.83
1896–1905	4.73	1.57	19.2	40.78	32.09	1.57	0
1906–1916	6.58	1.95	18.76	33.4	34.63	4.14	0.48

LIST OF KERRY SENIOR COUNTY CHAMPIONSHIP WINNERS, 1889–1934

	Senior Football Championship	Senior Hurling Championship
1889	Killorglin Laune Rangers	Kenmare
1890	Killorglin Laune Rangers	Kilmoyley
1891	Ballymacelligott	Ballyduff
1892	Killorglin Laune Rangers	Kilmoyley
1893	Killorglin Laune Rangers	Abbeydorney
1894	Ballymacelligott	Kilmoyley
1895	Ballymacelligott	Kilmoyley
1896	Tralee Mitchels, Cahersiveen (shared)	Abbeydorney
1897	Tralee Mitchels	Not Held
1898	County Board inactive, none played	County Board inactive, none played
1899	County Board inactive, none played	County Board inactive, none played
1900	Killorglin Laune Rangers	Kilmoyley
1901	Killarney Dr Crokes	Kilmoyley
1902	Tralee Mitchels	Kenmare
1903	Tralee Mitchels	Tralee Celtic
1904	Merged with 1905 championship	Tralee Celtic
1905	Final never played (Tralee v Cahersiveen)	Kilmoyley
1906	County Board inactive, none played	County Board inactive, none played
1907	Tralee Mitchels	Kilmoyley
1908	Tralee Mitchels	Tralee Mitchels
1909	Merged with 1910 championship	Merged with 1910 championship
1910	Tralee Mitchels	Kilmoyley
1911	Killorglin Laune Rangers	Tralee Mitchels
1912	Killarney Dr Crokes	Tralee Mitchels
1913	Killarney Dr Crokes	Abbeydorney
1914	Killarney Dr Crokes	Kilmoyley
1915	Not held due to backlog of games	Not held due to backlog of games
1916	Championship abandoned	Tullig
1917	Tralee Mitchels	Tubrid
1918	Ballymacelligott	Tralee Parnells
1919	Tralee Mitchels	Tralee Parnells
1920	Championship abandoned	Championship abandoned
1921	County Board inactive, not held	County Board inactive, not held
1922	Championship abandoned	Championship abandoned
1923	County Board inactive, not held	County Board inactive, not held
1924	Championship abandoned	Championship abandoned
1925	Tralee Selection	Tralee Selection
1926	Tralee Selection	Not Held
1927	Not held due to backlog of games	Not Held
1928	Rock Street	Rock Street
1929	Boherbee	Rock Street
1930	Rock Street	Championship abandoned
1931	Austin Stacks (Rock Street)	Austin Stacks (Rock Street)
1932	Austin Stacks	Causeway
1933	O'Rahillys (Boherbee)	Lixnaw
1934	Championship abandoned	Championship abandoned

APPENDIX III

LIST OF EVERY GAA CLUB/TEAM RECORDED IN KERRY 1884–1934

Club/Team Name	First Recorded	Location	Hurling Football or Camogie
27th Battalion National Army HC	1924	Tralee	H
Abbey Street FC	1918	Tralee	F
Abbeydorney	1888	Abbeydorney	H
Acres FC	1906	Tralee	F
Addergown FC	1925	Ballyduff	F
Addergown HC	1925	Ballyduff	H
Aghadoe	1900	Aghadoe	F
Aghatubrid	1902	Cahersiveen	F
Ahafoula	1911	Ballydonoghue	F
Annascaul Camogie Club	1929	Annascaul	C
Annascaul FC	1924	Annascaul	F
Annascaul Ex-Servicemen FC	1924	Annascaul	F
Annascaul Liberators	1889	Annascaul	F
Ardcast FC	1925	?	F
Ardfert	1893	Ardfert	H
Ardfert Camogie Club	1925	Ardfert	C
Ardoughter Shannon Rovers	1911	Ballyduff	F
Ardrahan	1902	Ardfert	H
Ashill Alderman Hoopers	1888	Ballymacelligott	F
Assassins FC	1930	Killarney	F
Atlantic Rangers	1893	North Kerry	H
Austin Stacks	1931	Rock Street	F
Ballinagal	1918	West Kerry	F
Ballinclogher	1930	Lixnaw	H
Ballinorig	1896	Tralee	F
Ballinskelligs William O'Briens	1889	Ballinskelligs	F
Ballinskelligs FC	1929	Ballinskelligs	F
Ballybunion	1889	Ballybunion	F
Ballybunion Corncrakes	1900	Ballybunion	F
Ballybunion Shannon Rovers	1909	Ballybunion	F
Ballycarberry	1889	Cahersiveen	F
Ballycarberry FC	1917	Cahersiveen	F
Ballyconry	1893	Lisselton	F
Ballydavid FC	1924	Ballydavid	F
Ballydavid St Brendan's	1905	Ballydavid	F
Ballydavid Isles of the Sea	1908	Ballydavid	F
Ballydowney FC	1927	Killarney	F
Ballydonoghue FC	1912	Ballydonoghue	F
Ballydonoghue Parnells	1933	Ballydonoghue	F
Ballyduff	1888	Ballyduff	H
Ballyduff Shannon Rovers	1912	Ballyduff	H
Ballyferriter	1889	Ballyferriter	F
Ballyfinnane	1901	Firies	F

Club/Team Name	First Recorded	Location	Hurling Football or Carmogie
Ballygrennan	1928	Listowel	F
Ballyhar	1891	Killarney	F
Ballyheigue	1888	Ballyheigue	H
Ballyheigue FC	1906	Ballyheigue	F
Ballylongford	1891	Ballylongford	F
Ballylongford Clan na Gaels	1907	Ballylongford	F
Ballylongford Liam Mellows	1933	Ballylongford	F
Ballymacelligott	1900	Ballymacelligott	F
Ballymacelligott Alderman Hoopers	1889	Ballymacelligott	F
Ballyrehan HC	1924	Lixnaw	H
Ballyseedy FC	1928	Ballyseedy	F
Banna HC	1927	Banna	H
Barraduff FC	1907	Barraduff	F
Barraduff Daniel O'Connells	1888	Barraduff	F
Barrow HC	1918	Ardfert	H
Behins FC	1926	Listowel	F
Beaufort	1929	Beaufort	F
Bedford FC	1933	Bedford	F
Blenerville FC	1924	Blenerville	F
Bog Road FC	1928	Kilgarvan	F
Boherbee FC	1918	Tralee	F
Boherbee Fianna HC	1928	Tralee	F
Boherbee HC	1906	Tralee	H
Boherbee Lower FC	1929	Tralee	F
Boherlahan	1929	Tralee	F
Bonane	1891	Kenmare	H
Boro Rovers	1929	Listowel	F
Brackhill	1929	East Kerry	F
Brian Borus	1889	Muckross	F
Brosna	1889	Brosna	F
Brosna FC	1933	Brosna	F
Caherdaniel	1902	Caherdaniel	F
Caheria FC	1929	Tralee	F
Cahersiveen HC	1902	Cahersiveen	H
Cahersiveen Mountain Rangers	1889	Cahersiveen	F
Cahersiveen O'Connells	1890	Cahersiveen	F
Callinafercy	1889	Milltown	F
Camp	1889	Camp	F
Camp Camogie Club	1929	Camp	F
Camp Liberators	1891	Camp	F
Camp FC	1933	Camp	F
Capa HC	1930	Kilflynn	H
Caragh Lake FC	1898	Killorglin	F
Cashen Rovers HC	1928	Ballyduff	H
Castlecove FC	1921	Caherdaniel	F
Castleisland Desmonds	1888	Castleisland	F
Castleisland Geraldines	1905	Castleisland	F
Castleisland Kruger's Own	1901	Castleisland	F

Club/Team Name	First Recorded	Location	Hurling Football or Carmogie
Castleisland Slashers	1893	Castleisland	F
Castleisland Shaughranus	1899	Castleisland	F
Castlegregory	1901	Castlegregory	F
Castlegregory Allen	1889	Castlegregory	F
Castlegregory Camogie Club	1929	Castlegregory	C
Castlemaine	1890	Castlemaine	F
Causeway	1895	Causeway	H
Causeway FC	1896	Causeway	F
Causeway Shannon Rovers	1924	Causeway	H
Celtic Hurling Club	1901	Tralee	H
Chapel Rovers	1933	North Kerry	H
Charles Stewart Parnells	1896	Boherbee	F
Charles Street United	1928	Listowel	F
Church Street	1889	Listowel	F
Churchill FC	1917	Churchill	F
Churchill HC	1917	Churchill	H
Civic Guards FC	1924	Tralee	F
Civic Guards HC	1924	Tralee	H
Clan na Gaels	1899	Ballylongford	F
Clahane FC	1900	Tralee	F
Cloghane FC	1930	Cloghane	F
Clounalour FC	1929	Tralee	F
Clounmacon FC	1927	Clounmacon	F
Coolbane FC	1925	Killorglin	F
Corcoran FC	1928	West Kerry	F
Cordal Wild Rovers	1889	Cordal	F
Counanna	1902	South Kerry	F
Craughdarrig FC	1927	Asdee	F
Craughdarrig Emmets	1903	Asdee	F
Crom a Boos	1901	Keel	F
Cromane FC	1925	Cromane	F
Cromane Sarsfields	1909	Cromane	F
Crossroads HC	1925	East Kerry	H
Crotta	1896	Kilflynn	H
Crotta HC	1930	Kilflynn	H
Crotta Camogie Club	1929	Kilflynn	C
Crotta FC	1900	Kilflynn	F
Cuas FC	1933	West Kerry	F
Cuas St Brendan's	1906	West Kerry	F
Cuas Isles of the Sea	1907	West Kerry	F
Curragh Camp Selection	1924	Tralee	F
Currans	1888	Currans	F
Curraugh FC	1896	Killarney	F
Curravough	1896	Tralee	F
Currow	1901	Currow	F
Currow Wolfe Tones	1912	Currow	F
Dalcassians	1906	West Kerry	F
Davitts FC	1890	Dingle	F
Derrynane	1889	Derrynane	F
Derrynane FC	1921	Derrynane	F

Club/Team Name	First Recorded	Location	Hurling Football or Carmogie
Dick Fitzgerald's Camogie Club	1933	Killarney	C
Dicksgrove FC	1928	Currow	F
Dingle FC	1888	Dingle	F
Dingle Allens	1891	Dingle	F
Dingle Camogie Club	1929	Dingle	C
Dingle Emmets	1906	Dingle	F
Dingle Gascons	1906	Dingle	F
Dingle HC	1906	Dingle	H
Dingle Maurice Quirke Guards	1907	Dingle	F
Dingle O'Husseys	1909	Dingle	F
Dingle Shamrocks	1892	Dingle	F
Dingle Wreckers	1903	Dingle	F
Doon	1889	Ballyheigue	F
Doon HC	1927	Ballyheigue	H
Dr Crokes	1887	Killarney	F
Dr Crokes Camogie Club	1929	Killarney	C
Dromid	1889	Dromid	F
Dromid FC	1929	Dromid	F
Dromlought	1911	Lisselton	F
Drumnacurra	1914	Causeway	H
Duagh	1890	Duagh	F
Dunquin	1907	Dunquin	F
Dysert HC	1930	Lixnaw	H
East Kerry FC	1930	East Kerry	F
East Kerry HC	1930	East Kerry	H
Erin's Hope	1889	Irremore	F
Éire Óg	1908	Dingle	F
Faha FC	1919	Killarney	F
Faranacarriuga	1906	?	F
Farranfore	1901	Farranfore	F
Farranfore Plunketts	1917	Farranfore	F
Feale Amateurs	1889	Listowel	F
Fenit Casement	1933	Fenit	F
Fenit FC	1926	Fenit	F
Fenit HC	1926	Fenit	H
Fermoyle	1918	Ballinskelligs	F
Fethard	1905	?	F
Foilmore Camogie Club	1929	Foilmore	C
Foilmore FC	1917	Foilmore	F
Foilmore Liberators	1891	Foilmore	F
Finuge	1900	Finuge	F
Finuge HC	1924	Finuge	H
Firies	1895	Firies	F
Firies FC	1933	Firies	F
Fossa FC	1926	Fossa	F
Fossa Parnells	1890	Fossa	F
Headford Camogie Club	1933	Headford	C
Headford FC	1924	Headford	F
Headford HC	1920	Headford	H
Hearty Shamrocks	1901	Castleisland	F

Club/Team Name	First Recorded	Location	Hurling Football or Carmogie
Holy Terrors	1889	Tralee	F
Home Rulers	1913	Killarney	F
Gaeltacht	1933	West Kerry	F
Gale Rovers	1930	Listowel	F
Garden Boys	1910	Tralee	F
Garrynagore HC	1918	Lixnaw	H
Gaum FC	1929	Killorglin	F
Gilpen Troopers	1895	Tralee	F
Gleann	1929	Listowel	F
Glenbeigh Rovers	1907	Glenbeigh	F
Glencar	1889	Glencar	F
Glenflesk	1902	Glenflesk	F
Glin Emmets	1898	Tarbert	F
Glouria	1912	Lisselton	F
Gneeveguilla	1914	Gneeveguilla	F
Goat Street FC	1926	Dingle	F
Grawn	1932	Killorglin	F
Green and Gold FC	1916	West Kerry	F
Greenville FC	1928	Listowel	F
Grey Street	1927	Dingle	F
Guhard	1893	Lisselton	F
Gunsboro FC	1918	Listowel	F
Inch Island Rovers	1908	Inch	F
Independents	1906	Listowel	F
Ironsiders FC	1929	Listowel	F
Irish Brigade Transvaal	1900	Killorglin	F
Irremore	1889	Listowel	F
Irremore and Lixnaw	1888	Listowel	F
Irremore St Patrick's	1903	Listowel	F
Jameson Raiders	1896	Tralee	F
J.D. Sheehan Volunteers	1889	Killarney	F
J.F. Fitzgerald XVII	1889	Cahersiveen	F
John E. Redmonds	1893	Tralee	F
John Mitchels	1933	Boherbee	F
John Street	1929	Dingle	F
Joubert's Choice	1901	Tralee	F
Keel	1889	Keel	F
Keel Geraldines	1891	Keel	F
Keel Sinn Féiners	1917	Keel	F
Keelduff	1908	Annascaul	F
Kilmalkedar	1934	West Kerry	F
Kells	1895	Cahersiveen	F
Kenmare	1888	Kenmare	F
Kenmare Camogie Club	1933	Kenmare	C
Kenmare Black Valley FC	1919	Kenmare	F
Kenmare FC	1906	Kenmare	F
Kenmare O'Connells	1888	Kenmare	H
Kenmare Shamrocks	1932	Kenmare	H
Kilcummin	1901	Kilcummin	F
Kilfenora	1932	Fenit	F
Kilflynn FC	1899	Kilflynn	F
Kilflynn HC	1918	Kilflynn	H

Club/Team Name	First Recorded	Location	Hurling Football or Carmogie
Kilcummin FC	1901	Kilcummin	F
Kilgarvan	1888	Kilgarvan	F
Kilgarvan FC	1917	Kilgarvan	F
Kilgarvan HC	1909	Kilgarvan	H
Kilgarvan Shamrocks	1888	Kilgarvan	H
Killahan	1905	Abbeydorney	H
Killahan, Abbeydorney	1885	Abbeydorney	H
Killocrim	1932	Listowel	F
Killarney Catholic Truth Society	1929	Killarney	F
Killarney College Street	1924	Killarney	F
Killarney Croadh na nÁirne	1905	Killarney	H
Killarney HC	1909	Killarney	H
Killarney High Street	1924	Killarney	F
Killarney Loch Lein HC	1911	Killarney	H
Killarney Main Street	1924	Killarney	F
Killarney New Street	1924	Killarney	F
Killarney Shamrocks	1889	Killarney	F
Kilmoyley Emmets	1888	Kilmoyley	H
Killoe The Raparees FC	1917	Cahersiveen	F
Killorglin Camogie Club	1933	Killorglin	C
Killorglin Celtic FC	1925	Killorglin	F
Killorglin Dashers	1907	Killorglin	F
Killorglin Harringtons	1889	Killorglin	F
Killorglin HC	1929	Killorglin	H
Killury, Rathoo	1885	Killury	H
Killury FC	1889	Killury	F
Kingstown HC	1908	Valentia	H
Knockeenduff FC	1929	Killarney	F
Knockanure FC	1928	Knockanure	F
Knockanure Volunteers	1889	Knockanure	F
Knockavata FC	1925	Killorglin	F
Knocknagoshel	1889	Knocknagoshel	F
Knocknagoshel FC	1933	Knocknagoshel	F
Knocknagree Camogie Club	1933	Rathmore	C
Knockeen FC	1930	Castleisland	F
Kruger's Own	1900	Tralee	F
Labasheeda Sarsfields FC	1919	South Kerry	F
Labasheeda St Patrick's FC	1919	South Kerry	F
Ladies Walk HC	1930	Ballyduff	H
Langford Street	1932	Killorglin	F
Laune Rangers	1888	Killorglin	F
Lauragh FC	1919	Beara Peninsula	F
League of the Cross Athletic Club	1889	Dingle	F
Lee Rangers HC	1924	Tralee	H
Legion FC	1929	Killarney	F
Leithruich FC	1930	?	F
Lerrig HC	1919	Ardfert	H
Lerrig Holy Terrors	1890	Ardfert	H
Lisivageen FC	1929	Killarney	F

Club/Team Name	First Recorded	Location	Hurling Football or Carmogie
Listowel Camogie Club	1925	Listowel	C
Listowel Church Street	1889	Listowel	F
Listowel GAA Athletic Club	1885	Listowel	–
Listowel FC	1888	Listowel	F
Listowel Feale Amateurs	1889	Listowel	F
Listowel HC	1906	Listowel	H
Listowel Na Gaedhna Fiadhaine	1903	Listowel	F
Listowel St Patrick's	1911	Listowel	F
Listowel Thomas Ashe	1933	Listowel	F
Listowel Wild Geese	1900	Listowel	F
Listowel Wolfe Tones	1916	Listowel	H
Lispole Emmets	1889	Lispole	F
Lispole St Johns	1897	Lispole	F
Lispole FC	1929	Lispole	F
Listry FC	1925	Listry	F
Listry Sheehans	1889	Listry	F
Lixnaw	1888	Lixnaw	H
Lixnaw Davis	1913	Lixnaw	H
Lixnaw FC	1890	Lixnaw	F
Lixnaw Redmonds HC	1913	Lixnaw	H
Lixnaw Sir Charles Russells	1889	Lixnaw	H
Lohar FC	1921	Waterville	F
Lough Lein Rangers	1889	Aghadoe	F
Lougher	1906	Inch	F
Lower Bridge Street	1932	Killorglin	F
Lower Town FC	1932	Killorglin	F
Lower Tralee	1916	Tralee	F
Meanus	1898	Killorglin	F
Mall United	1906	Tralee	H
Marhin	1933	West Kerry	F
Mastergeehy FC	1925	Waterville	F
Military HC	1925	Tralee	H
Milltown	1900	Milltown	F
Milltown Rangers	1889	Milltown	F
Milltown Shamrocks FC	1916	Milltown	F
Milltown Volunteers	1891	Milltown	F
Morley's Bridge	1928	Killarney	F
Moyeightragh	1931	Killarney	F
Muckross O'Connells	1890	Muckross	F
New Street FC	1930	Killarney	F
Newtownsandes	1900	Moyvane	F
North Kerry Rangers	1903	Abbeydorney	H
Oakpark	1906	Tralee	F
O'Brennan	1888	Ballymacelligott	F
O'Rahillys	1933	Strand Rd	F
Parnells FC	1910	Tralee	F
Parnells HC	1912	Tralee	H
Pearses HC	1933	North Kerry	H
Pick of the West FC	1921	West Kerry	F
Pioneers	1898	Tralee	F

Club/Team Name	First Recorded	Location	Hurling Football or Carmogie
Portmagee	1896	Portmagee	F
Quay FC	1916	Dingle	F
Rathea	1906	Listowel	F
Rathmore	1888	Rathmore	F
Rathmore Croad na nAíne	1905	Rathmore	F
Rathmore Pearses FC	1916	Rathmore	F
Rathmore HC	1918	Rathmore	H
Rathmore Pioneers	1912	Rathmore	F
Red Hughs	1889	Tralee	F
Renard	1902	Renard	F
Renard Holy Terrors	1917	Renard	F
Riversiders FC	1929	Tralee	F
Rock Street FC	1918	Tralee	F
Rock Street HC	1906	Tralee	H
Rock Street Shamrocks	1896	Tralee	H
Rock Street Slashers	1896	Tralee	F
Revenue Kilties	1908	Valentia	H
Saint Brendan's Seminary	1890	Killarney	F
Saleen Rovers	1905	Ballylongford	F
Scartaglin Flesk Rangers	1911	Scartaglin	F
Scartaglin Young Irelanders	1905	Scartaglin	F
Scrahan	1906	Castleisland	F
Shannon Rovers	1891	Causeway	H
Six Crosses FC	1933	North Kerry	F
Sneem	1898	Sneem	F
South Kerry FC	1930	South Kerry	F
Spa Road	1887	Tralee	F
Spa Road FC	1929	Tralee	F
St Brendan's	1910	Dingle	F
St Brendan's Camogie Club	1934	Blennerville	C
St Brendan's HC	1933	North Kerry	H
St Bridget's Camogie Club	1929	Tralee	C
St Finbar's	1934	North Kerry	H
St Patrick's Temperance Society	1895	Listowel	F
St Mary's Cahersiveen	1929	Cahersiveen	F
St Mary's Camogie Club	1929	Tralee	C
Steelroe Rovers FC	1925	Killorglin	F
Strand Street	1887	Tralee	F
Strand Street Emmets	1898	Tralee	F
Strand Street FC	1918	Tralee	F
Strand Street HC	1906	Tralee	H
Streets United	1907	Tralee	F
Sunhill Corncrakes	1907	Killorglin	F
Tahilla FC	1919	Sneem	F
Tarbert FC	1891	Tarbert	F
Tarbert Rovers	1902	Tarbert	F
Tarmon Emmets	1905	Tarbert	F
Templenoe	1903	Templenoe	F

Club/Team Name	First Recorded	Location	Hurling Football or Carmogie
Thomas Ashe HC	1920	Tralee	H
The Gods	1906	Tralee	F
Tralee Amateurs	1889	Tralee	F
Tralee Camogie Club	1925	Tralee	C
Tralee County Hall Selection	1920	Tralee	F
Tralee Dalcassians HC	1917	Tralee	F
Tralee Drapers	1893	Tralee	F
Tralee Emmets	1934	Tralee	F
Tralee Fianna FC	1924	Tralee	F
Tralee GAA Athletic Club	1885	Tralee	–
Tralee Gaelic League	1906	Tralee	F
Tralee Grocers	1893	Tralee	F
Tralee League FC	1919	Tralee	F
Tralee Mitchels	1887	Boherbee	F
Tralee Mitchels HC	1910	Boherbee	H
Tralee Printers FC	1911	Tralee	F
Tralee Railway	1914	Tralee	F
Tralee Rangers	1928	Tralee	F
Tralee Red Hugs	1890	Tralee	F
Tralee Robert Emmets	1907	Tralee	F
Tralee Rovers FC	1928	Tralee	F
Tralee Wolfe Tones	1934	Tralee	F
Tubrid	1903	Ardfert	H
Tullamore Ramblers	1914	Listowel	F
Tullig	1896	Kilflynn	F
Tullig Gamecocks	1916	Kilflynn	H
Tuogh FC	1925	Beaufort	F
Tuogh Parnells	1889	Beaufort	F
Tuosist FC	1902	Tuosist	F
Tuosist HC	1918	Tuosist	H
Tyromoyle	1895	Filemore	F
Upper Tralee	1916	Tralee	F
Valentia	1889	Valentia	F
Valentia HC	1905	Valentia	H
Ventry	1905	Ventry	F
Ventry Villagers	1907	Ventry	F
Waterville FC	1902	Waterville	F
Waterville Geraldines	1889	Waterville	F
Waterville HC	1902	Waterville	H
West Kerry FC	1930	West Kerry	F
West Ventry Mountaineers	1907	Ventry	F
Western Valentia FC	1933	Valentia	F
William O'Briens	1889	Ballinskelligs	F
William Street	1889	Listowel	F
Young Ireland	1911	Listowel	F

ESTIMATED NUMBER OF CLUBS AFFILIATED TO KERRY
COUNTY BOARD, 1885–1924

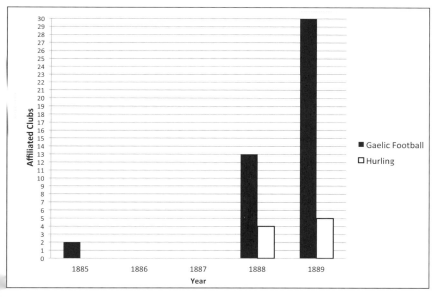

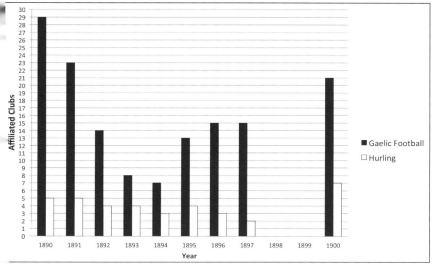

ESTIMATED NUMBER OF CLUBS AFFILIATED TO KERRY COUNTY BOARD

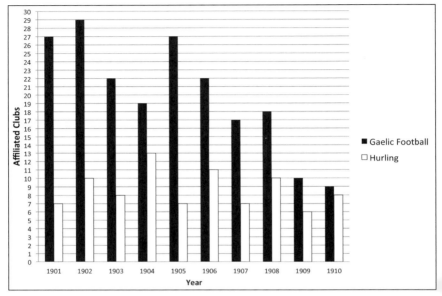

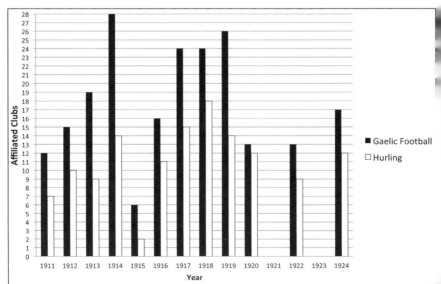

TOTAL NUMBER OF HURLING AND FOOTBALL COMBINATIONS
IN KERRY, 1885–1934

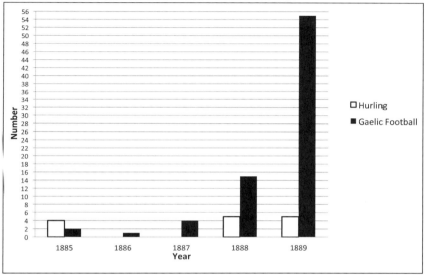

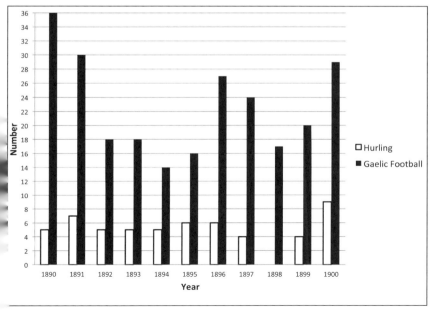

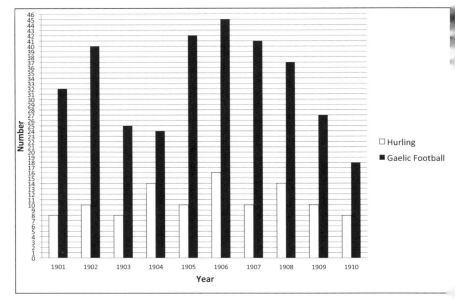

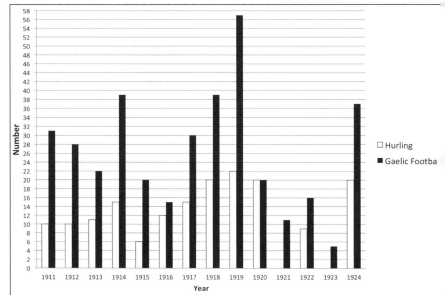

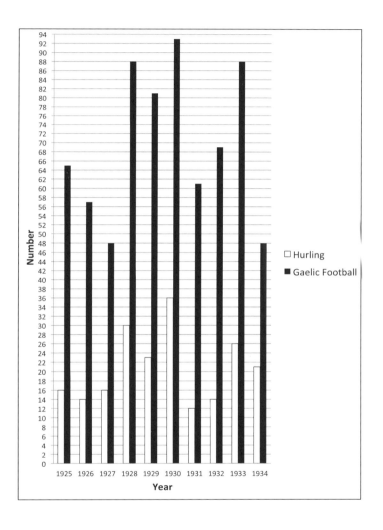

NUMBER OF TEAMS IN KERRY COUNTY CHAMPIONSHIP, 1889–1934

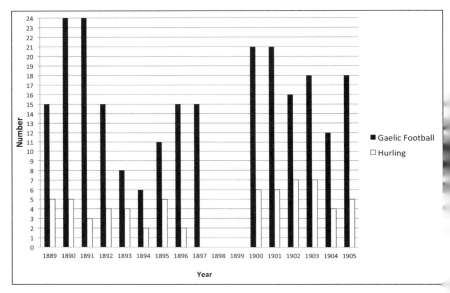

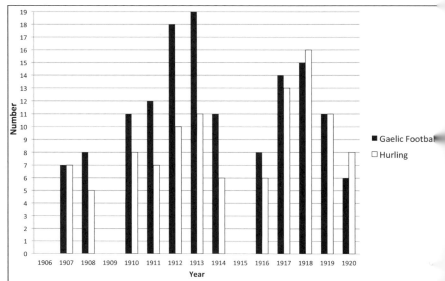

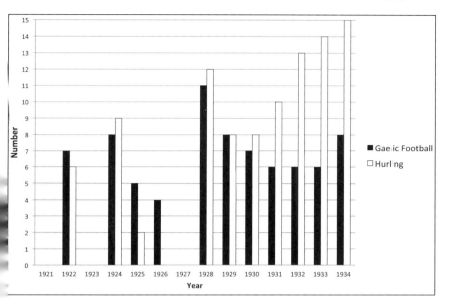

APPENDIX VII

GAA MATCHES REPORTED IN KERRY, 1885–1924

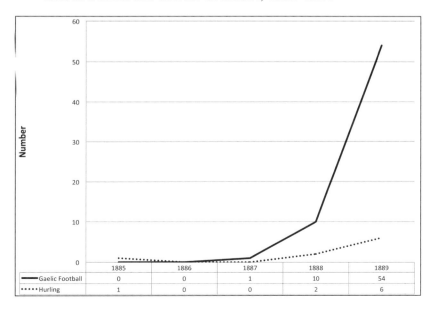

	1885	1886	1887	1888	1889
Gaelic Football	0	0	1	10	54
Hurling	1	0	0	2	6

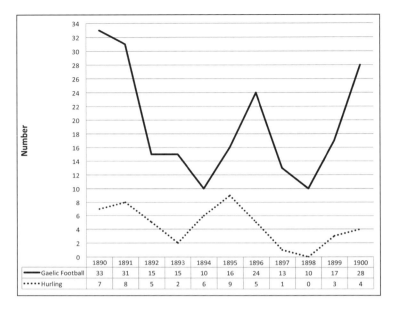

	1890	1891	1892	1893	1894	1895	1896	1897	1898	1899	1900
Gaelic Football	33	31	15	15	10	16	24	13	10	17	28
Hurling	7	8	5	2	6	9	5	1	0	3	4

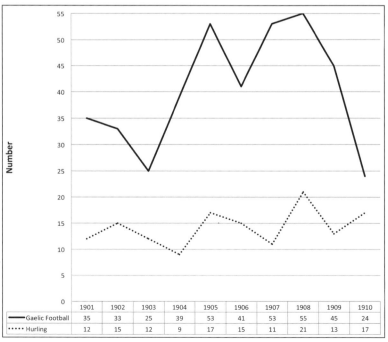

	1901	1902	1903	1904	1905	1906	1907	1908	1909	1910
Gaelic Football	35	33	25	39	53	41	53	55	45	24
Hurling	12	15	12	9	17	15	11	21	13	17

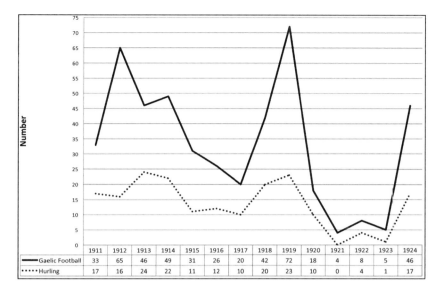

	1911	1912	1913	1914	1915	1916	1917	1918	1919	1920	1921	1922	1923	1924
Gaelic Football	33	65	46	49	31	26	20	42	72	18	4	8	5	46
Hurling	17	16	24	22	11	12	10	20	23	10	0	4	1	17

APPENDIX VIII

COMPARISON OF 'FOREIGN GAME' MATCHES REPORTED IN THE *KERRY SENTINEL* AND *SPORT*, 1891–1901

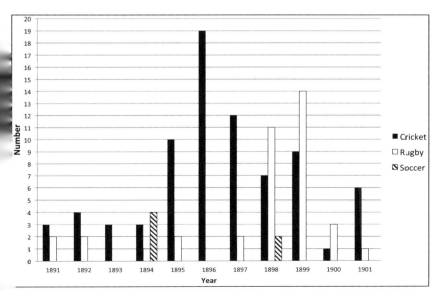

INDEX